# INVENTING AMERICAN EXCEPTIONALISM

Yale Law Library Series in Legal History and Reference

# INVENTING AMERICAN EXCEPTIONALISM

## THE ORIGINS OF AMERICAN ADVERSARIAL LEGAL CULTURE, 1800–1877

*Amalia D. Kessler*

Yale UNIVERSITY PRESS    *New Haven and London*

Published with support from the Lillian Goldman Law
Library, Yale Law School.

Yale University Press books may be purchased in quantity
for educational, business, or promotional use. For
information, please e-mail sales.press@yale.edu (U.S. office)
or sales@yaleup.co.uk (U.K. office).

Set in Scala type by IDS Infotech Ltd., Chandigarh, India.
Printed in the United States of America.

Library of Congress Control Number: 2016944171
ISBN: 978-0-300-19807-2 (hardcover : alk. paper)
ISBN: 978-0-300-22225-8 (paperback : alk. paper)

A catalogue record for this book is available from the
British Library.

This paper meets the requirements of ANSI/NISO
Z39.48-1992 (Permanence of Paper).

10  9  8  7  6  5  4  3  2  1

*For Adam, Stella, and Ari*

*We should scarcely like our enemies to call us a litigious people, and yet there is no nation where members of the legal profession more abound, or where Courts of Law are so crowded with litigants.*

*Something of this may be attributed to the facilities which are afforded to the bringing of suits at law, and to the comparatively light expense attendant upon their prosecution; but much more may be ascribed to a peculiarity of temperament. We are a keen, shrewd, energetic, business people, tenacious of our rights, even to the tenth part of a hair, and resolutely bent upon defending them. . . .*

"Courts of Conciliation," *Alexandria Gazette*, January 21, 1856, p. 2.

# Contents

# ACKNOWLEDGMENTS

In researching and writing this book, I benefited enormously from the wisdom and generosity of a great many people and institutions. A remarkable number of colleagues, both at Stanford and elsewhere, took the time to read the entire draft manuscript and provide me with detailed comments. Indeed, some read more than one draft! These include Jud Campbell, Kevin Clermont, George Fisher, Lawrence Friedman, Bob Gordon, John Langbein, Renée Lettow Lerner, Bernie Meyler, Judith Resnik, Norm Spaulding, Rachel St. John, Jim Whitman, and John Witt. I am also very grateful to the anonymous reviewers whose helpful feedback was secured by Bill Frucht, my wonderful editor at Yale University Press, and to Martin Schneider for excellent copyediting.

In addition to those who read the manuscript in its entirety, an even larger number offered insights and advice concerning particular portions of the text (and/or particular images) in the context of formal presentations or more informal exchanges. These include Bruce Ackerman, Laura Appleman, Keith Baker, Daphne Barak-Erez, Denis Baranger, Felice Batlan, Leora Bilsky, Binyamin Blum, Susanna Blumenthal, Margaret Boittin, Tomiko Brown-Nagin, Steve Bundy, Sarah Burns, Paul Butler, Amy Cohen, Charlie Donahue, Sharon Driscoll, Laurie Edelman, Malcolm Feeley, Katherine Florey, David Fontana, Willy Forbath, Tom Gallanis, Nuno Garoupa, David Gerber, Bill Gerdts, Philip Girard, Paul Goldstein, Risa Goluboff, Jim Gordley, Ariela Gross, Dan Hamilton, Ron Harris, Jill Hasday, Deborah Hensler, Steve Heyman, James Berry Hill, Dan Ho, Adam Hofri-Winogradow, Morty Horwitz, Bob Kagan, Linda Kerber, Roy Kreitner, Alexi Lahav, Pnina Lahav, Adriaan Lanni, Claire Lemercier, David Lieberman, Assaf Likhovski, Peter Lindseth, Screven Lorillard, Ken Mack, Leo Mazow, Chuck McCurdy, Tom McSweeney, Ralf Michaels, Kerry

Morgan, Cal Morrill, Alex Nemerov, Bill Novak, Josh Ober, Jim Oldham, Nick Parrillo, Moria Paz, Dylan Penningroth, Rogelio Pérez-Perdomo, Wilfrid Prest, Claire Priest, Sally Richardson, Noya Rimalt, Susan Rose-Ackerman, Issi Rosen-Zvi, Richard Ross, Yoram Shachar, Jed Shugerman, Reva Siegel, Nomi Stolzenberg, Eleanor Swift, Symeon Symeonides, Chris Tomlins, Avishalom Tor, Mark Tushnet, Amanda Tyler, Barbara Welke, Steven Wilf, and Caroline Winterer. So many have generously shared their knowledge and ideas with me that I fear I may have inadvertently neglected to thank some. My deepest apologies to anyone I mistakenly omitted.

I am also very grateful to the organizers and participants of the following workshops and speaker series to which I was invited to present portions of the book: the Australian and New Zealand Law and History Society Conference Keynote; the Berkeley Center for the Study of Law and Society Speaker Series; the Berkeley Civil Justice Workshop; the Berkeley Comparative Law and Economics Forum; the Chicago-Kent Law Faculty Workshop; the Duke Global Law Workshop; the George Washington Law School Works in Progress Series; the Haifa Law Faculty Workshop; the Harvard Law and History Workshop; the Hebrew University Legal History Workshop; the Illinois Legal History Program; the Institut Michel Villey/Paris II Speaker Series; the Iowa Legal History Workshop; the Ohio State/Moritz Law Faculty Workshop; the Osgoode Hall Law School Genest Global Faculty Lecture; the Stanford Humanities Center Works in Progress Series; the Stanford Law Faculty Workshop; the Tel Aviv Law and History Workshop; the Tel Aviv Law Faculty Workshop; the Tulane Law Faculty Workshop; the University of California Davis Law Faculty Workshop; the University of Connecticut Legal History and Culture Speaker Series; the University of Minnesota Legal History Workshop; the University of Minnesota Public Law Workshop; the University of Southern California Law, History, and Culture Workshop; the University of Virginia Legal History Workshop; the Willamette Law Faculty Workshop; the William and Mary Law Elmer J. Schaefer Workshop; the Yale Law Faculty Workshop; and the Yale Legal History Forum.

The amazing staff of the Stanford Law School Library contributed enormously to this project through their many efforts to assist me in locating and obtaining vital source materials. While I am hugely grateful to the library staff as a whole, I owe special thanks to Sonia Moss and Rich Porter. I also benefited greatly from the good counsel of James Folts, head of Reference Services at the New York State Archives. Many thanks as well to the research assistants who offered key help in tracking down sources: Mark Axelrod, Gilat Bachar,

Hannah Chartoff, Jon Connolly, Gea Kang, Amanda Klein, George LeBour-
dais, Jennifer Luo, Andy Schupanitz, Tommy Tobin, and Zain Yoonas. So,
too, I am indebted to the incredible Eun Sze, who, along with Ginny Clegg,
provided much-needed assistance in preparing the manuscript for submission, and to Jaya Chatterjee of Yale University Press, who helped a great deal
in this process as well.

Research for the book was supported, in part, through generous fellow-
ships provided by a number of organizations, to all of which I am tremendously grateful. These include a Charles A. Ryskamp Research Fellowship
from the American Council of Learned Societies; a research fellowship within
the Workshop on Common Law Legal Transplants hosted by the Institute for
Advanced Studies of the Hebrew University of Jerusalem; and a Violet Andrews Whittier Fellowship at the Stanford Humanities Center. I also owe a
great debt to two wonderful Stanford Law School deans, Larry Kramer and Liz
Magill, who supported my research in numerous ways, including by making
it possible for me to pursue these fellowship opportunities.

Portions of the material published here have appeared previously in different form: "Our Inquisitorial Tradition: Equity Procedure, Due Process, and
the Search for an Alternative to the Adversarial," *Cornell Law Review* 90 (2005):
1181–1275; "Deciding against Conciliation: The Nineteenth-Century Rejection
of a European Transplant and the Rise of a Distinctively American Ideal of
Adversarial Adjudication," *Theoretical Inquiries in Law* 10 (2009): 423–83; and
"Constructing an Ideal: Chancellor Kent, Justice Story, and the Surprising Revival of Equity in Early Nineteenth-Century America," *Annuaire de l'Institut
Michel Villey: L'équité et ses metamorphoses* 2 (2010): 107–27, Dalloz-IMV. Many
thanks to these journals' publishers for granting me permission to use some
of this material in this book.

Last but not least, my deepest thanks go to those without whom nothing
else would be possible. I am eternally grateful to my parents, Laure Aurelian
and Irving Kessler, for their unswerving faith in me and their extraordinary
enthusiasm for any and all of my endeavors. My husband, Adam Talcott, has
been my dearest friend and champion and a truly equal partner in all that life
has to offer. I cannot begin to thank him enough. The arrival of our beloved
children, Stella and Ari, has put a face (or rather two) on the future. As my love
for them grows each day that passes, so too does my longing for a world of
greater justice.

# Introduction

The notion that American legal procedure is adversarial (and, indeed, distinctively so) is such a given today that a statement to this effect can be found in just about every textbook and treatise on American law.[1] While some trumpet the virtues of adversarialism and others decry its vices, almost all are agreed that American procedure is quintessentially adversarial. But how precisely did this come to be? For the most part, the fact that American procedure is adversarial is assumed, such that the standard historical questions of how, when, and why are not posed. Given the vehemence of present-day arguments both for and against adversarialism—a vehemence evident in such recurring debates as those over tort reform and alternative dispute resolution—it is extraordinary that we have yet seriously to explore how the United States came to have such an adversarial legal culture.[2]

This book inquires into the origins of American adversarial legal culture and, in so doing, seeks insights not only into American legal procedure as such but also into the processes by means of which the new nation forged its identity in the turbulent decades before and during the Civil War and Reconstruction. In this crucial period, debates over the nature and purposes of procedure played a key (but now forgotten) role in defining American social structures and values and, as a result, national identity as a whole. The heated antebellum debates over procedural reform—long of interest to lawyers alone—have much to teach about how contemporary Americans made sense of (and sought to grapple with) the myriad difficulties stemming from such complex and transformative social processes as democratization, the market revolution, religious revivalism, and Reconstruction. But while much excellent work has been done in the field of procedural history, it focuses mostly on the evolution of procedural doctrine and largely fails to connect doctrinal change to external developments—other than (at best) those concerning the narrowly legal institutions (such as courts, judges, and juries) within which procedure is employed.[3] Likewise, although there is a substantial literature concerning how Americans formed a national identity in the decades following the Revolution—some of which is rightly focused on the important role of legal texts—none of it considers procedural law and practice.[4] The time is thus ripe substantially to broaden the analysis.

Toward these ends, this book traces the emergence of a national legal culture of adversarialism. Beginning with New York courts and procedure, it gradually expands its focus to consider the more far-flung regions of Florida and California, the Freedmen's Bureau courts of the Reconstruction South, and the neglected influence of European (and especially French) developments. In so doing, it weaves together the technicalities of procedural doctrine and practice with the socioeconomic, political, and cultural life of the nation. The end result is a broad-ranging exploration of the rise of American adversarial culture that encompasses such disparate voices as that of Frederick Jackson, a long-forgotten but once quite successful novelist who worried about the dangers of a seemingly new and impersonal market economy; Henry Vanderlyn, a self-aggrandizing lawyer from rural New York who imagined himself and his fellow lawyers as modern-day Ciceros responsible for the republic's very survival; and Walter Colton, a nativist evangelical minister who wrote a popular travel narrative describing his experience serving as an *alcalde* (or local judge) in Gold Rush–era California.

But before proceeding any further, we must first define the term *adversarial*. The notion of an "adversarial" legal system is itself an ideal type, constructed in opposition to the category "inquisitorial." As such, neither category represents any actual legal system (past or present) but instead reflects certain broad patterns or tendencies evident within particular legal systems. The distinction between the two ideal types was initially developed by continental jurists, who do not in fact employ the term *adversarial* but rather *accusatorial*. While a comprehensive history of the accusatorial/inquisitorial distinction has yet to be written, it appears that—dating as far back as the twelfth century—the terms were used to distinguish between criminal proceedings that had to be initiated by a private complainant (*processus per accusationem*) and those that a court official was authorized to initiate on his own volition (*processus per inquisitionem*). Much later, especially in the late nineteenth and early twentieth centuries, the distinction came to be used to contrast the

Anglo-American and continental European approaches to procedure. As deployed in this fashion, the terminology is painfully imprecise and elusive, such that, as Mirjan Damaška notes, "criteria remain uncertain for the inclusion of specific features into the adversarial and the inquisitorial types."[5]

Despite such imprecision, there is a tendency, in distinguishing between adversarial and inquisitorial systems, to focus on at least some subset of the following seven aspects of litigation, set forth in the magisterial *A History of Continental Civil Procedure*—a 1927 publication authored by leading scholars from the United States and Europe. These seven aspects of litigation include: (1) whether the court or the parties initiate the litigation and take the actions needed to move it forward; (2) whether the court or the parties determine the litigation's scope and content; (3) whether proceedings are conducted in public or in secret; (4) whether proceedings are conducted in writing or orally (and whether proof is written or oral); (5) whether the court deals directly with the parties and witnesses or indirectly, through intermediate agents; (6) whether the litigation is composed of discrete stages or (as required by the impanelment of a jury) consists of a single concentrated trial; and (7) whether the value of the proof is fixed formally by rule or determined rationally by free evaluation of the judge.[6]

Why focus on these seven aspects of litigation? An important part of the answer is that many appear to be functionally related. For example, a judge who is sufficiently powerful to initiate the litigation is likely capable of (and interested in) determining its scope and content as well. Moreover, a legal system that relies on powerful judges of this sort to control the litigation is one that would seem to require a large judicial staff in order to function effectively, since it imposes so much work on each individual judge, rather than on the parties. The large size of the judicial staff, in turn, makes possible a division of labor. Thus, individual judges, not responsible for ultimately deciding the case, can be assigned such tasks as recording the proof in writing for later review and intermediating between the deciding judge, on the one hand, and the parties and witnesses, on the other. That said, a few of these seven aspects of litigation appear to bear no necessary interrelation and are instead associated with one another primarily as a matter of historical accident. That a judge is powerful, for example, would seem to have no necessary bearing on whether the value of the proof is fixed formally by rule or determined rationally by free evaluation of the evidence. But during the key periods of medieval and early modern European legal history that provided the real-world examples underlying the formation of the two ideal types, the legal systems of continental

Europe embraced a quantitative approach to proof, such that comparative scholars later came to associate this approach with the inquisitorial type as a whole.[7]

In practice, because the models of adversarial and inquisitorial procedure are ideal types—derived from medieval and early modern European history—no procedural system today fully reflects either type. Indeed, because these types were based initially on criminal procedure, they are particularly poor approximations for civil justice in that there is no system of civil procedure in which the court is responsible for initiating the litigation. Nonetheless, we can differentiate between procedural systems on the basis of the extent to which they embody the seven features associated with either the adversarial or the inquisitorial model. And American procedure (including civil procedure) has long been recognized closely to approximate the pure adversarial type in its reliance on lawyer-controlled proceedings conducted orally and in public. Within this short list, it is the fact of lawyer control—the fact that the parties' lawyers are empowered to engage in adversarial battle, relatively unhindered by judicial supervision—that is given pride of place. Thus, a textbook account of "the American approach to adjudication" opens by stating that "[f]or more than 250 years American courts have relied upon neutral and passive factfinders to resolve lawsuits on the basis of evidence presented by contending litigants during formal adjudicatory proceedings"—a "method of resolving disputes . . . generally referred to as the adversary system."[8] The implication of these (quite typical) statements is that the United States has always had an adversarial approach to procedure and, moreover, that this approach is the only one that this country has ever adopted. In reality, however, as this book argues, the United States has had a very long history of employing not only adversarial procedure but also various forms of more judge-empowering, quasi-inquisitorial procedure—including, most importantly, the equity tradition borrowed from England but also, to a lesser extent, conciliation courts transplanted from continental Europe.

That many American states, borrowing from England, developed two distinct sets of courts and rules of law—those of common law and those of equity—is widely known, at least to lawyers. But precisely because of the assumption that American procedure is inherently adversarial, most scholars to date have failed to give serious thought to the ways in which law and equity procedure differed. Certain procedural differences between law and equity are commonly recognized, such as the fact that equity courts were endowed with distinctive remedial powers (most importantly, the power to issue injunctions and to order specific performance) and that equity pleading was not limited to the narrow forms of action that controlled at common law. But aside from such particularities, the general assumption has been (with few exceptions) that equity procedure, like common-law procedure, was (or rather must have been) fundamentally adversarial in nature.[9] A careful review of equity procedure suggests, however, that in certain fundamental respects, this body of procedure is better characterized as inquisitorial than as adversarial.

Equity procedure adopted many components of the inquisitorial type, including, most importantly, significant elements of judicial control (primarily as concerns fact-finding), a reliance on written proceedings, and a preference for undertaking these in secret. So too equity encouraged the judge to interact with the parties and witnesses through intermediate officers and composed the litigation in discrete stages. In some more limited respects, equity procedure also fixed the value of proof through formal quantitative mechanisms.[10] Indeed, the only ways in which equity procedure unmistakably followed the adversarial model was that it authorized the parties to initiate the litigation and to determine its scope and content. Given these limited but important respects in which equity embraced the adversarial model, I refer to its procedure as "quasi-inquisitorial," rather than inquisitorial.

Equity, moreover, was not the only American departure from adversarialism. From the time that the United States took possession of Florida in 1821 through the Civil War and Reconstruction, various American states and ultimately the federal government experimented with adopting some form of continental European conciliation court. This was an ideal type developed by the English jurist Jeremy Bentham based on the *bureaux de conciliation* established by the French revolutionaries in 1790. In the late eighteenth and early nineteenth centuries, several European countries and their colonies created conciliation courts. While these courts differed in a number of respects, they shared certain key features. Most importantly, they employed lay judges, selected because of their high standing within the local community, rather than because of any legal knowledge, to help reconcile disputants hailing from that same community. The expectation was that these judges would use their position of communal authority to persuade the disputants to agree to some kind of equitable, commonsense resolution in private, lawyer-free proceedings. Such conciliation proceedings did not approximate the inquisitorial model to the same extent as equity. For example, they shared with adversarialism a tendency to prioritize the oral over the written. But in the degree to which they empowered judges vis-à-vis the disputants, as well as their preference for closed-door proceedings, they came significantly closer to the inquisitorial end of the spectrum than did traditional common-law procedure.

That the United States employed such quasi-inquisitorial modes of procedure gives the lie to the oft-repeated notion that American legal culture has always been necessarily and exclusively adversarial. Indeed, it suggests that we have a procedural inheritance that in many ways looks much like the European practices that our courts and scholars have so long disdained.[11] In accounting for the origins of American adversarialism, we must therefore explain how the United States came to rely so extensively on adversarial procedures, thus abandoning (and, indeed, relegating to near-oblivion) these earlier, quasi-inquisitorial traditions. But the inquiry cannot end there. This is because there is much more to the standard refrain that American procedure is adversarial than simply a recognition that in various technical respects, it approximates the model of adversarialism. As Damaška observes, "On the Continent, lawyers continue to attribute to the opposition [between adversarial and inquisitorial systems] a more technical and descriptive meaning," whereas "[t]o Anglo-Americans . . . the two concepts are suffused with value judgments." In particular, he notes that "the adversary system provides tropes of a rhetoric extolling the virtues of liberal administration of justice in contrast to an antipodal authoritarian process."[12] As this suggests, the notion of an adversarial system of procedure extends beyond a particular set of procedural devices to include a broader array of political and social values intertwined with those devices. It is the complex intersection of legal doctrine, institutionally grounded practices, and social and political values that together form the American adversarial legal culture whose origins this book seeks to trace.

What are the "value judgments" that inhere in the notion of adversarialism? As Damaška observes, there is a longstanding discourse dating back to the English Revolution of the seventeenth century that associates key features of the common-law procedural tradition—including, most importantly, the right to a jury trial—with a governmental regime based on (and respectful of) liberty. When in the late nineteenth and early twentieth centuries the adversarial/inquisitorial distinction came to be used to differentiate between the Anglo-American and continental European legal systems, this inherited notion that the common law is liberty-promoting was grafted onto the category of adversarial procedure. But the promotion of liberty is only one of the political and social values with which adversarialism has been at times associated. In the American context, in particular, adversarialism also became part and parcel of a grand narrative of American exceptionalism. Pursuant to this prevalent discourse, the roots of adversarialism are acknowledged to derive from the English common-law tradition, but it was in the United States that they flourished most fully. From this perspective, the "competitive individualism" that underlies the United States' distinctively anti-statist, market-based society also contributed to its uniquely adversarial approach to litigation—though precisely how, when, and why this linkage occurred is left unexplored.[13]

While there is an established literature examining the origins of the idea of American exceptionalism, it has focused almost exclusively on claims concerning the country's supposedly unique political and socioeconomic underpinnings. As Jack P. Greene shows, assertions that Americans enjoy greater freedom and prosperity than their old-world counterparts and that they live in a society in which free (white) men were always formally equal under the law (rather than a hierarchical, corporatist order of ranks) date back well into the colonial period.[14] But the idea of *American legal exceptionalism* is one whose history—like that of adversarialism itself—has yet to be recounted. To tell the story of the rise of adversarialism in the United States is thus not only to describe the origins of particular procedural devices (many of which were borrowed from or developed independently in England) but also to explain how adversarial procedure as such came to be viewed as a distinguishing feature of American national identity—one distinct from, but nonetheless related to, prevailing notions of American political and socioeconomic exceptionalism.

Accordingly, we must stop accounting for adversarialism through ahistorical appeals to presumably innate American qualities like "competitive individualism" or by reference to the broad category of "Anglo-American" procedure (with the attendant implication that American procedure is necessarily adversarial because of its English, common-law roots). We must instead focus on the historical particularities of the American experience. This does not, of course, mean that English history is irrelevant. To the contrary, this book carefully examines the institutional structures and practices that New York Chancery inherited from England and touches on significant procedural developments in nineteenth-century England. So too, it argues that one important strand feeding into the nineteenth-century American embrace of adversarialism was the common law itself—especially the discourse dating to the seventeenth-century English Revolution, pursuant to which the English common law was proclaimed by parliamentarians and their Puritan supporters to be distinctively liberty-promoting, as compared with the Roman-canon law tradition that they associated with monarchists and "papists." That said, the American turn to adversarialism reshaped this longstanding discourse in important ways, expanding it into a new theory about the right kind of (universally applicable, adversarial) procedure. As this suggests, this book's forays into English legal history are deployed in service of studying the American experience—and broad generalizations about the Anglo-American tradition as such are studiously avoided.[15]

In inquiring into the origins of American adversarialism, we must confront, as an initial matter, the problem of method. For several decades now, legal historians have been engaged in a heated debate about the nature and causes of legal change and, relatedly, the relationship between law and society. On the one hand, internalists insist that legal change is primarily a product of developments internal to law and legal institutions as such. From this perspective, if we wish to understand developments in American procedure, we should immerse ourselves in legal treatises, court records, and the like with the goal of examining how changes in legal ideas and/or practices emerged within a largely self-enclosed system. In contrast, externalists believe that law and society are inextricably linked, such that there is no way to understand developments in law without relating them to socioeconomic, political, and cultural change more generally. While the dominant approach to legal history within the United States was once internalist, this began to change from the early 1970s onward, as the socio-legal approach, pioneered by James Willard Hurst in the 1950s, became increasingly influential. Externalism now reigns within the field as a whole, though the history of procedure remains in this respect an outlier. Much of the leading scholarship on the history of procedure is internalist, focusing on the complex interrelationship between procedural doctrine and legal institutions like the bench and the bar.[16] And while there are a number of important works that approach issues related to procedure from a more externalist perspective, these tend not to focus directly on procedure as such but instead on such peripheral, though important, topics as the legal profession or the law of evidence.[17]

Underlying the ongoing methodological debate is a powerful assumption, too rarely articulated or defended, that scholars must of necessity choose between the internalist and externalist perspectives. But why is such a choice necessary—or even (at least in some circumstances) appropriate? The underlying premise of this book is that neither the internalist nor the externalist approach alone can capture the entirety of the ways in which law evolves over time. The internalists are correct that there are aspects of legal ideas, institutions, and practices that are logically and structurally interrelated such that, for heuristic purposes, they can be usefully conceived as constituting a relatively enclosed, interconnected system. A system of procedure, in particular, is constructed as a set of interrelated doctrinal practices (ranging from modes of pleading to fact-finding to remediation) and institutions (including not least courts and the legal profession), all of which must come to bear in the process of adjudication. A change in any one component part is thus likely to ramify throughout the system. At the same time, it is clear that the doctrinal practices that constitute a procedural system do not emerge ex nihilo but are instead produced by particular persons in particular socioeconomic, political, and cultural contexts. These practices, moreover, are themselves purposefully designed to operate within particular contexts—namely, within particular sets of courts, as deployed by particular kinds of actors to resolve particular kinds of substantive legal claims (and all within a particular time and place). To understand procedural development, it is thus necessary to attend seriously to its interrelation with the broad range of people, ideas, and institutions implicated in both the production and application of procedure. And as we will see, in the context of the nineteenth-century United States, this inquiry touches on such disparate phenomena as conceptions of lawyering, political party politics, debates over the role of government in market-based society, and the proper place of race and racial status in shaping social and economic relations.

The insufficiency on its own of either the internalist or externalist approach is suggested by the existing scholarship concerning nineteenth-century American procedural reform, including especially codification. Focused largely on explaining the origins of the Field Code of Procedure of 1848, this literature posits two main accounts—one functionalist and the other materialist—neither of which is entirely satisfying. The traditional Whiggish or functionalist account adopts a largely internalist perspective, suggesting that the Field Code and its merger of the separate systems of law and equity represented the rationalization of procedure. The code, in other words, was a functional response to the problem of the costs and delays generated by existing procedural devices—such as those inherent in equity's written approach to the taking of testimony and in the jurisdictional conflict stemming from the existence of two distinct court systems and bodies of procedure.[18] But as revisionist critics have powerfully argued, the depiction of procedural reform as "rationalization" obscures the interests of those individuals—mostly lawyers—who were ultimately responsible for it.[19] In so doing, the traditional account suggests that there was a necessary and obvious path toward procedural reform—one leading to the code (and its oral, adversarial approach to procedure) and thus to the present day. There were, however, other possible paths. Indeed, as we will see, the primary reform advocated by New York governors and legislators from the mid-1830s onward was to augment the number of equity judges (thereby strengthening equity's quasi-inquisitorial foundations). To accept the notion that the code and its embrace of oral, adversarial procedure constituted rationalization is thus to avoid the essential question of how contemporaries (and especially contemporary lawyers) came to view adversarialism as the embodiment of procedural progress. Addressing this question, in turn, requires serious engagement with the multiple (including nonlegal) factors shaping lawyers' (and other actors') motivations and values.

In contrast to the traditional, Whiggish narrative, the revisionist account is more externalist, insisting on lawyers' professional and especially material self-interest. Rightly characterizing the traditional narrative and its theory of rationalization as an uncritical embrace of the arguments advanced by those antebellum lawyers advocating on behalf of codification, revisionist scholars have insisted, to the contrary, that the procedural reform embodied in the Field Code was simply a feint. In their view, antebellum lawyers adopted the mantra of procedural reform in order to distract the public's attention from the profession's failure to engage in meaningful, substantive reform of the law—of the kind that would have resulted, for example, in a redistribution of resources.[20] But the revisionist assertion that the legal profession's focus on procedure was a ruse assumes (like the Whiggish account that it criticizes) that the actual content of reform—namely, the code and its turn to adversarialism—was somehow a given. In so doing, it ignores the ways in which factors internal to the legal system may have shaped procedural development while positing an externalist account of lawyers' interests and incentives that is simplistic to the point of caricature.

In order to develop a richer, more satisfactory understanding of nineteenth-century procedural reform, we must move beyond the Whiggish and revisionist narratives of the Field Code, seeking to attend to developments both internal and external to the law as well as to the complicated interrelations between these. As concerns the internalist perspective in particular, our starting point must be to recognize that it is long past time to move beyond a fixation with codification as the defining feature of nineteenth-century procedural reform.[21] From the vantage point of the mid- and late nineteenth century rather than the present, the striking thing about the code is not that it undertook codification of the law but that it recognized and gave content to a theretofore unknown entity: procedure. Put differently, the code marked the invention of procedure as a distinct, coherent category, defined in antithesis to the substantive law.

That the category of procedure did not exist in any meaningful way before the mid-nineteenth century is difficult to conceive—and perhaps for this reason has received no scholarly attention. But while significant thought had been devoted previously to particular mechanisms that we would now characterize as procedural, it was only in this period that the overarching category of procedure came to be developed as a crucial and distinct component of any legal system. Indeed, until the late nineteenth century, standard American legal dictionaries did not even include the term *procedure*, containing entries instead for the more traditional (writ-based) notions of *pleading* and *practice*. As the United States Supreme Court observed in 1883, "[t]he word 'procedure,' as a law term, is not well understood, and is not found at all in Bouvier's Law Dictionary, the best work of the kind in this country."[22] Moreover, the 1897 edition of this dictionary, in finally defining *procedure*, was careful to emphasize that "[t]he term is, with respect to its present use, rather a modern one."[23]

While procedure as such came to be recognized as a distinct body of law only well into the nineteenth century, the processes leading to this development had deeper roots. During the late eighteenth and early nineteenth centuries, the common law was gradually transformed from a mass of procedural writs, granting the right to file suit under particular sets of circumstances, into a coherent system of substantive rights, grouped into such categories as contract and tort. The end result was that substantive rights under the law came to appear as distinct from the particular procedural mechanisms allowing for recovery—a notion that was then popularized through Jeremy Bentham's influential writings to this effect. So too, the disentangling of procedure from substance contributed to the emergence of a new, more purposive conception of the common law by means of which law came to seem increasingly like a tool for the promotion of particular policy objectives.[24]

How precisely this transformation from writ to right came to pass has been a subject of longstanding scholarly debate. Scholars like William Nelson and Daniel Hulsebosch emphasize the complexity and technicality of pleading under the traditional writ system and the resulting need for litigants to rely on counsel trained in such "legal science." This, in turn, resulted in widespread complaint that the system was overly expensive and suited only to the interests of lawyers. From this perspective, the effort to simplify pleadings was intimately linked to the emergence of substantive categories of law—either because (per Nelson) simplified pleadings made the underlying substantive law more readily apparent or because (per Hulsebosch) the emerging substantive conception of the law made the writ system appear unnecessary and costly. In contrast, John Witt argues that tort law in particular developed primarily as a result of efforts to reconcile the new problem of industrial accidents (and the resulting rise of nonnegligent harms to faultless victims) with the era's dominant free labor ideology.[25]

But while legal historians have devoted many pages to examining the rise of substantive law categories like contract and tort, little if any attention has been paid to the procedural side of this equation. If the separating out of writ from right meant the discovery of substantive law, then so too it meant the discovery of procedure. According to the now well-established historiography, lawyers who learned that writs were not inviolable and that adjudication served to frame substantive rights discovered the key role played by courts in framing such rights and thus in making policy. But what did this mean for their thinking about procedure? It is a central theme of this book that the nineteenth-century rise of the category of procedure created a set of conceptual (and practical) problems that contemporary lawyers and policymakers had little choice but to address. Confronted with the notion that there was a body of procedural law that necessarily operated alongside the substantive law that they were then in the process of developing, they asked themselves what the content of this law ought to be—an endeavor that required them to grapple with technical minutiae, but also to make important judgments of value and purpose.

As reflected in English legal thought to this day, the rise of the substance/procedure divide would lead to the view in Bentham's own country that procedure was merely the handmaiden of substance—a mechanism for greasing the wheels but nothing more. Nineteenth-century Americans, however, firmly rejected this approach.[26] Indeed, it was in the antebellum period, when lawyers first addressed the problem of defining procedure as such, that the distinctive American love affair with adversarial procedure took firm root. From this perspective, the true significance of the Field Code was not that it initiated a process of reform, which, as we will see, it did not, or even that it was a code. It was instead that it gave clear, legal recognition to the emerging concept of procedure—and that it did so by identifying procedure with the oral, adversarial tradition of the common law. The invention of procedure as a category was thus fundamentally intertwined with the embrace of adversarialism.

To understand how this came to be, I begin by recovering the neglected tradition of equity procedure, as developed in New York Chancery—the new nation's leading and highly influential court of equity. An examination of equity procedure, both in the books and in action, reveals that in fundamental ways this was a quasi-inquisitorial system. But as I then show, beginning around 1817, chancery came to embrace core aspects of the common law's adversarial mode of procedure, such that the later-enacted Field Code and its merger of law and equity were all but faits accomplis.

In explaining equity's turn to the oral and adversarial, I commence with a largely internalist story, arguing that there were certain inherited structural features of New York Chancery—including, most importantly, a disjunction between its quasi-inquisitorial logic and lack of a sizable professional staff—that predisposed it to instability, especially through lawyerly manipulation. These structural features alone, however, are insufficient to explain the court's early and mid-nineteenth-century turn to oral and adversarial procedure in that they were a feature of English Chancery dating back many centuries. Also important were socioeconomic and political developments—including the rise of an increasingly robust market economy and the growing democratization of politics—that encouraged more litigation, thus putting greater pressure on chancery's limited staff. But if such developments help explain why the reform of equity was vital, they do not in themselves account for the particular (oral and adversarial) direction of such reform. Toward this end, I point to a set of more immediate and contingent developments, once again internalist in nature. In particular, I trace how small changes in the approach to taking testimony before chancery officials known as masters ended up having unintended systemic consequences, leading ultimately to equity's complete adoption of the oral, adversarial methods of the common law.

But importantly, even such internalist change cannot be divorced from the broader socioeconomic, political, and cultural context. It was practicing lawyers themselves who introduced changes into equity procedure on a bottom-up, case-by-case basis. A complete account of equity's turn to oral, adversarial procedure must therefore grapple with the question of lawyers' motivations. These were, as it turns out, multiple and complex—including not only a strategic desire to win litigation but also a powerful impulse to pursue both professional and political authority. The period from the nation's founding through well into the nineteenth century was marked by a pervasive and severe public animosity against the legal profession, which led lawyers to search for ways to justify their claims to a continued professional monopoly. Drawing on the prevalent political discourse of civic republicanism and the contemporary obsession with classical oratory, they thus sought to develop procedure in ways that would augment both their professional standing and their political power. This effort, I argue, led lawyers to embrace the common law's oral, adversarial procedures—a set of devices that, quite unlike those of quasi-inquisitorial equity, enabled them to undertake grand public performances in defense of civic virtue.

Having examined how New York Chancery came to embrace the oral, adversarial techniques of the common law, I then turn to explore the broader values with which these techniques came to be invested. In so doing, I consider the ways that procedure implicates the interests and values not only of lawyers but also of nonlawyers. Especially to the extent that procedure is deployed in courts open to the public, lawyers have an incentive to use it in ways that resonate with the values and aspirations of the broader lay public. But more fundamentally, as anthropologists have long recognized, methods of dispute resolution—and thus procedure—provide an important window into a society's key ordering principles.[27] Such methods draw, in other words, on deeply rooted nonlegal values concerning questions like the optimal extent (and nature) of conflict as well as the sources of authority requisite to attain a socially legitimate resolution of the dispute. With an eye toward exploring the broader values with which nineteenth-century Americans (including nonlawyers) came to associate adversarialism, I examine an important but previously forgotten set of debates over whether to establish European conciliation courts. These debates, I argue, developed in such a way that, during a number of key moments, advocacy of adversarialism became intimately linked with demands for a largely unregulated market and the preservation of white supremacy.

Those who advocated for the establishment of conciliation courts, including many nonlawyers, hoped to deploy these institutions for the purpose of moderating the worst excesses of market-based society—especially in the context of labor relations. Through sustained efforts, these advocates achieved some victories in the decades just prior to the Civil War, including the enactment of various state constitutional provisions authorizing legislatures to create conciliation courts and a number of statutes that did so. But despite these accomplishments, such institutions did not take meaningful root in the antebellum United States. Opponents of conciliation courts successfully rejected them as incompatible with the American commitment to both political and market freedom. A nation that was distinctively liberty-oriented and market-based, they insisted, was one that employed a distinctively adversarial approach to social, economic, and (perhaps most importantly) labor relations—and, by implication, to legal procedure as well. In this way, arguments in favor of adversarialism came to be bound up with efforts to thwart government intervention in market relations.

The Freedmen's Bureau courts established throughout the Reconstruction South marked a significant partial exception to the otherwise prevailing failure of European-style conciliation courts to take root in American soil. As such, they constituted an important locus for debating the role of race and racial status in the formation of American labor (and, more generally, social) relations. Created to help integrate the newly freed African-Americans into Southern society and to reconfigure the latter on free labor foundations, the Bureau courts were understood by prominent Northern architects of Reconstruction to be a kind of conciliation court. White Southerners (and their Northern Democratic allies) appealed, in turn, to the defense of adversarialism developed in the years before the Civil War—especially in the debates over conciliation courts—to denounce the Bureau and its courts as fundamentally un-American. With the Supreme Court's decision in *Ex parte Milligan* disallowing the use of military tribunals to try civilians and the subsequent ratification of the Fourteenth Amendment, their campaign to dismantle the Bureau courts and to preserve their own racial supremacy would prove victorious. The restoration of adversarial justice would thereafter be framed as a triumph of due process.

In developing this account of the origins of American adversarialism, I draw on a varied and broad primary source base, encompassing both published and archival materials. These include the archival holdings of New York Chancery, published case reports, legal treatises, legal dictionaries, statutory law, judge-made procedural rules, lawyers' diaries (both published and unpublished), lawyers' biographies and autobiographies, newspaper reports, Gold Rush–era travel narratives, novels, and the records of Freedmen's Bureau agents. So too, I read these primary sources against a wide-ranging secondary literature concerning not only legal developments but also such key socioeconomic, political, and cultural developments as civic republicanism, the Albany Regency, the market revolution, religious revivalism, and postbellum Reconstruction.

The time frame covered extends roughly from 1800 through 1877. The turn of the century marked the rise of Jeffersonian democracy and an increasingly dominant political party system. These developments would significantly influence the staffing of chancery offices. At the same time, they sparked a host of demands for access to justice and critiques of elitist rule that would together serve to undermine chancery's legitimacy, especially its top-down, quasi-inquisitorial approach to procedure. On the back end, 1877 witnessed the close of Reconstruction and thus the definitive demise of the Freedmen's Bureau courts and their short-lived stand against adversarialism. In addition, this period marked a turning point in American legal culture more broadly. In the years after the Civil War and Reconstruction, corporations grew in wealth and influence, and the administrative state expanded to regulate the new challenges created by industrial society. As a result, the multi-purpose, litigation-focused lawyers of the antebellum period—working alone or in partnership with at most one or two others—were increasingly replaced with new kinds of specialist lawyers operating in large firms or government departments and prized less for their skills as litigators than as advisors and negotiators.[28]

As this time frame indicates, this is a book about the origins of American adversarial legal culture rather than a complete account of its history. As such, it extends back much further in time than the small body of scholarship to date that treats American adversarialism not as a given but instead as a product of particular historical developments. This scholarship—including notably the work of Robert Kagan and John Witt—emphasizes the centrality of the period immediately after the Second World War. More particularly, these scholars suggest that in the wake of the Great Depression and World War II, the United States was unique in translating public demands for activist government (common to much of the democratic, industrialized world) into adversarial procedural rights.[29] But as important as the post–World War II period was in the development of adversarialism today, the roots of the United States' distinctively adversarial legal culture lie in a much earlier period—one that, despite the changes wrought by intervening years, left a profound legacy. This book explores these earlier, nineteenth-century roots, locating the turn to adversarialism in a set of developments both internal and external to the law, including deep-rooted structural and cultural inheritances and more immediate and contingent occurrences.

It bears emphasis that, even as concerns the period covered, this book is not a complete account of the history of American adversarial legal culture for the further reason that it focuses exclusively on civil rather than criminal procedure. As between the two modes of procedure, it was criminal procedure that underlay the initial accusatorial/inquisitorial distinction. But in many ways, it is civil procedure that best embodies the adversarial ideal in that it presumes a battle fought between private and thus (at least theoretically) co-equal litigants—a battle in which the state is implicated only insofar that it seeks, through the figure of the judge, to mediate the dispute and enforce the law. Moreover, as a historical matter, some of the key nineteenth-century debates giving rise to adversarial procedure—debates that are the subject of this book—focused on civil, rather than criminal procedure, including in particular the procedure employed in chancery and in European conciliation courts. I make no claim, however, that these debates were the sum total of the developments that gave rise to an adversarial legal culture or that valuable insights might not also be gained from a study of criminal procedure.

As concerns geography, the book's primary focus is on New York but extends across the country as a whole—and even, to some extent, across the Atlantic. The reason for concentrating on New York is that the state exercised enormous socioeconomic, political, cultural, and legal influence in the antebellum period. In all these respects, New York came to fulfill the ambitions implicit in its late eighteenth-century moniker, the Empire State, and thus cannot be said to be representative of the nation as a whole. It is of interest, to the contrary, precisely because of the disproportionately significant role that it played in influencing developments elsewhere. As New York City became the country's leading center of commerce and banking, the state as a whole experienced extraordinary industrial development and rapidly expanding rates of urbanization and population growth. Likewise, nineteenth-century New York gave rise to many of the nation's leading newspapers and was the birthplace and longtime home of some of the most important literary figures of the era, including Walt Whitman and Herman Melville. So too, law that originated in New York spread outward to the rest of the country, such that a broad array of legal arenas, ranging from constitutional law to corporate law, came to be shaped by developments there.[30] Perhaps nowhere was this more the case than in the realm of procedure. Equity took root in American legal culture in no small part because of the influence of nineteenth-century New York Chancery and its leading light, Chancellor James Kent. Moreover, the Field Code of Procedure of 1848, which marked the decline of equity as a distinctive quasi-inquisitorial tradition, was itself copied by numerous jurisdictions (including many that had never known distinct systems of law and equity), leading to their common characterization as "code states."[31] In contrast to these code states, the federal courts ostensibly avoided the merger of law and equity until the enactment of the Federal Rules of Civil Procedure in 1938. But the Federal Rules of Equity and the case law interpreting these were profoundly shaped by developments in New York, such that as early as the mid-nineteenth century, federal equity had adopted core aspects of oral, adversarial procedure.[32]

That said, while the book opens with a focus on New York, the final chapters extend much further afield, considering debates over conciliation courts (and Freedmen's Bureau courts) that took place throughout much of the country—including in the newly acquired territories of Florida and California and thereafter across the Reconstruction-era North and South. As these chapters emphasize, the New York debates over procedural ordering were but one component of a much larger national discussion. And because contemporaries expressly framed this discussion by reference to European legal practice, we must also make a brief foray beyond the country's borders and across the Atlantic. Indeed, ironically, despite deep-rooted assumptions that adversarialism lies at the core of an exceptionalist American legal identity—assumptions whose origins this book traces—the reality is that our procedural culture has been influenced by seemingly alien European traditions.

The path connecting the late nineteenth-century zenith of adversarialism with which this book ends to the present day was in no way direct. But the developments traced below contributed in important ways to making American legal culture today distinctively adversarial. Moreover, the price that we have paid for this inheritance has been high. Although there are undoubted virtues to adversarialism, our excessive commitment to adversarial process has contributed to a crisis in access to justice, even while undermining the values of autonomy and publicity that as devotees of adversarialism we claim to be committed. I thus conclude with a brief reflection on the non-adversarial possibilities suggested by our own forgotten history of equity and conciliation courts. Whatever the precise path forward, the starting point, I argue, must be to abandon our longstanding (but constructed and contingent) assumption that due process and adversarial procedure are somehow one and the same.

# 1 • The "Natural Elevation" of Equity

## Quasi-Inquisitorial Procedure and the Early Nineteenth-Century Resurgence of Equity

Toward the end of the eighteenth century, an observer of the American legal landscape might well have predicted that the English tradition of equity as a distinct body of law and courts was soon to disappear in the newly established republic—along with other legal relics inherited from England's feudal and monarchical past, such as primogeniture and the fee tail. While courts of chancery had been established in several colonies (including most notably New York and South Carolina), these had long been viewed with suspicion. This wariness was a legacy of the seventeenth-century English Revolution, during which the conflict between parliamentarians and royalists manifested itself, in part, in an institutional struggle between courts of common law and courts of equity.[1]

Embracing the common-law courts as bastions of England's ancient constitution and thus its citizens' immemorial, customary rights (including rights to sovereignty), parliamentarians depicted equity courts as emanating from—and therefore tending slavishly to serve—the royal will.[2] This inherited notion that courts of equity promoted tyranny was reinforced in colonial America by the common practice of appointing the royal governor as chancellor—namely, the head of the Court of Chancery and thus the colony's primary equity judge. As animosity toward England and its monarchy increased in the decades leading up to the American Revolution, so too did enmity toward equity. Reflecting such enmity, the landmark Judiciary Act of 1789—in which Congress established the framework for the federal judiciary—provided that all federal courts were to conduct proceedings (and in particular, the taking of testimony) in the manner of courts of common law, rather than of equity.[3]

Surprisingly, while the fate of equity in the early republic seemed anything but rosy, this distinctive legal tradition experienced a remarkable rebirth in the first decades of the nineteenth century. Indeed, as we will see, by the mid-1830s, New York Chancery—the country's leading court of equity—had a docket that was so overburdened that complaints of delay were rampant. Admittedly, this renaissance was both limited in scope and short-lived. Some colonies and later states never developed independent, freestanding courts of equity. Moreover, among those that did, nearly all abolished them, most by the early twentieth century.[4] But however limited and brief, the renaissance of equity—especially in the highly influential state of New York—had profound consequences for the later development of the law throughout the nation. Even states that never created separate courts of chancery eventually adopted a great many principles of equity law and practice over the course of the nineteenth century—and in so doing looked in no small part to the achievements of New York Chancery.[5] Those states, including New York itself, that ultimately eliminated independent chancery courts opted nonetheless to retain many important elements of both the substantive and procedural law of equity (including, not least, the injunction and fact-pleading). As concerns procedure in particular, equity's powerful legacy is perhaps most evident today in the Federal Rules of Civil Procedure, which have been adopted as the basis of state rules in more than half the states and exert significant (though perhaps declining) influence in many others. As Stephen Subrin argues, these widely applied rules can be read in certain respects as evidence of "equity['s] triumph[]" over the common law.[6]

So how did the long-disfavored tradition of equity come to take such firm root? Surprisingly, given both the importance of equity and the well-established literature documenting colonial and early American animosity toward it, this question has received very little scholarly attention. To the limited extent that it has been examined, the explanation offered has been largely functionalist, emphasizing the needs of a growing commercial society.[7] Pursuant to this account, equity was of limited use in the early colonial period but became increasingly vital from about the mid-eighteenth century onward as a mechanism for facilitating commercial development.

That the period from the mid-eighteenth through the mid-nineteenth century was one of tremendous socioeconomic change is beyond cavil. The late colonial and early national periods witnessed a number of significant legal and economic developments that were in many ways precursors to the even more dramatic transformations experienced in the early to mid-nineteenth century. These included, perhaps most importantly, the increasing commodification of agricultural products and landed property and the rise of negotiable instruments, both of which played an important role in facilitating economic development, including what historians have described as a consumer revolution in the mid- to late eighteenth century.[8] As British merchants and manufacturers flooded American markets with large quantities of clothing, ceramics, glassware, and the like, a growing number of middling Americans were encouraged to purchase items once reserved for the elite—and, increasingly, to do so on credit.

Following on the heels of this consumer revolution and the rapid expansion in credit that it generated was what the historian Charles Sellers termed the "market revolution"—an interrelated series of changes in modes of production, employment relations, consumer practices, and methods of transportation that swept across the United States between the close of the War of 1812 and that of the U.S.-Mexican War. More recently, a number of historians, particularly Daniel Walker Howe, have challenged Sellers's moniker for this period, observing that a market-oriented economy had in fact already emerged, along with the mid- to late eighteenth-century consumer revolution. But while it is important to recognize the existence of continuities that tend to be obscured by the term *revolution*, there is nonetheless widespread agreement that this was a period that witnessed dramatic economic (and technological) change—resulting in the development of what Howe himself has called "The New Economy."[9] Spared the full brunt of English competition during the War of 1812 and the embargo preceding it, domestic production—particularly of textiles and shoes—grew extensively in the second decade of the nineteenth century and thereafter. This growth in domestic production was fueled by new methods of manufacturing, including the development of the factory system as typified by the newly established mill towns of New England like Lowell. Also of much importance was the emergence of the "sweating system," pursuant to which specified tasks were delegated to a dispersed group of workers, operating out of their homes, who produced component parts that were then gathered for subsequent assembly. Such developments in manufacturing were greatly facilitated by a series of remarkable transformations in technologies of transportation. These included, most significantly, the rapid diffusion of steamboats during the first decade of the nineteenth century, the explosion of canals on which they could operate (beginning with the 1819 opening of the first segment of the Erie Canal), and the emergence of the first railroads in the 1830s.[10]

In this increasingly complex and interconnected, market-driven economy, chancery and its distinctive procedure proved especially useful. Consider, for example, the sorts of chancery proceedings identified in 1838 as prototypical by Theodore Sedgwick Jr., a prominent Jacksonian lawyer. These included proceedings to "restrain the holder [of a promissory note] from fraudulently negotiating it," an issue vital to the burgeoning law of negotiable instruments and to the expanding credit market that these instruments served to fuel. Likewise, it was to chancery that creditors frequently looked for assistance in obtaining payment, including "payment out of . . . property mortgaged" and payment on "a judgment rendered in an action at law." So too, Sedgwick explained, chancery would enjoin a "co-partner . . . from misapply[ing] the joint property," a matter of great importance to business partners and thus of much significance in a period of tremendous commercial and industrial growth.[11] Indeed, as we will see, one of the reasons that chancery came under such withering public criticism from about the mid-1830s onward was precisely that it was so widely viewed as an institution in service of an increasingly wealthy commercial elite.

But while it is surely true that various claims and devices available in equity were useful for facilitating market development, there is good reason to believe that a purely functionalist account of its early nineteenth-century resurgence is incomplete. There were, after all, commercially successful states like Massachusetts and Pennsylvania that steadfastly resisted developing a distinct equity system. While Massachusetts incorporated aspects of equity law and procedure into its ordinary common-law courts, it did so on a piecemeal basis. And until Pennsylvania granted some of its common-law courts broad equity powers in 1836, it regularly deployed common-law actions in service of what were historically deemed equitable claims. So too, it developed common-law writs that served as the functional equivalents of such key equitable remedies as the injunction.[12] As this suggests, market success, while likely facilitated by equity, did not hinge on the embrace of the institution of chancery and the full panoply of equity rules and procedures. Explaining the rebirth of equity in early nineteenth-century America—at a moment when the deep-rooted animosity against it was powerfully reinvigorated by the Revolution—thus requires us to look beyond functional needs as such. We must also ask in whose eyes equity came to be viewed as desirable and why. Who, in other words, advocated for equity in the early American republic? And what led them to do so?

There were two figures above all others who took the lead in promoting the rebirth of equity: James Kent, chancellor of the New York Court of Chancery, and Joseph Story, associate justice of the United States Supreme Court. Two of the most celebrated jurists of the nineteenth century, these men made much of their contribution to American legal thought and practice through their work on equity. And while an important component of what drove their admiration of equity was their commitment to promoting the new country's commercial and economic growth, their fascination with chancery and its procedure cannot be pigeonholed in this manner.

As early as his own lifetime, Kent was widely credited with establishing equity on American soil, primarily as a result of his efforts as chancellor in shaping New York's highly influential Court of Chancery. Story, who played a key role in transmitting Kent's vision of equity across the nation (and beyond), was hailed as his natural successor—and thus in many respects, as a second founding father of the American equity tradition. However, such claims that American equity owed its existence entirely to the efforts of these two jurists were clearly overstated. Indeed, there is ample evidence that well before Kent's chancellorship, New York had already embraced key aspects of the traditional English model of equity. So too, there were states, like South Carolina and New Jersey, that had courts of chancery dating back to the colonial period and thus long preceding Kent.[13] But as it developed from the early nineteenth century onward, equity was indelibly marked by the influence of Kent and Story, who both played a decisive role in conceptualizing, systematizing, and most importantly, justifying it. At the same time, by so successfully identifying the nature and purposes of equity—and by aligning these with a particular elitist vision of social and political authority—these jurists helped to usher in a backlash against it that would soon thereafter contribute to the demise of core aspects of its distinctive procedural tradition.

## The English Treatise Tradition

The roots of New York Chancery lay in English practice, as transmitted to the new nation through an extensive treatise literature. And it was on precisely this literature that Kent and Story relied in developing their own highly influential model of an elitist, judge-empowering system of equity. In drafting his opinions as chancellor, Kent cited a number of different treatises, including most importantly, Geoffrey Gilbert's *Forum Romanum*,[14] Joseph Harrison's *The Practice of the Court of Chancery*,[15] Henry Maddock's *A Treatise on the Principles and Practice of the High Court of Chancery*,[16] and George Cooper's *A Treatise of Pleading on the Equity Side of the High Court of Chancery*.[17]

Published posthumously in 1758, *Forum Romanum* was written by Sir Geoffrey Gilbert—chief baron of the English Exchequer from 1725–1726 and known primarily for drafting the first major English treatise on the law of evidence. *Forum Romanum* was the starting point for all of the nineteenth-century treatises on equity, and especially those on equity pleading and practice. Indeed, as late as 1874, the editor of an American edition of the treatise proclaimed that, while more recent works on equity pleading and practice had come to be written, "[y]et the work of Gilbert has maintained the reputation of the highest authority down to the present day, and is referred to by the ablest writers on equity procedure, as well as by the most learned judges in their judicial opinions in chancery."[18] In practice, Harrison's, Maddock's, and Cooper's treatises were more commonly cited—perhaps in part because the first two of these appeared in American editions early in the nineteenth century, whereas Gilbert's work was not issued by an American publisher until 1874.[19] Notably, however, these more popular treatises—and especially Harrison's—relied heavily on Gilbert, paraphrasing (indeed, often copying wholesale) vast portions of his text.

As suggested by its title, Gilbert's treatise starts from the premise that equity procedure—and, in particular, the procedure followed by chancery, England's very first equity court—was based on that of the Roman-canon, civil law tradition. A great deal of the book is essentially an elaboration of its second chapter: "A Comparison of the Proceedings in the Civil and Canon Law With Those of the Courts of Chancery."[20] Whether and to what extent the substantive and procedural law of equity was influenced by the Roman-canon tradition has been a subject of longstanding controversy among scholars, but most today agree that at a minimum, chancery's "written procedure, as developed since the late fourteenth century, had a Romano-canonical inspiration."[21] For our purposes, the crucial point is that at the time that Gilbert's treatise was published and throughout much of the nineteenth century, it was commonly believed that equity was indeed modeled on the Roman-canon tradition. This belief dated at least as far back as the English Revolution, at which time the Roman-canon origins of equity were deployed as evidence of its alleged tendency to promote slavish subservience to royal (and "popish") authority. In line with this orthodoxy, Gilbert asserted that equity procedure derived from the Roman-canon law and was therefore radically different from the procedure applied in England's common-law courts. The emergence of English Chancery as a court of equity, he argued, "hath introduced a new process, and a new manner of trial, totally before unheard of."[22]

What precisely was this new manner of process and trial? Not surprisingly, given the view that equity emerged from the Roman-canon tradition, Gilbert described equity procedure in terms that emphasized the relative power of judges vis-à-vis lawyers—as, in short, quasi-inquisitorial. In thus depicting the quasi-inquisitorial nature of equity, Gilbert focused particular attention on equity's approach to trying questions of fact and in particular to gathering the evidence (and especially witness testimony) necessary for this purpose.

As described by Gilbert and later treatise writers, a suit in equity commenced when the plaintiff filed a bill of complaint, which required the defendant to appear and file an answer under oath. Thereafter, if the plaintiff sought to deny the defendant's factual assertions and to require that these be proved, he would file a "replication" or reply. The case was then deemed "at issue," and the parties could begin to gather proof—and, in particular, to examine witnesses. The party calling a witness would draft written interrogatories and the opposing party cross-interrogatories. The court would then appoint an officer responsible for presenting the written interrogatories and cross-interrogatories to the witnesses. If the witness lived in or near London, this officer was one of two examiners who worked as permanent court staff. In contrast, if the witnesses resided in the countryside outside of London, the court appointed private individuals, designated "commissioners," to take the testimony on a case-by-case basis—presumably because it was inefficient to require the busy examiners to travel to the witnesses. In either case, the court officer was required to read the interrogatories to the witnesses and then have his clerk record the answers. These answers were not to be taken down word for word but in a streamlined form, intended to eliminate extraneous commentary and redundancies. As summarized by Richard Newcombe Gresley, the author of a leading 1837 treatise on the law of evidence as applied in equity, "[a]fter hearing the interrogatory read over, the witness often enters into a long detail, part of which is, and part is not, admissible under the interrogatory; and from that narrative the examiner has to extract and shape a full, but pertinent answer to the questions on the record."[23]

After thus taking testimony, the examiner or commissioners would read the recorded narrative to the witness for approval. If the witness claimed that an error had been made in recording the testimony, then the examiner or commissioner was required to amend the deposition accordingly. Once witnesses approved of the narratives that were thus produced, they would "subscribe their Christian and surnames, or marks."[24] Thus proceeding, all the plaintiff's witnesses would be examined, followed by those called by the defendant. It was only after all witnesses in the case had testified that the record of the testimony could be revealed to the parties. At this point, the court would order its "publication"—a term of art meaning that the testimony could be disclosed to the litigants. Thereafter, no further examinations were permitted, absent some showing of extraordinary circumstances.

As concerns documentary evidence, witnesses could be ordered to produce all relevant (and non-privileged) materials: "The production of deeds, papers, etc. in the custody of a witness may be enforced at the examination of a witness, either at the examiner's office, or at the execution of a commission to examine witnesses. . . ."[25] Once all testimonial and documentary evidence was gathered, the parties presented it at a hearing, after which the judge would either enter a final decree, resolving the dispute, or an interlocutory decree, ordering further proceedings. The amount of evidentiary materials thus produced was often very extensive, such that the chancellor was incapable of singlehandedly reviewing all of it. Accordingly, to the extent that fact-finding proved burdensome, the chancellor referred disputed questions of fact to a master in chancery, whose fees were to be paid by the litigants.[26] As Harrison observed, "Upon hearing causes, all matters of account, and other matters (except in cases of very great weight, which are determined by the court,) are generally referred to a master. . . ."[27] As this language suggests, masters were frequently employed, and they were asked to report to the court on a wide variety of matters.

In pursuit of the fact-finding for which he was responsible, the master had authority to direct the necessary discovery, including, most importantly, ordering the parties and/or witnesses to submit to examination under oath. According to the treatise literature, such examinations were to take place as if the master were himself an examiner—namely, on the basis of written interrogatories and cross-interrogatories, which were not to be revealed to the parties until all testimony had been taken. If the witnesses lived some distance from London, the master was not to take the testimony himself but instead (as was also the case with examiners) was expected to delegate the task to a commission. As Maddock explained, "The master, whenever any subject occurs in which he wishes to have the examination of a witness, is authorized to take such examination . . . , and if he sees cause to direct a commission into the country, . . . the commission issues of course."[28] Based on the evidence thus garnered, the master would report his findings and recommendations to the chancellor, who, aided by the master's report, would "make an order absolute, and determine such matters. . . ."[29]

As established in this treatise literature, there were three key features of equity's approach to taking testimony that were thought to stem from the influence of the Roman-canon law and thus to distinguish it from that of the common-law courts—namely, its written nature, its focus on preserving secrecy, and its de-emphasis of the lawyers' role. In order fully to appreciate the distinctiveness of equity's approach, it is necessary to focus more closely on each of these in turn.

### THE WRITTEN NATURE OF THE TESTIMONY

Testimony in equity was largely a written affair. While the examiner or commissioner posed questions to the witness orally, he did so by reading interrogatories (or cross-interrogatories) that had already been prepared in writing by the parties' lawyers. Moreover, the witness's answers were themselves recorded in another written document, known as a deposition. Indeed, the ultimate findings of fact were to be made not by the master, examiner, or commissioners who saw the witnesses testify, but instead by the chancellor, whose only encounter with the testimony was through reading the written depositions. As Harrison was careful to emphasize, "[t]he constant and established proceedings of this court are upon written evidence, like the proceedings upon the civil or canon law. . . ." Similarly, Maddock insisted that "[t]he examination of witnesses [in chancery] is not viva voce, as at law, but proceeds by depositions in writing, and bears, in this respect, a resemblance to the course of the civil and canon law."[30]

### PRESERVING (PRE-PUBLICATION) SECRECY

Testimonial evidence in chancery was distinctive not only because of its written nature but also because it was taken privately or, as contemporary commentators frequently stated, "secretly." It was taken, in other words, in a closed room, rather than in open court, such that the parties, their lawyers, other witnesses, and ordinary members of the public would be unable to hear it. It was only after all the testimony in the case had been gathered and the court had ordered its publication that anyone other than the officers responsible for questioning the witnesses would finally learn of its content. As Gilbert observed in describing the practice of the Roman-canon courts which, he argued, chancery had embraced, "[t]he depositions thus taken before the judge were to be kept secret til publication. . . . " Likewise, Harrison claimed that depositions "are to be kept private, and no copy or abstract of them delivered till publication is past."[31]

Underlying this commitment to pre-publication secrecy was a particular vision of how to ensure the veracity of witness testimony—a vision quite different from that which animated the oral, public examinations of courts of law. Equity procedure was premised on the belief that it was less likely that a witness would mistake someone else's testimony for her own or be tempted to alter her testimony to make it consistent with (or explain away) that of others if she had no knowledge of what others had testified. This, in turn, required that all witnesses be examined in private. And since the parties might be tempted to deploy their knowledge of witness testimony for the purpose of procuring additional witnesses to concoct contrary testimony, equity also insisted that the parties, like the witnesses, be kept in the dark. As Gilbert explained, the reason that all depositions were to be kept secret until the court ordered publication was "because the parties should not bring false witnesses to disprove what had been sworn."[32]

There was, moreover, yet another reason why, in the logic of equity procedure, a secrecy-oriented approach to gathering witness testimony was deemed best suited to ensuring veracity. Pursuant to this logic, most witnesses were assumed to be honorable people who sought to testify truthfully and to the best of their recollection.[33] Such people, it was believed, would be most likely to testify accurately when given the opportunity calmly to reflect on what they remembered. This, in turn, suggested that they should testify in private—removed from the parties and other interested figures—and without the partisan pressure of an oral, lawyer-driven cross-examination. As Maddock asserted, "[f]or a rogue, a *viva voce* examination is the best; but for an honest man, depositions coolly and deliberately made, seem preferable."[34]

In line with this distinct, secrecy-oriented approach to ensuring the truthfulness of testimony, equity embraced a different method than that of the common law for dealing with testimony that was found to contain a falsehood. Because the witness in chancery had the time calmly to reflect in giving testimony, it was the established rule that, should it be determined that he had made a false statement, his entire testimony would be disregarded as likely perjurious. As Harrison insisted, "[i]f it appears a witness has deposed falsely in part, as where his depositions contain manifest contrarieties in any material point, his depositions are wholly to be rejected." The same point was made by Simon Greenleaf in his monumental treatise on the American law of evidence:

> [A]ccording to the course of chancery, the testimony of the witness is taken upon interrogatories in writing, deliberately propounded to him by the examiner, no other person being present; and where ample time is allowed for calm recollection, and any mistakes in his first answers

may be corrected at the close of the examination, when the whole is distinctly read over to him; there is ground to presume that a false statement of fact is the result either of bad design or of gross ignorance of the truth, and culpable recklessness of assertion; in either of which cases all confidence in his testimony must be lost, or at least essentially impaired.

In contrast, when a witness in a common-law court was determined to have testified falsely, it was the testimony only as to that particular matter that was disregarded. As Greenleaf explained, in common-law courts "the witness is not only examined orally, but is subjected to a severe and rapid cross-examination, without sufficient time for reflection or for deliberate answers, and hence may often misrepresent facts, from infirmity of recollection or mistake."[35]

But while equity determined that witnesses would be most likely to testify truthfully from memory when they were questioned in a calm and orderly fashion, it also insisted that they not be repeatedly examined. It was a well-established rule of equity that, absent special court authorization, a witness could be examined only once.[36] If witnesses were examined on more than one occasion, they might be tempted—having had the opportunity to reflect on their earlier testimony—to alter it in order to bolster the claims of one or the other of the litigants.

Equity developed a number of different techniques to ensure that all but the judicial officer responsible for questioning remained ignorant of the testimony until such time as the court ordered publication. First, examiners and commissioners were required to swear an oath that they would preserve the pre-publication secrecy of the depositions. Similarly, the clerks whom they employed to record the testimony were also required to "take an oath, not to deliver or make known, directly or indirectly" the contents of the depositions.[37]

Second, a special set of rules emerged for ensuring that testimony taken by commissioners (as opposed to examiners) was returned safely unopened to the court. Such rules were deemed necessary because testimony taken on commission was, by definition, gathered at a significant distance from the court, which in turn increased the risk that it might be tampered with in transit. Moreover, as we will see, the fact that commissioners were private individuals appointed to serve on a case-by-case basis meant that, for a variety of reasons, they were invested with a lesser degree of trust than the full-time examiners. Accordingly, it was established that once commissioners had examined all witnesses, they were required carefully to seal the depositions prior to returning them to court—and to do so in such a way that it would be immediately apparent whether anyone had opened them. Additional rules were developed to address the problem of hastily written (and thus frequently illegible) draft depositions produced in the course of recording witness testimony. The English treatise writers specified that these initial drafts were to be carefully stowed away so as to ensure that "no person see them until publication pass in the cause."[38]

A third, more complicated set of rules designed to ensure that testimony would remain secret prior to publication concerned the issue of when witnesses could be examined. The most important of these rules provided that once a court ordered publication of the testimony, no further witnesses could be examined absent special court order. In moving for more time to examine witnesses—or as the procedure was known, to "enlarge publication"—a party would have to establish that he and his lawyer had no knowledge of the testimony that had already been taken in the case. As Harrison explained, the party had

> to shew by affidavit that he has (as he is advised) a material witness or witnesses to examine, without whose testimony he cannot safely proceed to an hearing; and also shew satisfactory reasons to the court why he or they could not attend and be examined before publication; and moreover in this case the party making this application, his clerk in court and solicitor, joining him therein, must make oath, *"That they have neither seen, heard, read, or been informed of, any of the contents of the depositions taken in that cause; nor will be they see, hear, read, or be informed of the same till publication is duly passed in the cause;"* . . .[39]

The only clear exception to this general rule prohibiting the post-publication taking of testimony concerned testimony regarding witnesses' credibility—or, as it is commonly known, impeachment testimony. On motion, chancery would authorize the post-publication calling of witnesses for the sole purpose of procuring testimony concerning the credibility of others who had testified regarding the merits. The logic here was that "because the matters examined to in such cases were not material to the merits of the cause, but only relative to the characters of the witnesses," there was no risk that such impeachment testimony could be used directly to bolster or contradict prior testimony on the merits.[40] To the extent, however, that impeachment testimony did touch on the merits—by suggesting that a prior witness had lied in testifying as to a material fact in dispute—it would not be permitted post-publication. Impeachment witnesses, in other words, could challenge the credibility of prior witnesses only by suggesting that the latter had lied concerning matters that were not material to the case itself. As Maddock asserted, "after publication has passed, the court will . . . give the party liberty to examine witnesses by general *interrogatories,* as to the *credit* of the witness, and in contradiction of such facts sworn to by the witness, *as are not material to what is in issue in the cause;* for witnesses in that stage of the suit are not permitted to be brought to vary the case in evidence, by testimony that relates to the matter in issue, under the pretence of examining to credit only."[41]

The treatise literature suggests that in the period immediately after the court ordered publication, parties regularly sought witnesses to challenge not only the credibility but also the competency of (pre-publication) fact witnesses.[42] Under the law of evidence as it applied throughout the first half of the nineteenth century (somewhat differently in law and equity), a wide array of competency rules served to bar entire categories of individuals from serving as witnesses—including atheists, felons, and those deemed to have a financial interest in the matter.[43] Whether testimony concerning the competency of pre-publication witnesses ought to be treated like impeachment testimony, such that it would be permitted after publication had already passed, was a point of some dispute.

The difficulty here was that parties seeking testimony concerning competency could be motivated by entirely legitimate or illegitimate goals, and it was quite hard for a neutral observer to distinguish between the two. On the one hand, a party might seek post-publication testimony as to competency because he had not been aware, until he became acquainted with the pre-publication testimony, that a particular witness could be challenged on the grounds of competency. On the other hand, the party might be hoping to deploy such post-publication testimony to bolster or contradict testimony on the merits, thereby bypassing the strict prohibition on the post-publication acquisition of further testimony concerning material facts in dispute. Most treatise writers suggested that the best way for a court to resolve this dilemma was to inquire into whether the party seeking post-publication testimony concerning competency had been reasonably able to pursue such testimony prior to publication. If he had been, it could be assumed that he had sat on his rights (and thus lost them) or that his intentions were to evade the general prohibition on post-publication testimony. In either case, such a party's request to take post-publication testimony concerning witness competency ought to be denied. As Harrison explained, it was only if "the objection to the competency arose from a matter, that came to the knowledge of the party after the examination" that such additional testimony would be permitted.[44]

Post-publication testimony would be taken in much the same way as that gathered prior to publication—namely, by court officers relying on interrogatories provided by the parties. In the case of post-publication testimony, however, the drafting of interrogatories was preceded by the filing of "articles." These were a set of objections to a witness's credibility or competency, stated in positive form, rather than as a series of questions. A party filed articles with "the examiner or clerk in court," who in turn "annex[ed] them to the depositions impeached," thus providing the other side with notice of the particular objections to credibility and/or competency. Having thus filed articles with the court, the party seeking to impeach or exclude prior testimony would then draft "[i]nterrogatories adapted to the inquiry intended," which were "filed as in ordinary cases, and witnesses thereto examined either by commission or at the examiners' office; after which the depositions are to be published in the usual manner."[45]

### MINIMIZING THE LAWYERS' ROLE

A final distinguishing feature of the taking of testimony in chancery was that lawyers were to play a very limited role. Although they drafted the interrogatories and cross-interrogatories, it was court officials who were responsible for posing these to the witnesses. Moreover, the defining feature of such officials, in contrast to the parties' lawyers, was their neutrality. In describing the Roman-canon tradition on which, he claimed, chancery procedure was based, Gilbert asserted that "commissioners were . . . to be indifferent; for upon exception to the partiality of one of them, the court would supply his place by putting in another." Like the commissioners of the Roman-canon tradition, chancery commissioners were likewise "ministers of the court, and therefore must be impartial." Along similar lines, Harrison emphasized that "commissioners ought to be indifferent persons" and for this reason, commissioners were not permitted to be "of kin, or counsel or solicitor for [one of] the part[ies]," nor "his landlord or partner," or someone to whom "the party is indebted." Like commissioners, moreover, "the examiner is an officer of credit, and sworn, and so presumed to be impartial."[46]

The goal of ensuring that the court officials responsible for taking testimony be neutral led to the development of strict limitations on their ability to communicate with the parties. Harrison, for example, explained that in order to preserve his neutrality, "[t]he examiner, after the examination begun, ought not to confer with either party touching the examination, or take new instructions concerning the same. . . ." Equally important was the manner in which examiners and commissioners posed questions to witnesses during the examination itself. Because their function was to pursue the truth, they were required to pose interrogatories and cross-interrogatories in a calm, non-aggressive fashion. In Harrison's words, "it is the duty of the examiner gravely, temperately, and leisurely, to take the depositions of the witnesses, without any menace, disturbance, or interruption of them. . . ." Similarly, chancery officials were expected to rephrase and clarify interrogatories as needed in order to make them comprehensible to witnesses, thereby furthering the goal of procuring complete and truthful testimony: "The examiner is not strictly bound to the letter of the interrogatories, but ought to explain every other matter or thing which ariseth necessarily thereupon for the manifestation of the whole truth. . . ."[47]

Like examiners and commissioners, masters were deemed neutral court officers responsible for discovering the truth. But toward this end, they, unlike their colleagues, were invested with the independent power to pursue whatever additional discovery they deemed necessary to resolve the factual questions the chancellor had delegated to them. As a result, the master was not simply a passive audience for whatever evidence the parties chose to present. Having determined that "any particular points or circumstances" were "not fully proved," he could "direct the parties to draw interrogatories to such points or circumstances only" and then order the examination of witnesses regarding these points.[48] In all these respects, the equitable approach to gathering evidence (and especially witness testimony) described in the English treatise literature was one that minimized the role of lawyers vis-à-vis court officials. It was, in short, a judge-empowering, quasi-inquisitorial process.

## New York Chancery Procedure prior to Kent: Replicating the English Model

To what extent did early American equity courts actually embrace the judicially empowering, quasi-inquisitorial approach to procedure set forth in the English treatise literature? As generations of law-and-society scholars have taught, the law in the books often bears little resemblance to the law in action. And strikingly, when Kent first became chancellor in 1814, there was not even much law on the books. A smattering of case reports began to appear in the late eighteenth century, beginning with Ephraim Kirby's 1789 publication of a volume of Connecticut reports. But it was Kent himself who, soon after becoming chief justice of the New York Supreme Court in 1804, played a dominant role in establishing case reporting as a systematic practice—one rapidly copied by other jurisdictions.[49] So what did contemporaries actually encounter when they looked to American courts of equity—including, most importantly, Kent's own highly influential New York Chancery?

Kent and his supporters insisted that, at the time he became chancellor, it was as if chancery "had been a new institution," such that he was "left at liberty to assume all such English Chancery powers and jurisdiction as [he] thought applicable under our constitution."[50] The evidence, however, suggests that such grandiose claims were designed more to flatter Kent's sizable ego than to describe realities on the ground. While failing to adhere to every dictate of the treatise literature, New York Chancery—well prior to Kent— embodied the basics of the English quasi-inquisitorial model.

Chancery dated back in New York to 1683 and operated continuously from 1711 until the Revolution.[51] The court's existence thus long preceded the foundation of the American republic, let alone Kent's chancellorship. During much of the colonial period, chancery was quite controversial because of its association with a high-handed monarchy—an association that originated, as we have seen, in the seventeenth-century English Revolution and that was reinvigorated by the colonial practice of appointing the royal governor as chancellor. But despite such controversy, New York Chancery survived—and it did so for well over a century before Kent assumed the chancellorship. It beggars belief to suggest, as did Kent, Story, and their supporters, that the court somehow operated for all these years without having any real system of procedure.

The first systematic set of rules governing procedural practice in New York Chancery was issued not by Kent but by his predecessor, John Lansing Jr.[52] While Kent undertook to augment these rules—in multiple, repeat editions for which he took exclusive credit—the notable fact is that, in so doing, he preserved most of Lansing's rules. Thus, despite his insistence that no one ever cited to him "a single decision, opinion, or dictum of either of my two predecessors (Ch. Livingston and Ch. Lansing)," he relied extensively on Lansing's efforts. Lansing's rules, in turn, were clearly based on English Chancery procedure.

Like the procedure described in the contemporary treatise literature, Lansing's chancery rules contemplated a method of gathering evidence, and in particular witness testimony, that was quasi-inquisitorial in that it prioritized the written over the oral, sought to preserve (pre-publication) secrecy, and attempted to limit the role of lawyers. As in England, testimony was to be gathered on the basis of written interrogatories prepared by the parties, which were in turn to be read to witnesses by ostensibly neutral court officials. The rules thus refer to examinations of witnesses being conducted "either before an examiner or commissioners" and note that questioning is to take the form of "direct and cross interrogatories."[53]

Lansing's rules, moreover, reveal the same concern as the English treatise literature for ensuring the (pre-publication) secrecy of testimony. For example, they provide that witnesses are to be examined only once, so as not to give them the opportunity to change their testimony. Similarly, these early New York Chancery rules carefully regulate the timing of when testimony could be taken, focusing in particular on whether witnesses were examined before or "after publication has passed and the depositions [are] delivered." And as in the treatise literature, post-publication testimony was deemed permissible only to the extent that it concerned the credibility or competency of those who had testified prior to publication.[54]

Moreover, as in English Chancery, Lansing's rules provide for the court official who, perhaps more than any other, epitomized equity's traditional commitment to a strong judicial presence and to a proportionally minimal role for the parties' legal counsel—namely, the master in chancery. Indeed, the rules are replete with discussions of masters and their various duties. They explain how to proceed "when a matter is referred to a master to examine and report upon," how to go about "fil[ing] [exceptions] to a master's report," and how to serve process in proceedings requiring the parties "to attend a master."[55]

The most striking feature of these early New York Chancery rules, however—and the one that serves as the clearest indication that, well prior to Kent, the court had embraced English Chancery's traditional, quasi-inquisitorial system—is the many assumptions that they make. Lansing's rules, in other words, are full of definitional lacunae. Nowhere do they explain what an interrogatory is or what it means for publication to pass. Similarly, they fail to describe who the examiner is or how his role differs from that of commissioners. As this suggests, these rules were drafted by and for an audience of legal experts who were already familiar with the basic outlines of English equity's quasi-inquisitorial structure.

That New York Chancery embraced key aspects of English Chancery's quasi-inquisitorial methods well before Kent is also evident from the surviving case files. As Julius Goebel Jr. has shown based on an extensive review of Alexander Hamilton's papers, by the late colonial period "a *cursus cancellariae* resembling the[] models" of "the early English practice books" had clearly emerged, such that "practice [in New York Chancery], if not as complex as in England, was on a sound professional level." Moreover, as in England, the procedure employed in late eighteenth-century New York Chancery was in key respects "patterned after the [Roman-canon based] ecclesiastical procedure." This included the approach to taking testimony—namely, "questioning witnesses in secret with interrogatories prepared by counsel."[56]

While the archival records of New York Chancery from the period prior to 1800 are not nearly as complete and extensive as those dating from the nineteenth century, they too suggest that by the final decades of the eighteenth century, and likely well before, the court had borrowed core features of its English ancestor's distinctive procedural tradition.[57] Archival records reveal that, like its English counterpart, New York Chancery in this period relied on masters to assist with fact-finding.[58] So too, it employed both examiners and commissioners to take testimony privately on the basis of written interrogatories and cross-interrogatories. And these officials were required to preserve the secrecy of the testimony thus gathered (including from the parties themselves) until publication passed.[59]

As we will see, there were a number of ways that New York Chancery failed to comply with the many rules of the English equity tradition. But the evidence suggests that the court's overarching structure and logic were borrowed directly from its English counterpart—and well prior to Kent's ascension to the chancellorship. Accordingly, while Kent took great pleasure in proclaiming himself the founder of American equity, his role was more modest. He served, in essence, as a systematizer, advocating more rigorous adherence to all aspects of the English quasi-inquisitorial model and working assiduously (through his published reports and treatises) to publicize this model across the country. His efforts, in this regard, were a great success and helped to ensure that core components of equity would survive even after the formal mid-nineteenth-century merger of law and equity and the consequent disappearance of chancery as a distinct legal institution. But as we will see, the very success that Kent (and Story) achieved in systematizing and conceptualizing equity as a judge-empowering procedural tradition—one that operated in sharp contradistinction to the common law—also contributed to a lawyerly groundswell in favor of oral, adversarial procedure, thus serving to undermine the quasi-inquisitorial logic that they so admired. This, however, takes us too far ahead in our story. Before studying the backlash against it, we must first examine more closely Kent and Story's vision of equity as well as the reasons for its appeal.

## The Idealized Image of the Equity Judge

Kent and Story were, of course, two different people, such that their views on equity (as on all matters) necessarily differed to some extent. Overall, however, it is clear that, as concerns equity (and much else besides), they shared a common vision. At the heart of this common vision lay an idealized, heroic conception of the equity judge. For both men, it was an article of faith that the role of the judge in equity was quite distinct from that of his common-law counterpart. As Kent argued, "[t]he systems [of law and equity] were essentially different in their character, and relations, and objects; and each of them required a distinct preparation, and study, and qualifications."[60] Along similar lines, Story opined that "[a] man may be a great common law judge, but may have no relish for equity. The talents required for both stations are not necessarily the same; and the cast of mind and course of study adapted to the one, may not insure success in the other."[61]

Figure 1 Rembrandt Peale, *James Kent* (circa 1835). Courtesy of the National Portrait Gallery, Smithsonian Institute / Art Resource, New York.

W.W. Story.                                    Photo from Drawing.

Figure 2  Photograph of a drawing of Joseph Story (n.d.),
by William Wetmore Story, Record ID: olvwork260082,
Historical & Special Collections, courtesy of the Harvard
Law School Library.

As Kent and Story saw it, a defining feature of the equity judge—one that
clearly distinguished him from his common-law counterpart—was his refined
moral sensibility. Empowered with the authority necessary to enter a complex
judgment balancing the equities, the equity judge could not simply look to the
narrowly applicable legal rule but was instead required to rely to some degree on
moral intuition. It was for precisely this reason that those of "great mind" felt
"cramped and fettered" by the kinds of narrow pursuits that typified the common law and were drawn instead to equity.[62] Moreover, a powerful moral intuition was particularly vital for the equity judge because his jurisdiction had
emerged, in part, to provide justice where the common law and its writs had
failed to do so—in the many cases in which an otherwise just legal rule threatened to work an injustice due to power differentials, miscommunication, and

the like. As Story explained: "There are . . . many cases . . . of losses and injuries by mistake, accident, and fraud; . . . and many cases of oppressive proceedings, undue advantages and impositions, betrayals of confidence, and unconscionable bargains; in all of which Courts of Equity will interfere and grant redress; but which the common Law takes no notice of, or silently disregards."[63] Only a judge of high moral character could be expected to correct such wrongs and thus to ensure justice for the poor, weak, and abused—including minors, women, and the mentally ill. Similarly, an elevated moral sensibility was required for overseeing the many cases in equity that concerned fiduciary relations (such as trusts and partnerships) and that imposed a high duty of good faith.

The extent to which a refined moral character defined Kent's idealized conception of the equity judge is evident in his reflections on his own experience as chancellor of New York. In describing his approach to resolving equity suits, he emphasized his reliance on moral intuition: "I saw where justice lay and the moral sense decided the cause half the time, and I then set down to search the authorities until I had exhausted my books and I might once in a while be embarrassed by a technical rule, but I most always found principles suited to my views of the case. . . ."[64] Along similar lines, Story argued that "[t]he principles of equity jurisprudence are of a very enlarged and elevated nature. They are essentially rational, and moulded into a degree of moral perfection which the law has rarely aspired to."[65] As he elsewhere implied, it was precisely this aspiration toward "moral perfection" that ensured the "natural elevation" of equity courts and their judges, rendering them superior to their common-law counterparts.[66]

In thus emphasizing the equity judge's refined moral character, Kent and Story were at the same time careful to insist on the importance of a high degree of intellectual sophistication and rigor. The equity judge whom they described was not an untutored, natural man but was instead the product of great discipline and learning. The reason for this was that, contrary to popular belief, decisions in equity were not simply a product of the judge's personal conscience. As Kent insisted, courts of equity had become just as rule-bound as courts of law: "[Chancery] has no discretionary power over principles and established precedents; and . . . [it] has grown to be a jurisdiction of . . . strict technical rule. . . ."[67] Likewise, Story refuted the "often repeated" but nonetheless mistaken belief "that Courts of Equity are not, and ought not, to be bound by precedents; . . . but that every case is to be decided upon circumstances, according to the arbitration or discretion of the Judge, acting according to his own notions, *ex aequo et bono*."[68]

The greatness of equity lay precisely in that it combined a deep moral orientation with a commitment to rational predictability. And only a very particular kind of judicial character—one uniting elevated moral sensibilities, on the one hand, with intellectual acuity and discipline, on the other—was capable of achieving this complex, equitable balance. The prototype of such a judge was, of course, none other than Kent himself, whom Story lauded as the founder of American equity. According to Story, Kent possessed a rigorous mind and sense for justice that enabled him to look beyond legal formalities to the deeper animating (often moral) principles of the law: "It required such a man, with such a mind, at once liberal, comprehensive, exact, and methodical; always reverencing authorities and bound by decisions; true to the spirit, yet more true to the letter of the law; pursuing principles with a severe and scrupulous logic, yet blending with them the most persuasive equity;—it required such a man, with such a mind, to unfold the doctrines of chancery in our country, and to settle them upon immovable foundations."[69]

In insisting on the equity judge's unique blend of intellectual and moral capacities, Kent and Story drew on tropes of both the Enlightenment and the Romantic era. As men who bridged the eighteenth and nineteenth centuries, they created a portrait of the idealized equity judge (and thus of themselves) that merged Enlightenment conceptions of scientific and commercial modernity with Romantic notions of natural genius.

Like the enlightened *philosophe,* the equity judge devoted his great intellectual prowess, discipline, and learning to the pursuit of philosophical inquiry. As Story wrote of Kent's equity jurisprudence, "Look to the chancery decisions of New York. Where shall we find in our times . . . a more philosophical spirit than is displayed in the elaborate arguments of her late chancellor?"[70] In the view of both jurists, there was no better evidence of the equity judge's commitment to such philosophical, scientific inquiry than his embrace of the study of Roman civil law. Though a matter of some dispute among legal historians today, it was, as we have seen, widely believed well into the nineteenth century that equity (unlike the common law) derived in significant measure from this continental European tradition.[71] As Kent observed, "[t]he great body of the Roman or civil law . . . exerts a very considerable influence upon our own municipal law, and particularly on those branches of it which are of equity . . . jurisdiction."[72] Likewise, Story claimed that "from the moment when principles of decision came to be acted upon and established in [English] Chancery, the Roman law furnished abundant materials to erect a superstructure, at once solid, convenient, and lofty. . . ."[73] Because of equity's presumed roots in

Roman civil law, Kent and Story believed that a close familiarity with this tradition was essential for the equity judge. And the defining feature of this tradition—in sharp contrast to the primitive and arbitrary system of the common law—was its modern, scientific sophistication.

According to Kent and Story, there was much to be celebrated in the common law—including especially its distinctive commitment to preserving (interrelated) property rights and political liberties.[74] But the fact remained that the common law dated back to the Middle Ages and was thus a product of an ignorant, feudal, and monkish time. The baleful remnants of this unfortunate inheritance were evident in its great technical complexity, its mass of illogical and palpably false fictions, and the numerous premodern doctrines—such as rights of primogeniture and infeudation—that the several states had managed to overcome only by legislation. As Story opined, "the English common law . . . [was] churlish and harsh as was its feudal education."[75]

The primitive nature of the common law contrasted starkly with the comparative sophistication of the civil law tradition of continental Europe, which borrowed heavily from the law of the Romans. The world's most erudite and complete body of law, Roman law was created to serve a complex commercial society—ultimately, a commercial empire. Rediscovered by continental Europeans just as the Dark Ages were passing into memory and developed to heights of perfection in the early modern period, Europeanized Roman law, or civil law, embodied nothing short of civilization itself. In Story's words:

> Where shall we find more full and masterly discussions of maritime doctrines, coming home to our own bosoms and business, than in the celebrated Commentaries of Valin? Where shall we find so complete and practical a treatise on insurance as in the mature labors of Emérigon? Where shall we find the law of contracts so extensively, so philosophically, and so persuasively expounded, as in the pure, moral, and classical treatises of Pothier? Where shall we find the general doctrines of commercial law so briefly, yet beautifully, laid down, as in the modern commercial code of France? Where shall we find such ample general principles to guide us in new and difficult cases, as in that venerable deposit of the learning and labors of the jurists of the ancient world, the Institutes and Pandects of Justinian? The whole continental jurisprudence rests upon this broad foundation of Roman wisdom. . . .[76]

Unlike the common law, equity had wisely opted to borrow from this fount of Roman, continental learning.

As suggested by Story's language in praise of the civil law (including his references to its "maritime" and "commercial law" doctrines), the greatness of this legal tradition lay not only in its scientific sophistication but also in its commitment to deploying such wisdom toward the betterment of the human condition, especially through commercial development. In Story's view, the English tradition of equity had borrowed from the Roman civil law with an eye toward furthering precisely such modern, commercial ends. Rising to prominence during the Renaissance and expanding its power during the seventeenth-century age of commerce, chancery was created by modern commercial men—quite unlike the feudal legists who bore primary responsibility for the emergence of the common law. As Story explained, "[t]he law of contracts . . . in England"—much of which arose within chancery—"has been formed into life by the soft solicitudes and devotion of her own neglected professors of the civil law."[77] Working within this longstanding civilian tradition, the equity judge was the very embodiment of a man of modern, enlightened science seeking to deploy his sophisticated learning to promote commerce and thus human welfare.

Like all enlightened men of science, moreover, the equity judge did not work alone but instead participated in an international community of scholarship. Familiarity with the civil law tradition was thus not simply a marker of the equity judge's deep enlightenment. It was also a kind of lingua franca enabling him to converse across borders with the most important jurists of the civilized, continental European world. In this respect, the American equity judge continued to inhabit an Enlightenment republic of letters in which leading intellectuals engaged in an ongoing transnational conversation about great questions and ideas.[78]

As the very embodiment of his own ideal of the equity judge, Kent himself corresponded extensively with scholars abroad. And it was precisely his familiarity with Roman civil law that helped make such correspondence possible, since his European interlocutors quite naturally sought to share with him writings from their own legal tradition.[79] Well aware that participation in this transnational republic of letters required some familiarity with Roman civil law—and thus with the languages that served as its gatekeepers—Kent took great pride in his efforts to master these languages. As he recounted, in 1786, long before he was appointed to the bench, he was put to shame by Edward Livingston—a man who, because of his role in drafting the Louisiana Civil Code, was also to gain fame as one of the new nation's great civilians. Livingston evidently recited to Kent some passages from Horace in the original

Latin. Unable to follow, Kent was deeply traumatized and committed himself to mastering the great languages of the civilized world:

> [S]tung with shame and mortification for I had forgotten even my Greek letters[,] . . . I purchased immediately Horace and Virgil, a dictionary and grammar, and a Greek lexicon and grammar, and the Testament, and formed my resolution, promptly and decidedly, to recover the lost languages. I studied in my little cottage mornings, and devoted one hour to Greek and another to Latin daily. I soon increased it to two for each tongue in the twenty-four hours. My acquaintance with the languages increased rapidly. After I had read Horace and Virgil, I ventured upon Livy for the first time in my life . . . and I can hardly describe at this day the enthusiasm with which I perseveringly read and studied in the originals Livy and the Iliad. It gave me inspiration. I purchased a French dictionary and grammar and began French and gave an hour to that language daily.[80]

Although scholars have questioned the extent of Kent's fluency in foreign languages as well as his mastery of Roman civil law, it is evident that he gained sufficient competency to engage in dialogue with scholars abroad—and thus to embody his conception of the enlightened, equity judge. Writing to Kent from Berlin in 1838, Nicolaus Heinrich Julius, a noted advocate of prison reform, referred to himself as "only one of the most insignificant among the numerous foreign . . . worshippers continually presenting themselves at the shrine of the oracle of American law."[81] While clearly intended to flatter Kent's not insubstantial ego, these words reflected the extent to which the American jurist had indeed succeeded in gaining a reputation abroad—a product not only of his achievement in publishing the first major treatise on American law but also of his success in acquiring the legal and linguistic knowledge necessary to maintain contacts with European scholars. Those seeking to honor Kent as the very prototype of the equity judge thus made particular reference to his mastery of the learned civil law tradition. For example, when Hamilton College's Phoenix Society voted to make him an honorary member, they so informed him in a letter praising his long-established reputation as "the acute and learned Civilian."[82]

A man of enlightened, philosophical spirit, the equity judge was also for Kent and Story—and especially the latter—a kind of Romantic hero. Sixteen years Kent's junior (and thus more truly a man of the nineteenth century), Story described the equity judge by appealing to the Romantic discourse of genius, portraying him as an individual whose expansive mind and hypersensitive spirit set him apart from all others. While at first glance, the equity jurist would appear to be a mere pedant, burying his nose in books and scurrying after ancient wisdom, he was, in fact, the very prototype of the Romantic voyager, engaged in a perilous, personal quest for deeper knowledge and refinement.

It was in precisely such terms that Story characterized Kent, the great titan of American equity. Noting that Kent's "life has been devoted, sedulously and earnestly, to professional studies," Story went on to suggest that such study was nothing short of an adventure. Through his studies, Kent was required, like the hero of some *bildungsroman,* to "fathom[] the depths and search[] the recesses," to "trace[] back the magnificent streams of jurisprudence to their fountains, lying dark and obscure," to "pursue[]" knowledge "amidst the dust and the cobwebs," to "dare[] to examine," and perhaps most importantly, to "master[]."[83] Along similar lines, more than a decade later, Story concluded his *Commentaries on Equity Jurisprudence* by addressing himself to "the ingenuous youth" who was just setting out on the quest to master equity. Warning the youth not to imagine that a mere reading of the *Commentaries* was sufficient to prepare him for the journey ahead, Story depicted the totality of equity jurisprudence and learning as a "magnificent temple reared by the genius and labours of many successive ages."[84] It was through a similar combination of Romantic genius and steadfast discipline, he advised, that the young would-be master of equity might, like those before him, attain to heights of learned glory.

True to the Romantic ideal of the genius as a man of unique spiritual—and, in particular, artistic and literary—sensibilities, Story was careful to emphasize the aesthetic merits of the equity judge's written prose. Thus, in describing the commercial-law jurisprudence that Kent developed while serving as chancellor, Story observed that he "contributed to the[] beauty and perfection" of this body of law. Along similar lines, elite lawyers seeking to honor Kent on his eightieth birthday made a particular point of highlighting the refined literary and stylistic quality of his chancery opinions: "Nor is it merely as legal disquisitions that these decisions demand our praise, their literary merits are of the highest order," and "the occasional splendor of their eloquence" was nothing short of breathtaking.[85] Indeed, when asked to account for his emergence as one of the nation's greatest jurists, Kent himself emphasized the important role that literature had played in the development of his mental and moral capacities. Beginning in his early twenties, he observed, he "appropriated the business part of the day to law . . . [but] accorded evenings to English Literature in company with my wife." And "[f]rom 1788 to 1798," the year he was first appointed to the bench, he "steadily divided the day into five portions and allotted them to Greek, Latin, Law & Business, French and English varied literature." In this way, he developed his legal capacities in tandem with his literary sensibilities and "mastered the best of the Greek, Latin and French classics, as well as the best English and Law books at hand."[86]

Enlightened man of letters and Romantic genius—enjoying acute powers of scientific reasoning but endowed at the same time with refined moral and literary sensibilities—the equity judge was, in sum, nothing short of heroic. But why precisely was he so central to Kent and Story's shared vision of equity? What purposes, in other words, did these jurists hope to serve by creating such an idealized, heroic image of the equity judge? That the equity judge was particularly interested in (and attuned to the importance of) commercial law adds weight to the functionalist account of equity's early nineteenth-century resurgence. But Kent and Story's idealized conception extended well beyond a narrow focus on the equity judge's commercial-law expertise. To take full account of the many dimensions of their ideal of the equity judge, it is necessary to look beyond the (indisputably true but insufficient) fact that both men were strongly committed to a (largely Federalist) vision of commercial growth and prosperity. Their idealized image of the equity judge also presented them with a solution to a number of intersecting personal and political problems. These included the challenges posed to their career ambitions by their backward American origins and, most importantly, the increasingly democratic (and thus, to them, distasteful) thrust of American political life.

The image that Kent and Story created of the equity judge as a man of superior intellectual and moral capacities was in part a response to the fact that the United States was then a remote backwater of the civilized world. By developing an idealized image of the equity judge, and thus of themselves, these jurists sought to promote their own reputations both within and beyond the borders of the United States. Toward this end, they made great efforts to be recognized as the founding fathers of American equity and therefore as the very prototypes of the idealized equity judge. Kent, in particular, took great pride in insisting that he was the primary founder of American equity. Although as we have seen, this was far from the truth, he even claimed that prior to his chancellorship, equity as such hardly existed in the United States:

> In 1814 I was appointed Chancellor. . . . The person who left . . . [the office] was stupid and it is a curious fact that for the nine years I was in that office, there was not a single decision, opinion, or dictum of either of my

two predecessors (Ch. Livingston and Ch. Lansing) from 1777 to 1814 cited to me or even suggested. I took the court as if it had been a new institution and never before known in the world. I had nothing to guide me, I was left at liberty to assume all such English Chancery powers and jurisdiction as I thought applicable under our constitution. This gave me grand scope and I was only checked by the revision of the Senate or Court of Errors.[87]

In much the same way, Story—who became known through his judicial opinions and treatises as a great exponent of equity law and practice—sought to position himself as Kent's natural successor and thus as a cofounder of American equity. As Story's son would later report in a hagiographic account of his father's life that clearly gave voice to the elder Story's own self-conception, "To the united efforts of my father and Chancellor Kent the enlightened system of Equity, which now prevails in this country, is chiefly due. Kent, indeed, led the way, but he found in my father an equal coadjutor. They stood shoulder to shoulder in this work, and divide the honor between them."[88]

In developing and promoting an idealized model of the equity judge, Kent and Story understood themselves to be doing more than simply advancing their own career interests and ambitions. As they were well aware, the eyes of the civilized European world were watching to see what would become of the great American experiment in law and government. By creating an idealized image of the equity judge, which they themselves undertook to embody, they sought to elevate not only their own personal status but also that of the new nation as a whole. Offering one another the adulation that each evidently hoped to obtain for himself, they made a point of emphasizing the extent to which the other's writings—especially in equity—had gained acclaim across the Atlantic. Story, for example, observed in praise of Kent's chancery reports that they could easily rival the jurisprudential achievements of the English legal tradition. In Story's words, Kent's chancery reports were "a monument of [Chancellor Kent's] learning, industry and integrity, which will endure as long as the law shall be studied as a science . . . [and which] will not suffer in the comparison with those of the highest age of the British Empire."[89] Along similar lines, in proposing a toast in Story's honor, Kent emphasized the wonderful reputation that his colleague's treatises and judicial decisions had acquired abroad, particularly among European scholars intimately familiar with the great works of both the English and the Roman civil law traditions: "We have long been accustomed to receive with diffidence and submission the authority of Westminster Hall, and especially to contemplate with wonder, if not with despair, the massy piles of Gothic lore and court-law learning accumulated by the civilians of Europe. But some of the treatises as well as decisions of the gentleman to whom I have alluded, are well calculated to teach our trans-Atlantic teachers."[90] Thus, for both Kent and Story, the idealized image of the equity judge that they sought to create—and then claimed to embody—served as evidence not only of their own greatness but also of the fact that the nascent American legal culture and its institutions could rival those of the new nation's more powerful and established European ancestors.

But perhaps most importantly, Kent and Story's heroic conception of the equity judge was also a response to the perceived dangers of democratic rule. As represented by the Jeffersonian electoral victory of 1800 (and the consequent routing of the Federalists), the early decades of the nineteenth century witnessed a substantial democratization of the United States—a turn of events with which neither jurist ever fully reconciled himself. As Kent explained in 1828: "I had commenced in 1786 to be a zealous federalist. I read everything in politics. I got the Federalist almost by heart and became intimate with Hamilton. I entered with ardor into the federal politics against France in 1793 and my hostility to the French democracy and to French power beat with strong pulsation down to the Battle of Waterloo. Now you know my politics."[91] Pursuant to Kent's Federalist conception of good government, the survival and success of the republic hinged on the leadership of a select few men of extraordinary intelligence and virtue, who possessed not only the innate character but also the requisite property necessary to rise above the demands of faction and mass and to act in the best interest of the public as a whole. In his view, in short, "[a]ll theories of government that suppose the mass of people virtuous and able, and willing to act virtuously are plainly utopian and will remain so until the return of the Saturnian age. . . ."[92]

In contrast to Kent, Story's political leanings were, at least initially, more nuanced and complex. He began his life as a member of the Republican Party, and it was in fact in recognition of his service to that party that in 1811 he obtained his position as a justice of the United States Supreme Court. Story, however, quickly gained a reputation as a traitor to the cause. Devoted to promoting both a strong national government and extensive commercial development, he was described by none other than Jefferson himself as a "pseudo-republican" and would later profess loyalty to the Whig Party, decried by old-school Republicans as a reincarnation of the Federalists. Like Kent, moreover, he saw in Andrew Jackson's rise to power the fearful prospect of mass rule—or as he (and other critics) termed it, "the reign of king 'Mob' "— and he sought to deploy his position as Supreme Court justice as a mechanism for resisting the mounting democratic tide.[93]

For Kent and Story, the idealized, heroic image of the equity judge that they created was, in no small part, a response to the growing prospect (and reality) of mass democratic rule.[94] Appealing to the widely prevalent discourse of civic republicanism, both jurists took the position that the welfare of the new nation hinged on the preservation of virtue among the citizenry and that this, in turn, required the steadfast leadership of a select, public-minded elite. In their view, as the elected branches of government fell into the hands of the unwashed masses, the nation's only hope was for the judiciary to act as a backstop to the democratic onslaught. And while the judiciary as a whole might attempt to serve this function, equity courts were in the best position to do so. Free of the constraints posed by juries (in an era in which many still believed that jurors had the power to decide the law),[95] such courts were entrusted to judges who—as depicted by Kent and Story—possessed the moral and intellectual qualities requisite to serve as key leaders of the new republic. Accordingly, by developing and strengthening a distinct system of equity, they sought to empower the sort of elite, educated, and independent men—or in Story's words, " 'men of talent,' 'men of virtue,' the 'truest of true' "[96]—who, both jurists believed, ought to bear primary responsibility for guiding the helm of state. But as time would soon prove, their successful efforts to bolster equity would generate a backlash, leading lawyers to argue that they, rather than equity judges, were the nation's true civic republican elite.

## A Predominantly Procedural Conception of Equity

Why did Kent and Story settle on the equity judge as the institutional embodiment of their elitist, civic republican ideal of leadership? Part of the answer has to do with the way that the judiciary as a whole became a central focus of the deepening struggle between nascent political parties. After a hardfought and bitter electoral campaign, Republicans swept to power in the "Revolution of 1800," wresting control of both the presidency and Congress and causing ousted Federalists to seek refuge (and continued power) in the judiciary, the only non-elective branch of government. For Federalist-leaning jurists like Kent and Story, the appeal of the equity judge was thus, in part, of a piece with their broader attraction to any and all judicial institutions. Moreover, as Daniel Hulsebosch argues, Federalists were especially drawn to equity, because they viewed it as uniquely well suited to promoting the development of a truly national body of law.[97] But at least as important in explaining why Kent and Story were so taken with the idea of the equity judge was that their heroic image of this official was actually grounded in certain key features of chancery practice. Most importantly, the judge in equity was entrusted with extensive discretionary procedural power—power befitting these jurists' image of the equity judge as a man of superior moral and intellectual qualities.[98] It was precisely because the equity judge exercised so much discretionary procedural power that he was, in Kent and Story's view, ideally suited to provide the elite leadership that the new country so desperately needed.

Writing in the early to mid-nineteenth century, Kent and Story came of age as jurists just as the substance/procedure divide was beginning to take root within the common law and thus had yet to reshape traditional understandings of equity. They therefore made no clear distinction in their writings between the substance and procedure of equity. But if we review their work with this modern-day distinction in mind, it is clear that, in discussing equity, they focused almost entirely on procedural mechanisms rather than substantive rights. Indeed, as they saw it, the chancery judge's tremendous procedural powers were, in many ways, the defining feature of equity. That this is the case is evident perhaps first and foremost in Story's treatises on equity, which afforded him an opportunity to provide a comprehensive overview of the field.

Story wrote two master treatises on equity: *Commentaries on Equity Jurisprudence,* first issued in 1835–1836, and *Commentaries on Equity Pleadings,* published shortly thereafter in 1838. In concluding his preface to the first of these works, Story observed, "I hope . . . to find leisure to present, as a conclusion of these Commentaries, a general review of the Doctrines of Equity Pleading, and of the Course of Practice in Equity Proceedings."[99] As suggested by this language, as well as the quick succession in which the two treatises appeared, Story had evidently planned to write both books from the outset, viewing them as separate components of an integrated whole. That he sought to publish distinct treatises on equity jurisprudence, on the one hand, and pleading and practice, on the other, might suggest that his goal was to distinguish between the substantive and procedural law of equity. But to thus transpose our modern-day substance/procedure divide into the 1830s would be anachronistic and therefore misleading.

A brief review of Story's *Equity Pleadings* suffices to reveal that he had no conception of procedure as such. Like most other contemporary jurists (with the exception of Jeremy Bentham), he never employed the term *procedure* to describe the various formalities by means of which a cause of action was initiated and then made its way through court proceedings to final judgment.[100] Instead, he spoke of pleadings and practice—two components of litigation that he viewed as clearly distinct. Whereas pleadings constituted "the written allegations of the respective parties in the suit," or the means by which the parties brought their claims and defenses before the court, practice consisted of the proceedings by means of which these claims were then adjudicated. Story recognized that "[t]he principles, which regulate the pleadings, are sometimes . . . intimately connected with the practice of the Court," such that there was no way to discuss the one without alluding to the other. But he nonetheless concluded that these were distinct topics, which ought therefore to be treated separately. Evidently deeming pleadings to be of greater significance than practice, he decided to devote the treatise to the former and to leave the latter to another day, when he hoped "to find leisure to complete my original design by furnishing an elementary outline of the Practice of Courts of Equity, from the first inception of the cause, through all its various stages, to the execution of its final decree. . . ."[101] Committed to the notion that pleadings and practice were distinct subjects meriting distinct treatment, Story had in no way embraced the modern-day conception of procedure as the sum total of formal mechanisms necessary for the adjudication of a distinct set of substantive legal rights.

Just as Story's *Equity Pleadings* was by no means a treatise on procedure, so too his *Equity Jurisprudence* was not an account of the substantive law of equity. In the book's opening chapter, he endeavored to define "the true nature and character of equity jurisprudence." Rejecting as mistaken the prevalent view that equity was synonymous with "natural justice," he explained that "[i]n England, and in the American States . . . Equity has a restrained and qualified meaning." According to Story, this narrower, technical meaning of *equity* was far too complex to reduce to "direct definitions," and accordingly, a series of "explanatory observations" would have to suffice.[102] Strikingly, almost all of the "explanatory observations" that he then offered as a way of defining equity jurisprudence were procedural, rather than substantive, in nature. As this suggests, Story's conception of equity—much like the traditional writ-based conception of the common law—was predominantly procedural.

In his first "explanatory observation," Story noted that "Equity Jurisprudence may . . . properly be said to be that portion of remedial justice which is exclusively administered by a Court of Equity, as contradistinguished from that portion of remedial justice which is exclusively administered by a Court of Common Law." The content of equity, in other words, was *not* defined by reference to particular categories of substantive law. Instead, it was determined by a purely procedural hurdle—namely, the jurisdiction before which claims could be made. Equity jurisprudence was thus synonymous with those claims that—as a matter of the procedural law of jurisdiction—were to be brought before courts of equity. Moreover, as suggested by this same language, Story viewed equity as a form of "remedial justice"—as a set of procedural remedies for enforcing substantive legal rights or, in his words, "for the redress of wrongs, and for the enforcement of rights."[103]

That Story thus prioritized the remedial (and therefore the procedural) is also evident from his subsequent "explanatory observations," in which he continued to define the content of equity jurisprudence by reference to the various remedies that were available in courts of equity as opposed to common law. Common-law courts, he observed, required that all suits be filed pursuant to "certain prescribed forms of action," such that judgment would "be given for the plaintiff or for the defendant, without any adaptation of it to particular circumstances." The problem with this approach was that "there are many cases, in which a simple judgment for either party, without qualifications, or conditions, or particular arrangements, will not do entire justice *ex aequo et bono* to either party," and thus "[s]ome modifications of the rights of both parties may be required; . . . some adjustments involving reciprocal obligations or duties." Unlike common-law courts, Story emphasized, courts of equity were "not so restrained." Endowed with a procedural, remedial flexibility lacking in their common-law counterparts, equity courts were able to "vary, qualify, restrain, and model the remedy, so as to suit it to mutual adverse claims, controlling equities, and the real and substantial rights of all the parties." In addition, as Story was careful to observe, the distinctive ability of equity courts to craft such a nuanced remedy hinged on their unique procedural authority to call before them all interested parties. "[W]hereas Courts of Common Law are compelled to limit their inquiry to the very parties in the litigation before them, although other persons may have the deepest interest in the event of the suit," equity courts had the power to "bring before them all parties interested in the subject matter, and adjust the rights of all, however numerous."[104] In all these respects, therefore, equity jurisprudence was defined primarily by procedural considerations—and, in particular, by the distinctively flexible and broad scope of equity courts' remedial authority.

It was only after thus defining equity jurisprudence in procedural terms that Story finally suggested a more substantive definition—though here as well he began his "explanatory observation" by prioritizing procedural remedy over substantive right. As he argued, "[a]nother peculiarity of Courts of Equity is, that they can administer remedies for rights, which rights Courts of Common Law do not recognize at all. . . ." Equity jurisprudence, in other words, was defined not in the first instance by its recognition of a distinctive set of substantive legal rights, but instead by the fact that it afforded procedural remedies for the enforcement of such rights. Having yet again prioritized the procedural, Story then briefly identified a number of the substantive rights for which equity, unlike the common law, provided a procedural remedy. He highlighted, in particular, the law of trusts, as well as "losses and injuries by mistake, accident, and fraud" and "cases of impending irreparable injuries, or meditated mischiefs," which we would now view as falling largely within the law of contract and tort.[105]

Story's (partial) turn to the substantive, however, was but a momentary detour, followed by a set of further "explanatory observations" focused once more on primarily procedural considerations. Equity jurisprudence, he suggested, was characterized not only by the distinctive relief that it was able to afford, but also by its unique approach to litigation itself. Just as equity courts had far greater remedial authority than their common-law counterparts, so too they had far greater authority to seek evidence—including, crucially, the testimony of the parties themselves. Thus, while common-law courts obtain evidence "not from the parties, but from third persons, who are disinterested witnesses," equity courts "address themselves to the conscience of the defendant, and require him to answer upon his oath the matters of fact stated in the bill, if they are within his knowledge. . . ."[106]

Perhaps most importantly, common-law and equity courts also differed over the adjudicatory personnel responsible for conducting the trial. While common-law courts "proceed to the trial of contested facts by means of a jury," equity courts relied for judgment on a single judge—and it was precisely this reliance that made possible the distinctive procedural flexibility and authority that were the hallmarks of equity.[107] Moreover, as Kent and Story saw it, the equity judge was necessarily endowed with superior moral and intellectual gifts, since only an individual of such high character was able to gather all relevant evidence (including that provided by the parties themselves), adjudicate the claims of all interested persons (rather than merely those between one plaintiff and one defendant), and craft a remedy that was perfectly suited to the particulars of the case (finding neither for the plaintiff nor the defendant but instead balancing the equities, often through complex injunctive relief).

In short, underlying their idealized, heroic image of the judicial role in equity were the distinctive, judge-empowering procedural features of the equity tradition.

It was the profoundly procedural nature of Kent and Story's conception of equity that explains their otherwise puzzling assertions that the equity judge somehow embraced a commitment to both moral intuition and rational predictability. As we have seen, Story insisted that chancery was bound by precedent, and he therefore firmly rejected the notion that the chancellor "act[s] according to his own notions, *ex aequo et bono*." But at the very same time, he praised chancery, unlike the common-law courts, for "do[ing] entire justice *ex aequo et bono*." Though seemingly contradictory, these statements make much more sense when we recognize that both Kent and Story conceptualized equity in terms of (comparative) procedure. Put differently, these men rejected the view that the chancellor sought to impose his own arbitrary conception of a *substantively* just outcome on the parties—an assertion most famously associated with the seventeenth-century English jurist John Selden's quip that equity was determined by the size of the chancellor's foot. That said, as Kent and Story understood it, the chancellor did pursue the outcome that was *procedurally* just. Their notion of procedural justice was, in turn, shaped by comparison with the framework of the common law. As Story observed, a standard way of framing "the peculiar duty of a Court of Equity is, to supply the defects of the Common Law, and . . . to correct its rigour or injustice."[108]

The common law and its writ-based system of pleading allowed plaintiffs to file suit only to the extent that their particular complaint happened to fall within one of the established writs (or formulas) allowing for litigation. This resulted not only in many rightful claimants being denied a forum but also in holdings that were themselves unjust—as in situations where the plaintiff complied with the formal requirements imposed by the writ for obtaining relief, but where a broader examination would have revealed evidence of fraud or mistake suggesting that the defendant's obligation ought to be excused. So too, common-law pleading aimed at joinder of issue—namely, narrowing the dispute to a single question of law raised against a single defendant, thus simplifying the case for purposes of jury deliberation. And even in thus limiting the suit to two parties, the common law refused to consider any claims that the defendant himself might have against the plaintiff. Moreover, in adjudicating the dispute, the common-law courts disregarded key sources of relevant evidence because they disqualified the parties themselves from serving as witnesses and, more generally, lacked robust mechanisms for the discovery of proof. So too, in crafting a remedy, such courts were limited to ordering money damages—a resolution that might not always provide adequate compensation for past harm and afforded no protection against future or ongoing injuries.

In sharp contrast, as Story emphasized, equity encouraged plaintiffs to file open-ended narratives addressing all aspects of their injuries and utilized procedural mechanisms that facilitated the involvement of all interested parties. This made it possible for plaintiffs in equity to assert multiple claims against multiple parties and for others involved in the suit to assert their own related claims. Moreover, because equity was not constrained to enforce a given writ but concerned itself instead with the conscience of the parties, it was able to identify situations in which fraud, mistake, or the like suggested that a party ought to be released from an otherwise lawfully contracted obligation. At the same time, equity deployed powerful mechanisms of discovery aimed at bringing all relevant evidence before the court, including party testimony, thus increasing the probability that the suit would be decided in accordance with the actual facts. And in designing a remedy, equity was able to ensure specific relief by acting on the person of the defendant, whether by mandating specific performance of contracts to convey property or issuing injunctions to prevent continued and future injuries (like ongoing pollution to property). The net effect of equity's procedural particularities was that chancery could reflect on the extent to which the multiple parties involved in a given suit acted in accordance with both law and justice and adjust the equities accordingly. Such procedural maneuvering—aimed at delivering justice *ex aequo et bono*—hinged, in turn, on the distinctive power of the equity judge.

Contemporary readers of Story's treatises who were acquainted with the extensive English treatise literature on equity (and with contemporary New York practice) would have found very familiar his account of equity as a predominantly procedural system—one defined by the extensive authority confided to the judge. Such readers, however, may well have remarked that there was one important and distinguishing feature of equity procedure to which Story gave short shrift—namely, its approach to deciding facts, including in particular the taking of witness testimony. Story undertook no sustained discussion of this key topic, addressing it instead only in passing. For example, in noting that equity, unlike the common law, allowed for the examination of the defendant under oath, he observed that "the testimony of . . . witnesses . . . may be taken to confirm, or to refute, the facts . . . alleged" by the defendant in his sworn answer.[109] Such a generic statement failed to address (or even acknowledge) the very significant differences between the equitable and common-law approaches to gathering witness testimony. As we have seen, the common law relied on the oral presentation of testimony, whose veracity was to be tested by public, lawyer-driven cross-examination, while equity relied on written evidence, gathered by chancery officials in closed, private proceedings from which the parties themselves were excluded. Equity's approach to taking testimony, in short, was reminiscent of that employed in the quasi-inquisitorial systems of procedure that had developed in continental Europe. As such, it was yet one more powerful device in the equity judge's substantial procedural arsenal.

Why then did Story—a great advocate of preserving equity as a distinctive judge-empowering tradition—opt not to discuss this important aspect of equity procedure? The choice is particularly puzzling given that this was a topic of extensive commentary in the English treatise literature from which contemporary Americans (including both Kent and Story) derived much of their knowledge of equity procedure. Likewise, as we will see, the subject of witness testimony was one to which Kent devoted enormous attention when he became chancellor of New York in 1814. One possible explanation for Story's silence regarding witness testimony is that he considered the topic to be a matter of "practice," rather than "jurisprudence" or "pleadings," and thus more suited to discussion in the third treatise on equity that he intended to write but never did. At the same time, the topic may well have been one that he was all too glad to avoid, since by the time he wrote his treatises in the mid- to late 1830s, the traditional equity methods for taking witness testimony had become deeply contested. In the highly influential state of New York, lawyers on the ground had by then adopted significant elements of the common law's oral, adversarial approach to testimony. In this respect, while the publication of Story's treatises represented the high-water mark of American equity, his silence on the key topic of witness testimony served obliquely to denote the set of conflicts that were already then undermining core aspects of its distinctive quasi-inquisitorial mode.

## Kent's Efforts to Reinforce Equity's Traditional, Written and Secrecy-Oriented Approach to Taking Testimony

While Story eschewed any discussion of equity's distinctive approach to taking testimony, this was a topic to which Kent himself devoted considerable attention in his capacity as chancellor. Adopting a self-consciously didactic tone, he strenuously urged chancery practitioners to observe the many rules underlying English Chancery's traditional, written, and secrecy-oriented approach to witness testimony.

Ironically, it was in an opinion by means of which Kent unwittingly helped to open the door to oral, adversarial procedure—his 1817 decision in *Remsen v. Remsen*—that he provided one of his most complete accounts of the virtues of equity's traditional, quasi-inquisitorial approach to fact-finding. Secrecy, he explained, was the only sure way to prevent perjury. After publication passed and the parties became acquainted with the testimony, there was a serious risk that they would deploy this knowledge to manufacture additional testimony that would bolster or contradict that already taken. In his words, the reason why "examinations in chief are not permitted, after publication" is that "there is very great danger of abuse from public examinations, by which parties are enabled to detect the weak parts of the adversary's case, or of their own, and to hunt up or fabricate testimony to meet the pressure or exigency of the inquiry." For the same reason, once the court ordered publication, further testimony before the master was not allowed, unless directed by the court, and then only as to issues regarding which the witness had not previously testified.[110]

Similarly, in *Hamersly v. Lambert,* decided the same year as *Remsen,* Kent denied the defendants' request to take post-publication testimony and in so doing reaffirmed the fundamental importance of equity's secrecy-oriented approach to preventing perjury. As he explained:

> To allow this motion, after publication has passed, without good cause shown, and without a sufficient excuse for the delay, would be overturning the established course and practice of the Court, and setting a mischievous precedent. The rule not allowing evidence to be taken after publication, is founded in wisdom and sound policy. It is intended . . . to guard against the mischiefs which would result from holding out an opportunity to a party to supply a defect by fabricated evidence.

In so holding, Kent rejected the defendants' argument that they ought to be permitted to take further testimony because they had not seen the depositions already taken, and there was therefore no risk that they might be tempted to procure additional, false testimony. While this made sense in theory, the reality was that it was nearly impossible to determine whether parties claiming not to have seen depositions were, in fact, telling the truth: "The party, on such motions as this, does, indeed, make the usual oath, that *he has not seen, heard, or been informed of, nor will he see, hear, or be informed of, the contents of the depositions taken,* until publication shall be again duly passed; but such an oath ought not to be much encouraged. It is partly promissory: it may be difficult to be strictly kept, and is of dangerous and suspicious tendency."[111] Because of the difficulties inherent in policing party behavior and because the goal of maintaining pre-publication secrecy was so important, Kent held that motions to take post-publication testimony would be permitted only if the moving party could show good cause for the failure to take the testimony prior to publication. Since the defendants in *Hamersley* had failed to show such cause, Kent denied their motion.

Likewise, in his 1818 opinion in *Troup v. Sherwood,* Kent once again defended equity's longstanding policy of prohibiting post-publication testimony. The defendants in *Troup* took post-publication testimony before an examiner—ostensibly for the limited and permissible purpose of impeaching witnesses examined by the plaintiff prior to publication. They then moved for an order to pass publication of this impeachment testimony. But upon seeing the articles filed by the defendants, which stated their grounds for concluding that plaintiff's witnesses lacked credibility, the plaintiff objected to the defendants' motion. His main argument was that the defendants were challenging not simply the witnesses' general reputation for honesty but also their testimony as to particular material issues of fact. In thus challenging the specifics of the witnesses' testimony, the plaintiff argued, the defendants were seeking an opportunity to obtain additional testimony addressing the facts in dispute. In this way, they were attempting to use impeachment testimony for the purpose of doing an end run around the rule prohibiting post-publication testimony on the merits. Not surprisingly, Kent denied the defendants' motion to pass publication. Having reviewed both the articles and the interrogatories prepared by the defendants, he concluded that "[i]t is plain to perceive, that the interrogatories do go into the merits of the issue, under pretence of examining as to credit only." As he was careful to explain, "[t]his cannot be permitted; for it would be indirectly breaking down those ancient and salutary rules, which require the examination on the merits to be closed as soon as publication has passed."[112]

Kent reaffirmed the key importance of these principles of secrecy several years later in *Field v. Schieffelin,* a case in which one of the defendants moved for leave to file a cross-bill against the plaintiff, or as it is now known, a counterclaim. In denying the motion, Kent stated that the defendant improperly sought by means of "the cross-bill . . . to put in issue, and establish by proof, the very matters which have been already put in issue, and upon which proof had been taken and submitted to the judgment of the Court," thereby violating the prohibition on the post-publication taking of testimony. According to Kent, there were two ways to ensure that the filing of a cross-bill was not such an illicit attempt to pierce the veil of secrecy by taking additional (that is, post-publication) testimony. The first was to require the defendant to rely in the new pleading exclusively on testimony already taken in the case. Alternatively, a post-publication cross-bill might be authorized if the original hearing resulted in a default judgment, such that no testimony was ever taken, in which case "there can be no danger of abuse." But short of these two exceptions, once testimony in a case had been published, a cross-bill would not be permitted. To hold otherwise, Kent insisted, was to ignore human nature itself and thereby jeopardize the court's pursuit of truth. Alluding to an extensive body of eighteenth-century moral and political-economic thought focused on the role of self-interest and the passions in shaping social interaction, he claimed that the rule prohibiting post-publication cross-bills was "founded in sound policy, and in a just sense and deep knowledge of the seductions of interest, and the force and influence of the passions." By carefully attending to these aspects of human nature, he suggested, the rule made it possible "to prevent the danger of perjury."[113]

But Kent's most careful and extended defense of equity's quasi-inquisitorial approach to the taking of testimony appeared in February 1821, in opposition to proposed legislation intended "to alter the mode of taking evidence in the Court of Chancery." As summarized by the *Albany Gazette*, this bill was designed to "abolish[] the present mode of taking evidence in secret, on written interrogatories" and to replace it with the oral, adversarial methods of the common law. Toward this end, the bill required "the chancellor, either personally, to examine witnesses in public, *ore tenus*, or to direct an examiner, master, etc. to take such examination in like manner."[114] As we will see, this legislation, though seemingly radical, served largely to further developments that were already well underway as a result of lawyers' changing practices. Not surprisingly, Kent was deeply opposed to these developments and to the legislature's evident willingness to provide its stamp of approval. Accordingly, he wrote a report to the State Senate that criticized the bill and trumpeted the virtues of equity's traditional, secrecy-oriented approach to testimony.

Contrary to the assumptions of the common law, Kent argued, it was secrecy, rather than publicity, that provided the most effective means of preventing perjury. Accordingly, the most "serious objection to the new mode of examination proposed is the temptation it would hold out to abuse." The oral, public examination of witnesses would enable parties and their counsel to learn of the testimony given in the case and, to the extent that it proved in any way disappointing, to search for additional testimony to counteract it: "The parties, or their more sagacious counsel, would be enabled very early to detect the weak parts of their adversary's proof, or their own, and they could be induced to seek upon adjournment, for further testimony to meet the pressure and exigency of the case." It was to avoid precisely this temptation to suborn perjury that parties and their counsel were traditionally prohibited from being present and that "examinations in chief are rarely permitted, after the testimony on each side has been disclosed by publication." So too, "[i]t is for the same reason, that a witness who has been once examined in chief, cannot be re-examined before a master without a special order; and even then, not to any matter to which he had been before examined." Indeed, Kent insisted, the great wisdom of equity's traditional, written, and secrecy-oriented approach was such that "[e]ven during the period of the English commonwealth, when every part of the English constitution, except their jurisprudence, was laid in the dust, and when the commissioners, who took the place of the chancellor, undertook the reformation of the court, the present mode of examination of witnesses was preserved. . . ." Accordingly, he concluded, "it has become an axiom in [English] equity policy, that no proceeding can take place, of more dangerous import, than to permit parties to make out evidence by piece-meal, and after a discovery of the weakness of testimony, to allow them an opportunity to look out for witnesses to supply the deficiency." The end result of "[s]uch a course of practice" was "perjury and vexation."[115]

Given Kent's continued power and prominence, the proposed legislation was not enacted. But later that very year, a constitutional convention was called to revise many aspects of the original state constitution deemed to be anti-democratic, and as we will see, some delegates demanded the abolition of chancery in its entirety. Kent, himself a delegate, successfully rose in defense of the institution, pointing once again to the virtues of equity's distinctive written and secrecy-oriented approach to testimony. In so doing, he took the opportunity to address, if only briefly, a key point of institutional structure— namely, that equity's quasi-inquisitorial model required an extensive (neutral and professional) judicial staff to pose and record questions and otherwise oversee fact-finding.

Chancery, Kent observed, was better able than a common-law court to resolve legally and factually complex matters. This was in part because of the unique wisdom and sensibilities of the equity judge, as compared with the more limited capacities of the common-law judge and especially the jury. But at least as important in this regard was the fact that the equity judge was assisted by a body of expert judicial assistants, including, most importantly, masters in chancery:

> The subjects of equity jurisdiction were not proper for a jury, and therefore they ought to reside in a separate tribunal. . . . Nothing is more complicated than the investigation and settlement of accounts between partners in trade, and between factors and agents and their principals. It would be impossible in most cases, to bring such cases within the reach of a jury, and a jury would be utterly incompetent to bestow the time and labour requisite to examine them. Courts of law always refer such matters to reference, with or without the consent of parties, and the investigation can be as well, and perhaps much better, conducted before a master under the direction of the chancellor. The masters in chancery are sworn officers, whose habits, and study, and knowledge, fit and prepare them for such duties. The business is made a matter of distinct profession and science, and they will usually have the skill and capacity which such an exclusive employment creates.[116]

In short, as Kent implicitly recognized, equity's quasi-inquisitorial approach to evidence-gathering (and thus fact-finding) necessitated a staff of judicial officers ready to serve.

In thus describing equity's judicial staff as a set of public officers of "distinct profession and science," Kent in no way envisioned a modern-day civil service bureaucracy. Rather than salaried bureaucrats, what he had in mind was public-oriented elites—propertied men like himself, who embraced as their civic duty a lifetime of service on behalf of the commonweal. His was, in short, a civic republican conception of public office—one that trusted that the right kind of educated, elite, and (financially) independent men would naturally rise to the task at hand.[117] But with the emergence of party politics and the spoils system, this civic republican conception of public office was quickly becoming outdated.[118] As we will see, the offices of master and examiner in chancery became important pawns in the patronage politics underlying the early party systems. Having trusted in an elitist, civic republican conception of politics to ensure that the right kind of men serve as chancery's judicial staff, Kent thus failed to address one of the main, longstanding deficiencies of equity's quasi-inquisitorial model of procedure—namely, that chancery lacked the neutral professional staff required to implement equity's quasi-inquisitorial logic.

Kent's failure of vision in this respect would soon be reflected in an important shift in how civic republican discourse was deployed to characterize equity proceedings and personnel. While Kent had used this language to describe chancery's judicial staff, practicing lawyers increasingly appropriated it to describe themselves. In so doing, we will see, they helped give rise to an oral and adversarial vision of equity practice that was deeply at odds with Kent's quasi-inquisitorial conception of the institution and the civic elite at its helm. To understand how this came to pass, we must begin by examining the structural features of chancery—inherited from England—that functioned to destabilize equity procedure, thereby making it susceptible to various kinds of lawyerly manipulation.

## 2 · A Troubled Inheritance

The English Procedural Tradition and Its Lawyer-Driven
Reconfiguration in Early Nineteenth-Century New York

Just as Kent succeeded in conceptualizing and systematizing equity's distinctive quasi-inquisitorial logic, the procedural system he worked so assiduously to promote began to implode. This was due to the intersection of a set of longstanding structural features of chancery with more immediate and contingent developments. New York Chancery inherited from its English counterpart a profound structural tension—namely, a disjunction between its quasi-inquisitorial logic (which necessitated a large professional staff of judicial officers) and its choice to rely on a relatively small official staff, supplemented on a case-by-case basis by lay commissioners. This structural tension, in turn, created opportunities for lawyers to insert themselves into chancery proceedings in ways that contravened the court's traditional quasi-inquisitorial logic. As we will see, lawyers in the first decades of the nineteenth century began to be present in some proceedings before masters to take testimony, and for a number of reasons, Chancellor Kent, much to his later regret, authorized this practice in his 1817 decision in *Remsen v. Remsen*. The presence of lawyers in masters' proceedings then initiated a dynamic—a kind of chain reaction—pursuant to which lawyers came to exercise ever greater control over these proceedings. And once masters' proceedings were changed in this fashion, the logic of adversarialism radiated outward, extending to proceedings before examiners as well, such that by the 1840s these were transformed into miniature versions of oral, adversarial common-law trials.

But while New York Chancery's adoption of oral, adversarial procedure seems to have followed largely from incremental developments internal to the institution itself, lawyers were the moving force. Accounting properly for their motivations requires us, in turn, to consider the multiple factors—including resolutely externalist, cultural ones—that helped to shape these. As we will see, one such factor was lawyers' ambition to be perceived as embodying the classical ideal of the lawyer-orator as a Ciceronian civic elite. But so too, their turn to the oral, adversarial methods of the common law was likely influenced by the era's embrace of publicity in governance—an emerging transatlantic value most powerfully advocated by the English jurist Jeremy Bentham.

## The Conflict between English Chancery's Quasi-Inquisitorial Logic and Ad Hoc Institutional Structure

As John Dawson observed, English Chancery procedure was conceptually conflicted at its core in that it embraced a method for obtaining proof that necessitated an extensive judicial personnel, even while lacking one. Remarkably, throughout its entire history, English Chancery remained a one-judge court. Moreover, from the 1530s until its demise in the late nineteenth century, it employed only two examiners to take witness testimony. While there were more masters—a total of twelve—these too proved insufficient to assist the (lone) chancellor with his many fact-finding duties, especially as chancery's docket expanded from the sixteenth century onward. Like so many other English governmental institutions, chancery made an early and fateful decision to avoid creating a permanent bureaucracy of officeholders, opting instead to rely on lay commissioners appointed on a temporary, ad hoc basis.[1] The ad hoc, private nature of these appointments—including the fact that such individuals were usually nominated and compensated by the parties themselves— undermined the sense that they were neutral court officers responsible to the judge, rather than to the litigants. The logic animating equity procedure was thus fundamentally at odds with chancery's institutional structure—and this disjuncture, in turn, created the potential for lawyers to exercise greater control over the proceedings than the logic of equity ought to have allowed.

As described in the treatise literature, commissioners—private, lay individuals who were appointed to take testimony on a case-by-case basis—were nominated by the parties themselves, rather than by the court.[2] Each party was responsible for identifying four possible commissioners, two of whom would be struck from the list by his adversary. The remaining four would then be officially appointed by the chancellor. In theory, the fact that it was the court itself that was ultimately responsible for appointing the commissioners meant that the latter were neutral court officials, rather than partisan representatives of the litigants. As Gilbert explained, "though the commissioners are named by the party, yet that is but by way of proposal to the court, for they are the ministers of the court, and therefore must be impartial."[3]

In reality, the fact that the parties themselves selected the commissioners (and paid their fees) had a profound effect on the role that these individuals served. As Michael Macnair argues, commissioners in seventeenth-century English Chancery were often viewed not as "judicial officers" but instead as "somewhat suspect party nominees."[4] Indeed, the rules governing the conduct of commissioners are clearly premised on the assumption that these supposedly neutral court officers might be tempted to represent the interests of whichever party had selected and paid them. For example, they assume that a party's commissioners may try to inform him of the contents of depositions taken on behalf of his opponent—thus violating equity's fundamental commitment to (pre-publication) secrecy. For this reason, the treatise literature explains, commissioners who are present during an examination undertaken by another party's commissioners but who fail to examine witnesses themselves are thereafter strictly prohibited from undertaking further examination without a special court order so allowing. As Gilbert observed, the purpose of this rule was to ensure that when a commissioner was present but did not examine witnesses himself, the party who chose that commissioner would "not form his interrogatories upon the discovery made to his commissioners of what the other side examined to." The danger here was that "after having knowledge of all that his adversary hath proved, . . . [the party] may easily conceive what interrogatories to exhibit, and how to hit the bird in the eye. . . ."[5]

That commissioners were, in practice, often associated with the litigant who employed them, rather than viewed as neutral court officers, is also suggested by the differences between the rules that applied to them and those that applied to examiners. According to the treatise literature, examiners were entitled (prior to publication) to examine witnesses not only upon an initial set of interrogatories provided by the parties but also on new interrogatories, should these prove necessary. In contrast, absent specific court authorization to the contrary, commissioners were entitled to examine witnesses only on the initial set of interrogatories. The reason for this difference in treatment was, in part, that examiners were full-time court officials and, as such, had some independent authority to act. In contrast, commissioners were delegated to perform only a particular task—namely, examining witnesses on the interrogatories annexed to the formal letters of commission appointing them.[6] To examine witnesses on a second set of interrogatories was thus, as a technical matter, to exceed the bounds of the commission. More fundamentally, however, commissioners, unlike examiners, were prohibited from administering new interrogatories for fear that they might function as partisan advocates of the litigants who had selected them, revealing to "their" party the contents of the first set of interrogatories and depositions. As Gilbert explained, in the case of commissioners, "it is presumed that there has been a discovery made of the proofs, when the party is desirous to examine upon a new set of interrogatories." But no such presumption was made about the examiner, who as a full-time court official was "at the peril of his office to make no discovery of the proofs."[7]

A similar anxiety that commissioners might be partisan is evident in the rules governing when they, as opposed to examiners, could serve as witnesses. While the treatise literature addresses the possibility of commissioners serving as witnesses, it is silent concerning when and if examiners might testify. This suggests that, in practice, it was commissioners and not examiners who had the most occasion to testify. That this was so likely stems from the very nature of commissioners—from the fact that these were ordinary individuals, otherwise unassociated with chancery, chosen by the litigants because they knew and trusted them. There was, in short, a probability of some preexisting relationship between litigants and commissioners—and this, in turn, made it that much more likely that commissioners would also prove to be material witnesses. In such cases, there was a danger that commissioners, already partial to the party who had selected them, would attempt, in their capacity as witnesses, to promote that party's interests. And if, because they were commissioners, they had knowledge of what others had testified, they might be tempted in their position as witnesses to bolster or contradict such testimony. It was therefore crucial that a commissioner who was also to serve as a witness not be permitted, in his capacity as commissioner, to hear the testimony of other witnesses prior to testifying. As Gilbert cautioned, "A commissioner may be examined by the other commissioners, if he be examined first before any other depositions taken in the cause; but if any other depositions be taken in the cause, his depositions shall be suppressed, for if it were otherwise, a commissioner might lie in wait, and after having knowledge of the depositions, might by his oath contest the same."[8]

Despite the existence of these various rules designed to ensure that commissioners avoid any temptation to promote the interests of the parties who selected and paid them, the treatise literature reveals that they were at times honored more in the breach than in the observance. Indeed, as is so often the case with the law, the creation of (and insistence on) such rules was likely itself a reaction to the very practices that they were designed to prevent. Gilbert himself complained that it was common for commissioners who had observed an examination but failed to pose interrogatories to request a second commission. Commissioners, in short, were all too willing to do an end run around equity's traditional commitment to (pre-publication) secrecy: "[B]y common experience, it is but too often found that country commissioners publish and divulge all the evidence taken before them, and this even before publication, and that in such manner that it is rarely or ever to be detected, because they disclose it only to the attorney or solicitor who employs them, and who is their friend. . . ."⁹

As suggested by Gilbert's reference to commissioners revealing secret information to the attorneys who employed them, lawyers seem to have played an important role in leading commissioners to function more like partisan advocates than neutral officials. Lawyers sought to deploy their relationship to commissioners to their clients' advantage—as a means of evading those rules designed to ensure that fact-gathering would be conducted in a neutral, non-partisan fashion. Consider, in this vein, Gilbert's report of one late seventeenth-century lawyer's efforts to circumvent the rules mandating pre-publication secrecy. According to Gilbert, this lawyer endeavored to ensure that his adversary would discover, prior to publication, the contents of the depositions for which he (the conniving lawyer) had arranged:

> There was a memorable instance . . . in my Lord Sommers's time, where an artful solicitor got copies of his client's depositions, and immediately went away with them to the adverse attorney or solicitor, showed him the depositions, and, to make sure work of it, read them over to him. His adversary, being ignorant of the rule, told him they must notwithstanding have an opportunity to examine their witnesses; and soon after bringing his witnesses to the examiner's office, he was told they could not be examined, because publication was passed, and the depositions were copied and delivered out.¹⁰

In this way, the lawyer successfully took advantage of his adversary's unfamiliarity with equity procedure to prevent him from examining witnesses of his own.

Commissioners, moreover, do not appear to have been the only judicial officers in chancery subject to party manipulation. While we know remarkably little about those few individuals who served as examiners and were thus responsible for taking testimony on a permanent rather than ad hoc basis, extant research suggests that they too could at times operate more as partisan advocates than as neutral court officers. In his account of Elizabethan chancery, W. J. Jones notes that while "the Examiners claimed to adhere strictly to the code of public officers who dealt indifferently between litigants . . . complaints were often to be heard as to the manner in which the Examiners conducted their work." These included not only complaints that they evidenced "the sort of slipshod incompetence which might be expected from an understaffed office" but also concerns about the propriety of their conduct. As Jones observes, "[s]ome litigants in Chancery revealed themselves to be fearful of a dishonest Examiner" who had produced an inaccurate narrative of the witness's testimony (perhaps to advantage one side over the other in return for an improper financial award).

Although masters in Elizabethan chancery held their positions on a permanent rather than ad hoc basis, the effort to make ends meet required them to seek work elsewhere as well. Thus, they provided assistance to other courts that, like chancery, were influenced by the civil law tradition (such as Admiralty, Requests, and the ecclesiastical courts) and offered expert legal consultation on matters of international and commercial law. So too, they accepted unofficial contributions from the chancery litigants whom they served, leading many to question their neutrality.[11] Moreover, because both masters and examiners charged fees for the services they provided, they were long suspected of undertaking unnecessarily numerous and lengthy proceedings with an eye toward increasing their incomes, thus contributing to the sense that these chancery officials were not the fair-minded professionals that they were supposed to be.[12]

As suggested by these examples, there was a profound tension between the quasi-inquisitorial logic of equity and its ad hoc institutional structure. This tension, in turn, enabled lawyers eager to promote their clients' interests to intervene in the proceedings in ways that subverted equity's quasi-inquisitorial foundations. In this respect, English Chancery itself produced some of the potential for its own subversion by adversarial forces.

## New York Chancery's Inherited Structural Tensions

The tension between English Chancery's quasi-inquisitorial logic and ad hoc institutional structure was inherited by its New York counterpart. Until 1823, when the state legislature augmented the number of judges authorized to hear first-instance suits in equity by creating eight circuit judges, New York

Chancery had only one judge—namely, the chancellor. While the state as a whole had many more than the two examiners and twelve masters on which English Chancery had long relied, these officers were selected, supervised, and paid in such a way that, as in the case of their English counterparts, there was reason to doubt their professionalism and neutrality. Moreover, New York Chancery continued to make extensive use of lay commissioners appointed on an ad hoc, case-by-case basis. As in England, these individuals appear to have operated at times largely outside court supervision, responsive more to the parties who nominated them than to the judge himself.

The deck was thus arguably stacked against New York Chancery and its traditional quasi-inquisitorial methods. Indeed, as rising population growth, commercial activity, and democratization put ever more pressure on the court's docket, perhaps it was inevitable that something had to give. But while reform of some kind was likely unavoidable, the same cannot be said for the particular nature of the reform pursued. The structural disjunction responsible for the court's instability could have been resolved by increasing the size of chancery's staff rather than by embracing oral, adversarial procedure. And as we will see, serious efforts to augment the number of chancery officials were in fact made for quite some time. Given the centuries-old failure of English Chancery to adopt a large and permanent judicial staff and the inherited American anxiety about too many officeholders and placemen, it is certainly doubtful that New York could have ever developed a large, European-style judicial bureaucracy. Still, it may perhaps have increased chancery's staff sufficiently to permit the institution to continue to function in a quasi-inquisitorial mode, even if with less than perfect efficiency. But even if we conclude that the deck was so stacked against quasi-inquisitorial equity that its demise was all but inevitable, it is important to understand the particular way in which New York Chancery came to adopt oral, adversarial procedure. As we will see, the path taken in New York was itself distinctive and would, in turn, contribute to Americans' uniquely intense and self-conscious embrace of adversarialism.

## APPROACHES TO FACT-FINDING

New York Chancery managed to function with relatively few officers partly because its need for factual inquiry, while significant, was nonetheless limited. A review of 466 chancery cases decided between 1801 and 1847 reveals that relatively few—only 142, or roughly one-third—involved the taking of testimony.* In about two-thirds of the cases, the lawsuit was resolved either on purely legal grounds (in which case the court relied primarily on the pleadings and argument of counsel) or, if a factual determination was necessary, that determination was made entirely on the basis of written documentation (sometimes as assessed and reported by a master in chancery).

What accounts for this? One possible explanatory factor is the significant proportion of cases reviewed (61%) in which the bill of complaint was taken *pro confesso*. In these 285 cases, the defendant opted not to file an answer (or sometimes even to appear at all) and was thus deemed to have admitted the allegations in the complaint. Moreover, in an additional 26 cases, or 6 percent—all involving multiple defendants—some defendants filed an answer, while others opted not to do so, such that the bill was taken *pro confesso* as to the latter. The practice of the defendant admitting the complaint thus played a role in about two-thirds of the cases examined.[13]

Upon first glance, the frequency of bills taken *pro confesso* would seem to explain the limited need for factual investigation. In many legal systems, including modern American federal practice, the defendant's failure to file an answer often (though not necessarily) results in a default judgment in favor of the plaintiff, thus obviating the need for fact-finding.[14] But many early and mid-nineteenth-century New York Chancery suits in which bills were taken *pro confesso* did not, in fact, result in default judgments and instead necessitated some factual investigation, including the examination of witnesses.

Consider, for example, suits to foreclose on and sell a mortgaged property, which constituted a remarkably large proportion of the 466 cases reviewed— namely, 279 cases or approximately 60 percent of the total.[15] In such suits, the defendant's failure to file an answer was deemed an admission that there was a lawfully contracted mortgage and that payments were in arrears. But a precise determination of how much the defendant owed was understood to require a more particular investigation and the production of proof. As the New York Chancery explained in 1824, "The bill when confessed by the default of the defendant, is taken to be true in all matters alleged with sufficient certainty: but in respect to matters not alleged with due certainty, or subjects which from their nature and the course of the court, require an examination of details, the obligation to furnish proofs, rests on the complainant."[16] Accordingly, foreclosure suits were almost always referred to a master, whose

* For details concerning the archival records examined and the sampling method employed, see the appendix.

responsibility it was to calculate the exact amount owed on the mortgage—a factual determination that required him to examine a significant amount of documentation and on occasion to take testimony as well.[17]

Another question that commonly arose in foreclosure suits and that chancery delegated to masters (even when the bill was taken *pro confesso*) was whether the mortgaged property was of sufficient value to cover the debt. Unlike the determination of the amount owed on the mortgage, which could often be based exclusively on written documentation, such assessments of current market value were much more difficult to make. Indeed, some masters simply refused to provide any estimate. As one noted, "I have no Data whereby to ascertain the value of the said mortgaged premises."[18] Others responded by assessing the value of the property without providing any explanation of their methodology. As master John G. Spencer obliquely observed, his calculation was based on "the best evidence I can obtain."[19] Yet others relied entirely on personal knowledge: "I the said master have a general knowledge of the nature, situation and value of the said mortgaged premises having viewed the same. . . ."[20] But many masters opted to take testimony.[21]

Suits involving defendants who were minors constituted another type of litigation in which factual determinations proved necessary, even when the bill was taken *pro confesso*. Dating back to its English origins, chancery long prided itself on the protective role that it assumed vis-à-vis minors. Drawing on this tradition, New York Chancery insisted that proof of the facts alleged in the complaint be furnished when the defendants were minors, even if they had failed to file an answer. In cases where a plaintiff sought to foreclose on and sell a mortgaged property (in order to recoup his debt), these principles were deemed to require, in particular, that "the plaintiff . . . prove his debt before the master" and that the master make a "special report" concerning "whether a sale of the whole, or only of a part, and what part of the premises will be most beneficial" to the minor defendants.[22] The archives reveal that these principles were respected in practice, such that the court regularly undertook factual investigations in cases involving minor defendants, even when the bill was taken *pro confesso* against them. Moreover, such factual investigations often entailed the taking of testimony.[23]

But it was a third kind of suit, those for divorce, that imposed the greatest fact-finding burden in cases where the defendant did not file an answer. As initially enacted in March 1787, the New York statute authorizing divorce was quite limited in scope, applying only in cases of adultery. As revised in April 1813, the statute was expanded to cover cases of cruel treatment by the husband. Both statutes, however, provided that where the defendant failed to file an answer and the bill was taken *pro confesso,* chancery was nonetheless required to refer the case to a master to take proof of the plaintiff's allegations.[24] In so ordering, the legislature sought to prevent the parties from colluding to obtain an otherwise unlawful consensual divorce. The end result of this requirement was to force the master to undertake significant factual investigation. And unlike suits for foreclosure, where much of the relevant evidence could be obtained through documentation, the same was not the case in suits for divorce. In divorce suits, a master might examine a marriage certificate to confirm that the parties had been legally married to one another, such that a divorce was actually necessary. But as described below, the key question raised by most such suits—namely, whether the defendant had committed adultery—could be answered only on the basis of (often extensive) witness testimony.

That so many complaints in early and mid-nineteenth-century New York Chancery were taken *pro confesso* thus played some role in reducing the need for extensive factual investigation, but not as significant a role as we might have otherwise imagined. Probably more important in accounting for the fact that testimony proved necessary in only one-third of the cases that I reviewed is that, to the extent that there were disputed questions of fact, these could often be resolved entirely on the basis of written documentation.[25] As noted, about 60 percent of the 466 cases examined were foreclosure suits, and the dominant question in these suits—namely, the amount owed on the mortgage—could typically be answered by reviewing paperwork. Indeed, in only about 18 percent of the foreclosure suits was it necessary for the court to obtain witness testimony. So too, many other types of lawsuit were commonly resolved without recourse to testimony. Of the twenty suits concerning the distribution of an estate, there were only six in which testimony was taken. Of the remaining fourteen, twelve raised factual questions that were disposed of entirely by means of writings and two were confined to legal issues, thus avoiding questions of fact entirely. Similarly, of the 51 suits focused primarily on obtaining injunctive relief (to prevent waste, to disallow the execution of a common-law judgment, and so forth), there were only 21 (or 42%) in which witnesses were called to testify. Only five of the thirteen suits filed regarding trusts required the taking of testimony. And of the four suits aimed at obtaining accountings, in only half was witness testimony solicited. Moreover, in suits designed to obtain a partition of property, the court often delegated the question of where precisely to divide the land to a commission of lay individuals familiar with the property, thereby obviating the need for witness testimony as such.[26]

But while chancery managed to avoid a good many factual questions—and particularly those requiring the taking of testimony—the fact remains that in a not insubstantial one-third of the 466 cases reviewed (or 142 cases), some form of testimony was taken. Who precisely was responsible for doing so? Unfortunately, the surviving records are such that in 17 percent of these 142 cases, it is impossible to determine which court officers took the testimony. But since there is no reason to assume that the absence of identifying information would be skewed more toward one type of officer than another— and since there is no more complete source of data—it makes sense to rely, however cautiously, on the information we do possess. This information is that in 15 percent of the 142 cases, the testimony was taken by commissioners and in 12 percent by examiners. A very sizable proportion—on the order of 58 percent—relied on masters.[27]

What accounts for the far greater frequency with which masters were appointed to take testimony than either commissioners or examiners? The most likely answer is that, as noted above, there were many situations in which the court itself required the taking of testimony, and in these circumstances, it always appointed a master—though on occasion, the master would then opt to rely in part on commissions and/or an examiner. In contrast, commissioners and examiners were typically employed in those cases in which it was the parties themselves who decided to seek testimony. That there were relatively few such cases is likely due to the fact that the taking of testimony was a time-consuming and expensive proposition, which parties therefore preferred to avoid. Avoidance, however, was not always possible.

## TESTIMONY-TAKING AND THE COMPROMISED NEUTRALITY OF CHANCERY OFFICERS

Whether undertaken by commissioners, examiners, or masters, the practice of taking testimony brought to the fore the deep-rooted tensions between chancery's quasi-inquisitorial logic and ad hoc institutional structure. Dating, as we have seen, well back into the English tradition, commissioners were long viewed as suspiciously akin to party agents, rather than neutral court officers. Not surprisingly, given the extent to which New York Chancery borrowed from its English counterpart, there are indications that its commissioners were at times similarly compromised.

Consider, for example, *Bell v. Manning*, an 1828 suit that suggests that, like their English counterparts, New York lawyers sometimes nominated as commissioners individuals with whom their clients were personally acquainted and whose loyalties they hoped to exploit. The plaintiff's claim was that he had been duped through a fraudulent conveyance of property. In an effort to disprove this allegation, one of the defendants, Robert Manning, moved for the appointment of a commission to take the testimony of witnesses living out of state in New Jersey. The plaintiff opposed the motion, arguing that the proposed commissioner was, in fact, a close relative and business associate of the defendant's: "[T]he said Randolph Manning is the only commissioner proposed in the said petition, . . . he is a nephew of the said Robert Manning. . . , and . . . the said Randolph Manning has been in the office of the said Robert Manning the principal part of the time since he commenced his clerkship as a student at law and now is an associate in the office of the said Robert Manning in the City of New York. . . ."[28] For these reasons, the plaintiff insisted, the proposed commissioner could not be expected to be neutral and thus could not be trusted with the task of taking testimony. While I have been unable to locate the court's ruling on the defendant's motion, the fact that the defendant so brazenly sought to obtain the appointment as a (supposedly neutral) commissioner of his own nephew and law partner suggests that at least some early nineteenth-century New York lawyers were eager to exploit equity's reliance on lay officers for adversarial advantage. It was, moreover, not only these lay officers but also the examiners and masters who worked for chancery on a more permanent basis who were subject to such lawyerly manipulation.

Unlike commissioners, both examiners and masters in New York were appointed for a fixed term of years, rather than on a case-by-case basis. As a result, suggested Joseph W. Moulton in his 1829 account of New York Chancery practice, they possessed "a statutory rank as judicial officers."[29] It would be misleading, however, to assume a sharp division between lay commissioners, on the one hand, and professional examiners and masters, on the other. While examiners and masters served for a term of years and (unlike commissioners) were all lawyers,[30] they almost never worked as full-time court officers. Instead, likely because they knew that their appointment to chancery was only temporary, most continued to engage in regular legal practice. This in turn meant that they never came to view themselves first and foremost as (neutral) judicial officers. At the same time, their continued legal practice created possibilities for them to deploy their judicial positions toward partisan and self-serving ends. That these possibilities were, indeed, acted on—in ways deemed to subvert the ends of justice—is strongly suggested by the New York legislature's 1824 enactment of a statute directing that "[n]o master or examiner in chancery shall act as such . . . in any cause or matter in which he shall be solicitor or counsel, or which shall be prosecuted, defended, or in any manner managed or directed by any solicitor or counselor with whom such master or examiner shall be directly or indirectly connected in business."[31]

Also tending to undermine the perceived professionalism, expertise, and neutrality of both examiners and masters was the highly politicized nature of the appointment process. As of the commencement of Kent's chancellorship in 1814, these officials were, like many other government officers in New York, selected by the Council of Appointment. Created by the Constitution of 1777 as one of several institutional mechanisms designed to limit popular democratic government, the Council—consisting of the governor and four senators—was endowed with vast powers of appointment. But with the unanticipated rise of political parties and the emergence of the spoils system for distributing public office, the Council came to be a locus of party conflict and was also widely criticized as undemocratic. Accordingly, the state constitutional convention of 1821 abolished the Council, delegating most non-elective appointments to the control of the governor (upon consent of the Senate).[32] The offices of master and examiner in chancery, which became central to the debate over political patronage and the spoils system, were among those whose disposition was expressly regulated by the new constitution. As provided in the Constitution of 1821, "[t]he governor shall nominate, and with the consent of the senate, appoint masters and examiners in chancery. . . ."[33] Under the system of tight party discipline developed by the Albany Regency—the country's first and arguably most influential political party machine—this new arrangement served to all but guarantee that this leading group of Democrats (who remained in control of state politics until the elections of 1838) would have exclusive say over the appointment of both masters and examiners.[34]

Because of the way they were appointed, masters and examiners quickly became tainted through their association with the spoils system. Indeed, even before the 1821 constitution changed the method for appointing masters and examiners, New York newspapers were filled with complaints that there were far too many such officers because these positions were distributed to party loyalists as a form of political spoils. As the New York Columbian queried in 1817, " 'How long shall the system continue of multiplying the divisions of office . . .? Must we have . . . fifty-six masters in chancery to do the business of six?' " As the article asserted, "Such multiplications are a mockery of common

sense, shifts to create partisans." The end result of appointing so many unnecessary officers was to augment partisan spirit—and at the cost of worsen-
ing the quality of those in office: "[A]s for the masters in chancery—it is not
*every one* who can be well qualified for the duty, because it requires long study
and practice. A *capable few* would be *serviceable* to the community; whilst
a multitude are perhaps rather an inconvenience than otherwise."[35] So too,
long after the 1821 constitution was enacted, similar complaints continued
to emerge. As late as 1838, the *Jamestown Journal,* a Whig paper, complained
that Governor William Learned Marcy—one of the last titans of the Albany
Regency—dispensed the positions of master and examiner as patronage
designed to solidify party loyalty. In its words,

> We have seldom witnessed a more glaring instance of executive usurpa-
> tion or a grosser outrage upon the moral sense of this community, than
> the recent appointment of Surrogate and Masters and Examiners in
> Chancery for this county, by the Governor and Senate of this State. . . .
> Gov. Marcy and his corrupt clique in the senate . . . appointed their par-
> tisans to office. . . . [T]hese veteran expounders of the law saddle the
> people of this county with offices which the laws do not sanction, and
> which the interests of the community do not require.[36]

Under pressure to respond to these concerns, the legislature repeatedly considered enacting laws to reduce the number of masters and examiners.[37] Pursuant to legislation passed in 1827–28, New York City was limited to five masters
and two examiners and all other counties to no more than three masters and
three examiners.[38] But despite this legislation, the number of such officers allowed by law was soon thereafter expanded. On April 25, 1829, the legislature
authorized the appointment of ten masters and three examiners in New York
City and five masters in Albany.[39] And on April 13, 1835, it passed a statute permitting the appointment of one additional master in every county, except for
the city and county of New York.[40] The number of such officers thus continued
to grow. While part of the reason for this growth was the expansion of chancery's docket (especially during the 1830s), the continued incentive to appoint
such officers as a form of political spoils also bore significant responsibility.

The demand for such spoils was, moreover, very high. As observed by the
narrator in Melville's "Bartleby the Scrivener," the position of "Master in
Chancery" was "very pleasantly remunerative."[41] Masters and examiners were
authorized to charge litigants statutorily determined fees for each of the
activities they undertook in their official capacities.[42] But it was widely be-

lieved that they performed unnecessary services as a way of charging additional fees—a practice that cast doubt on their status as supposedly fair-minded court professionals. As argued by Theodore Sedgwick Jr. in an 1838 pamphlet concerning *Delays and Arrears of Business in [New York] Chancery,* "practitioners in . . . courts [like chancery] where [fees] are taken, will bear me out in the assertion that . . . [fees] tend indefinitely to increase the delays and expenses of litigation."[43] So too, lawyers quickly recognized that holding office as a master or examiner—while continuing in practice—served not only as an additional source of income but also as a valuable advertisement, increasing their recognition within the legal profession and among the public more generally. At the same time, by holding such offices, lawyers could help fulfill their status ambitions, striving to embody the contemporary civic republican ideal of the lawyer as the quintessential, public-minded citizen.[44] The urgency with which lawyers pursued office-holding—including the positions of master and examiner—is suggested by a July 23, 1823, article in the *Ithaca Journal,* which reported that "[w]e know of an Attorney in this state, who is solicitor and Examiner in Chancery, senior Judge of the court of Common Pleas, Surrogate of the county, Post-Master, President of the Village Trustees, together with about half a dozen offices in Church and State, which are less profitable but perhaps equally honorable."[45]

For all these reasons, while the quasi-inquisitorial structure of equity conceived of masters and examiners as neutral, professional court officers, the process by which they were appointed and paid often belied such lofty notions. In the eyes of many contemporaries, those who obtained these positions were little more than party hacks, chosen because of their political loyalties and eager to promote themselves (by padding their pocketbooks and reputations) rather than to serve the ends of justice. While there were no doubt many well-qualified men who held these positions, the archival evidence suggests that there was some truth to these widespread contemporary perceptions. Those holding office in chancery did at times exhibit less than professional behavior—and such lapses were exploited by lawyers eager to serve their clients and, in turn, to augment their own procedural power.

## THE CASE OF THE DRUNKEN EXAMINER

Perhaps no case better showcases the dangers—and temptations—posed by chancery's reliance on a limited and relatively uncontrolled staff than *Bennet v. Woodcock.* Filed in 1821, this case, like so many early nineteenth-century chancery suits, concerned the disputed ownership of land. The plaintiff, Silas Bennet, sought specific performance of a contract for the sale of land against the defendant, David Woodcock, a prominent Ithaca lawyer who would go on to serve as a representative to the U.S. Congress just a few short months after the suit was filed against him. Testimony in the suit was taken by an examiner named William Lupton who was initially hired by the plaintiff but whom the defendant—eager to save costs—thereafter decided to employ as well.[46] While the parties opted to use the same examiner, this in itself did not ensure that testimony would be taken in a neutral, expert fashion, free of adversarial influence. Indeed, *Bennet* highlights the extent to which examiners could operate outside institutional constraints, thus becoming subject to adversarial capture and lawyerly manipulation.

Lupton, as it turns out, was an admitted drunkard—and this provided an opportunity for the defendant and his counsel, dissatisfied with the testimony Lupton had recorded, to challenge its validity and attempt to enter new evidence in the record. According to the defendant, David Woodcock, Lupton became extremely intoxicated when taking testimony on his behalf, and as a result, failed correctly to record testimony addressing his central defense. This defense was that the plaintiff, upon abandoning possession of the land in question, had "given up the idea of keeping said property and concluded to have nothing more to do with it." As Woodcock explained, he had expected that two witnesses, Emery Brown and Peter Brown, would testify to this effect, and he was therefore shocked to discover that, according to the depositions prepared by Lupton, they had stated precisely the opposite. Woodcock thus concluded that, because Lupton was drunk, he had failed properly to record the testimony.[47] As a result, Woodcock moved to suppress the depositions taken by Lupton on his behalf and to appoint a commission to take testimony, or alternatively to examine the witnesses himself "viva voce . . . upon the hearing of this cause."[48]

Not surprisingly, Lupton flatly denied that he was drunk while taking the testimony of Emery Brown and Peter Brown. Although he acknowledged that he had consumed alcohol when taking the testimony of later witnesses, he insisted that this had in no way impaired his ability accurately to record such testimony:

[T]his deponent does declare that for a long time previous to the taking of the testimony of the said Emery Brown and Peter Brown he was not in any wise affected by spirituous liquors, that this deponent has a distinct and perfect recollection of his situation and conduct and knows that up to the 16th day of September on Saturday, he had not indulged himself in the improper use of spirituous liquors, that although subsequent to that period, this deponent with the humility which the occasion demands of him, and with a regret which none can feel with more poignancy than himself, declares that he did indulge in the use of liquors to excess, and so much so that appreciating his own weakness, he declined doing any business, and that although his reserve might have been affected injuriously by the intemperate use of liquors while taking some of the subsequent testimony, he is notwithstanding confident that his mind was not impaired.

Moreover, according to Lupton, the defendant had been entirely aware that he was drinking and had failed to express any concern at the time.[49]

Seeking to preserve the credibility of testimony favorable to his cause, the plaintiff, Silas Bennet, argued, like Lupton himself, that the defendant had known about Lupton's alcohol consumption and had said nothing about it. Had Lupton been in any way impaired, suggested the plaintiff, the defendant would surely have observed this fact and reported it at the time.[50] The plaintiff, moreover, filed affidavits of various witnesses, all of whom insisted that Lupton had been sober while serving as an examiner in the lawsuit in question.[51] The defendant and his lawyer, John A. Collier, responded by insisting that they had been unaware at the time that Lupton was taking testimony that he was intoxicated.[52] In addition, Collier procured the affidavits of several witnesses—including, the owner of "a tavern . . . about twenty-five yards from the hostel . . . where the said Lupton was taking the testimony of the witnesses"—all of whom claimed that they had observed Lupton during the period that he was taking testimony and that he had appeared to be highly intoxicated.[53]

Ostensibly, the extensive affidavit testimony submitted by both parties concerned only the narrow question of whether Lutpon had, in fact, been intoxicated while serving as examiner. In reality, however, this dispute over Lupton's state of mind provided an opportunity for defense counsel to resubmit testimony concerning the material facts of the case, thus enabling him to circumvent the longstanding rules prohibiting repeat testimony. Consider, for example, the affidavit of Emery Brown, submitted on behalf of the defendant. Brown began by observing that "the said William Lupton esquire appeared to this deponent to be an intemperate man and that at the time of said examination he appeared to be under the influence of strong drink. . . ." It was precisely because

Lupton was so intoxicated, insisted Brown, that he had misrecorded Brown's testimony. As reported by Lupton, Brown had testified that "he has not at any time heard the said complainant say that he had abandoned the idea of keeping the said property." But according to Brown, nothing could be further from the truth: The testimony "thus taken down is not as the deponent did testify on the said examination;" rather, he "testif[ied] that he had heard the said complainant say that he intended to give up said property and have no more to do with the same."[54] In this way, the defendant and his lawyer were able to transform testimony that was supposed to address the narrow question of whether Lupton was intoxicated into an otherwise unavailable opportunity for their witnesses to testify once more (after publication had passed) concerning a question of material fact—namely, whether the plaintiff had expressed any intent to abandon the land in dispute.

That the defendant thus sought to reexamine witnesses whose testimony disappointed him—in violation of equity's longstanding prohibition of repeat testimony—did not escape the plaintiff. Indeed, Bennet suggested that the defendant had manufactured his supposed concerns about the accuracy of the depositions for precisely this purpose. In addition, he claimed, the testimony given by the defendant's witnesses on reexamination—in their affidavits alleging that Lupton had misrecorded their words—ought not to be trusted, since the defendant exercised significant power over them. According to Bennet, "Levi Brown, Emery Brown, and Abner Howland do and have for several years resided on the property in dispute in this cause, the said Browns in the employment most of the time of the defendant David Woodcock and . . . have been in some degree dependent on said Woodcock. . . ."[55] That these witnesses were so dependent on the defendant suggested that the latter had the power to force them to recant their testimony and thus to perjure themselves. It was precisely to avoid such a temptation to procure false, manufactured testimony that equity had long prohibited repeat testimony. But Lupton's lack of professionalism and the absence of any oversight over his activities had provided defense counsel with an opportunity to circumvent this prohibition.

Notably, it was a very particular kind of repeat testimony that the defendant and his lawyer sought to obtain—testimony in the nature of an oral, adversarial cross-examination. As the defendant's lawyer, John A. Collier, reported to the court, he had expected, based on what his client had told him, that Emery Brown and Peter Brown would testify that they had heard the plaintiff say that he had intended to abandon the land in dispute—and he had drafted his interrogatories accordingly. He was thus shocked when, after publication had passed, he obtained copies of their depositions stating the opposite. But by the time he saw the depositions and discovered what Emery Brown and Peter Brown had actually testified, it was too late to take any further testimony. This would not have been the case in a common-law trial, where Collier might have rebounded from this surprise by cross-examining the Browns. In this light, Collier's challenge of Lupton as a drunkard is perhaps best viewed as an effort to obtain the benefits of an immediate, oral cross-examination of the kind available in the common-law courts. As this suggests, and as we will soon explore at greater length, lawyers of Kent's era were searching for ways to import into equity what was fast becoming a defining feature of common-law procedure. In this pursuit, they sought to exploit the weaknesses inherent in equity's procedural and institutional structure—most importantly, its delegation of extensive responsibilities to an insufficient, nonprofessional, and largely unsupervised staff whose primary contacts were with the parties and their lawyers rather than with the court itself.

Ultimately, Chancellor Kent ruled against the defendant, holding that the testimony taken by Lupton was permitted to stand. Like the plaintiff, he expressed doubt that the witnesses who sought to impugn the testimony were acting of their own accord, given their dependence on the defendant. As he observed, the "[d]efendant has had a full opportunity of tampering with Brown, who is one of his workmen at his mills, and evidently a man pliable to the defendant's views." In addition, however, Kent placed great stock in the fact that the defendant lived in Ithaca and had spoken with Lupton regularly while the latter was conducting the examinations. The plaintiff pointed to this fact— and to the defendant's failure to complain at the time—as evidence that Lupton had not been intoxicated. Kent agreed. But he also emphasized that when Lupton was undertaking the examination of the defendant's witnesses, he was serving as the defendant's "own agent." Because the "[d]efendant was present and in constant habits of intercourse with the examiner," the defendant "should have discharged him, if he thought [him] incapable."[56]

That Kent concluded that Lupton was best viewed as the defendant's agent is a remarkable fact—and one that bears emphasis. In the English treatise literature in which Kent immersed himself and whose precepts he was committed to implementing, neutrality was supposed to be one of the defining features of the examiner's expert, professional identity. Yet, like the lawyers whom, as we will see, he roundly criticized for failing to adhere in all respects to equity's quasi-inquisitorial structure, Kent succumbed here to the adversarial forces encouraged by the deep structural tensions of equity. In this sense, much like the treatise literature on which he relied, he exhibited contradictory attitudes toward chancery's judicial staff—categorizing them as neutral court officers but also recognizing them to be partisan agents. That such a strong advocate of equity's quasi-inquisitorial structure was able to lapse into an argument so deeply at conflict with this structure highlights the profound nature of chancery's inherited tensions and the extent to which these could be manipulated by lawyers seeking partisan advantage. In no aspect of early nineteenth-century New York Chancery practice was this dynamic clearer—or more portentous—than in proceedings before masters.

## Proceedings before Masters

As was the case with commissioners and examiners, early nineteenth-century masters sometimes failed to conform to strict standards of professionalism, exhibiting a laxity in the enforcement of equity's quasi-inquisitorial structure. But in the case of masters, the deviations from equity's traditional rules appear to have been more significant and fateful. That commissioners and examiners were a largely unprofessional and unsupervised staff made it possible for lawyers to identify creative ways to promote the interests of their clients in proceedings before these court officers—as in the case of the drunken examiner Lupton. But the archival evidence suggests that in major respects—as concerns, in other words, their core testimony-taking functions—both commissioners and examiners largely played by the rules. Thus, prior to the enactment of the April 17, 1823, statute, which authorized these officers to engage in the oral, public examination of witnesses, commissioners and examiners continued to take testimony secretly on the basis of written interrogatories and cross-interrogatories.

To the extent that the testimony taken by commissioners and examiners has been preserved, the extant files often include copies of both interrogatories and cross-interrogatories as well as separate depositions for each witness that list seriatim the witness's responses to each individual interrogatory.[57] Moreover, in the case of commissioners, who, unlike examiners, were appointed on a case-by-case basis, the pre-1823 files often contain copies of the commission appointing them to serve and specifying that they were to examine each of the witnesses secretly ("examine each of them apart") and "upon . . . interrogatories."[58] So too, both the commissioners and the clerks they employed "in taking, writing, transcribing, or ingrossing the . . . depositions" were required to swear an oath prior to taking testimony, by means of which they promised that they would "not publish, disclose, or make known . . . the contents of all or any of the depositions of the witnesses . . . until publication shall pass."[59]

But while commissioners and examiners appear to have abided by chancery's core structuring principles, the same cannot be said for masters. Even before Kent issued his 1817 decision in *Remsen* authorizing masters to take testimony orally, most such officers appear already to have been in the habit of doing so. Moreover, while the evidence in this respect is less clear, it seems that with some regularity, they took such testimony in the presence of parties and their counsel. Once their presence was sanctioned by *Remsen*, lawyers increasingly began to undertake responsibility for questioning themselves, gradually displacing masters from center stage.

## AN EARLY AND FATEFUL DEVIATION: ORAL EXAMINATIONS AND PARTY PRESENCE

Despite the inherited English treatise literature, which dictated that testimony before masters be taken privately on the basis of written interrogatories and cross-interrogatories, the archival evidence suggests that, even prior to Kent's 1817 decision in *Remsen*, this was not the practice of New York Chancery. Of the 244 cases reviewed that were decided before 1823, there were 36 (15%) in which masters arranged for the examination of witnesses in proceedings before them—and 15 of these were decided before 1817. A review of these fifteen cases, cross-checked against a more informal perusal of other files,[60] reveals not a single case in which testimony before masters was taken on the basis of interrogatories.[61] So too, not surprisingly, the twenty-one cases decided from 1817 to 1823 do not include any in which masters relied on interrogatories.

How do we know that masters did not rely on interrogatories? How, in other words, do we detect an absence? The answer, in short, is by comparing the files prepared in these thirty-six cases with those from cases (involving testimony before commissioners or examiners) in which it is clear that interrogatories *were* used. As noted, in those cases in which commissioners or examiners took testimony, the surviving files often contain copies of the individual interrogatories and cross-interrogatories posed as well as two sets of depositions for each witness, listing seriatim responses to interrogatories and cross-interrogatories. In contrast, in all thirty-six cases in which masters were responsible for taking testimony, the case files contain no record (or even mention) of interrogatories or cross-interrogatories. Moreover, in reporting testimony to the court, masters constructed a single continuous narrative for each witness rather than two separate sets of seriatim responses to numbered interrogatories and cross-interrogatories. Given these differences in the reporting of testimony, it seems all but certain that masters did not rely on written interrogatories and cross-interrogatories to question witnesses. Their examinations were instead oral.

That oral examinations in proceedings before masters were common prior to Kent's decision in *Remsen,* and even to his arrival on the bench, is also suggested by the published record. In deciding *Remsen,* Kent himself made a point of observing that while "[t]he books assume the practice to be settled, that the parties and witnesses are to be examined before the master upon written interrogatories[,] . . . [t]he practice with us, as I have reason to believe, has been more relaxed, and oral examinations have frequently, if not generally, prevailed."[62] Taking a more definitive stance, master and treatise-writer Murray Hoffman insisted in 1824 that masters in New York Chancery had always departed from the traditional written approach of their English counterparts. In his words, "[O]ral examination has . . . been the practice of our court as long as its rules can be traced."[63]

What accounts for this deviation from equity's traditional commitment to relying on written interrogatories, including in proceedings before masters? As we will soon see, Kent concluded in *Remsen* that it would be more efficient to take testimony orally, rather than on the basis of written interrogatories, since this would obviate the need to pose interrogatories that had been drafted in advance and thereafter proved to be irrelevant. Perhaps practicing masters and lawyers had already come to this conclusion. The more difficult question is how precisely such oral testimony was taken. Who, in other words, bore primary responsibility for questioning? Was it the master himself or the parties? And to the extent that the master was responsible, did he take testimony privately, outside the presence of the parties and their counsel? Or did he allow the parties and their counsel to be present—and perhaps even assist— during questioning?

The evidence as a whole suggests that masters were responsible for conducting oral examinations themselves. That the master recorded a single narrative for each witness suggests that one person—namely, the master himself—bore primary responsibility for the questioning. If the parties' lawyers had themselves undertaken oral examination in the style of the common law, one would expect to see two separate narratives—one reflecting the direct examination and the other the cross-examination. That masters were responsible for undertaking witness examination is also suggested by the language many used to describe their efforts. For example, in an 1814 divorce suit, *Sackridger v. Sackridger,* master Samuel Andrews reported to the court that Mrs. Lucy Wheeler "appeared before me" and was "examined by me under oath by me duly administered." Moreover, in concluding his report, Andrews observed that he had "particularly enquired into the circumstances attending the transaction sworn to by Lucy Wheeler," thus further suggesting that it was he, rather than counsel, who was responsible for examining the witness.[64]

How did masters manage to assume responsibility for questioning? Unlike the parties and their lawyers, they lacked familiarity with the case, other than from reading the pleadings and motions filed, and so presumably would have found it difficult to master the facts necessary for undertaking oral witness examination. An at least partial explanation is afforded by the limited nature of masters' inquiries in most cases. As we have seen, foreclosure suits represented a large proportion of the chancery docket,[65] and in such disputes masters were typically required to focus on only two quite narrow questions—namely, how much debt remained outstanding and whether the mortgaged property was of sufficient value to cover this debt upon sale. Similarly, suits for divorce and those for separation of bed and board (constituting a smaller, but not insubstantial proportion of the docket)[66] were ones in which the master had to focus on one or at most two questions: whether the defendant had committed adultery and/or engaged in abuse. Moreover, in cases in which there were complex factual questions to be resolved, witness examination was usually undertaken in proceedings before examiners or commissioners, prior to reference to a master. Masters were brought in at the end—after the testimony in chief was collected and publication passed—in order to wrap up smaller points of contention. Given the limited nature of the fact-finding for which they were responsible, masters were able to examine witnesses orally, even though they were much less familiar with the case than were the parties themselves.

Although masters' reliance on oral testimony contravened chancery's tradition of employing written interrogatories, it did not undermine the core policy goals that lay behind the court's commitment to secrecy—as long, that is, as masters continued to be responsible for questioning and to undertake it privately, outside the presence of the parties and their counsel (or anyone else). The reason for the court's traditional commitment to written interrogatories, rather than oral questions, was that, as concerns the evidentiary heart of complex disputes, it was impossible for court officers to learn enough about the case to question witnesses effectively without the assistance of counsel. Since the officer required such assistance—and since the parties and their counsel could not (consistent with the court's commitment to pre-publication secrecy) be present to hear the testimony given—the solution was to have the parties and their lawyers draft written questions in advance. Thus, to the extent that factual inquiries were sufficiently limited in nature that masters could grasp them without party assistance, there was no reason in principle why masters could not proceed orally.

That said, the archival evidence contains hints that masters in early nineteenth-century New York Chancery did at times deviate from the strictures of quasi-inquisitorialism in ways that posed a serious challenge to the institution's core values—and, in particular, its embrace of the virtues of secrecy. More particularly, parties and their counsel were sometimes present during the master's oral examination of witnesses. For example, in an 1814 suit for the separation of bed and board, master Sterling Goodenow reported that testimony was taken "in presence of the solicitor for the complainant," though he also emphasized that it was he himself who "proceeded . . . to examine" the witnesses.[67] Why were parties and their counsel thus allowed at times to be present? The answer, one suspects, is convenience. Although masters retained the quasi-inquisitorial discretion to identify and call witnesses, this task was assigned as a preliminary matter to the parties and their counsel. To the extent that parties and their lawyers were responsible for identifying witnesses, it was a relatively small step from there to attending the witness examinations. Moreover, even in those cases in which the factual inquiry before the master was relatively narrow, it surely helped the master to have someone more familiar with the case readily available during the examination to provide additional information.

How often were lawyers permitted to be present while masters examined witnesses? Unfortunately, the nature of the archival evidence does not allow for any definitive response to this question. There are very few reports in which masters expressly acknowledged the presence of counsel, but of course such silence does not necessarily mean that counsel was absent. Indeed, to the extent that both masters and lawyers knew themselves to be acting in contravention of equity's traditional rules of secrecy, they would have had an incentive not to acknowledge that lawyers were present, even when they were. The only thing we can conclude for certain is that there were at least some cases in which lawyers attended masters' examinations of witnesses, and this, in turn, provided an opening through which they could seek to exert greater control over the proceedings—most importantly, by beginning to question witnesses themselves.

## KENT'S MISCALCULATION: *REMSEN V. REMSEN*

*Remsen* raised the question that New York Chancery had long managed to avoid—namely, whether masters were required to examine witnesses on the basis of written interrogatories taken secretly, outside the presence of the parties and their counsel. The parties in the suit appeared before master James Hamilton, who was ordered by the chancellor "to take and state an account between the[m]." In this context, "it was urged by the counsel for the defendant, that . . . the testimony . . . be taken by the master in writing, privately, upon interrogatories; and that the depositions so taken should not be disclosed, until the whole evidence of both parties was taken."[68] When master Hamilton ruled in the defendant's favor, the plaintiff objected to the master's report, leading to an appeal directly to the chancellor. In a decision that he had good reason thereafter to regret, Kent overruled Hamilton, holding that masters in New York Chancery were free to take testimony orally before both the parties and their counsel. While this was a fateful decision, providing the first legitimized in-road of oral, adversarial procedure into equity's quasi-inquisitorial structure, this was in no way Kent's goal. He was focused instead on trying to make equity procedure more efficient and thus less costly.

In the traditional, written, and secret mode, lawyers—knowing that they would not themselves be present—had to anticipate all of the responses that each witness might offer and then draft follow-up questions for every one. As a result, much time was spent drafting (and then posing) questions that ultimately proved to be off point. As Kent explained, "it seems almost impossible to reduce the requisite inquiries to writing, in the first instance, and to know what questions to put, except as they arise in the progress of the inquiry." Oral examinations would, in Kent's view, address the "many inconveniences" that stemmed from equity's traditional approach. By making it possible to respond on the spot to new or unexpected information produced by a witness, oral examinations would proceed more quickly than written ones and avoid irrelevant lines of questioning. Accordingly, Kent held that "the requisite proofs ought to be taken on written interrogatories, prepared by the parties, and approved by the master, or by *viva voce* examination, as the parties shall deem most expedient, or the master shall think proper to direct, in the given case. . . ."[69]

In thus holding that, for the sake of efficiency, it was permissible to bend equity's traditional commitment to examining witnesses on the basis of written interrogatories, Kent need not have abandoned the related but nonetheless distinct principle that all such questioning was to be done secretly. He might have held, in other words, that an oral examination, just like a written one, was to be conducted by the master outside the presence of the parties and their counsel. Indeed, as Kent observed, secrecy of examinations was of fundamental importance, far outweighing the merely technical consideration of whether such questioning was to be undertaken orally or on the basis of written interrogatories. In his words, the practice of masters undertaking oral examinations was "a question merely of convenience, and does not involve any principle of policy, or of right; . . . [but] whether examinations shall be secret, and to what extent they shall be carried, suggests much more important considerations." Nonetheless, despite his belief in the critical importance of secrecy, Kent ruled that "the testimony may be taken in the presence of the parties, or their counsel (except when by a special order of the Court it is to be taken secretly); . . ."[70]

Why was Kent willing to abandon equity's traditional commitment to prepublication secrecy by allowing lawyers to be present? In part, he may have believed that the goal of making chancery procedure more efficient would be best served not only by allowing testimony to be taken orally but also by permitting parties and their counsel to be present. Even though the scope of masters' factual inquiries was typically quite limited, the fact that they were strangers to the case necessarily meant that they were at a disadvantage vis-à-vis the parties in gaining the knowledge required to examine witnesses effectively. Kent may therefore have concluded that the benefits to be gained by deviating from strict principles of secrecy were worth the cost. But at least as important in explaining Kent's willingness to permit masters to take oral testimony in the presence of parties and their counsel is that, to at least some extent, this reflected existing practice. As we have seen, masters usually took witness testimony orally, and they did so at times in the presence of parties and their counsel. If testimony before masters was sometimes taken orally in the presence of the parties' lawyers, Kent may have concluded that the wisest course was to sanction this practice. To attempt to enforce compliance with the traditional rule mandating secret examinations, only then to fail, would have cost him considerable credibility.

That this was Kent's reasoning is suggested by his insistence that oral testimony be allowed only in proceedings before masters and not in those before examiners and commissioners. When the legislature proposed draft legislation in February 1821 that would have required oral examinations in proceedings before all chancery officials, Kent firmly opposed it—despite having allowed such testimony in proceedings before masters a mere four years earlier. In Kent's view, the risk of perjury (and thus the need for secrecy) was much smaller in proceedings before masters than in those before examiners and commissioners because masters took testimony on a relatively narrow set of issues, after the testimony in chief (before examiners and commissioners) was already taken. Indeed, he sought in Remsen to encourage this division of labor, specifying that the parties ought to "make their proofs as full, before publication, as the nature of the case requires or admits of, to the end that the supplementary proofs, before the master, may be as limited as the rights and responsibilities of the parties will admit."[71] Nonetheless, even if the scope of inquiry before masters was limited, the publicity of testimony necessarily entailed some risk of perjury. Kent's effort to draw a firm line between these types of proceedings may thus have been less a matter of principle than a pragmatic recognition of the reality of contemporary practice. It was, in short, only before masters, rather than before examiners and commissioners, that testimony was then taken orally (and sometimes in the presence of parties and their counsel).

Even while authorizing parties and their counsel to be present in masters' proceedings for the examination of witnesses, Kent remained quite concerned that this would undermine the veracity of testimony. He thus identified a number of procedures designed to limit this risk. These included, as noted above, requiring the parties to take the bulk of the testimony before examiners or commissioners, prior to the reference to a master. In addition, Kent seems to have believed that the longstanding prohibition on repeat testimony would help to obviate any serious risk of perjury generated by lawyers' presence. It was primarily when parties were able to question witnesses repeatedly (and over a long period of time), he argued, that opportunities arose to seek favorable testimony and to suborn perjury: "If examinations are protracted from day to day, for any length of time, there is very great danger of abuse from public examinations, by which parties are enabled to detect the weak parts of the adversary's case, or of their own. It is to guard against this abuse, that examinations in chief are not permitted, after publication. . . ." As long as each witness testified only once and did so rapidly (ideally in one session), the fact that such testimony was no longer taken secretly—that parties and their counsel knew what had been said—would not pose any real danger. Accordingly, he ruled, "when an examination is once begun before a master, he ought, on assigning a reasonable time to the parties, to proceed, with as little delay and intermission as the nature of the case will admit of, to the conclusion of the examination, and, when once concluded, it ought not to be opened for further proof, without special and very satisfactory cause shown."[72]

Kent thus concluded that, even though he was authorizing masters to undertake oral examinations before the parties and their counsel, he was not really overturning equity's longstanding commitment to secrecy. As he explained, the approach he set forth in *Remsen* represented a compromise between the goals of efficiency and secrecy, thus "unit[ing] convenience and despatch with sound principle and safety."[73] Kent's calculation, however, would turn out to be mistaken—and deeply so. By opening the door to lawyers in proceedings before masters, he helped initiate a process whereby lawyers would profoundly reconfigure the nature and purposes of equity procedure, ultimately demolishing its quasi-inquisitorial structure in favor of a newfound commitment to the virtues of oral, adversarial process.

## THE LAWYER'S ROLE: FROM PRESENCE TO CONTROL

Despite Kent's expectations, the evidence suggests that lawyers who were present in proceedings before masters often—and, indeed, increasingly—sought to control them by assuming responsibility for the examination of witnesses. The process by which lawyers came to exercise such increased control did not occur in an orchestrated or linear fashion. To the contrary, the archival record reveals plenty of outliers. Procedural practice, in short, was sufficiently fluid that individual masters and lawyers could significantly shape proceedings to suit their own tastes. That said, there was an overarching pattern or progression in the way that masters' proceedings were conducted over time—one leading to the oral, adversarial methods of the common law.

In exploring these transformations in masters' proceedings, it is useful to confine ourselves to one particular kind of lawsuit, thereby setting aside the substantive-law variable and homing in on the specifically procedural dynamics. For these purposes, divorce suits are particularly attractive because they, unlike many other types of lawsuit, always required masters to report testimony. As we have seen, the New York legislature authorized divorce only for fault, primarily in cases of adultery. Well aware that couples might be tempted to collude to manufacture the requisite fault, the legislature provided that in cases where the defendant failed to file an answer and the bill was taken *pro confesso,* chancery was required "to refer the . . . [case] to a master in chancery, with directions to take the proof of the adultery charged."[74] Toward this end, the master was required to examine witnesses. In contrast, as we have seen, in many other types of cases no testimony was required, or it was taken exclusively by examiners and commissioners (prior to reference to a master).

Divorce suits are an appealing object of study for the further reason that they marked a clear departure from the otherwise applicable norm that when the master took testimony, he was required to spare the chancellor the burden of reviewing extensive evidentiary materials. Toward this end, he was expected to make findings of fact that referred only generally to the underlying evidence on which these were based. As explained in Daniell's *Pleading and Practice,* a prominent late nineteenth-century treatise, the master "does not, unless under special circumstances, detail the evidence upon which he proceeds in making his report" but at most "generally refers to it."[75] While treatises from earlier in the century did not specify that masters were to avoid detailing the evidence in their reports, there are indications that such a norm also operated in this earlier period. For example, in his 1824 treatise *The Office and Duties of Masters in Chancery,* Murray Hoffman—himself a master in New York Chancery—published examples of masters' reports in which the master noted simply that his findings of fact were based on "the testimony of A. B. and C. D., witnesses produced before me."[76] Moreover, archival evidence from the early nineteenth century similarly suggests that masters often reported little more than their core findings.[77] It is thus suits for divorce, in which masters were required to take and report testimony—and in which the evidence supporting a finding of adultery was often highly circumstantial and detailed—that provide the most fruitful source for examining changes in masters' proceedings.

These changes are evident first and foremost in the way that masters drafted their reports. During Kent's chancellorship, masters generally reported testimony in a manner designed to reflect and in turn reinforce their extensive power and discretion in fact-finding. In contrast, by the 1840s, they sought to minimize, and indeed erase, their own presence. As masters receded into the background, it was the parties (or rather their lawyers) who came to the fore. The end result was a record of the testimony before masters that came increasingly to resemble a written version of the oral, adversarial testimony taken at a common-law trial.

As a starting point, consider *Mabee v. Mabee,* filed in 1815, toward the very beginning of Kent's chancellorship. Appointed "to take the proof of adultery charged in the complainant's bill of complaint with an opinion thereon," the master reported the testimony of two witnesses. The following excerpt should provide a good indication of the master's style: "The said Orrin Woodens testified that the said parties were residents of the said county with whom the said witness was well acquainted. That the said John Mabee lived separate from the said Patty Mabee his wife. That he took one Caty Brock to live with him in his house as his wife some time in the fall of 1812, and has from that time down to the present period lived with her as his wife." Having reported all the testimony in this fashion, the master concluded, "in my opinion the said testimony is satisfactory to establish the charge of adultery in the said bill of complaint."[78]

Highly condensed and without much factual detail, the testimony reported by the master in *Mabee* could lead to but one conclusion—namely, that the defendant had committed adultery. Indeed, the voices of the witnesses are subsumed within that of the master, who summarizes what he has heard instead of reporting their exact words. The witnesses are, moreover, made to speak in the third person, with the first person reserved for the master himself, who thus becomes the central subject of the narrative. In a very real sense, this narrative style not only signals the master's substantial power in gathering and assessing testimony but also constructs it. This is because the master's report contains no information that would permit the chancellor reading it to engage in probing review. The chancellor therefore had little choice but to defer to the master's judgment.

In the years just before and during Kent's chancellorship, masters also demonstrated (and exercised) their control over testimony by relying on their own personal knowledge of witness character. This is precisely what Samuel Andrews did when serving as master in the 1814 *Sackridger* divorce suit. As in *Mabee,* Andrews's report of the testimony taken in the case is terse, offering little if any basis for the chancellor, later reviewing it, to differ in his assessment of whether the defendant had committed adultery. But while Andrews failed to disclose most of the factual specifics raised in the testimony, he made a point of emphasizing that he had personal knowledge of "the character of the witness"—presumably derived from the fact that they were both residents of Kingsbury, a relatively small farming and mill town in Washington County.[79] The master thereby highlighted his control and made it all but impossible for his judgment to be questioned.

Similarly, in an 1821 suit for divorce, master Jacob Hoighton relied primarily on two witnesses—John H. Godfrey and Jacob Hutchins—to support his conclusion that the defendant had committed adultery. But as Hoighton explained, he took the testimony of two additional individuals to determine whether Godfrey and Hutchins were themselves reliable witnesses: "Samuel Barret and Abel Wilcox of Ellicott aforesaid have been sworn and examined by me as to the character of the said John H. Godfrey," and "Abel Wilcox has also made oath before me that he is acquainted with the said Jacob Hutchins." As Hoighton reported, Barrett and Wilcox testified that both Godfrey and Hutchins are men "of truth and veracity." But what about the character of these character witnesses? The possibility of infinite regress was avoided by the testimony of the master himself. In Hoighton's words, "[t]he said Barrett and Wilcox are persons with whom I am acquainted and believe to be men of truth and veracity." The master's finding that adultery had been committed thus rested ultimately on his own personal—and unreviewable—knowledge of the character witnesses.[80]

Another device for signaling and bolstering the master's control over the fact-finding process was to emphasize the importance of witness demeanor in assessing the veracity of testimony. Consider, for example, an 1818 divorce suit in which master Joseph B. Lathrop relied on the testimony of two witnesses to conclude that the defendant had committed adultery. In support of this conclusion, Lathrop observed that "from the examination of the witnesses aforesaid I believe them entitled to credit and that the parts set forth in the said depositions are true." Although Lathrop failed to explain exactly why he believed that the witnesses were entitled to credit, their demeanor while testifying was evidently such that he was able to determine "from the examination" (rather than from any personal knowledge of their character) that they were reliable.[81] Like a master's reliance on his personal knowledge of witness character, such emphasis on witness demeanor was essentially unchallengeable since the chancellor—not present during the taking of testimony—had little choice but to take the master at his word.

As time passed, masters' reports began to change in ways that suggest a growing involvement by lawyers in the proceedings—and, in turn, increased resistance to deferring to the master's discretionary judgment and power. One important manifestation of this trend was a striking switch in the use of the first- and third-person pronouns. Masters had long used the third person to describe witnesses' testimony, reserving the first person for themselves and thereby suggesting that they were the central, dominant actors in the proceedings. But by the 1840s, this practice was transformed, such that masters came to report all testimony in the first person. Consider, for example, the 1843 divorce suit filed by Abigail Rexford against her husband, Edmund, in which master George W. Rathbun reported the testimony of a witness by the name of Thomas P. Pike:

> I reside in the city of Schenectady, am over twenty five years of [age], . . . I know Edmund Rexford, have known him for two years previous to his leaving the city of Schenectady. He left this city a year ago last summer. [I] know a girl by the name of Ruth Ann Grovenbury who resided at the city of Schenectady at the time and previous to Rexford's leaving this city. She was reputed to be a common prostitute. About two months before Rexford left the city and in the spring of 1842 I went into his barber's shop in this city to get shaved. It was about seven o'clock in the evening. Rexford and Ruth Ann Grovenbury were there alone. Rexford had his arm about her waist or bosom. They had an obscene point and were talking, laughing and joking about it. . . . I saw him in Syracuse sometime in September 1842. He enquired of me then about Ruth Ann Grovenbury and said she was one of his "old coveys." This was in his barber's shop at Syracuse. There was a room back of the barber's shop and I saw two females who appeared to be living there. . . . I told him that I heard he kept a woman of ill fame. He answered "you do not suppose I live without women." The appearance of the room back of the shop indicated a house of ill fame.[82]

As recorded by the master, this testimony differs from that reported in early nineteenth-century cases like *Mabee* not only in its use of the first person but also in the level of detail—as exemplified by particular turns of phrase ("old coveys") and the specification of physical circumstances ("Rexford had his arm about her waist or bosom"). Here, in other words, the reliability of the testimony is suggested not by the master's personal knowledge of the witness and assessment of his demeanor but instead by the master's report of circumstantial details, as provided by the witness himself, speaking in the first person.

This transformation in the way masters reported testimony was not the result of any legislative or judicial mandate. That said, as concerns the shift to the first person, it is important to consider the possibility of English influence. An English statute enacted on August 28, 1833, provided that "all depositions of witnesses examined in the High Court of Chancery shall hereafter be taken in the first person."[83] According to a contemporary English authority on the law of evidence, this statute was understood to apply only to depositions "taken before the Examiners" but was thereafter extended to "'all depositions'" by a court order of May 1845.[84] Given the attention that leading American (and especially New York) lawyers paid to contemporary English legal and political developments, the question arises whether New York masters' switch to the first person was motivated by a desire to copy English practice. American versions of a number of British treatises on chancery practice did make brief mention of both the 1833 statute and the 1845 rule, so at least some New York lawyers and chancery officials were likely familiar with these.[85] But most of these treatises were published after New York masters in chancery had already begun recording testimony in the first person.[86] It therefore seems implausible that the shift away from the third person was primarily a product of direct English influence. More probable is that there was a set of developments common to both New York and England that contributed to the embrace of first-person testimony in both jurisdictions. Especially relevant in this regard was the growing concern, explored below, with promoting publicity in governance, including through the courts.

As concerns New York in particular, it seems to have been lawyers themselves who were responsible for transforming the way that masters in chancery recorded testimony—including but not limited to the shift to the first-person pronoun. While there are no definitive indications concerning who precisely was responsible for questioning witnesses, the newly detailed nature of the testimony recorded suggests that it was lawyers who began to do so, seeking in part to elicit responses that would be helpful to their clients. They thus became eager to ensure that these responses would be recorded as accurately and completely as possible—namely, by having the master take down the actual language employed (including, not least, the first-person pronoun).

In line with this trend toward increased lawyer control was the tendency of masters' reports from the 1840s to evince a new and apparently lawyer-driven focus on the admissibility of evidence, both oral and written. For example, in an 1845 divorce suit, master William McMurray reported the testimony not only of those witnesses claiming to have seen conduct suggestive of adultery but also of those called solely to verify that a document was what it purported to be—or to use the technical term, to authenticate it.[87] In particular, he reported the testimony of Thomas E. Velmilyen, who was called for the narrow purpose of verifying the signature on the parties' marriage certificate. According to McMurray's report, the following exchange took place between the witness and some unidentified interlocutor, most likely the plaintiff's lawyer:

> Look at paper marked "Exhibit No. 1" purporting to be a copy of a record of the Dutch Church of Claverack, signed by Ira C. Boise and state

whether you are acquainted with the hand-writing of the said Ira C. Boise and whether you believe said Exhibit No. 1 to be in the hand-writing of the said Ira C. Boise.

I am acquainted with the hand-writing of Ira C. Boise and I believe "Exhibit No. 1" to be his hand-writing.[88]

The master's decision thus to transcribe word for word the details of how a foundation was laid for admitting the marriage certificate into evidence marked a clear departure from the usual, more informal practice, whereby masters relied on documentary evidence as they deemed appropriate and without having to establish its formal admissibility. It is thus a measure of the extent to which proceedings before masters had come to mirror lawyer-dominated common-law proceedings. The plaintiff's lawyer, questioning the witness, drives the narrative set forth in the master's report, and the only function of the master is to create an authentic, easily reviewable record of the proceedings.

What accounts for lawyers' interest in thus exerting greater procedural control? It is common to explain lawyers' behavior by reference to their strategic interest in winning litigation, and this was, of course, an important interest. Lawyers likely concluded that a more detailed and accurate report of the testimony—one that did not hinge on the master's personal knowledge and assessments—offered more grounds for appealing from unfavorable decisions (or opposing appeals from favorable ones). But as concerns divorce suits, in particular, most were, in fact, uncontested, such that narrowly strategic interests of this kind likely played little direct role.[89] This suggests that lawyers also sought to gain control over masters' proceedings as an end in itself. More particularly, as we will soon see, they had powerful incentives to present themselves as modern-day Ciceros, engaged in public-serving advocacy—and this, in turn, required them to exercise substantially more (and more visible) procedural power than equity's quasi-inquisitorial methods had traditionally allowed. But before examining how this came to pass, it is necessary to consider how changes in proceedings before masters radiated outward, thereby transforming the entirety of equity procedure.

## From Masters' Proceedings to Equity Procedure as a Whole

The presence of lawyers in proceedings before masters quickly came to transform other proceedings in chancery as well. Although Kent insisted in *Remsen* that there were important differences between proceedings before masters and those before examiners, such that parties and their counsel could be present in the former but must be excluded from the latter, this was not a distinction able to bear weight in practice. Once it became lawful for lawyers to appear in proceedings in which masters were taking testimony, it came to seem natural that they should also appear in the other proceedings in which chancery gathered testimony—most importantly, those before examiners. The end result was the unraveling of the entirety of chancery's secrecy-based logic and its replacement with a new, oral, and adversarial conception of procedural justice.

## PROCEEDINGS BEFORE EXAMINERS AND COMMISSIONERS

In February 1821, toward the end of Kent's chancellorship, a bill was proposed "to alter the mode of taking evidence in the Court of Chancery." As reported by the *Albany Gazette*, the purpose of this legislation was to "abolish[] the present mode of taking evidence in secret, on written interrogatories." Toward this end, the bill required "the chancellor, either personally, to examine witnesses in public, *ore tenus*, or to direct an examiner, master, etc. to take such examination in like manner."[90]

The most complete account of this draft legislation appears in a report penned by Chancellor Kent upon the request of the New York Senate—a report that was thereafter widely published in contemporary newspapers. According to Kent, the core purpose of the bill was to replace equity's traditional written, secrecy-oriented approach to taking witness testimony with the common law's oral, public approach:

> The substance of the bill is, that the Chancellor shall either personally examine, *ore tenus*, witnesses in Chancery, or appoint some proper officer or person to do it, and that the officer or person to be appointed, shall take notes of the testimony in the manner practiced by a judge at *Nisi Prius*, and report the same to the Chancellor: and that it shall be lawful for the parties by their counsel to attend every such examination, and put questions, *ore tenus*, and also to examine witnesses, at the same time, touching the competency or credibility of any other witness. . . .[91]

Evidence-taking would, in short, proceed much as at *nisi prius*—a quintessential practice of the common-law courts, whereby judges delegated from a central court rode circuit to convene and preside over a jury trial. In this sense, the proposed legislation can be read as an effort to extend to all chancery proceedings Kent's more limited holding in *Remsen* that testimony taken before masters could proceed in the oral, adversarial fashion of the common law, and in the presence of the parties. Indeed, it went a step further, authorizing what Kent had sought to eschew—namely, lawyers' active participation in the process of examining witnesses.

According to Kent, lawyers' desire to exert greater procedural control in chancery proceedings was the driving force behind the legislation. More particularly, he suggested, lawyers complained that equity's quasi-inquisitorial approach to testimony deprived them of the opportunity to undertake cross-examination: The "objection to . . . [equity's traditional] mode of taking testimony . . . *which seems principally within the purview of the present bill . . .* is, that the parties are not present by their counsel, to question and cross-examine the witnesses, *viva voce,* and by discovery of what is proved on one side, to be enabled to meet it by countervailing proof on the other."[92] In other words, having successfully imported the oral, adversarial methods of the common law into chancery through their own bottom-up efforts, lawyers were also interested in promoting legislation that would formally authorize such a change and, in the process, extend it to all chancery officials, rather than just masters. Given the extent to which the New York legislature was then dominated by lawyers, this was relatively easy to achieve.[93]

Not surprisingly, Kent himself—long committed to reinforcing the traditional structure of equity—strongly opposed the proposed legislation, and given his continued power and prominence, it did not pass. But this would not be the case for long. In 1823, Kent stepped down from the bench, pursuant to a constitutional provision mandating that judges retire at the age of sixty.[94] That very year, on April 17, the New York legislature enacted a statute that endowed circuit judges with first instance jurisdiction in equity. In so doing, this statute also sought to achieve the main goals of the failed legislation of February 1821. In particular, it established that when circuit judges sat in equity, they were to take testimony pursuant to the oral, public, and lawyer-driven practices that had traditionally operated at law: "[T]he mode of proof by oral testimony, and the examination of witnesses in open court, shall be the same in all the courts of the said circuit judges, in the trial of causes in equity, as in the trial of actions at common law." Only if "special causes" were shown were circuit judges to permit testimony to be taken by "an examiner or commissioner." Moreover, unlike traditional equity practice, which insisted on secrecy in the gathering of testimony—and thus prohibited parties and their lawyers from being present—the April 17 statute provided that any testimony taken by an examiner or commissioner had to be "in the presence of the parties or their counsel, who shall be allowed to examine and cross-examine the witnesses." As for those cases pending before the chancellor himself, rather than before a circuit judge, these too were to approximate common-law proceedings in that "the respective parties and their counsel, shall have a right to be present and cross examine . . . witnesses."[95]

Despite the new statutory requirement that, absent a showing of "special causes," all testimony was to be taken directly before the circuit judge or chancellor himself, archival records demonstrate that most testimony continued to be taken before examiners or commissioners. That this was the case was openly acknowledged fifteen years later by a commission appointed by the New York legislature to undertake judicial reform.[96] As explained in the commissioners' report, circuit judges (by then renamed vice chancellors) hardly ever heard oral testimony and instead continued to rely on examiners: "Although [testimony] may be taken orally before the Vice-Chancellors, if they think proper to make a special order for that purpose, or the Chancellor so directs, it is understood that in point of fact it is very seldom done under the existing system of Vice-Chancellors."[97] The commissioners' language here is particularly telling in that it mischaracterizes the April 17, 1823, statute. Pursuant to the statute, the default rule was for testimony to be taken orally before the vice chancellor, such that testimony was to be taken before examiners or commissioners only upon a special showing. But according to the three-man commission, a "special order" was required to take testimony "orally before the vice-chancellor," thus suggesting that the default rule was for examiners or commissioners to take testimony. As this mischaracterization of the statutory language indicates, the law in action—though deviating radically from the law in the books—came to dominate so entirely that it was assumed to be the official, governing law. Along similar lines, case law concerning the Act of April 17, 1823 describes the statute as imposing a single requirement—namely, that testimony before examiners and commissioners be taken orally in the presence of parties and their counsel. That the statute also—and indeed, as a primary matter—sought to ensure that all testimony be taken directly before the chancellor or circuit judge was simply forgotten.[98]

Subsequent attempts to eliminate the intermediation of examiners and commissioners in the taking of testimony proved equally unavailing. Like the legislators of 1823, the three commissioners charged with devising a plan for judicial reform in 1838 sought to bring witnesses directly before the finder of fact—though they hoped this would be a jury. This selection of the jury as fact-finder was in line, we will see, with a burgeoning rhetoric that criticized chancery by drawing on and updating centuries-old tropes of the jury-reliant common law as uniquely liberty-promoting. But to the extent that it proved impossible to frame an issue proper for jury decision, the commissioners recommended a return to what the Act of April 17, 1823 had attempted but failed to achieve—namely, that the judge himself be responsible for hearing oral testimony taken by lawyers via direct and cross-examination.[99] In line with this recommendation, a statute enacted on April 18, 1838, provided that, when the chancellor or vice chancellor determined that a case was not suitable for jury decision, "the testimony to be given shall be given orally before the chancellor or vice-chancellor who hears the cause, except when the witness resides more than one hundred miles from the place of trial or out of the state, or is unable to attend. . . ."[100] Yet, as with that portion of the Act of April 17, 1823 directing that the chancellor or circuit judge hear oral testimony himself, the Act of April 18, 1838 quickly proved to be a failure, such that it was repealed just one year later, on May 2, 1839.[101]

While both the statute of April 17, 1823, and that of April 18, 1838, failed in the effort to require chancery judges to hear oral testimony themselves, archival evidence reveals that the fallback requirement that testimony before examiners be taken in oral, adversarial fashion (with lawyers present and undertaking cross-examination) was readily implemented. In particular, the archives contain numerous examiners' reports noting that it was the parties' lawyers who were responsible for questioning witnesses. Indeed, by the 1840s, certain examiners—in an effort to save themselves the time and effort involved in drafting handwritten depositions—began to use pre-printed forms, which expressly stated that counsel (not the examiner) was responsible for undertaking oral examination of the witness.[102] So too, these examiners' reports of the testimony typically included both direct and cross-examinations for each witness.[103]

As lawyer-driven examination and especially cross-examination became an increasingly common and important component of proceedings before examiners, lawyers began seeking to undermine their opponents' efforts to take testimony by objecting as frequently as possible.[104] This new practice of making evidentiary objections, in turn, placed pressure on examiners to capture the exact language used by the witnesses, since rulings on such objections might easily hinge on a particular turn of phrase. As a result, the depositions created by examiners began increasingly to resemble a verbatim transcript of an oral, common-law trial. Consider, for example, *Malcomb v. Malcomb*, a lawsuit filed in 1841, in which Charles sued his brother Stephen, claiming that they had formed a partnership to run a farm and that Stephen had thereafter failed to comply with his partnership obligations. The new practice of raising extensive evidentiary objections and the concomitant pressure to create a precise, verbatim record of the testimony is clearly reflected in the following excerpt from examiner Van Vechten's report of a cross-examination undertaken by counsel for the defendant:

> Question: Did Charles work on the farm the same as the other men and Stephen did? . . . Answer: He did but I considered him boss as much as Stephen. Mr. Yates counsel for the defendant objected to the taking down of the last part of witness's answer, as it was irrelevant. Objection allowed by the examiner. Mr. Doolittle counsel for complainant insisted upon the whole answer's being taken down. It was so taken, subject to the objection.[105]

As recorded in Van Vechten's report, it was this adversarial exchange between the lawyers that became the focal point of the narrative, reducing the examiner himself to little more than a scribe. Indeed, while the examiner formally retained the power to rule on the lawyers' objections, even this was highly circumscribed in that the pressure to create a complete and accurate record—one permitting review (and thus reversal) by the chancellor—required the examiner to authorize a recording of the witness's "whole answer," despite his ruling that the "last part" ought to be struck as "irrelevant."

As the parties' lawyers came increasingly to occupy center stage, examiners receded into the background. As in the case of masters, examiners began to record testimony in the first person, making the witnesses (under lawyer examination), rather than themselves, the true subjects of the narrative. While this move from the third person to the first did not occur without difficulty—a fact reflected in the striking way that certain examiners shifted back and forth between the two pronouns, evidently confused about which was appropriate[106]—the trend was clear. Indeed, it too was reflected in pre-printed deposition forms.[107]

Why was the statutory requirement that testimony before examiners be taken in oral, adversarial fashion implemented, even while the provision that it be taken directly before the finder of fact remained a dead letter, not to be enforced until the 1846 constitutional convention abolished chancery and its entire judicial staff? This piecemeal implementation of the law likely followed from the fact that the requirement that testimony before examiners be taken in oral, adversarial fashion codified developing practice, whereas the requirement that it be taken before the chancellor or circuit judge did not. In particular, as we have seen, masters in the years before 1823 had already begun taking testimony orally, and Chancellor Kent confirmed the permissibility of this practice in his 1817 decision in *Remsen*—at which time he also allowed lawyers to be present. This development suggested that it was both logical and permissible for other chancery officials to permit oral examinations in lawyers' presence— a practice that the April 17, 1823, statute expressly authorized. But while these developments shifted procedural power from masters and examiners to lawyers, they also led these chancery officials to assume an important role as the neutral umpires responsible for recording all testimony and ruling on evidentiary objections. The attempt of the 1823 and 1838 statutes to all but banish masters and examiners from the examination of witnesses thus went significantly further than practice itself had evolved.

The legislature's failure to impose change from above was due, at least in part, to the fact that masters and examiners had a vested interest in preserving their positions as a source of additional income and status. To the extent that they ceased to be involved in the taking of testimony, they would lose a significant justification for their existence. They therefore had a strong incentive to resist any efforts to do away with their intermediation in witness examination. In contrast, they had relatively little reason to resist the embrace of lawyer-driven, oral examination. Masters and examiners were all lawyers, and most continued to practice law while holding office, if only because the highly politicized nature of the appointment process meant that they might easily lose their positions when new elections ousted their political patrons from office. As reported by Godfrey Thomas Vigne, an English barrister who visited New York in 1831, "I observed that 'Mr. A., master in chancery,' was almost as frequently to be seen on the door, as the names of a counsellor and solicitor."[108] Focused on preserving a successful legal practice, masters and examiners had little motivation to resist a change in procedure—namely, the turn to oral, adversarial examination—that they enjoyed in their capacity as lawyers and that continued to ensure them an important income stream in their capacity as chancery officials. In theory, of course, they might have developed a more status-based, nonpecuniary interest in resisting this change in that it deprived them (qua chancery officials) of their quasi-inquisitorial power to control witness examination. But the very fact that they continued to practice as lawyers—and that their terms of office were often short—meant that they never developed the kind of strong professional identity as chancery officers that might have lent itself to the emergence of such an interest.

The self-interest of masters and examiners coincided, moreover, with certain practical institutional limitations that made any effort to eliminate the intermediation of these officers difficult, if not impossible. Even with the addition of circuit judges (later identified as vice chancellors), chancery did not have enough judges for these to assume exclusive responsibility for hearing all testimony in equity. As Murray Hoffman remarked in his 1839 treatise on chancery practice, a key difficulty with the April 18, 1838, statute was that, in practice, it "amounted almost to a suspension of the collection of testimony, in new causes, for the period of one year."[109] Without the intermediation of masters and examiners, there were simply not enough judges to take testimony, and equity thus ground to a halt. It was only in 1846 that it finally became possible—at a constitutional convention, rather than a legislative session—to do away with these longstanding chancery officials and their intermediary role in taking testimony.

## CONSEQUENCES OF THE SHIFT TOWARD ORAL, ADVERSARIAL PROCEDURE

Having radiated outward from proceedings before masters to those before examiners, the influx of oral, adversarial procedure proceeded to reshape numerous other aspects of equity procedure. This was in part because a procedural system is an interconnected whole, such that a change to any one component puts pressure on the entire system, thereby encouraging changes throughout. But the way in which the turn to oral, adversarial testimony came to remake so much of equity procedure also reflects the extent to which equity's quasi-inquisitorial approach to witness examination lay at the heart of chancery's entire procedural system. Indeed, as John Dawson argued, the roots of the distinction between the common law and civil law date back, most fundamentally, to a set of distinctive choices made in the Middle Ages about how best to go about taking testimony.[110]

One of the most important consequences of the new dominance of lawyers in chancery proceedings was a significant increase in cost and delay. As we will soon see, complaints about the inefficiency of chancery procedure became widespread by the 1830s, but the procedural system that was the object of these attacks was not, in fact, the quasi-inquisitorial tradition of equity. The source of the problem was, to the contrary, the influx of oral, adversarial procedure—especially as grafted onto a system that continued to rely on judicial intermediaries to take testimony on behalf of the ultimate finder of fact.

Consider, for example, *Burch v. Kent,* a long-running suit for specific performance of a contract to convey real estate, which was finally decided by Chancellor Walworth in 1842.[111] Among the many witnesses called before examiner
Virgil D. Bonesteel was the hapless Silas Washburn, a laborer who regularly
hired himself out to work on farms and lay stone walls. Called as a witness for
the defense, Washburn ended up testifying multiple times over a three-day
period in January 1839—first on direct examination by counsel for the defendant, then on cross-examination by counsel for the plaintiff, followed by re-
direct, re-cross, and lastly re-re-direct.

Examiner Bonesteel is all but erased from his own report of the testimony,
appearing only insofar as necessary to swear in the witness and record his
testimony (along with counsel's objections). The focus is instead on the lawyers' adversarial debate with one another, which continues across numerous
pages of (handwritten) text. Particularly striking in this regard is the debate
that ensued when the defense counsel, undertaking the second of three examinations of Washburn, "took the witness aside to converse with him"—a
colloquy that never could have happened pursuant to equity's traditional rules
of secrecy, which barred parties and their counsel (as well as anyone else)
from attending the witness examination. As reported by Bonesteel,

> [T]he counsel for the complainant objected and the [defense] counsel
> insisted that he had a right to talk with the witness either in this room or
> out doors or anywhere else with a view to ascertain from him whether he
> has such a knowledge of facts pertaining to the case as to make it worth
> while to examine him at all in relation thereto and having ascertained
> that he does not know anything as to the points inquired of him he fore-
> bears examining him on the points enquired about. The counsel for the
> complainant insists that the defendant's counsel did ascertain that the
> witness knew about the point but found it to be unfavorable and there-
> fore declines questioning him on that point. To which the defendant's
> counsel says that the representations of complainant's counsel are ut-
> terly untrue; to which the complainant's counsel replies that his repre-
> sentations are true and that he can prove them by the witness and several
> other persons present; to which the defendant's counsel says he cannot
> prove it by the witness or any body else.

The absurdity of this detailed, play-by-play recording of the lawyers' respective
arguments—all completely unrelated to the material facts in dispute in
the litigation—highlights the extent to which the examiner had lost control

over the proceedings, having ceded all power to the lawyers. Given free rein to examine and reexamine witnesses, raise unlimited evidentiary objections, and coach witnesses on the side, they caused proceedings (as well as the reports documenting these) to drag on ad infinitum. The examiner, in turn, was unable to make any definitive rulings himself and thus focused merely on transcribing the lawyers' objections and antics for review by the chancellor. Accordingly, when "[t]he counsel for the complainant . . . objected to any further examination of witness by the counsel for defendant," the examiner's only move was to record the objection before allowing defense counsel to proceed with his examination.[112]

The hybrid blending of oral, adversarial witness examination with chancery's quasi-inquisitorial tradition of relying on an intermediary judicial staff to record the testimony for later review by the finder of fact served, moreover, to undermine both the legal and equitable approaches to ensuring testimonial veracity. The influx of oral, adversarial testimony into chancery eliminated the court's ability to rely on (pre-publication) secrecy as a mechanism for discouraging perjury. But at the same time, contemporaries quickly concluded that the common-law reliance on cross-examination to serve as a lie detector was misplaced in the context of chancery's lengthy and noncontinuous proceedings. Cross-examination was expected to reveal witnesses' mendacity by shining light on contradictions in their testimony and on any awkwardness in their demeanor. In ways, however, that we have long since forgotten, the truth-probing effects of cross-examination were believed to hinge on the element of surprise. Indeed, contrary to the present-day view that surprise is inherently unfair, early and mid-nineteenth-century lawyers thought that it was essential for promoting veracity. Only if witnesses were surprised by the questions posed by the cross-examiner would they be forced to be truthful, since they would lack the time to prepare a credible lie. So too, lawyers themselves had to be surprised by witnesses' testimony under cross-examination, because otherwise they would be tempted to find additional witnesses to explain away testimony detrimental to their case.

Traditional common-law procedure ensured that both witnesses and lawyers would be surprised by requiring a single concentrated trial and by denying any prior opportunity for discovery. And because (unlike today) common-law trials were typically fairly short, rarely extending beyond two days, witnesses usually testified in one sitting.[113] Moreover, the need to have all witnesses for both sides available to testify in a single continuous proceeding ensured that lawyers would have no time to procure additional witnesses able to explain away harmful testimony provided under cross-examination. But while cross-examination's utility in detecting and deterring perjury was believed to hinge on the surprise made possible by a single, short, and continuous trial, equity proceedings were neither single, nor short, nor continuous. It was partly on these grounds that Kent had opposed the February 1821 draft bill requiring the oral, lawyer-driven examination of witnesses in chancery. As he explained, the reason why common-law courts were able safely and effectively to adopt such an adversarial approach was that, quite unlike chancery, their proceedings were traditionally both short and continuous: "In trials at common law, before a jury, the mischief" of inducing lawyers "to seek upon adjournment, for further testimony to meet the pressure and exigency of the case . . . cannot well arise, because the cause is heard, and the verdict taken at one sitting, and all undue opportunity for ranging at large and getting up suppletory proof, is precluded."[114] In contrast, because equity proceedings did not take the form of a single concentrated trial—a form necessitated in the common-law courts by the impaneling of a lay jury—they were regularly adjourned and rescheduled, enabling a flexibility that, whatever its other benefits, could all too easily be manipulated for the illicit purpose of procuring false testimony.

In the wake of chancery's embrace of oral, adversarial witness examination, contemporaries became increasingly worried that Kent had been prescient in warning of the dangers of perjury. Chancellor Reuben Walworth thus deployed his authority to create and revise rules of practice to attempt to restrict the ability of lawyers to manipulate the process of evidence-gathering. In the chancery rules that he issued in 1829, he created a new Rule 83 providing that: "Before the commencement of the examination of any witnesses, . . . the parties respectively shall deliver to each other . . . the names of the several witnesses intended to be examined. . . . And no other witnesses shall be examined by either party, without special permission of the court, on sufficient cause shown. . . ."[115] As Walworth explained in an 1832 opinion addressing the new rule, its purpose was to force parties to disclose all witnesses *before* they heard any testimony, thus limiting their ability to benefit from knowledge of the testimony provided for the purpose of identifying additional, more favorable witnesses:

> After the passing of the statute, authorizing the examination of witnesses openly before the examiner or commissioner, it was found that part of the evils which had been anticipated were actually produced by

this change in the practice of this court. When the principal witnesses had been examined, the parties respectively were in the habit of protracting the closing of the proofs, to endeavor to fish up testimony to contradict the depositions of the witnesses who had been examined against them. By the course of proceeding, garbled conversations and much useless matter, wholly irrelevant to the issue in the cause, were frequently introduced. There was also reason to apprehend it sometimes led to subornation of perjury. The object of the 83rd rule was to remedy this evil, as far as practicable, by requiring the parties to interchange lists of their witnesses . . . before the taking of the testimony was commenced.[116]

Similarly, in 1844, an assistant vice chancellor reaffirmed that the purpose of Rule 83 was to address the new risk of perjury that followed from chancery's turn to oral, adversarial examination and cross-examination. As he observed, "[t]he principal object of the 83rd rule, was to cut off the opportunity for parties to fish up testimony after the witnesses in the cause had been partially examined; an evil to which suitors were exposed, by the change from secret examinations on written interrogatories, to the oral examinations now in use."[117]

Given modern-day anxieties regarding discovery abuse, there is a striking familiarity in these concerns about (and proposals for addressing) the misuse of out-of-court witness examinations for purposes of perverting the truth. This sense of déjà vu is no mere coincidence. It is instead a product of the fact that current discovery practice—concerning most especially depositions—replicates in many ways the approach to taking testimony that came to dominate in New York Chancery during the years between the 1817 decision in *Remsen* and the 1848 enactment of the Field Code. While the path from past to present was by no means direct, the mode of taking testimony that came to dominate in New York Chancery during this period—namely, an out-of-court proceeding in which lawyers conducted oral examination and cross-examination before an officer whose only function was to record what was said—appears to be an important progenitor of modern-day deposition practice, as set forth in the highly influential Federal Rules of Civil Procedure.[118] As this suggests, core aspects of our concerns with discovery abuse date all the way back to New York Chancery's early and mid-nineteenth-century embrace of oral, adversarial witness examination and, more particularly, to the hybrid procedural form that dominated until the Field Code abolished both masters and examiners, ushering in a primarily adversarial mode of procedure. Thereafter forgotten, the potential dangers of such procedural hybridity would resurface in 1938, when the drafters of the Federal Rules merged law and equity and, in so doing, created modern discovery.[119]

On a more mundane level, the new presence and involvement of parties and their counsel in the examination of witnesses made many aspects of traditional equity procedure superfluous. This was the case, for example, for the complex series of rules designed to ensure that testimony taken by commissioners would remain secret prior to publication. Archival records reveal that in the years after 1823, the oaths sworn by commissioners and their clerks no longer included language committing these officers to the preservation of pre-publication secrecy, requiring them instead simply to promise that they would proceed "without partiality to any or either of the parties."[120] Similarly, Chancellor Walworth ruled in 1841 that chancery would no longer enforce the long-standing rules designed to ensure that testimony taken by its officers would be returned to the court carefully sealed and therefore unseen by the parties. As he put it, "as the practice of taking the testimony in secret has been abolished in this state, it is only necessary now that the court should be satisfied the depositions are genuine, and that they have not been altered since they were sworn to by the witnesses."[121]

But perhaps the most significant consequence of the shift to oral, lawyer-driven examinations was the rise of a new conception of what procedural justice entailed. As such examinations became increasingly common, so too they became the norm, such that the traditional, written, and secrecy-oriented approach came to seem unfair. Consider, in this regard, *Reid v. Peters,* a creditors' suit filed in March 1845 to collect on debts owed by the defendant, John Peters. According to the defendant, his key witness was his brother, William Peters. But unfortunately for John, William lived in Philadelphia, and because of a combination of illness and professional obligations, he was unable to travel to the defendant's home in Sanford, New York, until mid-July 1847. Since the period for taking testimony in the case had already closed, John moved for an order that would reopen the proofs and "extend[] the time for such examination until the 15th day of July next."[122]

In order to justify his request for an extension of the time to take testimony, John had to suggest that there was no way to obtain William's testimony other than by waiting for him to reappear in New York around mid-July. But this was not an argument that he could easily make, because there *was* another mechanism available—namely, a commission to take testimony out of state. While examiners were authorized to operate only within state boundaries and thus could not take William's testimony until such time as he arrived in New York, commissions were designed to acquire the testimony of witnesses who lived at a distance, including out of state. John therefore had to explain why a commission was not a viable option. Part of his argument was to insist that it would likely take until mid-July to procure and execute a commission, such that there were no time savings to be gained by this device. But the more important reason why he could not rely on a commission was that "he is advised by his said counsel and believes true that it would be impossible to do justice to deponent's cause by examining the said William Peters by a commissioner."[123]

John failed to specify how precisely the taking of testimony by out-of-state commission would result in an injustice that would be avoided by the in-state examination of the witness, presumably before an examiner. But as contemporaries well understood, the core difference here concerned whether testimony was to be taken on the basis of written interrogatories or by means of oral examination by the parties' lawyers. While the Act of April 17, 1823 and the case law interpreting it provided that testimony before a commission might be taken orally by the parties' lawyers,[124] this does not appear to have occurred with any frequency. Well into the 1840s, most commissions to take testimony—especially out of state—continued to rely on written interrogatories. To do otherwise was likely cost-prohibitive. For John Peters to argue that "to do [him] justice," the court must authorize the in-state examination of the witness, rather than force him to rely on an out-of-state commission, was thus to argue that examination by means of written interrogatories was inherently unjust. Put differently, the process he was due was oral and adversarial. It is, of course, possible that John's arguments were instrumental in the narrowest sense of the term—namely, that he had failed to take testimony in a timely manner and was now looking for any excuse to justify his tardiness. Indeed, the plaintiffs' lawyer made precisely this point. But while John Peters may have had these instrumental reasons for insisting that he could not obtain justice from a commission, the fact that he (and his lawyer) deemed this to be a plausible argument is in itself significant because it suggests that they were not alone in their belief in the superiority of oral, adversarial procedure.

That procedural fairness would thus come to be viewed as synonymous with oral, adversarial procedure was not an outcome anyone anticipated in the early years of the nineteenth century, when certain masters allowed lawyers to be present during witness examinations and when Kent sanctioned this practice in his 1817 decision in *Remsen*. Yet, in ways that no one expected or intended, these developments—driven by lawyers' eagerness to exercise more procedural control—initiated an incremental series of changes that led to the near-complete transformation of equity into an oral, adversarial system of procedure. New York Chancery's embrace of such procedure thus followed largely from developments internal to the institution itself. Importantly, however, lawyers' motivations for seeking increased control were themselves profoundly shaped not only by strategic interests in winning litigation but also by broader cultural values and aspirations, including, as we will soon see, the classical ideal of the lawyer as orator-statesman. But before examining the role of this classical ideal, we must pause to acknowledge the possibility of another cultural influence that may have played some part in lawyers' embrace of the oral, adversarial methods of the common law—one on which we have already touched briefly in passing.

As we have seen, during the early decades of the nineteenth century, both English Chancery and New York Chancery adopted the first-person pronoun for recording witness testimony. Roughly contemporaneous, these developments appear to stem in some fashion from the era's new and widespread commitment to publicity in governance. The eighteenth century witnessed the rise of what Jürgen Habermas famously termed the "bourgeois public sphere"—namely, various new fora of civil society (such as coffee houses, clubs, and salons) in which citizens across a broad range of social ranks could gather and debate matters of public interest. The defining and novel feature of these institutions was that they departed from the structuring logic of the Old Regime—namely, the effort to replicate a hierarchical status quo—and sought instead to promote (relatively) egalitarian communicative exchange, in the service of truth instead of power. Since Habermas first articulated this category several decades ago, it has been subject to extensive critique. Nonetheless, it has proven enormously influential, leading to many works considering, inter alia, the connections between the rise of the Habermasian public sphere and the late eighteenth-century democratic revolutions.[125] In an important contribution to this literature, Judith Resnik and Dennis Curtis argue that the eighteenth-century commitment to institutions of democratic publicity profoundly shaped the court systems that emerged in the wake of the French and American revolutions. As epitomized by the extensive writings of Jeremy Bentham, courts in this period were conceived as an important set of institutions for facilitating democratic self-governance—ones that would function as intended only to the extent that their proceedings were public. As Resnik and Curtis detail, this Benthamite commitment to publicity in general—and to public courts in particular—was multi-pronged. Publicity was thought to promote accuracy in adjudication, encourage judges and other officials to act in accordance with the law, educate the citizenry about the law, and foster the law's legitimacy.[126]

Bentham's conception of the courtroom as a powerful institution of democratic self-governance implied the need for extensive procedural reform aimed at promoting greater publicity in judicial decision-making. Among the reforms that he advocated was the embrace of oral interrogation (including cross-examination), as opposed to what he called "the epistolary mode." The epistolary or written mode, used in chancery, among other institutions, suffered from many deficiencies, he claimed, not the least of which was that witnesses were made to speak in the third person, rather than the first. Bentham offered a number of different arguments for why the first-person pronoun was superior to the third. One was that it would help prevent unnecessary verbosity and thus "voluminousness." More importantly, he suggested, using the first person was essential for promoting two goals—truth and clarity—that were themselves key to developing and maintaining a robust, democratic public sphere. First-person testimony would promote truth by forcing deponents to take responsibility for their own words: "When a man speaks in his own person, he considers what he has to say to be his own discourse, and himself to be in the highest degree responsible for it." At the same time, use of the first person encouraged the related, but distinct, virtue of communicative clarity, avoiding "ambiguity and obscurity, and thence unintelligibility." Drawing an express parallel between the use of the third-person pronoun in the taking of testimony and "on the occasion of epistolary correspondence for the trivial purposes of common life," Bentham decried the practice as having "been among the inventions of cold pride, to keep inferiors and intruders at a distance."[127] Pronoun selection, in sum, had a profound effect on the structuring of communicative relations, such that a shift to the first person was vital for sustaining a public sphere in which individuals could meet as respectful equals, jointly engaged in the project of democratic self-governance.

Bentham's discussion of the epistolary mode of interrogation and the virtues of the first-person pronoun appear in his *Rationale of Judicial Evidence*, which was first published in 1827. It is thus possible that his views on these matters played some role in informing thinking and practice on both sides of the Atlantic. More likely, as was so often the case with Bentham, he gave voice—and clear conceptualization—to patterns of thought and value judgments that were themselves just on the cusp of emergence, reflecting views that would soon become widespread.[128] Either way, it seems clear that the shift to first-person testimony was linked not only to New York lawyers' increased control over masters' proceedings but also to a broader set of transnational (Benthamite) concerns regarding the rise of democratic governance. In this, there was no contradiction. Claiming to be a virtuous civic elite responsible for preserving the foundations of the republic, New York lawyers were able to demand the expansion of their own power while at the same time insisting that their actions in this regard were vital for sustaining the new, democratic nation. But before delving deeper into lawyers' motivations, we must take a step back and examine the Field Code of Procedure of 1848. Long hailed as the crowning glory of nineteenth-century procedural reform, responsible for a supposedly revolutionary merger of law and equity, it was in fact little more than a fait accompli.

# 3 • The Non-Revolutionary Field Code
## Democratization, Docket Pressures, and Codification

In the 1820s and 1830s, governors, legislators, constitutional convention delegates, and opinion leaders of various stripes launched a massive campaign against the institution of chancery, pointing in part to Kent and Story's highly judge-empowering conception of the court to decry it as a bastion of elitist rule. Given the rise of the political party machine known as the Albany Regency and the remarkable democratization of politics that followed, these men were eager to demonstrate their populist credentials. Lambasting chancery as an elitist institution—partly because of its quasi-inquisitorial procedural approach—was an effective means of doing so. This sustained legislative attack, in turn, contributed to a perceived need for institutional and procedural change. It thus helped to legitimate the procedural transformations that lawyers themselves had undertaken while also removing the political and doctrinal stumbling blocks that might have stood in their way. As a result, when the Field Code of Procedure was enacted in 1848, it was by and large a fait accompli, reflecting changes that had already occurred, rather than, as so long assumed, initiating reform.

## Democratization and Its Discontents: The Rise of the Albany Regency and the Campaign against Chancery

While there was a centuries-old tradition of hostility to chancery, such hostility resurfaced with a vengeance in the late 1810s as a result of the Albany Regency's remarkable rise to power. The empowerment of the Regency followed from and contributed to an extraordinary democratization of politics in New York—and, as a result of that state's preeminence, in the nation as a whole. Such democratization was reflected in various reforms undertaken by the 1821 constitutional convention, including important expansions of suffrage and the abolition of powerful governmental institutions (such as the Council of Appointment and the Council of Revision) that were widely viewed as tools of an aristocratic elite. After the convention, a series of statutory enactments served further to broaden suffrage (for white men) and to reform property law by eliminating those elements (like the persistence of a system of feudal tenure) that were historically associated with a society of orders. But while the rise of the Regency led to significant transformations in law and governance, Gregory Alexander is right to caution that "the rhetoric of democratization greatly outpaced the . . . actual effects" of constitutional and legislative reform.[1] It would be a mistake, however, to assume that rhetoric is unimportant. Indeed, the Regency would lose its stranglehold on New York political life only in 1838, when the Whigs gained control over both the governorship and the state assembly by adopting the populist rhetoric and electioneering techniques of their Democratic adversaries.[2] This was a political climate, in short, in which politicians had much to gain by signaling their commitment to democratization. And one particularly effective way of doing so was by complaining about the elitist nature of chancery and its procedure.

From the early republic through to the middle decades of the nineteenth century, lawyers and the legal system as a whole—including not only equity but also the common law and its courts—were subject to great public opprobrium on the grounds that they were antidemocratic institutions, lacking in transparency and operating for the exclusive benefit of a wealthy elite. As Perry Miller famously observed, the young nation was characterized by a profound "antilegalism"—one expressed in "the widespread hostility of ordinary Americans to the very concept of law." But while a great many early Americans rejected all law and legal institutions as an inheritance of their British oppressors, tending to undermine their hard-won liberties, chancery was subject to an especially high degree of distrust and animosity. This was due, in part, to the way that equity became associated with tyranny during the English Revolution—an association that the recent colonial experience served powerfully to reinvigorate. As Stanley Katz argued, "no colonial legal institution was the object of such sustained and intense political opposition as the courts dispensing equity law."[3] But so too, the nature of equity procedure as a quasi-inquisitorial system managed by a lone and powerful judge made the institution particularly suspect. Indeed, Kent's very success in relying on such procedure to develop the image of chancery as a bastion of elitist rule all but invited a response from his Democratic opponents, thereby ensuring that the rise of the Albany Regency would lead to a backlash against equity.

In complaining about the elitism of chancery and its procedure, critics drew on the longstanding discourse linking equity with authoritarian (and thus antidemocratic) rule—in contrast to the supposedly more liberty-promoting common law. Just as this discourse was used to undermine the power of royalists in seventeenth-century England, so too in nineteenth-century New York, it was deployed to thwart political enemies deemed elitist—first by Democrats against their Federalist and Whig opponents and then by chastened Whigs eager to regain the upper hand.

## THE REACTION AGAINST KENT'S QUASI-INQUISITORIAL VISION OF EQUITY

Aggressively promoted by Kent as a bulwark of elite (Federalist) rule, chancery and its procedure quickly fell within the crosshairs of the ascendant Democrats and, not long thereafter, those of the rising Whigs as well. In the early years, when the Albany Regency was just coming into power and Kent himself continued to serve as chancellor, enmity against the institution and its procedure followed from (and indeed was all but synonymous with) hatred of the forceful judge with whom it was so widely associated.

In his role as chancellor, Kent reached a number of decisions that proved to be highly politically contentious, resulting in several reversals by the Court of Errors. Created by the state's initial 1777 constitution, the Court of Errors was empowered to reverse decisions issued by chancery and the supreme court and was staffed by both legislators and judges, including the chancellor himself. Not surprisingly, given that so many of its judges were legislators, the court reversed quite a few of Kent's decisions that seemed out of step with the prevailing democratic winds—including, for example, those in which he staunchly protected the interests of creditors.[4]

Kent garnered significant enmity, however, not solely because of some of his decisions as chancellor but also due to his role (as chancellor) within the state's Council of Revision. Established by the 1777 constitution, the Council of Revision was a purposefully antidemocratic entity, composed of the governor, the chancellor, and the three judges of the supreme court (or any two of them). It was charged with reviewing all legislation passed by the legislature and was authorized to revise or veto it. The legislature was then required to consider the views expressed by the Council, and unless both houses passed the initial legislation once again—this time by a two-thirds majority of each house—it was not to become law.[5] Kent self-consciously utilized his position as a member of the Council to wage a counterattack against the rising forces of democracy, explaining to his brother Moss that his goal was to "enter my feeble protest against several violent bills coming from our Jacobin legislature and governor." He thus devoted himself to quashing, inter alia, all legislation that in his view threatened to impair property rights—whether by abridging the dower-rights of the widows of much-hated loyalists or by authorizing entities incorporated for public ends (like building aqueducts) to seize land by means of eminent domain.[6]

So great was the animosity Kent sparked as chancellor that in his final years in office, the Democrat-controlled legislature voted several times to reduce his annual salary, cutting it by more than 50 percent in a period of just seven years.[7] And when the New York Constitutional Convention met in 1821, several of Kent's Democratic opponents sought to abolish chancery, in no small part because they so hated him. Erastus Root, the delegate who initially called for abolition, groused that he was tired of hearing Kent lauded as a "branching oak," since if the metaphor held true, it was not because he provided shelter to those in need but instead because he "cast a baleful political pestilence" around him, "carr[ying] death and desolation to the extent of [his] atmosphere."[8]

But while animosity against chancery followed in significant measure from hatred of its chancellor, the two were not perfectly coextensive. When the constitutional convention met in 1821, Democrats like Root were well aware that pursuant to a provision retained from the state's first constitution, Kent was required to retire from the bench at the age of sixty, a mere two years later. Had their animosity against chancery stemmed solely from their hatred of Kent, there would have been little incentive to abolish the institution as a whole. That said, Kent himself—by conceptualizing chancery as a bastion of elite rule, designed to protect the nation from the forces of democracy—played an important role in generating hostility toward the court. Moreover, because his elitist conception of equity was a profoundly procedural one, grounded in the court's quasi-inquisitorial tradition, the democratic turn against chancery manifested itself largely as a turn against its traditional, judge-empowering model of procedure. For example, in the debates over chancery in the 1821 constitutional convention, Jacob Radcliff, a Democratic former supreme court justice and New York City mayor, observed that "In Great-Britan [sic], the chancery court was an immense power, wielded by the king; and in this country it was enormous, and unlike any thing else in our government and institutions. It was inexpedient that such powers should be lodged in any individual, whatever might be his talents and integrity."9 Along similar lines, Melancton Wheeler, a newly minted Democrat (and former Federalist), insisted that chancery's "exuberant [procedural] powers [ought to be] somewhat circumscribed" because they were far too extensive to be entrusted to a single judge in a democratic society.10

In casting chancery procedure as excessively judge-empowering and thus antidemocratic, opponents drew on the longstanding discourse, dating back to the English Civil War, that depicted chancery as tending to promote royal and "popish" supremacy. As we have seen, this was a discourse that tarred chancery—and other equity courts—as the Roman-canon law–based creations of the king (and his "papist" supporters) and thus as a tool for promoting absolutist rule. Pursuant to this discourse, royal attempts to aggrandize power manifested themselves in part in the efforts of equity courts to deprive common-law courts (loyal to Parliament and people) of their rightful jurisdiction. Drawing on this centuries-old language, Wheeler insisted that "[t]he court of chancery, as at present organized in England, is founded in usurpation." The powers that chancery had accrued were not only excessive in and of themselves but, at least as troubling, had been obtained at the expense of the common-law courts, which chancery and its civilians were bent on dominating, along with Parliament itself: "[Chancery] has drawn to itself, by gradual encroachments upon the precincts of the common-law courts, a jurisdiction of immense extent"—and this despite "the long and arduous struggle maintained by our Saxon ancestors, in defence of the common law . . . against the attempts of their Norman conquerors to introduce the civil law, which they and their monkish followers had engrafted upon the Pandects of Justinian."11

According to Wheeler, the English Civil War forced civilians to abandon their hope of controlling the common-law courts, but this simply made them all the more attached to chancery, which they viewed as a base from which to insinuate themselves into the fabric of state and society: "[W]hen the clergy were driven from the courts of common law, they held fast to the office of chancellor, which they claimed as their own . . . and from this beginning, the chancery court of England, and of this state, have extended their jurisdiction to most cases which arise out of the private controversies of mankind." Along similar lines, Erastus Root carried this narrative of jurisdictional "usurpation" forward into the colonial context, observing that chancery in New York "was a power assumed by the governor and council without right, against which the legislature had uniformly and strongly protested, and which had been kept up by usurpation ever since."12

From the perspective of chancery's opponents, there were several good reasons for drawing on this traditional language of jurisdictional usurpation. The very act of "usurping jurisdiction" was itself a synecdoche for undemocratic rule: Just as courts of equity (particularly chancery) exercised unlawful jurisdiction stolen from the people's common-law courts, so too government as a whole had been hijacked by aristocratic elites. In addition, this narrative of usurpation served—as it always had—as a means of highlighting the procedural differences between common law and equity, thereby suggesting that the latter endowed the chancellor and his staff with excessive powers. Most obvious among these procedural differences was that the common law relied on a jury, while equity was a one-man court.

Precisely because chancery was located in Albany—and held at best two sessions annually in New York City—it was necessarily remote.[13] Many litigants thus either had to pay for their lawyers to travel to Albany or instead hire additional counsel in Albany to supplement the services provided by local counsel. As a Senate committee complained in February 1823, there were portions of the state that were "heretofore almost virtually excluded [from chancery jurisdiction], arising from the peculiar structure and practice of the court of chancery, and its location."[14] Many chancery critics hoped that, by creating circuit judges whom the legislature was authorized to endow with equity jurisdiction, the new constitution of 1821 would make chancery more accessible. The legislature acted on its new constitutional authority by promulgating the statute of April 17, 1823, and to some extent, the reform was successful. Thus, after 1823, complaints about the remoteness of equity jurisdiction largely subsided—though, as contemporaries widely recognized, the fact that the chancellor (in Albany) had appellate jurisdiction over every case was itself a significant cause of expense and delay.[15] But while critics thereafter ceased to focus on chancery's geographical remoteness, they continued to complain that the court was excessively costly, such that it remained inaccessible.

Also troubling to chancery's critics was its distinctive approach to taking testimony. The common law constrained judicial power by having witnesses examined by lawyers orally and in public, but equity provided for the written, secret examination of witnesses by court personnel. As delegate Wheeler observed during the 1821 convention, it was the great virtue of the English common lawyers that they managed to "preserve[ ] from the rude grasp of popish civilians the trial by jury, [and] the right of examining witnesses *ore tenus*. . . ."[16] Less than two years after the convention, critics drew once again on the centuries-old discourse linking chancery and its procedure to absolutist rule when the state legislature debated the legislation that would eventually be enacted on April 17, 1823. As we have seen, this statute, as ultimately enacted, augmented the number of judges authorized to hear suits in equity by creating eight circuit judges endowed with first-instance equity jurisdiction. In addition, it directed that all testimony in equity be taken "as in the trial of actions at common law"—namely, through oral, lawyer-driven examination and cross-examination before the deciding judge himself. But as initially drafted, the proposed legislation contained no provisions concerning testimony.[17] Accordingly, a number of legislators insisted that more radical reform was needed—and, in particular, reform of chancery's approach to witness examination.

Complaining that the proposed legislation permitted equity's traditional, written, and secret approach to persist, Wheeler renewed his insistence that this approach was intimately linked to chancery's long history of "violence and usurpation." "[I]n [chancery's approach to] the investigation of truth," he claimed, "much of the form, and of the practice, of the monastick, or civil law is retained."[18] This was a powerful argument, resonating not only with the longstanding English discourse about the allegedly Roman-canon (and thus tyrannical and "popish") roots of equity procedure but also with new, more local fears of the foreign that were developing in these years of rising Catholic immigration and concomitant nativism. Along similar lines, Wheeler's Democratic colleague in the Senate, John Cramer, also argued that the 1823 statute ought to proscribe chancery's traditional "method of taking testimony, which has been one of the most crying evils to which the state has ever been subjected." In his view, the secrecy of examinations tended to wreak injustice: "The ingenuity of man could not devise a worse system, than the one practiced by our courts of chancery; when a man is shut up in a master's chamber and presented with a set of interrogations, with time to deliberate and prepare his answers, without any one to witness his apparent feelings or emotions. Here the most artful villain may be made to appear to the best advantage."[19] Such calls for more radical reform were evidently persuasive, in that the statute, as ultimately enacted, directed that chancery abandon the traditional, quasi-inquisitorial approach to testimony and instead embrace the oral, adversarial methods of the common law.

## THE WHIG VICTORY AND THE PERSISTENT (BUT RECONFIGURED) CRITIQUE OF CHANCERY

From the late 1830s onward, critics of chancery continued to draw on the longstanding discourse associating equity with absolutist (undemocratic) rule as a means of decrying the excessive procedural powers invested by chancery in a single judge. But there were some notable differences from the way this discourse had been employed in the late 1810s and 1820s. During Kent's chancellorship and immediately thereafter, criticisms of chancery were directed largely by Democrats at Kent himself and his Federalist vision of elite rule. In contrast, the later critique of chancery was widely voiced by both Democrats and Whigs. And while this critique was aimed at the sitting chancellor, Reuben Walworth, it also extended well beyond him. More particularly, the once generic criticism of chancery as elitist and thus undemocratic was refined to address two particular developments that were both widely perceived as challenges to the nation's democratic experiment—namely, the rise of the spoils system of party politics and the market revolution.

In the wake of the financial panics of 1837 and 1839, the Whigs began to embrace many of the populist views and techniques of their Democratic adversaries, and thus they too began complaining about chancery's excessive procedural powers. For example, in January 1839, the newly elected Whig governor, William H. Seward, called in his annual message to the legislature "for dividing the power and responsibilities of the chancellor." As he explained, "[t]he powers of the court of chancery are too vast . . . to be vested in a single individual." Moreover, as compared with that of other courts, "its process [was] more searching and potential" and therefore in need of significant restraint.[20] Shortly thereafter, the Whig members of the legislature published an "Address . . . to the People of the State of New York" in which they echoed Seward's concern that chancery "with its vast powers . . . still remains vested in a single individual."[21] Since meaningful legislation was not forthcoming, Governor Seward declared once again in 1841 that chancery's "power[s] were too great to be reposed in a single judge."[22]

Similar arguments about the need to constrain the excessive procedural powers invested in chancery were made by public intellectual and Democratic senator Gulian C. Verplanck in a series of speeches before the New York Senate in May 1839, all of which were widely reprinted in the press. Using much the same language as his Democratic predecessors and as Governor Seward and his Whig colleagues, he complained that the chancellor's "power is too much for any one man." According to Verplanck, the "powers" of the equity judge "are great and undefined—its process strict and searching," much like that of "an arbitrary judge in a half-civilized country, a Mandarin or a Cadi."[23] In addition, he decried chancery's "mode of taking testimony" as "the very worst ever devised"—not simply because it was "dilatory [and] expensive" but also because it "open[ed] a door to the grossest perjuries and the vilest frauds."[24]

Just as personal animosity against Kent had earlier contributed to animosity against the institution he headed, so too the widespread dislike of his successor, Reuben Walworth, exacerbated anxieties that chancery was endowed with excessive procedural power. Biographical accounts of the long-seated chancellor, many written soon after his death, are replete with anecdotes relating his predilection for offending the lawyers who argued before him—for example, by interrupting them and critiquing their performances.[25] As noted by the well-heeled Manhattan lawyer George Templeton Strong in a diary en-

Figure 3  Rembrandt Peale (American, 1778–1860),
*Chancellor Reuben Hyde Walworth* (1788–1867), (probably
1835), oil on canvas, $30\frac{3}{16} \times 25$ in. (76.68 × 63.5 cm). Layton
Art Collection, Inc., Gift of Mrs. Jenkins. Courtesy of
Milwaukee Art Museum, L1925.1. Photographer credit:
P. Richard Eells.

try from June 1839, a visit to chancery was an opportunity "to see the lawyers tortured by the Chancellor." According to Strong, Walworth "exhibits his smartness by snubbing the lawyers most outrageously."[26] While Walworth's treatment of lawyers in an imperious, high-handed manner surely stemmed in no small part from his sizable ego, it also fit squarely within the longstanding tradition of the powerful, domineering equity judge that Kent had done so much to revivify. In this way, distaste for Walworth contributed to the persistent and growing concern that chancery was entrusted with too much power. But by the late 1830s, the traditional critique of chancery and its procedure as generally undemocratic was further refined, such that the court came increasingly to be criticized because of its association with both the spoils system and the market revolution.

### "Patronage" and the Spoils System

By the late 1830s, the perennial assertion that the chancellor was endowed with too much authority came frequently to be directed at what were widely called his "patronage" powers. Critics complained, in particular, that the chancellor had exclusive control over the appointment of the court's register and assistant register, whose job it was (along with the clerks they oversaw) to register court documents and, perhaps most importantly, to oversee "the receipt, investment, payment and expenditure of monies brought into court."[27] That these registers oversaw the vast sums of money regularly deposited with the court was in itself widely viewed as grounds for concern in that, as Senator Verplanck opined, these men were appointed by (and reported to) the chancellor such that, for all intents and purposes, the chancellor himself controlled these sums.[28] Even more troubling, the registers appeared to be raking in the cash for relatively little talent or effort. As Verplanck argued, thus echoing an opinion common at the time, the "income of [these] officers whose duties require no high talents, and upon whom nothing beyond clerical responsibility is imposed, . . . [is] excessive." The problem was that these officers received a statutorily determined fee for every service they performed. And while each one of these fees was relatively low, it was widely agreed that the fee system "holds out a premium to multiply rules, orders, motions, and all the forms of courts, no matter how troublesome to suitors, provided they may be profitable to clerks and judges."[29]

Because the appointment of the register and assistant register was within the chancellor's exclusive control—and because these officers stood to earn such large sums of money—critics of chancery complained that the chancellor possessed worrisome powers of patronage. Verplanck, for example, asserted that it was dangerous "to decorate the office of chancellor with such a share of patronage as may tempt him to use it to provide for friends and dependents."[30] In so arguing, he alluded to the widely known and much-criticized fact that Walworth had opted to appoint family members as both register and assistant register. As the Whig publication the *Albany Evening Journal* observed in April 1839, there was great danger in "the immense and rapidly increasing money patronage and power which exists in the Court of Chancery—a patronage and power wielded by *one* man for the exclusive benefit of *one* Family! The Chancellor has appointed his Son-in-Law Register, and his Brother Assistant Register of the Court of Chancery, thus concentrating the vast patronage of that office in his own family! This is following too rapidly 'in the footsteps' of Monarchy."[31]

As troubling as such self-serving appointments were, the reality was that the chancellor's allegedly "vast" powers of patronage were in fact limited to the register and assistant register (and their clerks). So why were contemporaries so deeply concerned that the chancellor's ability to appoint these officers would lead "rapidly" to "monarchy"? As suggested by the mismatch between the appointment powers and their feared consequences, the debate over the chancellor's patronage powers implicated one of the era's much broader political debates—in particular, the debate over the rise of organized party machines (as exemplified by the Albany Regency) and, relatedly, the spoils system. The Albany Regency's remarkable rise to power was enabled in no small part by the masterful way that its leadership dispensed political offices to electoral supporters, thus giving rise to what became known as the spoils system. Pursuant to this system, loyal party members were awarded political office and were then, in turn, required to contribute a portion of their earnings to the party machine. While in theory, the party should have been indifferent as to whether officers were paid fees for their services or a fixed salary, the political reality was that it was easier to disguise a large total income paid through fees. Offices paid in the form of fees thus provided political party machines with a larger base to be assessed. As a result, the fee system as a whole—and most especially, the existence of high-income offices paid through fees—came to be associated with political machines and the spoils system on which they depended.[32] In these respects, New York Chancery and its two registers clearly fit the bill.

But while the spoils system was an irrefutable fact of political life in this period, its legitimacy remained questionable, contributing to the eventual rise of a modern-day civil service. More particularly, the civic republican discourse of the American Revolution continued to resonate (though by no means unchallenged) during the antebellum period, such that the notion that government offices would go to party hacks rather than a virtuous civic elite remained troublesome. As suggested by the term "Albany Regency"—derisively devised by the Whig newspaper publisher and politician Thurlow Weed—the Whigs claimed that the Democrats had undermined the foundations of democratic rule by imperiously controlling and distributing all political offices from their centralized party machine. Having long attacked the Democrats and their spoils, the Whigs—newly empowered in 1838—were especially eager for any opportunity to undermine their rivals' capacity to distribute patronage while also demonstrating (often contrary to reality) that they themselves would operate differently.[33] One easy way to pursue both goals was to challenge Walworth's patronage powers (along with those of other high judicial officers, like the justices of the supreme court).

Accordingly, upon first entering office, Governor Seward charged the legislature with investigating "[t]he fees of the clerks of the supreme court and the register, assistant register, and clerks of the court of chancery." As he opined, "[t]o lavish [compensation] upon public favorites is anti-republican, wasteful and demoralizing. . . ."[34] Acting on Seward's lead, a committee of the state assembly concluded that "[t]he almost princely incomes received by several of these officers . . . are repugnant to the true principles and proper practice of republican economy."[35] The Whig-dominated legislature thereafter transformed chancery's registers and clerks (as well as the clerks of the supreme court) into salaried officers. But despite such reforms, the Whigs continued to complain that chancery was a source of "enormous patronage."[36] Moreover, as late as 1841, Governor Seward declared in his annual message that chancery's "patronage" was "too great to be reposed in a single judge."[37] As this suggests, criticizing the chancellor's patronage powers was at least as much about tarnishing political opponents as antidemocratic as it was about pursuing actual institutional reform.

### Creditors' Bills and the Market Revolution

In much the same way that the longstanding critique of the chancellor's excessive power came to be directed at his control over "patronage," so too by the late 1830s, the assertion that chancery had gained its jurisdiction by usurping that of the common-law courts came to be directed at its jurisdiction over what were commonly called "creditors' bills." Not to be confused with the older equitable device designed to enable creditors of a deceased debtor to collect from the estate, this newer form of creditors' bill was created by the New York legislature when it systematized its legislation in the Revised Statutes of

1830. According to contemporaries, these newly established creditors' bills quickly became a sizable component of the chancery docket. As Murray Hoffman explained in his 1839 treatise on chancery practice, "Bills by judgment creditors have become since the passage of the Revised Statutes, of great importance, and embrace a large proportion of the business of the court."[38] Similarly, in his 1838 publication concerning delays in chancery, the prominent Jacksonian lawyer Theodore Sedgwick Jr. argued that adjudicating disputes commenced by the filing of such bills had "become one of the most important functions of this court."[39]

The purpose of a creditors' bill was to enable someone who had been issued a judgment from a common-law court ("a judgment creditor") to enforce that judgment in equity. As explained by Senator Verplanck, creditors' bills were widely used because they allowed judgment creditors to benefit from chancery's discovery powers and thus to identify property "concealed or assigned" by the debtor that could be used to satisfy the judgment. If the plaintiff was successful, chancery would appoint a receiver to take title to the debtor's goods, both personal and impersonal, thereby preventing the debtor from disposing of them and ensuring that they could ultimately be used to pay off the debt. According to Verplanck, the primary beneficiaries of this new form of action were commercial creditors: "[W]e have (what I believe is carried to a far greater extent in this State than was ever dreamt of any where else), the habit of collecting commercial debts by what are called creditors' bills."[40]

Why was there such a proliferation of creditors' bills filed by (often commercial) creditors in the late 1830s? The financial panics of 1837 and 1839 were largely responsible. In the wake of these panics, countless New Yorkers, including many businessmen, found themselves unable to pay their debts. As banks collapsed and payments ground to a halt, creditors rushed to file suit, since the first to obtain a judgment and to execute on it was deemed to have a lien on the debtor's property (and other creditors were prohibited from pursuing the debtor until that first creditor was satisfied). On securing judgments in the common-law courts and failing successfully to execute on them, creditors filed creditors' bills in chancery, seeking to discover any property hidden by their debtors.[41] As a result, when New Yorkers like Verplanck complained from the late 1830s onward about chancery's usurpation of the common-law courts' jurisdiction, the image that loomed in their minds was that of the equity receiver, imperiously ferreting out the poor debtor's remaining property and distributing it to his creditors. In an era when both Democrats and Whigs vied to prove their populist credentials, this was not an image that was conducive to support for chancery and its procedural powers. Moreover, creditors' bills were no outlier. The nature of chancery jurisdiction more generally—in particular the fact that, as Verplanck observed, the court tended to adjudicate "complicated causes"—meant that the suits brought before it often implicated "immense pecuniary interest[s]."[42] Chancery thus came to be tarred as an institution of and for a wealthy (especially commercial) elite.

But while chancery was generally associated with the wealthy (and thereby labeled "undemocratic"), creditors' bills, in particular, proved especially distressing. This was, in part, because, as we have seen, the number of such bills filed appears to have grown significantly in the wake of the financial panics of 1837 and 1839. Equally significant, however, was that this type of lawsuit seemed to highlight the worrisome byproducts of market change—including, perhaps most importantly, the novel ease, in light of the rapid expansion of networks of commerce and credit, of doing business with strangers. There were enormous advantages associated with this newfound capacity to engage in trade beyond local networks of family and community. These included, not least, more and greater opportunities to earn profits and increased access to credit and goods, even for those in the lower social ranks and for those who lived in the remote countryside.[43] But as the panics of the late 1830s taught, there was also a significant downside. A world in which such large numbers of people were interconnected through expansive networks of credit was one in which the effects of business and bank failures could not be limited to a few conniving speculators but were instead ramified throughout large swaths of the population. The creditors' bill—as the device par excellence for seeking to obtain payment on debt—came to symbolize the plight of the unfortunate debtor, caught in a trap that was not of his own making and thus subject to the cruel whims of an impersonal market economy. And by extending its extraordinary procedural powers of discovery in the service of such lawsuits, chancery was complicit, helping to unravel the neighborly, communal relations lying at the core of civic virtue and thus democratic governance.

The extent to which creditors' bills came to represent the perils of an increasingly market-driven order and its impersonal credit-based economy is strikingly apparent in a novel published in 1841 by a now-forgotten author, Frederick Jackson. Appearing over a decade before the publication of *Bleak House,* Dickens's far more famous critique of English Chancery, *The Victim of Chancery, or A Debtor's Experience* (rightly) has no place in the canon of American literature and, even in its day, received no attention in the nation's leading journals.[44] But while ignored by the elite press, it was widely reviewed—and praised—in publications aimed more at the middling classes.[45] There is thus good reason to conclude that, perhaps even more than a work of superior artistic merit, it bears reading as a reflection of contemporary public opinion.

The book recounts the hardships suffered by Mr. Adams, a formerly prosperous New York City merchant, in the aftermath of the panic of 1837. As depicted by the novel's omniscient narrator, the panic is a "commercial revolution" that leaves Adams, along with a "great number" of others, "fated, by means not within their control, to meet a reverse in their worldly circumstances." As banks collapse and debtors fail to make payments, Adams—through no fault of his own—is "obliged to suspend business." While there are many decent and honorable merchants who feel his pain, the increasingly market-oriented nature of society has generated "a class of wealthy men in New-York" who seek to "use . . . their power . . . for the sole purpose of taking advantage of" others' misfortune.[46]

Among such dishonorable men is one of Adams's creditors, named (in Dickensian fashion) Mr. Heartless, who rushes to file suit and obtain a judgment in his favor from a common-law court. Of a similar nature is a vicious lawyer, aptly named Mr. Gouge, who—unlike respectable men of his profession—identifies potential clients by examining the judgments entered in the local court of common pleas and the superior court. In this way, Gouge finds and contacts Heartless. The two then agree that the lawyer will pursue collection of the debt, in return for "half of whatever he might get"—and with an eye toward encouraging Adams's wife to surrender the "little property, received from her deceased father's estate."[47]

With no regard for the well-being of Adams (and his wife and children) or of Adams's many other rightful creditors, Gouge and Heartless turn to chancery to pursue their cruel ambitions. As advised by his law partner—named (with sledgehammer-like subtlety) Mr. Gammon—Gouge proceeds "immediately to *file a creditor's bill of discovery.*'" As a result of this filing, Gammon explains, the court will issue an injunction "lock[ing] up any property . . . [Adams] may chance to have in his hands, *whomever it may belong to!!,*" thus enabling the plaintiff to harness chancery's vast procedural powers for the purpose of forcing a settlement. As the narrator details for those of his readers who were fortunate enough not to know,

> when an injunction is served on a debtor, on the filing of what is termed "a creditor's bill in chancery," the debtor is deprived of the right to part with a dollar in money, or a dollar's worth of any thing he may have in

his possession, until the said injunction is removed, and it is sometimes held over him for years. The law does not provide him with the liberty even to buy bread for his family; and if he does so, he is subject to the tender mercies of the court, to say how much he may reasonably eat.

Moreover, because those who violate an injunction do so in contempt of court, they will be "punish[ed] with fine and imprisonment." This is no idle threat, since chancery afforded powerful procedural mechanisms for obtaining discovery from the debtor-defendant. Most importantly, "the attorney for the plaintiff may call the debtor up, and examine him . . . before a 'master in chancery,' as often as he pleases, and compel him, on his own oath," subject to the court's contempt power, "to give *evidence against himself,* contrary to all rule of law and justice in criminal cases."[48] In this way, the merciless nature of the impersonal marketplace is compounded by chancery's all-too-ready willingness to deploy its enormous procedural power on behalf of heartless creditors.

As Gammon predicted, Gouge's filing of a creditors' bill is quickly rewarded with the issuance of an injunction restraining Adams from disposing of his and his wife's property. A receiver is then appointed and Adams directed "to deliver every thing he has into the hands, of that receiver." Aiming thus to "induce an offer of settlement," Gouge and Heartless proceed to collect the furniture in Adams's house, which he assigned "as a security to his creditors." Though the furniture is worth only "the paltry value of a few hundred dollars[]," these merciless men are willing to do anything necessary to subjugate their prey, even "turn[] a man and his family out of doors." Having successfully obtained an injunction, they then seek every means possible to create delays and thereby ensure that it remain in force, such that Adams "would be driven by the law's delay alone . . . to contrive some means to pay the debt." Toward this end, Gouge is able to rely on chancery's painfully slow process for procuring testimony. In the narrator's words,

The plaintiff may call up the defendant whenever he pleases, and ask a thousand frivolous questions with no other benefit, and perhaps with no other view.—Testimony in chancery is always taken down in writing, and the lawyer's costs are taxed by the number of lines he writes. Mr. Adams was called up some twelve or fourteen times, and detained nearly the whole day and evening for examination, and a good ream of foolscap written over in taking down the questions and answers, and in making the duplicate and triplicate copies required by the lawyer, the "master," court, etc. . . .

The end result of this highly effective strategy is that "more than six months were spent holding . . . [Adams] in this state of trial, vexation, and suspense, without any progress being made towards the consummation of the suit, or anything being elicited worthy of continuing it."[49]

Despite the endless delay and resulting penury of his family, Adams continues to resist settlement. Gouge thus decides to examine Adams yet again, and in so doing, asks whether he has received any money since first being served with the injunction. Refusing to answer with a simple yes or no, as both would fail to capture the whole truth, Adams responds that he has received "[n]one that I considered as due." The fact was that, after being served with the injunction, Adams received money from his brother, to whom he had previously lent funds to assist in buying a farm. As Adams had been very wealthy at the time, "he took no security or obligation for it, but told his brother, if he never needed it, he would never call for it." When Adams's brother learned of Adams's difficulties, the brother "voluntarily refunded the money." Because this was a loan of money without security—essentially a gift—from Adams to his brother, and then again from the brother back to Adams, it does not fall within the scope of the injunction, which applies only to obligations owed to Adams as of the date of its issuance. The chancellor determines, however, that by declining to respond to the question with a simple yes or no, Adams is in contempt of court. "[N]ow in the eye of the law a condemned criminal—he was . . . [therefore] incarcerated with felons."[50]

While Gouge and his allies expect that imprisonment will force Adams finally to "make some compromise by paying the debt," he continues to resist, insisting that it is not right to pay Heartless before his other creditors. Adams thus languishes for many weeks in prison, waiting to procure testimony from his brother that will confirm his explanation of the money the latter had given him. Here too, however, chancery's approach to taking testimony served to encourage further delay. Since the brother lives in Indiana (and thus far from the New York–based examiners), the normal way of procuring the testimony is through a commission. But as Mrs. Adams learns upon consulting with a lawyer, this process is very time-consuming because "the questions to be proposed would all have to be taken down in writing." Moreover, the lay "commissioners to whom . . . [the commission] was sent, might not attend to it immediately."[51] Given these difficulties, Mrs. Adams concludes that she has no choice but to go to Indiana to collect the evidence herself. There she finds a judge who immediately appoints commissioners to take the brother's testimony, and she locates letters between Adams and his brother discussing the nature of their transaction. Even with all of this evidence, it still takes weeks to secure Adams's release from prison since chancery is so slow to schedule hearings. Ultimately, it is only by means of a writ of habeas corpus—issued by a common-law judge—that Mrs. Adams is able to force her husband's release.

While released from jail, Adams is still subject to the injunction and, as a result, "[h]is prospects as a merchant" remain "cut off forever." But with the assistance of an honorable merchant who fortuitously comes to learn of the misdeeds of Gouge and his allies, Adams finally obtains the evidence required to demonstrate that "the suit [against him] was a malicious one." He thus moves for a hearing to dismiss the suit—at which Heartless and his attorney fail to appear. Given the plaintiff's default, Adams's motion for dismissal is granted and the injunction finally dissolved. Adams is therefore at long last free to resume commercial activity. But commerce, he concludes, has been transformed of late into an increasingly impersonal and heartless endeavor. Based on "his own experience of the changes and chances of commerce," he determines that he no longer wishes to be a merchant and opts instead to move his family to Indiana. There "his sons [w]ould become 'lords of the soil,' rather than take their chance of becoming masters of finance." Relieved to abandon New York and the commercial activities he had pursued there, Adams proclaims himself comforted by the knowledge that the persecutions he suffered "could have been sustained . . . in no other court in America, but *the court of chancery of the State of New-York*."[52]

Adams and his family are able to flee from the market and its heartless pursuit of profit—and from the chancery court that served to sustain and encourage this self-serving ethic—but not all were so lucky. As the narrator takes pains to observe, "hundreds of cases" in chancery are "continued from year to year, serving for no other purpose" than to facilitate the cruelty of the new and impersonal market economy by "encourage[ing] the strong to oppress the weak" and by "depriv[ing] families of their support." Rehearsing the now-familiar list of criticisms against chancery and its procedural powers, the narrator concludes that the court served these destructive purposes by, inter alia, "assum[ing] jurisdiction which properly belongs to our law courts, and thus overturn[ing] their authority, . . . monpoliz[ing] power, and . . . overturn[ing] our institutions, by destroying the very first principles of them, the right of a trial by jury."[53] In this way, the centuries-old critique of chancery as usurping the jurisdiction of the common-law courts, tending toward the centralized monopoly of power, and destroying the civic foundations of liberty was harnessed and retooled to address a new set of anxieties particular to mid-nineteenth-century America rather than mid-seventeenth-century England. As deployed in this new context, chancery was allied not with royal despotism but instead with new commercial and financial elites whose boundless pursuit of profit threatened to undermine the civic bonds undergirding the still new American democracy.[54]

## MOUNTING DOCKET PRESSURES AND
### THE PROBLEM OF DELAY

From the mid-1830s onward, the most persistent complaint about chancery was that it was no longer able to keep pace with the growing amount of litigation filed. As with other critiques of the court, the problem of expanding dockets and resultant delays was framed as a challenge to democracy—as a challenge, in short, to ensuring equal justice for all. Eager to demonstrate their commitment to democratization, politicians of all stripes spoke widely of the need to remedy delay.

That chancery was no longer able to keep up with the growing equity docket was a point made by New York governors in their annual messages to the legislature almost every year from 1834 until 1846, when the constitutional convention ordered the merger of law and equity. In January 1834, Governor William L. Marcy, a Democrat, complained that "our present [judicial] establishment, though adequate to the public exigencies when first organized, now needs to be enlarged," as a result of "the rapid increase of this State in population, and the still more rapid augmentation of its business transactions, both of which greatly multiply the labors of the judiciary."[55] When the legislature failed to act, Marcy repeated his assertion that reforms were needed to address the problem of overburdened courts (including, prominently, chancery) every year of his governorship through to 1838.[56] These points were renewed by Marcy's Whig successor, William H. Seward, in his 1839, 1840, and 1841 messages to the legislature.[57] So too Seward's Democratic successor, William C. Bouck, complained in his 1843 message that "the court of chancery is so overburthened with business, that injurious delays are experienced in the administration of justice."[58] And when Bouck was succeeded by another Democrat, Silas Wright, in 1845, he too remarked that "years of experience have proved that the labors of no one man are equal to the discharge of the duties and the dispatch of the business" of chancery.[59]

In bemoaning the burden of rising litigation rates—especially in chancery—New York governors echoed widespread public concern, as reflected in contemporary newspaper reports and other publications.[60] But there was one work in particular that galvanized public attention to the problem of burgeoning dockets and ensuing delays in chancery—namely, the 1838 publication by Theodore Sedgwick Jr. of a pamphlet entitled *A Statement of Facts in Relation to the Delays and Arrears of Business in the Court of Chancery of the State of New York*. As suggested by its title, the pamphlet argued that litigation rates in chancery had expanded to the point that the court's limited judicial staff was completely overwhelmed. Based on a survey of the number of bills of complaint filed each year in chancery proper, as well as in the various circuit courts, Sedgwick concluded that rampant delays were not "owing to some temporary cause" but were instead the result of "the regular increase of the business of the court, which indeed might be presumed to keep pace with the growth of state."[61]

Appearing just a handful of years after Sedgwick had published a series of widely read articles attacking the injustice of monopoly—and calling for an end to all forms of government-sponsored privilege—his pamphlet on chancery arrears framed the problem of delayed justice as yet another form of bad government. But while monopoly arose when government exceeded its proper bounds, the severe delays in chancery followed from New York's failure to comply with the minimalist mandate of "effectually protect[ing] the citizen or subject in the enjoyment of his person and property." Thus presented by one of the state's (and nation's) leading Democrats, the problem of chancery delays was powerfully framed for the public as one of access to justice and therefore likely—like monopoly itself—to result in the unequal treatment of citizens. As Sedgwick complained, "every moment is precious as gold dust, to the distressed suitors."[62] But the pain of delay was not felt equally by everyone: For all but the very wealthy, justice delayed was justice denied.

Not surprisingly, given its well-known author, Sedgwick's pamphlet was widely discussed in contemporary newspapers and served as a call to action for those advocating reform in the state legislature. For example, the January 19, 1839, edition of the *Albany Argus*, a Democratic paper, published a laudatory review of the pamphlet, observing that "[w]hatever may be the diversities of opinion in relation to improvements or reforms in the organization of our courts, none exists, we believe, touching the fact that suitors are now subjected, from the necessities of the case, to great delays."[63] Likewise, in April of that year Senator Verplanck called for reform to chancery to alleviate "the monstrous delay and intolerable evils of our present Equity System" and in so doing, cited Sedgwick's work as offering ample "proof of [such] delays and grievances."[64] And just a few months before, in February 1839, a group of fifty-two Manhattan lawyers—including Sedgwick himself—petitioned the legislature to complain about "the arrears of equity business."[65]

Given the extensive, repeated nature of the calls for reforming chancery in order to remedy the problem of delay, mounting docket pressures would seem to be a likely causal factor in the court's turn toward oral, adversarial procedure. The assertion that expanding dockets helped to motivate nineteenth-century procedural reform is made so often that it is all but a truism.[66] And complaints of delay were indeed legion. But while docket pressures clearly played an important role in encouraging procedural reform as a whole, there are good reasons to doubt that they bore meaningful responsibility for the embrace of oral, adversarial procedure in particular.

Consider first the timing. The turn to oral, adversarial procedure began during Kent's chancellorship—roughly in the wake of his 1817 decision in *Remsen*. But it was only in the mid-1830s, almost two decades later, that complaints about excessive chancery business and, as a result, intolerable delays began to abound. That docket pressure had not yet become severe during Kent's chancellorship was a point made by Sedgwick himself, who in analyzing the number of bills filed in chancery concluded that "Chancellor Kent did all the business that came before him, and did it promptly." In contrast, he observed, a comparison of "the statistics of the court, in the days of that officer, and at present" proved that the press of business had since mounted to such an extent that "no one person can at present adequately discharge the duties of the Chancellor of this State."[67] Thus, as a basic matter of timing, the turn toward oral, adversarial procedure does not appear to be directly linked with the (later arising) anxiety about docket pressures.

Once litigation rates were recognized as a serious problem, efforts to address it did lead to calls for procedural reform, including various legislative and constitutional proposals. But the reforms suggested by politicians and commentators in no way advanced the adoption of oral, adversarial procedure. Concerns that chancery was overburdened led instead to demands for an increase in its judicial staff—and thus for reinforcement of the court's judge-empowering, quasi-inquisitorial underpinnings.[68] For example, Governor Marcy called in 1834 and 1835 for the creation of additional vice chancellor's courts throughout the state.[69] And in 1837, he advocated "for the appointment of an additional number of equity judges, to be located in different parts of the State," all of whom would possess concurrent jurisdiction with the chancellor and appeals from whom would go before a new court of review.[70] Likewise, in his 1839 message to the legislature, Governor Seward urged his listeners "to reorganize the court of chancery with such addition of chancellors as shall be necessary to decide originally all causes to be brought in that court."[71] Refining this argument in his 1840 message, Seward called specifically for "the appointment of three chancellors, with coordinate powers."[72] And in his 1843 message, Governor Bouck observed that it was imperative to "enlarge the present system, so as to meet the public wants."[73] When the legislature still failed to act, Bouck's primary recommendation in his messages of 1844 and 1845 was again to increase the number of judicial staff in chancery by appointing "two or more additional officers, having co-ordinate powers with the Chancellor."[74] Similarly, the three-man commission established by the legislature on May 15, 1837, "to digest and report a Judicial and Equity System" advised that the main problem with chancery was "the utter inadequacy of the force provided for the despatch of the business to be done" and that the primary remedy was therefore to increase the number of its judicial staff. The commissioners recommended, in particular, the appointment of five chancellors, each responsible for a separate district and with appeals to go before a court consisting of any three of them.[75] Shortly thereafter, in addressing the problem of mounting litigation rates and consequent delays, Sedgwick urged the adoption of the commissioners' report.[76]

Bowing to this pressure, the legislature repeatedly considered proposals to augment chancery's judicial staff. And on a few rare occasions, it acted. As early as 1831, it appointed a vice chancellor for the First Circuit (encompassing New York City), who was to be responsible exclusively for deciding cases in equity. As explained by Senator Benton, this legislation was motivated by the fact that chancery "[b]usiness [in the First Circuit] had accumulated to such a degree that to obtain justice it required a longer time than was allotted for man to live."[77] Thereafter, in 1839, a vice chancellor was appointed in the eighth circuit and an assistant vice chancellor in the first.[78] Moreover, as we have seen, the legislature repeatedly augmented the number of masters and examiners—though its reasons for doing so stemmed at least as much (if not more) from the goal of distributing political spoils.

Aside from these limited actions, the state legislature proved to be paralyzed—due in no small part to the sharp partisan rift that then obtained between Democrats and Whigs. As Erastus Root complained in the Senate in January 1840, he had no more patience "for this matter of playing off from party to party the blame of existing evils" in chancery.[79] It bears emphasis, however, that the many proposals for reform that the legislature debated (and ultimately did not enact) from the mid-1830s until the constitutional convention of 1846 all focused first and foremost on increasing the numbers of judges in chancery.[80] Indeed, in 1844, a mere two years before the convention met, the legislature voted to pass a constitutional amendment that would augment the number of chancellors by creating "a court of chancery, to be composed of a chancellor and three associate chancellors."[81] But pursuant to the then operative Constitution of 1821, an amendment was to be sent to the public for ratification only if passed by two successive legislatures—and the legislature of 1845 failed to act.[82] Accordingly, while the intensive focus on litigation rates and ensuing delays did lead to demands for reform, the reform pursued was not the embrace of oral, adversarial procedure but rather a fortification of chancery's quasi-inquisitorial foundations in the form of an increase in its judicial staff.

Although the traditional written and secret approach to taking testimony had already fallen largely by the wayside by the time that anxieties about docket pressures became commonplace in the mid- to late 1830s, some contemporaries argued that the problem of delay followed from the fact that the embrace of oral, adversarial procedure was incomplete. In particular, the examination of witnesses—though oral and lawyer-driven—continued to take place before masters, examiners, and commissioners rather than directly before the finder of fact. As Democratic senator Daniel Dickinson complained in 1838,

> More injury to the community—heavier costs to the lawyers—and longer delays in suits—grow out of the present mode of taking a witness before an examiner, and requiring that officer to endeavor to put his testimony on paper, which the chancellor is obliged to wade through and digest as well as he can, instead of receiving it from the lips of the witness . . . —than any other evil which it is proposed to remedy.[83]

In the view of critics like Dickinson, eliminating the role played by intermediate judicial officers in the taking of testimony would greatly streamline the examination process and thereby mitigate the problem of delay.

Similarly, the three-man commission appointed by the legislature in May 1837 concluded that, while understaffing was the primary cause of delay, the court's approach to taking testimony also bore some responsibility: "One of the principal causes of the great delay and accumulation of business in the court of chancery is believed to be the immense labor and consumption of time necessarily employed in analyzing the undigested and confused mass of

depositions in which the facts of the cases in that court are too often buried. . . .
[S]everal weeks are frequently consumed in taking testimony before an
examiner. . . ." The solution, they recommended, was to have testimony presented directly before a jury responsible for fact-finding, or if this proved impossible, before the chancellor himself—thus avoiding the need to draft
lengthy depositions that would have to be reviewed by the finder of fact.[84]

Influenced by the commissioners' report, Governor Marcy recommended
in 1838 that the legislature adopt it in its entirety, including those provisions
designed to render "an important change in the mode of taking testimony."[85]
While the legislature declined to act on much of the commissioners'
report—including its primary recommendation to augment the number of
chancellors—it did enact legislation on April 18, 1838, declaring that testimony was henceforth to be taken before a jury and, if not, before the chancellor or vice chancellor. But as we have seen, this was repealed just one year after
its enactment.[86] Complaints thus persisted that equity's approach to testimony bore some responsibility for the problem of overburdened dockets. As
this suggests, oral, adversarial procedure was not embraced as a solution to
the problem of delay but was instead—when combined with the chancery tradition of relying on intermediate officers to take testimony—an important
contributing factor.

While there appears to be little direct connection between expanding litigation rates and the turn toward oral, adversarial procedure, docket burdens do
help explain the rising pressure to abolish the positions of master and examiner. By the mid-1830s, the shift toward oral, adversarial procedure had largely
occurred as a matter of practice—a shift in practice that, as we will see, was
bolstered by a new ideological commitment to adversarialism as an end in and
of itself. Given this newfound commitment to oral, adversarial procedure (especially in the examination of witnesses), the obvious solution to the problem
of delays in witness examination was to do away with the other variable in the
equation—namely, chancery's reliance on masters and examiners. This was
the logic of the short-lived statute of April 18, 1838, whose main effect, if
meaningfully implemented, would have been, as Sedgwick remarked, to ensure that "the examiner's office, will be effectually abolished."[87] While that
statute proved to be all but dead on arrival, the constitution of 1846 succeeded
where the earlier legislation had failed, forthrightly abolishing both masters
and examiners.[88] This, in turn, helped pave the way for the formal merger of
law and equity through the much-celebrated Field Code of 1848.

# A Fait Accompli: The 1846 Constitutional Convention and the Field Code

When New York's third constitutional convention met in 1846, it appointed commissioners to codify the state's approach to practice and pleadings. The end result was the appearance, two years later, of the Field Code of Procedure, long praised for initiating a supposedly revolutionary merger of the formerly distinct traditions of law and equity. But notwithstanding the familiar paeans, there was little about the code that was revolutionary. As we have seen, it was lawyers, litigating in chancery on a case-by-case basis, who were responsible from roughly 1817 onward for importing the oral, adversarial methods of the common law into equity and thereby instigating the merger of the two. For the most part, the Field Code itself simply ratified what lawyers themselves had already accomplished.

## ABOLISHING MASTERS, EXAMINERS, AND CHANCERY ITSELF

The 1846 constitution specified that there was to be a single Supreme Court "having general jurisdiction in law and equity," thus abolishing chancery. In so doing, it provided further that "testimony in equity cases shall be taken in like manner as in cases at law,"[89] thereby enshrining lawyers' now decades-old embrace of (oral, adversarial) common-law procedure. But what precisely was required to achieve this goal? Although testimony in equity had long been taken in the oral, adversarial fashion of the common law, it was not taken directly before the finder of fact but instead before masters, examiners, and commissioners responsible for creating a written record of the testimony for subsequent judicial review. The Acts of April 17, 1823 and April 18, 1838 mandated that all testimony be taken directly before the trier of fact, but as we have seen, this requirement was never implemented.

Seeking to succeed where their predecessors had failed, delegates to the constitutional convention reiterated that all testimony was to be taken in the oral, adversarial manner of the common law. In order to guarantee that it would henceforth be taken directly before the finder of fact, they abolished the key personnel responsible for recording written testimony outside the court-room—namely, masters and examiners.[90] Strikingly, while the delegates disagreed about various aspects of procedural reform, they were all but unanimous in their view that the masters and examiners had to go. There was thus almost no debate on the topic. Delegates simply rehashed the argument, repeatedly urged by critics of chancery from the 1830s onward, that equity's approach to testimony bore significant responsibility for the rise of intolerable delays and therefore required remediation. As insisted by John W. Brown, a Democratic lawyer from Orange County, if testimony were taken orally before the fact-finder, then "[g]entlemen would see that vast masses of irrelevant matter, which now find their way into the depositions taken before an examiner would be rejected."[91]

Because agreement on this point was so widespread, the vote on whether to enact a constitutional provision establishing that "[t]he testimony in equity cases shall be taken in like manner as in cases at law" was unanimous. While the vote on whether to abolish the offices of master and examiner was not quite unanimous, it was nearly so—with eighty-eight voting in favor and only five against.[92] Why was it only in 1846, and not earlier, that the decision was finally made to abolish masters and examiners? Some may have believed that the legislature lacked the authority to eliminate these offices since they were enshrined in the then-applicable constitution of 1821.[93] That said, the legislature clearly had the power to propose constitutional amendments, and it failed to enact an amendment abolishing these offices. This failure, in turn, was likely due to persistent concerns that chancery lacked sufficient judges to hear all testimony as well as to the lobbying power of the prominent lawyers who served as masters and examiners and who were reluctant to lose this important source of income and status. But why would these concerns have dissipated to such an extent that it suddenly became possible in 1846 entirely to do away with masters and examiners?

As regards the longstanding concern that chancery judges would not be able to hear all testimony themselves, this was mitigated by the decision to restructure the court system and thereby increase the total number of judges.[94] Some delegates, moreover, anticipated that—as would, indeed, be the case—a court possessing jurisdiction in both law and equity would be able to employ juries to hear cases once deemed to lie within the exclusive purview of equity. But as for the lobbying power of masters and examiners, there is no reason to believe that it had meaningfully diminished by 1846. Indeed, in insisting that "[t]he office of Master was entirely unnecessary," delegate Ansel Bascom, a lawyer and onetime Democrat who had become a Whig in 1840, paused to note that "this horde of officers, distributed throughout the state," formed a powerful lobby that had long proved effective in thwarting legislative efforts at reform, including efforts to reduce their fees.[95]

While the influence of "this horde" did not simply disappear in the intervening years, it was bypassed through the calling of the constitutional convention. The convention was dominated by the radical Barnburner faction of the Democratic Party—a group of anticorruption reformers that arose in the 1840s in opposition to the practice of party insiders (both Democratic and Whig) using political patronage and other favors as a means of enacting self-serving legislation.[96] Because the Barnburners dominated the convention— and because they so hated political patronage—arguments for preserving masters and examiners were understood to be hopeless. Both of these offices were long viewed as being all but synonymous with the spoils system of party politics. As delegate Conrad Swackhamer, a Democratic artisan or "mechanic" from Kings County, noted in demanding the abolition of masters and examiners, "all these officers were well calculated for the promotion of political objects, and afforded good berths for partizan leaders."[97]

Although delegates easily agreed that testimony in equity was to be taken in the manner of the common law (and thus that masters and examiners ought to be abolished), they had a more difficult time reaching consensus on other aspects of procedural reform. The debate over whether to preserve chancery as a distinct institution was one in which arguments on both sides were actually voiced—though here as well the outcome (in favor of abolition) appears to have been a foregone conclusion. While some delegates expressed opposition to abolishing chancery, they also indicated that they were well aware of being, in this respect, on the losing side of history. For example, William G. Angel, a Democratic lawyer from Allegany County, asserted that the jurisdictions of "law and chancery . . . should be kept separate." But "inasmuch as the demolition of the court of chancery has become so great a favorite with this Convention, and inasmuch as they assert that they are only reflecting the will of the people in this respect, I would consent to vote for the adoption of a Constitution that provided for vesting the law and equity powers in the same court."[98] Similarly, delegate Lemuel Stetson, a Democratic lawyer from Clinton County, acquiesced in the creation of a single unified court on the grounds that "the Convention generally regarded . . . with disfavor" his preferred policy of preserving "separate courts and separate jurisdictions."[99]

That the abolition of chancery seemed all but inevitable is hardly surprising given the withering criticisms to which the institution was subjected from about 1820 onward—and with growing intensity by the mid-1830s. As we have seen, critics drew on the centuries-old discourse associating equity with royal and "popish" tyranny to decry New York Chancery as antidemocratic. So too, in arguing for the abolition of chancery at the 1846 convention, delegates turned to this same language. Delegate Samuel Richmond, a farmer from Genesee County, thus noted that "it was a general remark now that the chancellor had more power than the Autocrat of Russia."[100] Likewise, delegate Swackhamer described chancery as "a compound of aristocracy and despotism," arguing that "[i]t had its origin from behind the throne of kings."[101] And Henry Nicoll, a Democratic lawyer from New York City, insisted that in its origins, English Chancery was

> the mere creature of royal prerogative. It took its hue from the palace, and fostered and encouraged, it soon became no mean part of the judicature of England. Twin-sister to the star chamber, and too often acting not in furtherance of the common law, but in strict opposition to its rules, and in the exercise of an arbitrary discretion, it shared in many respects with that tyrannic tribunal in the odium of the people. The early chancellors were in most instances either soldiers or churchmen, and the system in vogue in the court, so far as it may be said to have been a system, was founded on the unpopular models of the civil and the canon laws.[102]

Even delegate Shepard, who claimed that there ought to be "a separate administration of equity jurisprudence, either by a different court, or by different, particularly designated, judges of the same court," felt compelled to make clear that he did "not stand upon this floor the advocate of the present court of chancery." The reason for this, he explained, was that he had "a hearty detestation of the one man power," for "[i]n a republican government, no man, however high his character or commanding his intellect, should be permitted to wield the patronage—the coercive power—the might and controlling influence of such a tribunal."[103]

In addition to decrying chancery as an agent of tyranny, delegates calling for its abolition renewed claims that it had grown excessively powerful by usurping jurisdiction. Delegate Swackhamer, for example, observed that chancery had long been "insidiously grasping power and usurping authority" and that, as a result, "millions of property and the rights and happiness of thousands of our citizens depended on the *dicta* of this *one man* power." Likewise, in referring to chancery, delegate Richmond exclaimed that "[h]e would give to no body the power to erect such courts as could usurp such powers, and encroach on the rights of the people so infamously as this court has done." So too delegate Bascom complained that chancery had acquired excessive "power and jurisdiction," partially as a result of "usurpation."[104]

As a number of delegates noted, chancery's excessive power resulted not only from unlawful usurpation but also from legislative grants of authority. Bascom pointed in particular to various forms of chancery jurisdiction extended by the legislature that tended to assist creditors, corporations, and other agents of wealth and power. These included "[t]he power to compel discovery and assignments by judgment debtors [namely, jurisdiction over creditors' bills], power to foreclose mortgages, partition lands, to aid rail road corporations in obtaining rights of way—a power over banks and incorporations. . . ."[105] In short, as was the case with earlier critics, delegates tarred chancery as an institution that exercised its excessive power in service of a wealthy elite whose rise to power and prominence was intimately linked to market change. Not surprisingly, given the continuity and vehemence of such language, those delegates favoring the preservation of chancery as a separate court quickly reached the conclusion that theirs was a hopeless cause.

## WHETHER TO CREATE A SINGLE UNIFORM MODE OF PROCEDURE

While delegates managed to agree that it was time to abolish chancery as a separate institution, they were unable to reach agreement on whether the existence of a single court for both law and equity implied (or ought to imply) a single uniform mode of procedure for both law and equity cases—or whether, as in the federal court system, two distinct modes of procedure ought to be preserved. Views on this matter appear to have tracked views on the prior question of whether to establish a single unified court combining both law and equity. Those delegates who called for a single court argued that this implied the creation of a single mode of procedure, whereas those who opposed such a unified court (but consented to it because they believed it was inevitable) also opposed the creation of a single mode of procedure. Consider, for example, the position of Arphaxed Loomis—a Democratic lawyer from Herkimer County and member of the convention's judiciary committee who would go on to help draft the Field Code. Loomis defended the committee's proposal to "bring into one tribunal the jurisdictions of law and equity" and, in so doing, noted that "he did not hesitate to say that he believed this would produce a perfect blending of the two in the course of practice."[106] In contrast, delegate Angel observed that, while he was willing against his better judgment to "consent to vote for the adoption of a Constitution that provided for vesting the law and equity powers in the same court," he would not compromise on the subject of whether to unify procedure: "I regard it as highly dangerous that the distinction between the proceedings at law and in equity be abolished."[107]

Underlying this dispute concerning whether to adopt a unified mode of procedure was an even more fundamental (though never fully crystallized) disagreement concerning the nature of procedure and its relationship to substantive law. Those delegates who urged a single mode of procedure had come to view procedure as a set of practices, distinct from the substantive law, whose primary purpose is to facilitate the just and efficient application of that law. This essentially modern conception of procedure suggested that it was possible to disentangle the procedural mechanisms by means of which claims were historically filed in law and equity from the underlying substantive law—and that, once this was done, a unified mode of procedure could be created. Put differently, the dividing line between law and equity was procedural and thus in no way necessary or inherent. Along these lines, delegate Charles O'Conor, a Democratic lawyer from New York City, supported his demand for "one simple, uniform and harmonious mode of practice" by insisting that the differences between law and equity were purely procedural and therefore subject to change. As he asserted, "The difference between law and equity, and the only difference, was in the form of pleading and the remedies. The principles of law, applicable to both, were the same. . . . There was no difference except in the form of getting into court and getting out of it."[108] So too, delegate Kirkland, who differed from O'Conor only in that he favored a more gradual progression to a unified mode of procedure, claimed that "[t]he difference between 'law' and 'equity' is a difference in the *remedies,* and *substantially* in nothing more."[109]

In contrast, those delegates who opposed creating a unified mode of procedure continued to adhere to the older framework pursuant to which there was no sharp delineation between substantive and procedural law. From this perspective, a legal claim was an inchoate amalgam of substantive rights and procedural maneuvers—an amalgam that was characterized perhaps first and foremost by its procedural form. This, in turn, suggested that the differences between law and equity were inherent and therefore immutable. As delegate Shepard argued, "there is a marked and decided difference between the great substantial parts of law and equity jurisdiction—a difference resting not solely in the will of the Legislature—nor in any great degree dependent on or controlled by it, but existing in the unalterable nature of things themselves."[110] Similarly, delegate George A. Simmons, a Whig lawyer from Essex County, asserted that "the division of remedies into legal and equitable, is founded on a natural distinction, and that it is [therefore] impracticable to blend them under a common code of procedure, or to administer them by the machinery of courts similarly organized."[111]

As this debate over whether to unify law and equity procedure suggests, one of the most significant—and yet remarkably unappreciated—achievements of the 1846 constitutional convention (and the Field Code to which it gave rise) had nothing to do with merger as such but instead with the emergence of a modern conception of procedure. Stated differently, the Field Code's creation of a unified body of procedure bridging the divide between law and equity (and relatedly, between pleadings and practice) marked a key moment in the rise of "procedure" as the sum total of rules—distinct from the substantive law—required to initiate and move forward litigation. But as of the 1846 convention, this modern conception of procedure had yet fully to triumph. Delegates were thus unable to decide whether to adopt a unified mode of procedure for both law and equity. This question and a host of narrower ones—such as what form pleadings were to take and whether cases were to be tried before judges or juries—were left unresolved. They were delegated to the legislature and to the three commissioners, whom pursuant to constitutional dictate, the legislature was required to appoint with directions "to revise, reform, simplify and abridge the rules and practice, pleadings, forms and proceedings of the courts of record of this State."[112]

The legislature's selection of the three commissioners appears to have taken place in predictably partisan fashion, such that an understanding was reached that two were to be Democrats and one a Whig. As a Whig newspaper complained, "We regret to see that the appointment of commissioners to codify the laws and revise the practice and pleadings of the Courts, in this state, has been drawn into the party vortex."[113] The Democrats selected two prominent lawyers, Nicholas Hill and Arphaxed Loomis (himself, as we have seen, a member of the 1846 constitutional convention). After extensive debate, the Whigs chose as their candidate another prominent lawyer, David Graham. And on April 8, 1847, the legislature enacted a statute that formally appointed these three as commissioners.[114]

Relatively little of the debate concerning the appointment of the commissioners appears to have turned on the core question of what kind of procedural reform each would favor, focusing instead on such matters as the salary that they would be paid. At least some legislators, however, did address the question. Ansel Bascom, for example, favored the appointment of Theodore C. Peters over David Graham, because "he had yet to learn that . . . [Graham] was in favor of, or had faith in the practicability of, the particular form that he, Mr. B thought was demanded"—namely, the establishment of "a like mode of procedure . . . for what had been distinguished as legal and equitable causes." Similarly, a Whig assemblyman named Blodgett argued in favor of appointing Peters, rather than Graham, on the grounds that only the former was "in favor of substantial and truthful legal reform."[115]

The relative lack of attention to the policy preferences of the candidates was likely due to the fact that, with no fanfare, the April 8, 1847, statute appointing Hill, Loomis, and Graham as commissioners also resolved the key question that had been left undecided by the constitutional convention—namely, whether the establishment of a single court with jurisdiction in both law and equity implied the creation of a similarly unified model of procedure. The statute concluded in the affirmative and provided, moreover, that as part of this move toward a single unified mode of procedure, the common law's distinct forms of action were also to be eliminated: "[I]t shall be the duty of the said commissioners to provide for the abolition of the present forms of actions and pleadings in cases at common law; [and] for a uniform course of proceeding in all cases, whether of legal or equitable cognizance."[116] As the *Rochester Advertiser* observed in an article reprinted in the *Spectator,* this language "is the great reform, what Cromwell [referring to the final, monarchy-defeating battle of the English Civil War] would have called the 'crowning mercy.' "[117] So what was the origin of this remarkable statutory language? And what accounts for its inclusion, with apparently little, if any, debate, in the statute appointing the three commissioners? The language seems to have been copied verbatim from a February 1847 petition, drafted by David Dudley Field and signed by fifty members of the New York Bar, concerning the content of the proposed "act appointing Commissioners."[118]

That the language from this petition was included in the statute stemmed in no small part from the prominence of the many lawyers who signed it, including not only Field himself, but also such notables as Theodore Sedgwick Jr., Charles O'Conor, and William T. McCoun, vice chancellor for the First Circuit.[119] The legislative decision to mandate a unified mode of procedure likely also followed, however, from the fact that the 1846 constitution itself played a role in further undermining the traditional conception of procedure as inseparable from substance. As we have seen, the debate over whether to create a unified mode of procedure turned in significant measure on a deeper underlying division over the very nature of procedure. In particular, those who embraced a modern conception of procedure as the sum total of rules (distinct from the substantive law) that are necessary to pursue litigation also believed that it was possible (and desirable) to create a single mode of procedure that would unify law and equity. While the convention delegates failed to decide on whether to adopt such a unified procedural approach, the constitution that they promulgated tended in this direction in that it mandated the appointment of one set of commissioners to reform "the rules of practice, pleadings, forms and proceedings of the courts" and a completely separate set "to reduce into a written and systematic code the whole body of the law of this state."[120] Put differently, the very decision to appoint two distinct sets of commissioners implied a sharp division between procedure and substance, thus stacking the deck in favor of a unified mode of procedure.

## THE NON-REVOLUTIONARY NATURE OF THE CODE

Once appointed, the commissioners got off to a rocky start. On September 18, 1847, the state assembly passed a resolution requiring them to report on their progress.[121] Two days later, a mere five months after he was initially appointed, Hill resigned, explaining that he was strongly opposed to his fellow commissioners' view that it was "expedient to abolish the whole of the present practice and rules of pleading in courts of record and to substitute a system entirely new. . . ."[122] Shortly thereafter, on September 25, Loomis and Graham, the remaining two commissioners, issued their report and, in so doing, announced their intention to adopt "an entirely new system." Thereafter, on September 29, the legislature selected David Dudley Field as Hill's replacement.[123] The politics behind this selection are a bit mysterious in that Field was evidently deemed too radical to be initially selected as a commissioner just five months earlier. But perhaps given Hill's reasons for resigning, legislators had by this time concluded that they needed to name a person of like mind with the remaining two commissioners if progress was to be made. That this is indeed what happened is suggested by Loomis's later assertion that Field was appointed on his suggestion.[124]

As usually recounted, the Field Code of Procedure was the brainchild of David Dudley Field himself—one that emerged from his head ex nihilo (or perhaps as a result of his travels in Europe in 1836–1837, when he first encountered the (codified) civil law).[125] According to Roscoe Pound, "In preparing the Code of Civil Procedure Field had nothing to build on. He could not codify common-law and equity pleading and practice as they stood in New York in 1847. . . . Field had of necessity to strike out new lines, and with little

to guide him but his legal learning and the instinct of a practical lawyer. . . ."
So too, Alison Reppy writes of Field's "solitary struggle for legal reform," describing his achievements (including, most prominently, the Field Code) as
the end product of his "almost single-handed . . . crusade." And Charles M.
Cook argues that Field's "almost solitary, promotion of codification" ensured
that when the Field Code was finally enacted, the latter "made a distinct break
with the past."[126]

That Field played a crucial role in the enactment of the code is clear. In the
months leading up to, during, and following the constitutional convention of
1846, Field—long a promoter of procedural reform—became particularly active in drafting articles, pamphlets, and petitions on the subject for the attention of delegates, legislators, and the public at large. Moreover, as we have
seen, he was responsible for writing the February 1847 memorial to the legislature that provided the language, later inserted into the April 8, 1847, statute,
directing the commissioners to create a "uniform course of proceeding." Indeed, he provided a detailed outline of what such a uniform course of proceeding would entail in his earlier, January 1, 1847, pamphlet entitled *What Shall
Be Done with the Practice of the Courts?*[127] It is thus evident that Field's activism
and framing of the issues played a major role in making the subsequent drafting and enactment of the code politically feasible. As a conceptual matter,
however, it is doubtful that Field deserves the encomia with which he has long
been honored for creating the procedural code—and equally doubtful that the
code itself was truly revolutionary. While contemporaries, including the code
commissioners themselves, often spoke of the code as revolutionary, they had
incentives to present it in this light and lacked the historical perspective that
would enable them easily to recognize the extent to which such claims were
exaggerated.

The core change wrought by the code was the creation of a single uniform
mode of procedure. Such procedure was uniform in two distinct senses, only
one of which is commonly appreciated. The first, well-recognized kind of uniformity was the transsubstantive nature of code procedure, as represented,
most importantly, by its transcendence of the traditional law/equity divide.[128]
The second, unappreciated kind of uniformity inhered in the very nature of
the code as a system of "procedure"—a set of rules, in other words, that
bridged the longstanding divide between pleading and practice. The code's
embrace of both kinds of uniformity marked a significant turning point—one
that profoundly shaped the subsequent development of procedural law
throughout the United States. But uniformity in both these senses did not

simply emerge out of the blue or, as is commonly argued, from the genius of David Dudley Field. The code, in other words, was not so much a revolutionary beginning as a logical endpoint—the culmination of a set of longstanding historical developments.

As concerns the transsubstantive nature of procedure, this kind of uniformity was the outgrowth of a set of developments within chancery that were long in the making. As Field himself argued in *What Shall Be Done with the Practice of the Courts?*, the key development leading to the emergence of such a uniform mode of procedure was equity's embrace of the common law's oral, adversarial approach to testimony. Once the approaches to taking testimony were the same in the two jurisdictions—a development finalized by the 1846 constitution's express mandate to that effect and the consequent abolition of masters and examiners—it became possible (and indeed logical) to imagine a uniform method of trial. This, in turn, suggested the possibility of a uniform mode of pleading. In Field's words, "the Constitution enjoining the taking of testimony in . . . [equity] cases in like manner as at law, must lead to a similar mode of trial. When a mode of trial is found for cases in equity similar to that used in cases at law, it will then be seen that the pleadings in the two classes of cases can be framed in the same way."[129] Put differently, New York Chancery's embrace of an increasingly oral, adversarial approach to testimony from roughly 1817 onward—a development that has long been neglected in the scholarly literature—goes far toward explaining the merger of law and equity and the consequent rise of a new ideal of uniform, transsubstantive procedure.

Also contributing to the emergence of uniformity of this sort was the long chain of developments leading to the rise of a modern conception of procedure as a body of rules distinct from the substantive law. As we have seen, the notion that procedure and substance were distinct played an important part in causing many delegates at the constitutional convention of 1846 to conclude that the differences between law and equity were purely procedural and therefore subject to change. Similarly, the code commissioners predicated their effort to create a single uniform mode of procedure on the modern notion that procedure and substance were distinct. As they observed, the traditional notion that "distinct [legal and equitable] modes of procedure should exist" followed from the fact that, prior to the 1846 constitution, "the jurisdiction of law and equity . . . [was] vested in separate and distinct courts." The existence of distinct jurisdictions with distinct personnel gave rise to distinct procedural practices—but this was merely an accident of history. Now that a single court had been established, it was possible to create a unified mode of procedure transcending the traditional law/equity divide without in any way interfering with "the [substantive] rights of parties." This was because procedure was "the mere means by which those rights are to be ascertained and enforced."[130]

Likewise, the commissioners defended their decision to develop "an entirely new system" of procedure by pointing to the fact that "[t]he system of procedure by which law is administered, differs from the law itself." The substantive law, they argued—or, in their words, "the law itself"—is "a body of elementary rules founded in the immutable principles of justice, drawing their origin from the obligations which divine wisdom has imposed upon the relations to each other in which he has placed his creatures." In contrast, procedural law is "a body of prescribed rules, having no source but the will of those by whom they are laid down, and invented by human ingenuity, as the mere means or forms by which rights are to be enforced and justice administered." Given this important difference between substance and procedure, the commissioners concluded that, while "[it] may be a hazardous experiment, with a careless hand to innovate upon" substantive law, "the peril of an unsuccessful effort at reform is not so alarming" in the case of procedural law.[131]

Like its transsubstantive nature, the second kind of uniformity that characterized code procedure—that it was a set of rules of "procedure," encompassing the traditionally distinct categories of pleading and practice—was also the product of longstanding historical trends, rather than a revolutionary development. The code represented the culmination of the gradual process whereby common-law writs came to be viewed as distinct from the underlying rights whose adjudication they enabled—a development encapsulated in the legislative command to the three commissioners "to provide for the abolition of the present forms of action and pleadings in cases at common law."[132] Once the forms of action were abandoned, such that pleading would henceforth be transsubstantive, it became possible to view pleading as intimately connected, not with particular (substantive) legal claims but instead with the rules of "practice" that structured the adjudication of a properly pled claim. As Field explained, "The question whether there shall be a uniform course of proceeding ... amounts to this: Shall there be a uniform mode of stating the allegations of the parties [namely, pleading], taking the proofs, and deciding the questions?"[133] His answer was, of course, yes. The enactment of the code thus marked the endpoint of a long process leading to the birth of "procedure."

While the core features of the code were formed by developments long in the making and thus in no way revolutionary, the precise contours of the "course of proceeding" that it laid out were more contingent on immediate circumstances, including the direct influence of the commissioners them-selves. Even some of these more fine-grained choices, however, followed from longer, more deeply rooted processes. Although scholars today debate whether the Field Code adopted more elements from the common law or from equity, this disagreement turns, in part, on the definitional question of which precise features are most important for distinguishing between these two procedural traditions. If we focus on the key, adversarial components of orality, publicity, and lawyer control, there is a good case to be made that, as Stephen Subrin has observed, the Field Code leaned more toward common law than toward equity[134]—a fact surely linked to the extensive assault on equity in the decades immediately preceding the code's enactment. Indeed, as envisioned by the commissioners, there were only two main elements of equity procedure that would be retained in the new, uniform procedure. And the first of these—equity's transsubstantive approach to pleading—was one as to which the commissioners had essentially no choice, given the legislature's command that they dispense with the common law's many distinctive forms of action.[135]

The second element of equity procedure that the code commissioners opted to retain was equity's distinctive set of remedies—including, most im-portantly, the injunction. These would henceforth be available in any case (whether formerly deemed legal or equitable) in which they seemed best suited to vindicating the injured party's rights. As the commissioners ex-plained, "It is a leading feature of our proposed plan, to require in all cases a judgment adapted to the established rights of the parties; and we can see no difficulty in incorporating into it, as a portion of an uniform system of prac-tice, a form of execution which shall adapt itself to the judgment."[136] While the commissioners might in theory have eliminated equitable remedies—and perhaps had some incentive to do so in that they epitomized the much-criticized procedural power of the equity judge—this was never in fact pro-posed, not even by equity's most vehement critics. Equity's power to enjoin had developed many centuries earlier, and parties were long accustomed to relying on it. Moreover, the rise of an increasingly complex and interconnected market made the injunction that much more valuable. As we have seen, from the 1830s onward, creditors' bills came to constitute one of the most sizable components of equity jurisdiction. Enabling a judgment creditor to identify property hidden by his debtor, these bills were premised on the court's power not only to order discovery but also to enjoin the debtor (or person in posses-sion) from selling or otherwise disposing of the property in question. More generally, injunctions played a key role in suits directed at preventing injury to

property, including actions to stay waste and to prohibit infringement of patents and copyrights. So too, they were vital in regulating relations among business partners (and as the corporate form became increasingly dominant,
among corporate shareholders and directors), helping to ensure compliance
with core duties of fair dealing.[137] Accordingly, while chancery and its tremendous power to enjoin were subject to extensive populist critique as tools of
oppression in the hands of elites—including, most especially, the new financial and industrial elites—the fact remained that important segments of the
expanding market-driven economy relied on the injunction, and those who
benefited were unwilling to forgo its use.

Aside from pleading and remedies, the code commissioners largely eschewed the traditional procedural mechanisms of equity.[138] Perhaps most importantly, they greatly reduced the court's powers of discovery. While the
parties in equity had traditionally been responsible for drafting interrogatories
themselves, court officers—especially masters—had significant power to
shape the examination by directing a line of questioning. In contrast, under
the Field Code, all witness testimony was to be taken in open court, and thus
exclusively by the lawyers, unless the witness did "not reside within one hundred miles from the place of trial" or was "unable to attend." Moreover, even
in these exceptional circumstances, such testimony was to be taken orally, by
lawyers themselves (in front of a judge based near the witness's place of resi-
dence), and thus in no way meaningfully shaped or constrained by the kind of
top-down, quasi-inquisitorial control traditionally exercised by masters.[139]

At the same time, the code commissioners extended the right to a jury trial
to many cases that had once fallen within the exclusive purview of the equity
judge. Henceforth, this quintessential common-law institution was to be used
for deciding "issue[s] of fact" in every case (whether previously deemed legal
or equitable) seeking "the recovery of money only, or of specific real or personal property"—and thus in most litigation.[140] That said, as Renée Lettow
Lerner observes, the commissioners (in accordance with the dictate of the
1846 constitution) were careful to specify that parties had the option of waiv-
ing trial by jury and proceeding instead with a bench trial. So too, the jury
could be waived in favor of a reference to lay decision-makers, termed referees, who were to be appointed on an ad hoc, case-by-case basis.[141] Thus, while
the Field Code seems at first glance to mark the unassailable triumph of the
jury, the reality was more complex.[142]

Overall, however, it is clear that code procedure was in many key respects
common-law procedure. As such, it valorized the lawyer-driven (jury) trial—a

single concentrated event, focused on the taking of witness testimony by means of oral examination and cross-examination by the lawyers themselves. That the code thus embraced a model of procedure that put lawyers front and center followed quite naturally from the fact that it was a set of lawyer-driven developments—including, most importantly, the turn to oral, adversarial procedure—that underlay the enactment of the code. But to the extent that the code marked the coming to fruition of these developments long in the making, it is now important to turn to the question of what motivated lawyers to act as they did.

If we wish to understand the shape taken by mid-nineteenth-century procedural reform—and, in particular, lawyers' embrace of oral, adversarial procedure—it is necessary to develop a richer, more contextualized account of their motivations than that provided by either of the standard narratives of the Field Code. The traditional Whiggish account of the code as an all-but-inevitable end product of frustration with accumulated procedural irrationalities—as the outcome, in short, of rationalization—ignores the key question of what motivated the lawyers who, as we have seen, were largely responsible for the turn to adversarialism. At the same time, the revisionist suggestion that the code and its procedural reform were intended merely to forestall demands for material (redistributive) change relies on an account of lawyers' motivations that is so caricatured as to beggar belief. The time has thus come to explore the cultural foundations of mid-nineteenth-century procedural reform.

# 4 • Cultural Foundations of American Adversarialism
## Civic Republicanism and the Decline of Equity's
## Quasi-Inquisitorial Tradition

To the extent that it was lawyers themselves, practicing in chancery, who bore substantial responsibility for transforming equity proceedings into the oral, lawyer-driven process that typified the common law, what motivated them? Why, in other words, did early nineteenth-century lawyers seek to change a model of procedure that appears until then to have functioned, though at times imperfectly, largely undisturbed?

Lawyers embraced adversarialism—including, most importantly, oral and public witness examination and cross-examination—because they were eager to exercise more procedural control. As we have seen, one motivation underlying this desire for greater procedural control was the belief that it would assist them in winning litigation. But as important as these strategic interests were, it would be a mistake to assume that they alone were responsible for lawyers' embrace of adversarial procedure. Such an assumption relies on a myopic conception of procedure—one that fails to take into account the important ways that procedure related to the contemporary interest in (and, indeed, obsession with) oratory. This myopia, in turn, generates an artificially narrow and constrained conception of the range of lawyers' professional interests and motivations.

In order properly to contextualize lawyers' turn toward adversarialism, it is necessary to begin by recalling the remarkable fact of their early and mid-nineteenth-century rise to power and prominence. From the early republic onward, the legal profession was subject to fierce popular hostility. Longstanding criticisms of lawyers as avaricious sowers of ill will came to meld with new post-revolutionary fears that the legal profession's adherence to the niceties of the (English) common law threatened to undermine the nation's hard-won liberty. The end result was the emergence of numerous calls radically to simplify the legal system so as to obviate any need for lawyers. Yet remarkably, despite these severe challenges, lawyers in this period succeeded in gaining an important stronghold in social and political life, such that by the time of his visit to the United States in the late 1830s, Alexis de Tocqueville would famously describe them as the American aristocracy.[1] While lawyers had always held a disproportionate share of political offices from the very founding of the republic, they increased this already sizable share during the antebellum period. During the 1790s, on the order of 45 percent of the members of the U.S. House of Representatives were lawyers, but by the 1840s and 1850s, this number had increased to 67 percent.[2] And strikingly, between 1823 and 1861, 58.1 percent of those who were named speakers in state legislatures had begun their careers as lawyers.[3]

How did this happen? How, in other words, did lawyers succeed in transforming themselves into Tocqueville's American aristocracy? One important and neglected factor is their contribution to the development of what they (and others) came to view as a distinctive American procedural culture—one premised on adversarialism and thus ensuring that lawyers would play a very active (and visible) role. To make sense of this history, we need to begin by examining the contemporary interest in oratory and its important linkages to civic republican political thought.

## Civic Republicanism and Antebellum Procedural Culture

For the past several decades, scholars across a range of fields—including history, literature, and law—have puzzled over the remarkable fact that early nineteenth-century Americans came to conceive of themselves as *Americans,* bound together by a shared national identity. As these scholars have rightly emphasized, there was nothing obvious or inevitable about the emergence of such a shared identity.[4] As of the founding, the various peoples who would come to think of themselves as Americans were divided by important regional, local, and religious—not to mention racial—differences. Indeed, as Carolyn Eastman notes, "[t]he one identity that most white Americans had previously shared—their Britishness—was now precisely what they were *not.*"[5]

Drawing on Jürgen Habermas's influential notion of the bourgeois public sphere and Benedict Anderson's conception of the nation as an imagined community, a variety of scholars have traced the way that communicative exchange (both printed and oral) served to give rise to the concept and practice of an American public. As Americans talked to and with each other about the public that they were interested in forming, they ended up calling this national public into being. In this process, print culture and oratory were deeply interconnected and mutually reinforcing; many contemporaries understood reading to be an oral exercise, while quite a few publications (like schoolbooks and newspapers) devoted substantial space to presenting speeches.[6] That said, oratory as such had a special place in contemporary political culture because of the prominence of civic republican thought.

Scholars have extensively debated the relative importance of civic (or classical) republicanism in late eighteenth- and early nineteenth-century American political culture—as compared, most especially, with some combination of individualist liberalism and Protestant millennialism.[7] But whatever the precise nature and scope of its impact, it is beyond cavil that civic republicanism was one of the founding era's defining ideologies. And though historians once believed that the influence of ancient Greece and Rome began to wane in the early national period, recent research suggests that quite the opposite was the case. If anything, the classical world grew in importance as American citizens grappled to structure and preserve the new republic that they had created.[8] This was, at any rate, certainly the case among lawyers.

As a number of scholars have argued, including most notably Robert Gordon, antebellum lawyers embraced a model of the lawyer-statesman that was rooted in the discourse of civic republicanism.[9] Pursuant to this discourse, republican government—or government by the people—was always in danger of collapse because its survival hinged on the preservation of virtue among the citizenry, which in turn was subject to the constant threat of corruption. Only a citizenry that was virtuous and thus devoted to the public welfare, over and above narrow, private self-interest, would make the kinds of sacrifices (of wealth, time, and ultimately life itself) necessary to sustain self-government.

As it emerged in the Renaissance and early modern period, in the midst of rising commercial development and prosperity in Western Europe, the discourse of civic republicanism identified commerce—or the pursuit of private wealth—as the primary threat to virtue. The plasticity of this discourse was such, however, that any threat to national unity—including both regional and religious sectionalism—could be depicted as a threat to virtue.[10] The dramatic commercial growth that the United States experienced from the 1820s onward, along with intensifying debates over slavery and the proliferation of religious sects following the Second Great Awakening, combined to fuel continued anxieties that private interests would undermine the public good.

Civic republicanism thus remained a defining discourse and ideology—one to which orality was key.

Embracing the language of republicanism, early nineteenth-century law-yers conceived of themselves as key civic leaders who played an essential role in preserving virtue, thus enabling the new republic to survive. Consider, for example, the comments of David Hoffman, a professor of law at the Univer-sity of Maryland, who published a highly influential text concerning the study and practice of law in 1817, which was then reissued in expanded versions in 1836 and 1846.[11] According to Hoffman, the lawyer was "the assertor of right, the accuser of wrong, the protector of innocence, and the terror of crime." Devoted to vindicating virtue, he "obtain[ed] over society a large and legitimate control"—one that he always exercised with an eye toward "becom[ing] in it a more useful member."[12]

Whether in the assembly or the forum—the legislature or the courtroom—lawyers in the new United States, as in ancient Greece and Rome, would de-ploy oratory to guide their fellow citizens toward wise and just self-governance. Indeed, because vital social and political decisions were made by both legisla-tures and courts (and because ancient lawyer-statesmen traditionally argued before both), the kind of oratory that American lawyers sought to develop was often described as "forensic"—a term that while usually used to refer to court-room argument was also not infrequently deployed to describe legislative (and other political) debate.[13] As argued in an article published in the 1824 edition of the well-respected *North American Review* and widely reprinted thereafter, the fact that the constitutionality of the law was subject to discussion in both legislatures and courts gave rise in the United States to "a new style of forensic eloquence, in which the enlarged views and liberal arguments of the statesman are happily blended with the minute accuracy and strict logic of the lawyer."[14] So too a November 1827 edition of New York's *Evening Post* insisted that "[t]he people of the United States, as a nation, are remarkable for the possession of the talent of eloquence in legislative debate and at the forum." As the article concluded, "Our peculiar institutions, the freedom of discussion secured to us by the laws, the jealousy with which public and private rights are guarded, all create a demand for this talent and accordingly it is supplied."[15]

While this republican conception of lawyers as the nation's natural leaders was a product primarily of the professional elite—namely, college-educated individuals, many of whom leaned Federalist-Whig in their politics[16]—there is good reason to conclude that its influence extended further down the ranks. The republican image of the lawyer was widely propagated in contemporary legal textbooks and treatises, as well as in newspapers and magazines, as a model to which would-be lawyers might aspire. So too, it was captured in visual images, such as Cephas Thompson's portrait of William Wirt (fig. 4) in which the famed Virginia lawyer and orator is depicted in a classical pose, complete with toga. Moreover, the institutional context of American legal practice—the fact that all licensed lawyers were authorized to litigate (unlike in England's divided profession) and that there was a wealth of local courts in which they might do so—helped to ensure that the more humble members of the profession could imagine themselves as belonging, if only at the fringes, to a distinctive republican elite. Indeed, as Maxwell Bloomfield observes, even to the extent that non-elite lawyers were more concerned with making ends meet than with establishing themselves as national leaders, the fact that success in litigation hinged so much in this period on the display of powerful

Figure 4  Cephas Thompson, *William Wirt* (circa 1809–10).
Courtesy of the National Portrait Gallery, Smithsonian
Institute / Art Resource, New York.

rhetorical skills meant that the lesser lights of the profession were necessarily concerned to some degree with emulating the high culture and values of their more prominent contemporaries.[17]

Whether and in what ways civic republican ideology shaped antebellum lawyers' experience of the profession have long been subject to scholarly debate. There is widespread agreement that civic republicanism significantly influenced the antebellum ideal (though less so the reality) of legal pedagogy. Pursuant to the then-dominant model, the law was part and parcel of a broader liberal arts education, such that legal study was, at least in theory, commenced only upon completion of extensive reading in the Western canon of moral and political thought.[18] Much less clear is how civic republicanism shaped legal practice itself. To the extent that scholars have explored this question, they have focused almost exclusively on one aspect of practice—one that in the antebellum period itself had yet to be clearly defined as such: namely, professional ethics. According to a widespread line of thought, civic republicanism lent itself to an ethical code of lawyering pursuant to which the lawyer was required to advocate only those matters that he deemed consonant with the public good. In this view, it was only in the aftermath of the Civil War, with the emergence of large corporate interests and a newly organized bar specially attuned to these, that there arose the modern-day expectation that lawyers zealously advocate on behalf of clients without regard to broader questions of justice.[19] But as Norman Spaulding has persuasively argued, the notion that civic republicanism translated in any clear, direct way into precise principles of legal ethics—let alone ones requiring lawyers to place their own conception of the public good above their clients' interests—is more myth than reality. The antebellum period was marked by multiple competing conceptions of lawyers' ethical obligations, all of which were at times justified by recourse to the language of civic republicanism.[20] But that does not mean that civic republicanism was without implications for legal practice. These were, however, in the realm of procedure, rather than ethics.

Civic republicanism fostered a particular model of lawyerly self-presentation—ways that lawyers could display themselves as the virtuous citizens and statesmen that they claimed to be. Put differently, this discourse and ideology offered a kind of script by means of which lawyers could "perform" (in Erving Goffman's sense)[21] the role of virtuous civic leaders. In thus providing a set of norms for lawyerly self-display, civic republicanism greatly influenced what lawyers sought to do in the courtroom and, as a result, helped give rise to a new, unified conception of what procedural justice entailed—one premised on the oral, adversarial methods of the common law rather than the quasi-inquisitorial methods of equity. But because scholars have long assumed that Anglo-American procedure is necessarily oral and adversarial—thus neglecting the longstanding tradition whereby courts of law and equity operated according to two very different procedural models—they have failed to date to recognize these profound procedural developments.

That the imperative of republican self-display played an important role in the formation of antebellum procedural culture does not mean that this was the only factor responsible for the American turn toward adversarial procedure. Lawyers also embraced adversarialism because they believed that it would prove strategically valuable, helping them to win litigation. Moreover, as discussed below, no account of the nineteenth-century rise of adversarialism would be complete without an exploration of its important roots in contemporary struggles over both the market revolution and racial hierarchy. But however important these other factors, it is clear that antebellum lawyers' civic-republican self-conception also played a significant role in shaping procedural practice, thus contributing to the decline of the distinctive (quasi-inquisitorial) tradition of equity and the consequent embrace of merger.[22]

There are a number of reasons why antebellum lawyers were so drawn to the classical republican model of lawyering, all linked in important ways with issues of professional identity, status, and power. In the early and mid-nineteenth century, the longstanding critique of lawyers as hired guns eager to obfuscate the truth and sow dissension—all with an eye toward augmenting their fees—resulted in a growing body of anti-lawyer literature and renewed efforts to limit the power of the bar. These efforts, in turn, contributed to such developments as the widespread loosening of requirements for entry into the profession, the revision of statutory law (and later codification) aimed at increasing transparency, and the decreasing technicality of procedure (as exemplified by the simplification of common-law pleading).[23] Eager to resist this public critique and the challenges it posed, lawyers grasped at ways to present their specialized knowledge and guild power as being in the public interest—a goal for which the republican model of the lawyer as a virtuous, public-serving elite seemed tailor-made.

The expanding size of the legal profession made possible by the loosening of barriers to entry led to increased tensions within the bar itself—especially as those of lower social standing joined the ranks. Traditional elites (including particularly those who identified as Federalist-Whigs) sought ways to resist what they perceived to be an onslaught of the rabble.[24] Here too, the discourse of republicanism provided a ready-made language for insisting on their own superiority as the elite guardians of civic virtue.

As the size of the bar expanded and pressures to compete increased, lawyers also found themselves hounded by a growing insistence that they were merce-naries. Pursuant to a longstanding English inheritance (common to continental Europe as well), the practice of law was not supposed to be a mere trade sullied by the pursuit of monetary gain but instead an honorable calling suited to gen-tlemen. This, in turn, meant that lawyers were not, in theory, permitted to ac-cept fees for their services—though they were entitled to accept an honorarium, should the client choose to offer one. But as the nineteenth century progressed, the economic realities under which lawyers operated were such that they be-came increasingly embedded in the market, openly charging fees and often suing to recover them.[25] The dissonance they thus experienced as a result of the widening gap between self-image and actual practice was helpfully mediated by their embrace of a republican model of lawyering. Acting the part of Cicero urg-ing the defense of virtue on the public stage was, in part, a way of hiding from the harsh reality that money-making was a key professional concern.

Lawyers seeking for these various reasons to embody the classical model of the profession as a virtue-promoting, civic elite found the procedural tools of the common law to be enormously helpful. While there were a number of dif-ferent stages on which nineteenth-century lawyers could (and did) seek to dis-play their commitment to public service—including, not least, legislative debates and political party meetings—it was the courtroom that for centuries lay at the core of lawyers' professional identity. Engaging in courtroom oratory, lawyers were able to display their passion for vindicating virtue and assailing injustice and, in so doing, appeal to their listeners' corresponding sentiments. So too, cross-examination afforded them a powerful tool for dramatically dis-tinguishing between virtue and vice. And the common-law tradition ensured that there would be a substantial audience of citizens available to witness such lawyerly display—including jurors, members of the general public, clients, and fellow lawyers. By way of contrast, many of these mechanisms were un-available in the quasi-inquisitorial tradition of equity.

In thus embracing core aspects of the common-law tradition as vital for producing the republican lawyer who would preserve and promote the new nation's freedom, nineteenth-century Americans drew in part on the discourse of the seventeenth-century English Revolution, which identified the common law as distinctively promotive of liberty. As we have seen, it was this same dis-course that was so effectively used by New York legislators and constitutional convention delegates to decry equity as authoritarian. But the nature of the legal system in nineteenth-century New York, as compared with contemporary England, was such that this discourse about the common-law approach to adjudication was quickly transformed into one about adjudication tout court. In England, the common-law courts remained until the mid- to late nineteenth century but one component of a broader patchwork of institutions, each claiming jurisdiction as the inherited privilege of a distinct authority (royal, manorial, ecclesiastical, and so forth) and served by its own distinct practitioners. Thus, even as the common law came increasingly to be conceived as the law of the English land (and people), it also continued to be viewed to some extent in jurisdictional terms.[26] In contrast, in nineteenth-century New York, there was no corporatist tradition undergirding the court system, and the state was therefore able to claim general jurisdiction for its courts—before all of which the same generalist lawyers were able to practice. In this context, the inherited discourse about the liberty-promoting effects of the common law found a welcome but transformative home. Not linked in the same way to a particular set of courts and their personnel, this discourse expanded into a much broader series of arguments about the proper (adversarial) approach to adjudication— one to be utilized by the parties and their lawyers in any and all proceedings in which they might find themselves.

## ORATORY

Inspired by the ancients and their model of republicanism, antebellum Americans deemed public speaking, or oratory, to be crucial in exhorting the citizenry to virtue. It was thus considered essential knowledge for all citizens. Students studied rhetoric or oratory, along with the history of the ancient world, from their earliest schooling through to college.[27] And speech-making was deemed vital in those spheres thought to have the greatest influence on communal life—namely, religion, politics, and law. Contemporaries thus devoted a great deal of energy to observing and critiquing the oratorical performances of clergymen, politicians, and lawyers. But in an age when lawyers commonly aspired to serve in politics—and when, even more than today, a great many politicians were in fact lawyers—it was law, in particular, that was thought to be the pathway to civic leadership. Accordingly, lawyers paid especially close attention to mastering the art of oratory.[28]

American lawyers embraced Cicero, the revered lawyer-statesman and orator of ancient Rome, as a model to emulate. Looking especially to his speeches resisting tyranny, they sought to make themselves in his image (and voice). As Robert Ferguson notes, "[John] Adams and his club of lawyers . . . read Cicero aloud, hoping to lead the Massachusetts bar to a 'Purity, an Elegance, and a Spirit, surpassing any Thing that ever appeared in America.' "[29] In so doing, early Americans—and especially lawyers—engaged in what Christopher Looby calls a "politics of ventriloquism," hoping that by "adopt[ing] not only the moral and political sense of [Cicero's] philosophy but the whole paralinguistic apparatus of [his] tone, gesture, cadence, and pronunciation," they would be able quite literally to channel him.[30] In their efforts to emulate Cicero, these lawyers not only learned and delivered his speeches but also committed themselves to acting in his image. They thus deployed oratory in the courtroom, legislature, and any number of other public fora—ranging from political party meetings to stump speeches to July 4 festivities—as a means of reminding fellow citizens of their obligation virtuously to serve the republic.[31]

As law professor David Hoffman observed, the centrality of oratory or "eloquence" to the legal profession was such that "[t]he student scarce needs to be reminded by any remarks of ours, of the importance of this branch of his legal accomplishments."[32] He advised students searching for "instruction in the arts of rhetoric, and for models of oratory" to study the classical texts of Cicero and Quintilian. Similarly, in his inaugural address upon becoming Dane Professor of Law at Harvard in August 1829, Joseph Story emphasized that the "perfect lawyer" was one who mastered "the power of eloquence" and that only such an individual could achieve "excellence in the highest order of the [legal] profession."[33] The notion that lawyers must model themselves on the great citizen-orators of the ancient world was so deep-rooted and widespread in the antebellum period that, in May 1842, noted diarist and New York City lawyer George Templeton Strong mockingly described his first courtroom performance as concluding with "a speech, Demosthenian as to eloquence [and] sledgehammer-like as to force."[34] A man of biting wit, Strong's decision to deride his "debut in Court" by self-deprecatingly referring to his own "Demosthenian . . . eloquence" highlights the extent to which the lawyerly role came to be equated with an ideal of classical oratory.

While early and mid-nineteenth-century Americans believed that lawyers' oratory was particularly important in the new United States, they were, in fact, not alone in their obsession with eloquence and the ancient model of the lawyer-statesman. A deep respect for classical oratory (particularly among lawyers) was widely shared among Western European nations in this period, including most importantly Great Britain and France.[35] Indeed, to some extent,

American lawyers imbibed a respect for oratory from their English counterparts, whose legal system they often sought to emulate. English ideas about the importance of oratory for the successful lawyer made their way into the American consciousness through numerous publications (and republications), including in the popular press.[36]

Like the American public more generally, however, American lawyers had a complex relation to all things English—seeking to prove their worth by mastering English ways while at the same time trying to distance themselves from anything associated with the old empire. Accordingly, even while embracing the English ideal of the lawyer-orator, early nineteenth-century American lawyers self-consciously sought to develop their own unique national style of oratory. Reflecting this determination, contemporary newspapers commented extensively on the nature of American "forensic eloquence" and anxiously queried whether it was able to match the quality of its European (and especially English) counterparts.[37] But whether they criticized or praised the state of American eloquence, early and mid-nineteenth-century commentators—especially lawyers—agreed that the development of a distinctive national style of forensic oratory was vital to the broader project of nation-building.

Embracing a rhetoric of national cultural difference that had its roots in Montesquieu and that flourished widely in the middle decades of the nineteenth century, Hoffman claimed that "[t]he people of each nation . . . are physically, mentally, and politically characterized from each other; their circumstances, in all of these respects, are sufficiently different to produce a correspondent variation in the style of their oratory." Careful observation of American public life—including "not only the pulpit, the bar, and the senate, . . . but [also] the conversation of daily life"—revealed certain tendencies indicative of the distinctive (and, in Hoffman's view, superior) features of American oratory. In his words, "our forensic oratory differs widely from that of England, and, indeed, from that of all the continental nations, and . . . the scale greatly preponderates in our favour. . . ."[38]

The superiority of American oratory derived first and foremost from the fact that it called on the passions and was in this sense far truer than its English counterpart to the model of ancient Greece and Rome. As antebellum Americans (and especially lawyers) were well aware, the classical six-stage model for developing a persuasive argument included an appeal to the listeners' emotions, known as the "pathetic part."[39] Attempting to emulate the ancients, American lawyers self-consciously worked to cultivate what Hume, in his late eighteenth-century critique of English oratory, described as the classical world's unique "vehemence of thought and expression."[40] In thus seeking to deploy impassioned oratory, lawyers were moreover very much in line with the ethos of Romanticism that was so pervasive during the first half of the nineteenth century and with the evangelical culture of "theatrical sermonizing" that emerged from the Second Great Awakening.[41] Accordingly, as Hoffman reminded law students, one of the advocate's most powerful weapons was his passion, which if honestly conveyed to the jurors could not help but sway them toward the cause of virtue: "Ardour in debate is often the soul of eloquence, and the greatest charm of oratory. When spontaneous and suited to the occasion, it becomes powerful."[42] Similarly, legal biographies and autobiographies, a popular genre in the era, consistently emphasized their subjects' capacity for oratorical feeling.[43]

Drawing on Hume's critique of the English orators as dry, dull, and unfeeling, Hoffman observed that "the English are proverbially ineloquent." "Substantial, considerate and calm," the "English standard of eloquence exercises none of the sublimer faculties of the mind." In contrast, Americans' oratory, while still not fully developed, was more finely attuned to the important role of pathos in argument. In this respect, it was more comparable not only to the oratory of the ancients but also to that of England's (not so friendly) neighbors the Irish and the French. But while American oratory, like its Irish and French counterparts, was more attentive to the role of passion and feeling, it was superior to these, because it was also duly grounded in logic and reason. It was, in short, "that happy medium between the florid and the severe, the passionate and the grave, which seems to mark the growing character of American eloquence."[44]

In arguing that in their appeal to pathos Irish and French orators were superior to their English counterparts, Hoffman was in no way alone. Indeed, ironically, the criticism of contemporary British oratory as excessively dull and dry in comparison with that of the ancients, as well as that of the Irish and the French, was itself prototypically British.[45] Nonetheless, this view was widely shared among antebellum American lawyers, who embraced the development of an oratory that appealed to feeling partly as a means of marking the new American nation as distinct and independent from that of the British. So too, the use of impassioned oratory had the advantage of highlighting the commonalities between Americans and another nation that bravely sought independence from British control—namely, the Irish. Indeed, in celebrating the passionate nature of Irish oratory, antebellum Americans looked especially to the orators associated (to varying degrees) with Ireland's recently failed revolution against the British—to barristers like John Philpot Curran, Henry Grattan, and Charles Phillips. Early nineteenth-century American newspapers were filled with reviews and advertisements of books containing these men's speeches.[46] As noted in one such article, the publication of a volume containing Curran's speeches was of great value "[t]o the citizens of America in general," but especially "[t]o the gentlemen of the bar," who would thus have available for "their study and imitation, the productions of a man who is thought to excel all his contemporaries in the powers of forensic eloquence."[47] Moreover, in seeking to laud American lawyers' forensic oratory, contemporary publications regularly drew parallels to these Irish greats. Thus, for example, William Wirt was described as "the Curran of America."[48]

But however common, comparisons between American and Irish forensic oratory were necessarily fraught in that it was unthinkable that American lawyers should slavishly imitate any other nation's oratorical style—including even that of the fiercely independent Irish. These tensions are evident perhaps first and foremost in an 1804 essay entitled "On Forensic Eloquence" believed to have been written by Wirt.[49] Reflecting on the recent publication of Curran's speeches, Wirt observed that "[t]heir merit will no doubt secure to them an extensive and rapid circulation in America; nor would it be a matter of surprise, if they soon produce a striking effect on the American bar." While remarking that much of this influence would be for the good, Wirt was also careful to observe that "I should be sorry that a single man of genius . . . should assume [Curran] as the standard of forensic eloquence and form himself on the models which that orator has furnished."[50] A nation's mode of oratory, he explained, is intimately linked to its experience and character, such that the Irish approach would necessarily ring false in the American context.

The project of building a distinctive national oratory was one to which numerous individuals contributed—including even such disempowered groups as women and native Americans.[51] But lawyers pursued it with particular relish. In so doing, they promoted their own social and professional ambitions while at the same time helping to generate and propagate the notion of a distinctive American identity. In this respect, scholars to date have been right to point to the important role of the law in giving rise to a sense of national identity, but their tendency to focus almost exclusively on published legal literature is misplaced.[52] As important as case reports, treatises, and the constitution itself were in creating the concept of an American people and culture, lawyers' oratory was vital as well. And remarkably, as we will see, lawyers' efforts to develop a distinctive style of forensic oratory also played a transformative role in shaping procedural practice.

## CROSS-EXAMINATION

As the antebellum ideal of forensic oratory emerged, it came to consist not simply of (often lengthy) speech-making but also of the associated practice of witness examination and especially cross-examination—a practice that came into full flourishing only in the late eighteenth and early nineteenth centuries. Indeed, cross-examination was embraced as a core component of a mode of forensic oratory imagined as distinctively American—one that enabled lawyers to undertake highly dramatic republican self-display by virtuously bringing to light those malefactors who had engaged in perjury and were otherwise unworthy of the public trust. This is not to suggest, of course, that cross-examination itself was a uniquely American practice. But while cross-examination emerged on both sides of the Atlantic, the motivations behind its adoption, as well as the cultural meanings attached to it, were not themselves uniform.

The early history of Anglo-American cross-examination remains obscure, but recent scholarship suggests that, contrary to longstanding assumptions, lawyer-driven, adversarial cross-examination was actually relatively new as of the beginning of the nineteenth century. As John Langbein has shown, it was only over the course of the eighteenth century (by about the 1780s) that cross-examination in the modern sense—namely, the questioning of adverse witnesses by counsel—became a common feature of English criminal practice. Until this period, defense counsel were largely absent from ordinary felony trials. In contrast, civil litigation was dominated by lawyers well before the eighteenth century, leading scholars to assume that cross-examination must have initially arisen in the civil rather than the criminal arena. But as recent research suggests, quite the opposite appears to have been true.[53]

Because law reporting did not become systematized until the end of the eighteenth century, we know surprisingly little about trial practice prior to this period.[54] Much has been learned, however, from studying the first eighteenth-century treatises on the law of evidence. In contrast to modern-day evidence treatises, which devote extensive attention to the prohibition of hearsay—a prohibition now justified on the grounds that such testimony is not subject to cross-examination—treatises published throughout the eighteenth century say little concerning this topic. To the limited extent that they do address it, they offer as a basis for the prohibition the fact that such testimony is not presented under oath, rather than the fact that it is not subject to cross-examination. Thus, by implication, as of the late eighteenth century, cross-examination had yet to become a central feature of English civil trials.[55]

Although we tend to view cross-examination as a necessary or inevitable feature of common-law adjudication, it therefore seems likely that it was, in fact, a relatively late development.[56] That it was something of a novelty helps to explain the widespread enthusiasm for it in the early nineteenth century. Numerous legal biographies, novels, and newspaper articles celebrated the art of cross-examination and the lawyers who had mastered it. But novelty was not its only appeal. One argument commonly made in favor of cross-examination was that it helped in distinguishing truth from falsehood. Yet, as Langbein has suggested in the English context, it would be a mistake to assume that lawyers (and the public at large) all naively assumed that cross-examination would flawlessly serve the falsehood-detection function for which it was ostensibly designed.[57] In the first half of the nineteenth century, many English and American lawyers expressed great skepticism in this regard. As these critics complained, cross-examination was frequently used not to establish the truthfulness of testimony but rather to manipulate it, thereby helping the examining counsel win his case.[58] For example, in 1832, Benjamin L. Oliver, a self-described "counselor at law," lauded cross-examination, insisting that "[t]he advantage of this mode of examining a witness, in detecting a concerted story . . . is very great." In so arguing, however, he also bemoaned the fact that there were lawyers who made it "a frequent practice" to engage in cross-examination in a manner that was both "unfair and ensnaring."[59] Thus, while recognizing that cross-examination could serve as an important engine of truth, Oliver also acknowledged that it was sometimes abused to promote obfuscation.

To the extent that many lawyers doubted the ostensible truth-promoting properties of cross-examination, why was this (relatively new) practice so readily—indeed, enthusiastically—embraced? One reason is that cross-examination could prove strategically useful in litigation—either by bringing the truth to light or more cynically, as some recognized, by muddying the waters. That cross-examination was desired for such strategic reasons was precisely what Chancellor Kent suggested, in claiming that the main "objection" to traditional equity procedure was that "the parties are not present by their counsel, to question and cross-examine the witnesses, *viva voce,* and by discovery of what is proved on one side, to be enabled to meet it by countervailing proof on the other."[60] But however important these strategic interests were, a review of contemporary writings by and about American lawyers suggests that this was not the only reason why cross-examination proved so popular in this period.

Obsessed with developing a distinctive mode of American forensic oratory, many lawyers came to believe that cross-examination should be an important component of such oratory, assisting lawyers in their efforts to serve as a Ciceronian civic republican elite. This is not to suggest that but for the influence of civic republicanism, the practice of cross-examination would not have emerged. To the contrary, in England itself, republican discourse extended well back into the early modern period, but cross-examination did not arise until the late eighteenth century—a gap in time that negates any simplistic causal relation between the two. But once cross-examination had arisen, certain distinctive features of the legal landscape in the nineteenth-century United States encouraged lawyers to embrace this new practice as an aspect of oratory and thus as a mechanism of republican self-display. In England, only a select elite of barristers could argue in court and undertake cross-examination, and the judges before whom they appeared exercised significant power, thus constraining these lawyers' ability to steal the limelight. In contrast, all American lawyers were free to litigate, and they had a wealth of local courts in which they could do so—courts in which the judges overseeing the proceedings were on the whole comparatively weak.[61] Anxious about preserving their status and market share in a way that English barristers were not—and able to undertake cross-examination much more easily, frequently, and freely than their English counterparts—American lawyers were uniquely eager and able to engage in cross-examination as a form of republican self-display.

During the antebellum period, cross-examination was thus widely described as a key component of the emerging ideal of a distinctively American (and republican) legal oratory. The reasons for this were, in part, mundane. As John Quincy Adams explained in his *Lectures on Rhetoric and Oratory,* delivered at Harvard between 1806 and 1809, the examination and cross-examination of witnesses was a facet of "judicial oratory" because these devices served to elicit the evidence that would thereafter form the basis of the lawyer's argument.[62] But more fundamentally, to examine and cross-examine witnesses was to undertake legal oratory in the sense that such questioning drew on the same talents necessary for great speech-making. Both practices required the advocate to possess and display intelligence, eloquence, and, most importantly, pathos. As David Paul Brown insisted in 1843, "[t]here is often more eloquence—more mind—more knowledge of human nature displayed in the examination of witnesses, than in the discussion of the cause to which their testimony relates."[63] Similarly, Hoffman advised his readers that

> Great knowledge of the human character, the art of adapting his manner
> to its varieties, penetration, equanimity, amiableness, clearness of expres-
> sion, etc. are requisite in extracting the precise truth from witnesses. . . . It

is an art, in which there may be a considerable display of genius; and often more strongly commands the admiration of intelligent observers, than elaborate and eloquent speaking.[64]

Perhaps most importantly, like a good jury speech, cross-examination high-lighted the lawyer's passionate commitment to pursuing virtue and trampling vice. As John Finlay argued, Curran's cross-examinations were key to his abil-ity, when speaking to a jury, to "appear[] as if designed by providence to be the refuge of the unfortunate, and the protector of the oppressed."[65] By thus high-lighting the antebellum lawyer's role as a leader devoted to promoting the public good, cross-examination served the all-important function of republi-can self-display.

That lawyers embraced cross-examination at least as much because of what it implied about their own character as for what it revealed about the witnesses they questioned is suggested by a telling comment made by the lawyer Benja-min Oliver. Oliver complained that some lawyers, in undertaking cross-examination, "waste the time and patience of the court, jury and witnesses, by asking a thousand frivolous and unmeaning questions, which have no bearing on the merits of the cause." Such cross-examination, he concluded, was done "without any other object than the gratification of the examiner's vanity, in having all eyes directed towards him during the examination."[66] It was in no small part because the practice of cross-examination thus displayed the lawyer as a crusader for virtue that it became such a central component of the na-tion's emerging procedural culture.

## PUBLIC PROCEEDINGS: JURORS, COMMUNITY MEMBERS, CLIENTS, AND FELLOW LAWYERS

Implicit in the emerging ideal of the American lawyer as a great forensic orator was the notion that there was an audience for his argument—one that would witness and attest to his republican self-display. Pursuant to the logic of such display, this audience was to serve as a stand-in for the citizenry as a whole, inspired to virtue by the virtuous conduct of the lawyer himself.

The jury, in particular, was embraced as a key component of the lawyer's audience. The centrality of the jury stemmed in part from the fact that the ancient lawyer-statesmen on whom American lawyers sought to model them-selves argued before juries. As in the classical world, early Americans viewed the jury as the voice of the citizenry, such that to argue before a jury was to argue before the citizenry itself. In thus glorifying jury argument as a core component of republican self-government, and one derived from the ancient world, American lawyers borrowed from a long tradition of English thought. As Blackstone argued in his *Commentaries on the Laws of England*—a book that served as a key text for American students of law and politics throughout the nineteenth century—"the trial by jury ever has been, and I trust ever will be, looked upon as the glory of the English law" because it has "secured the just liberties of this nation for a long succession of ages." Moreover, England had in this respect learned from the classical republics of the ancient world: "Rome, Sparta, and Carthage, at the time when their liberties were lost, were strangers to the trial by jury."[67] This longstanding conception of the jury as a bastion of liberty was reinforced in the American colonies, where juries were used to nullify unpopular British laws. As a result, during the founding era, civil jury provisions were included in most state constitutions as well as the later federal constitution.[68]

That the United States thus constitutionalized the civil jury—the institution that was in many ways the centerpiece of the adversarial, common-law approach to procedure—would seem in itself to constitute a significant and early thumb on the scale in favor of adversarialism. To the extent, in other words, that juries were historically (and also to some extent functionally) associated with other aspects of adversarial procedure (including, most importantly, orality and publicity), then perhaps the American embrace of adversarialism was all but set in stone as of the nation's founding? While this account seems intuitive, it neglects the fact that, in reality, the widespread constitutionalization of the civil jury had remarkably little effect on preserving the institution's actual power and usage.

In contrast to colonial and late eighteenth-century judges, who embraced a jury-empowering "jurisprudence of common sense," nineteenth-century American judges were much more learned in the law. As the century progressed, they began to wrest control away from juries in an effort to augment their own authority and to establish the legal predictability necessary for rational market activity. Accordingly, they created a newly rigid distinction between law and fact and claimed the sole right to decide questions of law, relegating the jury to questions of fact, subject to the judge's legal instructions.[69] Nineteenth-century courts—together with legislatures—also developed a number of other mechanisms for undermining the civil jury. Indeed, as Renée Lettow Lerner demonstrates, they began doing so as early as the beginning of the century—at the very same time that jury argument was being widely celebrated as a defining feature of the new republic's procedural culture. These mechanisms included permitting parties to waive their right to a jury, providing a jury only on appeal from non-jury summary proceedings and upon the incurring of substantial costs, granting motions for a new trial after a jury verdict had been entered, and expanding the judges' authority to direct the verdict as a matter of law.[70] The constitutionalization of the right to a civil jury thus did little in practice to maintain the institution's power—a fact suggesting, in turn, that it in no way necessitated or implied the burgeoning American commitment to adversarialism.

It bears emphasis, however, that while nineteenth-century litigants were afforded incentives to avoid jury trial—and those juries that were convened were increasingly stripped of their power—it was only in the twentieth century that judges developed powerful tools, like summary judgment, for keeping cases entirely out of jurors' hands.[71] There was thus no shortage of juries, which continued to be convened in civil cases throughout the nineteenth century and before whom lawyers might argue. Even while the power of these juries was diminished,[72] the very fact of arguing before one (and being seen to do so) could thus continue to exert symbolic force, demonstrating the lawyer's republican commitment to promoting virtue. The jury therefore remained an important mechanism of republican self-display.

The jury, moreover, was not the only courtroom audience for the antebellum lawyer-orator. As Judith Resnik and Dennis Curtis have emphasized, both the United States Constitution and a significant number of early state constitutions sought to guarantee the broader public's access to (at least some) courtroom proceedings.[73] And many individuals sought to make full use of this right. In an age before the emergence of radio and television, which serve to bring urban culture to remote, rural areas, many people viewed the courtroom as their primary source of entertainment. In small towns throughout the new nation, large segments of the community regularly attended court sessions to experience the drama of litigation and to keep informed about such local happenings as marital disputes and conflicts over property. Those who attended, moreover, were in no way shy about expressing their approval or disapproval of what lawyers had to say.[74]

The way in which jury trials brought together the entirety of the community is suggested by A. Wighe's remarkable painting *Trial by Jury* (fig. 5), in which those individuals directly involved in the proceedings appear to comingle with a broad panoply of local characters, ranging from the neighborhood waif drawing on the floor to a well-mannered dog, eager to join in the festivities. Indeed, even in big cities like Manhattan, members of the public paid close attention

Figure 5  A. Wighe, *Trial by Jury* (circa 1849). Courtesy of the Museum of Art, Rhode Island School of Design, Providence. Photographer credit: Erik Gould.

to court proceedings—especially when these involved figures of some fame or notoriety.[75] In this, they were aided by local newspapers, which frequently printed synopses of the legal arguments made in interesting courtroom battles, sometimes under the heading "forensic eloquence."[76] Thus, even though members of the public lacked the authority to issue a formal verdict, they constituted yet another group whom lawyers might try to sway.

Lawyers' desire to impress the broader public in attendance was fanned, in part, by their awareness that many clients selected a lawyer to represent them (including in transactional matters) by observing courtroom litigation.[77] But in addition to thus attempting to attract new clients, lawyers also sought to demonstrate their efficacy and loyalty to those clients whose matters they were actually litigating, many if not most of whom would have been present in the courtroom. For all these reasons, the community itself, regularly attending court sessions, provided lawyers another opportunity to engage in republican self-display.

But as detailed below, it was one particular segment of the public whom antebellum lawyers were most eager to impress—namely, their fellow lawyers. Lawyers' self-anointed status as civic leaders encouraged them to view each other's judgment as being of paramount importance. In addition, lawyers cared so much about the opinion of fellow lawyers because they were often personally acquainted with one another. Because of the relatively small size of the bar as well as the common practice of traveling together to court—and residing and dining with one another while there—antebellum lawyers in a given area tended to know each other.[78] And familiarity bred competition. Accordingly, lawyers' efforts to engage in republican self-display were aimed, in significant measure, at one another—a fact that helped ensure that such self-display would become a defining feature of the new nation's procedural culture.

## The Example of Henry Vanderlyn

The imperatives of republican self-display that so shaped antebellum procedural culture—and that came to be viewed as fundamentally incompatible with the traditions of equity—can be garnered from a range of sources, including the textbooks, lectures, and articles examined above. But they are perhaps best understood by examining lawyers' actual lived experience of the law, as related in a personal diary. Of course, no individual lawyer's experience can be said to be representative of the legal profession in its entirety, not least because the nature of practice varied across regions. Moreover, even within a given locale, as the century progressed, the bar became increasingly differentiated between elites, the rank and file, and those who barely managed to make ends meet.[79] Nonetheless, if we wish to explore the professional sensibilities that shaped procedural practice, the study of a lawyer's diary—cross-checked against what we know to be generally true of contemporary legal practice and values—affords especially useful information.[80]

Given the crucial role played by the state of New York and its lawyers in shaping the development of American law in this period, the diary of the lawyer Henry Vanderlyn is of particular interest. Vanderlyn was a resident of Oxford, New York, a small town in Chenango County, located toward the south-central part of the state. During the thirty-year period between April 1827 and March 1857—a period that includes some of the crucial decades in which, as we have seen, many of the procedural changes leading to the merger of law and equity occurred—he kept a diary on an almost daily basis.[81] The seven volumes of this diary, each running several hundred pages long, provide a remarkably thorough and detailed account of antebellum legal practice and professional identity. Yet, surprisingly, they have been all but ignored by legal historians to date.

Oxford, the town in which Vanderlyn spent almost the entirety of his professional life, was small and rural. According to a gazetteer published in 1824, Oxford's population as of that date was "near 1000 inhabitants" in the incorporated town (or 2,317, if residents of the surrounding countryside were included). About 80 percent of these people were farmers, with the remaining 20 percent consisting largely of "mechanics," or small-scale artisans, as well as a handful of individuals engaged in more extensive wholesale commerce.[82] Although many regions of central and western New York state expanded greatly as a result of the new economic opportunities generated by the construction of canals from the mid-1820s onwards, Oxford does not appear to have been one of these. Opened to traffic in 1837, the Chenango Canal passed through Oxford, thus providing an important outlet for the agricultural activity (especially dairy farming) in which local farmers engaged.[83] But Oxford itself never became a great manufacturing center.[84]

As a relatively small, rural town dependent largely on agriculture, Oxford was distinct from those areas of the state that experienced rapid urbanization and industrialization during the antebellum period. Vanderlyn's legal practice must therefore be distinguished from that of his city-dwelling counterparts. While Vanderlyn's clients were mostly farmers pursuing agricultural interests, the city lawyer's clientele consisted primarily of merchants and traders.[85] That said, it is Vanderlyn's rural experience of the law and legal practice that typified that of the legal profession in the first half of the nineteenth century. In 1820, only 11.7 percent of New York State's population lived in cities. While the percentage increased dramatically over the following decades—reaching 39.3 percent in 1860—more than half the population continued to live in rural areas until after the Civil War.[86] In this sense, the experience of most lawyers in antebellum New York was likely more akin to that of Vanderlyn than to that of another, more famous lawyer and diary-keeper—the consummate Manhattanite, George Templeton Strong.

More importantly, the differences between rural and urban legal practice ought not to be exaggerated. As credit practices became more sophisticated in the first half of the nineteenth century and the frontier shifted westward, land came to be valued increasingly as an instrument of investment, leading many wealthy urbanites to make land purchases. At the same time, the expanding market in negotiable instruments, facilitated by the emergence of a growing number of banks, entangled rural farmers in the same kinds of networks of credit in which urban merchants found themselves, often linking both groups together.[87] Urban and rural lawyers could thus expect to confront many of the same questions stemming from their common involvement in land and credit transactions. The great differences between rural and urban legal practice were to emerge primarily in the years after the Civil War, when industrialization and the rise of the business corporation transformed the nature of elite urban practice, leading to the formation of the large corporate law firm. Prior to this development, almost all lawyers, both rural and urban, worked alone—or occasionally in partnership with at most one or two others. And all lawyers tended to be generalists, engaging in both litigation and office work—though it was the former on which they mostly depended to attract clients of any kind.[88]

For all these reasons, Vanderlyn's experience of the law bears significantly on the more general question of antebellum legal practice in New York. But like all diaries, his must be read with a critical eye, since we have no way of assessing the validity of many of the details of his account. In particular, we must resist the temptation to read his diary as a fully transparent and accurate record of his experiences. Like many other diary-keepers before and since, Vanderlyn sought to make a favorable impression on future (and even contemporary) readers. As recounted in his diary, he often read portions of it to colleagues, friends, and family members. Moreover, he kept two sets of diaries at the same time—one of which he seems to have written with particular attention to the impression that it would make on others. As he explained, one set of diaries "contains my more extended and matured thoughts, while the fleeting occurrences of each day" are recorded in the other.[89] A careful reading suggests that he self-consciously drafted the first set—that containing his "more extended and matured thoughts"—with an eye toward winning readers' approval. Indeed, it was from this set of diaries that he most commonly read excerpts to listeners.

That the Vanderlyn diaries—and especially this last set—were written at least in part to impress an audience does not, however, mean that we must discount them as a valuable source of information. To the contrary, to the extent that Vanderlyn was trying to convey his worth as a lawyer to readers (both real and imagined), he drew on his understanding of what was likely to be meaningful to them. Thus, even though we cannot take his diaries entirely at face value, we can learn a great deal from them about commonly held views of lawyers and legal practice in the antebellum period—unless we have reason to believe that Vanderlyn was out of touch with contemporary mores. Fortunately, however, there is no basis for such a belief. Vanderlyn's detailed account of his life and legal practice credibly suggests that he achieved considerable success as a lawyer, practicing for over forty years, during which he represented numerous clients and became acquainted with many of the era's most prominent lawyers and politicians. A 1906 book entitled *Annals of Oxford, New York*—published more than forty years after Vanderlyn's death—reports that "[t]he term 'Count' clung to him through life from his great suavity and gentlemanly manners . . . , which rendered him a great favorite in the social reunions of the bench and bar during term time."[90] Given the success Vanderlyn enjoyed—and the social standing he, in turn, acquired—it seems highly unlikely that his perceptions of contemporary mores were in any way meaningfully askew. There is thus every reason to read his diary (including those portions directly aimed at impressing contemporaries) as a largely accurate reflection of the (idealized) self-conception and public image of the antebellum lawyer.

This idealized self-conception was not, of course, the only one possible. We can, in fact, identify hints of an alternative, more critical self-conception, but these moments of doubt were largely suppressed and therefore left far fewer traces in the historical record. In Vanderlyn's case, for example, all mention of his numerous efforts to be paid by clients are buried in brief discussions contained in those diaries that he devoted to "the fleeting occurrences of each day" (and from which he did not read to visitors).[91] The focus below is thus on the idealized, republican self-conception of the lawyer—one that is not only more readily detected in the sources but that also played a key role in shaping contemporary procedural practice. This ought not to blind us, however, to the important frictions that followed from lawyers' embrace of adversarialism as a form of republican self-display.

As suggested by Vanderlyn's attempt to avoid acknowledging the reality of when and how he was paid, the republican, public-serving model of the lawyer fit at times uneasily with an adversarial approach to adjudication whose functioning ultimately depended on the lawyer's willingness to hire himself out for a fee. Indeed, despite Vanderlyn's insistence that his role as lawyer was to pursue the cause of virtue, the content with which he invested this category appeared to shift along with his clientele—such that the virtuous litigant might one day be the duped creditor and the very next (in a different litigation) the unfortunate debtor. But by grounding his idealized self-conception on his case-by-case procedural pursuits—on the oratory he displayed in a particular opening or closing argument or in a particular cross-examination—Vanderlyn was able largely to blind himself to what might otherwise have seemed to be glaring contradictions between the positions he advocated from one moment to the next. Lawyers like Vanderlyn, in other words, did not promote republican, communitarian values through their practice but instead treated practice (and, in particular, procedure) as providing a script for republican self-display. This script facilitated their efforts to ignore those aspects of practice that did not entirely square with their virtuous self-image, while also helping to generate the kinds of professional success that were readily translated into material wealth, as well as social and political capital.

## EARLY LIFE AND MOVE TO OXFORD

Henry Vanderlyn was born on April 21, 1784, in Kingston, a city in Ulster County, located along the Hudson River between Albany and New York City. From all appearances, he came from a typically upper-middle-class family from this town. Of Dutch descent, his father was, in his words, a "skillful physician" and "man of letters." His paternal uncle John, taken under the wing of Aaron Burr, acquired no small fame in both the United States and Europe as a painter in the neoclassical style so popular in the early nineteenth century.[92] After attending the local academy, Henry moved to Schenectady in 1800, at the age of sixteen, to commence two years of study at Union College.[93]

While Henry's older brother Peter went into his father's line of work, becoming a physician himself, Henry, as the younger child, opted for a different path, deciding to become a lawyer. In the spring of 1802, he commenced the first of three clerkships that he would pursue in his effort to acquire the requisite legal knowledge and skills. Dissatisfied with both of the clerkships that he undertook in Kingston, he moved to New York City in March 1805 to begin a third, in the office of Roger Strong and Ogden Edwards, after which he finally determined that he was ready to enter practice on his own. In November 1805, he was licensed by Chief Justice Kent to practice as an attorney before the New York Supreme Court, and he began searching for a town in the relatively uninhabited Western part of the state where he might commence law practice without significant competition. After seeking the advice of, among others, several members of the state legislature, he settled upon Oxford, to which he moved in May 1806, at the age of twenty-two.[94]

As recollected by Vanderlyn in the spring of 1827, his decision to move to Oxford was the key to the success he thereafter achieved as a lawyer because it enabled him to become a good orator. While often asked during his clerkships

Figure 6  John Vanderlyn (American, 1775–1852), *Henry Vanderlyn* (circa 1815), oil on canvas, 26 $\frac{5}{8}$ × 21 $\frac{1}{2}$ inches. Courtesy of the Saint Louis Art Museum, Bequest of Edith J. and C. C. Johnson Spink 29:2014.

to assist in the trial of small matters before justices of the peace, "so great was my timidity and bashfulness, [that] I never dared to open my lips, and had got an idea that I could not become an extempore speaker." Fortunately for his later professional development, the move to Oxford left him entirely on his own, such that "necessity and pride urged me to burst the shell, and I went through the trial of an action of trespass in a Justice's Court." Because a lawyer's success depended first and foremost on his skills within the courtroom, Vanderlyn credited his move to Oxford for all his subsequent achievements in the law:

> Had I remained in Kingston it is most certain that I should not have dared to burst the chains of my timidity, and I should have been . . . unknown and unimportant. . . . Because without the talents of an advocate, I should have been without business and consequently without

ambition. Thus I am indebted for all I have been and may be in my profession to the resolution of commencing my career among strangers in
this new part of the state.[95]

To be a lawyer, in short, was to be an orator.

Vanderlyn's lifelong obsession with oratory, however, was not simply a
product of his recognition that it was key to obtaining professional success in
the narrow material sense. His desire to succeed as a lawyer was itself part of
a deeper republican longing to be perceived as a key civic leader, devoted to
promoting the welfare of the new American republic. It is this civic republican
worldview, pursuant to which oratory was an essential tool for guiding and
prodding one's fellow citizens to virtue, that shaped his self-understanding as
a man and a lawyer. If we are to comprehend the profound ways that civic republicanism influenced his conception of procedural justice, we must therefore begin by stepping back and surveying how it shaped his self-understanding
more generally.

## EDUCATION

Like so many of his generation, Vanderlyn embraced a civic republican
ideal of education as a core foundation of citizenship. Only those who were
properly educated in the liberal arts and were thus exposed to the Western
tradition of moral and political thought—including that of the ancient world—
could be expected to fulfill their civic obligation virtuously to devote themselves to the public good. And a core component of this civic republican ideal
of education was its focus on oratory. It was through oratory that a student
demonstrated his mastery of knowledge—and most importantly, proved his
capacity to engage in the essential civic function of governance, which required the better sort to assume the responsibility of guiding their fellow citizens by means of persuasive argument. Those of superior talent and virtue,
who had mastered these foundational elements of the Western tradition,
might then study to become lawyers and thus to implement those principles
of moral and political virtue necessary for the republic to thrive.

Vanderlyn's civic republican conception of education as a foundation of
citizenship—including, the view that legal study was key to the formation of
an elite civic leadership—is captured by a lengthy newspaper clipping that,
with evident admiration, he pasted into his diary on November 27, 1846. This
article was a reprinting of a letter written by famed South Carolina lawyer and
politician Hugh Legaré in October 1841, shortly before his death, "in reply to

the inquiries of a young, Carolina planter relative to the studies best adapted to qualify him to play a useful and honorable part, as a public man, in the affairs of his native land." Legaré's response was that the young man should first pursue a broad liberal arts education, focusing on the classics, and then study to become a lawyer: "The sort of education you would give yourself is that of the citizen of an ancient commonwealth—which always fitted him to 'perform all the offices, public and private, of peace and war.' . . . This being assumed, you must begin by making yourself a *lawyer,* and a thorough one."[96]

Embracing the civic republican conception of education to which Legaré gave voice, Vanderlyn devoted a significant amount of time and energy to improving schooling in Oxford. He claimed to have taken the lead in founding an "infant school," opened on June 1, 1831, which was designed to be of "superior usefulness to children." But his greatest pride stemmed from the role he played as treasurer and member of the executive committee of the local academy, which was reopened in 1821, after having been "entirely abandoned for a period of 16 years," and which was lauded by an 1860 gazetteer as an institution that "for many years bore the highest reputation of any academy w[est] of the Hudson."[97] While frequently complaining that Oxford's other leading citizens lacked his willingness selflessly to devote himself to the virtuous cause of education, he remarked with pride that his efforts on behalf of the academy proved "how much happiness the exertions of a single individual are able to dispense among the publick." As he contentedly concluded, the knowledge of having served the public good was "a better reward than the gratifications of appetite or selfish desire."[98]

Lacking any children of his own, Vanderlyn sought to implement his republican pedagogical philosophy through his role as doting uncle to the four children of his younger brother, a farmer named Gerardus, or Garry. Vanderlyn lived with Garry and his family and, as portrayed in the diary, came to serve as the family's financial and moral head. As de facto patriarch, he was deeply attentive to the schooling of his brother's children—and especially to that of the two oldest sons, Henry and Peter. Like his father before him, Vanderlyn focused on the development of his nephews' oratorical skills, tutoring them at home and cheering their performances in the public examinations held as part of their schooling at the local academy. He took particular pride in his nephews' successes in declaiming famous political speeches, such as "the best peroration of Daniel Webster's speech on the union against nullification."[99] So too, Vanderlyn regularly sought his nephews' company at the two events that showcased the importance of oratory in republican self-governance and in which he himself enthusiastically participated: political party meetings and litigation.[100]

## POLITICS

Like many lawyers, Vanderlyn had a complex, love-hate relationship with politics—and, in particular, party politics. Having imbibed classical republican principles, he was firmly of the view that a leading, virtuous elite ought to take a dominant role in political affairs, helping to guide the masses (through powerful oratory) to virtuous self-governance. So too, he believed that lawyers' distinctive capacity for forensic oratory made them best suited to serve as such an elite. At the same time, the emergence of an increasingly fractious system of party politics seemed to augur the rise of a dangerous new class of civic leaders, who—instead of being independent agents virtuously serving the broader public good—were beholden to political party bosses and their patronage.[101]

Vanderlyn himself was actively involved in party politics throughout much of his life. Until William Seward, then a Whig senator from New York, spoke out against the Compromise of 1850—designed to prevent the onset of civil war—he was a deeply devoted Whig. But from 1850 onward, he divorced himself from that portion of the Whig Party that would soon form the new Republican Party and aligned himself instead with those (Whigs and Hunker Democrats) who called for the formation of a new Union Party. At all times, however, regardless of party affiliation, he kept apprised of political events and lionized those leaders who, through their oratory, exhorted the nation toward virtue—understood by Vanderlyn to mean the preservation of the union at any cost. Moreover, for many years, he actively participated in the local political party meetings—first Whig and then pro-Union—that took place in advance of elections and that became increasingly agitated as the issue of slavery proved ever more divisive.

As Vanderlyn would record both at the time and thereafter, one of the great highlights of his life was the period that he spent in Washington, D.C., during the fall and winter of 1836–37. The resident of a small, rural town, he was awed by the comparative grandeur of the nation's capital and its civic elite. But the primary thrill afforded by this sojourn was the opportunity to observe Congress in session and thus to witness the oratory of the nation's greatest statesmen. As he recounted in a letter to a friend, "What a luxury it is to see and peruse the interesting countenances of messieurs Webster, Clay, Crittenden, Calhoun, Rives, and Preston. I became acquainted with each of these distinguished

statesmen and orators and witnessed day after day the flights of their eloquence." But it was not only national politicians and their oratory that interested Vanderlyn. Equally concerned with state and local matters, he recorded,
for example, that on October 8, 1852, he attended a series of speeches given by
then-governor Horatio Seymour and a number of lesser lights in the neighboring town of Norwich. Rather than reflecting on the substance of what he heard,
he devoted most of his attention to commenting on each speaker's distinctive
rhetorical style, noting that one was "dull [and] heavy," while the other was full
of "vim and zeal."[102]

Although an avid consumer of political oratory, Vanderlyn was concerned
first and foremost with his own speech-making abilities. As he later recounted,
he made his first speech at a political meeting quite late in life—on August 27,
1834, when he was already fifty years old. The occasion was a meeting of Whig
Party members held at General De Forrest's, a hotel and tavern in Norwich.
According to Vanderlyn, he had not planned to give a speech but only to participate in organizing the group. Persuaded, however, that the fate of the republic was deeply threatened by Jacksonian demagoguery, he spontaneously
rose to his feet to deliver a powerful speech against the dangers of corruption:
"I was induced by the great occasion without any preparation and contrary to
my previous determination, to address the meeting and succeeded to make an
impressive speech on the corruptions and usurpations of our present rulers."
Evidently inspired by this initial success in "discharg[ing] the duty of a freeman and a patriot," Vanderlyn thereafter repeatedly made speeches at the political party meetings held in advance of elections.[103]

But while actively involved in party politics, Vanderlyn repeatedly
proclaimed—especially after (or in anticipation of) Whig losses suffered at the
hands of the Albany Regency—that he would cease all such involvement and
focus exclusively on the law. For him, as for so many influenced by civic republican thought, party politics were deeply troubling in that they seemed to demand a loyalty to private or sectional interests over and above the public good.
As he observed, "the pleasing vision of a patriotic people moving in unison for
the public good I must hereafter look upon as a thing seldom, very seldom to
be realized." The law, in contrast, seemed to offer the promise of a form of
neutral, nonpolitical expertise that might be exercised in service of the public
good without regard to narrow, sectarian interests.[104]

Pursuant to this republican model of the law, it was precisely because the
lawyer was an independent agent—not beholden to particular parties and
their patronage—that he was able to act as a virtuous citizen promoting the

public good. Accordingly, Vanderlyn took great pride in his decision (unlike many other lawyers, including colleagues and friends) not to run for political office and to decline partisan appointments. Prior to becoming an ardent Federalist and then Whig, he explained in his diary, he had supported the campaign of Morgan Lewis for governor of New York. As a reward for this support, he was appointed to serve as master in chancery—a position that he shortly thereafter lost when Daniel Tompkins was elected as the next governor. This experience led him to conclude that he was

> unfitted for a mere shifting politician and preferr[ed] to follow the independent dictates of my own judgment, rather than obey the selfish dictates of aspiring office hunters. This course has been invariably pursued by me to the present day and I have never repented of my voluntarily remaining as a private citizen. I have been the better able to pursue my profession which has brought me the blessings of independence in mind and property and enabled me to be useful to my relations and fellow men and I have seen most of my professional brethren in Chenango pursue with zeal the phantom of popularity after some office and while doing so relax their studies and their professional ambition and in the end they were disappointed and neglected as a politician and as an advocate. Hence they are generally poor and idle. Every young man should depend on his profession only and seek for eminence in that; and not turn aside to bluster in politicks and spend his time in retailing the political lies of the day, in attending and addressing publick meetings, all which will shortly end in poverty and disappointment.[105]

As this language suggests, Vanderlyn's motives in declining office were not entirely as virtuous as he liked to suggest and stemmed, at least in part, from more pedestrian concerns—including, most importantly, a belief that he could earn substantially more money focusing full-time on the practice of law. But such material interests could (and did) coexist with more purely ideological ones.[106] Vanderlyn's very self-conception as a virtuous republican lawyer hinged on his independence from potentially corrupting influences—and this, in turn, made political party loyalties quite troubling. While he overcame these concerns to the extent that he became actively involved in party politics from 1834 onward, he made no effort to pursue public office and in fact declined an appointment as master in chancery in 1840.[107]

For Vanderlyn, then, the practice of law was valuable because it enabled an escape from politics—but not just any escape. While permitting a retreat from sectional, partisan interests, law shared with politics a concern with actively promoting the public good. And it required of its practitioners many of the same talents and skills, including "forensic oratory." This commonality between politics and law—one that led many lawyers to seek and excel in political office—was reinforced in the antebellum period even at the level of physical space. Especially in the undeveloped parts of the state (and nation) to the west, civic infrastructure remained relatively primitive, and it was thus the courthouse that often served as a meeting place for large numbers of politically engaged citizens. As Vanderlyn observed, sessions of the common pleas and circuit courts (and after 1847, the newly formed supreme court) were regularly punctuated by political activity of various kinds, focused on such matters as temperance, canal construction, and the presentation of dueling party speeches.[108] For the many community members who attended the courthouse to listen to the same group of lawyer-orators deliver speeches on both political matters and lawsuits, it must indeed have seemed that, as lawyers like Vanderlyn eagerly insisted, they were the new nation's natural leaders.

## LAW

For Vanderlyn, like so many others, the law constituted an opportunity to pursue virtue, while eschewing the corrupting dangers of party politics. The product of centuries of moral and political refinement, the law represented the accumulated wisdom of the ages as well as the distinctive genius of the American people. As such, it provided the essential tools for constructing the new social and political order. In this sense, all legal work—including not only courtroom argument but also transactional practice—served the cause of virtue. But in reality, however valuable a lawyer's office work might be, it was courtroom argument that came to serve as the foundation of his identity, because only it enabled him to engage in republican self-display and thus to prove his virtue (to himself and others). Such self-display, in turn, profoundly shaped commonly held conceptions of the lawyer's courtroom role and, as a result, procedural justice.

The extent to which Vanderlyn viewed courtroom argument, including both speech-making and cross-examination, as key to his professional identity is suggested by the way he recorded his legal activities in his diary. As a careful reading of his diary makes clear, Vanderlyn spent a great deal of time and effort assisting clients in transactional matters. He helped business partners draw up partnership agreements, settle their accounts, and dissolve their partnerships. He drafted deeds for the transfer of interests in real estate, and he prepared judgment bonds to secure extensions of credit, particularly through negotiable instruments like promissory notes. But while Vanderlyn's office work was an essential part of his professional practice and vital to his financial security, it was in no way central to his self-definition as a lawyer. In contrast to his courtroom performances, to which he frequently devoted many paragraphs or even pages of his diary, such transactional matters are generally relegated to a few brief lines.[109] Moreover, these brief accounts of his transactional business appear primarily in those volumes of his diary devoted to preserving only the "fleeting occurrences of each day." The volumes in which he recorded his "more extended and matured thoughts"—and from which he most often read to others—largely gloss over such transactional matters, focusing instead on lengthy accounts of litigation.

Because it facilitated his efforts at republican self-display, Vanderlyn's courtroom performance came to lie at the heart of his self-conception as a lawyer. But only certain kinds of courtroom activity—those associated with the procedural mechanisms of the common law, rather than equity—enabled such self-display. These procedural mechanisms were, most importantly, jury argument and oral, adversarial cross-examination—in a public forum. As lawyers like Vanderlyn came widely to embrace these mechanisms as the epitome of procedural justice, a legal culture emerged that was increasingly inhospitable to the alternative traditions of equity.

In many ways, Vanderlyn's account of his legal practice reads as an extended reflection on the importance of jury argument, cross-examination, and public proceedings. Looking back on his life at the age of forty-three, he happily recalled his many successful jury arguments, observing that those in which he took the most pride were in lawsuits concerning "fraudulent sales." By helping to protect the hapless creditor from the snares of the wily and self-serving debtor, Vanderlyn contentedly reported, he proved himself to be a civic leader devoted to (and capable of) preserving the law and order so essential for the new republic to thrive: "The desire to defeat these schemes and punish the conspirators and restore the sense of justice in the community induced me whenever they fell in my way to hunt down the villains who expect to thrive by fraud upon the property of others."[110] As he emphasized, the pursuit of virtue came at a cost—one that he was selflessly willing to pay: "In thus fearlessly breaking up these nests of deceit I have made myself some enemies and undergone much fatigue, . . . and anxiety. . . ." However costly these endeavors, the rewards were also great, consisting primarily of moral satisfaction and professional acclaim but also, he acknowledged, of significant financial gain: "I have been rewarded by the consciousness of duty and the sense of justice, and even in a pecuniary view the success of my exertions had been well rewarded. My station as an advocate has also been elevated in the county."[III]

It was through oratory—especially oratory that revealed the speaker's own passion for justice—that the lawyer was able to vindicate virtue in the courtroom and, not insignificantly, display his own virtue. As Vanderlyn observed on February 16, 1828, thus drawing a lesson from the ancient orators he so admired, pathos was the key to great oratory: "The warm emotions of the heart are at the bottom of all true oratory and he who has not much sensibility and much kindness can never become an eloquent speaker. Judge of Pliny by what is known of him in his Letters and he must have been a grand and pathetic speaker." Accordingly, Vanderlyn's diary is filled with detailed accounts of those occasions when he managed to convey through his courtroom speeches his own moral indignation and outrage. On October 12, 1830, for example, he described a suit that he brought at the Common Pleas Court in Norwich on behalf of Samuel Garnsey, who was suing his agent, William Bush, "to recover . . . the proceeds of 14 barrels of cider" that Bush had agreed to sell on his behalf. As recorded by Vanderlyn, he closed the suit by calling on the jury to join him in promoting the cause of virtue and punishing the corrupt:

> I had made no preparation for any display, but was in full possession of all the facts. I began in a plain and simple way and gradually warmed into zeal as I proceeded without any consciousness that I was doing anything extraordinary. I introduced insensibly a good deal of action into my delivery and many vivid images of the defendant's depravity and falsehood, the value of integrity and the paramount duty of a jury to support fair dealing and to punish guilt and prevarication. I lifted up the curtain which hid defendant's depravity from view and laid him bare to the eyes of the jury.

As he happily concluded in reflecting back on his week at court, "I am . . . much pleased with the result of my last week's operations and humbly thankful to God for my exertions in the cause of honesty against fraud. It will increase my zeal for virtue and add perhaps something to my usefulness as a man and a citizen."[112]

As Vanderlyn understood it, great courtroom oratory hinged not only on the lawyer's opening and closing arguments to the jury. At least as important was his ability to examine witnesses—and most especially, to cross-examine them. Like the opening and closing arguments, examination and cross-examination were the means by which the lawyer used his words, tone, and gestures to convey himself and his message to his audience. Thus, in describing one of his lawyer heroes, Elisha Williams from the town of Hudson in Columbia County, Vanderlyn depicted cross-examination as but one facet of the latter's genius for courtroom oratory:

> This renowned advocate has been lord of the ascendant at the bar for the last 27 years. . . . He was formed by nature for a great and accomplished orator. His appearance is commanding, his voice excellent, and his delivery graceful: He possesses the rarest endowments of the mind, an extensive knowledge of human nature, and all its concerns, the readiest wit and cutting satire. He is unequalled in America as an advocate before a jury. There he is in his element and seems to feel that he has no competitor. He marshalls the facts of the most complicated suit with the power and facility that is astonishing to every audience. His entire self-command and confidence gives him the perfect control of all his energies and enables him at his will to resemble the rushing torrent or the gentle and placid stream. In cross-examining witnesses, one of the most important duties of an advocate, he is very successful. His mind has a vision capable of embracing the most extensive subjects and he goes through the most extended speeches with an order and a lucidity and with an eloquence that I have never elsewhere witnessed.[113]

Cross-examination was central to courtroom oratory, however, not only because it drew on the same basic skills (of intellect, eloquence, and passion) so essential to good speech-making but because it too aimed to vindicate virtue. Indeed, cross-examination was perhaps the lawyer's most potent and dramatic tool for pursuing (and thus displaying his own commitment to) virtue.

Consider, for example, the role that cross-examination played, according to Vanderlyn, in enabling him to win a lawsuit that he viewed as one of the highlights of his career. As he described it, the *Achorn* suit entailed "much toil and anxiety in ferreting out the hiding places of fraud and deceit." Vanderlyn's clients in this case were three women (represented by their husbands), who were suing their step-mother, Jemima, for fraudulently "g[e]t[ting] old Achorn to make a will and devise to her ¼ of all his real and personal estate during her widowhood."[114] As depicted by Vanderlyn, Jemima was the very image of a woman without virtue. Lacking in both scruples and chastity, she married Andrew Achorn, even though she herself was already married, with the goal of obtaining his valuable property. Toward this end, "[s]he employed Benjamin Birdsall, an unprincipled villain of Green (who happened to be a commissioner to acknowledge deeds) to come with a deed ready drawn to Achorn's and in a moment of excessive drunkenness got his signature to the deed." According to Vanderlyn, the wicked stepmother's carefully laid plot would have borne fruit, but for his brilliant cross-examination, which brought to light her many deceptions. As Vanderlyn gloated, "Birdsall was sworn as a witness to support the deed. I was 6 days engaged in cross-examining him and completely succeeded in involving this infamous villain in a dozen or more flat and positive contradictions and perjuries."[115]

The centrality of courtroom oratory (including both speech-making and cross-examination) to Vanderlyn's self-conception as a lawyer stemmed from its utility as a mechanism for republican self-display—a means, in other words, of showcasing the lawyer's republican commitment to the pursuit of virtue. It was therefore essential that an audience be available to witness the lawyer's courtroom exertions. As Vanderlyn observed in October 1831, "[T]o understand a cause well in all its various views and all the topics connected with it is essential to an advocate. Then, if he has genius or eloquence, the zeal and spirit excited by debate before an audience will awaken those secret and mysterious powers of eloquence and argument, which are apt to create surprize and admiration."[116] The antebellum proliferation of local courts (including low-level justices of the peace) helped to ensure that all lawyers would have some audience to witness their efforts—one more readily available than that provided, for example, by the relatively distant state legislature. This audience consisted not only of the judge and jury, who had the power to decide the case, but also of attending members of the public, including clients themselves and, perhaps most importantly, fellow lawyers.

By persuading the jurors and other members of the public that he was a great orator—passionately devoted to pursuing justice—Vanderlyn hoped not only to win the case but also to establish his own virtue and thus his entitlement to a position of civic leadership. In the relatively small rural communities of antebellum America, the notion that a lawyer's successful jury argument might translate into civic authority was no mere abstraction. Lawyers who argued before local juries were frequently arguing before some individuals (in the jury and the audience) whom they knew personally, or at least by reputation. This was certainly true of Vanderlyn. In describing his successful closing in the *Garnsey* suit, he thus happily observed that "Mr. John Adams, a shoemaker and Mr. Balcom, son of Col. Balcom, both of Oxford were on the jury."[117] And in a December 21, 1848, suit before the newly established supreme court at Norwich, Vanderlyn expressed joy that there was a large audience in attendance—including at least one neighbor—all of whom admired his performance: "I never made so good a speech all agree and considering the ordinary speeches of our courts, this will long be remembered as a handsome display of forensic eloquence. My neighbor, C. A. Hunt, who was present, was overjoyed at its resounding effect on the defendant and on the admiration of the large audience."[118] So too, lawyers regularly argued before their clients, for whose approval they were of course particularly eager. Thus, for example, in January of the same year, Vanderlyn made a point of remarking that his closing was "a brilliant and well reasoned argument [made] to the great satisfaction of . . . my client."[119]

But while Vanderlyn cared a great deal about how members of the jury, the general public, and clients assessed his oratory, it was the judgment of his fellow lawyers that mattered to him most of all. He thus usually made a point of noting which lawyers attended the court sessions at which he argued and what they thought of his performances. For example, on January 23, 1848, he recorded with pride the many lawyers from the surrounding area who were present to witness his triumph defending a suit before the supreme court at Norwich: "I made the closing speech before a goodly number of lawyers from abroad, among whom were Gordon, Parker, Palmer, More and Wheeler of Delaware, Becker, Chatfield, Lathrop, Fery, and Sturges of Otsego, etc. I . . . made a brilliant and well reasoned argument. . . . There was not besides in this cause any good speaking and no good law argument during the first week."[120] Indeed, according to Vanderlyn, his fellow lawyers held his courtroom oratory in such high esteem that there were occasions when, even though he had not intended to address the jury, they called on him to do so—and he could not resist their demands. This is precisely what happened, he claimed, in a February 9, 1836, lawsuit in which he was serving as co-counsel: "I intended not to address the jury but several members of the bar insisted on my summing up and I rose and addressed the jury in a style, zeal and manner exceeding I think any of my former efforts. Such I believe was the general impression."[121]

The importance that Vanderlyn placed on how his fellow lawyers assessed his courtroom efforts at republican self-display was reinforced by the fact that he knew most of these individuals personally, or at least by reputation. Although the bar expanded significantly in the period leading up to the Civil War, it remained relatively small, such that most lawyers in a given region knew one another—especially in the rural areas where the majority of the population continued to live. When Vanderlyn first moved to Oxford in 1806, there was only one other lawyer in town.[122] While over twenty years later the number had grown, it could still be counted on two hands. As Vanderlyn recorded in his diary in October 1827, there were then six lawyers living in Oxford (including Vanderlyn himself), but only he and one other "do all the heavy business in this place." Of the remaining four, one no longer practiced law, a second was a judge and thus "does little or no law business," and a third "lives on the property got by his wife and relations." The fourth was a former student of Vanderlyn's who had unwisely opened his own office in town, only to abandon it and the town one year later. As for the neighboring towns within the county, Vanderlyn reported that each had between one to three lawyers. And as late as June 1846, he claimed that "[t]here are now 49 attorneys in the county."[123] Thus, while Vanderlyn, like other lawyers of the period, complained of increasingly bitter competition in law practice, there were sufficiently few lawyers within his general locale that he could easily be (more or less) acquainted with all.

In addition to the relatively small size of the bar, the structure of the antebellum judiciary further served to ensure that lawyers in a given region would come to know one another personally. Because of the relative difficulty of travel in this era, courts typically did not sit every day of the week but instead periodically, in sessions. This enabled lawyers from the surrounding areas to travel to court—often together—and stay in town until the session was completed.[124] In an age when travel was relatively slow and at times (especially in winter conditions) dangerous, such travel provided plenty of opportunity for bonding on the road. Even the relatively short eight-mile distance from Oxford to Norwich—which, as the county seat, housed both the common pleas court and (after 1823) the circuit court—could easily take an hour when traveling by horse-drawn carriage; in poor conditions, that time might double. Vanderlyn's diary thus includes many accounts of the fellow lawyers with whom he traveled to court in frequently difficult circumstances. Moreover, once lawyers arrived at the courthouse, they generally stayed together at the same inn, sharing meals and even bedrooms. And since there was often little else to do in town, they spent many hours chatting. Writing in his diary in January 1844, Vanderlyn described his experience talking with fellow lawyers who attended court at Norwich as the best possible entertainment: "I enjoyed myself in merriment and laughter more so than at an opera." Indeed, Vanderlyn so enjoyed his time with fellow lawyers at court that even when he decided in his late sixties to stop litigating cases, he continued to attend court sessions for the entertainment that they provided.[125]

Personally acquainted with so many of the lawyers who observed his court-room arguments, Vanderlyn—like a great many of his professional peers—viewed the legal profession as a kind of brotherhood.[126] In bemoaning the lack of communal feeling among the clergymen representing the various Christian sects established in Oxford, he argued that these clergy could learn much about true brotherhood from the example of lawyers. While there was a long tradition of stigmatizing lawyers as self-interested disrupters of harmony seeking to profit from conflict, the reality, insisted Vanderlyn, was that the legal profession was the very model of fraternity: "No social visits nor brotherly love exists between [members of the village clergy] as among the members of the bar."[127] But with brotherly love came brotherly competition, such that Vanderlyn invested enormously in persuading his fellow lawyers, above all others, of his merits as a great courtroom orator and, by implication, a man of virtue.

The status anxieties that followed from lawyers' sense of brotherhood were exacerbated by their (exaggerated but deeply felt) concern that, due to Jacksonian reforms loosening requirements for entry into the profession, the size of the bar was expanding, thus increasing competition. As early as October 1827, Vanderlyn bemoaned the growing number of men who, though lacking the skills of their more elite predecessors, were being licensed to practice law: "A crowd of desperate adventurers were at work in every part of the state in breeding lawsuits and pillaging the pockets of hard earned industry." Twenty years later, in December 1847, such complaints reached near fever pitch:

> Great change in admitting attorneys to practice in courts. The late session of the legislature at Albany passed a law that any one licensed or not licensed, black or white, male or female, might act as attorney and counsel in all our courts. No examination is necessary. . . . [There is reason to fear] that these continued and radical changes will prove very injurious to the public and to all litigants who intrust their business to these new and ignorant men who will now rush into the practice. Our state has been woefully degraded and injured. . . .[128]

For Vanderlyn, this degradation of the profession was personified by Abial Cooke, a Democratic lawyer from the neighboring town of Norwich, whom he depicted (in prototypically Whig fashion) as one of the new breed of pandering and talentless men elevated to power by the nation's recent democratic turn:

Cooke a lawyer of Norwich appeared this morning in court in a pair of old shoes that were of the coarsest, thickest bull hide leather being never blackened. They were white and hard as granite. I never saw a teamster or slave in coarser shoes. This is all affectation, to become popular among the vulgar, upon whose votes he depends to be elected to Congress, for which he has a big ambition. Sometimes he wears an old coat with large steel buttons and a miller's hat to catch the notice of the common people. He has some talents, no industry and no law knowledge and delights in the conversation of barrooms or in stories and caricatures which raise a horse laugh.[129]

As suggested by Vanderlyn's focus on Cooke's desire for public office, the threat posed by Cooke and others like him was not simply competition in the narrow, material sense, though that of course mattered. Equally troubling was a feared loss of status—a fear, in short, that the public would cease to be able to distinguish between those lawyers who were worthy of its esteem and those who were not. Put differently, while Vanderlyn might not want to be elected, he nonetheless wished to be recognized as someone worthy of election—unlike his vulgar competitor Cooke. And as he understood it, the courtroom art of republican self-display was tailor-made for the pursuit of such recognition. Through such display, Vanderlyn assured himself, his distinctive virtue would shine forth, and others would recognize his superiority to Cooke—a man "of low habits, great indolence and ignorance of the affairs of government and qualified only for a pettifogger."[130] As this suggests, the legal fraternity itself (and the competition for power and status within it) provided a key motivation for lawyers to engage in republican self-display, thus helping to ensure the triumph of a procedural culture dominated by public oral argument and adversarial cross-examination.

## Reconceptualizing Procedural Reform: The Decline of (Quasi-Inquisitorial) Equity and the Emergence of (Oral, Adversarial) "Procedure"

Seeking to justify their claims to social and political leadership, antebellum lawyers rushed to engage in the republican self-display that would prove their devotion to the cause of virtue and thus to the welfare of the republic. In this way, the discourse and ideology of civic republicanism, while failing to translate into the kinds of rules of professional ethics for which scholars have searched, did specify the contours of the lawyer's courtroom role. The result, in turn, was to generate a unified, overarching model of procedural justice, the defining features of which were public jury argument, including adversarial cross-examination. To the extent that modes of adjudication failed to comply with this model, they began to seem undesirable—even illegitimate—in ways that had never before been the case.

The extent to which antebellum lawyers came to embrace a single model of procedural justice, characterized by public, oral argument and cross-examination, is suggested by Vanderlyn's descriptions of the many proceedings before arbitrators or referees in which he was involved (either as counsel or as arbitrator/referee).[131] One might have expected that arbitral proceedings would be characterized by significantly less procedural formality than courtroom adjudications. Indeed, the established wisdom is that such proceedings were frequently employed by merchants (at least until the early nineteenth century), precisely because they afforded a mode of dispute resolution that was both faster and cheaper than formal litigation.[132] But while the scholarly literature has focused largely on commercial arbitration, the extrajudicial proceedings described by Vanderlyn often had nothing to do with merchants' disputes and concerned instead the broad range of parties and matters that came before the state's formal judicial institutions.[133] Moreover, Vanderlyn's accounts of such proceedings suggest that they unfolded much like ordinary common-law litigation—but for the absence of a jury.

Vanderlyn's April 22, 1828, account of the "Whitehall arbitration," for example, reads very much like his descriptions of the many lawsuits he litigated, and he in fact repeatedly referred to the proceedings as a "trial." The events leading to this "trial" commenced the previous fall, when the complaining party, William Whitehall, traveled from his home in Smithville, a town in Chenango County, to New York City. As Vanderlyn explained, "[d]uring his absence, his brother-in-law Mr. Oakley Beebe conspired with his sister, the wife of Mr. Whitehall, to plunder all his personal effects of the value of about $460 and to elope from his bed and board (as the phrase is) and to take with them the two infant children of Mr. W[hitehall]." In this alleged conspiracy, Beebe and Mrs. Whitehall were assisted by the two "Defendants, who came to the dwelling house of Mr. W[hitehall] in the night with two wagons to transport the goods to Syracuse to the house of one Van Tapel, the father of Oakley Beebe's wife."[134] Seeking damages for trespass, Whitehall had initially filed suit in the supreme court, but perhaps in an effort to save costs, the parties ultimately agreed to arbitration.

Held in Oxford, the arbitration proceeded in nearly all respects just like a formal litigation. While the deciding arbitrators were private individuals empowered by agreement of the parties, rather than public officers acting in the name of the state, all three appear to have been lawyers, and one (John Tracy) was in fact the first judge of the county's Court of Common Pleas. The parties, moreover, were all represented by counsel—with Vanderlyn and his friend James Clapp representing the plaintiff and Simon Throop representing the defendants. As Vanderlyn described it, "this arduous trial" lasted approximately four days—running from April 17 through April 21—and was attended by much of the local community, including no doubt many people from the town of Smithville, eight miles away, who were very curious about their neighbors' troubled domestic affairs.[135] In Vanderlyn's words, "Great excitement prevailed among the people which induced the attendance of a large audience from day to day." Precisely where the arbitration was held is unclear, as there was no courthouse in Oxford. But given the substantial audience in attendance, a sizable venue must have been selected—and based on Vanderlyn's reports of other arbitrations in town, it seems likely that this was the local inn and tavern (Perkins' Hotel). Notably, however, throughout his report of the proceedings, Vanderlyn referred to the "court" and "court room" as the physical space in which the arbitration took place.[136]

Vanderlyn's tendency thus to lapse into the belief that he was actually arguing in court was encouraged by the fact that the proceedings themselves seem to have followed the ordinary course of common-law adjudication—commencing with opening statements, followed by the parties' respective presentation of sworn witnesses (who were duly examined and cross-examined), and ending with closing arguments. Moreover, as in much ordinary litigation, the lawyers' "courtroom" oratory, including speech-making and cross-examination, appears to have dragged on for hours. Vanderlyn noted that his cross-examination of the defendant's main witness—Oakley Beebe—lasted for six hours. Similarly, defense counsel's closing argument "consumed 6 hours," while Vanderlyn and Clapp each presented an approximately two-hour closing on behalf of the plaintiff.[137]

As in his accounts of the many ordinary lawsuits he argued, Vanderlyn made a particular point of emphasizing his oratorical triumphs, including, most importantly, his brilliant cross-examination: "On Saturday a.m. Oakley Beebe was sworn a witness for defendants. This villain stepped glibly on his direct examination through a train of prepared falsehoods. I began his cross-examination before dinner and continued it 6 hours. He staggered under the weight of his guilt and evinced great trepidation and guilt. At last we drew from him his full agency in the plot and his having procured the assistance of defendants to carry it into execution." Milking the drama of the moment for all it was worth, Vanderlyn ended the cross-examination by instructing his client, Whitehall, "to go to justice [of the peace] Wheeler and procure a warrant for the arrest of Oakley Beebe for larceny."[138]

According to Vanderlyn, his dramatic and successful cross-examination of Beebe was followed by a masterful closing argument, which served, like all great republican oratory, to advance the cause of virtue—here defined as encompassing the interests not only of his client, but also his own: "As Mr. T[hroop] had opened upon me his battery of abuse, I felt it my duty to expose him before the court and audience, and I was pleased with the success of my exertions on behalf of an injured old man. I returned home with gratified feelings, built up a fire in my office, eat [sic] a piece of pie, and smoked a cigar and then retired to bed contented and happy."[139] Vanderlyn's assessment of his (and his co-counsel's) success was evidently accurate, as about two weeks later, the arbitrators found for Whitehall, ordering the defendants to pay his costs from the initial supreme court filing, as well as the costs of the arbitration and $225 in damages for trespass.

But it was not only arbitrations that came to be characterized by the now-dominant features of the common-law trial. Even more dramatic was the transformation of equity. It was here that the imperatives of republican self-display (and the model of procedural justice to which they pointed) had the greatest impact. The logic of the republican model of procedural justice suggested that it was necessary to dispense with core aspects of longstanding equity practice. Particularly troubling was the fact that witnesses in equity were traditionally examined by a judicial officer outside the presence of counsel or any other members of the public—a practice that denied lawyers the opportunity to undertake oral, adversarial cross-examination and to do so before representatives of the public at large, including not least their clients.

Once testimony was taken, chancery did allow for oral argument, thereby providing lawyers the opportunity to make opening and closing statements before an audience—though, significantly, not a jury. But, in practice, this opportunity was not available to most New York lawyers. Because there was a single Court of Chancery, located in Albany (with occasional sessions in New York City), most lawyers had to travel a substantial distance to argue before it—a proposition that was rarely feasible as a matter of cost.[140] For this reason, they either had to hire local counsel in Albany to undertake oral argument on their behalf or rest satisfied with submitting the case on written arguments. The 1823 decision to endow circuit courts with first-instance equity jurisdiction ensured a more readily available forum, such that many more lawyers could thereafter undertake oral arguments in equity themselves. But the option to appeal meant that it was the argument before chancery—which most lawyers could not make—that might ultimately prove decisive.[141]

This disjunction between traditional equity practice and the new imperatives of republican self-display is an important reason why New York lawyers were so eager to appear in proceedings before masters and examiners—and in so doing, to undertake oral, adversarial examination and cross-examination. But what about the timing? How, in other words, do we explain the fact that, despite the prevalence of civic republican discourse in the founding era, chancery practitioners did not embrace oral, adversarial procedure until the early decades of the nineteenth century? This is no easy question. But it seems likely that at least part of the answer has to do with the democratization of politics, society, and the legal profession that began after 1800. Although many barriers to entry into the bar would not be removed until the Jacksonian era, the first decades of the nineteenth century witnessed an expansion of the profession.[142] With this expansion came new pressures to compete—pressures that made adversarial procedure and the republican self-display that it facilitated particularly appealing.

At the same time, it is probable that Kent's efforts clearly to conceptualize (and firmly to root) the quasi-inquisitorial underpinnings of equity made the nature of equity practice suddenly much more visible and therefore intolerable. As we have seen, Kent embraced an elitist conception of equity and its procedure, which he framed in civic republican terms—as a way of promoting the establishment of a select group of powerful (and Federalist) judges who would devote themselves to serving the public good. But Kent's very success in linking equity to this elitist social and political vision contributed significantly to legislators' growing animosity against chancery. So too, while harder to document, this same vision likely inspired similar sentiments among practicing lawyers—especially given the high percentage of legislators who were themselves lawyers. Rejecting Kent's effort to identify a narrow group of (Federalist) equity judges as the nation's civic republican elite, lawyers as a whole claimed the republican mantle of leadership for themselves. Accordingly, despite the earlier predominance of civic republican thought, it was not until the early nineteenth century that the imperatives of republican self-display first emerged.

In thus transforming the way in which testimony was taken in equity, antebellum lawyers like Vanderlyn were able to ensure that these proceedings would provide them with the opportunities for republican self-display that they had come to view as the defining feature of their role as lawyers. Accordingly, Vanderlyn's descriptions of equity proceedings for the taking of testimony are nearly indistinguishable from his accounts of the examination and cross-examination of witnesses in common-law trials (or for that matter, in arbitrations and references).

Consider, for example, Vanderlyn's account of the *Achorn* suit in which he so prided himself for proving the misdoings of the wicked stepmother, Jemima, who had fraudulently sought to obtain a large share of her husband's property, thus wronging his rightful heirs. Though only a careful reading of his account would so indicate, this was, in fact, a suit filed in chancery. And the key turning point in the case, which ultimately ensured the victory of the plaintiffs, was Vanderlyn's oral, adversarial cross-examination of Birdsall, the rogue commissioner to acknowledge deeds, who assisted Jemima in her evil plot: "When the suit in chancery was commenced by me in August 1825 no evidence was known to us by which the fraud could be proved but time unfolded to me many circumstances of deep suspicion, and at last on the cross examination of Ben Birdsall the author of the crime, I drew from him so many contradictions as completely established his perjury and this gained our cause." Because the suit was in equity, this cross-examination did not take place in the open courtroom but before a court-appointed commissioner: "[W]e produced and examined 30 witnesses to sustain our cause before John Tracy Jr. who was appointed a commissioner for that purpose."[143] But while the taking of testimony did not occur in open court, there is every reason to suspect that a sizable audience was in attendance. In particular, although Vanderlyn does not specify where the *Achorn* testimony was taken, his account of other suits in equity suggests that, given the large number of witnesses called, it was probably taken in Perkins' Hotel, the local inn and tavern—and therefore before a significant crowd.[144]

Even though it was filed in chancery, the *Achorn* suit thus provided Vanderlyn with an opportunity to engage in oral, adversarial cross-examination that was all but indistinguishable from that afforded by common-law proceedings. In Vanderlyn's view, in fact, it was this chancery suit that epitomized the benefits of cross-examination in uncovering fraud and thereby promoting the interests of virtue:

> In the course of this cause as well as on former occasions, I have been
> most forcibly reminded that there is a providence who controuls unseen
> the conduct of the guilty, whereby they are made against their will to

divulge their own guilt, which when perpetrated was unknown to human eyes or tongues other than their own. They seem to be left without a polar star to conduct them through the dark labyrinth of guilt. They are like the tempest lost vessel without guide or rudder. A sort of madness perverts the faculties of a guilty man and deprives him of common sense and prudence and drives him with his eyes open down the precipice.[145]

As this language suggests, lawyers like Vanderlyn came to embrace a uniform conception of what procedural justice entailed—one that provided maximal opportunity for their own republican self-display—such that traditional distinctions between law and equity ceased to make sense.

Vanderlyn was keenly aware, however, that in one key respect, the *Achorn* suit, as a chancery proceeding, denied him the full potential for republican self-display that a common-law adjudication would have afforded. Residing well over one hundred miles from Albany, Vanderlyn had to hire a local, Albany-based lawyer to undertake the oral argument before chancery once the taking of testimony was completed. This lawyer was the well-respected Harmanus Bleecker—a former Federalist member of the U.S. House of Representatives who would later become the American ambassador to the Hague.[146] In order to assist Bleecker, Vanderlyn devoted a great deal of time and effort to preparing a written argument for the latter's perusal:

> About the month of March 1827, I began to draw my written argument for the use of the counsel who was to argue the cause before the chancellor. It contained an abstract of the pleadings and the evidence to unfold the fraudulent means whereby the deed was obtained. I critically analyzed the answer of Jemima, which was full of falsehoods and contradicted by numerous witnesses. I probed the testimony of Birdsall and took each perjury contained in it seriatim and exposed it naked to view. I finished my argument the latter end of July 1827. . . .

As Vanderlyn noted in his diary with evident pride, Bleecker thereafter reported that this written argument was brilliant and that he, Bleecker, had relied on it extensively in making an oral argument to the court: "The papers were luckily safely delivered to Mr. B[leecker] and the cause argued on the 6th of September 1827. Immediately after I received a letter from Mr. Bleeker [*sic*] complimenting my full and excellent argument as he was pleased to call it, and which had been of great service to him. He mentioned that he had spoken all that was contained in my argument, with further suggestions of his own."[147]

Such assurances that his argument came before the court, if only indirectly, provided Vanderlyn with some consolation for what he had missed, but this vicarious thrill was no substitute for the real deal. It was only with the abolition of chancery in 1846 and the establishment of a single supreme court with jurisdiction in both law and equity—and multiple branches scattered throughout New York's counties—that lawyers like Vanderlyn were ensured a meaningful opportunity to undertake oral argument themselves in the large category of suits previously deemed equitable.

But well before New York's third constitutional convention was held and the decision was made to adopt "a uniform course of proceeding in all cases"[148]—and a single set of courts in which such uniform procedure might operate—a great many of the state's lawyers had come to conceptualize procedure in such a way that, in retrospect, these developments hardly seem surprising. Many lawyers of course resisted merger in the belief that such a seemingly radical transformation would run counter to a long tradition of the gradual, incremental refinement of the law over time—a tradition thought to lie at the heart of the distinctive Anglo-American legal genius.[149] Along these lines, George Templeton Strong responded to the (self-aggrandizing) statements of the Field Code commissioners that they intended to create an entirely new body of procedural rules by sarcastically observing in Burkean fashion that "all existing law and usage [was] to be swept away and a new system created *in vacuo* by these enlightened and modest jurists." Moreover, some elite lawyers no doubt feared that such officially sanctioned procedural changes might destroy the partial monopoly that they had acquired over suits in chancery, thus undermining a significant source of income. And others, like Strong himself, worried that by "reduc[ing] . . . legal practice to a Hottentot standard of simplicity and despatch," the code would open up law practice to any and all comers, thereby decreasing "legal emoluments."[150] But while the decision to create a uniform mode of procedure struck many contemporary lawyers as a dramatic turn of events, the reality was that they themselves had laid the groundwork for this development through their persistent efforts to engage in republican self-display (thus giving rise to an implicitly unified model of—oral and adversarial—procedural justice).

Indeed, it was not uncommon for lawyers in New York to argue for a uniform mode of procedure, modeled on that of the common law, at least as far back as the early 1840s, if not earlier.[151] Vanderlyn, like many of his professional peers, fully supported such demands. As he noted in his diary in December 1843, he heartily approved of a speech made by Michael Hoffman, a member of the assembly, "in favor of calling a state convention to remedy the defects of our present constitution." Hoffman urged among other things that "the court of chancery . . . be either abolished or its powers greatly limited and its practice to conform to the suits at law." Similarly, in March 1844, Vanderlyn pasted into his diary an article from that month's *New York American,* which described intolerable delays in chancery and with which, Vanderlyn reported, "I entirely concur." His response to this article was that "a remedy may be provided or the court abolished as a nuisance and the powers now vested in chancery be transferred to the courts of law where rules of equity and rules of law can be decided by one rule of action according to the course of the common law." And in January 1847, having read "a pamphlet written by David D. Field esq. of N.Y. on an entire reform of our mode of pleading in suits and a uniformity of proceeding in courts of law and equity," he concluded that "[t]here is much in it to commend as there is in truth, much nonsense to correct in our present system of practice." In particular, he observed, "[t]he above mentioned uniformity of proceeding in both courts and the abandonment of our forms of action are what I have been advocating for a long while."[152] For lawyers like Vanderlyn, in short, there was nothing particularly revolutionary about the Field Code. It was, as we have seen, a fait accompli—the logical end result of developments long in the making, including in particular the rise of a procedural culture premised on lawyers' republican self-display.

To argue that antebellum lawyers' embrace of oral, adversarial procedure (like the concomitant rejection of equity's distinctive, quasi-inquisitorial tradition) was partly a product of the cultural imperative of republican self-display is not to suggest that more material considerations were of no consequence. How then should we account for these? One possibility is that the turn toward adversarial procedure stemmed at least in part from an objective difference in the profitability of common-law and equity proceedings. But given the great variation among New York courts and types of cases filed, it would be difficult, if not impossible, to reach any definitive conclusions about relative profitability. That said, the large amount of paperwork involved in most equity litigation, as well as the lengthy nature of such proceedings, suggests that these cases could be quite profitable. While lawyers did not play a dominant role in traditional, quasi-inquisitorial equity proceedings, they were nonetheless important actors, able to charge significant fees for their services.[153] Moreover, the substantive content of many disputes falling within equity jurisdiction— including, as we have seen, disputes over property and matters of agency and trust—was such that these cases often (though by no means always) involved wealthy litigants arguing over substantial financial interests.[154] It thus seems unlikely that lawyers rejected traditional equity practice because, as an objective matter, proceedings at law were more profitable than those in equity.

Another alternative is that, whether objectively true or not, lawyers believed that common-law proceedings were more profitable—and, in particular, that the adversarial procedure of the common law could be deployed to help win litigation, either by ferreting out the truth or by obfuscating it. That some lawyers were motivated in part by such narrowly strategic interests seems clearly to have been the case. But then what do we make of the story that antebellum American lawyers told themselves and others about why adversarial procedure was desirable? Pursuant to this story, adversarial procedure was vital to the efforts of lawyers, as the new nation's civic republican elite, to promote the public good. Was this account mere window dressing—an effort by lawyers to justify their choices to themselves and others and thus at best a form of false consciousness, disguising deeper, materialist motivations? The question itself seems misplaced in that the notion of false consciousness assumes that it is possible clearly to disentangle status-based and material motivations. But in the nineteenth century, as today, social respect was meted out in part in material rewards, while wealth contributed to high social standing.

For antebellum lawyers eager to establish themselves—and fretting about popular hostility to the legal profession, as well as the effects of Jacksonian reforms thought greatly to expand bar admissions—the deeply influential and widespread discourse of civic republicanism offered a means to garner social and professional esteem, along with the wealth commonly associated with the latter. It provided a cultural script whereby lawyers could present themselves as modern-day Ciceros. Seeking to adhere to this script, lawyers turned to oral, adversarial procedure, and in so doing, they elevated their social standing and advanced their careers, thereby accruing both psychic and material rewards. In this way, civic republicanism profoundly shaped contemporary understandings of the nature and purposes of the emergent category of "procedure," linking it from the outset to a culture of adversarialism. Conceived (largely by lawyers) as the byproduct of a uniquely American mode of oratory, this adversarial culture would, in turn, come to be embraced by many nonlawyers, as part of an effort to advance a distinctively market-oriented conception of the nature of American social, economic, and (perhaps most especially) labor relations.

# 5 • Market Freedom and Adversarial Adjudication

## The Nineteenth-Century American Debates over (European) Conciliation Courts and the Problem of Procedural Ordering

Eager to engage in republican self-display, early nineteenth-century American lawyers embraced core techniques of common-law procedure, especially oral jury argument and cross-examination in a public forum. Valued by lawyers because they facilitated republican self-display, these techniques also came to be viewed (both by many lawyers and by the public more generally) as fostering a form of socially beneficial competition. This adversarial competition between warring litigants was, in turn, vaunted as vital for preserving and promoting a distinctively American commitment to freedom, encompassing both political liberty and free enterprise.

That adversarialism was a product both of a civic republican ideal of lawyering and of efforts to promote a market-oriented conception of American society is initially difficult to comprehend. There are, after all, profound tensions between republican, communitarian values, on the one hand, and a market-based order, on the other. But this seemingly contradictory parentage appears less odd when we recall that lawyers paid much more attention to looking like Cicero than to ensuring that their professional activities in fact conformed to republican ideals of justice. As we have seen, engaging in republican self-display was a way for lawyers to augment their status and power—a goal on which they were especially focused given the widespread public animosity against lawyers, the competitive anxieties unleashed by the loosening of barriers to entry into the profession, and the dissonance between such market pressures and the continued insistence that lawyers should not seek monetary compensation. But however useful it was, civic republicanism was not the only available ideology by means of which lawyers could present themselves as serving the public welfare (and thereby claim both guild power and social and political authority). This was an era in which competing social and political ideologies vied for dominance—a more republican, communitarian model against a more individualist, libertarian one.[1] And many lawyers eager to promote their professional authority simply embraced the available rhetorical tools, with little attention to the question of logical consistency. That said, as we will see, there were also lawyers who, even while sharing the view that adversarialism and a market-based order were integrally linked, resisted the full-on embrace of both. The support of nonlawyers was thus crucial for the ultimate triumph of the view that the adversarial conflict between private parties was a valuable, public-serving end in and of itself.

It was not discussions of equity, but instead an entirely distinct set of debates—concerning, in particular, whether to adopt what Jeremy Bentham influentially termed conciliation courts—that provided the context in which the adversarial courtroom clash of conflicting interests came to be praised as a valuable (market-promoting) public good. In the first half of the nineteenth century, proposals for the establishment of such courts emerged from various quarters in the United States. The ensuing debates were part and parcel of a much broader and now-forgotten transnational discussion concerning conciliation courts—a fact in itself surprising given the prevailing view that it was only after the Civil War that Americans began seriously to consider the possibility of transplanting institutions from abroad.[2] As commonly depicted, the conciliation court was a lawyer-free realm in which a respected local authority figure relied on his stature within the community to persuade the parties to agree to a compromise, derived from his own sense of justice rather than the formal rule of law.

In the United States in particular, debate over whether to adopt conciliation courts came to serve as a foil against which Americans (both lawyers and nonlawyers) constructed their own procedural culture. Those advocating for the establishment of conciliation courts claimed that they were an important mechanism for restoring social stability in the wake of dramatic economic (and technological) change. More particularly, these courts were thought to attenuate the harsh effects of an increasingly market-driven order by protecting the weakest members of society, including especially workers. But the ultimately victorious opponents of conciliation courts insisted that these institutions fostered deference to the judge, rather than to the rule of law, and prized communal harmony over and above the competitive assertion of self-interest. For these reasons, they concluded, conciliation courts were suited to primitive peoples and to the inhabitants of hierarchical old-world societies, rather than to modern, freedom-loving, and market-oriented Americans. In this way, a disagreement over procedure was transformed into a debate on the very nature of American identity.

## *Bureaux de Conciliation*: Bentham and the French Experiment

During the nineteenth century, a number of continental European countries (and their colonies) experimented with some form of conciliation court—including, France, Spain, Denmark, and Prussia. While there were significant differences between the various institutions of this ilk that were established across the globe, such entities shared certain core similarities. The leading such institution—the one underlying Bentham's notion of the conciliation court as an ideal type—was the *bureau de conciliation* instituted by the French revolutionaries in 1790, knowledge of which was disseminated, in part, through Bentham's influential writings on conciliation courts and natural procedure.

Established in 1790 by the Constituent Assembly of revolutionary France, the *bureaux de conciliation* were required to attempt to reconcile disputants in a wide range of civil matters. Only if such efforts failed was litigation to proceed. The conciliation proceedings themselves were to be an informal, lawyer-free affair, relying largely on oral pleadings and taking place in secret, outside the public's view—namely, in the presence only of the parties and court personnel. These courts were to be staffed by a newly created group of officers known as justices of the peace, each of whom was to be assisted by two *assesseurs prud'hommes* (literally, assistant wise men). As initially contemplated, both the justices of the peace and the *assesseurs prud'hommes* were to be mere amateurs, lacking any legal training, and elected by all eligible voters in the district.[3] The expectation was that voters would select locals of any profession who had become known to the community for their wisdom and virtue. As articulated by a deputy to the Constituent Assembly, "any good man, even one with little experience, can be a justice of the peace."[4] Remarkably, even after Napoleon reconfigured these courts to eliminate the *assesseurs prud'hommes* and to ensure that judicial selection would henceforth reside in his hands alone, nineteenth-century French justices of the peace continued generally to be locals, born in the region where they served and described by one historian as "small-scale notable[s] close to the peasantry."[5] Such local bigwigs were expected to rely on their standing within the community, rather than any legal knowledge per se, to conciliate intra-communal disputes.

In addition to the *bureaux de conciliation*, the French established a number of other judicial institutions in this period that relied heavily on community leaders to promote informal conciliation and therefore came to be lumped together with the former. Most importantly, the Napoleonic regime created a set of labor courts, known as *conseils de prud'hommes*, that paralleled the *bureaux de conciliation* in certain key respects. Designed to help quell the extensive labor strife that emerged in the wake of the Napoleonic Wars, these courts were staffed by lay judges (usually the leading manufacturers in the community, elected by their peers) and were required to prioritize informal conciliation over formal adjudication.[6] Along similar lines, the revolutionaries and the Napoleonic regime opted to retain a set of merchant-run courts (*juridictions consulaires*) that dated back to the sixteenth century. Renamed *tribunaux de commerce*, or commercial courts, these institutions also relied on elected lay judges—in particular, leading local merchants—and tended to place a heavy emphasis on informal conciliation.[7]

As of the late eighteenth and early nineteenth centuries, the French had thus established a number of different institutions that could be (and were) commonly described as conciliation courts. In these waning days of French influence, many European countries opted—either on their own initiative or under military compulsion—to adopt some form of conciliation court within their own borders. As we will see, Spain first established a version of the French *bureaux de conciliation* in its Bayonne Constitution of 1808, which was drafted by Napoleon himself shortly after he put his brother Joseph on the Spanish throne. And the ultimately more influential Cádiz Constitution of 1812 preserved and augmented this French-inspired institution. Similarly, courts akin to the French *conseils de prud'hommes* were created in the Rhineland when the region fell under French rule in 1795, and a version thereof was then preserved when the territory came under Prussian control in 1815.[8] Moreover, in 1795, the Danish decided on their own initiative to establish a set of conciliation boards akin to the *bureaux de conciliation*, which were staffed entirely by laymen and charged with attempting to conciliate most civil disputes.[9]

Despite the pervasive nature of French influence, the particular form taken by the conciliation courts established in each country was shaped by local practices and traditions. Indeed, in France itself the *bureaux de conciliation*—though conceived as revolutionary—were in many ways the direct descendents of the abolished seigneurial courts of the Old Regime, which had commonly relied on traditions of deference within the village community to promote informal, equitable conciliation rather than formal, legal adjudication.[10] Similarly, as we will see, the Spanish *juicio de conciliación* drew on a long tradition of local judges, or *alcaldes,* serving as conciliators. As suggested by these French and Spanish examples (among others), medieval and early modern European judges often failed to distinguish clearly between their roles as conciliator and adjudicator.[11] And it was this tradition of judicial conciliation that helped the conciliation courts established in the late eighteenth and early nineteenth centuries take root. Such courts, however, were different from their predecessors in that their very establishment stemmed from an effort clearly to delineate between conciliation and adjudication. In the age of revolution, as countries throughout the West became increasingly committed to establishing governments based on the formal rule of law—rather than the personalized justice embodied in the medieval and early modern king—the notion of state-sponsored conciliation suddenly proved troubling in a way that had never before been the case. No one gave clearer (or more influential) voice to these concerns than Jeremy Bentham.

Bentham devoted a great deal of attention to discussing the virtues and vices of conciliation, including in particular the French (and French-inspired) conciliation courts, and his writings on these institutions, as on many other matters, proved highly influential. Indeed, he bears primary responsibility for creating the notion of a conciliation court as an ideal type, thus eliding differences between the various institutions of this sort created across Europe and its colonies. While continental European legislators (including the French) failed in practice to implement many of his suggestions, his writings on the topic came to be widely viewed as the starting point for discussion.[12] In addition, as we will see, Bentham's work on conciliation courts greatly influenced a major English promoter of institutional and procedural reform, Lord Chancellor Henry Brougham,[13] whose advocacy of such institutions helped inspire mid-nineteenth-century New Yorkers to consider adopting them.

Bentham thus played a key part in spurring discussion of conciliation courts throughout the nineteenth-century Western world—and he contributed, in particular, to launching what would prove to be the most important American debate on the subject. But while fostering debate over such institutions, Bentham himself never suggested that these were clearly worth establishing. To the contrary, he was at once deeply attracted to and repelled by the notion of conciliation courts.[14] And the confused and conflicting attitudes that he expressed would, in turn, characterize subsequent American thinking about such institutions—though, like Bentham, nineteenth-century Americans would largely opt against the establishment of such courts.

In Bentham's view, conciliation courts had the potential to be useful—helping disputants avoid the substantial financial and psychic costs of litigation. But at the same time, they were potentially dangerous in that their secret, lawyer-free proceedings proved most effective when disputants willingly deferred to the wisdom of an authority figure. According to Bentham, this raised the possibility that conciliation courts were fundamentally incompatible with a society premised on individual freedom and the rule of law—precisely the kind of society that he hoped to establish throughout the world. Many Americans—and especially those eager to promote an increasingly market-driven order—would, in turn, draw on this logic, adding to Bentham's concern with promoting individual freedom and the rule of law, the goal of facilitating market competition. The American commitment to political liberty and free enterprise, they insisted, did not permit the establishment of an institution that encouraged deference to the person of the judge, rather than compliance with the rule of law, and that valued communal harmony more than the competitive assertion of self-interest. From here it was a short step to developing an account of adversarial adjudication as a vital bulwark of American liberty, both political and economic.

## Market Revolution and Procedural Change

The period from roughly 1815 to 1848 witnessed, as we have seen, a broad array of interrelated changes in modes of production, employment relations, consumer practices, and methods of transportation. Confronted with such dramatic changes as the emergence of factories, canals, and railroads as well as the new labor relations and patterns of mobility to which the latter gave rise, Americans spent much of the first half of the nineteenth century struggling with the question of how to respond. Should they resist these changes or embrace them? And what did these changes mean for their political, personal, and professional identities, as well as for the social relations that undergirded them?

The First and Second Party systems were shaped in no small part by differences in approach to market change. Federalists and later Whigs embraced the rise of an increasingly market-driven order, arguing that continued commercial growth would expand the nation's wealth and power and thereby benefit all. In contrast, Republicans and thereafter many Democrats decried these developments on the grounds that they generated dangerous inequalities of wealth and a passion for private gain that threatened to subvert virtue and undermine the republic. When the Second Party system collapsed in the 1850s, the reconfiguration of party structures turned significantly on the problem of slavery and free labor—and thus, once again, on issues linked in important ways with market society.

But it was not only Americans' political identities and structures that were put in question by new market forces. The profound economic transformations of the period also threatened major changes to workplace and family relations, thus raising difficult questions about how to restructure key building blocks of the social order. As concerns the workplace, the rise of factories and the sweating system led to a growing divide between those who produced consumer goods and those who financed their production and sale. While master artisans once lived and worked alongside the journeymen they trained, the new systems of mass production presumed an owner who would supply capital to procure labor, which, in turn, took place outside his home. The end result was to displace production from the home and to replace the kinds of paternalistic bonds that linked masters and journeymen with a new culture of impersonal discipline.[15] The nature of workplace relations thus became a key source of contemporary anxiety.

Such anxiety was fueled by the concomitant decline of the self-sufficient yeoman farmer. For the many Americans who operated small family farms, producing not only their own food but also the basic woolens and other items required to survive, the rise of an increasingly modern integrated market economy undermined their self-sufficiency. Where once they were able to rely largely on their own handiwork, supplemented by practices of barter, they now depended on the market, for which they produced cash crops and to which they turned for most household items and farming tools. As farming families struggled to remake themselves in the new economic mold, growing numbers of their children found themselves obligated to work in the new forms of manufacturing, contributing to the rise of an urban and rural underclass.[16] To the extent that the nation had been founded on the basis of a civic republican ethic pursuant to which the preservation of political virtue was thought to hinge on economic independence (as best represented by land ownership), the rise of a class of people who appeared to be so utterly dependent on others was deeply troubling to many. Concerns about such dependence were, moreover, exacerbated by a set of fears particular to the new urban environment. As cities expanded with growing numbers of people who were strangers to one another, many became anxious about the seeming fluidity of social identity and the difficulties of knowing whom to trust.[17]

Market developments in the period served, however, not only to remake workplace relations and the urban landscape but also to reconfigure the family itself. For those lucky urban families who managed to attain middle-class status, becoming business owners responsible for managing the labor of others or working in a professional or clerical capacity, the new separation of workplace and home led to a profound reconfiguration of the latter. The home came to center around the immediate nuclear family. And women, confined to a home from which business had been excised, began to focus primarily on managing domestic affairs—a task for which they were lauded as uniquely suited. The fundamental rethinking of gender identity and core familial relations that ensued would, in turn, lead to the rise of a new "cult of domesticity."[18]

The extent to which these disruptions of key social relations proved deeply troubling to many Americans is suggested by scholarship on the origins of nineteenth-century religious revivalism—most especially during the heated decades from roughly 1815 to 1845. As Paul E. Johnson and Mary P. Ryan argue, the market revolution helped to fuel the Second Great Awakening, such that it was in those regions of the country where the social order was most profoundly reconfigured by economic change that evangelicalism achieved its greatest number of converts. Among these was the famed burned-over district of central and western New York, so named for its population's remarkable susceptibility to spiritual conflagration and rebirth. According to Johnson, the appeal of evangelical religion was that it provided a new means of exerting social control over workers recently freed by the separation of home and workplace from the watchful eye of the master's domestic supervision. Ryan, in contrast, suggests that it was not so much the reconfiguring of master/worker relations but instead the remaking of gender relations that spurred revivalism. Pointing to the disproportionate role played by women in promoting religious fervor and conversion, she shows how evangelicalism (aided by the cult of domesticity) enabled mothers to instill in their sons the discipline and affect necessary to obtain middle-class employment and standing, thus helping to ensure that the family as a whole would preserve its position in an increasingly competitive marketplace. While disagreeing over the precise mechanisms by means of which market change translated into religious revivalism, both scholars agree on one key point: Evangelicalism was at least in part a reaction to—and thus a measure of—the profound tensions stemming from the myriad ways that the market revolution transformed fundamental social relations, including those of both work and family.[19]

While extensive scholarly attention has been paid to the consequences of market change in restructuring the order of both workplace and home, little thought has been devoted to its possible effects on procedural ordering.[20] As a set of mechanisms designed to resolve disputes between members of society and thus to restore (or reconfigure) the social fabric, all systems of civil procedure necessarily draw on some vision of a normative social ordering. While rarely articulated in any express fashion, this vision helps to structure the procedural system and to give it meaning. Indeed, it is precisely because dispute-resolution procedures offer such a fascinating window into a society's basic ordering principles that they have proven a valuable resource for legal anthropologists.[21] It should thus come as little surprise that, in disrupting core social relations, the reconfiguration of the antebellum market also problematized procedure. Put differently, one of the many ways that Americans of this period grappled with the question of how to restructure their society in light of the profound economic and technological changes that they were experiencing was to debate the nature and purposes of their procedure.

Among contemporary lawyers, the question of how to define procedure was already front and center because the separation of writ from right led to the emergence of procedure as a distinct category of law, requiring for the first time clear definition and content. But this effort to give shape to a distinctive body of procedural law was a technical matter, primarily of interest to lawyers. While lawyers' efforts to engage in republican self-display were hardly technical—and did have a transformative effect on procedural culture—these were, as we have seen, substantially directed at fellow lawyers, involving non-lawyers only insofar as an audience was requisite for such display. In contrast, the effort to grapple with the meaning and nature of market change ended up involving a much wider swath of Americans in procedural thinking. And it was the conciliation court that served as the primary focal point for this broader public discussion. But in part because of the unfortunate tendency to approach the history of procedure from an exclusively internalist perspective, scholars to date have neglected this important set of debates.

As we will see, the antebellum debates over conciliation courts spanned several decades and geographical regions, such that they defy easy classification. The major American debates over conciliation courts took place in Florida and California at the moment that these territories were acquired, respectively, in 1821 and 1848, and in New York, during the state's 1846 constitutional convention. In Florida, advocates of conciliation courts tended to focus on disputes over debt, arguing that such institutions were better able than ordinary courts to arrive at mutually beneficial compromise solutions that would ensure the creditor's recovery, even while protecting the debtor from being forced into abject penury. The arguments made for conciliation courts in California, in turn, were penned largely by middle-class Eastern transplants who suddenly found themselves serving as conciliation court judges. As a result, they highlight the institution's benefits for the conciliation judges themselves—namely, enabling these men to escape the burdensome strictures of middle-class male identity while also offering a means of propagating the reform ideals associated with religious revivalism and the latter's critique of an expanding market order. This revivalist thrust was also significant in the New York debates. But in New York, the religiously infused arguments in favor of conciliation courts tended to emphasize the urgency of ameliorating the growing tensions between capital and labor, as reflected in workers' burgeoning efforts to organize. As we will see, in the wake of the Civil War, it was this framing of the conciliation court as a form of governmental intervention in the labor market that would come to dominate contemporary understandings of the institution.

Despite significant variation in the arguments made for and against conciliation courts, there was, nonetheless, a dominant theme animating these debates. This was the question of the appropriate relationship between law and economy—a question sparked in no small part by the dramatic social, economic, and technological transformations of the period. Those who advocated for the adoption of conciliation courts voiced a more regulatory, even paternalistic conception of the role of the law in relation to economic developments. They insisted that such courts ought to intervene in credit relations (in Florida); in the kinds of immoral conduct, like consuming alcohol and gambling, that threated bourgeois market rationality (in California); and in labor disputes (in New York). In contrast, those who opposed conciliation courts claimed that the remarkable socioeconomic transformations then occurring were a net social positive, thus obviating the desirability of governmental intervention of these various sorts.

There is a vast literature exploring the complex relationship between law and economy in the nineteenth century. While the size and complexity of this literature is such that there is little clear consensus, most scholars would agree that the period prior to the Gilded Age ought not to be characterized as one of laissez-faire. Throughout much of the century, state and local governments actively regulated and shaped economic activity, whether by investing extensively in public infrastructure, delegating to private corporations the power of eminent domain, or remaking the law of contract and tort with an eye toward promoting what James Willard Hurst famously described as "the release of energy." Indeed, the very institutions that we associate with the free market—including, not least, private property itself—were themselves the product of intensive legal construction, rather than some preexisting fact of nature.[22] At the same time, even while government intervention in the economy (as well as other spheres of society) remained common—and even as an older discourse justifying such intervention as an exercise of police power in service of the public welfare persisted—this was also an era that developed and became increasingly committed to principles of "freedom of contract," understood to undergird a society premised on largely unregulated market individualism. Thus, as Harry Scheiber argues, the nineteenth-century American approach to law and economy was "one of continuous and creative tension between competing validating canons," juxtaposing a continued tradition of police power and public rights, exercised in the name of the common good, against a burgeoning devotion to the ideal of an unfettered market and the protection of private individual rights.[23]

Those who argued against conciliation courts on the grounds that they ran counter to a distinctive American commitment not only to political liberty but also to free enterprise were among the many in the antebellum era who urged the second of these two competing canons—namely, an individualist, free-market model of social and economic organization. Their insistence that the United States embraced a largely unregulated free market was, in other words, not a transparent description of social fact but rather a gambit in an ongoing battle over the nature of the emerging market order and the role of the law in relation to it.

## The Spanish Inheritance

It was in the highly influential state of New York, during the constitutional convention that gave rise to the Field Code, that the American debate over conciliation courts would reach its full flowering. But this was not where the debate began. While mid-nineteenth-century New Yorkers considered the possibility of transplanting conciliation courts from abroad, an earlier generation of Americans—those who had settled in territorial Florida approximately two decades earlier—confronted the question of whether to preserve an institution of this kind that had taken root under Spanish law. This question then reemerged around the middle of the nineteenth century, when the United States gained control of California.

## FLORIDA

In March 1821, shortly after the United States acquired Florida from Spain, Congress established a set of mechanisms for territorial governance, including a legislative council consisting of the governor and thirteen other members appointed annually by the president. In addition, it created two superior courts and invested the legislative council with the authority to create inferior courts as it deemed necessary. The legislative council quickly acted on this authority, establishing justices of the peace, circuit courts, and county courts in August and September 1822. But some months later, in June 1823, the council significantly reconfigured the territorial judiciary, abolishing the circuit courts and endowing the county courts with the jurisdiction that the latter had possessed.[24]

It was in this same month of June, as the council was considering various reforms of the territory's judicial apparatus, that a bill was proposed to establish "courts of conciliation."[25] Because legislative records from the period were not published, many details of the proposed legislation remain unknown. Fortunately, however, a weekly newspaper based in St. Augustine—the *East Florida Herald*—published a running commentary on sessions of the legislative council while also offering a forum for members of the local community to air their views. Although the paper's reports of the legislative debates concerning conciliation courts are quite terse, they afford a broad overview of the basic purposes of the bill as well as the community's divergent reactions to it.

The bill provided that all who sought to litigate would be required first to appear before "any magistrate" who would, in turn, function as a conciliation court. If the conciliation proved successful, the judge would record its terms, which would then become enforceable like any court order. If it failed, the parties were free to file suit. As concerns the nature of the conciliation proceedings, discussions in the *Herald* suggest that these were to be secret and lawyer-free and that no written record was to be kept.[26] And while the surviving legislative history is quite sparse, the idea for such an institution seems to have derived from Spanish law, which borrowed in this regard from the French *bureaux de conciliation*.

In 1808, just a few days before Napoleon placed his brother Joseph on the Spanish throne, he convened an Assembly of Notables in the town of Bayonne with instructions to write a new constitution for the Spanish monarchy. Initially drafted by Napoleon himself, this document drew on contemporary French law and practice. Accordingly, the Bayonne Constitution eliminated all seigneurial jurisdictions and replaced these with a hierarchy of state-run courts—including at the very lowest level, a conciliation court (*tribunal de paci-ficación*) staffed by conciliation judges (*jueces conciliadores*). In practice, as the Napoleonic Wars continued, the Bayonne Constitution remained largely a dead letter, its authority extending only so far as French troops happened to be present at any given moment.[27] But however limited the influence of this initial constitution, it was followed a few years later by the enactment of a second constitution, destined to play a more important and lasting role in the organization of Spanish government and society—namely, the Cádiz Constitution of 1812.

The Constitution of 1812 was promulgated by the national legislative assembly (or *Cortes Generales*), which had organized in opposition to French rule—with an eye toward reestablishing Ferdinand VII to the throne of a liberalized monarchy. Drafted in the Spanish town of Cádiz, where the *Cortes* was hiding from French forces, this constitution, like its Napoleonic predecessor, was based significantly on French sources, though the extent of French influence remains a subject of scholarly debate. Like its predecessor, the Cádiz Constitution established a requirement of pre-litigation conciliation that appears to have derived largely from French law. While the Bayonne Constitution remained silent as to how precisely conciliation was to proceed, the Cádiz Constitution provided much more guidance. In particular, it established that the *alcalde* or local judge of each town was to serve as a conciliator, along with two "good men" (*hombres buenos*) named by each party. Having heard the parties' respective allegations, as well as the "report of his associates" (namely, the *hombres buenos*), the *alcalde* was to suggest a resolution that seemed to him "appropriate for ending the litigation." Further details of this conciliation process were then specified in implementing legislation, issued on October 9, 1812.[28]

The parallels between the *juicio de conciliación*, or conciliation process, established by the Cádiz Constitution and the French *bureaux de conciliation* were extensive. Like the French *justices de paix*, the *alcaldes* were required to attempt conciliation in almost all civil suits and no litigation was to be filed absent such a (failed) attempt. Moreover, just as the *justices de paix* were (at least originally) to be elected by local members of the community and to be assisted by two *assesseurs prud'hommes*, so too, the *alcalde* was to be an elected official aided in all conciliation proceedings by two *hombres buenos*. Most importantly, the Spanish *alcalde*, like the French *justice de paix*, was not expected to apply the law. Indeed, like the *justice de paix*, he was not supposed to possess legal training of any kind. In the eyes of both the French revolutionaries and the authors of the Cádiz Constitution, the essential prerequisite for serving as a conciliating judge was not legal knowledge as such but instead one's standing in the local community. In the words of the nineteenth-century Spanish jurist José de Vicente y Caravantes, such a judge was trusted as "a prudent and impartial person of good faith and sound advice."[29] In this respect, just as the French *bureaux de conciliation* drew on an older tradition of local deference to the seigneurial judge, so too the Spanish *juicio de conciliación* called on the familiar figure of the respected local *alcalde*. Dating back to the Moorish occupation of the Iberian peninsula, the *alcalde* was a member of the town council (*cabildo* or *ayuntamiento*) in charge of municipal government and endowed with a broad array of executive, administrative, and judicial powers. Responsible for maintaining peace and order, *alcaldes* were long accustomed to mediating local disputes—a role that was formalized through the conciliation requirement imposed by the Constitution of 1812.[30]

The Cádiz Constitution was enforced sporadically in the nineteenth century, recognized as applicable law during periods of liberalization and deemed null during periods of absolutist retrenchment. Moreover, even during those moments in which the Constitution was, in theory, in force, it did not reach everywhere to the same extent. Those regions at the outskirts of the empire that would eventually become core components of the United States—including both Florida and California—remained largely unsettled military outposts throughout Spanish occupation. Accordingly, formal law and administration were slow to develop in these areas. As concerns Florida, in particular, while it long had its own municipal government, this appears to have been a relatively ad hoc institution that for centuries did not include *alcaldes*. Nonetheless, as M. C. Mirow has recently argued, the Constitution of 1812 was eagerly embraced and faithfully applied in Spanish Florida, and this, in turn, led to the establishment of local *alcaldes*. Given the military's prominence, these, in turn, came to share their authority—including the authority to conciliate—with military officers known as *capitanes de partido*, or district captains.[31]

The *capitanes de partido* were established pursuant to a royal decree of 1786 that sought to apply the new French system of administrative intendancies to New Spain. As developed by the Bourbon monarchy that then ruled both France and Spain, this system was designed to replace unaccountable venal officeholders with salaried royal officials (the intendants and their subordinates) who would comply more readily with royal command. Among the new officials established pursuant to the 1786 decree were *capitanes de partido*, who were endowed with substantial local authority. But while replacing many former venal office-holding officials, the 1786 decree provided that local *alcaldes*, responsible for municipal governance and dispute resolution, would continue to operate in towns with a Spanish population of (an unspecified) sufficient size. Accordingly, from the late eighteenth century onward, *alcaldes* and *capitanes de partido* coexisted in much of New Spain, such that there was substantial jurisdictional overlap and competition between the two offices. Once *alcaldes* took root in Florida around 1812, they and the *capitanes de partido* appear to have shared (and competed over) the jurisdiction to oversee conciliation proceedings.[32]

As this history suggests, when the legislative council of Florida debated whether to adopt conciliation courts in the summer of 1823, the institution that it had in mind was the Spanish *juicio de conciliación*—a formalization (inspired by the French *bureaux de conciliation*) of the longstanding practice of *alcaldes* serving as conciliators. While most members of the council were of Anglo-American descent, a good many had spent time living in Florida prior to its acquisition by the United States and thus had some opportunity to become familiar with local Spanish institutions like the *juicio de conciliación*. Consider, for example, William R. Reynolds, the councilman responsible for introducing the conciliation courts bill. Born in Pennsylvania, Reynolds had come to live in East Florida during the American occupation of 1817 and 1818, when he served as the interpreter and private secretary to Captain John R. Bell. Trained as a lawyer, he was likely interested to some extent in local legal institutions. And since he had lived for a number of years in Spain, he was fluent in Spanish—a skill that helped in acquiring knowledge of such practices as the *juicio de conciliación*.[33] Along similar lines, council members probably became familiar with the local tradition of conciliation proceedings through their acquaintance with those English speakers—including both Americans and men of British descent—who themselves served as *alcaldes* and *capitanes de partido*. Serving in this capacity, such men quickly became familiar with the *juicio de conciliación*—knowledge of which they were then able to transmit to the growing number of American émigrés, including those who served on the legislative council. And notably, Edmund Law, one of the original members of the legislative council, had himself served as the *alcalde* of St. Augustine.[34] In proposing the establishment of conciliation courts in June 1823, Reynolds and his supporters were thus arguing for the preservation of a (French-derived) institution that had operated under Spanish rule.

While the *Herald* unfortunately did not report on the arguments made within the legislative council itself, it published throughout the summer of

1823 a series of letters to the editor penned by leading local residents arguing either for or against the proposed legislation. These provide an overview of the contours of the debate within the community (and thus, in all likelihood, within the council as well).

For the most part, the debate over conciliation courts tracked the two sides of Bentham's conflicted analysis of such institutions. Proponents of the courts pointed to their utility in resolving disputes quickly and efficiently without recourse to litigation and lawyers—and without the lasting enmity that these tended to generate. In so arguing, they advocated the virtues of paternalism: People, in short, needed to be saved from their own worst instincts, including the instinct to waste time and money on unnecessary litigation. In contrast, opponents claimed that conciliation courts threatened liberty by denying people immediate access to litigation and, more importantly, by subjecting them to the personal influence of the conciliating judge rather than to the rule of law. As these opponents insisted, (informal) conciliation courts were to be contrasted with (formal) adversarial adjudication, a practice that they depicted as serving two distinct but related goals: establishing predictability and promoting competition.

As concerns predictability, formal adjudication (as distinct from informal conciliation) ensured the development and application of a clear, consistent body of law. This, in turn, enabled individuals to predict the consequences of their actions, thus facilitating the maximal exercise of freedom within limits set only by the rule of law while also establishing the foundations for sustained market growth. The problem with conciliation courts, however, was not simply that they encouraged a case-by-case exercise of discretion that hindered the establishment of predictable (and thus market-promoting) rules. At least as troubling was that they also encouraged a mentality of deference that was itself contrary to the spirit of freedom and free enterprise. As the opponents of conciliation courts came to conclude, a dispute-resolution process suited to a market-based society was one that encouraged the aggressive, competitive assertion of self-interest. For this reason, the antithesis of the conciliation court was not simply formal adjudication but in particular formal, *adversarial* adjudication.

Among the primary advocates of conciliation courts in the *East Florida Herald* was George J. F. Clarke, who wrote under the pen name "A Native Floridian." Born in Florida to an English father and an Irish mother during the brief period from 1763 to 1783 that the territory was under British rule, Clarke was one of the biggest landowners in the area and a leading figure in the community. Having served as a trusted advisor to the Spanish governors and

Figure 7   Unidentified artist, *George John Frederic Clarke*
(n.d.). Courtesy of the St. Augustine Historical Society
Research Library.

remained loyal to Spain during the uprisings that preceded American annexation, he believed that there was much to be admired in Spanish law and governance. Most importantly, the Spanish understood the virtues of paternalism. According to Clarke, Spanish law was animated by a deep-seated belief that the administrative might of the state ought to be deployed to promote equity, or substantive justice, for all citizens in all aspects of their daily lives. Its hallmark, in short, was "great equity and moderation."[35] And to the extent that equity of this kind could be purchased only at the expense of predictability and (a formalistic conception of) individual liberty, these were sacrifices well worth making.

Clarke argued that it was precisely this disposition toward benevolent, paternalistic oversight that distinguished the Spanish civil law tradition from that of the Anglo-American common law. While the common law continued to order imprisonment for debt and to subordinate wives to their husbands pursuant to the rule of coverture, the civil law had rejected these traditions in favor of more "enlightened" and "equitable" practices. So too, conciliation courts—derived from Spanish law—were intended to promote equity: "[E]quity was the first object; benevolence the second. . . ." Because the purpose of such courts was to "open[] a new, short, and cheap road to equity," they were to use "every reasonable persuasive and inducement towards an amicable compound of the parties"—a clear reference to the civil law tradition of "amiable composition."[36] This meant that if the parties had to be pushed against their will into attempting conciliation, such a mild deprivation of liberty was perfectly acceptable. Only in this way could the government ensure that parties would not through error or passion commit large psychic and financial resources to pursuing litigation that they would ultimately lose or whose value, even if victory followed, failed to justify the costs. Accordingly, Clarke emphasized, in the days of Spanish rule, "every endeavor . . . w[as] used in order to bar against the greater evils consequent on the delays, expenses, toils, animosities, etc. of a lawsuit." And this "parental regard of the Spanish government" was a "beautiful feature" of Spanish law, which the proposed conciliation courts admirably sought to reestablish.[37]

Writing under the pen name "Youlee," Moses E. Levy was another advocate of conciliation courts who appealed to the virtues of paternalism and to the limits of formalist notions of liberty. A Jewish merchant and later planter, Levy was born in Morocco in 1782, moved to the Danish West Indies in 1800, and then left for Cuba in 1816. Once settled in Cuba, he began to purchase large tracts of land in Florida, to which he moved in July 1821, around the time that the territory was formally annexed to the United States. Developing large sugar plantations (even while decrying the evils of the slave labor that he at least initially employed), Levy became a prominent local figure and wrote regularly for the press. Among the issues he advocated in his writing was judicial reform, including the adoption of conciliation courts—institutions that he likely first encountered in their Danish variety while living in St. Thomas.[38]

In Levy's view, like Clarke's, conciliation courts were fundamentally paternalistic institutions in which the paternalistic requirement that disputants attempt conciliation was matched by a similarly paternalistic mode of proceeding. Lacking legal training of any kind, the conciliation judge did not resolve the dispute by imposing the law, but instead by using his common sense to urge an equitable outcome that would be mutually acceptable to the disputants. He was, in short, to "use no argument but such as the equity and circumstances of the case may dictate and a sense of justice and conciliatory feelings may allow of." And crucially, it was his status as a trusted community leader—as "[a] man of longstanding, tried probity, and possessing the respect and good will of the public"—that helped ensure that the parties would be swayed by his good counsel.[39]

Like Clarke, Levy emphasized that substantive justice was ultimately more important than formal freedom. Although opponents of the conciliation courts complained that they forced people to conciliate against their will, this was a non sequitur in that conciliation would prove effective only if both parties willingly embraced the judge's recommended resolution. Should the conciliation fail, the parties "are at liberty to pursue whatever course they please," including litigation. More importantly, the supposed freedom to litigate was often little more than a formalist illusion since, in reality, adjudication was far too expensive to be readily available to all. As Levy observed, the notion that conciliation courts threatened "*free access* to courts of justice" was absurd, since litigation in the ordinary courts was anything but free. Those who argued in this vein took "no account of the vexatious delays, and often ruin, a poor or an ignorant and unfortunate client is exposed to" in the ordinary courts.[40]

Such arguments for the preservation of conciliation courts as a form of state paternalism did not emerge in a vacuum. Although Florida itself was largely undeveloped at the time that it became a territory of the United States in 1821, the market developments already underway in the North were beginning to exert pressure in the South. Indeed, recent research suggests that, even though the Northeast was the primary locus of industrialization and urbanization, the market revolution also made significant headway in the South. As Jonathan Daniel Wells argues, the antebellum South witnessed the emergence of a sizable and growing white middle class whose members earned their livelihood by entering the classical professions and by developing local banking and industrial concerns. Through their connections with family and friends in the North—as well as the growing circulation of newspapers and journals published in the North—these men and women came to embrace many of the values associated with their Northern counterparts. Believing for the most part that the institution of slavery could be made compatible with core aspects of a market-based society, they argued on behalf of greater industrialization and the development of the infrastructure necessary to support it. And like Northerners, they experienced significant anxieties stemming from the social rupture and dislocation associated with market change—anxieties that, in turn, manifested themselves in Southern variants of the cult of domesticity and religious revivalism.[41]

At the time of Florida's annexation, those who rushed into its borders were familiar with the extraordinary economic developments then beginning to transform the North.[42] As these men and women imagined and debated the kind of society that they hoped to create, a key question was the extent to which similar developments ought to be encouraged (or resisted) in this newly established territory. The debate over conciliation courts was thus in no small part a debate over the virtues and vices of a market-based social order. In the view of those advocating the preservation of such courts, the paternalism that these institutions facilitated would serve as a vital check on the acquisitive self-interest that threatened to undermine the social fabric.

Consider in this respect a letter to the editor of the *Herald,* penned under the initials "Y. C." According to Y. C., conciliation courts were vital for ensuring that the creditor's interest in the immediate, predictable recovery of his debt would not trump more humanitarian considerations, such as the well-being of the unfortunate debtor. Formal, adversarial adjudication, as undertaken by the recently established County Court of St. John, "drove the greater part of the poor Floridian from their homes and deprived the city of a large proportion of its inhabitants." Among the examples Y. C. offered in support of this claim was "the case of the unfortunate Waterman," whose ten slaves were seized to recover a debt of $1,200 and who, in addition, had to pay $1,400 in costs and fees. Attempting to leave Florida and seek his fortune elsewhere, Waterman ended up drowning, and "his orphan children are now compelled to grind with their own hands, the corn which charity affords them." The greatest horror of this turn of events, Y. C. argued, was that it was entirely avoidable. In contrast to the county court, a conciliation court would have recognized that there was a way to respect the creditor's right to recovery, even while affording the debtor some solace. In particular, a conciliating judge could have proposed that Waterman "assign to the creditors four of his best negroes, the value of which would have more than covered" his debt. Evincing (unsurprisingly) no concern for the slaves themselves, Y. C. observed that, had this approach been adopted, Waterman's "crop might have been gathered by his remaining negroes, [and] his life might have been spared to his now widowed wife and orphan children."[43]

As suggested by Y. C.'s insistence that a conciliation court would give due attention to the interests of both debtors and creditors, those advocating the establishment of conciliation courts were no opponents of commerce and commercial prosperity as such. Indeed, from the little we know of men like Clarke and Levy, such an attitude would have been in conflict with their own substantial business interests as large plantation owners (and, in Levy's case, a onetime merchant as well). For men of this kind—those with sufficiently great wealth and social standing to have their letters published by the *Herald*— the goal was not to eradicate commerce but rather to attenuate its possibly destructive impact, thereby shoring up the foundations of the social order. Accordingly Clarke, like Y. C., insisted that there was no necessary contradiction between conciliation courts and commercial prosperity. In support of this claim, he pointed to the operation of conciliation courts in Florida prior to its annexation by the United States, discussing, in particular, Philip R. Yonge, who had been appointed to serve as *capitán de partido* in 1813:

> The practical utility of these courts was well exemplified at Fernandina under Judge Philip R. Yonge, while the Spanish constitutional government was in force in a part of 1813 and 1814, and at a time when vast foreign shipping and commercial business was going on at that place. In about fifty important cases awarded in this manner, some of them involving very large amounts of property, not eight of them appealed to a course of law. How great then must have been the savings in litigations, delays, fatigues, dissentions, and expenses![44]

Conciliation courts were thus perfectly compatible with a form of moderated free enterprise.

While advocates of the conciliation courts appealed to the virtues of these paternalistic institutions in attenuating the potentially destructive impact of a market-based order, opponents decried the evils of paternalism and insisted that these courts were fundamentally incompatible with the foundations of a free society. In so doing, they constructed an argument linking together adversarial adjudication and American identity that would reach its full fruition two decades later in the New York Constitutional Convention of 1846. Underlying this argument was a particular vision of American freedom—one grounded not only on political liberty but also on free enterprise.

Consider in this regard the writings of someone who published in the *Herald* under the pen name "Amicus Curiae." Amicus Curiae assaulted the proposed conciliation courts on two related grounds—that they were of civil law origin and that they threatened to undermine freedom, especially the freedom necessary for a vibrant commercial republic. Relying on the longstanding association in the Anglo-American world between the continental civil law and the twin evils of despotic rule and "popish" domination, he suggested that the notion of conciliation courts is "absolutely at variance with the principles of the common law" and "must originally have been engendered in the brain of some ignorant and conceited monk." That this was the origin of these institutions, he argued, was evident in the fact that they were so contrary to the American spirit of liberty. In forcing would-be litigants to attempt conciliation against their will, the proposed legislation was not only morally reprehensible but also a contradiction in terms, "for nothing surely can be less conciliatory than to compel a man to take counsel and advice, whether he will or not."[45]

This threatened assault on liberty, Amicus Curiae warned, would have significant social and economic consequences. Florida was in its infancy and required an influx of men and capital if it was to aspire to the agricultural and commercial development that would enable it to assume its rightful place among the older, more established states. But men of means would refrain from moving to Florida and risking their wealth without the guarantee of a speedy and reliable legal system that would adjudicate their rights and affirm their property interests in a clear, predictable fashion. In Amicus Curiae's words,

> It is in vain and idle to boast of our soil and our climate—to count upon the *physical* advantages of this Territory, as inducements to men of respectability and property to come and settle in it, if we have no *moral* inducements. . . . Let us show to the world, and convince our neighbors, that in Florida, the laws and administration of Justice afford complete security and protection to the person and property of every individual.

To adopt institutions that were so clearly detrimental to commerce was to reject enlightened modernity in favor of primitive barbarity: "If . . . in this Territory, we are already tired of the *common law*, let us say so at once—abolish it *in toto* and borrow from the *Moors* and *Hottentots*."[46]

Similar arguments were voiced by "Verus," another opponent of conciliation courts whose identity remains unknown. Like Amicus Curiae, Verus argued that to compel individuals to submit to conciliation was to impinge on their liberty in a manner better suited to primitive, barbaric times than to civilized modernity. As Verus wrote, "Shall we compel an individual to enter into a specious and hollow agreement mistermed amicable, and to undergo the *ordeal* of conciliation, when we have tribunals where the laws are administered, with system and science. . . ."[47] Moreover, like Amicus Curiae, Verus claimed that grave economic consequences would follow from such a deprivation of liberty. But while Amicus Curiae criticized the conciliation courts for failing to establish the legal predictability necessary for market activity, Verus took the argument one step further. According to Verus, Florida needed not merely formal adjudication but in particular formal, *adversarial* adjudication.

Drawing on a market-based conception of social relations, Verus argued that the main virtue of adjudication under the traditional common-law model was precisely that it facilitated open, adversarial conflict between competing interests. In sharp contrast to those who praised conciliation because it helped to quell animosities, Verus claimed that there was nothing so terrible about the fact that adjudication sometimes promoted "a degree of ill will . . . among individuals." To the contrary, the adversarial battle of wills was vital in a free, competition-based society, which would thrive only to the extent that the best ideas (political, economic, and otherwise) proved victorious. In Verus's words, litigation "contributes to keep up a salutary agitation in the body politic, which at all times requires a pretty severe degree of exercise for its health, and is therefore measurably benefitted by those wholesome contentions among individuals which the operation of good laws most generally produce." By means of adversarial adjudication and the "wholesome contentions among individuals" that it facilitated, "the barriers of right and wrong, continue to be discriminated, and the highest interests of society are thereby upheld and preserved." In contrast, conciliation did not permit the competition necessary to ensure that the best men and ideas would rise to the top. Valuing the comfort of social harmony over and above the rigors of competition, conciliation could easily lead to wrongful outcomes that, taken together, would be detrimental to social flourishing, including economic development: "[B]y the plan of conciliation, it is plainly implied, that a party to a controversy, who perhaps has a valid claim against another, may by an appeal both to his good nature and prudence, or by playing upon his fears of expense, be induced to compound between justice and expediency, and be reconciled to a wrong. . . ."[48]

Ultimately, it was these arguments in opposition to conciliation courts—and in favor of a wholehearted embrace of a market-based social order—that won the day. Thus, on June 28, the legislative council voted against the enactment of the conciliation courts bill. This conclusion, however, was far from foregone. As described by the *East Florida Herald*, the debate leading to the vote was a "hard struggle," and the vote itself was close—six to four. And in what appears to have been an attempt to throw a bone to those who had unsuccessfully advocated for the establishment of conciliation courts, the legislative council enacted on July 2, 1823—just a few days after the defeat of the conciliation courts bill—"An Act to Provide for the Conciliation of Private Controversies."[49]

Pursuant to this statute, "in all causes of action within the jurisdiction of the Justices of the Peace," the parties were required to "appear before said Justice each accompanied by an arbitrator chosen by himself and the said arbitrators thus appointed shall under the direction of the justice of the Peace . . . endeavor to conciliate the parties." Thus, as in the Spanish model of the conciliation court, the justice of the peace was to be aided by two private persons, selected as "arbitrators" by each of the parties. Significantly, however, the July 2 legislation applied only to those relatively small disputes that came within the jurisdiction of the justices of the peace. And unlike the proposed conciliation courts bill, which seems to have contemplated a lawyer-free proceeding, the July 2 legislation specifically provided that a party might appear through his "attorney." Most importantly, while in the conciliation court model, the failure to attempt conciliation served as a bar to filing suit, the July 2 legislation specified that in such cases, the matter was to proceed directly to trial.[50] Thus, while seeming to defer in at least some respects to the wishes of those who had advocated for the preservation of conciliation courts, the July 2 legislation sounded the death knell of the (French-derived) Spanish model.

## CALIFORNIA

Before turning to mid-nineteenth-century New York, where the debate over conciliation courts and adversarial procedure was most fully developed, it is important to consider another region inherited from the Spanish Empire, where nineteenth-century Americans encountered conciliation courts— namely, California. As part of Mexico and prior to that the Spanish Empire, California inherited a tradition of conciliation proceedings that was more firmly established than that of Florida. But despite this tradition, no legislative effort to preserve such proceedings emerged around the time that California became an American state in 1850—likely because, as described below, the newly established state judiciary quickly ruled that conciliation courts were incompatible with American legal culture. Nonetheless, as a result of the burgeoning literary market for contemporary accounts of California just before and during the Gold Rush—much of it penned by respectable, middle-class easterners—the new state served as an important locus for transmitting knowledge of conciliation courts across the nation. The dominant (and influential) image of such institutions created by this literature was that they were suited only to primitive, deferential peoples lacking the independent spirit necessary for governing themselves through the fixed, predictable rule of law and for engaging in productive market competition.

Because the function of conciliation was long understood to be a core component of the *alcalde*'s responsibilities, it seems probable that judicial conciliation proceedings were first established in California in 1779, at the time that the region's Spanish governor created local *alcaldes*. The *alcalde*'s role as a conciliating judge was then formalized as a legal requirement in the Cádiz Constitution of 1812. While enforcement of this constitution was in abeyance after the return to absolutist rule in 1814, it came back into force in 1820 during a brief period of Spanish liberalization. Shortly thereafter, when Mexico gained its independence in 1821, the Cádiz Constitution was deemed to be applicable law, until such time as it was superseded.[51]

The first Mexican constitution, enacted in 1824, continued the tradition of requiring pre-suit conciliation proceedings, but without setting forth any specifics. These were finally established in legislation enacted on March 20 and May 23, 1837. Borrowing many aspects of French law—including the Napoleonic administrative structure of regional prefectures—the March 20 legislation created a new set of officials entitled *jueces de paz,* or justices of the peace, apparently inspired by the French *justices de paix.* As directed by this legislation, *jueces de paz* were henceforth to perform many of the judicial duties (including conciliation) that had been previously entrusted to *alcaldes* alone. *Alcaldes* were to exercise their authority primarily in large towns, while *jueces de paz* were to operate both within smaller rural villages and within particular urban neighborhoods. As for the conciliation procedure that these officers were to follow, this was detailed in the May 23 statute, which adopted in large measure the language of the Cádiz Constitution and its implementing legislation of October 9, 1812. As David Langum demonstrates, these conciliation proceedings proved extremely successful, resolving on the order of 85 percent of the disputes that came before *alcaldes* and *jueces de paz.*[52] Such proceedings were therefore well established—and quite popular—when the United States gained control over California in 1848, in the wake of the U.S.-Mexican War.

During this period, it was generally understood that, pursuant to established principles of international law, Mexican law governing private relations was to remain in force until such time as Congress or the new state legislature was to act. In the view of many contemporaries, this principle extended to the law governing civil proceedings. For this reason, the appendix to the published report of the debates at the California Constitutional Convention of 1849 reprinted large excerpts of the Mexican statutes of March 20 and May 23, 1837—including those portions mandating conciliation. As explained in an introduction to the appendix authored by Henry Halleck, the lawyer and army officer who came to serve as California's military secretary of state and who played a substantial role in drafting the state constitution, the decision to reprint these Mexican statutes stemmed from the fact that "some months will necessarily elapse before the existing government and laws of California can be changed."[53] Until such time, Halleck suggested, these statutes were to remain in force.

Not surprisingly, given the belief that the March 20 and May 23, 1837, statutes remained good law, contemporary litigants continued to invoke them. When lawsuits were filed without first attempting conciliation before an *alcalde,* many litigants sought dismissal by pointing to Mexican law. As the California Supreme Court observed in *Von Schmidt v. Huntington,* a March 1850 decision addressing precisely such a motion for dismissal, "this point has been frequently made heretofore."[54] Moreover, the evidence suggests that it was not only defendants eager for dismissal who demanded adherence to traditional practices of conciliation. The various accounts of life in California published by recent migrants from the eastern United States who were elected to serve as local *alcaldes* reveal that, even after the American invasion of 1846, such officials continued to devote a substantial amount of time to reconciling disputants.[55]

But while there is good reason to believe that conciliation court proceedings were well rooted in California at the time of annexation, no legislative debate concerning their preservation—of the kind that took place in territorial Florida—appears to have arisen. The California Constitution of 1849 authorized the legislature to establish "tribunals of conciliation."[56] But this provision was adopted on the recommendation of the Convention's Judiciary Committee and without any reported debate. The Judiciary Committee, in turn, seems to have taken this language directly from the New York Constitution of 1846—one of a few state constitutions from which the California drafters borrowed heavily. It is thus unclear precisely what those who voted in favor of the conciliation courts provision had in mind. Although it is probable that at least some believed that they were authorizing the legislature to enact Spanish-style conciliation courts, there is no direct evidence to this effect.[57] The legislature itself, moreover, never attempted to establish such courts.

The absence of any meaningful legislative debate on the preservation of conciliation courts is likely attributable to the fast action of the newly created

California Supreme Court. Just months after the legislature first met in December 1849, the Court ruled in *Von Schmidt* that the conciliation tradition had been superseded by American law. This case arose as a dispute between co-owners of a joint stock company established to undertake gold mining in California. The defendants moved to dismiss on the grounds that the plaintiffs had not attempted conciliation as required by prevailing Mexican law.[58] The trial court, in turn, denied the motion and ultimately ruled in the plaintiffs' favor, leading the defendants to appeal. On appeal, the defendants argued, inter alia, that the trial court erred in denying their motion to dismiss the suit for failure to attempt conciliation. The California Supreme Court upheld the lower court's decision, ruling that disputants were henceforth not required to comply with the conciliation provisions of Mexican law.

Although the California Supreme Court did not elaborate on the basis of its holding in *Von Schmidt,* its core logic was strikingly reminiscent of one of the central claims of those who had opposed conciliation courts in territorial Florida about two decades earlier—namely, that however well suited such courts were to other cultures, they had no place in the American legal system. In the Court's words,

> Notwithstanding the importance which seems to be attached to the trial of *conciliacion* by Spanish and Mexican writers . . . and even conceding that it may operate beneficially in the nations for which it was originally designed, still, amongst the American people it can be looked upon in no other light than as a useless and dilatory formality, unattended by a single profitable result, and not affecting the substantial justice of any case.

What, precisely, was so wrong with these institutions in the American context? Unlike the Floridians who had claimed that conciliation courts rendered a deprivation of liberty, the California Supreme Court was more restrained in its criticism, insisting simply that the institution had become obsolete, such that it was invoked only by defendants seeking dismissal: "[S]ince the acquisition of California by the Americans, the proceeding of *conciliacion* has, in all cases, been deemed a useless formality by the greater portion of the members of the bar, by the Courts and by the people; . . . it has, in fact, passed into disuse and become obsolete."[59]

Despite this language, it seems highly unlikely that obsolescence was the real basis of the Court's decision. As described above, there is good reason to believe that there was a robust, functioning system of conciliation proceedings that operated through 1848. That there was some diminution in interest in these proceedings at the time of annexation is, of course, possible. Those of Mexican origin may have been reluctant to seek conciliation before newly elected American *alcaldes*. And recent American migrants may have been uncomfortable with proceedings that struck them as alien. Moreover, according to at least one scholar, the nature of the disputes that arose became increasingly complex at this time—presumably as a result of economic development—and this, in turn, led to a decrease in (but not the disappearance of) conciliation proceedings.[60] But even if there was some decline in the number of conciliation proceedings that took place, the notion that they suddenly became so neglected as to be rendered obsolete is an exaggeration—more an indication of the California Supreme Court's aspirations than of the facts on the ground. The Court, however, was not unique in its view that there was something fundamentally un-American about the Spanish tradition of conciliation courts. This same belief was widely espoused in the many narratives of life in California penned by recent migrants from the eastern United States—including, interestingly, by those who themselves served as *alcaldes*.

The authors of these narratives drew a distinction between formal adjudication and *alcalde* justice (as epitomized by the requirement of conciliation) that parallels in many ways the distinction that Max Weber would draw—more than a half-century later—between (modern) formally rational legal systems and (primitive) kadi justice. In Weber's framework, modern, Western legal systems are characterized by a trend toward formal rationality—namely, the development of fixed legal rules that are to be applied in all cases of a similar type, thus generating clear, predictable results regardless of the identity of the particular judge. Weber contrasted such legal systems with kadi justice, an ideal type based on (but in no way limited to) the Islamic law judges of the Muslim world. According to Weber, kadi justice is characterized by the judge's effort to achieve equity in the particular case without regard to the issue of predictability. As such, it is a form of personalized justice, whose legitimacy hinges largely on the judge's high status within the community and his concomitant ability to give voice to communal norms and values, while also securing deference to his own individual judgments. As Weber explained, kadi justice "display[s] a peculiar co-existence of strict traditionalism and of arbitrariness and lordly discretion."[61] The distinction between modern, Western adjudication and kadi justice is thus not reducible to the opposition between formality and informality or predictability and unpredictability but also concerns forms of deference. While modern, rational legal systems are premised on deference to the (abstract) rule of law, kadi justice is premised on deference to the (particular) rule of men.

Along similar lines, Americans describing the Mexican legal system that they encountered in California drew a distinction between the personalized, case-specific, and irrational justice rendered by *alcaldes* (a Spanish derivation of the Islamic kadi) and the abstract, broadly applicable and rational justice of formal, American adjudication. As David Langum argues, American expatriates disdained the *alcalde* system and its emphasis on conciliation, because they associated it with kadi justice—or rather, in his words, because of its "paternalistic nature" and its tendency to undermine "certainty and predictability in the law."[62] But while Langum is correct that such criticisms were common, he neglects the evidence that many Americans—including those who themselves served as *alcaldes*—were also deeply enamored with the institution that they criticized. Indeed, Langum misleads in characterizing the American encounter with Mexican law as a "collision" of "legal values"—as a conflict between "the embodiment into law of individualism, enshrined as a norm by Anglo-Americans" and "the paternalism, communalism, and spirit of conciliation embodied into law by Mexican Californians."[63] This characterization implies that American legal culture, as a kind of platonic ideal, came into necessary, inevitable conflict with its Mexican counterpart—and it thereby obscures the extent to which the former was itself in flux and subject to significant internal contestation. Contemporary Americans, engaged in a series of profound internal debates concerning such core issues as national identity, market change, and religious revivalism, came to construct their own American legal culture in relation to the alien people and practices that they encountered in California, repelled by but also attracted to various aspects of Mexican law.

While it is difficult to draw a great many generalizations from the narratives written by the various Americans who served as *alcaldes* in that the authors differed along any number of dimensions (including, not least, age and professional background), certain commonalities are nonetheless striking. In particular, such authors suggested that preserving the office of the *alcalde* was a temporary expedient, in deep tension with the American commitment to the rule of law, even as they also savored the unrestrained authority that they themselves were able to wield while serving in the office. Moreover, their reasons for savoring this unrestrained authority appear to have been linked in important, though differing, ways with the profound social and cultural tensions stemming from recent market developments.

Consider first the account penned by Stephen J. Field, which in certain respects seems to embody the type of Gold Rush narrative studied by Brian
Roberts.[64] As Roberts observes, contemporary eyewitness accounts of life in
California around the time of the Gold Rush—accounts that still form the basis of much of our understanding of this period—were written primarily by
East Coast transplants of middle-class origins. While many of these authors
sought to depict themselves as simple, rugged men in no way bound by the
niceties of civilization, the very fact that they were literate individuals capable
of publishing such successful works serves as an important reminder that, for
the most part, they were not as down and out as they liked to suggest. To the
contrary, the unrestrained, rough persona developed by these men was a literary construct—one that represented a rebellion against the bourgeois strictures (of gender identity, work ethic, religion, and the like) that they had
imbibed as young men growing up in the East in an era of rapid market expansion. In this respect, the literature of the Gold Rush is a metric of the extent to
which the new middle class produced by the market revolution had become
firmly established and institutionalized.[65]

Although Field made no pretense of being unlearned, his account of his
experiences in California is strikingly consistent with Roberts's depiction of
the Gold Rush narratives as a form of bourgeois rebellion. Field was himself
the very prototype of middle-class manhood then taking shape in the eastern
United States. The son of a minister, he was born in Haddam, Connecticut, on
November 4, 1816, and studied at Williams College before apprenticing in law.
Having begun his career in the law office of his brother, David Dudley, he
would go on to become a justice of the United States Supreme Court and, as
such, the iconic defender of "liberty of contract."[66] Field thereby played a vital
role in establishing the legal framework that facilitated the remarkable economic growth of the Gilded Age—and a key component of his jurisprudence
was a commitment to an ideal of fixed and (at least facially) neutral rules of law
that he believed would maximize liberty by ensuring a level and predictable
playing field. In this sense, Field's "liberty of contract" was a kind of liberty
that could be found only within the binding constraints of law. In contrast, the
office of the *alcalde* offered him the frisson of a very different, primitive, and
manly sort of liberty—namely, freedom from law itself.

After a brief stint working for his brother, Field returned from the tour of
Europe requisite for young American men of means of his generation and encountered the news that gold had been discovered in California. In December
1849, he opted to join the hundreds of other lawyers from across the country

Figure 8  Unidentified photographer, *Justice Stephen
Johnson Field* (circa 1865–80). Courtesy of the Library of
Congress.

who migrated to California in this period, seeking to try their luck not in gold
mining but instead in the interrelated arenas of law and politics. Field's gamble
quickly proved to be a wise one, as on January 18, 1850, just a few weeks after
arriving, he was elected *alcalde* of Marysville, a newly established town near
Sacramento.[67]

For Field, serving as an *alcalde* provided a chance to assume a heroic, larger-
than-life authority within the local community. Pointing to the multiplicity of
roles—judicial, executive, and legislative—traditionally played by *alcaldes,* he
noted of his tenure in office that "until I was superseded by officers under
State government, I superintended municipal affairs and administered justice
in Marysville with success . . . [such that] [i]t was the model town of the whole
country for peacefulness and respect for law." As he described it, a significant
part of what made his role as *alcalde* such a thrill was precisely that it departed

so much from the norms of lawfulness to which he was accustomed. By combining distinct forms of governmental power in a single office, the institution
of the *alcalde* violated basic principles of separation of powers and threatened
to aggregate more power in a single person than was compatible with democratic rule. As Field explained, whatever the extent of the authority exercised
by *alcaldes* under Mexican rule, the fact that such officers were the main governmental institution preserved under American occupation meant that "they
exercised almost unlimited powers." The vertiginous sense of being freed
from the constraints of law that Field experienced as an *alcalde* was magnified
by the fact that, to whatever (in his view limited) extent Mexican *alcaldes* had
been expected to apply the law, their American successors simply had no
knowledge of the law that they were to apply. In Field's words, "I knew nothing
of Mexican laws; did not pretend to know anything of them; but I knew that
the people had elected me to act as a magistrate and looked to me for the preservation of order and the settlement of disputes; and I did my best that they
should not be disappointed."[68]

It was in his official role as conciliator, however, that Field seems to have
taken the greatest pleasure: Here he was lawfully authorized to depart from
the law. As he later recollected, conciliation was among his primary duties as
*alcalde,* and accordingly, he served "as arbitrator in a great number of controversies which arose between the citizens." In such cases, the parties "generally
came to my office together" without counsel, and for the most part, "[t]he
whole matter was disposed of without any written proceedings. . . ." According to Field, he resolved a broad array of disputes in this way, including those
concerning employment, commercial contracts, and marital relations. As for
the manner in which he proceeded, he made no reference to the Spanish and
Mexican tradition of calling upon two "good men" to assist in his efforts. But
as was the case with his Spanish and Mexican predecessors, he seems to have
relied extensively on his high standing in the community to encourage deference to his conciliatory judgment. As he remembered it, he needed only to
offer his commonsense opinion regarding what justice required for the disputants quickly to recognize the wisdom of his recommendation and to defer to
it. Thus, for example, in the case of a couple seeking "relief from the bonds of
matrimony," he "heard their respective complaints, and finding that they had
children . . . , persuaded them to make peace, kiss, and forgive; and so they left
[his] office arm-in-arm. . . ."[69]

Field's memory was, no doubt, self-serving and selective. But his insistence
that locals readily deferred to his wisdom helps explain the satisfaction he

experienced serving as *alcalde* and the image of this institution that he there-after conveyed to fellow Americans. In language highlighting the etymological and institutional link between the Muslim kadi and the Spanish *alcalde,* he recalled: "I carried out my conception of the good Cadi of the village, from which term (Al Cadi) my own official designation, *Alcalde,* was derived."[70] As this suggests, Field's conception of his role as *alcalde*—and especially as a conciliator—partakes of the ideal of "legal primitivism" that, as Steven Wilf argues, was deeply appealing in this era because it served as "an *alter-id* for Victorian Anglo-America."[71] As a man who embodied ideals of middle-class respectability, Field experienced in his brief service as *alcalde* a liberating release from the constraints of bourgeois legal (and market) rationality. Yet, at the same time—and, indeed, for this very reason—he concluded that the office of the *alcalde* was a primitive institution, in no way suited to the modern United States.

A different sort of narrative was penned by another man who came to serve as *alcalde* in this period: the Reverend Walter Colton. Born in Rutland, Vermont, on May 9, 1797, Colton pursued training in theology and then moved to Washington, D.C., to work as a preacher and as an assistant editor on a new missionary newspaper. In his clerical capacity, he came to know President Andrew Jackson, who took a liking to him and appointed him a navy chaplain. In that role, Colton was sent to California, where on July 28, 1846, Commodore Robert Stockton named him *alcalde* of Monterey just a few weeks after the American flag was first raised in the town. Shortly thereafter, on September 15, he was elected to the same position by a vote of the local community. After serving in California for three years, during which time he also established the first American newspaper in the territory, he returned to the East Coast and published a narrative describing his experiences that came to be extremely popular and was reissued in several editions.[72]

While Field experienced his time as an *alcalde* as a youthful rebellion against the strictures of his own middle-class identity, Colton—a middle-aged man at the time of serving in the office—viewed the position as providing an opportunity to fulfill the revivalist ideals to which he had long committed himself. An evangelical, nativist minister who was a founding member of the American Protestant Association—an organization devoted to "oppos[ing] the progress of Romanism in this country"[73]—Colton relished the opportunities afforded by his work as an *alcalde* not only to curb such vices as dancing, gambling, and drinking spirits[74] but also to bring American (Protestant) values of self-control and self-governance to what had been a predominantly Catholic

Figure 9  Unidentified artist, *Walter Colton* (n.d.).
Courtesy of The Bancroft Library, University of
California, Berkeley.

community.[75] But while his service as an *alcalde* represented the fulfillment
(rather than the rejection) of his long-term values, the revivalist project that
inspired his actions was itself, as we have seen, partly a reaction to market
change. In this sense, his experience as an *alcalde,* much like Field's, was profoundly shaped by the dramatic socioeconomic transformations of the era.
Moreover, like Field, he too had conflicting views of the *alcalde* system. While
he celebrated the power with which he was endowed as an *alcalde,* rejoicing in
the many opportunities it afforded him to pursue his evangelical goals of social reform and purification, he also feared that the granting of such personalized, discretionary authority to a single officer was antithetical to the American
(Protestant) way of life and law.

   In addition to deploying his authority as an *alcalde* to attempt to root out
various kinds of vice, Colton utilized it to promote his vision of good Christian

relations. For this reason, he—much like Field—appears to have viewed his role as a conciliator as the most gratifying. As he described it, such peacemaking called not for legal expertise but instead for the clerical wisdom (or charisma) so central to his own professional identity as a preacher. For example, he depicted with great self-satisfaction his ability to reconcile two washer-women who were on the verge of coming to blows. According to Colton, the women were fighting over access to a pool of water in which to do their washing and, unable to resolve their dispute on their own, "rushed down to the office to have their difficulties settled." Like Field, Colton proceeded simply. He listened to each party's account of the conflict and then formed an opinion as to where justice lay, which he then persuaded the parties to embrace. In Colton's words,

> Both . . . [women] commenced talking at the same time; and their stories ran together like two conflicting rivulets forced into the same channel. There was plenty of tumult and bubble. When these had a little subsided, I began cautiously to angle for the truth—a difficult trout to catch in such waters. But one darter after another was captured, till I had enough to form some opinion of those that had escaped. These we discussed till bitter feeling, like biting hunger, became appeased. The rest was very easily settled. Both went away declaring either margin of the pool good enough, and each urging on the other the first choice.

Evidently so moved by his success that he found it necessary to express himself in verse, Colton observed:

> How gentle is forgiveness! And how sweet
> To feel the severed heart flow back again
> To one we loved, estranged by hasty words![76]

But while taking enormous pride in his role as the conciliating *alcalde,* Colton, like Field, suggested that such personalized justice was contrary to the American way. Exercising a vast array of judicial, legislative, and executive functions, the *alcalde* operated to a remarkable extent outside the bounds of law. As Colton explained, "an *alcalde* under the Mexican law, has a large scope in which to exercise his sense of moral justice." Indeed, especially "[i]n minor matters the *alcalde* is often himself the law." For this reason, among others, Colton concluded that "[t]here is not a judge on any bench in England or the United States, whose power is so absolute as that of the *alcalde* of Monterey." The great problem with entrusting so much power to a single person was that there was no guarantee that all men would be able to be at once "absolute" but also "upright, impartial, and humane." Such personalized justice also tended to breed subservience within the citizenry. As he remarked, the mere sight of the *alcalde*'s cane, which traditionally bore the insignia of the office, was sufficient to cause locals to defer to the officeholder's judgment: "The authority of that baton they always respect. How comfortable it is for one to carry his moral power on the top of his cane."[77] But while such deference was useful to Colton in his efforts as *alcalde* to curb vices like gambling, he did not believe that a passive citizenry was suited to a free, Protestant country like the United States; such subservience was instead characteristic of Catholic nations.

Referencing a heated contemporary debate between Protestants and Catholics concerning the correct reading of a New Testament passage regarding the patriarch Jacob, Colton noted that the deference extended to the *alcalde*'s cane "almost justifies the Roman Catholic exegesis—and Jacob worshipped the top of his staff."[78] This Catholic translation of the biblical text—deployed to legitimate the use of crucifixes and other religious icons—was deemed by Protestants to be a misreading designed to promote (impermissible) image worship.[79] Pursuant to a well-established Protestant tradition, such image worship was said to go hand in hand with a Catholic tendency toward mindless subservience—to officers of both church and state. As Colton wrote in an 1844 pamphlet, published shortly before his departure for California, the Catholic Church promoted the " 'mental vassalage of the common people' " and, for this reason, ought to be relegated to countries, unlike the United States, "where men have never tasted freedom, and never exercised the rights of their moral nature."[80]

By thus linking deference to the *alcalde*'s cane with the Catholic tradition of image worship, Colton made it abundantly clear that there was no place for *alcaldes* in the United States—a nation that, as he argued in his 1844 pamphlet, was a "Protestant land," in which "the spirit of the Protestant faith pervades the very genius of its institutions."[81] In this respect, the institution of the *alcalde* posed, for Colton, an unresolved dilemma. While the power that the *alcalde* exercised could be utilized to promote Protestant revivalist ideals, so too this power (and the deference to authority that it tended to encourage) were fundamentally incompatible with these very same ideals.

Penned by respectable middle-class Americans who briefly served as *alcaldes*, these Gold Rush narratives, among others,[82] helped to develop (and propagate across the country) conflicting conceptions of the *alcalde* and his conciliating role. On the positive side, the institution promised a welcome reprieve from the increasingly triumphant logic of the market and the middle-class culture to which it gave rise as well as an opportunity to pursue evangelical ideals of peacemaking and reform (whose urgency was itself a by-product of market change). The more dominant message, however, was that the *alcalde* system and its practice of case-specific, equitable conciliation were fundamentally incompatible with the American commitment to market-oriented (and Protestant) liberty.

## The New York Debates

While the debates over whether to preserve conciliation courts in Florida and California played an important role in steering Americans toward adversarial procedure, their influence was necessarily limited by the fact that these regions remained at this time relatively remote backwaters. It was a separate set of discussions that took place in New York—a state that lay at the heart of the twin developments of market revolution and religious revivalism and whose legal system was arguably the most influential in the country—that proved decisive in the American embrace of adversarialism. These discussions (over whether to transplant conciliation courts from abroad) began within institutions of civil society—in newspapers, lectures, and sermons—and came ultimately to center on the state constitutional convention of 1846.

### ORIGINS OF THE DEBATE: LORD BROUGHAM AND RELIGIOUS REVIVALISM

What were the origins of the New York debates on conciliation courts? It is tempting to look to disputes over the *juicio de conciliación* in Florida and California as possible points of departure. Contemporaneous reports of the debates regarding conciliation courts within the legislative council of territorial Florida did appear in a few newspapers published in the Northeast.[83] These debates, however, do not seem to have received extensive coverage. It is thus far from clear that delegates to the New York Convention more than two decades later had any knowledge of them. As concerns the discussions that took place in California—including the various narratives published by American *alcaldes*—these arose upon the close of the U.S.-Mexican War in 1848 and therefore played no role in shaping debates at the convention, which was held two years earlier.

That said, delegates to the convention were clearly aware of the existence of conciliation courts within the Spanish Empire. Delegate Charles Kirkland, for example, observed that "[s]everal years ago [conciliation courts] were established in Denmark, in Prussia, in France, and in Spain, and in all the countries where they had been in operation, they had uniformly been pronounced to be sources of the greatest blessings to the people."[84] But as this statement suggests, delegates do not seem to have had any particular interest in the *juicio de conciliación* as such, and instead (like Bentham) viewed the Spanish example as part of a broader European pattern. The New York debates on conciliation courts thus appear to have arisen largely independently of those in Florida and California—though strikingly, they followed much the same course, leading to an ultimate rejection of these institutions and a concomitant embrace of adversarialism.

What, then, were the origins of the New York debates? An initial flurry of discussion arose in the early years of the nineteenth century as a result of an article published in the highly influential *Edinburgh Review*—a Whig journal advocating legal and political reform that enjoyed widespread readership on both sides of the Atlantic.[85] This 1803 article provided an extensive review of the first account of the Danish conciliation courts to appear in the mainstream European press: Jean-Pierre Catteau-Callville's *Tableau des états danois* (*Portrait of the Danish States*). As suggested by its title, Catteau-Callville's book offered a broad overview of Danish political and social life, but as part of this analysis devoted significant attention to the conciliation courts. In Catteau-Callville's view, these courts had achieved great success in persuading litigants to settle outside of the ordinary court system, thus sparing them the costs and delays of litigation: "A short experience has sufficed to convince the government of the utility of this institution. During the three years that preceded that of its establishment, 25,521 lawsuits were filed in the trial courts; during the three subsequent years, the number was only 9,653; a difference thus of 15,868."[86] In its review of the book, the *Edinburgh Review* presented a comprehensive account of the various chapters but focused at some length on the discussion of conciliation courts, lauding them, like Catteau-Callville himself, for the rapid and cheap justice that they provided.[87] The portion of the review concerning conciliation courts (and only that portion) was thereafter copied verbatim in numerous American newspapers across the East Coast, including at least two in New York.[88]

As suggested by this extensive publication of articles in praise of the Danish conciliation courts, such institutions struck a chord in early nineteenth-century American political culture. They appealed to the many Americans of the period who were deeply resentful of the increasingly powerful (and long disdained) legal profession.[89] Consistent with this pervasive anti-lawyer sentiment, some contemporaries called for the development of modes of dispute resolution that would eschew reliance on lawyers. Among such proposals were demands for a return to earlier, native traditions of informal dispute resolution, including the Quaker-derived Pennsylvania custom of relying on laymen to serve as peacemaking referees and the use of merchant-run arbitral tribunals in New York and South Carolina. According to Morton Horwitz, practices of this kind came under attack in the early nineteenth century as state courts sought to restrict the independent power and discretion of lay arbiters.[90] But not all contemporaries were pleased with this chain of events. Jesse Higgins of Philadelphia, for example, argued in an 1805 tract for a reinvigoration of traditional practices of *"reference, adjustment, or arbitration,"* which he claimed were approximations of "the ancient trial by jury, before the same was innovated by judges and lawyers."[91]

The early nineteenth-century appeal of the European conciliation court was precisely that it seemed to offer another, untried—and thus perhaps more fruitful—avenue for challenging the growing power of the legal profession. As argued, in a July 5, 1805, article published in the *Enquirer* of Richmond, there was a great need for conciliation courts, because "the governor, the judges, the lawyers and all the advocates of antiquated institutions have avowed their approbation and extended their support to the whole routine of courts of law, their multifarious forms, their counsellors, their numerous, learned and disciplined judges."[92] But such calls for the establishment of European conciliation courts bore no fruit. After the brief discussion spurred by the *Edinburgh Review* article, conciliation courts largely disappeared from the public eye until the 1840s. It was this later discussion, culminating in the debates of the New York Constitutional Convention of 1846, which was to have a more lasting influence—though this too has now been all but erased from memory.

What happened to bring European conciliation courts back into public debate in the 1840s? And why did this second round of discussion prove so much more influential than the first? One important reason for the rediscovery of conciliation courts in this period (and for the sustained attention they received at this time) was the influence of England—and, in particular, the Whig Party's reforming chancellor, Lord Henry Brougham. From the late 1820s onward, Brougham launched a concerted campaign to establish conciliation courts within England. This campaign, in turn, proved (like most things English in this period) to be of significant interest to contemporary Americans.

Greatly influenced by Bentham, Brougham argued for an extensive restructuring of the judiciary. Beginning with a famous speech to Parliament in 1828 and continuing well into the 1850s, he called for the simplification of court procedure with an eye toward decreasing the costs and delays associated with litigation and thus opening the justice system to more than a privileged, wealthy few. Included as a key component of his plans for procedural reform was a proposal—evidently inspired by Bentham—to establish conciliation courts.[93] Observing that "[s]uch a tribunal exists in France, under the name of *Cour de Conciliation;* in Denmark it exists; and for certain mercantile causes in Holland also," Brougham argued that such a court ought to be created in England as well.[94]

More a politician than a philosopher, Brougham evidently did not share (or at least failed to express) Bentham's doubts about the virtues of conciliation courts and in particular the latter's anxieties that such institutions might work to subvert the rule of law. Never pausing to consider how precisely conciliation would be achieved, Brougham suggested that conciliation judges would oversee public, lawyer-assisted proceedings aimed at pacifying the litigants and thus encouraging them to comply more readily (and at a lower cost) with the formal letter of the law. In his view, all that had to be done to ensure that conciliation courts would not undermine legal rights, and thus the rule of law, was to guarantee as a formal matter the voluntary nature of the decision to participate in conciliation proceedings and to abide by any proposed compromise.[95]

However superficial Brougham's analysis, and despite the fact that he ultimately failed in his campaign to establish conciliation courts, his advocacy of such institutions received widespread attention in both the English and American press, including perhaps most importantly in the highly influential journal of which he was a founding editor—namely, the *Edinburgh Review*. New Yorkers, especially elite lawyers and politicians, appear to have taken particular note. Henry Vanderlyn, for example, devoted a diary entry in the summer of 1837 to the subject of "Courts of Reconcilement for Hearing and Advising"—an "experiment," he remarked, that "has been tried in many countries." While Vanderlyn expressed some skepticism regarding the efficacy of such courts, he observed that they were "recommended in England by Lord Brougham" and were thus a topic of discussion in "the Ed. Review."[96] Likewise, about a decade later, a delegate to the 1846 New York Constitutional Convention urged that "the subject of conciliation courts was worthy of more consideration than some gentlemen seemed willing to bestow upon them" and, in so doing, emphasized that such courts "had received great consideration in England."[97]

But while Americans in this period were predisposed carefully to follow (and sometimes to imitate) English legal and political developments, it was a set of circumstances internal to the United States (and especially to New York) that ultimately explains why a good many contemporary New Yorkers were so taken with the notion of establishing conciliation courts. As we have seen, anxieties stemming from market change helped give rise to the Second Great Awakening—a nationwide phenomenon, but one that centered on certain regions, including most importantly the burned-over district of central and western New York. These anxieties, in turn, were greatly exacerbated by the Panic of 1837. Now thought to have originated in the international movement of specie, rather than, as long believed, in Jacksonian policy, the panic and its consequences were severe. As banks throughout the United States failed, credit quickly dried up, and the country entered a severe depression, rivaling in various respects that which took place between 1929 and 1933. Although the economy began to revive in 1838, the following year witnessed yet another set of bank runs, sometimes termed the Panic of 1839. Accordingly, full recovery did not begin until 1843. While scholars today disagree about the extent of unemployment and whether reductions in wages had a significant impact on real incomes, it is clear that, however we quantify the hardships suffered, many at the time lost their jobs and, as a result, were unable to feed and clothe themselves and their families.[98] The magnitude of the suffering is powerfully captured in an 1837 lithograph entitled simply "The Times" (fig. 10), which depicts a city devastated by bank runs, begging, and drunken idleness, as the local pawnbroker—Shylock Graspall—rakes in a fortune.

Although large urban centers like New York City appear to have borne the brunt of the depression, the relatively prosperous communities of upstate New York were not immune. As Jan Saltzgaber writes of Seneca Falls, while the depression did not "wreck[] the prosperity of the community, [it] slowed the pace of development, transformed the character of enterprise, and tempered optimism with caution."[99] For contemporaries, increasingly bound together by vital but precarious relations of credit, the anxiety that they were subject to the merciless whims of anonymous market forces was greatly exacerbated by the financial panics of the late 1830s and the ensuing depression.[100] And not surprisingly, there is evidence that religious revivalism (at least of certain stripes) proved particularly appealing in the period immediately after the panics. This was clearly the case, for example, of the highly influential Millerite movement, which, as Michael Barkun explains, "crested as the economy hit bottom."[101] Painted in 1839, J. Maze Burbank's depiction of a religious

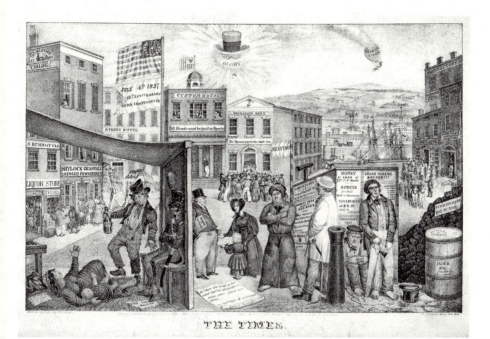

Figure 10  Unidentified artist, *The Times* (1837). Courtesy of the American
Antiquarian Society.

camp meeting conveys the remarkable power of revivalism at this moment, showcasing how itinerant preachers were able to stir large throngs into paroxysms of piety (fig. 11).

Consumed with religious fervor, evangelicals responded to the radical socioeconomic transformations occurring all around them (including the panics and their aftermath) by promoting various kinds of Christian social reform. Seeking to temper the spirit of self-interest that had fueled the speculative fever thought to underlie the panics of 1837 and 1839, they argued that people must significantly curb their appetites. Reformers thus called for temperance, sexual purity, and hard work. So too, they drew on a long tradition of Christian thought that associated peacemaking with the virtuous abnegation of self to denounce the instinct for dominance and vengeance that led to litigation, pleading instead for the promotion of communal reconciliation and harmony. Accordingly, when New Yorkers learned about conciliation courts in this period, they did not conceive of them (as they had in the very early years of the nineteenth century) simply as a means of limiting the power of much-hated

Figure 11  J. Maze Burbank, *Religious Camp Meeting—An Oldtime Camp Meeting* (1839). Courtesy of the New Bedford Whaling Museum.

lawyers—though such anti-lawyer sentiment likely remained a motivating interest for some. These courts were instead now viewed primarily as one component of a broader (and highly influential) revivalist reform agenda, aimed in no small part at the dangers posed by market change.

Foremost among the evangelical leaders who preached about the importance of creating conciliation courts was the renowned Presbyterian minister Robert Baird. At the precise moment that the New York Constitutional Convention met in 1846, Baird was engaged in a well-received and much-reported lecture tour that sparked considerable American interest in conciliation courts—particularly in those areas of the country, like significant portions of New York, that had been touched by the Second Great Awakening. Baird had gained fame in both the United States and Europe through the 1842 publication (and subsequent reissuings and translations) of *Religion in America*, in which he sought to explain and justify the role of religious revivalism in American social and political life. Having thus established an international reputation, Baird began in 1844 and 1845 to tour the United States, presenting a series of lectures on the impressions of continental Europe (and especially Scandinavia) that he had gained while traveling to advocate for world temperance reform and for the establishment of an international evangelical alliance. As reported in contemporary American newspapers, one of the key points that he made in this tour, which continued well into the 1850s, was how much he admired the Danish conciliation courts.[102] According to Baird, such courts were evidence of a "high state of civilization."[103]

Given the centrality of New York (and its burned-over district) in fueling the fires of religious revivalism, as well as the leading role that the state and its legal system had long played in national life, those seeking the establishment of European-style conciliation courts concluded that the 1846 convention was tailor-made for their purposes. Calls were thus quickly issued for the convention to create such courts. For example, on May 9, a few weeks before the convention was to meet, the *Friends' Weekly Intelligencer* of Philadelphia presented an overview of Baird's Scandinavian lecture, which it concluded by calling on "our New York friends . . . [to] take a lesson, now they are about revising their Constitution from . . . [the] Danish . . . Court of Conciliation. . . ."[104] Such demands for the establishment of conciliation courts were evidently heard by those attending the convention. As observed by delegate John Miller, a farmer from Cortland County, "The attention of the people had been called to th[e] subject [of establishing conciliation courts]; they had earnestly desired to have them to try them; there was a great demand for them throughout the State" and "[t]he president of the Convention himself had been addressed on this subject through the newspapers by able persons who took a deep interest in the subject."[105]

## THE CONSTITUTIONAL CONVENTION OF 1846

Inspired by such demands, a number of delegates to the New York Constitutional Convention called for the establishment of conciliation courts by pointing to their success on European soil. While those delegates arguing in favor of conciliation courts had no clear, precise model on which they agreed, they envisioned an institution whose core features replicated those of the various French and French-derived courts that together constituted Bentham's ideal type of the European conciliation court. As delegate Charles Kirkland, a Whig lawyer from Oneida County and a member of the convention's Judiciary Committee,[106] insisted, such institutions would operate not by enforcing a universally applicable legal rule but instead by "endeavor[ing] to induce [the parties] to adjust their difficulties amicably." Given this conception of the courts' mission, such delegates resisted any involvement of lawyers in the proceedings—either as judges or as advocates. Since the law was not to be decisive, lawyers were unnecessary. As Kirkland emphasized, "none but the parties themselves" were to appear before the judge.[107] So too delegate Alvah Worden—a Whig lawyer from Ontario County and also a member of the Judiciary Committee[108]—observed that there are no "counsel or attorneys employed" in European conciliation courts.[109]

Because those advocating the establishment of conciliation courts viewed them as a method for achieving flexible compromise outside the formal bounds of the law, they also opted against publicity in such proceedings—a decision that is all the more remarkable in that it was precisely this convention that achieved near-universal agreement on the importance of eliminating those aspects of equity-court proceedings that had traditionally occurred behind closed doors. By enabling litigants to shield their dispute from public view—and thus to preserve their dignity—conciliation courts would provide a further incentive to compromise. And since formal law was not to govern such proceedings, there was no need for publicity as a means of constraining the judge to enforce the law or of educating citizens about its content and application. Delegate Kirkland thus noted that "[t]he Courts sit with closed doors. . . . As an absolute rule, nothing that passes in the Court is divulged by the members of it, and is forbidden as evidence in the Courts of law." Similarly, delegate Ansel Bascom, a lawyer from Seneca County, cited approvingly the fact that in Danish conciliation courts, judges "cause contending parties . . . to come before them in private. . . ."[110]

While advocates of conciliation courts never identified precisely how a compromise would be reached in such lawyer-free and secret proceedings, they placed great emphasis on the parties' willingness to defer to the judge's personal wisdom and discretion. Delegate Bascom, for example, remarked that the Danish conciliation courts worked by persuading parties to "submit to the influence of the conciliators." And delegate Worden, evidently trusting in people's tendency to show deference to elders, suggested that each conciliation court ought to consist of "two of the eldest justices" from the town in which the court was to be established. In addition, he argued, community sentiment itself—and, in particular, "the moral sense of the community in favor of a peaceful adjustment of difficulties"—could be harnessed as a further tool in encouraging parties to submit to judicial influence and thus to forgo the assertion of their formal legal rights.[111]

For those delegates advocating the establishment of conciliation courts, one of the great virtues of these institutions was that, by persuading disputants to reconcile, they would prevent (or at least decrease the amount of) formal litigation and thus save parties the associated costs and delays. As delegate Kirkland asserted, "The object of the tribunal . . . was to prevent litigation." For this reason, both Kirkland and, at a later date, his colleague, Conrad Swackhamer, an artisan, or "mechanic," from King's County, emphasized that three years after the Danish conciliation courts were established in 1795, they had served to reduce the total number of cases brought to trial from over twenty-five thousand to fewer than ten thousand—a piece of data likely garnered from Catteau-Callville's book, as reported in the *Edinburgh Review* and then reprinted throughout the American press. Similarly, delegate Worden claimed that conciliation courts, by tending toward "the suppression of litigation and . . . the adjustment of controversies, would do much towards repressing . . . the costs and vexation attendant upon long and protracted legal controversies, which often had no other result than the ruin of those engaged in them."[112]

In the view of those arguing for conciliation courts, however, litigation was problematic not only because of the costs and delays that it entailed. At least as troubling was the fact that to litigate was nakedly to assert self-interest and thus to encourage conflict and the concomitant disruption of communal harmony. The core problem, in short, was, as one delegate put it, "the spirit of litigation" itself. Like Robert Baird, advocates of conciliation courts appealed to the centuries-old Christian ideal of peacemaking. In this vein, delegate Swackhamer, quoting from Jesus's Beatitudes, observed:

> The highest honor is tendered to those who soothe the passions of men.—"Blessed are the peace-makers, for they shall be called the children of God,"—The principles were founded in the Christian spirit of kindness and peace. Friendly advice and kind words would very often accomplish what the law could not obtain—it would not only secure justice, but calm the anger of man. It was like the morning dew, the summer shower, it cooled and tranquilized the burning passion, leaving freshness and beauty in place of darkness and waste.

Similarly, delegate Bascom urged that conciliation courts "were in consonance with the great doctrine of Christianity, that before we should turn over our offending brother to the judge, we should exhaust every reasonable effort for reconciliation."[113]

As this expressly Christian language suggests, religion was a key influence on at least some of the delegates who urged the establishment of conciliation courts. This is not to claim, however, that every proponent of these institutions at the New York Convention was himself an evangelical Christian. As Jane Rendall argues, the evangelical spirit of reform was so pervasive and influential in this period that even those Christians (like Unitarians and Quakers) who fiercely opposed revivalism were shaped by its reforming zeal.[114] Take the example of Ansel Bascom, a delegate who, as we have seen, advocated the establishment of conciliation courts on the grounds that they accorded with principles of Christian brotherhood. A lawyer from Seneca Falls, as well as a member of the Convention's Judiciary Committee, Bascom was no evangelical, but he aggressively campaigned on behalf of those causes to which he was ideologically committed, such as temperance, abolitionism, and women's rights. Moreover, as Judith Wellman observes, Bascom and many of his "civic-minded" neighbors in Seneca Falls contributed money to build local churches—including churches run by denominations to which they did not belong—because they believed that Christian religious institutions of all sorts were vital for creating an orderly, moral community.[115] As the example of Bascom suggests, a commitment to Christian social reform—while sparked in no small measure by the Second Great Awakening—was widely shared in this period, including by those who were not themselves evangelical Christians. And for the many who were moved by this reforming spirit, the notion of establishing conciliation courts seemed like the logical extension of their other commitments to remaking—and thereby moralizing—the social order.

Because the demand for conciliation courts was spurred, in no small part, by this broader, religiously infused reforming zeal, there was a certain imprecision in the claims of those delegates to the New York Convention who advocated for their establishment. While insisting that such institutions would contribute to brotherly love, these delegates said remarkably little about their precise contours, thus failing to address such key questions as where they would be located and what the scope of their jurisdiction would be. It is clear from their comments, however, that—in line with the era's pervasive commitment to Christian social reform—many believed that conciliation courts would provide a (partial) solution to the conflict and disruption that followed from recent market developments, including urbanization and industrialization. By emphasizing reconciliation over victory, these institutions would temper the spirit of aggressive self-interest that was undermining traditional community structures, like the household economy that once joined masters and workers together under a single familial roof.

Consider, for example, Bascom's proposal. Bascom argued that, because conciliation courts were an untried experiment, they ought to be introduced at first only in those places where they were most needed. This meant, most importantly, New York City—the center of the urban industrial revolution that the state was then experiencing: "In the great commercial emporium of the State and the Union, with its thousands of questions of difference constantly arising, not only among its own citizens but among those who congregate for business purposes at that great mart of commerce, there was a necessity for a tribunal where differences could be more promptly and equitably adjudicated upon, than was possible by the existing courts." Of particular concern to Bascom were those urban-industrial disputes that touched on employment and thus class relations and that thereby raised the frightening possibility of mass social upheaval. Accordingly, he was careful to specify that conciliation courts were not necessary for disputes between New York City merchants, who already had their own "tribunal of arbitraments"—presumably a reference to the New York Chamber of Commerce, which had provided merchants with arbitration services since 1768.[116] A conciliation court was needed instead for the "immense number of questions arising between employers and contractors, artizans and merchants, owners and builders, for which no provision was made; [and] questions arising too between city and country dealers of every description. . . ."[117]

Lest anyone mistakenly conclude that he viewed such disputes as petty squabbles, Bascom was careful to point out that he "did not desire the court to settle mere justices of the peace quarrels," but instead "the large quarrels."[118] The reason, in other words, for creating special conciliation courts to address the new sources of urban litigation was not to spare the ordinary courts the burden of ostensibly trifling matters but to the contrary, to ensure that disputes implicating the foundations of the communal order would receive their proper due. Left unstated, since this background was so obvious to Bascom and his contemporaries, was New York City's recent history of labor turmoil. The late 1820s witnessed the short-lived emergence of the Working Men's Movement among the city's craft workers. As Sean Wilentz has argued, this was the first time that workers "organized across trade lines, looked beyond their immediate grievances to the deeper causes of political and social inequality—and then . . . took their conclusions into politics."[119] Shortly thereafter, with the formation of the General Trades Union in 1833—an organization estimated to have included at its peak between 20 to 30 percent of the city's white male workforce—Manhattan experienced a brief period of labor activism, including a number of significant strikes marked by occasional violence. While the union movement collapsed as a result of the Panic of 1837, workers' frustration and anger did not disappear but was instead driven into other channels, including movements for lower-class temperance and nativist reform. Indeed, by 1850, just a few short years after the meeting of the constitutional convention, militant unionism would return to the city, culminating in substantial labor unrest, including several major strikes.[120] As this background suggests, Bascom's likely aspiration was that conciliation courts might play some role in mollifying the growing tensions between capital and labor generated by market change by providing a mechanism for negotiation that would help to remedy injustice, while also forestalling workers' militancy.

Other advocates of conciliation courts, while also concerned about the dangers of social upheaval implicit in urban industrial life, questioned the capacity of such institutions to thwart these and argued that conciliation courts ought to focus instead on conflict between small-town neighbors—conflict of the kind that characterized the rural countryside. For example, delegate Worden expressed grave "doubt[s] whether [conciliation courts] could be made applicable to the state of things existing in our State, and the nature of the various dealings between individuals, or to all the questions that arise of our extensive mercantile transactions." More generally, he saw great "difficulties in making [this system of courts] applicable to the entire state, and to controversies arising between citizens residing in different portions of it." Conciliation courts were instead best suited to disputes between individuals living within the same "town" or perhaps the same "county." Used in this way, he suggested, such courts would be a means of fighting a rearguard action, helping to preserve those rural neighborly communities that he imagined had not yet succumbed to the forces of market change. The purpose of the proposed conciliation courts, he thus concluded, was to resolve "neighborhood difficulties—personal controversies—that now disturb communities, and call in aid courts and juries."[121]

Along similar lines, delegate John Taylor, a Democratic lawyer from Tioga County,[122] insisted that conciliation courts would help to preserve a neighborly ideal of small-town life. Such courts, he opined, would attract "[t]he better part of the community, men who are not litigious in their habits," and this in turn, would result in a culture where, eventually, "in a certain class of cases, men would be regarded as disposed to be quarrelsome who would not submit their differences with their neighbors to this amicable mode of settlement." While Taylor did not specify the types of cases that he imagined would be best suited to conciliation, he, like Worden, seems to have envisioned these courts as designed to restore neighborly relations. In his view, harmony in the local neighborhood would redound to the benefit of society as a whole, such that he "doubted not [that the conciliation courts'] influence would be most salutary in neighborhoods and society generally."[123]

But whether they imagined the locus of the conciliation court as the big city of Manhattan or the small rural town, the delegates supporting the establishment of such institutions envisioned them as a device for quelling the unrest and disruption that accompanied the rise of an increasingly market-driven order. In so arguing, these men did not seek radically to challenge the market foundations of society. As was the case with those who had advocated conciliation courts in territorial Florida a few decades earlier, these later New York proponents were themselves men of means and stature who profited in various ways from the market-based economy. Bascom, for example, earned a living not only as a lawyer and landowner but also as an industrialist, helping to found the Seneca Woolen Mills in 1844. He was a successful entrepreneur—but one who, as Jan Saltzgaber writes, immersed himself "in the life of the [Seneca Falls] village through a strong sense of personal dedication and moral obligation."[124] So too Alvah Worden gained fame as a lawyer by arguing an 1839 case before the New York Supreme Court, *Griffith v. Reed,* which came to be widely cited as a leading precedent in the emerging doctrine of negotiable instruments—a body of law that proved crucial in promoting the rapid and extensive circulation of credit.[125] As one of his biographers noted, the thrust of his argument in *Griffith* was to emphasize the vital importance of bills of exchange in facilitating market activity and thus "the effect of the decision to be made on the commercial relations of the country."[126] These were not the arguments of a man who was virulently opposed to market-based society. Likewise, John Taylor devoted his career not only to the practice of law and politics but also to business. Indeed, he worked in the two sectors that lay at the heart of the ongoing market revolution (namely, banking and railroads), concluding his long career by serving as the president of two different railroad companies.[127] For such men, the purpose of advocating the establishment of conciliation courts was not to eradicate, but rather to temper, the market mechanisms that had so profoundly restructured the communities in which they lived. They did not aspire to a radical redistribution of resources. But they did feel a paternalistic sense of obligation to the community—a kind of noblesse oblige—that (fueled in part by the era's revivalist and reforming ethic) motivated them to search for means of curbing the worst excesses of modern market society.

Like the proponents of conciliation courts, those delegates who opposed these institutions were driven largely by their views as to how market change was transforming the landscape of New York state. But for these men, the social conflict—and thus litigation—threatened by recent socioeconomic developments did not represent an evil to be bemoaned but instead a source of productive change. The formal adjudication of legal rights in established courts of law was vital, they argued, for a country that embraced freedom and free enterprise and that was reaping the rewards of both in the extraordinary economic growth that it was then experiencing. As asserted by Richard Marvin, a Whig lawyer from Chautauqua County who would thereafter be repeatedly elected as a state judge,[128]

> [I]n a free country like this, there would always be litigation. A country where every man was the equal of his fellow-man, where every citizen had a right to prefer his complaints and demand a patient hearing, where everyone enjoyed the right of launching upon the great ocean of enterprise his little ship whose flag was entitled to respect, where the relation of lord and vassal did not exist; where freedom was the birthright of all, in such a country and among such a people, there would be litigation. Men would defend their rights from all encroachments.[129]

To seek a world without litigation was to attempt to return to the Old World of Europe, still moored in its feudal heritage, where deference to authority hindered the assertion of the productive self-interest that was so essential to promoting a successful market and that, in turn, spurred both competition and conflict.

Just as their predecessors in territorial Florida had argued, the New York opponents of conciliation courts insisted that the problem with these institutions was not simply that, by operating on a case-by-case basis, they undermined the certainty and predictability essential for rational market activity. At least as troubling was that by deterring litigiousness (or the adversarial assertion of self-interest) conciliation courts also jeopardized the individualist and enterprising values so key to American (commercial) liberty. In the words of delegate Ambrose Jordan, a Whig lawyer from Columbia County and member of the Convention's Judiciary Committee[130]: "Such courts belonged only to a despotic government, where the people were ignorant, and had a superior class over them, and not for our free Yankee population; who consider they are competent to judge for themselves in such matters." Jordan thus concluded that the very notion of establishing conciliation courts was beneath contempt. The decision whether to create such institutions should be left to the legislature, which as a constitutional matter was free to enact any number of misguided statutes and could even "provide that old women might talk over these matters at a tea table, or that some very wise heads, some few extraordinary old gentlemen, might advise their neighbors not to be cross or litigious."[131] As this highly gendered language suggests, Jordan associated conciliation courts with a backward, premodern—indeed, pre-commercial—society in which everyone knew and deferred to the neighborhood elders. Such a social order was, of course, to be contrasted with the free and manly society of modern New York, where litigation was necessary to encourage the spirit of independence and enterprise so vital for free government and a free market.

While Jordan was especially vociferous in expressing the view that conciliation courts would undermine not only the rule of law but also the independent spirit so essential for preserving the American way of life, he was not alone among his colleagues in voicing such concerns. Consider, for example, the words of Henry Nicoll, a Democratic lawyer from New York City who would go on to gain fame in combating the corruption of Tammany Hall, only to die shortly thereafter amidst accusations of embezzlement.[132] Nicoll stated that he was willing to permit the legislature to create conciliation courts as an experiment, but he expressed grave doubts as to the likelihood of their success. To the extent that such courts had proved effective in continental European states, he suggested, this was because these other nations did not share the American spirit of political freedom and free enterprise: "Where these tribunals have existed, and have been a benefit, a far different state of society prevailed from what was to be found in our country—here we were politically, if not socially, equal. No man regarded another as his superior, or perhaps as more capable than himself." Nicoll's colleague, delegate John W. Brown, a Democratic lawyer from Orange County and a member of the Judiciary Committee, agreed, suggesting that "[i]t could clearly be demonstrated that such courts had no affinity with our institutions." Similar comments were made by James Forsyth, a Whig lawyer and onetime judge from Ulster County whose life, like Nicoll's, was to end in disgrace, when he fled to England to escape charges of forgery.[133] Forsyth claimed that he "opposed the system of conciliation courts in any form as unsuited to our system of government."[134]

Ultimately, because sentiment both for and against conciliation courts was so fierce, a number of delegates to the New York Constitutional Convention proposed a compromise position: They would support the establishment of such institutions, but only if they departed in significant ways from the traditional secrecy-oriented and lawyer-free model. Delegate Nicoll, for example, expressed grave doubts as to whether conciliation courts were suited to the freedom-loving citizenry of the United States but stated that he was willing to attempt the experiment, as long as the conciliation judges were themselves lawyers. In thus insisting that the conciliation judges be "men in whom the people had confidence in respect to matters of law," Nicoll betrayed his hope that conciliation courts—despite their name—would focus more on enforcing the letter of the law than on promoting equitable compromise.[135] And since a proposal to limit the number of lawyers who might serve as conciliation court judges was thereafter firmly rejected, there were evidently many others who shared Nicoll's aspiration.

Another approach to tackling the perceived dangers posed by conciliation courts was attempted by Robert Morris, a Democratic lawyer from New York City who had recently served several terms as mayor.[136] Morris argued that the proposed constitutional provision authorizing the establishment of conciliation courts ought to include language that would require these institutions to apply formal law and procedure: "Such tribunals shall be governed by the law of the land and the evidence in the case." But he then withdrew the proposal prior to a vote.[137] That he did so is a reflection of the substantial support that existed at the convention for the traditional European model of the conciliation court, with its secret, lawyer-free proceedings, oriented toward equitable compromise, rather than the strict enforcement of the letter of the law. In addition, Morris (and the other opponents of conciliation courts) likely concluded that such a withdrawal was politically pragmatic, since victory could be more easily achieved simply by postponing the decision—or rather, delegating it back to the legislature. Accordingly, the convention agreed on a constitutional provision that authorized the legislature to establish conciliation courts but was otherwise largely silent as to the structure and function of such institutions: "Tribunals of conciliation may be established, with such powers and duties as may be prescribed by law; but such tribunals shall have no power to render judgment to be obligatory on the parties except they voluntarily submit. . . ."[138]

In this way, die-hard advocates of conciliation courts could continue to envision these as traditionally conceived—as the secrecy-oriented and lawyer-free institutions described by Bentham. At the same time, their opponents could rest confident that, if the legislature did act, the conciliation courts that it established would not necessarily differ greatly from the ordinary, lawyer-based, and rule-bound civil courts. Indeed, the only substantive feature of these institutions on which delegates managed to reach agreement was on the importance of their proceedings being voluntary in Brougham's narrow, formalist sense of the term.

## The Failure of Conciliation Courts to Take Root and the Narrative of American Exceptionalism

While the 1846 constitution failed to take decisive action, proponents of conciliation courts were convinced that it would not be long before the state legislature acted on its newly granted authority to create such institutions. Calls for legislation establishing conciliation courts thus emerged from many different quarters throughout the decade following the promulgation of the constitution. Newspaper articles demanding such legislation were penned by a wide variety of interests, including merchants, Unitarians, and farmers.[139] And in their "annual messages" to the state legislature, several New York governors issued similar calls that were evidently heard throughout the country. For example, when in January 1850, Governor Hamilton Fish proposed the establishment of conciliation courts, a leading Philadelphia newspaper expressed the "hope that New York will try these [c]ourts . . . , and let the rest of the Union see how they work."[140] Along the same lines, a letter to the editor of the *Boston Cultivator* wondered "if our Governor would not do well to follow the example of Gov. Fish, of New York, and recommend a Court of Conciliation. . . ."[141] Indeed, looking to New York, many states considered the possibility of establishing conciliation courts, and some—like Indiana, Ohio, Michigan, Wisconsin, North Dakota, and, as we have seen, California—enacted similar constitutional provisions.[142]

In the end, however, little came of all this activity. With few exceptions, most state legislatures failed to act on the new constitutional provisions authorizing them to create conciliation courts.[143] In New York itself, legislation establishing conciliation courts was proposed several times, including in 1847 and 1855, but it repeatedly failed to pass.[144] Unfortunately, there is little extant legislative history concerning this proposed legislation. But the available evidence suggests that one of the main reasons for the legislature's failure to act was the persistent view that conciliation courts were fundamentally un-American—suited only to despotic or feudal regimes, where the populace tended toward subservience.

Consider, for example, the following letter examined by the New York State Senate in its deliberations over the conciliation courts bill proposed in 1847. Penned in December 1846 by Steen Bille, Denmark's chargé d'affaires to the United States from 1826 to 1854,[145] the letter responded to a request by conciliation court advocate and constitutional convention delegate John L. Stephens to provide "any information . . . respecting the institution of 'Conciliation Courts' " in Denmark. Not surprisingly, Bille waxed enthusiastic over the institution, insisting that it had proven highly effective in decreasing litigation rates. He emphasized, however, that "[t]he success of an institution of this kind is altogether dependent upon the character of the commissioners, to whom the mediation shall be committed," noting that what was especially important was "weight of character with the community" and the ability "to command respect and confidence with the parties."[146]

Precisely because conciliation courts so depended on the ability of the commissioners to command deference and the willingness of the parties to defer, Bille was not confident that these institutions would prove as successful in the United States as they had in Denmark. As he explained, whether conciliation courts would work in the United States was "a matter of doubt, considering the great disparity existing between the two countries, both as regards the form of their governments and the character of their people." In particular, he observed,

> The people of this country seem . . . to be over-jealous of any interference with the management of what they are disposed to call their own affairs, and cannot therefore be supposed to look upon the above institution with as much favor as it really deserves at their hands. I apprehend, on the contrary, that they will find their *personal appearance* before the commissioners within *closed doors,* and the *discussion of their conduct* in the special matter before them, in favor of a compromise on the score of expediency, both in a legal and moral point of view, to be an interference with their independence, a mastery over them, to which they will not willingly submit. . . .[147]

A successful diplomat who ended up serving in the United States for almost thirty years, Bille paid close attention to American politics and political culture. Accordingly, in suggesting that Americans were likely to balk at the prospect of being forced to defer to authority, he gave voice to a set of arguments framing conciliation courts as inherently un-American that had become by this time remarkably commonplace and widespread. And given the legislature's failure to establish conciliation courts, it would seem that it shared these concerns about whether the institution would thrive on American soil.

While the legislature debated, the Field Code commissioners acted. In particular, the final 1850 draft of the code provided for the establishment of conciliation courts. The draft, however, was never enacted by the legislature, which promulgated only the initial 1848 version of the code. Moreover, the draft code's provisions concerning conciliation courts were proposed at the recommendation of only two of the three commissioners—namely, David Dudley Field and Arphaxed Loomis.[148] And notably, these two commissioners vacillated between the traditional secrecy-oriented and lawyer-free model of the conciliation court described by Bentham and the more formalist, public, and lawyer-based version advocated by Lord Brougham.

On the one hand, the commissioners expressed great interest in the traditional European model of the conciliation court. They argued that the lesson to be drawn from the European experience with such institutions was that it was crucial to their success that they be controlled by judges who possessed significant persuasive influence over the parties. They therefore emphasized that conciliation court proceedings in Norway were "a mere form, because the judges are inferior magistrates, without influence over litigants." So too, in France the *bureaux de conciliation* had "almost entirely . . . [failed] in the large towns, and especially in Paris, where the justices of the peace, having in general little knowledge of the persons who come before them, can exercise but a feeble influence."[149] On the other hand, the very fact that the efficacy of conciliation courts seemed to hinge on the judges' persuasive influence was troubling to the code commissioners, as it confirmed fears that these institutions might subvert the formal rule of law, while also fostering a submissive mindset. For this reason, the commissioners agreed that conciliation courts ought to be empowered not only to encourage the parties to embrace some kind of equitable compromise and thereby reconcile but also to impose the strict letter of the law through summary proceedings akin to arbitration.

As outlined in the draft code, should the parties request conciliation, the conciliation court would seek to settle their dispute by helping them reach a compromise, negotiated without concern for whether this should happen to coincide with the result dictated by the law.[150] The parties could, however, opt instead for a kind of arbitration proceeding, whereby they would "submit their matters in difference to the court, and agree to abide the judgment."[151] While the draft code does not define exactly what this procedure would entail, its emphasis on the vital importance of conciliation court judges' knowing the law suggests that (like much arbitration today) this was to be a means by which the court would apply the law, but pursuant to a more informal (and thus speedier and cheaper) procedure than otherwise available. As explained by the code commissioners, it was precisely because it was so crucial that conciliation court judges be legal experts that they had opted against appointing justices of the peace to the task, as some at the 1846 Constitutional Convention had proposed.[152] The conciliation courts were instead to be staffed by New York county-court judges—themselves professional lawyers.[153]

Given that the 1850 draft of the Field Code thus hesitated fully to embrace the traditional European model of the conciliation court and in fact flirted significantly with Brougham's more formalist, rule-based model, it is not surprising that the "tribunal of conciliation" that was briefly established during the Civil War—and that appears to have been inspired by the 1850 draft code—reflected the same hesitation. Established in Delaware County between 1862 and 1865, this court was to be headed by the local county-court judge and to offer litigants a choice between conciliation, or instead a highly simplified model of formal adjudication. Indeed, as suggested by the Report on the proposed tribunal drafted by the New York Assembly's Judiciary Committee, those advocating for its establishment seem to have been entirely uninterested in its capacity to promote conciliation and envisioned it instead as a means of providing cheap and rapid formal adjudication.

According to the Committee Report, the delegates to the 1846 Constitutional Convention who agreed on a provision authorizing the legislature to establish conciliation courts were inspired by "similar tribunals [that] existed in several of the countries of Europe." However, the Report emphasizes, these delegates were well aware that "in consequence of the forms of government, habits, and institutions in Europe differing so essentially from those of our own, . . . all the features and peculiarities of those tribunals could not be adopted here." As the Report never once discusses how the tribunal of conciliation would actually promote conciliation, it would appear that, in the Judiciary Committee's view, conciliation itself was—despite the court's name—precisely such a "feature[] and peculiarit[y] . . . that could not be adopted here." The Report's focus was, instead, on the court's ability to provide cheaper, more accessible formal adjudication in a county that was "one of the largest . . . in the state," and where—because of the great distance between inhabited areas and the limited transportation infrastructure—parties seeking to "attend court with their witnesses" could not do so "without great pecuniary sacrifice."[154] In this respect, the relative strength of the tribunal of conciliation was that, in contrast to New York's ordinary state trial courts, which held trials only at the county seat, it would hold trial "in the town where the majority of the witnesses reside and where the interests of the parties may require that such trial be held."[155]

As I have been unable to locate any records that the court produced, it is impossible to determine how it actually functioned during its brief existence.[156] It would seem highly unlikely, however, that the institution embraced a conciliation function that it was never really intended to serve. The creation of the tribunal of conciliation in Civil War New York was thus in no way an exception to the general failure of the European model of the conciliation court to take root in the nineteenth-century United States.

Later, in the early twentieth century, a successful movement for the establishment of small claims courts would, in turn, draw on this longstanding interest in European-style conciliation courts—an interest that led to many of these institutions being called courts of "small claims and conciliation." Like many nineteenth-century advocates of conciliation courts, the Progressive-era reformers (especially lawyers) who pressed for the establishment of courts of small claims and conciliation viewed them as a means of affording access to justice to the marginalized—especially the growing mass of immigrant poor then flooding American cities. To the extent that these courts initially achieved some success in this regard, this appears to have been, in no small part, a product of the decision to employ as judges members of the very same immigrant community from which the disputants themselves hailed. Such judges were able to rely on their high standing within the local community to encourage deference to their views, thus affording what an earlier generation of Americans had termed *alcalde* justice. But as with the nineteenth-century efforts to establish conciliation courts, Progressives' aspirations for the small-claims-and-conciliation courts would ultimately be disappointed. While the courts survived, they came to serve as what are in effect collection agencies for businesses—a far cry from the ambitions of those who promoted conciliation courts as vital for protecting the interests of a growing underclass.[157]

Despite the widespread and fairly long-running nature of the American debates over conciliation courts, the efforts of their proponents thus came to naught. What accounts for this failure? Given that these courts originated in Europe and were repeatedly cast as suited to un-American, authoritarian regimes, one possibility that comes to mind is that the mere fact of their European roots was in itself sufficient to doom them. As of the mid-nineteenth century, but for a brief flourishing of democracy in 1848, Europe remained a continent of monarchies. Moreover, the legal systems of continental European nations were associated with the Roman-canon, civil law tradition, which, dating back to the seventeenth-century English revolution, was linked in political and legal discourse with despotic rule, in contrast to the supposedly more liberty-oriented Anglo-American common law. Such longstanding antipathy toward European legal systems was exacerbated by the rise of nativist, anti-Catholic sentiment in the wake of the dramatic 1840s expansion of already sizable rates of immigration. It seems clear, however, that anxieties about conciliation courts rested on more than such general antipathy toward continental European government and law. After all, during the antebellum period, many advocates of legal reform actually looked to Europe and, in particular, to France, as a model for how the law could be simplified by means of codification.[158] And while there were nativists, like the Reverend Walter Colton, who associated conciliation courts with authoritarian rule, others who made this association (and thus suggested that these institutions were fundamentally un-American) expressly repudiated nativism.[159]

Another possibility is that lawyers were responsible for the failure of conciliation courts to take root in the United States. As traditionally conceived, conciliation courts obviated any need for lawyers, either as counsel to the disputants or as judges. It might thus be expected that such institutions would not be appealing to a growing and increasingly powerful legal profession. The evidence does not, however, support the conclusion that lawyers as a group were to blame for the failure to establish these institutions, or even that their views were determined primarily by a desire to preserve a powerful guild monopoly. Anxieties about conciliation courts were voiced not only by lawyers but also by nonlawyers like Colton. Moreover, to the extent that lawyers took the lead in the debate, they were well represented on both sides of it. Those delegates to the New York Constitutional Convention who favored conciliation courts were themselves primarily lawyers.[160]

How then do we make sense of the fact that despite repeated calls for their establishment, conciliation courts enjoyed such little success in the United States? Some insight can be gained by comparing the demand for conciliation courts with other contemporary calls for social reform. As we have seen, advocacy of conciliation courts during the 1840s—most especially in New York but also to some extent in California—was understood to be part of a broader reform agenda sparked by revivalist fervor. So why did other components of the revivalist reform agenda, including most notably temperance, achieve considerably more success?

The push for temperance differed from the demand for conciliation courts in at least two key respects. First, the former gave rise to a mass movement, while the latter did not. Despite the solidly middle-class origins of those who initially called for temperance, members of the working class—as represented by those who formed the Washington Temperance Society (popularly known as the Washingtonians)—also came to lend their enthusiastic support.[161] While working-class men resented the patronizing intervention of the middle-class women who promoted temperance, they themselves came to believe with the onset of depression in the years after 1837 that, in Sean Wilentz's words, "alcohol made hard times worse and [thus] had to be avoided."[162] As advocated by these men—and linked to programs for helping the unemployed find work and providing much-needed food and clothing to their families—temperance was a form of self and group empowerment. In contrast, interest in conciliations courts emerged from (and never spread beyond) lawyers, entrepreneurs, and others of middling and elite status. The demand for conciliation courts as a state-sponsored institution was not an agenda that could be readily translated into individual and communal action. And even if it could, its appeal to working men and women was limited. After all, the call for conciliation courts as a check on competitive forces was no radical cri de coeur—no demand for a significant restructuring of social and economic relations or for the redistribution of resources—but instead a plea for moderation. Moreover, even among the many working men and women who themselves had no radical ambitions and sought only moderate reform within existing structures, the operational principle of these courts was a benevolent paternalism not likely to be of significant appeal. Resentful of the middle-class do-gooders who promoted temperance, workers and their families were not eager to embrace a court designed in many ways to institutionalize such noblesse oblige.

Even if the demand for conciliation courts never blossomed into a full-blown social movement, these institutions might have been established through legislation if the lawyers who dominated state legislatures throughout much of the nineteenth century had been sufficiently committed to the cause. This was not, however, the case. Thus, a second and perhaps more important way that calls for conciliation courts differed from those for temperance is that many of the middling and elite types who advocated the latter with unswerving conviction harbored serious doubts as to the feasibility of the former. As we have seen, Stephen J. Field and Walter Colton both relished their service as *alcaldes,* but their pleasure was tempered by the nagging concern that this office permitted the aggrandizement of far too much discretionary power to be suited to the freedom-loving (and Protestant) United States. So too, some of the delegates to the New York Constitutional Convention who argued in favor of conciliation courts felt obliged to acknowledge that there was a link between these institutions and authoritarian rule. Conrad Swackhamer, for example, noted that aside from its admirable adoption of conciliation courts, Denmark was "in all other respects an arbitrary government."[163] And similar views were voiced by those Americans who examined the subject of conciliation courts from a more neutral, academic perspective. For example, Francis Lieber—a leading political thinker of the antebellum period, now remembered primarily for drafting what became the first modern code of military conduct—was a strong proponent of conciliation courts, but he also observed that these institutions might be better suited to despotic regimes than to the free and democratic United States. In Lieber's view, "[w]herever [conciliation courts] have been tried in modern times, they have been found of the greatest benefit to the people, for instance, in Prussia and Denmark." But while he praised such courts for "produc[ing] a signal decrease of litigation and diminution of expenses," he insisted that what he termed "the principle of arbitration cannot be called a characteristic of liberty, for as a characteristic it belongs rather to the patriarchal government, and courts of arbitration may flourish in despotic states."[164]

Underlying these frequent references to conciliation courts as being suited to hierarchical, authoritarian regimes was an important, though inchoate comparative insight—namely, that it was far from clear where to locate extralegal discretionary authority within the relatively flat American social and political structure. Even to the extent that nineteenth-century European countries, like France and Spain, experimented (albeit sporadically) with democratic-republican government, they continued to be profoundly shaped by traditions of corporatism and hierarchy that dated back many centuries. As we have seen, the conciliation courts, while conceived by the French Revolutionaries as radically new, were in fact based on institutional structures—such as the French seigneurial courts and the Spanish *alcaldes*—that had deep (though in the French case, recently severed) roots. To the extent that these institutions—and their post-revolutionary successors—succeeded in promoting conciliation, this was not because they were formally authorized to do so as a matter of law but instead because disputants were long accustomed to deferring to their authority. Indeed, it was widely recognized in the nineteenth century that the *bureaux de conciliation* were far less successful at reconciling disputants in Paris than they were in the rural countryside. This was understood to be precisely because it was impossible to sustain the justices' customary authority and the communal pressure to defer in a large and increasingly anonymous urban environment.[165]

Although much (indeed, most) of the United States remained rural in the mid-nineteenth century, American society was relatively flat as compared with its European counterparts. There were, of course, important differences of wealth in the United States, but (with the important exception of race) there was no seemingly natural, historically rooted elite. So too, American society was much more mobile, such that customary, communally grounded authority was harder to sustain over the long run. The upshot of these differences was that it was far from clear where to locate the authority of the conciliation judge in the American context. Those delegates to the New York Constitutional Convention who supported the establishment of conciliation courts were thus unable to reach agreement on who ought to be appointed as conciliation judges—though they readily concurred that it was vital that such individuals be able to inspire deference.

Some suggested that justices of the peace were the logical choice, since they were local figures well known by members of the community and accustomed to resolving disputes in a relatively informal fashion, rather than in strict accordance with the rule of law.[166] Even in so arguing, however, these delegates acknowledged the problematic fact that justices of the peace were frequently the object of much disdain, such that it was far from clear that they possessed the force of character required to induce deference. As Conrad Swackhamer admitted, an essential prerequisite to his proposal that justices of the peace be made conciliation judges was that a way be found to "elevate their character." Others suggested that conciliators ought to be elected—on the theory, presumably, that such men would by definition have the trust of the community.[167] But in so arguing, these delegates failed to define the particular communities of voters entitled to elect any given conciliating judge. Would voting occur at the level of the state, the county, the municipality, or some other sub-group? In ignoring these questions, delegates avoided the key overarching problem of identifying a communal source of authority for the elected conciliation judges— one that would ensure deference to their discretionary judgments.

As advocates of the conciliation courts struggled to identify a workable solution and thus to overcome their own concerns about whether these institutions could in fact be effectively transplanted to American shores, their opponents solidified the link between adversarial adjudication and American identity. The inability to outline a clear method for implementing conciliation courts was itself proof positive, they suggested, that these institutions had no place on American soil. Convention delegate Ambrose Jordan, for example, poked fun at the inability of the courts' proponents to specify who would be entrusted with conciliatory authority by jesting that such authority might be granted to "old women . . . at a tea table" or a "few extraordinary old gentlemen" in the neighborhood.[168] The absurdity of these suggestions, he implied, sufficed to demonstrate the infeasibility of successfully transplanting European conciliation courts: America's unparalleled combination of political and economic freedom necessarily implied adversarial adjudication.

The extent to which adversarialism thus came to be tied to American identity as a whole was reflected, in turn, even in the arguments of those advocating the establishment of conciliation courts. Consider, for example, a letter to the editor entitled "Courts of Conciliation" that was published in the *Baltimore Post* and then reprinted in a January 1856 edition of the *Alexandria Gazette*. While strongly urging the creation of conciliation courts—noting that it was "unquestionable" that they "could accomplish a large amount of good"—the author observed that he would "not undertake to decide" whether the "quiet decisions" of these courts "would prove satisfactory to the great army of litigants with which suits at law have become a passion." The problem, he explained, was the very nature of Americans as "a litigious people." As he noted, "[w]e are a keen, shrewd, energetic, business people, tenacious of our rights, even to the tenth part of a hair."[169] Adversarialism was an offshoot of the same spirit of independence that had given rise to the Revolution and that—as manifested in the country's extraordinary economic growth (and geographic expansion)—was rapidly transforming the United States into the world's predominant commercial empire. It was—or rather, had by this time become—a defining feature of national identity and as such provided important evidence of the country's manifest destiny.

But while the fate of the conciliation courts seemed to be all but sealed in the years just before the Civil War, the ensuing cataclysm—including, most especially, the plight of the recently freed African-American community— would force the country to confront the extent of its newfound commitment to adversarialism. For a very brief moment, in the heart of Reconstruction, it seemed possible that, at least under certain extreme conditions of inequality and injustice, this commitment might give way.

# 6 • The Freedmen's Bureau Exception

## The Triumph of Due (Adversarial) Process and the Dawn of Jim Crow

The problem of reconstructing the South was one that consumed much thought in the North as the Civil War was drawing to a close. As Republicans and War Democrats committed to emancipation struggled with the question of how to proceed, they agreed on the need to establish some kind of federal agency responsible for this monumental task, thus giving rise to what would become known as the Freedmen's Bureau. Such agreement, however, did little to resolve the more difficult question of how exactly this agency and its officers should function.

From the Northern perspective, victory in the war served to vindicate the virtues of Northern free labor over the Southern slave system. But while the North and its ideology were triumphant, Northerners soon concluded that getting Southerners—both white and black—to absorb the core tenets of the free labor approach would be no easy task. Generations of African-American men forced into dependency and denied the right to marry and form families of their own would have to learn how to exert self-discipline in the workplace and patriarchal authority at home. So too, African-American women needed to develop the womanly virtues of domesticity deemed so essential for becoming proper helpmates and thereby ensuring familial success. Similarly, Southern whites, trained by slavery to view labor as degrading, had to learn the virtue of hard work. Long accustomed to controlling their workforce through violence, they needed to be taught that the interests of capital and labor were in harmony, such that it was in their own best interest—just as much as that of their former slaves—to respect freedom of contract.

As Northern politicians, military officers, and contemporary commentators grappled with the question of how to pursue such a vast project of social reform, one model to which they turned was that of the conciliation court. The appeal of this institution to would-be reformers stemmed, in part, from the way it was conceptualized in the years before the war. As we have seen, antebellum proponents of the conciliation court were of the view that it would somehow address the profound social tensions stemming from the market revolution—including, perhaps most importantly, the growing conflict between capital and labor. From the Northern perspective, the postbellum South embodied this conflict in the starkest possible form, pitting white landowners against a mass of penniless, recently freed slaves who had only just acquired ownership of their own bodies. As it became clear that freedpeople would be denied the forty acres and a mule that they had initially been promised, the potential for interracial, interclass warfare loomed ever larger, thus increasing the appeal of the conciliation court as a device for quelling labor disputes and thereby promoting social stability (without redistributing property).

Moreover, many of the individuals responsible for first envisioning and then establishing the Freedmen's Bureau—including its courts—were themselves men who had imbibed the religiously infused reformist ambitions of the Second Great Awakening. As we have seen, it was precisely those most influenced by such reformist aspirations—often but not always themselves evangelicals—who tended to be drawn to the model of the conciliation court in the decades preceding the Civil War. Not surprisingly, it was these same kinds of people who, in the wake of Emancipation, were particularly attracted by the idea that the Freedmen's Bureau courts would serve as conciliation courts. For these men, the utility of the conciliation court model was in part an untested article of faith, grounded in some combination of their belief in the inherent wisdom of the free labor ideals that they sought to promote, the innate subservience of African-Americans, and not least, the capacity of righteous men (like themselves) to hasten the day of salvation.

At least as important, however, in causing the Northern architects of Reconstruction to embrace the conciliation court was that it obscured the question of power. As they imagined it, Bureau courts functioning as courts of conciliation would not apply the law in a heavy-handed, top-down fashion. Instead, they would persuade the parties to embrace an equitable resolution, thereby obtaining the buy-in of locals in the Northern effort to remake the South on free labor foundations. The Bureau courts, in other words, would not force Southerners to embrace Northern free labor ways but rather engage in a form of pedagogy, teaching both freedpeople and whites to recognize the indisputable superiority of a free-contract regime and its associated cult of domesticity.

How precisely the Bureau judge would manage to convince Southerners to embrace his point of view was not a question on which these Northerners focused attention. Steeped in free labor ideology, they assumed that its core tenets were self-evident truths.

But what seemed self-evident to Northerners was recognized by white Southerners as a foreign set of values, sought to be imposed on them by force in the wake of their defeat. The very fact of having lost the war caused white Southerners to observe a key feature of the conciliation court model that was never made explicit by its proponents—namely, that the institution's successful operation hinged on its ability to draw on underlying communal structures and norms. While there were many different varieties of conciliation court that operated throughout Europe and its colonies—and indeed, within any one country— they all derived their authority from the fact that their judges were local elites serving as respected representatives of the community (or communities) from which the disputants themselves hailed. It was these communal (indeed, corporatist) underpinnings that encouraged disputants to defer to their judgment, which was itself understood to be grounded not in the law but instead in deep-rooted, communal norms. Although the courts established by the Freedmen's Bureau throughout the South also drew on communal norms, these norms were the free labor values of the Northern conquerors, rather than the values of the Southerners (white or black) whose disputes the courts sought to resolve. Thus, to the extent that the Bureau courts managed to gain adherence to their judgments, these white Southerners insisted, it was simply by means of force.

Drawing on a commitment to adversarialism developed in part through the debates over conciliation courts in the years prior to 1861, Southerners decried the Bureau and its courts as fundamentally un-American and mounted what would prove to be an ultimately successful campaign to dismantle them. With the Supreme Court's 1866 decision in *Ex parte Milligan* and the subsequent ratification of the Fourteenth Amendment, this powerfully reasserted commitment to adversarialism would be rendered all but synonymous with due process.

## Envisioning the Bureau: Robert Dale Owen and the American Freedmen's Inquiry Commission

On March 16, 1863, Secretary of War Edwin Stanton appointed the American Freedmen's Inquiry Commission to outline procedures for facilitating the former slaves' transition to freedom. The Commission, in turn, proposed the creation of a Freedmen's Bureau—a quasi-judicial, quasi-administrative agency conceived as a centralized version of the various freedmen's programs that had been established by the military in its efforts to provide African-Americans with food and employment. As ultimately established by statute on March 3, 1865, the Freedmen's Bureau would serve as one of the country's first large-scale social welfare agencies—distributing vast quantities of food, clothing, and other necessities; supervising the operation of numerous hospitals; and creating a broad array of educational institutions. In addition, the Bureau devoted enormous time and energy to the distinct but interrelated tasks of stabilizing the Southern labor market and providing justice to the former slaves.[1]

Despite the wide variety of goals that the Bureau was expected to pursue, its central, defining mission in the eyes of many supporters was to remake labor relations in the South, such that these would conform to Northern free labor principles. This was a matter not only of ideology but also of economics. Revitalizing the Southern agricultural economy was essential if the South and the nation as a whole were to recover from the devastation of war. As the *New York Times* opined in December 1865, "the relation of Labor to Capital—of the freedmen to their former masters" was at the heart of Reconstruction, and it was the Bureau's primary mission to intervene in these relations so as to prevent "fearful collisions ... between the ignorant freedmen and governing race, bringing calamity and disorganization to the land."[2] Because the vital mission of remaking the Southern economy was so intimately linked to the question of labor—and, in particular, to disputes between white planters and African-American laborers—Northern advocates of the Bureau as an instrument of Reconstruction devoted substantial attention to the role of Bureau-run courts in promoting dispute resolution (including, most especially, in interracial labor disputes).

## THE COMMISSION'S REPORTS

The three members of the American Freedmen's Inquiry Commission— all either abolitionists or reformers of one kind or another—were Gridley Howe, James McKaye, and Robert Dale Owen. After visiting the Union-occupied South to collect the testimony of such diverse individuals as white army officers, slaveholders, missionaries, free blacks, and former slaves, they submitted two joint reports to Secretary Stanton outlining their plan for a "provisional organization" devoted to "the improvement, protection and employment" of freedmen.[3] While these reports were submitted on behalf of the commission as a whole, they appear to have been written largely by Owen, who served as the committee's chairman.[4]

The two reports, dated June 30, 1863, and May 15, 1864, respectively, emphasized that the primary mission of the governmental organization that would later come to be known as the Freedmen's Bureau was in essence pedagogical. Former slaves had to be taught to view themselves "as men from whom, in their new character of freedmen, self-reliance and self-support are demanded."[5] As this emphasis on "self-reliance and self-support" suggests, the new men that the commissioners envisioned themselves as helping to create were to be modeled on the contemporary middle-class ideal of the self-made man—one possessing the combination of independent spirit and self-control required to function effectively as a political citizen and (risk-bearing) economic actor in the increasingly democratic and market-driven American society.[6] For the commissioners, it was not the former slaves' ability to engage in political citizenship that was of paramount importance—though in their final report they did call for the freedmen to be granted both "civil and political" rights.[7] Much more important was teaching freedmen to become self-sufficient participants in the country's free labor economy, such that they would not view themselves as "fostered by charity, dependent for a living on government or benevolent associations."[8] Success in this endeavor would definitively demonstrate the superiority of free to slave labor and, in so doing, would establish that the United States was worthy of respect among the civilized nations of the world—a claim long in doubt during slavery's reign in that, as the final report observed, "the grade of civilization in a nation . . . is the degree of estimation in which labor is held there."[9]

As outlined primarily in the first report, the Bureau would serve this broadly pedagogical function by undertaking activities on a number of different fronts, including by providing medical care and promoting "enlightened instruction, educational and religious." In addition, the report emphasized the importance of making plans for the "temporary provision" of courts responsible for adjudicating all cases involving freedpeople. The necessity for such institutions was due, in part, to the fact that throughout much of the South ordinary, state-run courts had "ceased to hold their sessions." More fundamentally, however, these courts would serve an important educational function, teaching African-Americans "the important lesson that the obedience which, as slaves, they paid to the will of a master, must now be rendered by them, as freedmen, to established law."[10]

This pedagogical role would be best fulfilled, the report concluded, if the Bureau agent charged with developing a temporary system of justice functioned as a conciliation court: "It should be specially recommended to the department superintendent, in the settlement of all personal difficulties between these people [the freedpeople], to act as arbitrator rather than as formal judge, adopting the general principles governing courts of conciliation." As for what precisely such "general principles" were, the report remained silent, evidently assuming that, given the contemporary interest in conciliation courts, these were widely understood. But in line with the antebellum understanding of these institutions, the report urged that the conciliation judge need not possess formal legal knowledge as such but must instead be a good man, widely respected for his sound judgment—a man of "comprehensive benevolence and humanitarian views." With such men at the helm, the Bureau and its courts could not but triumph: "[I]t is confidently believed by the Commission that if [the government agent] shall succeed in gaining the confidence of the freedmen under his charge he will, with rare exceptions, be able amicably and satisfactorily to adjust such difficulties without further resort to law."[11]

Ironically, as this language suggests, the system of courts intended to teach freedpeople "obedience . . . to established law" was expressly designed to ensure dispute resolution "without . . . resort to law." As in the Benthamite model of the conciliation court, the Bureau agent was to exercise a kind of patriarchal authority to resolve the conflicts that emerged among those "under his charge," seeking to promote equitable compromise, rather than to enforce the strict letter of the law. This, in turn, would help ensure that the freedpeople would "not . . . [be] encourage[d] . . . to become litigious."[12] But as emphasized in the final report, the role of the Bureau and its courts would be strictly "temporary," guided by the view that "[t]he sooner the[] [freedpeople] shall stand alone . . . the better both for their race and ours."[13] The proposed conciliation courts, in other words, would operate as a kind of way station on what Henry Maine, just two years earlier, famously called the path from status to contract.[14] In this respect, by framing Bureau courts as a temporary expedient, expected to cease operations as soon as freedpeople were fully integrated into a newly reconstructed, free labor–based Southern economy, the commissioners implicitly embraced the core conclusion that had emerged from the antebellum debates regarding conciliation courts: A free market society required adversarial procedure. In the interim, however, a quite different, judge-empowering procedural form was needed.

Interestingly, while the commission was quite insistent that all disputes between freedpeople be resolved by means of conciliation courts, it was far less clear about how to handle interracial disputes. Its only comment on such disputes was that when they were of some "difficulty" and were tried by either a military court or "any regularly established legal tribunal" in the state, the Bureau agent was "to act as friend and adviser for the freedman," even "employ[ing] legal counsel" when necessary.[15] As this language suggests, the commission assumed—without explanation—that significant interracial disputes would proceed before military or state-run courts rather than before the proposed Bureau-run conciliation courts. Given the commission's concern with remaking the Southern economy on a free labor basis and the intimate connection between this goal, on the one hand, and the resolution of (interracial) labor disputes, on the other, its silence in this regard is surprising. But this may well have been a strategic choice aimed at forestalling Southern whites' arguments that the proposed Bureau was an unconstitutional assertion of federal government power.

While the commission was in this respect restrained in its demands, it pulled no punches when it came to framing the moral necessity of establishing a Freedmen's Bureau along the lines it proposed. As the commissioners understood it, the civil war was "the mark of Divine condemnation" for the evil of slavery—an evil for which the United States had yet fully to atone. The proposed Freedmen's Bureau, in turn, offered a path to redemption: "God is offering to us an opportunity of atoning, in some measure, to the African for our former complicity in his wrongs."[16] For the commissioners, the Bureau was nothing short of a (Christian) mission—a chance to spread God's word and saving grace. Although the primary author of the commission's reports, Robert Dale Owen, was late to embrace both Christianity and abolitionism, he did eventually do so. And well before his conversion, he was indelibly marked by the powerfully religious and reformist impulses of the age—impulses that he shared with a great many of the individuals and groups calling for the establishment of a Freedmen's Bureau.

## ROBERT DALE OWEN AND THE "GREAT QUESTION" OF DISPOSSESSED LABOR

Devoted as a young man to secular, utopian communalism, Robert Dale Owen died—much to the chagrin of his erstwhile freethinker friends—a fervent advocate of Christian spiritualism.[17] But throughout his many years as a public intellectual and later politician, he enthusiastically committed himself to the search for a better, promised world—either in this life or beyond the veil. At the core of his demands for reform was what he described in 1844 as "a Great Question" that stands "unanswered, before the world"—namely, the question of "wealth and its distribution" in an era in which workers had been transformed into nothing more than "a commodity in the market."[18] Having concluded from the failure of his youthful communalist ambitions that property redistribution was, at least in his lifetime, no solution, he instead supported various modes of educational and legal reform—including not least, the establishment of conciliation courts.

The eldest son of famed industrialist and social reformer Robert Owen, Robert Dale was born in Scotland in 1801 and had a complex relationship with his father and the latter's communalist commitments. Through his mid-twenties, he largely embraced his father's worldview—including, most importantly, the latter's utopian ambition to establish small, self-sufficient ru-

Figure 12  Unidentified photographer, *Robert Dale Owen* (circa 1847). Courtesy of the National Portrait Gallery, Smithsonian Institute / Art Resource, New York.

ral communities in which all property would be communally owned. Thus, soon after Robert Owen purchased the town of New Harmony, Indiana, in 1824 with an eye toward developing it into his ideal communalist society, Robert Dale eagerly crossed the Atlantic to participate in building the new community.[19] In January 1826, he was elected to serve as a member of the seven-person committee responsible for drafting "a Constitution of Government for the New-Harmony Community of Equality."[20] In line with his father's view that communalist living would obviate all social conflict, the constitution that Robert Dale helped to write largely presupposed the harmony that he and his compatriots so eagerly sought. Reserving the question of dispute resolution until near the end of the document, the constitution provides simply—and obliquely—that "[a]ll misunderstandings that may arise between the members of the Community, shall be adjusted within the Community."[21] Aside from thus prohibiting community members from bringing their intracommunal disputes to extra-communal, formally established courts of law, this provision provided little guidance concerning how these disputes were to be decided. The only clear direction was that such disputes were to be "adjusted," meaning that an equitable compromise was to be reached without regard to the formal rule of law.[22]

Robert Dale's faith in his father's communalist ideals would soon, however, be shattered, forcing him to explore other routes—besides the redistribution of property—for addressing the growing problem of alienated labor. Just two weeks after the enactment of the New Harmony constitution, the community's assembly voted to entrust governance entirely to Robert Owen. Thereafter, town lots began to be sold to private owners, and the local mill adopted a wage system. Moreover, despite the constitutional requirement that all intra-communal disputes be "adjusted within the Community," one of the main conflicts that contributed to New Harmony's collapse culminated in the spring of 1827 with Robert Owen filing suit in the local circuit court against William Maclure, a famous geologist and a co-founder of New Harmony.[23] While the suit was eventually settled through arbitration, its filing highlighted for Robert Dale the failure of his father's utopian ideals. Reflecting back on his life many years later, he insisted that, despite whatever "partiality" he felt toward his father, he was no "disciple" of Owen's. His father had allowed himself to become "engrossed by the exciting delusion that he was about suddenly to revolutionize society and reform the world," but the time for communal ownership of property had not yet arrived.[24] Other approaches had to be found for addressing the problem of a growing underclass.

Having rejected his father's commitment to rural communalist living, Robert Dale embraced instead a set of policies that were, broadly speaking, pedagogical in nature. Like the evangelicals whom he (as a freethinker at that time) scorned, his ideas for bettering the lives of the poor were solidly middle-class. He was a great proponent of temperance, thrift, and hard work, arguing that workers must be taught to pull themselves up by their own bootstraps. However tepid these ideas may in retrospect seem, Robert Dale gave them real force by helping to create the short-lived but highly influential Working Men's movement that emerged in New York City in 1829. In particular, he worked as editor of two of the major newspapers that would vie to serve as the voice of the new movement. So too, he joined Fanny Wright (his coeditor at the *Free Enquirer*) in establishing a "Hall of Science" in an old Baptist Church in lower Manhattan. There, he and Wright developed an extensive lecture series for the local community, while also offering a deist Sunday school, a library for adults, and a free medical dispensary. In these ways, Robert Dale played a major role in developing the institutional infrastructure that enabled the rise of the "Workies" as a political force in the city—one that achieved meaningful success at the polls until it shortly thereafter imploded as a result of internal schism.[25]

Despite his disappointment over the Workies' collapse, Robert Dale continued to call attention to the problem of dispossessed labor.[26] But the ultimate failure of the Working Men's movement taught him the limits of self-help and the importance of government intervention—not to redistribute property (a goal he had by this time abandoned) but rather to create the conditions under which working people would be able to help themselves. Accordingly, he returned to New Harmony to forge a new life as a Democratic state politician, serving first in the state legislature and thereafter in Congress. In this capacity, he was a major advocate for the state's investment in local infrastructure, arguing for the developments of canals and turnpikes that would serve previously isolated portions of the state, like his own Posey County. So too, he demanded government investment in education, calling at the state level for funding public schools and the state library and thereafter, at the national level, drafting the legislation to establish the Smithsonian Institution. Along similar lines, he promoted legal reform, arguing that it was vital for leveling the playing field and otherwise ensuring workers (and women) a fair shot. He is best remembered today as a passionate supporter of married women's right to hold property independently of their husbands. But in addition, he advocated a panoply of legal reform measures aimed at reducing procedural costs and thereby promoting greater equality—including the merging of law and

equity, the drafting of a simplified code of procedure, and not least, the establishment of conciliation courts.[27]

As far back as his years serving as coeditor of the *Free Enquirer,* Robert
Dale had argued that lawyers and the lawsuits they generated were an important factor in exacerbating social injustice. In his view, the legal system had
become "complicated" and "expensive," thus depriving the poor of access to
justice. What was needed was precisely what he had envisioned some years
earlier in drafting the constitution of New Harmony—namely, a mode of dispute resolution that was focused not on legal rights as such but instead on
promoting "peace, harmony, and kindness." But because "three-fourths of our
legislators and governors have risen to their situation through the law," legislative efforts to promote legal reform were all too often stymied.[28] Heeding his
own call that legislators be selected "elsewhere than from among lawyers,"
Robert Dale contributed as both a member of the Indiana Constitutional Convention of 1850 and then as a state congressman to the enactment of core legal
reforms. Appointed as chairman of the constitutional convention's Committee on Revision, Arrangement, and Phraseology, Robert Dale bore primary
responsibility for ensuring that the new constitution cohered as a single intel-
ligible whole, such that, as one contemporary commentator observed, "he had
something to do, by way of revision or otherwise, with almost every section of
it."[29] Thereafter, while serving in 1851 and 1852 as a member of the state
House of Representatives, Robert Dale was elected as head of the legislature's
joint Committee on Revision, charged with implementing the constitutional
reforms enacted by the convention.[30]

In establishing conciliation courts, Indiana was influenced—like so many
other (especially Western) states—by recent developments in New York. Copying nearly verbatim the language from New York's 1846 Constitution, the Indiana provision authorized the state legislature to establish "[t]ribunals of
conciliation," if it so chose, and specified that these tribunals would possess
"such powers and duties as shall be prescribed by law." Moreover, as in New
York, these courts were to have "no power to render judgment to be obligatory
on the parties, unless they voluntarily submit their matters of difference, and
agree to abide the judgment of such tribunal or Court."[31] Whereas the New
York legislature would wait well over a decade before finally establishing a
conciliation court—and then only for a brief, three-year period in Delaware
County—the Indiana legislature acted quickly upon the new constitutional
authorization. On June 11, 1852, it passed legislation that borrowed from the
(never enacted) 1850 Field Code provision authorizing the establishment of

conciliation courts. As in the Field Code, the Indiana statute delegated conciliation authority to regularly sitting judges and, in particular, to the higher-status judges of the courts of common pleas, rather than to justices of the peace. So too, as in the Field Code, the statute developed two procedural tracks between which parties could choose—conciliation proceedings, in which the decision whether to reconcile was left to the parties, or a form of arbitration whereby the parties agreed to abide by "a judgment, in favor of one against the other in settlement of their differences."[32]

Although Robert Dale Owen does not appear to have been the primary champion of the constitutional provision concerning conciliation courts or the subsequent legislation creating these courts, the dominant role he played in drafting the Constitution and the Revised Statutes of 1852 was such that we can be certain of his intimate familiarity with the institution. While his name is absent from the roster listing votes on the constitutional and legislative provisions that were ultimately enacted, his voting record in the preceding debates suggests that he favored the establishment of conciliation courts.[33] Moreover, the "address to the electors of the State" outlining "the changes proposed in the amended Constitution," which he appears to have authored, makes a point of highlighting the provision authorizing the legislature to establish conciliation courts.[34] Accordingly, many would associate Indiana's attempt to create such institutions with "the influence of Robert Dale Owen, to whom the best part of the early legislation of that state was due."[35]

But as with the dissolution of New Harmony, the fate of the conciliation courts legislation enacted by the Indiana legislature in 1852 was such as to temper enthusiasm. As early as 1857, the legislature began considering bills to repeal the statute, and while repeal would not occur until November 1865, such calls were heard repeatedly until then.[36] Legislative records give little indication of the concerns leading to repeal, but other more or less contemporaneous texts suggest that the primary problem was that conciliation courts were "little resorted to," such that the legislation establishing them was "practically a dead letter in the statutes."[37]

While we unfortunately have no record of how Robert Dale Owen made sense of Indiana's largely failed conciliation courts experiment, it is likely that he viewed it much as other (white) contemporaries did. As the editors of the *Chicago Inter-Ocean* observed in November 1887, the problem with the Indiana legislation was that the people's "temper" was "too hot for conciliation, so that the courts were unused."[38] This conclusion was in line with Robert Dale Owen's own experience from his early days at New Harmony—an experience

that taught him that even those ideologically committed to principles of harmony were often unable to avoid litigation. It was in line, moreover, with the
rhetoric of adversarialism that emerged in the debates over conciliation courts
in Florida, California, and New York: It was simply not in the character of the
American people to subordinate their own interests in deference to the wisdom of a conciliating judge. As observed by a delegate to the Indiana constitutional convention of 1850, the difficulty faced by advocates of conciliation
courts was that so many contemporaries "labor[ed] under the impression that
they would not be considered men of spirit, if they did not go to law, and fight
it out in the court house" and "bleed most freely" from "their pockets."[39]

It may well have been this lesson, that conciliation courts would not prove
effective among self-assertive, white Americans, that informed Robert Dale
Owen's telling decision, in authoring the reports for the American Freedmen's
Inquiry Commission, to provide that important interracial disputes were to go
before ordinary or military courts rather than before Bureau agents acting
as conciliation judges. As explained in the commission's final report, white
Americans, including even Southerners, were characterized as a "race" by
"great force of character, much mental activity, [and] an unflagging spirit of
enterprise," as well as "a certain hardness, a stubborn will." Such a strong-willed
and self-assertive people could not be expected willingly to defer to the mere
opinion of any man. In sharp contrast, the report concluded, was the "African
race," which excelled in "the virtues of humility, loving kindness, [and] resigna-
tion under adversity." While this was "not a race that will ever take a lead in the
material improvement of the world,"[40] its tendency toward meek submission—
the fact, in other words, that it "resembl[ed] a child . . . seeking and needing, for
a season, encouragement and direction"[41]—made it the ideal subject of conciliation court proceedings. But as the war came to a close and the urgency of resurrecting the Southern economy on a new free labor basis intensified, the Bureau
and its agents quickly discovered that it was precisely those interracial disputes—concerning especially labor—that Robert Dale had left to the ordinary
and military courts that most desperately called for Bureau intervention.

## Refining the Vision: Oliver Otis Howard
## and the Problem of Labor

In January 1863, about two months before Secretary Stanton established
the American Freedmen's Inquiry Commission, the first bill to establish what
would eventually become the Freedmen's Bureau was proposed in the House.

More than two years would pass before legislation was finally enacted on March 3, 1865. But throughout these debates, congressmen had copies of the commission reports before them, and these, in turn, played an important role in shaping the legislation.[42]

## THE FREEDMEN'S BUREAU LEGISLATION AND HOWARD'S THREE-JUDGE MODEL OF THE BUREAU COURT

That the commission reports proved influential in shaping the first Freedmen's Bureau bill is hardly surprising, given that the senator who took the lead in advocating the Bureau's establishment—namely, Charles Sumner from Massachusetts—was largely responsible for creating the commission in the first place. Appointed in January 1864 as chairman of the Senate's Committee on Emancipation, Sumner had encouraged his good friend, Secretary Stanton, to appoint the commission and helped select the three commissioners, all of whom were close friends of his. Indeed, it was to Sumner that Robert Dale Owen and his fellow commissioners appealed for funding, access to restricted areas, and the like, and Sumner seems to have learned of the commission's findings well before the War Department did. Sumner, moreover, sought to deploy the commission reports to maximum political effect, insisting that several thousand copies be printed for public distribution. As John G. Sproat concludes, Sumner's Committee on Emancipation was "the legislative counterpart of the administration's Inquiry Commission."[43]

The Radical Republican vision of the Bureau—voiced by Sumner in the Senate and Thomas D. Eliot, chairman of the House's Committee on Freedmen's Affairs—was borrowed in large measure from Owen's reports. Although the House and Senate bills differed in certain respects—including, most importantly, on the question of whether to house the Bureau in the Department of War or the Department of the Treasury—they were quite similar overall.[44] In particular, both bills embraced the pedagogical approach outlined by Owen and his fellow commissioners—including the emphasis on Bureau agents serving as conciliation judges. Reported by Eliot on December 22, 1863, the House bill directed Bureau agents to serve "as arbitrators . . . bring[ing] to conciliation and settlement all difficulties arising between freedmen."[45] So too, the Senate bill, reported by Sumner on May 25, 1864, specified that Bureau agents were to function as "advisory guardians" to freedpeople, including by "do[ing] what they can as arbitrators, to reconcile and settle any differences in which freedmen may be involved whether among themselves or between themselves and other persons."[46] It was this language that was embraced nearly verbatim in the February 2, 1865, bill reported by the conference committee that was established to reconcile the House and Senate versions and on which both Eliot and Sumner sat.[47]

As it turned out, Eliot, Sumner, and their allies on the conference committee overreached. More particularly, the conference committee bill resolved the dispute over where to house the Bureau by making it into its own department. So too (and quite unlike Owen and his fellow commissioners), it adopted an expansive conception of the Bureau's conciliatory function, providing that it was to extend to "differences of all kinds where the freedmen are parties"— including disputes between whites and freedpeople.[48] Writing in the early days of emancipation, Owen had been able largely to ignore the labor disputes that pitted white planters against African-American laborers—and on which revitalization of the Southern economy at least partially hinged. But the ensuing months brought home the lesson, at least to Radical Republicans like Eliot and Sumner, that if the Bureau was to have a meaningful chance of remaking the South on a free labor basis, it had to exercise jurisdiction in such necessarily interracial cases. The powerful Bureau that they envisioned was, however, immediately attacked as an unconstitutional extension of the federal government's authority, which created vast opportunities for graft and replaced the yoke of slavery with a new form of government-imposed tyranny.[49]

As finally enacted on March 3, 1865, the first Freedmen's Bureau bill was much terser than the conference committee bill and studiously avoided all language of guardianship, focusing instead largely on questions of personnel and pay structure. With regard to the Bureau's actual purpose and function, the legislation noted simply that the Bureau was to be located within the Department of War and that the secretary of war had authority to direct "issues of provisions, clothing, and fuel, as he may deem needful." In addition, the legislation provided that the Bureau commissioner "under the direction of the President" could set aside abandoned land in the South "for the use of loyal refugees and freedmen."[50] No mention whatsoever was made of questions of justice and dispute resolution. But while the statute was silent on these matters, the man appointed to head the Bureau would quickly remedy the deficiency—and in so doing, he turned to the conciliation court model initially outlined by Robert Dale Owen.

In May 1865, soon after the Freedmen's Bureau was established and Lincoln was assassinated, President Andrew Johnson appointed Oliver Otis Howard as the Bureau commissioner charged with overseeing the operations of the new agency.[51] Given the many lacunae in the legislation creating the Bureau, Howard would play an especially vital role in shaping the agency and its sense of mission. In the process, he, like Owen before him, drew on the ideal type of the conciliation court. That he did so may at first glance be surprising in that the two men were in many ways dissimilar. Though eager to distance himself from his famous father and thus insistent that he did not share the latter's penchant "to revolutionize society and reform the world," Owen derived much of his sense of identity from his persistent efforts—through both his writings and political activities—to undertake ambitious projects of social reform.[52] In contrast, Howard was a military man and devout evangelical Christian, led by professional orientation and religious belief to think of himself as pursuing a life of simple service. As he depicted it, his position as Bureau commissioner was one into which he had been thrust by duty—both to his military superiors and to God.[53] Yet, despite their differences, the two men shared a similarly spiritual and reformist bent—one characteristic in many ways of the age of the Second Great Awakening. In Owen's case, as we have seen, this expressed itself in a deep-rooted and self-conscious commitment to social reform, undertaken first with an eye toward secular communalism and later within a framework of Christian spiritualism. Howard, in contrast, was a committed, lifelong evangelical. Believing himself to be a simple solider of Christ, he was inspired by his faith to spare no effort in spreading the Word, thereby hastening salvation.

Born in Maine in 1830, Howard was trained at West Point and went on to become a general in the Union Army, heading the Army of the Tennessee. In his mid-twenties, while serving as a second lieutenant in Florida, he attended a Methodist camp meeting in Tampa and underwent a conversion experience that would lead him, as he later reported, seriously to consider devoting his life to "the ministry of Christ" and "preach[ing] the Gospel of Peace."[54] Although he ultimately opted against this path, his religiosity was such that he came to be known as the "Christian Soldier." He was frequently either lauded or ribbed for his evangelicalism, as expressed through, inter alia, a deep commitment to temperance and refusal to utter profanity. While not an abolitionist as such, he had exhibited sufficient kindness and sympathy toward African-Americans in his role as a Union general that, once the Freedmen's Bureau was established, staunch abolitionist Henry Ward Beecher would be among the prominent anti-slavery figures who advocated for his appointment as Bureau commissioner.[55]

For Howard, the Freedmen's Bureau and its project of reconstructing the South were nothing short of a mission in the Christian sense of the word—

Figure 13 Unidentified photographer, *General Oliver
Otis Howard* (circa 1855–65). Courtesy of the Library
of Congress.

one in which he eagerly welcomed the involvement of his fellow (Christian)
citizens. As he stated in an August 1865 speech to the Maine Freedmen's
Relief Society, "I believe that . . . God sent us forth to liberate this oppressed
race." Toward this end, he told the crowd, "[t]he Bureau has to depend upon
voluntary associations for a great deal of its work." Together, the Bureau and
Christian associations would educate both blacks and whites about how to live
in freedom, teaching the former "the rights and duties of liberty" and the latter
"how to get more of the spirit of Christ" and thereby "substitute love for
hate."[56] In practice, just as Howard anticipated, the Christian abolitionist
organizations that had called for the establishment of the Freedmen's Bureau
in the first place ended up supplying it with crucial funding and personnel.
Indeed, the American Missionary Association (AMA)—founded in 1846 as
a coalition of abolitionist groups and headed by Howard's dear friend

George Whipple—even went so far as to offer its missionaries as Bureau agents. As the "Christian solider" heading the Bureau, Howard was the linchpin connecting the governmental agency and its largely military staff to a much broader network of Christian organizations and their profoundly religious missionary ideology.[57]

Upon his appointment, one of the first acts of the thirty-four-year-old commissioner was to issue a circular on May 30, 1865, establishing that his assistant commissioners were to "adjudicate, either themselves or through officers of their appointment, all difficulties arising between negroes themselves, or between negroes and whites or Indians." Most likely in deference to President Johnson's wishes, Howard was careful to specify that the Bureau's adjudicatory power was limited in nature, extending only to those areas where state courts were not functioning or where, as was more commonly the case, these courts, though operational, denied African-Americans the right to testify.[58] Aside from this limitation, the circular defined the Bureau's judicial power in expansive terms, providing—as had Eliot and Sumner—that Bureau agents would hear not only disputes between freedpeople but also interracial ones. That Howard adopted this expansive definition of the Bureau courts' jurisdiction was likely because he (like Eliot and Sumner before him) recognized the numerous difficulties—including labor disputes—confronting military authorities seeking to remake the Southern economy on new, free labor foundations. In addition, there are indications that Howard was familiar with the long-running legislative debate that led to the enactment of the first Freedmen's Bureau bill and sought to model his approach on the Radical Republicans' failed legislative efforts.[59]

Like Robert Dale Owen before him, Howard conceived of the Bureau courts' role in resolving labor disputes as fundamentally pedagogical in nature. As he insisted in December 1865, ignorance was the major challenge to implementing a free labor market in the South. While African-American laborers held "too exalted notions" of "justice and privileges," white planters were characterized by a "want of practical knowledge of any other system than the one under which [t]he[y] ha[ve] been brought up." It was the responsibility of the Bureau courts to teach both sides the virtue of free labor, thereby promoting "mutual confidence between the white employers and the colored employees."[60]

How precisely were the Bureau courts to serve this crucial pedagogical role? Although the May 30 circular offered no indication of how Bureau agents were to adjudicate disputes involving freedpeople, Howard would have occasion to provide more particular guidance, he later recalled, "[q]uite early in my administration"—in the fall of 1865.[61] Not surprisingly, the model to which he turned was that of the conciliation court. But as we will see, it was a very particular kind of conciliation court that he had in mind—one whose origins lay in France but not in the *bureaux de conciliation* that undergirded Bentham's ideal type.

As contemporary newspapers reported, Howard devoted part of October 1865 to "making the tour of Virginia," meeting with locals and trying to develop a plan for Bureau operations, including most importantly, the Bureau's role in resolving labor disputes.[62] It was during this tour that, as the *Norfolk Post* announced, Howard first described a "proposed Court of Conciliation."[63] Around this time, as he later recollected, he met with "a small assembly of planters" just outside Charlottesville. These men "appeared quite in despair how to make or execute contracts with ex-slaves" and pestered him with questions about how they were to prevent freedpeople from "running off and leaving a crop half gathered." Howard's response was to propose the organization of "a court" consisting of three judges: "My agent being one member may represent the Government; the planters of a district can elect another, and the freedmen a third." With "every interest" thus "fairly represented," a Bureau court that was so constituted would be able, he believed, to resolve labor disputes in a manner deemed legitimate by all, thereby assisting in the broader project of remaking the Southern economy on a free labor basis.[64]

About a year later, Howard reaffirmed his commitment to this three-judge model of the Bureau court, but in a somewhat more formal fashion. By this time, many Southern states, eager to oust the Bureau courts of jurisdiction, had repealed their legislation denying African-Americans the right to testify. But determined to preserve white supremacy, they also enacted Black Codes that served largely to re-create the conditions of slavery, pursuant to the formal language of free contract. As a result, by the summer of 1866, the Bureau courts had all but disappeared from the South, even as the possibilities for freedpeople to obtain justice in Southern courts grew no better or even worsened. In desperation, Howard searched for a way to restore the Bureau courts' jurisdiction, ultimately relying for this purpose on the Second Freedmen's Bureau Bill, enacted on July 16, 1866. This statute authorized the president to prescribe rules that would invest the Bureau with jurisdiction over cases implicating freedpeople's enjoyment of their civil rights. Determined to restore the rebel states to normal relations with the rest of the Union as soon as possible, President Johnson himself had no interest in acting on this authority, as Howard well knew. But Howard relied on the mere existence of this statutory authorization to draft a circular concerning the scope of Bureau agents' adjudicatory power and to send the latter to Bureau agents across the South—a circular whose authority was, of course, contingent on presidential approval that never arrived.[65]

In addition to outlining the Bureau courts' jurisdiction, Howard's September 19 circular sought to formalize the guidance concerning the courts' organizational structure that he had provided more informally during his tour of Virginia in October 1865. Bureau courts, he now reaffirmed, were to "be composed of three members, . . . one of whom shall be an officer or agent of this bureau, and the other two citizens of the county in which the court is organized."[66] Although Howard failed to specify that the two citizen-members of these courts were to be selected as representatives of the white planters and African-American laborers, respectively, the continuity with his earlier proposal—and, as discussed below, the actual composition of those three-judge Bureau courts that were established—suggests that there can be little doubt of his intentions.

From where did Howard derive this idea of a three-judge Bureau court? The tendency in the scholarly literature has been to assume that the Bureau courts were simply a kind of military commission—an offshoot of the largely ad hoc military tribunals created by the Union army to try those individuals (including civilians) deemed to "afford[] aid and comfort to rebels."[67] But while the Bureau was housed within the War Department, such that the Bureau courts derived their ultimate authority from the military, it would be a mistake to assume that Bureau courts and military commissions were one and the same. As we have seen, the initial (and influential) decision to establish a Freedmen's Bureau well preceded the much-contested decision to house the agency within the War Department. Moreover, once established, the Bureau developed its own chain of command. Thus, even though it relied on military officers to serve as its agents, those acting on its behalf were largely understood to serve in a distinctive capacity.[68]

So too, there are evident differences in how Bureau courts and military commissions were conceptualized. Admittedly, a number of leading military officials during the Civil War sought to ensure that military commissions would consist of at least three judges—a clear parallel to Howard's model of the three-judge Bureau Court. Generals-in-Chief Winfield Scott and Henry Halleck issued orders to this effect, and Judge Advocate General Joseph Holt issued an opinion so holding. But none of these men viewed the three-judge commission as ideal, specifying instead that more judges would be preferable.

In accordance with this preference, there is some evidence that Civil War military commissions "were most commonly constituted with five members," although three-judge commissions were "not unusual." These commissions, moreover, were all typically composed entirely of military judges. In contrast, Howard viewed the three-judge Bureau court not as some baseline to be preserved but instead as the very prototype of justice for which to strive. And in his model, only one of the three judges was to be a military officer; the other two were to be civilians.[69]

If we wish to understand Howard's idea of the three-judge Bureau Court, we must broaden our perspective to extend beyond the narrow confines of military justice as such. A committed evangelical who seriously considered devoting his life to preaching Christ's "Gospel of Peace" and who reconciled himself to his military role in the Civil War only because of his hope that "God would still use me for the promotion of his cause, and for the glory of his great name,"[70] Howard understood the Bureau and its courts to bear primary responsibility for resurrecting a newly harmonious nation. At the same time, the fact that he was an evangelical suggests that he was likely familiar with the widespread contemporary discussion of the conciliation court—an institution that, as we have seen, proved especially attractive to evangelicals and those who shared their reformist ambitions. It was thus natural for Howard to turn to the model of the conciliation court in his effort to design the Bureau courts that he viewed as vital for national reconciliation and regeneration.[71]

That said, Howard's three-judge court differed in key respects from the traditional model of the conciliation court developed by Bentham on the basis of the French *bureaux de conciliation*. The Benthamite model presumed a single judge who would be able to speak for the community as a whole, deploying his position as a communal authority figure to give voice to (and thereby reaffirm) the community's shared values. In contrast, Howard's three-judge model assumed that the disputants hailed from two distinct, conflicting communities—that of the white planters and that of the African-American laborers—such that no single judge could claim to speak for both. But while Howard's three-judge court differed in important respects from the traditional Benthamite model of the conciliation court, it was not pulled out of thin air. To the contrary, the parallels between Howard's proposed Bureau court and another institution then widely identified as a type of conciliation court—namely, the French labor courts, or *conseils de prud'hommes*—are such that it seems all but certain that his knowledge of the latter played an important role in shaping his approach.

## CONCEPTUALIZING THE FRENCH LABOR COURTS AS A
## FORM OF CONCILIATION COURT

The *conseils de prud'hommes* were established by the Napoleonic regime in the early nineteenth century in order to help quell the labor strife that emerged in the wake of the Napoleonic Wars. The first labor court was created in Lyon on March 18, 1806, and a modified version thereof was then established throughout France pursuant to a decree of June 11, 1809. But while of relatively recent origin, these courts resembled in many ways the corporatist institutions designed to regulate labor and commercial activity under the Old Regime.[72] Most importantly, their judges were elected much like guild leaders once were—namely, by the people whose disputes they were to resolve and whose activities they were to regulate.

Pursuant to the June 11, 1809, decree, the electorate for each *conseil* was to consist of the manufacturers and workers falling within the court's jurisdiction, all of whom were to join together in a general assembly to elect the courts' judges. But as was the case with the guilds and their leadership, not all who were involved in manufacturing were to have equal representation. While the decree established no fixed number of judges on any given court, it specified that there was always to be one more manufacturer serving as judge than the sum total of workers who served in this capacity.[73] The deck was thus stacked in favor of capital over labor. With the passage of time and the heightened labor strife generated by increased industrialization, the electoral rules were changed, such that in 1853 the general assembly of electors was divided into two distinct electoral colleges—one consisting of owner-manufacturers and the other of workers, with each responsible for electing its own representatives to the court.[74]

Despite such changes in the courts' structure, one feature remained constant. In much the same way that Old Regime guilds sought to resolve labor disputes by promoting compromise and reconciliation, rather than formal adjudication, so too the *conseils* were required to attempt to conciliate the disputants.[75] Staffed by lay leaders elected to temporary terms of office by the very communities whose disputes they were asked to resolve, these courts were not expected to apply the law. Instead, their judges were to use their communal authority to pressure the disputants toward compromise. The *conseils* thus came to be viewed as another sort of conciliation court.

While Bentham himself does not appear to have referred to the *conseils de prud'hommes* as conciliation courts, the link was made the very year he died, by none other than John Bowring—the polymath merchant who would go on to fame as, inter alia, a member of Parliament, editor of the utilitarian *Westminster Review*, and perhaps most importantly, Bentham's official literary executor, charged with editing a complete edition of the latter's collected works. In 1831, shortly after the July Revolution inspired hopes of liberalization among English radicals, the British and French agreed to pursue trade negotiations with an eye toward reducing tariffs. Bowring was selected by the British Board of Trade as one of two British representatives to the mixed commission charged with undertaking such reform. In this capacity, he spent much of the period from 1832 to 1834 touring the French provinces and meeting with numerous merchants, manufacturers, local politicians, journalists, and even some workers.[76]

In 1832, during the same period that he was serving as the Board of Trade's commissioner in Paris, Bowring was called to testify before a Select Committee appointed by the House of Commons to report on the English silk trade. As part of its investigation, the committee called on Bowring to describe what he had learned about France's famed silk production, as well as the French-English trade in silk. In this context, Bowring briefly discussed the *conseils de prud'hommes*—and in so doing, described the institution as "a court of conciliation."[77] But as another witness concluded, because the committee was focused primarily on helping English silk manufacturers compete abroad, the *conseils* were of little direct relevance to its inquiry.[78] It was a few years thereafter, when Parliament's attention turned from foreign competition to domestic labor turmoil, that Bowring would come out strongly in favor of adopting an English variant of the French labor courts. And in the process, he developed a more complete and influential account of why, in his view, the institution was best described as a form of conciliation court.

Spurred by a variety of factors, including the rise of the putting out system and the power loom, weavers were among the many English artisans who experienced a severe decline in status and earning power in the early decades of the nineteenth century. In the midst of repeated strikes, often brutally repressed, they petitioned the House of Commons for assistance, including a minimum wage. In response, in 1834, the House appointed a Select Committee, including none other than Bowring himself, which was charged with reviewing the weavers' petitions. Concluding that "the distress which the Petitioners described as so extreme, is fully verified by the Witnesses," the Committee recommended the enactment of a minimum wage.[79] But the proposed legislation was firmly rejected by the House in 1835 and repeatedly thereafter through the end of the decade. The committee thus proposed a number of other measures to relieve the weavers' suffering, including the development of methods of dispute resolution that would forestall strikes and attenuate labor militancy. In this context, it highlighted the "very valuable" testimony provided by Bowring "respecting industrial institutions in France . . . of which he has had much recent experience"—namely, the *conseils de prud'hommes*.[80] In recommending their establishment in England, the Select Committee would be among the first of many, in both England and the United States, who would thereafter advise the transplantation of this French institution as a means of addressing the problem of industrial labor strife.

Asked to provide testimony concerning "any attempts which have been made for the purpose of relieving the distress of the hand-loom weavers in Lyons, or elsewhere," Bowring pointed to the *conseils de prud'hommes*, noting that "[t]his tribunal was a highly popular one" and that, in his view, "something like it might advantageously be established in this country." According to Bowring, the *conseils* "settle[] almost every question . . . by amicable interference" and are thus appropriately categorized as a type of "court of conciliation." Drawing on and expanding Bentham's notion of the conciliation court, Bowring insisted that, like the *bureaux de conciliation,* these labor courts did not oversee "the administration of justice so much as the administration of benevolent feeling." As a result, he asserted, disputes before the labor courts were "almost invariably decided to the satisfaction of the parties," and the courts themselves were "objects of great affection among the weavers."[81]

In the decades that followed, as tensions stemming from industrialization continued unabated, others in England also called for the development of a local variant of the French labor court, now expressly defined as a type of conciliation court. For example, in 1855, William Alexander Mackinnon, a Whig member of Parliament, recommended the appointment of a select committee charged with developing a proposal for such an institution. The committee report, issued in 1856, concluded that "the formation of Courts of Conciliation in the country, more especially in manufacturing, commercial, and mining, districts, would be beneficial." But despite widespread press coverage, Parliament failed to act.[82] Thereafter, in response to a massive strike and lockout in the London building trades in 1859–60, Lord Henry Brougham, former chancellor and then member of Parliament, renewed his longstanding plea for the establishment of conciliation courts, advocating this time for the labor variant identified by Bowring.

Deploring the strikers for making demands that were "utterly absurd and . . . inconsistent with justice as well as common sense," Brougham expressed the hope that "out of these calamities a very great good might come which he had long been anxious to obtain." More particularly, he observed, "[h]e had always regretted that certain alterations of the law which he had often propounded had not yet been effected—he meant Courts of Reconcilements." In his view, "[i]t was impossible to read the annual report of the French Courts of Conciliation without wishing to see some analogous provisions in our own law brought to bear upon these combinations and disputes which were some-times carried to a great extent between master and man." In so arguing, he fo-cused particular attention on the "Conseils des Prud'hommes," which he claimed—citing an 1850 French government report—"satisfactorily settled without any litigation" on the order of 96 percent of the disputes brought before them.[83] Reported in the press, Brougham's speech spurred the appointment of yet another select committee, which, in 1860, approved the report issued by its predecessor four years earlier.[84] Thereafter, in 1861, draft legislation was pro-posed to establish an English variant of the *conseils de prud'hommes,* but it failed to pass.[85] Finally, in 1867, a statute establishing Equitable Councils of Concilia-tion was enacted—though it would prove largely a dead letter.[86]

Throughout these decades, as the English debated the merits of adopting some version of the French *conseils de prud'hommes*—framed expressly as a form of conciliation court—Americans paid close attention. For example, in 1844, the Philadelphia-based *Friends' Weekly Intelligencer* published an article that had appeared eleven years earlier in *The Penny Magazine*—a British Whig magazine aimed at educating the lower classes.[87] Pointing to "the evidence given by Dr. Bowring on the Silk Trade," the article called for the establish-ment of French-style *conseils de prud'hommes,* described as "court[s] of concili-ation." In the article's words, these would "promot[e] and continu[e] cordial good will between masters and workmen."[88] Similarly, the Albany-based pa-per, the *Mechanic's Advocate,* published an article in February 1847 that praised the French *conseils de prud'hommes* as "a paternal jurisdiction" focused on the "amicabl[e] settle[ment]" of disputes. According to the article, "[p]ettifogging and litigatious disputation find no field there for display," and as a result, the court was known for "its cheapness." These "Councils of Wise Men, or as they are now termed, Courts of Conciliation," had produced "incalculable good ef-fects" in France and thus ought to be tried in New York as well.[89]

So too, as the British Parliament considered the possibility of enacting some form of French-style labor court, American newspapers followed these debates closely. The London correspondent of the *Daily National Intelligencer,* based in Washington, D.C., reported in June 1860 that "the select committee appointed to consider the best means of settling disputes between masters and workmen" had just recently printed a report recommending "the establishment of voluntary courts of conciliation." And in May 1861, the *Scientific American* and the *American Railway Review,* both published in New York, reported on the legislation then pending before Parliament to establish what they described as "Workmen's Courts of Conciliation," modeled on the French "courts called *prud-hommes.*" The following month, *Street and Smith's New York Weekly* also discussed the proposed English legislation concerning "Courts of Conciliation" and argued that "[s]omething of this kind is a desideratum in this country, and would prevent much difficulty, injustice and hard feeling, if properly conducted."⁹⁰

Given the widespread coverage of the French labor courts in the contemporary American press—coverage that expressly defined the institution as a type of conciliation court—it seems very likely that Howard's three-judge conception of the Bureau court was modeled on the *conseils de prud'hommes.* Like the *conseils,* Howard's model court was designed to resolve disputes between owners (white planters) and laborers (their former slaves). Moreover, like the *conseils,* it sought not to impose the rule of law but instead to conciliate the disputants by persuading them to embrace an equitable compromise. As in the *conseils,* the main mechanism for promoting conciliation was a reliance on judges who were community leaders, selected by, and thus representing the interests of (white) owners, on the one hand, and (African-American) laborers, on the other.

Strikingly, Howard was not the only person concerned with the problem of Southern labor relations who, in 1865, embraced the model of the *conseil de prud'hommes* as part of the solution. On March 17, 1865, African-Americans in New Orleans held a meeting in Economy Hall, home to one of the city's leading black mutual aid societies, to discuss the issuance of orders by General Stephen A. Hurlbut, then commander of the Department of the Gulf, aimed at regulating labor relations.⁹¹ As provided in General Order No. 23, all "[v]oluntary contracts . . . made between Planters and Laborers" were to be submitted for review to a military officer designated the "Superintendent of the Bureau of Free Labor." The order specified, moreover, that all contracts were to award the freedmen not only monetary compensation (at precise rates indicated for different categories of workers), but also "wholesome rations, comfortable clothing, quarters, fuel, and medical attendance."⁹² In response to the issuance of this order, African-Americans in New Orleans penned a series of resolutions opposing the order as a perpetuation of slavery. As described in the African-American newspaper, the *New Orleans Tribune,* the resolutions emphasized that, unlike freedpeople, free white laborers were "not *compelled* to take food and clothing as a part of [their] wages" and were not placed under the control of "a special Bureau which perpetuate[s] the discrimination between castes and races."[93]

Having thus rejected Hurlbut's approach to regulating labor relations, the assembled African-American community demanded instead a process that would give them more of a voice in determining how their own labor was to be contracted out. And the institutional mechanism to which they turned was the *conseil de prud'hommes*. It was perfectly acceptable, they argued, for labor disputes to be decided as an initial matter by military officials, but these decisions ought to be appealable to "a Tribunal of Arbitrators, composed partly of freedmen, to decide in the simplest but in the most equitable way."[94] When Hurlbut dismissed this recommendation as "impracticable," the *New Orleans Tribune* published a lengthy article defending the proposed tribunal on the grounds that it was but an offshoot of the French *conseil de prud'hommes*, then widely viewed as the ideal institution for addressing the problem of conflictual labor relations:

> The meeting asked for a mixed tribunal, a "Court of Labor," partly composed of freedmen, and therefore formed of representative[s] of both interests, capital and labor. . . . It is the plan devised and carried out with great success in all countries where capital had taken sway over labor and had to be safely counterpoised. It is the system followed in most of Germany, in France—where it is known under the name "Prud'hommes," and given as a model by the most eminent jurists of all the nations—in Italy, in Switzerland and in many other States of Europe. It is the system which has lately attracted attention in British Parliament, with a view to have it extended to England. . . . The proposal was not the hollow conception of some freeman—or freedman—; it is a system found to be not only *practicable*, but desirable and fruitful, in all countries where capital overwhelms the rights of labor.[95]

That the African-American community of New Orleans also looked to the *conseil de prud'hommes* as the solution to reconstructing the Southern labor market underscores the likelihood that it was this French institution—nearly ubiquitous in the contemporary press—that underlay Howard's three-judge model of the Bureau court.

That both Howard and the African-American community of New Orleans looked to the *conseil de prud'hommes* does not, however, mean that they shared identical conceptions of the institution. While the freedpeople embraced this model of the conciliation court with the expectation that it would serve to empower them, Howard himself adopted a much more paternalistic approach. For the freedpeople, it was self-evident that those whom they elected as their representatives on the court would themselves be African-American. In contrast, Howard presumed that freedpeople would select white "citizens" to serve as their judicial representatives. In proposing the three-judge court to white planters in Virginia in the fall of 1865, he assured them that "[i]n nine cases out of ten the freedmen will choose [as their representative on the court] an intelligent white man who has always seemed to be their friend."[96] As implemented in practice, the Bureau courts assumed a number of different institutional forms. But to the extent that Howard's three-judge model was attempted, it was his paternalistic approach that won the day, rather than the more self-empowering version advocated by the freedpeople of New Orleans. In this respect as well, the Bureau courts hewed closely to the model of the *conseil de prud'hommes,* which as we have seen, long guaranteed owner-manufacturers at least one more representative on the court than was available to workers.

## The Bureau Courts in Practice

To what extent were the Bureau courts—as they actually operated—a type of conciliation court? Given the extent of Bureau court activity, this is a question of no small importance. While new research suggests that, in implementing Reconstruction, the Bureau and its agents were significantly outnumbered by ordinary army officers and servicemen,[97] the fact remains that the Bureau was widely recognized by contemporaries—including freedpeople themselves—as playing a vital role in the effort to remake the South.[98] And the Bureau courts, in turn, were a key component of this broader effort. Although they operated for only about four years, Howard estimated that they resolved on the order of one hundred thousand disputes during each of these years.[99]

Assessing whether the Bureau courts in fact functioned as conciliation courts turns out, however, to be remarkably difficult. One reason for this difficulty is that there is no single model of the conciliation court against which to compare the Bureau courts. As we have seen, nineteenth-century Americans believed that both the *bureaux de conciliation* and the *conseils de prud'hommes* were types of conciliation court, but there were important differences between these institutions. Moreover, courts established outside of

France—on the model of one or the other of these two institutions—varied in significant respects from their French antecedents. For example, it was often noted that the Danish conciliation courts, though modeled on the *bureaux de conciliation,* preserved far greater secrecy in their proceedings than did their French counterparts.[100] Similarly, the industrial courts created in late nineteenth-century Germany—and based on the *conseils de prud'hommes* that were first established in the Rhineland under Napoleonic rule—differed from their French predecessors in employing as judges not only representatives of owners and workers but also a neutral, third-party chairman.[101] To complicate matters further, even as concerns the original French *bureaux de conciliation* and *conseils de prud'hommes,* there appear to have been some significant differences between the law in the books and the law in action. Most importantly, while these institutions were originally conceived as ones in which disputants would represent themselves without legal assistance, lawyers quickly found ways to involve themselves.[102]

Despite such variability, there were certain common features shared (to a greater or lesser degree) by all these institutions, leading them to be categorized by lawyers, politicians, and commentators across nineteenth-century Europe and the United States as variants of a single ideal type: the conciliation court. These courts all relied on lay judges, lacking legal training, who were appointed not for their legal expertise but instead because of the position of authority that they occupied within the (relevant) local community—a community from which one or both of the disputants hailed. Relatedly, the judges were not expected to apply the law as such, but instead to rely on their authority within the community to persuade the disputants to embrace an equitable compromise. These common features, in turn, stemmed from the courts' shared roots in early modern European corporatism. As we have seen, the *bureaux de conciliation*—though conceived as new—were offshoots of the pre-revolutionary seigneurial courts that were owned and operated by noblemen as a badge of status and in which judges long relied on traditions of deference within the local peasant community to encourage disputants to reconcile. Likewise, the *conseils de prud'hommes* resembled Old Regime guilds, which permitted groups of merchants and artisans to engage in significant self-regulation, including conciliation-oriented dispute resolution. Moreover, the variants of these institutions that were established throughout Europe and its colonies took root, in no small part, by drawing on local corporatist practices—including, in the case of the Spanish Empire, the centuries-old tradition of *alcalde*-based municipal governance (and dispute resolution).

Armed with this minimalist definition of the conciliation court, it is still no easy task to assess the extent to which the Bureau courts in fact conformed to the definition. While there have been numerous studies of Bureau operations across the South, including those of the Bureau courts, these have focused little, if any, attention on questions of procedure as such. While scholars have relied extensively on Bureau court records as a way of gaining access to the voice of freedmen and women seeking to navigate Reconstruction, they have given little thought to the procedural pathways through which this voice was channeled. We have no answers to such basic questions as whether (and if so, how often and in what circumstances) disputants before the Bureau courts employed lawyers; whether Bureau-court proceedings were conducted in public or private; and how and by whom witnesses were examined.[103] Accordingly, despite the substantial size of the existing secondary literature, none of it is directly on point—though it is possible to glean from it many relevant insights.

A final reason why it is so difficult to determine the extent to which Bureau courts in fact operated as conciliation courts is the enormous variation that existed between (and even within) individual courts. In practice, despite Howard's aspirations, the various courts established by the Bureau across the South were not all structured identically. It was in Virginia, under the authority of Assistant Commissioner Orlando Brown, that Howard's system of three-judge courts was most widely established. In September 1865, Brown issued a circular providing that in each subdistrict of the state, a Bureau court would be created consisting of the Bureau agent and two men selected "from among the citizens," one by local whites and one by freedmen. This court was to "adjudicate upon all difficulties that may arise between the whites and the freedmen, or among the freedmen themselves, including crimes committed by the freedmen in which the penalty does not exceed imprisonment at hard labor for a period of three months or a fine of one hundred dollars." The three individuals constituting this court were also required to "aid and assist the freedmen in making contracts" and to "see that all able to work are properly and profitably employed."[104]

Even in this one state, however—and despite the clear wording of the circular—there was significant variability in Bureau court proceedings. The evidence, for example, suggests that the full court did not always sit. According to a reporter writing for the *New York Herald* in March 1866, the Bureau court in Richmond was typically staffed by only two judges—namely, "the two judges who represented the two colors"—and the Bureau agent himself was called in only "[w]hen the two differ in opinion."[105] Likewise, the Register of

Correspondence kept by Superintendent Thomas Franklin Philip Crandon, serving as Bureau agent in Gordonsville, Virginia, reveals that there were occasions when one of the two "civil members of the court" failed to attend, such that the dispute was resolved by the remaining member and the Bureau agent.[106]

Outside of Virginia, three-judge Bureau courts operated, but they exercised more limited jurisdiction, leaving many disputes involving freedpeople to single-judge Bureau courts (and military tribunals). For example, in October 1865, General Rufus Saxton, the assistant commissioner for South Carolina and Georgia, issued a circular ordering Bureau agents in each district to create three-judge boards staffed by the Bureau agent and two "citizens"—one chosen by local whites and one by freedmen. These boards were charged with "arrang[ing] equitable contracts between the employers and employees for the labor of the freedmen."[107] In the same month, General Howard issued an order directing that in certain, more limited places in coastal South Carolina and Georgia, where land was being restored to pardoned Confederates, such three-judge boards were to "aid in making contracts" between the restored landowners and local African-American residents. So too, these boards were required to "adjudicate all difficulties that may arise between the whites and the freedmen, or among the freedmen themselves." As demonstrated by Bureau records, these orders to establish such three-judge courts were in fact implemented.[108] Elsewhere in the South, efforts were made to channel disputes into three-judge Bureau courts but on an even more limited and case-by-case basis. For example, in Florida, in January 1867, the assistant commissioner directed that labor disputes be resolved by three-member arbitral boards that, rather than serving as standing courts, were to be selected by the parties themselves for the dispute in question. According to the Bureau agent in Jackson County, Florida, about one-fourth of the labor contracts entered in early 1867 contained provisions for such arbitral boards.[109]

Bureau records reveal, moreover, that agents sometimes exercised their discretion to assemble such three-judge panels for purposes of deciding a particular case. Consider, for example, a conflict that arose between a Georgia freedwoman by the name of Ann Brown and her employer's wife in February and March 1867. The employer, J. M. Culpepper, complained to the local bureau agent that Brown was "useing profane Language and . . . failing to do her work." Brown, in turn, claimed that Culpepper "beat me and abused me by throwing me down and choking me and kicking me at the same time his wife had hold of my hair with both hands." Faced with these competing claims of failure to abide by the contractual obligation and cruel treatment, the Bureau agent responded by creating a three-person panel consisting of himself and two other men—one chosen by Brown and the other by Culpepper. This panel, in turn, urged a compromise position aimed at teaching the planter that violence was improper in a free labor regime and the freedwoman that freedom was no license to be lazy and disrespectful. Culpepper was thus found guilty, but Brown was awarded only a "nominal fine of Ten (10) Dollars" since she "committed the first breach of the peace by shaking her fist in the face of Mrs. Culpepper."[110]

To the extent that Bureau courts did not adopt this three-judge model, they followed the single judge approach initially envisioned by the American Freedmen's Inquiry Commission. Here too, however, there was quite a bit of regional variation. In most states, Bureau agents—themselves military officers, lacking legal training—served as Bureau-court judges. But in Alabama, Mississippi, and Louisiana, Bureau agents invited state magistrates to serve as Bureau court judges, contingent on their agreement to apply the law equally to—and admit the testimony of—freedpeople. As a result, Bureau courts in these states were often staffed by local (and legally trained) Southern white judges. In South Carolina, in turn, but for the limited three-judge Bureau courts just mentioned, military tribunals initially retained jurisdiction over all but the most serious suits involving freedpeople. It was not until June 1866, when a Bureau agent assumed control over military forces in South Carolina, that a broad network of Bureau courts was officially established there.[111]

Just as the structure and staffing of the Bureau courts varied across the South, so too did the scope of their jurisdiction. Howard's initial circular of May 30, 1865, specified simply that, as long as Southern state courts continued to deny African-Americans the right to testify, assistant commissioners serving as Bureau agents were to "adjudicate either themselves or through officers of their appointment, all difficulties arising between negroes themselves, or between negroes and whites or Indians . . . so far as recognizable by military authority, and not taken cognizance of by the other tribunals, civil or military, of the United States."[112] As this was interpreted in practice, military courts retained jurisdiction over serious criminal matters—like murder, rape, arson, and burglary—while civil disputes and more minor criminal matters were delegated to the Bureau courts. How precisely these distinctions were drawn varied, however, from state to state. For example, Bureau courts in Mississippi were granted jurisdiction over particular types of dispute, including "petty cases such as theft, disobedience, and breach of the peace" and "cases of cruelty and abuse of freedmen." In contrast, Bureau agents in Tennessee were simply informed that "differences between freedmen and others (or between themselves) will be adjudicated by officers and agents of this Bureau."[113] In addition, Bureau courts' jurisdiction varied with the passage of time. As we have seen, on September 19, 1866, Howard issued a circular seeking— without presidential authorization—to reestablish Bureau courts to address the injustices that freedpeople were experiencing in Southern state courts. This circular defined the Bureau courts' jurisdiction in terms much more precise than his initial language from the previous year—limiting it to civil matters valued at $300 or less and criminal matters in which the punishment was less than a $100 fine or thirty days of hard labor. But since assistant commissioners in only three states (South Carolina, Florida, and Arkansas) actually implemented Howard's circular, its impact was relatively limited.[114]

To such differences in the structure and jurisdiction of the Bureau courts must also be added differences in procedure. There were no statutes or military orders that addressed the procedural mechanisms to be employed by the Bureau courts. Thus, especially given that the majority of Bureau court judges were not themselves legally trained, variability was, here as elsewhere, the norm. As the *New York Herald Tribune* observed in May 1866, "[t]he Bureau is a good or bad institution according to the personal character of the agent who administers it; it varies in every county and changes with every change of officers."[115]

In line with the ideal type of the conciliation court, Bureau court records suggest that a great many disputes were decided without the involvement of lawyers.[116] And not surprisingly, the fact that parties often represented themselves lent itself to considerable procedural informality. Testimony, for example, appears to have been admitted without regard to formal admissibility under the rules of evidence. As Superintendent Crandon advised a subordinate in December 1865, "My opinion is, all testimony bearing on the case should be allowed, and the Court should judge of its reliability."[117] Likewise, when in the spring of 1866 General Joseph S. Fullerton asked a Savannah lawyer whether "any attention was paid [by the local Bureau court] to the rules of evidence in taking testimony," the lawyer responded, "none whatever."[118] The accuracy of these assertions is suggested by the numerous Bureau court records that recount the testimony provided by disputants and witnesses without regard to basic evidentiary rules of competency or relevance.

Along similar lines, Bureau court records suggest that many disputes were brought before agents not through the filing of formal, written complaints but instead through more informal, oral channels. For example, a Bureau agent based in Vicksburg, Mississippi, reported to his superiors in April 1866 that, as directed, he had traveled to the town of Friars Point to "examine into the condition of the surrounding districts." Upon so doing, he visited the plantation owned by James A. Peace and discovered that the freedpeople who had contracted to serve there as laborers were refusing to work "in consequence of Mr. Hogan (who was formerly an overseer) being employed to superintend . . . the plantation." Having learned of this labor dispute through his own informal observations and conversations with the freedpeople involved, the agent intervened with an eye toward promoting settlement. He reviewed the laborers' contracts and, finding that these were satisfactory, proceeded to lecture them on "their duty in faithfully observing their obligations, also the importance of their obedience to, and showing respect for whoever their employer chose to employ as their superintendent, so long as no injustice or cruelty is practiced towards them." Thereafter, he reported, "they all seemed to be well satisfied and promised to go to work again; which I find since by inquiry they have done."[119]

Less clear is the extent to which the Bureau courts adhered to the Benthamite model of secrecy in proceedings. Many Bureau records describing agents' efforts informally to settle disputes make no mention of who was present. The aforementioned Bureau agent in Vicksburg, Mississippi, for example, observed that he had successfully settled a dispute between two freedmen that arose when one "whipp[ed] the child" of the other. As he explained, the freedmen were "arraigned before me . . . and I gave them some advice and received their promise that they would faithfully conduct themselves in a proper manner hereafter."[120] Whether anyone else was present during this brief proceeding is not clear from the report—though the informal nature of the encounter suggests at least the possibility that it was conducted in private.

But while Bureau courts often operated without lawyers and on the basis of considerable procedural informality, there were also plenty of Bureau court proceedings that adopted a more adversarial approach—including, not least, representation by legal counsel. While lawyers were never formally barred from Bureau court proceedings, it is clear that those who first envisioned the institution imagined them as absent. As we have seen, Robert Dale Owen, the lead author of the American Freedmen's Inquiry Commission reports, was quite antagonistic to lawyers, arguing that they did nothing but "sow dissensions" and thereby augment costs. Moreover, the Commission's only mention of legal counsel was in the context of those cases too serious to be relegated to the Bureau courts. So too, Howard's circulars concerning the operation of the

Bureau courts made no mention of lawyers representing the disputants. Indeed, implicit in his three-judge model of the court was the notion that it was the judges themselves—one selected by the local planters and the other by the freedpeople—who were to serve in this representative capacity. But despite such assumptions, the evidence suggests that (white) lawyers sometimes made their way into Bureau court proceedings. For example, in a March 1866 article concerning the Richmond Bureau court, the *New York Herald Tribune* reported that "[l]awyers . . . at first were reluctant to practice in a 'nigger court' " but "they now attend without any hesitation, and eagerly gather fees from the disputing clients of either color."[121] So too, numerous newspaper reports of Bureau court proceedings in Savannah and Nashville mention the involvement of counsel, sometimes even identifying the individuals who served as such and describing the "rather amusing cross-firing" that ensued from their adversarial interventions on behalf of their clients.[122] Similarly, Crandon explained to a subordinate in December 1865 that "Counsel is admitted to the [Bureau] court, the same as in any other court."[123]

Given that lawyers were at times involved in Bureau-court proceedings, it is not surprising to discover that procedural informality was not always the rule. While some disputes were brought before Bureau agents in an informal, oral fashion, others were presented as more formal, written complaints. Indeed, some Bureau agents, like Superintendent Crandon, required plaintiffs to submit written complaints—perhaps because they were too busy pursuing their many non-judicial, Bureau-related obligations to hold regular court hours.[124] Bureau-court records suggest, however, that written complaints, while not infrequent, were themselves typically quite simple and short factual narratives, free of legal jargon. For example, in the aforementioned dispute between Ann Brown and her employers, the Culpeppers, Brown submitted a very short document, signed with her mark, in which she detailed in a few brief sentences the nature of the abuse that she had suffered at their hands.[125]

Another quite common feature of Bureau-court proceedings that ran afoul of the Benthamite model of the conciliation court and that may well have stemmed, in part, from the not infrequent practice of disputants relying on legal counsel was their highly public nature. Neither Owen nor Howard—nor any of the circulars establishing Bureau courts—expressly stated that these courts' proceedings were to take place privately outside public view. The failure to do so may simply reflect that (likely for pragmatic, political reasons) no effort was made to create documentation specifying the nature of Bureau-court proceedings. But whatever the explanation for such silence, it is clear that in practice, many Bureau-court proceedings took place in public, thus departing from the ideal type of the conciliation court.

As a reporter for the *New York Herald* observed in March 1866 in describing his visit to the Richmond Bureau Court, "[i]n the street fronting the court door, a mixed crowd of blacks and whites, in good and bad garbs, awaited the settlement of their claims or the satisfaction of their curiosity." Not content to remain outside, this crowd pushed into the courtroom itself: While "[t]here is, in theory, no respecting of persons before the court—no distinctions because of color; yet, except when called within the bar to plead or to give testimony, the blacks remain beyond it, and the whites push, as a matter of course, into the precincts of the lawyers."[126] Similarly, as the *Savannah Daily Herald* reported on February 27, 1866, the courtroom was "densely packed with negroes and negresses," such that it was only when "[t]he judge threatened to bring the spectators up singly and require of them their papers showing their means of living" that the crowd finally dissipated.[127] Strikingly, moreover, in at least certain cities, newspapers eager to return to their longstanding practice of reporting on daily court activity published regular accounts of Bureau-court proceedings. In this way, newspapers like the *Savannah Daily Herald* and the *Augusta Chronicle* ensured that the public able to gain access to such proceedings would include not only those who managed to make it into the courtroom but also a much larger community of readers.

Given the tremendous variation in the structure, jurisdiction, and most importantly procedure of the Bureau courts, what, if anything, can we conclude about the extent to which these courts conformed to even a minimalist definition of the conciliation court? In other words, were the Bureau courts staffed by lay judges (1) who were appointed because of their position of authority within the community from which one or both of the disputants hailed and (2) who focused not on applying the law, but instead on encouraging the disputants to embrace an equitable compromise? In the case of those few states where the Bureau judges were themselves local Southern magistrates, the answer is clearly no. So too, in those cases where the disputants were represented by legal counsel, this fact in itself ran counter to the ideal type of the conciliation court. But what about those more common Bureau-court proceedings in which the agents serving as judges were military officers—sometimes, though not always, joined by two lay judges, one selected by the planters and the other by the freedpeople? To the extent that disputants appeared before these lay judges without legal counsel, the proceedings arguably conformed to the conciliation court model in certain key respects.

As historians have demonstrated, most Bureau agents serving as judges shared a common identity and set of values. They were largely white, Northern military men, steeped in the ideology of free labor. And it was these free labor values, rather than the law as such, that shaped their decisions, both in disputes between freedpeople and in those between freedpeople and whites. For example, it was Northern ideals of gender roles, born of the cult of domesticity, that the Bureau sought to impose in resolving familial disputes between freedmen and women—by insisting that male farm laborers be paid more than their female counterparts or that husbands provide for their families, as a way of institutionalizing the male role as primary breadwinner. So too, they sought to resolve labor disputes in ways they deemed necessary to teach both white planters and African-American laborers the virtues of a free labor system, even when this required contravening established principles of law. For example, to protect freedpeople against the risk that they would work the entire year only to be denied proper payment at the time the crops were harvested, agents devised a novel legal solution. The freedpeople were said by virtue of their labor to possess a lien on the crops, such that these could be seized and sold by the Bureau agents who would, in turn, retain on their behalf an amount requisite to pay their salaries. Similarly, Bureau agents assuaged the anxiety of white planters that their former slaves would simply refuse to work by ordering specific performance of labor contracts—a remedy traditionally denied in contracts for personal services.[128]

For Bureau courts like these, the primary goal was to implement Northern free labor values rather than to enforce the law as such. But while these courts relied on lay leaders to implement community values, they differed from the traditional model of the conciliation court in one vital way: The community whose values they sought to reinforce was not that of either of the disputants but instead that of a third-party outsider. Indeed, this was largely true even in the case of the three-judge courts, which were expressly designed to give voice to white planters and African-American laborers by including representatives of each on the court.

Unlike the *conseils de prud'hommes*, which appointed only employers and employees as judges, the three-judge Bureau courts included a third party— the Northern Bureau agent—as the courts' chief officer and tiebreaker.[129] As a reporter for the *New York Herald* stated in March 1866, whenever the representatives of the whites and the freedmen sitting on the Richmond Bureau court "differ in opinion, the President of the court is called and the whole case has to be gone over again," such that the Bureau agent, serving as president, had the final say.[130] Moreover, it was the values of the Bureau agent and the Northern white community from which he hailed that proved decisive in the selection of the judge representing the freedmen. Howard's expectation that freedmen would almost always select white men to serve as their representatives was realized through Bureau agents' careful regulation of judicial elections—regulation that sought to ensure not only the proper racial identity of those ultimately selected but also their adherence to proper norms of (Northern, middle-class) conduct.

Consider, for example, the role played by Bureau agent Crandon in the November 1865 election of a judge to represent the freedpeople of the Culpeper, Virginia, subdistrict. When a certain N. Snyder proved to be the choice of "a large majority of the Colored men," Crandon opted to disregard the electoral results. The problem, explained Crandon, was that "he (Snyder) was living with a prostitute negress" and "on this account, and because of his general immorality, he was not recognized by any respectable man." This, in turn, meant that "this man was entirely unfit for the position and that his reputation was such in the community that no respectable man would consent to be associated with him in the formation of the Court." That a "large majority" of African-Americans had, to the contrary, concluded that Snyder was perfectly fit to serve as their representative evidently did not weigh into the analysis. Indeed, when pressed by Crandon to choose another representative, the freedpeople of Culpepper continued to adhere to their original choice. As they observed, quite trenchantly, "[t]he fact that [Snyder] lived in a state of prostitution with a negress" meant merely that he "did a little more publicly what nearly every Southern man did privately, and that therefore he ought not to be objectionable on that account."[131]

But despite the freedmen's insistence that they stood behind the choice of Snyder, Crandon refused to permit it: "Not willing that the interests of the colored people should be compromised by being represented by a man of Snyder's reputation, I called another meeting of the more prominent colored men of the Town. I presume there were 30 or 40 present. . . . I advised the Colored men who were assembled to select another man to represent them, and told them my reasons." Thus pushed, they at last "acquiesced, and chose a Mr. Geo. Williams who from the first was the favorite of a number of the more prominent colored men, and was the second choice of Mr. Snyder's supporters. On this I set aside the election of Mr. Snyder. . . ." According to Crandon, Williams—in sharp contrast to the disgraced Snyder—was a "perfect gentleman." From Crandon's perspective, the decision to set aside the freedmen's choice of representatives followed naturally from the tutelary nature of the relationship between the Bureau and the freedpeople assumed to be under its charge. To the extent that freedpeople themselves did not yet understand what was in their best interests, Crandon himself, as Bureau agent, would show them—teaching them, in the case of Mr. Snyder, that no Northern man of middle-class standing would "knowingly and voluntarily be brought into official relations with whoremongers and miscegenationists."[132]

Whether of the one-judge or three-judge sort, the Bureau courts were, at the end of the day, offshoots of the Northern military victory and occupation. While the conciliation court model was premised on the notion that the judge would appeal to his position of authority within the community to inspire deference to his equitable judgment and thereby reinforce communal values, the Bureau courts did not attempt to reinforce but instead to transmute such values. An institution that was in many respects conservative in nature was thus deployed for radically transformative purposes. To the extent that the courts could rely on the reality or at least threat of military action to back up their decisions— which was not always the case, and increasingly less so as time progressed— they could be effective. But when they were, this was not because they were acting as conciliation courts harnessing local communal norms but instead because of the threat of force. The American experience had thus proven once again that, deracinated from any corporatist, communal structures and traditions, the conciliation court model could not meaningfully sustain itself.

However flawed the initiative, the effort to establish Bureau courts on the model of the conciliation court represented a nascent, though never fully theorized, recognition of the limits of the then-dominant adversarial model. Contrary, in other words, to what James Oakes has argued, the ultimate failure of the Bureau courts was not a product of its agents' blind faith that "the invisible hand of laissez-faire liberalism" would suffice to remake the South.[133] As men like Owen and Howard as well as many individual Bureau agents understood, decreeing an end to discrimination and trusting in private litigation—facilitated by adversarial procedure—was no panacea. The actual legal rules in place in the South continued to be deeply racist—especially as Black Codes proliferated. And lawyer-driven adversarial procedure was too expensive for most freedpeople to afford. Moreover, especially in interracial disputes, such procedure's presumption of equality of arms was palpably false. What was needed was a powerful judge who had the discretion to depart from procedural niceties and the rule of law in order to do substantive justice instead. But how to justify such discretion?

One option was the traditional model of quasi-inquisitorial equity—a model that allowed for a powerful and highly discretion-laden judicial figure. But this was not a model that was readily available as of 1865, when traditional equity of this kind had long since been dismantled. In contrast, what was available was the conciliation court model, which also allowed for a powerful, discretion-laden judge but claimed to ground this authority in some vague notion of consensus-oriented pedagogy. Indeed, this model was not only available but also appealing. Besides the fact that the conciliation court was of longstanding interest to the evangelical and reformist groups that ended up playing such an important role in funding and otherwise supporting the Freedmen's Bureau, it had the additional virtue of obscuring the question of power. By framing judicial authority as merely an exercise of equitable, commonsense-based persuasion, the model of the conciliation court enabled Northerners to imagine that true Reconstruction could somehow be achieved without the further use of force. White Southerners themselves, however, were under no such illusions.

## Conflicting Conceptions of the Bureau Courts

Once the Freedmen's Bureau was established and its agents began to serve as judges, commentators from both the North and the South filled the pages of contemporary newspapers and magazines with pieces concerning the new courts. While views of the Bureau courts varied even within a particular region, there were, nonetheless, certain commonalities in the opinions expressed—at least among Northern Republicans, on the one hand, and Southern whites (and their Democratic allies), on the other. The Northern Republican press discussed the courts in terms that largely tracked the model of the Bureau court as a conciliation court—as a kind of pedagogical institution grounded in consensus-building equity and common sense—developed by Owen, Howard, and the individual Bureau agents seeking to implement their vision. In contrast, white Southerners and the Northern Democrats supporting them described the Bureau courts as profoundly un-American institutions by means of which Northern Bureau agents denied disputants the core protections of adversarial procedure with an eye toward imposing their own personal prejudices on a subjugated population.

What about African-Americans themselves? There is a sizable secondary literature devoted to examining how freedpeople experienced the Freedmen's Bureau and its courts. As this literature demonstrates, freedpeople were, for the most part, favorably disposed toward the Bureau courts. In utilizing these institutions, they sought strategically to deploy Northern ideals of free labor and domesticity as a way of persuading Bureau agents to decide in their favor. For example, many successfully demanded back wages by asserting that they owned their own labor and thus had to be compensated when they expended it on others' behalf. So too, freedwomen encouraged Bureau agents to order absconding men to provide them with financial support by appealing to Northern conceptions of the male breadwinner.[134] But while regularly turning to the Bureau courts to promote their interests—and, in the process, demonstrating a sophisticated awareness of how best to draw on Northerners' ideological presuppositions—freedpeople eschewed the tendency of whites (both Northern and Southern alike) to frame the institution as a conciliation court. Premised on a pedagogical approach that was itself deeply paternalistic, the conciliation court model embraced by Northerners had little appeal to African-Americans seeking to assert their own independence and dignity.[135] It was thus largely in disagreements between (Northern and Southern) whites that the model of the Bureau court as conciliation court would be further developed and debated.

## THE NORTHERN REPUBLICAN PERSPECTIVE

Discussions of the Freedmen's Bureau within the white, Northern Republican press tended to start from the assumption that, as we have seen, also shaped the thinking of both Owen and Howard—namely, that the Bureau's most vital function was to remake the Southern economy on a foundation of free labor. As the *New York Times* argued in June 1865, the problem of "settl[ing] . . . the labor status of the emancipated slaves and their transformation into industrious, thrifty and intelligent citizens" lay at the heart of Reconstruction. So too, the *Times* described the process by means of which this transformation was to be pursued in largely pedagogical terms, emphasizing that it was not only African-Americans but also Southern whites who required substantial reeducation. "[T]he negro" had to be taught to abandon "his own exaggerated ideas of freedom"—including the notion that freedom entailed the right not to work. But the "planters and landowners" had to be trained to "meet their emancipated slaves with a liberal and commendable spirit, with no longings for the overseer's lash."[136] Similarly, a July 1868 issue of the New York–based *Harper's Weekly* praised the soon-to-be-abolished Freedmen's Bureau as "the conscience and common-sense of the country," which "taught the freedmen

Figure 14  Alfred R. Waud, *The Freedmen's Bureau* (1868). Courtesy of the Library of Congress.

that they are citizens" and "taught the late master class that all men have rights which must be respected." In an accompanying sketch, entitled simply "The Freedmen's Bureau" (fig. 14), the Bureau officer is depicted as the embodiment of the voice of reason, calmly but forcefully standing between warring mobs of Southern planters, on the left, and freed laborers, on the right.[137]

Like Owen and Howard, many Northerners believed that the Bureau courts in particular had an especially important role to play in the process of reeducating the South. Consider, for example, the following account of a dispute heard in late August 1865 by General Clinton B. Fisk, the Bureau's assistant commissioner in Tennessee, which appeared in largely identical form in numerous newspapers throughout the North.[138] As several of these articles emphasized in introducing their reports of this dispute, the Bureau court's role was educational. For example, the *Bangor Daily Whig and Courier* explained that "courts of justice established by Gen. Fisk, Assistant Commissioner of the Freedmen's Bureau" were providing "the white men of Tennessee" with "lessons . . . of a very emphatic description" concerning the fact that "the colored men have rights which they are bound to respect." Along similar lines, the *Independent* remarked that "the cases which came before Gen. Fisk for adjudication . . . were made the means of impressive lessons."[139]

The particular dispute so widely reported by the Northern press concerned a Southern planter named Abernethy, described as "[a]n old and highly respected citizen of Giles county," Tennessee, and thus representative of traditional Southern ways. Unable to accept that his former slaves were now free, Abernethy had "refused to pay his colored laborers the wages he had agreed to pay them." As a result, "two of the most intelligent of his employés came into the Freedmen's Court, mak[ing] oath to the contract and to the fact of non-payment." Based on this complaint, "an order was . . . issued to bring the venerable patriarch into court to answer." Shocked by the news that anyone would dare lay a hand on the old aristocrat, Abernethy's "neighbors, of course, were greatly excited." He was thus accompanied to "Gen. Fisk's headquarters by a respectable body of old citizens, whose woe-begone countenances indicated the deep disgust and horror which swelled their chivalrous bosoms."[140]

Having thus reveled in the shaming of these honor-obsessed Southern gentlemen before Northern military officers and their Bureau Court, the reporter went on to describe the colloquy that ensued between the defendant and Assistant Commissioner Fisk. After Abernethy indicated his affront at being dragged before the Bureau Court, Fisk evidently explained that "[t]wo *citizens* of Giles county, *neighbors* of yours . . . have appeared and made oath to a very grave complaint against you." Upon learning that the complainants were named Joseph and Paul Abernethy, Abernethy expressed incomprehension: "[T]he old gentleman's eyes fairly bulged out, and he looked the very picture of amazement," exclaiming "them aren't my neighbors, them's my niggers!" Fisk responded, in turn, by calmly rebuking the pupil: "You are mistaken, Mr. A, . . . there are no such persons in Tennessee now as 'your niggers.' Joseph and Paul Abernethy are citizens of Tennessee." Continuing with his admonishment of the old planter and the slave system he represented, Fisk then remarked that one of the plaintiffs "claims even a nearer relation to you" than fellow citizen, "and the striking resemblance he bears to you gives countenance to the claim."[141]

Deeply shamed by this public chastising—including the revelation that he had fathered (at least) one of his own slaves—Abernethy "covered his face with his hands, bowing his head for some time." Forced to confront his own guilt—not only in the labor dispute at hand, but more importantly, in the profound exploitation (including sexual) that slavery represented—Abernethy immediately abandoned his opposition to the Bureau court's jurisdiction. Indicating his newly submissive posture, he quietly asked Fisk how the latter intended to proceed, and the judge responded by proclaiming his intent to promote equity over and above the rule of law: "I am going to do *justice*." Justice here was, moreover, quite clear: If "you owe these men the amount they claim, . . . you must pay it." Encouraged by the Bureau agent's force of character to recognize what justice clearly required, "[t]he old gentleman came down at once, acknowledged the debt, and promised to call and settle it the next day." The account thus ended neatly with the triumph of free labor and its prime symbol, the contract: "The next day [Abernethy] came, paid the debt in full, and entered into a written contract with his employés for the future."[142]

Presented in a highly stylized and sentimental form, this account of the Abernethy dispute—published widely across the Northern press—is of questionable accuracy, though the basic facts are sufficiently similar to those of many cases reported in official Bureau records that they appear on the whole plausible. That said, the sentimental, indeed melodramatic nature of the rhetoric employed to report the dispute clearly signals the effort to use the case as a vehicle for presenting a moral lesson—namely, the superiority of free over slave labor. As for how the Bureau court was able to achieve its transformative goals, the newspaper reports suggested that all that was needed was for the judge, as teacher, to point to the just outcome—one assumed to be consonant with Northern, free labor values. As in all melodrama, good necessarily triumphed over evil—thus making it all but inevitable that Abernethy would come to recognize the error in his ways. Awash in melodramatic theatrical and literary productions and in an evangelical culture of oratory and writing that appealed to many similar narrative techniques,[143] contemporary (Northern Republican) Americans embraced this sentimental account of the Bureau court in much the same way that so many of their compatriots were drawn to the idealized depiction of the conciliation court.

The Abernethy case was unique in the extent to which it received such widespread press coverage. Moreover, its resolutely optimistic, melodramatic conclusion that the Bureau court's mere admonitions would suffice to establish a free labor contract regime in the South would prove harder to sustain as time passed and the extent of the challenges confronting the Bureau became increasingly clear. Even so, the Northern Republican press continued gleefully to report on cases before the Bureau courts in which Northern judges taught white Southerners the virtues of free labor. In July 1866, for example, the *New York Times* correspondent in Mississippi reported on a labor dispute heard by the Bureau agent stationed in the town of Grenada. According to the reporter, "[t]he planter made the first statement, and was followed by one of the colored men, who flatly contradicted some of his statements." The Bureau court ultimately found for the African-American laborers, thus forcing the planter with "a thin, cadaverous face" to honor his contractual commitments. But at least as important as this substantive victory was the procedural pathway leading to it. In the reporter's words, "[t]he idea of a negro contradicting a white man so bluntly in Mississippi is new. . . ."[144] By means of the procedural equality extended to the freedmen—the right, in short, to contradict their former masters—white planters were taught the important lesson that the labor contracts they had entered with the freedmen were, qua contracts, a recognition of fundamental equality under the law. What enabled this procedural collision of interests, however, was not an adversarial system overseen by a neutral, disinterested judge but to the contrary, a Bureau court staffed by a military officer from New Hampshire, who deployed his authority to teach the disputants the meaning of equality under the law—including by encouraging freedmen to speak freely.

The idea that the Bureau courts would have a transformative effect in reconstructing the South—not through brute force, but instead by means of pedagogical persuasion—continued to dominate Northern thinking on such matters, even after the enactment of Black Codes in late 1865 and early 1866 demonstrated that Southern resistance would be fiercer than many had imagined. And in the minds of many influential Northerners, this conception of the Bureau courts remained intimately linked to the model of the conciliation court. That this was so is evident perhaps first and foremost from a remarkable article concerning conciliation courts that appeared in the January 1866 volume of the *North American Review*.[145] Widely viewed at the time as a quintessential institution of the Northern elite, the *North American Review* was read throughout much of the United States. Moreover, the contents of this particular volume—including the article discussing "courts of conciliation"—were extensively advertised.[146] Published anonymously, this article was ostensibly a review—more than a half-century after its initial 1803 publication—of a book by Andreas Bjørn Rothe concerning the Danish conciliation courts. As suggested by the oddity of the decision to review a book so many decades after it first appeared, Rothe's work served merely as a point of entry for broaching the article's real purpose. This, in turn, was to provide a not-so-veiled defense of the proposed Second Freedmen's Bureau Bill, then pending before Congress and, by extension, the preservation of Bureau-run conciliation courts in the Reconstruction South.

The Second Freedmen's Bureau Bill was an attempt by the Republican-controlled Congress to augment the powers of the Bureau and thus to thwart President Johnson's efforts quickly to return Southern governments to power. As proposed by leading congressional Republicans, the bill would, among other things, expand the Bureau courts' jurisdiction to encompass all claims of deprivation of civil rights. Drafted in December 1865, the proposed legislation was debated in January 1866 and passed in early February, only to be vetoed by Johnson. While Congress succeeded in overriding the veto on July 16, 1866, the legislation thus enacted left it to the president to issue the rules and regulations governing the Bureau courts' activities—an undertaking that President Johnson was none too eager to pursue. Thus, as we have seen, despite the eventual passage of the bill and despite Howard's ongoing efforts to resist state-court jurisdiction, Bureau courts in many states had transferred much of their jurisdiction to civil authorities by the spring and summer of 1866.[147]

It was in January 1866, as the Second Freedmen's Bureau Bill was under congressional debate and the survival of the Bureau courts therefore in significant jeopardy, that the *North American Review* published its article reviewing Rothe's book concerning the Danish conciliation courts. Observing the existence of widespread transatlantic interest in conciliation courts during the first half of the nineteenth century, the article began by noting that attempts to establish such institutions had not all fared equally well. In both England and New York, conciliation courts had never really taken root. While such courts were successfully established in various continental European countries, they differed in their ability to promote conciliation. The most effective, the article asserted, were those established in Denmark, where the "writers speak[] with great pride and satisfaction of their success."[148]

What was the reason for the distinctive success of the Danish conciliation courts? Here the article's answer was precisely what Bentham might have predicted. Conciliation courts worked well in Denmark because the poor peasant population that they served was so lacking in sophistication, so infantile in attitudes and behavior, that the conciliation judges, intervening as kindly fathers, were easily able to reconcile the disputants. Echoing Bentham's account of conciliation courts as modeled on the patriarchal household, the article remarked:

> Disputes arising among such a rude peasantry cannot often be of much detail or complication. They must be as easy of settlement as the quarrels of servants or children. How different are the questions which come before the courts in this country! Springing as they often do out of the most involved transactions in a highly civilized state of society, they

present a variety of incident and a multiplicity of detail, to unravel which
demands patient and skillful examination.

The childish nature of the peasant class meant not only that its disputes could
be easily comprehended and an appropriate compromise quickly identified
but also that disputants could be readily persuaded to embrace this compromise. As the article observed, "To give the institution [of the conciliation court]
its effect, the suitors must look up to the opinion and advice of the judge as
only an ignorant and dependant people can look up, with a readiness to yield
their opinions and wishes to one whom they personally revere as higher than
themselves." The peasant class of Denmark constituted precisely such a guile-
less and subservient people because the "remains of the feudal system" continued to operate in Denmark, "to a greater extent . . . than in any other nation
of Western Europe." Danish society was thus still based on a "distinction between classes," such that those elites who served on the conciliation courts—
"[t]he grand bailiff who holds the court in the country, or his deputy, who is
often the clergyman of the parish"—were "invested with a temporal or spiritual power" that endowed their advice "with the weight of a command to [their]
tenants or parishioners."[149]

Having undertaken an extensive analysis of European conciliation courts—
and especially those of Denmark—the article concluded by expressly addressing why these ought to be of interest to American readers. Lest these readers
had somehow failed to draw the not-so-subtly suggested conclusion themselves, the article explained that "there is one part of the United States where
we think [these courts] might be established with success"—namely, "in those
States lately in rebellion, and especially for causes to which the Freedmen are
parties." Indeed, "[i]t is with special reference to their probable utility in such
cases, and to the important aid which they might afford in the reorganization
of society at the South on its new foundation of freedom, that we have thought
fit at this time to call attention to their working and methods." That conciliation courts could play such an important role in reconstructing the South
stemmed from the fact that African-Americans were comparable to the continental European peasantry. Like European peasants, only recently freed from
the bonds of feudal obligation, American freedmen were in desperate need of
paternalist protection:

> The situation of the recently enfranchised slaves presents many of the
> features which have made these courts successful among the peasantry
> of Denmark. They are a poor people, an agricultural people; their deal-

ings are confined to their own neighborhood; their quarrels are generally about simple matters; they have just been freed from slavery, and
have many of its trammels still hanging about them. Though an irasci-
ble, they are a very placable people, and when they do respect one of the
lately dominant race, they will submit to his opinion and advice with a
readiness which exceeded the docility of any European peasantry.

Accordingly, the article concluded, "it would be hard to find a combination of
circumstances more favorable to the usefulness of Courts of Conciliation"
than those that then pertained in the American South.[150]

Notably, while insisting on the suitability of conciliation courts for remaking the South on a "new foundation of freedom," the article entirely ignored
the problem of what to do with white Southerners—an omission that is particularly glaring in light of the widespread contemporary view that it was labor
disputes that lay at the heart of Reconstruction and thus at the core of the
Bureau courts' jurisdiction. Moreover, the article's silence in this respect is
paired with a telling insistence that conciliation courts had no place "even in
the most rural districts of the Northern States." Mature, self-assertive, and
industrious, the Northern white population of the United States could never
be expected to compromise legal rights merely out of deference to the conciliation judge: "The least elevated and educated Yankee holds his opinions on
matters affecting his own purse and person too tenaciously, and with too
much independence, to be ready to surrender them at the advice of any one,
even though he be a justice of the peace or the parish minister."[151]

Where did this leave white Southerners? Pursuant to free labor ideology,
Southern planters were lazy and effete. Accustomed to thriving on the labor of
others, they lacked the manly Northern virtues of self-discipline and enterprise. At the same time, the racial privilege from which they benefited was
such that, unlike African-Americans, they could not be readily compared to an
infantile and docile, serf-like peasantry. Much like Robert Dale Owen and his
colleagues on the American Freedmen's Inquiry Commission, the article thus
implicitly recognized what Howard and his agents sought studiously to
ignore—namely, that the conciliation court model presumed the existence of
underlying communal structures and norms that encouraged deference to the
court's judgments. The long tradition of slavery (combined with what these
men took to be African-Americans' innate tendency toward meek submission) provided precisely the requisite set of deference-promoting structures
and norms. But the same could not be said of Southern whites. In this way, the
article obliquely pointed to what was in fact to become the primary obstacle to

the Bureau courts' ability meaningfully to reconstruct the South: Southern white opposition.

## THE PERSPECTIVE OF SOUTHERN WHITES AND THEIR ALLIES

What Northern Republicans viewed as the educational (and Christian) mission of the Bureau and its courts was in the eyes of Southern whites and their Northern Democratic allies nothing more than an unlawful exercise of force. As depicted in an 1866 campaign poster urging the election of Hiester Clymer as the Democratic (and white supremacist) governor of Pennsylvania (fig. 15), the Freedmen's Bureau, sustained by military might, was engaging in a form

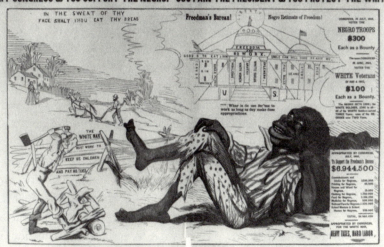

Figure 15  Unidentified artist, *The Freedman's Bureau! An Agency to Keep the Negro in Idleness at the Expense of the White Man. Twice Vetoed by the President, and Made a Law by Congress. Support Congress & You support the Negro, Sustain the President & You Protect the White Man* (1866). Courtesy of the Library of Congress.

of mass theft, stealing from white planters, now forced to hard labor, as well as from the American taxpayers as a whole—and all with the goal of encouraging the newly freed slaves to remain idle. According, moreover, to those who shared this perspective, the Bureau courts were key to implementing such an illicit use of power. As suggested in September 1865 by the *Daily Phoenix,* a newspaper based in Columbia, South Carolina, the supposed "Court of Conciliation" was more accurately characterized as a "Court of Aggravation." So too, the *Jackson News* described the Bureau and its courts as " 'an inquisition' and 'an oppression.' "[152]

From the Southern perspective, the core problem with the Bureau courts was precisely the feature that the courts' Northern supporters most emphasized—the fact that, like all conciliation courts, they were essentially extralegal. As the *Patriot,* a Pennsylvania-based Democratic newspaper, argued in February 1866, the Bureau courts were extralegal in two distinct but interrelated senses: They were both "irresponsible and unknown to the laws."[153] They were "unknown to the laws" in that they were not created pursuant to democratically legitimate legal processes but were instead imposed by military force. And they were "irresponsible ... to the laws" in that their judges failed to apply the rule of law and instead decided cases based on their own prejudices—including, most importantly, their hatred of Southern whites and their concomitant desire to subordinate the latter to their former slaves.

The argument that there was no lawful, constitutional basis for the Bureau courts was widely made both by Southern whites and by sympathetic Democrats to the North. As the *Memphis Daily Avalanche* argued in January 1866, the Bureau courts were "extra-judicial tribunals" that were being "foisted upon" the white people of the South "by the strong arm of the military authorities."[154] Along similar lines, North Carolina's governor, Jonathan Worth, argued that same month that the Bureau and its courts were "at once anomalous and inconsistent with the ancient constitutional authority of the several States."[155] Pursuant to this reasoning, the U.S. Constitution delegated most litigation, both civil and criminal, to state rather than federal courts. Moreover, to the extent that it authorized (quite limited) federal-court jurisdiction, this was to be exercised by those courts contemplated by Article III of the Constitution (establishing "the judicial power of the United States"), rather than by tribunals that, whatever their name, were operated by an agency housed in the War Department and staffed largely by military personnel.

As white Southerners understood it, the establishment of Bureau courts exceeding the federal government's limited constitutional authority constituted a massive and dangerous power grab on the part of Radical Republicans in Congress. So argued, for example, Montgomery Blair, a prominent Maryland-based Democratic lawyer and politician who had served under Lincoln as postmaster general but was vehemently opposed to radical Reconstruction. According to Blair, the Bureau and its courts represented an attempt "to supplant the State governments of the South by an arbitrary tribunal apparently in the interests of the negroes" but in reality aimed at establishing a "consolidated dictatorship"—a "new form of Congressional Government, which was absolved from all obedience to the principles or practice, or forms of the Constitution or laws of the State or National Government."[156] As the war receded in memory, the same point was made in even more inflamed tones by the Democratic Party as a whole, which stated in its July 1868 platform—about five months before the Bureau would be officially dismantled—that the Republicans had sought through their military commissions and Bureau courts to "subject[] ten States in times of peace to military despotism and negro supremacy."[157]

From the argument that the Bureau courts lacked a legal foundation there followed a second set of criticisms about the lawless manner in which they functioned. These arguments were much broader and more diffuse in nature, with different critics emphasizing different aspects of the court's ostensibly extralegal approach. Despite such differences, however, the overall thrust of the argument was clear: The Bureau courts failed to deliver due process. And due process, in turn, was conceptualized in adversarial terms. As stated in the Democratic Party platform of 1868, the result of the despotic rule achieved by the Bureau and its courts was that "military trials and Star Chamber inquisitions" had replaced "constitutional tribunals."[158]

In what ways was the Bureau courts' approach assimilable to that of Star Chamber and its inquisitorial procedure? The Democratic platform, like most arguments criticizing the Bureau courts for failing to deliver lawful, due process, was short on specifics. Moreover, as we have seen, the available evidence concerning how Bureau courts actually functioned in practice indicates that, contrary to the platform's assertion, a good many (though by no means all) of these courts adhered to core aspects of adversarialism—including, not least, the use of dueling lawyers responsible for presenting witnesses and developing the case. Reality aside, however, the decision to frame Bureau court procedure as a form of militarily imposed inquisitorial process enabled critics effectively to tap into the centuries-old tradition linking Anglo-American liberty to adversarial, common law–based procedure—a tradition that, as we have seen, was revived and strengthened in the decades leading up to the Civil War.

To the extent that critics pointed to specific features of Bureau-court proceedings that failed to comply with an adversarial model of due process, the main one on which they focused was precisely the critique repeatedly leveled against conciliation courts in the antebellum period—namely, the existence of an excessively powerful judge whose very existence threatened the core adversarial value of party empowerment. The excessive amount of power committed to Bureau-court judges was said to follow from several different features of Bureau-court proceedings. First was the fact, lamentable in itself as a violation of core, adversarial traditions, that the Bureau courts operated without a jury. As the Democratic platform of 1868 complained, the Radical Republicans and their Bureau had "nullified . . . the right of trial by jury" in the South.[159] Along similar lines, Montgomery Blair argued that "[t]he Freedmen's Bureau tried and decided everything in regard to the subjects committed to it, without . . . [a] jury. . . ." Another factor contributing to the excessive power of the Bureau-court judge was that, as Blair noted, cases were decided "without appeal." But most important of all in causing the Bureau-court judge to overpower the litigants was the fact that he was in no way constrained by the rule of law. Given free rein to shape proceedings and decide cases however he saw fit, the Bureau-court judge necessarily denied disputants the opportunity meaningfully to intervene in the process, leaving them to shoot blind. Blair, for example, bemoaned that the Bureau courts engaged in trials "without any fixed rules of law or evidence."[160] So too, Henry W. Slocum—a former commander of the Department of the Mississippi and soon-to-be Democratic congressman from New York—complained in October 1865 that in these courts, "[t]he usual forms adopted in our courts of justice to ascertain the facts in the case are discarded."[161]

According to white Southerners and their Northern Democratic allies, the fact that the Bureau courts were not required to apply the law, either substantive or procedural, meant that their decisions were based on little more than the judges' prejudices—including, most importantly, their prejudice against Southern whites. Thus, the many articles complaining about Bureau-court proceedings that were published by Southern and Democratic newspapers all discuss interracial disputes and focus, in particular, on the injustices allegedly suffered by white disputants. As Robert Dale Owen and his fellow commissioners had correctly intuited, Southerners would have little difficulty accepting the Bureau courts' jurisdiction over freedpeople; it was these courts' effort to decide disputes involving whites that was the real problem.

According to a November 1865 article published in the *Richmond Sentinel,* the danger that Bureau judges would deploy their unregulated authority to act on the animus they felt toward Southern whites was particularly great in the case of Bureau courts (like those of Virginia) that had been established along the lines of Howard's three-judge model. In the *Sentinel*'s view, the very structure of such courts exacerbated the problem of bias against white litigants: "The judge selected by the negroes seems often to regard himself as advocate and protector rather than arbiter. The representative of the Freedmen's Bureau is liable to share the same sentiment. The third umpire is often inexperienced, and is liable to be constantly outvoted."[162]

Even in the case of the more typical one-judge Bureau courts, the fact that the judges had no obligation (or ability) to apply the law was said to encourage these men to make decisions based entirely on their hatred of Southern whites. So claimed an article originally published by the *Nashville Dispatch* and then reprinted in Georgia's *Columbus Daily Enquirer.* Gleefully reporting the May 1866 decision by Assistant Commissioner Fisk to dismantle the Freedmen's Bureau court in Nashville, the article complained that "that anomaly known as the freedmen's court" was so biased in favor of the freedmen that it encouraged them to press mere "fancied grievances." In contrast, the article concluded, the state courts "are not the mere registry of the prejudices of the judge" but are instead "conducted upon the great principles which underlie the jurisprudence of the country."[163]

Along similar lines, the *New Orleans Times* called in October 1865 for the dismantling of the Freedmen's Bureau and its courts by citing a recent speech by General Slocum, in which the latter claimed that Bureau judges decided cases based on their anti-Southern prejudices rather than the law. According to Slocum, the fact that the typical Bureau judge was "a young man from a Northern state, not educated as a judicial officer, and often not possessing a single qualification for the discharge of such duties," resulted in an environment in which freedmen and women were encouraged to make frivolous claims, designed solely for the purpose of cruelly shaming their kind and honorable former masters. In his words, "Half the negroes in . . . [the area] are at once seized with a desire to see the Yankee military judge and to see how their masters or mistresses would act on being brought before him. Complaints are made against the kindest and best people in the country." As the article concluded, Bureau judges sought to deploy their excessive power with an eye toward establishing "a spurious ebony supremacy," and in so doing, they "rendered their names hateful."[164] The *Crisis*—an Ohio-based paper published by the Copperhead faction of Northern, anti-War Democrats—agreed, asserting in May 1868 that each day brought further accounts of "some white men dragged before some officer of the Negro Bureau, to be insulted, fined and imprisoned for having dared to deny the justice of some claim made upon them by their colored fellow citizens."[165] Overpowered by the Bureau courts and their judges, Southern whites were being cowed into silence, hesitant to assert their core rights and interests.

In the very worst cases, Southern newspapers suggested, the fact that the Bureau judges were empowered to act on the basis of their antipathy to whites, rather than required to enforce the law, resulted in nothing short of tragedy. This was precisely the point made by the *Little Rock Evening Republic* in a June 8, 1867, piece entitled "Tragedy at Pine Bluff." The article reported the murder near Pine Bluff of one William Mahoney—"a young man, about 22 or 23 years old; kind, courteous and quiet in his manners and respected by all his neighbors and acquaintances," who "leaves a widowed mother to mourn the untimely death of a good and affectionate son." According to the article, this paragon of white, Southern male virtue was murdered by a freedman in his employ whom he had fired for negligence. Despite having been fired, "[t]he negro hung around the premises, abusing Mr. M. and offering to fight him until he drove him off the place." Undeterred and unembarrassed, the unnamed laborer rushed to the local Bureau court to file a complaint against his former employer. But instead of teaching him his proper place, the Bureau agent serving as judge encouraged the laborer "to go and bring the stick with which he claimed he had been beaten." Thus emboldened, the laborer returned to Mahoney's house, and when the latter, "desiring to avoid a difficulty, ordered him to go away," the laborer responded with murderous rage. In an act of cowardice and cruelty, the laborer waited until Mahoney's back was turned and then "struck [him] on the head fracturing his skull," causing the "unfortunate gentlemen" to die that very night.[166] As the article implied, but for the Bureau court's encouragement of the freedman's false claim and concomitant failure to afford the white planter a meaningful voice in the proceedings, the innocent and virtuous young man would still be alive.

As time would soon tell, it was this Southern perspective on the Bureau courts that would prove triumphant. For white Southerners and their Northern Democratic allies, the problem with the Bureau courts was precisely what antebellum critics had long insisted was wrong with conciliation courts: They were extralegal. As such, they not only violated core commitments to the rule of law as an end in itself but also gave rise to excessively powerful judges whose domination of the proceedings denied (white) disputants the opportunity to assert their own rights and interests. The end result was a violation of due (adversarial) process.

## From the Bureau Courts to Jim Crow

On April 2, 1866, President Johnson issued a proclamation providing that "the insurrection which heretofore existed in the [Southern] States . . . is at an end." In the preamble, he was careful to note that

> standing armies, military occupation, martial law, military tribunals, and the suspension of the privilege of the writ of habeas corpus are, in time of peace, dangerous to public liberty, incompatible with the individual rights of the free citizen, contrary to the genius and spirit of our free institutions, and exhaustive of the national resources, and ought not, therefore, to be sanctioned or allowed, except in cases of actual necessity, for repelling invasion or suppressing insurrection or rebellion.[167]

As Brooks D. Simpson observes, Johnson appears to have been in a rush to issue this proclamation, such that it was a surprise to his cabinet. Simpson hypothesizes that one motivating factor may have been Johnson's knowledge that the Supreme Court was about to decide *Ex parte Milligan* the very next day—a case that tested the lawfulness of military courts' jurisdiction over civilians during times of peace and thus, by possible implication, the lawfulness of the Bureau courts themselves.[168]

*Milligan* did not directly concern the Bureau courts, which operated solely in the South, but instead arose out of the judgment of an Indiana-based military commission. In late 1864, Lambdin Milligan, a civilian who was a Democratic critic of the war, was tried and convicted by a military commission in Indianapolis for planning an uprising in the state that was intended to free Confederate soldiers and to kidnap the state's governor. But while *Milligan* concerned a military commission, rather than a Bureau court, many contemporaries (including not least Southern whites themselves) considered the Bureau courts to be a kind of military tribunal—one of the many to which the South had been subjected in its defeat. Although men like Robert Dale Owen and Oliver Otis Howard had looked to the model of the conciliation court in designing and implementing the Bureau courts, the fact that the Bureau was housed within the War Department meant that the ultimate authority for its activities lay with the military. Moreover, despite the Bureau's efforts to distinguish between Bureau agents and military officers by creating distinct chains of command, the nature of Southern white opposition was such that military intervention was often required to enforce the Bureau courts' decisions. The Supreme Court's adjudication of whether it was permissible for a military commission to try a civilian thus seemed to have direct implications for the Bureau courts as well.

Ultimately, the Supreme Court overturned the verdict, holding that the military commission did not have jurisdiction to try Milligan and that he therefore had to be released. The precise grounds for this holding were not, however, revealed by the Court until December. Accordingly, its implications for the continued survival of the Bureau courts remained unclear throughout the remainder of 1866.[169] In the interim, Johnson vetoed the Second Freedmen's Bureau bill, relying on the same broad language about the unconstitutionality of military tribunals being used against civilians in times of peace that he had employed in the preamble to the April 2 proclamation of the cessation of insurrection. According to Johnson, there was grave "danger, in representative republics, of conferring upon the military, in time of peace, extraordinary powers"—of the sort committed to the Bureau courts. Moreover, given that Southern state courts had reopened and were (as a formal matter) applying the same law to African-Americans as to whites, "it is believed that ample protection will be afforded [the freedman] by due process of law without resort to the dangerous expedient of 'military tribunals,' now that the war has been brought to a close." Drawing on the critique of the Bureau courts that was by then well developed in the South (and among its Northern Democratic allies), Johnson concluded that

> it will be better to trust the rights, privileges, and immunities of the citizen to [ordinary civil] tribunals . . . presided over by competent and impartial judges, bound by fixed rules of law and evidence, and where the right of trial by jury is guarantied and secured, than to the caprice or judgment of an officer of the bureau, who, it is possible, may be entirely ignorant of the principles that underlie the just administration of the law.[170]

While, as we have seen, Congress thereafter overrode Johnson's veto, the legislation left it to the president to decide whether and when Bureau agents might exercise jurisdiction in cases concerning equal rights under the law—a decision that, as one historian notes, was "a bit like allowing the fox to guard the chicken coop."[171]

When the Supreme Court finally issued its written opinion in *Milligan* in December, a majority of the justices embraced Johnson's broad-brushed approach: Military commissions were an impermissible departure from constitutionally enshrined norms of due process. The five-person majority opinion, authored by Justice David Davis, held in sweeping language that, pursuant to the constitution, civilians could be tried by military courts only when "in foreign invasion or civil war, the courts are actually closed, and it is impossible to administer criminal justice according to law." The minority opinion, written by Chief Justice Salmon P. Chase, concurred that Milligan could not be tried by the military commission but grounded the decision on much narrower reasoning. According to Chase, the problem with Milligan's trial by military commission was not that it could never be constitutionally authorized but instead that Congress had in fact failed to authorize it here.[172]

Davis's majority opinion left open the possibility that the decision might have been different if the military commission in question had been based in the South, noting that because Indiana had never seceded, there was never any justification for military tribunals there, whereas "during the late Rebellion [martial law] could have been enforced in Virginia."[173] But contemporaries understood that together Johnson and the Court had signaled a clear intention to shut down radical Reconstruction—including the Bureau courts. As Secretary Stanton complained, *Milligan* struck "at the roots of the Freedmen's Bureau law, . . . leading directly to its entire abrogation, as well as other legislation looking to the protection of loyal men, white and black, by the Federal Government, from the persecution of the disloyal and rebellious, whose bogus State power is thus confirmed to them." Accordingly, as both John Witt and Aziz Rana argue, *Milligan*—long remembered in triumphalist terms as a leading case establishing core civil liberties—takes on quite a different moral cast when we recall the forgotten political context of the decision. For contemporaries, *Milligan* was not some abstract statement on civil rights, including due process. It was instead a test case on the constitutionality of radical Reconstruction, implicating most especially the use of the Freedmen's Bureau and its courts to remake the South.[174]

On March 2, 1867, shortly after the Court issued its opinion in *Milligan,* Johnson cited the decision to justify his veto of the first Military Reconstruction Act. That act divided the ten unrestored rebel states into five military districts and provided that the military commanders of these districts could try defendants in military tribunals if they concluded that the state courts had failed to take action against those who abused the rights of freedpeople. In vetoing the bill, Johnson cited *Milligan* to support his argument that the proposed statute would violate the constitution by "deny[ing] a trial by the lawful courts and juries to nine millions of American citizens, and to their posterity for an indefinite period." "This bill," he claimed, "sets aside all process of law, and makes the citizen answerable in his person and property to the will of one man."[175] While Congress immediately overrode Johnson's veto, the fact that it was the president who was charged with appointing the district commanders and that Bureau agents could not act without these commanders' prior authorization limited the Bureau's ability to pursue those who committed "outrages" against freedpeople.[176]

Even so, the Reconstruction Act provided a key authorization for the continued use of military force (including courts) in the South and thus quickly became a focal point of Southern white resistance. Shortly after the Act's passage, two white men in Mississippi were tried in military commissions pursuant to its authority. William McCardle was convicted for inciting insurrection and Edward Yerger for killing a Union soldier. In challenging their convictions before the Supreme Court, McCardle and Yerger both raised the issue that *Milligan* itself had left undecided—namely, whether the use of military tribunals to try civilians in peacetime might be allowed in the rebel states themselves. Fearful that the Court, following the logic of *Milligan,* would hold the Act's authorization of military proceedings unconstitutional, Congress and the recently elected Republican president, Ulysses S. Grant, managed in both cases to prevent the Court from reaching a decision on the merits.[177] But even though the Reconstruction Act was spared judicial review, military Reconstruction proved short-lived. According to the statute itself, once the ten unrestored states drafted and ratified state constitutions enfranchising the freedpeople and, in addition, ratified the Fourteenth Amendment to the U.S. Constitution, they would be restored to the Union.[178] Thus, by the time *Ex parte McCardle* and *Ex parte Yerger* were decided in 1869, military Reconstruction was all but at an end.

How then should we assess the Freedmen's Bureau's success in promoting its goals? The final balance sheet is mixed. To the extent that the Bureau focused on revitalizing the Southern economy, it largely succeeded. So too, as a matter at least of legal form, the Southern labor market was in fact reconfigured on free contract foundations. But as concerns the Bureau's effort to guarantee African-Americans true freedom and equality, the institution was far less successful.

While scholars remain divided on the question, the dominant view today is that the Bureau and its courts advanced the interests of freedpeople beyond what would have been possible if they had been left entirely to the jurisdiction of the Southern states but nonetheless fell far short of achieving real equality. In many cases—and especially those involving disputes between freedpeople, or where a freedman was charged with a criminal offense against a white victim—it seems likely that the Bureau courts afforded freedpeople justice that they would not have been able to obtain in Southern state courts. So too in the case of labor disputes, it appears that the Bureau courts were sometimes able to protect freedpeople from the very worst abuses. Furthermore, a number of historians have suggested that the very fact that the Bureau courts afforded freedpeople some opportunity to assert their rights and interests was in itself significant in providing them with a new sense of empowerment and control.[179]

That said, there were also many cases between freedpeople and white planters in which the latter were able to use the Bureau courts to their own advantage—securing settlements from those they cowed into deference, sometimes with the assistance of Bureau personnel. Accordingly, to the extent that the Bureau courts helped to stabilize the Southern agricultural economy, they did so in no small part by reinstituting (through the formal mechanisms of free contract) a system by means of which a dominant white planter class was able to exploit a subordinated African-American community.[180] Finally, however much success the Bureau and its courts may have achieved over time, the triumphant Southern (and Northern Democratic) opposition to these institutions—as ultimately reflected in *Milligan*—foreclosed their long-term survival. Thus, however well intentioned many Bureau agents were—and despite the fact that quite a few freedmen and women were able to deploy the Bureau courts to their advantage in particular cases—the bottom line remains the same: The reign of the Bureau courts was replaced with that of Jim Crow.

But while the Military Reconstruction Act failed meaningfully to preserve and empower the Bureau and its courts, it did achieve its stated goal of encouraging the ten unrestored states to ratify the Fourteenth Amendment. As of July 9, 1868, the Amendment had been ratified by the legislatures of the requisite three-fourths of the states. Protecting all U.S. citizens against state deprivations of "life, liberty, or property, without due process of law," the Fourteenth Amendment was imagined by its principal framer, Republican Congressman John Bingham, as a means of protecting the rights of freedpeople without further resort to the laws of war. In this sense, as John Witt argues, the Reconstruction Act—while premised on the powers claimed by the North as victor pursuant to the laws of war—"also set in motion the return of constitutional normalcy." With this return to constitutionally authorized courts and law, the precise scope and nature of the due process enshrined in the Fourteenth Amendment would soon become subject to extensive litigation and debate. What kinds of state action would be deemed to infringe due process rights? Was the amendment concerned only with protecting the former slaves? Or as Justice Field would insist in his prescient 1873 dissent in the *Slaughterhouse* Cases, did it also guarantee the (substantive) right of all citizens to participate freely in the market? Moreover, to what extent did the due process clause permit the federal government to intervene in private relations?[181]

These were among the many questions that courts, commentators, and litigants would struggle to resolve in the decades following the enactment of the Fourteenth Amendment and whose resolution has in certain respects continued to be revised to the present. But there was one meaning of due process on which the country had largely come to agree by 1868—the year that saw the ratification of the amendment and, by December, the withdrawal of most Bureau agents from the South. This was the notion that due process was synonymous with adversarial process. Put differently, the Fourteenth Amendment's proclamation of the right to due process brought to a close the brief moment of possibility opened up by the establishment of the Freedmen's Bureau courts—a moment in which it was possible to imagine that, at least under certain conditions of extreme inequality, the country's commitment to adversarial procedure would give way to a judge-empowering flexibility focused on promoting substantive justice rather than guaranteeing procedural form. In the wake of the amendment and Justice Field's *Slaughterhouse* dissent, a form of "substantive due process" would be born. But as it emerged full-fledged in the early days of the twentieth century, this would serve as a limit on state action to protect the oppressed (especially workers), rather than—as envisioned by those advocating a conciliation court model of the Bureau courts—as affirmative grounds for state intervention. Robert Dale Owen's "Great Question" thus remained "unanswered, before the world."[182]

# Conclusion

## The Question of American Exceptionalism and the Lessons of History

In tracing the nineteenth-century origins of the American commitment to adversarialism, this book has focused both on developments in procedural practice and on the rise of the *idea* of legal exceptionalism—namely, how and why Americans came to think of themselves as having a distinctively adversarial legal culture. This analysis, in turn, raises a number of important questions, including, as an initial matter, the accuracy of the nineteenth-century American perception that the United States then possessed a distinctively adversarial legal culture.

There is, moreover, the question of legacy. More particularly, in what ways are the developments traced in this book related to present-day American legal culture? And are there any lessons that we ought to derive from this history? While a definitive resolution of these questions lies well beyond the scope of these pages, their importance is such that it is impossible to conclude without at least briefly considering them.

## A Brief Excursus on Continental Europe and England

There is a wealth of literature considering whether American legal culture today is distinctively adversarial. Although there is good reason to conclude that some of the claims commonly made about excessive adversarialism in the United States are exaggerated for political purposes,[1] the weight of the evidence suggests that the United States is indeed different from other democratic industrialized nations. As Robert A. Kagan argues, the American approach to resolving disputes and making public policy more generally is best characterized as "adversarial legalism." By this he means a tendency to rely on "formal legal contestation," rather than more informal processes of dispute resolution or negotiation, and to structure this legal contest so as to encourage "litigant activism." The end result is a process dominated by the parties themselves, battling through their lawyers, rather than one controlled by (more neutral) judges or other government officials. In contrast, otherwise comparable nations in the developed world tend to rely more on informal processes of dispute resolution and negotiation. Moreover, to the (not insignificant) extent that they also employ formal legal contestation, these proceedings typically endow judges and other government officials with more control vis-à-vis the parties and their lawyers than is the case in the United States.[2]

Kagan's account of American adversarial legalism focuses primarily on establishing, as a descriptive matter, the comparative distinctiveness of the current approach to dispute resolution and policymaking in the United States. But he also devotes some attention to the question of causation. Adversarial legalism, he suggests, is a relatively recent phenomenon, arising from a mismatch between, on the one hand, new public pressures for government intervention that arose in the twentieth century (especially after the Second World War), and on the other, inherited governmental structures that reflect a deep-rooted fear of concentrated state power. Because Kagan's exploration of adversarial legalism focuses primarily on developments in the relatively recent past—such as government efforts to regulate the new risks associated with mass society—it is hardly surprising that his causal account devotes particular attention to the period from about the mid-twentieth century onward. So too, John Witt's discussion of how and why Americans deployed the tradition of the common law to develop a system for the private administration of social welfare—contributing to the emergence of what Kagan describes as adversarial legalism—focuses on the post–World War II rise of the modern personal injury bar and its campaign for liberalized tort law.[3] But the history recounted in this book presses us to look further back in time. It was in the nineteenth century that Americans first came to view themselves as being distinctively committed to resolving their disputes through formal, legal proceedings dominated by lawyers engaged in adversarial contestation. So to what extent was their self-understanding accurate?

While a comprehensive comparative account of nineteenth-century civil procedure is well beyond the scope of this book, a brief survey of the available evidence suggests that contemporary Americans were largely accurate in their assessment of their own procedural distinctiveness. By the close of the Civil War and Reconstruction, American legal culture, in other words, appears to have been distinctively adversarial in its emphasis on resolving disputes through formal, lawyer-dominated proceedings—ones that were, moreover, more oral and public than the traditionally court-controlled, written, and secret procedures associated with the inquisitorial model. Adversarialism (and the ideology of adversarial exceptionalism) were thus built into the structures that Kagan and Witt's mid-twentieth-century Americans inherited as they struggled to respond to new public pressures for government action.

As this suggests, there were important path dependencies that followed from the choices made during the period studied in this book. These are highlighted most starkly by the comparison between the United States and England. Both countries undertook similar kinds of reform—including, most importantly, the merger of law and equity and the concomitant adoption of a uniform set of courts and procedure premised largely on the oral, adversarial methods of the common law. There were, nonetheless, important differences in how they went about doing so, and these, in turn, resulted in the emergence of procedural regimes that, despite surface similarities, differ in a number of key respects. But before turning to England, it is important briefly to consider the procedural cultures of continental Europe, frequently described by nineteenth-century Americans as "despotic" or "feudal." As we have seen, it was these continental systems that Americans had foremost in mind when insisting on their own distinctive commitment to adversarialism.

## CONTINENTAL EUROPE

Drawing any generalizations about civil procedure in nineteenth-century continental Europe is quite difficult in that there were significant differences between the procedural systems that were operative in various countries. Moreover, countries like Germany and Italy were relatively late to unify, such that procedure remained largely decentralized, and thus geographically variable, for much of the century. That said, from a bird's-eye perspective, it is clear that, as of 1800—and continuing well into the nineteenth century—there were important differences between continental European civil procedure as a whole and its American variants. While the United States began the nineteenth century with a divided legal and procedural tradition—that of law, on the one hand, and equity, on the other—countries like France and the not-yet-unified German nations knew no such divide. And despite the significant differences among the many procedural systems that continued to operate across Europe, these all reflected the continued influence of the Roman-canon law tradition.

From roughly the twelfth through the fifteenth centuries, core swaths of continental Europe came to embrace Roman-canon procedure, as disputants opted for arbitrations governed by its rules and thereby contributed to a bottom-up reshaping of norms of procedural justice. At the same time, key appellate courts—including the royal *parlements* in France and the *Reichskammergericht* or imperial court in Germany (then the Holy Roman Empire)—fell under the control of learned civilians, who deployed their judicial authority to impose Roman-canon procedure on the growing number of inferior courts brought within their appellate jurisdiction.[4] Roman-canon procedure, in turn, was largely inquisitorial, exhibiting strong tendencies toward court control, a reliance on written documentation, and a preference for gathering witness testimony outside public view. Indeed, as we have seen, it is continental European procedural practice during the medieval and early modern periods that underlies the more recent creation of the category of "inquisitorial" as an ideal type.

Although the French Revolution had a dramatic impact on numerous aspects of the legal systems of France and Europe as a whole—leading, most importantly, to the establishment of formal equality under the law—it had remarkably little effect on civil procedure as such. For the most part, Napoleon's Civil Procedure Code, enacted in 1806, "retain[ed] the general system of the [royal Civil Procedure] Ordinance of 1667, without important change."[5] Although a number of significant changes were introduced into criminal procedure, including not least, the establishment of a criminal jury, French civil procedure throughout much of the nineteenth century preserved its predominantly Roman-canon, quasi-inquisitorial form. The French procedure code of 1806 proved, in turn, to be highly influential. Imposed by the Napoleonic troops who conquered the German states west of the Rhine, the French code remained in force long after the French defeat in 1815. Indeed, it was only in 1877, when the newly unified German Empire enacted its own civil procedure code, that the French code ceased to be applicable law. The 1806 code was, moreover, adopted by (or significantly influenced developments in) a number of the states that constituted the German Confederation established in 1815 by the Congress of Vienna. There too, it continued in force until 1877. While some German states preserved a more local, Germanic form of civil procedure, this too had been shaped to a significant degree by the Roman-canon procedural tradition, such that, if anything, this local procedure was even more extreme in its embrace of core features of inquisitorialism.[6] There is thus good reason to conclude that throughout much of the nineteenth century, the American approach to civil procedure was distinctively more adversarial than its continental European counterparts.

If we step back from the particulars of courtroom procedure to consider the values with which procedure was infused, it becomes clear that in this respect as well, there were important differences between the nineteenth-century United States and continental Europe. Consider the example of France—a country in which, as in the United States, lawyers played an important role in fomenting late eighteenth-century democratic revolution. In both countries, lawyers came to view themselves as essential in promoting liberal, democratic society—a goal that they claimed to further partly through their mastery of legal (and political) oratory. But despite these parallels, there were key differences in how nineteenth-century French and American lawyers understood (and sought to undertake) their public-serving roles. These differences, in turn, highlight the extent to which the American lawyer's heroic self-conception was distinctively linked to an adversarial model of procedure.

Dating back to the Old Regime, French lawyers sought to promote what they took to be the public good through collective action and through participation in highly political cases, implicating core constitutional questions. French lawyers' tendency to act as a collective or *corps* was a product of the nation's inherited corporatist past and was facilitated by the relatively small number of lawyers who—prior to the unification of the legal profession in 1971—were authorized to serve as barristers, representing clients in court.[7] In contrast, American lawyers remained largely unorganized until the first modern bar associations arose in the 1870s.[8] In the absence of such formal organization, they nonetheless managed to develop a sense of professional identity—one that was, moreover, focused on their distinctive capacity to promote the public interest. What made this possible was, in no small part, adversarialism. The remarkable degree of control that American lawyers exercised over litigation made it easier to imagine that even ordinary, run-of-the-mill disputes implicated matters of great import, such that every case—and not just grand constitutional matters—afforded opportunities to engage in republican self-display. Moreover, the relatively open and competitive nature of American legal practice—the fact that the ability to litigate was not restricted to an elite few and that the bar as a whole expanded as the century progressed—increased the pressure on lawyers to deploy adversarial procedure as a means of investing even minor matters with civic weight. Their efforts in this regard were facilitated by the increasingly widespread view, among lawyers and nonlawyers alike, that American (political and economic) liberty hinged on the availability of adversarial dispute-resolution mechanisms that encouraged all (white, male) individuals to engage in the aggressive, competitive assertion of rights.

## ENGLAND

As of about 1800, the legal systems of England and of important parts of the United States (especially New York) were remarkably similar—including, not least, the jurisdictional division between courts of law and equity. There were, moreover, English counterparts to most of the core nineteenth-century procedural developments traced in this book. As in New York, so too in England, separate common law and chancery courts were (eventually) merged into a single institution, directed to apply a uniform body of procedure. And in both jurisdictions, this unified body of procedure was premised on the common law's lawyer-driven, oral, and public approach to examining (and cross-examining) witnesses rather than equity's court-controlled, written, and secrecy-oriented methods.[9] So to what extent, if any, were nineteenth-century American procedural developments unique?

While there are important overarching similarities in the patterns of American and English reform, these also mask some significant differences.[10] Perhaps most importantly, English lawyers' embrace of cross-examination (and of oral, adversarial testimony as a whole) appears to have been less deep-rooted and far-reaching than that of their New York counterparts. In New York, the period from about 1817 to 1848 witnessed the wholesale adoption of oral, adversarial examination—though such testimony continued to be presented before intermediate judicial officers like masters and examiners, rather than directly before the finder of fact. The Field Code of 1848 dispensed with such intermediate officers. In so doing, it directed that all testimony be taken orally in open court, unless witnesses resided far from the court or were otherwise unavailable to testify at trial. In contrast, contemporary English reformers embraced a system in which written, out-of-court records of the testimony continued to play a key role. Indeed, in contemporary England, affidavits (or sworn, written statements) displaced to some extent oral, adversarial cross-examination.

That English Chancery, as reformed from the 1850s onward, relied on affidavit evidence much more than the newly established New York Supreme Court is suggested by David Dudley Field's evident surprise in learning of this English practice. In 1851, the English Chancery commissioners appointed by Parliament to undertake procedural reform decided to investigate developments in New York, including by interviewing Field. In so doing, they asked him whether the New York Supreme Court "ever proceed[ed] by affidavit in any proceeding," especially those (such as accountings) that had previously been within the purview of chancery. For Field, this question was so surprising that he found it confusing and inquired whether his interlocutors were referring to "affidavits of the parties"—namely, affidavits submitted by the parties themselves in support of a motion (such as one for an injunction). The commissioners answered in the negative, explaining that they were referring to "affidavit evidence generally," including witness testimony. To this Field replied definitively: "No, we take very little of that. . . . [T]here is nothing but oral examination."[11] As this suggests, written accounts of the testimony of the sort that once dominated in New York Chancery played relatively little role in the state's new supreme court but continued to be of great importance in (reformed) English Chancery.

Indeed, while Kent's 1817 decision in *Remsen* opened the floodgates to oral, adversarial testimony, the same does not appear to have been true of the English counterpart to this decision—namely, an 1828 chancery rule authorizing the master "to examine any witness viva voce."[12] As the English Chancery commissioners noted many years later in their 1852 report, "[t]he common practice [in proceedings before masters] is to proceed by affidavit." Accordingly, the commissioners—even while recommending that "the existing system of examining witnesses upon written interrogatories should be abolished"—did not favor the wholesale adoption of oral, adversarial testimony. Instead, they proposed a combined approach that would encourage reliance on both oral testimony and affidavits.[13] This recommendation was enshrined (and given more precise contours) in a July 1852 statute that allowed either party to give notice of intent to take evidence orally. But if no such notice was given, the default rule was that the parties were to proceed by affidavit.[14]

Over the course of the following decades, various legislative changes were made regarding English Chancery's approach to taking testimony. But despite such ongoing tinkering, the applicable rules continued to give pride of place to affidavit evidence.[15] In merging law and equity and creating a unified supreme court, the Judicature Acts of 1873 and 1875 and the new rules issued pursuant to them shifted the balance somewhat more toward oral over written testimony. As a contemporary treatise writer explained, pursuant to the new rules, "[t]he case is in general tried upon evidence given *viva voce*." This default rule was, however, subject to two significant exceptions: (1) if the parties "agreed to try it on affidavits," or (2) if the court itself issued an order "allowing the affidavit of certain witnesses to be used."[16] These exceptions threatened to swallow the rule itself, extending well beyond the narrow circumstances in which the Field Code allowed written statements to replace oral testimony—namely, the witness's inability to attend the trial due to death, distance, or the like.

This brief survey of English procedural reform, though by no means complete, suggests that, while English lawyers, like their New York counterparts, turned to oral, adversarial procedure (including not least, cross-examination), their enthusiasm for it simply did not run as deep. Why was this so? The answer likely has to do with the fact that, while late eighteenth- and early nineteenth-century English barristers aspired to a model of "patriotic eloquence" that they associated with certain leading lights of the profession, the civic republican ideal of the lawyer-orator never took root in England to the same extent that it did in the United States. As in France—and quite unlike the United States—the English legal profession was divided, such that only a select elite of barristers could undertake courtroom pleading and argument. Indeed, barristers worked assiduously over the course of the eighteenth century to sharpen the boundaries distinguishing them from attorneys, thus further narrowing their ranks. As a result, nineteenth-century barristers' high status was relatively secured, such that they lacked the same motivation as their American brethren to engage in self-promoting (republican) display.[17]

Moreover, even within this select group of barristers, a number of factors constrained their ability to present themselves as embodying a Ciceronian model of public-serving advocacy. By about 1800, a combination of declining litigation rates and their own successful efforts to distinguish themselves from attorneys meant that barristers were representing a much narrower segment of the population than had been the case in the seventeenth century—primarily a wealthy, landed (rather than commercial) elite. At the same time, barristers' elevation to the bench came increasingly to depend on aristocratic patronage and crown preferment. As David Lemmings concludes, "the Roman ideal" of the lawyer was thus "translated into an emphasis on barristers' elite status and associations, rather than social responsibilities." Further limiting the utility of the civic republican model of the lawyer-orator was the eighteenth-century rise of parliamentary supremacy, which had the effect of depriving the common-law courts of their historical role in deciding matters of constitutional law—thereby eliminating an important forum in which barristers might display their patriotic virtue.[18] Finally, when undertaking ordinary civil (and criminal) litigation, English barristers encountered judges who, on the whole, were far more powerful than their American counterparts.[19] Accordingly, even barristers who practiced in the common-law courts—and thus as a formal matter, enjoyed the same procedural powers as American lawyers—operated under greater constraint, such that they did not have the same opportunity to deploy procedure as a mechanism of republican self-display.

There is thus good reason to conclude that, despite overarching similarities, the United States and England took different paths to the merger of law and equity and that the resulting procedural regimes differed in some important ways. Indeed, as we will see, these nineteenth-century differences have but further ramified with the passage of time. But while nineteenth-century American legal culture was (and has remained) more adversarial than that of England, the fact remains that there were significant parallels between U.S. and English procedural reform. So what accounts for these?

Given the extent to which early and mid-nineteenth-century Americans closely followed English developments, including perhaps especially in the law, one possibility that comes to mind is that New Yorkers copied reforms already taking place in England. But the timing of key reforms suggests that, if anything, it was England that copied New York and not vice versa.[20] The decisions to permit oral testimony before masters and then before examiners, to abolish masters and then examiners, to establish a unified court combining law and equity, and to create a single unified body of procedure were all made in New York well before they were made in England.[21] Moreover, the various commissioners designated by Parliament to undertake procedural (and substantive) law reform in mid- and late nineteenth-century England paid very close attention to developments in New York—with an eye toward possible borrowing. For example, those appointed in 1850 to "inquire into the process, practice, and system of pleading in the court of chancery" asked David Dudley Field a whopping 171 separate questions concerning "the provisions and operation" of the Field Code.[22] So too, the Judicature Commission of 1869, whose recommendations led directly to the merger of law and equity, sought the testimony of one of the New York Code commissioners.[23]

The parallels between New York and English procedural reform were likely also a product of underlying dynamics common to both jurisdictions. New York and English Chancery each began the nineteenth century with a quasi-inquisitorial approach to procedure that was fundamentally at odds with its lack of an extensive and professionalized judicial staff. While this disjuncture between procedural logic and institutional structure was in no way new, nineteenth-century economic and political developments common to both jurisdictions exacerbated the resulting tensions. The rise of an increasingly commercial and then industrial economy, combined with the push toward ever more democratic, egalitarian politics, led to increased demands on judicial systems in both New York and England. The end result was to exacerbate the problem of delay as well as to heighten the perception that such delays were intolerable. Similarly, the jurisdictional divide between law and equity dated back many centuries and had often produced jurisdictional conflict and confusion, as well as the delays inherent in these. But the high volume of litigation generated by the nineteenth-century economy, combined with new demands for broader, more democratic access to justice, made the resultant delays that much more abhorrent.

But while these developments helped to generate a perceived crisis in chancery (thereby encouraging reform), the way that contemporaries framed this crisis—and thus sought to act in response—turned significantly on issues of more local, immediate salience. In New York, in particular, the turn against chancery (especially from about 1830 onward) was spurred by a set of anxieties that were themselves intimately linked to a burgeoning commitment to democratization—including, most importantly, anxieties about the spoils system of party politics and the market revolution. So too, in England, as Michael Lobban suggests, the initial impetus to reform chancery was tied to local circumstances, such as the perduring animosity between Tories and Whigs.[24] Local circumstances of this kind—such as the distinctively American imperative of republican self-display—played a vital role, moreover, not only in creating the perception that chancery was in crisis but also in shaping the nature of reform. Put differently, structural features of both New York and English Chancery, as well as political and economic developments common to both, may have contributed to the sense that reform was necessary, but they did not resolve the separate question of what such reform would entail.

Another development common to both New York and England that may have played a role in leading both jurisdictions to undertake broadly similar approaches to procedural reform was the emergence of substantive law categories like contract and tort and the resulting shift from writ to right. This shift occurred in both New York and England—and in both jurisdictions it had the effect of problematizing the category of procedure, raising a host of new and pressing questions. Most importantly, what was the content of this new concept of procedure? And in what ways did its emergence necessitate the rethinking and reform of the existing (common-law and equity) traditions of pleading and practice? That such questions arose in both jurisdictions did not,

however, predetermine how they would be answered. As with the longstanding disjuncture between chancery's institutional structure and procedural
logic, more is needed to explain the particulars of the reforms ultimately embraced.

A final factor that may help account for broadly similar patterns of procedural reform in both New York and England is the rise of a new concern with
promoting publicity in governance—a concern that, as we have seen, was expressed most prominently in Bentham's writings. While Bentham's direct influence on legal reform is not easy to establish (and, indeed, remains a subject
of scholarly debate),[25] it is clear that the overarching pattern of reform in both
the United States and England took precisely the shape that he proposed—
including, most importantly, the elimination of equity's written and secrecy-
oriented approach to taking testimony, the merger of law and equity, and the
creation of a single system of procedural rules (entitled in New York a *code*).[26]
Bentham, in short, appears to have been a kind of barometer of legal and political culture—a man who was uniquely able to recognize and conceptualize
a rising commitment to values of democratic publicity that was just then taking root on both sides of the Atlantic and to forecast what these new political
values implied for the law. But while these common values surely played a role
in the turn away from written and secrecy-oriented, quasi-inquisitorial procedure in both New York and English Chancery, the paths taken in the two systems differed in a number of key ways. And as we will see, the legacy of these
differences has been of enduring significance, such that American procedure
continues to be profoundly (and uniquely) shaped by an ethos of adversarialism that often serves to thwart efforts to promote rational reform and, most
fundamentally, access to justice.

## Legacies of the Nineteenth-Century Rise of Adversarialism

That American legal culture was distinctively adversarial as of the close of
the Civil War and Reconstruction and remains so today does not mean that
there was a straight line connecting the past to the present. Indeed, the late
nineteenth-century zenith of the adversarial ideal also marked the beginning
of its decline. But even as social, economic, and political developments led to
demands for more expert and efficient procedure than the traditional adversarial model could readily deliver, the enduring legacy of adversarialism was
such that the search for alternatives proceeded in haphazard fashion, in ways
that encouraged powerful groups to promote their own interests, rather than

those of the public as a whole. The end result has been the emergence of dispute-resolution mechanisms that tend to undermine the very values of party autonomy and publicity to which adversarialism aspires or, even worse, to deny injured claimants any remedy at all.

## COUNTERVAILING TRENDS

The postbellum period witnessed the emergence of powerful corporate interests, which helped give rise to a new kind of lawyer and legal practice. As we have seen, throughout much of the nineteenth century most lawyers practiced alone or in small partnerships with at most one or two others. So too, they were generalists, engaging in litigation of all varieties, while also undertaking extensive transactional work. But the emergence of powerful, new banking, insurance, and railroad interests led to the growth of more specialized expert lawyers focused exclusively on the problems of particular sectors of the economy or even particular corporations. As a result, corporations began to employ their own general counsel; lawyers began serving on corporate boards of directors; and by the 1890s, large, multi-lawyer firms focused on corporate defense began to develop in New York City.[27] At the same time, the rise of such powerful corporate interests was met by an expansion in the scope of the regulatory state. At an accelerating pace, American states in the late nineteenth century created railroad commissions, charged with regulating the growing railroad industry. Soon the federal government followed suit, establishing the Interstate Commerce Commission in 1887. Shortly thereafter, it began targeting corporate cartels and monopolies through the Sherman Antitrust Act of 1890.

These developments in the private and public sectors were mutually reinforcing. Just as corporate expansion led to new regulatory efforts, such efforts, in turn, encouraged corporations to undertake new kinds of defensive maneuvers and planning, which likewise called for legal expertise. In this emerging world of legal practice, lawyers played a vital part, but one that was quite different from the litigation-centered model of the immediate past. These new kinds of lawyers were, in the words of James Willard Hurst, "master[s] of fact" and "administrators of social relations." Their function was to provide clients with expert guidance on such matters as how to cultivate new markets and avoid regulation (or, in the case of government lawyers, pursue regulation). So too, they assisted with negotiations, whether in service of facilitating a corporate merger or overcoming complex regulatory hurdles. And while litigation continued to be one component of their tool kit, it was increasingly demoted in stature. Even when undertaken, its goal might simply be to clear the path for settlement and thus for a renewed round of negotiation.[28]

From about the 1890s onward, this new conception of the lawyer as expert would be given powerful voice by Progressive jurists, who advocated for the expansion of the administrative state with an eye toward ensuring that social scientific expertise would guide policymaking. In line with (and to some degree anticipating) these Progressive demands, the expanding administrative agencies of the time—institutions like the Military Pension Bureau—undertook dispute-resolution proceedings premised on what Jerry Mashaw describes as "inquisitorial processes," requiring government "[a]djudicators . . . to establish the facts in a disinterested fashion, not as adversaries." Thus, for example, the Pension Bureau began relying extensively on medical expertise, in the form of three-physician boards, to determine whether veterans were entitled to payment for injuries related to their military service. And in all proceedings before the Bureau, the government itself appeared unrepresented—though claimants remained entitled to representation by counsel.[29] The end result of these various developments was that the lawyer's heroic, adversarial image as a public-serving advocate and orator had to make room for a new conception of the lawyer as a specialized, expert technician.

In line with these developments, the last half-century or so has experienced a dramatic decline in civil litigation, such that, as John Langbein observes, "we have gone from a world in which trials, typically jury trials, were routine, to one in which trials have become 'vanishingly rare.'"[30] The reasons for this development are multi-causal and complex, but one important factor has been the opposition—especially of business interests—to procedural mechanisms thought to undermine certainty by empowering non-expert judges and (especially) juries and to encourage coercive settlement in the face of high, lawyer-driven discovery costs.[31] The end result is a system in which private settlement has become the norm, such that in a great many cases the public has no way of knowing what has been decided or why.[32] Moreover, many businesses have simply opted out of the court system entirely—including increasingly in disputes with consumers and employees. Such disputants are regularly forced into binding, mandatory arbitration proceedings, which in many ways turn the ideal of adversarial litigation on its head. Far from promoting individual autonomy and choice, these proceedings deny consumers and employees any control over choice of forum as well as the ability to obtain representation by counsel. So too, they impose significant constraints on the procedural devices available to such disputants, typically denying them the capacity to undertake witness examination and cross-examination, make oral arguments, or engage in discovery. And like the increasingly ubiquitous practice of settlement, they take place in secret, behind closed doors.[33]

## CONTINUED INFLUENCE

While the late nineteenth and early twentieth centuries witnessed the emergence of powerful trends countervailing the new dominance of adversarialism, the legacy of the history recounted in this book proved, nonetheless, to be tremendously powerful. It is well beyond the scope of these pages to trace the precise linkages between the nineteenth-century rise of adversarialism and the present day. That such linkages exist is, nonetheless, clear. The continued centrality of adversarial procedure to American legal culture is evident perhaps first and foremost in the distinctive structure of the American law school curriculum. In both continental European and English law schools today, civil procedure is relegated to secondary status. Students are not required to take the course at all or are asked to do so only toward the end of their schooling, after topics deemed more important have been covered.[34] On this view, mastery of procedure is merely a technical skill to be developed in apprenticeship, early in the lawyer's career, rather than a field worthy of serious scholarly attention.

The United States could not be more different. Throughout American law schools, civil procedure is taught as a required first-year course, always in the first semester—a practice that dates back to the 1870s creation by Harvard Law School's Christopher Columbus Langdell of the very first modern civil procedure course. That students be exposed to civil procedure from their very first day of law school is deemed essential for conveying the view that law is not a neutral science composed of abstract principles lying dormant in some treatise but instead a form of difficult, contested policymaking, implicating the heartfelt interests of real flesh-and-blood people.[35] And notably, even though modern-day lawyers serve a policymaking function across a wide variety of fora—including not only traditional courtrooms but also legislative committees, administrative law hearings, alternative dispute resolution proceedings, and settlement negotiations—the civil procedure course focuses almost exclusively on adversarial courtroom litigation. Moreover, for a great many procedure scholars of the last several decades—including perhaps most especially those whose views have been shaped by Yale Law School's highly influential Owen Fiss and Judith Resnik—the lawyer qua litigator continues to be framed as a warrior on behalf of the public good.[36] Indeed, the available evidence suggests that American legal scholars, lawyers, and judges are distinctive in their strong support for the use of public interest litigation to shape policy, thus helping to sustain the country's unique reliance on such litigation to undertake regulatory aims that would elsewhere be consigned to the administrative state.[37]

So too, we can see the legacy of the nineteenth-century rise of adversarialism in some of the arguments commonly made on behalf of adversarial procedure today—including, most importantly, the notion that lawyer-controlled, adversarial procedure is better than its court-controlled, quasi-inquisitorial counterpart at promoting the autonomy (and thus dignity) of the individual. Monroe H. Freedman, for example, asserts that "the phrase 'adversary system' is synonymous with the American system for the administration of justice." In his view, this system "serves as a safeguard of personal autonomy and respect for each person's particular circumstances . . . thereby giv[ing] both form and substance to the humanitarian ideal of dignity of the individual."[38] While infused with references to dignity and humanitarian law characteristic of the late twentieth and early twenty-first centuries, this language justifies adversarialism in much the same way that nineteenth-century Americans did. It insists on the unique capacity of adversarial procedure to promote individual freedom and suggests that the United States is defined by (and thus distinctive in) its commitment both to adversarialism and to the individualist ethos that this procedural model implies.

While less common, there are also occasional defenses of adversarialism today that continue to be framed explicitly in terms of economic liberty. For example, Richard Posner draws an express parallel between adversarial process and the free market, suggesting that both give proper respect to principles of individual freedom and choice by deploying competition as the central allocative mechanism. In his words, adversarial "legal process, like the market, is competitive"; indeed, "[t]he adversary system, with its rules against ex parte contacts, its elaborate rights of cross-examination, and its rituals of partisanship, places the tribunal in the position of a consumer forced to decide between the similar goods of two fiercely determined salesmen." Along similar lines, Frank B. Cross argues that "the American system of adversarial legalism is an aspect of classical freemarket liberalism."[39]

Although such claims about the values implicit in adversarial process can be traced more or less directly back to the nineteenth century, the same cannot be said of the defense of adversarialism that is perhaps most common today—namely, that it is superior to inquisitorial modes of procedure in detecting the truth. In support of this assertion, proponents insist that the truth is best achieved when the ultimate finder of fact serves as a neutral, passive observer, and the parties (or rather their lawyers) are empowered to make the best possible case for themselves. While these truth-based arguments on behalf of adversarialism have become so familiar that one legal scholar even refers to them as "the original ideology" justifying adversarial procedure, the history here is, in fact, far more complicated—and ironic—than we have imagined.[40]

Although the practice of cross-examination was long defended as truth-promoting, there were also many who expressed skepticism about such claims. Moreover, cross-examination itself was but one device within a broader procedural system—and, as we have seen, the overall turn toward oral, adversarial procedure in nineteenth-century New York Chancery was not hailed as the triumph of truth but instead widely decried as tending toward its subversion. Contemporaries worried, in particular, that the use of oral, adversarial witness examination and cross-examination in a system that permitted testimony to be collected in writing outside the courtroom and then revealed to the parties—a system that, in many respects, anticipated modern discovery—was distinctively prone to encouraging falsehood. That our nineteenth-century ancestors had these fears does not, of course, mean that they were right, or even if they were, that their concerns apply equally to the present day.[41] But the fact that the architects of the procedural system that we have inherited—one that combines oral, adversarial procedure with discovery practices drawn from equity[42]—doubted its capacity to promote the truth should at least give pause to those who defend the current version of American adversarialism on these grounds.

Yet perhaps the greatest legacy of the nineteenth-century rise of adversaralism is that least easy to measure—namely, our collective failures of imagination. While this is not the place to provide a full accounting of the costs and benefits of adversarial procedure, the book would be incomplete without at least some reflection on the price of our continued attachment to American adversarial exceptionalism. In the context of civil justice, in particular, the most important price that we have paid concerns access to justice. As numerous commentators have bemoaned, there is good reason to believe that Americans as a whole have less access to justice—and thus are more likely to internalize harms that ought as a matter of law to be remedied—than their counterparts in other democratic, industrialized nations. The end result, as Deborah Rhode observes of the United States, is that "[a]ccording to most estimates, about four-fifths of the civil legal needs of the poor, and two- to three-fifths of the needs of middle-income individuals, remain unmet."[43]

One way to frame this disparity in access to justice is as an unfortunate offshoot of the remarkable success of the American adversarial system. To the extent that numerous individuals once marginalized because of race, gender, or socioeconomic class have come today to view the courts as a public forum within which they are empowered to pursue their rights under the law, the new (and overwhelming) demands being placed on the legal system can perhaps be viewed as reason for celebration.[44] But even while applauding the fact that we have a created a legal culture in which many more people than was once the case understand themselves to have a voice worthy of respect under the law, we must nonetheless acknowledge the reality of the burdens thereby placed on the court system. Part of the solution is surely to invest more re-sources—an approach whose utility is bolstered by comparative data suggesting that the United States spends less on its public justice system than do European nations. Strikingly, however, there is reason to believe that our relative failure to invest is itself a product, in Gillian Hadfield's words, of "the extraordinary extent to which [in comparison with other countries] the [American] bar and judiciary wield exclusive authority for shaping the cost and market structure of legal goods and services."[45] Thus, even if the problem is, at least in part, one of resources, it may well have arisen due to the disproportionate public power wielded by the legal profession—power that, as we have seen, is in itself intimately linked to the country's deep-rooted tradition of lawyer-driven adversarialism.

Relatedly, in many other countries civil litigants are guaranteed counsel, such that those who cannot pay for a lawyer are, nonetheless, afforded one. In contrast, in the United States, only criminal defendants are guaranteed counsel regardless of ability to pay. As a matter of logic, there is no necessary link between our commitment to adversarial procedure, on the one hand, and our failure to guarantee civil counsel, on the other. Indeed, while we never enacted a right to civil counsel of the sort that governs elsewhere, we devoted many more resources to providing legal aid to the poor prior to a series of spending cuts that began in the 1980s.[46] That said, as we have seen, adversarial court-room proceedings have long been envisioned as a structural parallel to private market transactions, imagined as free of government involvement. Although this early (and to some extent enduring) model of adversarialism in no way necessitated our parsimonious approach to civil counsel today, it does suggest a predisposition to frame litigation as a private matter in which the government need and ought not to concern itself—including by providing counsel.

There are also more direct and immediate ways in which the American commitment to adversarialism serves to hinder access to justice in this country. In systems that empower judges to play a greater role in the fact-finding process—for example by calling witnesses themselves (including experts)—disparities in the quality of legal representation are less likely to affect the outcome of the adjudication.[47] The American tendency toward an extreme of adversarialism thus exacerbates the injustices that follow from our failure to guarantee civil counsel. But perhaps most fundamentally, the American commitment to a lawyer-based model of adversarial justice means that we have left far too many social ills to the court system for resolution. The end result has been a series of interest-group driven efforts to avoid formal litigation—whether through settlement or forced arbitration—that, as noted above, have caused us to undermine the very values of autonomy and publicity to which, as devotees of adversarialism, we imagine ourselves to be committed. Even worse, a great many claimants are left with no forum at all in which to seek redress.

In contrast, in countries less wedded to adversarialism, it has been easier to engage in rational reform aimed at developing alternative, non-litigation-based (and nonlawyer-based) approaches to dispute resolution of benefit to the public as a whole. England, for example, has developed a range of institutional mechanisms for helping people address such common difficulties as landlord-tenant conflicts, alleged overcharging by service providers, and tax disputes. These include government ombudspersons empowered to investigate and resolve a wide variety of complaints and various (national and local) advice bureaus that employ nonlawyers to provide guidance concerning how best to address such complaints. The evidence suggests that, while in no way perfect (and subject to recent funding cuts), these non-adversarial, nonlawyer-based institutional mechanisms solve a great many problems in England that would simply go unaddressed in the United States, in no small part because of the high cost of accessing the courts. A legal system that is less ideologically committed to adversarialism is one in which, over time, lawyers have not succeeded in enforcing the same kind of monopoly claim to all matters of civil justice and in which due process is not imagined as necessarily synonymous with the adversarial trial. In contrast, in the United States, our persistent adherence to lawyer-driven adversarialism is such that we have ended up developing a two-track system—one in which an idealized model of (expensive) adversarial justice is available to a few and the claims of a great many are simply left unremedied.[48]

## Learning from the Past

While the history recounted here does not provide a clear, step-by-step blueprint for change, it can—and should—help to free our imaginations as to what might be possible. The nineteenth-century origins of American legal exceptionalism can—in at least two key ways—play an important part in dismantling our continued adherence to the ideology of adversarialism.

First, while we imagine that adversarialism is a legacy of the nation's founding (or even its colonial roots), such that alternatives are all but impossible, this book has shown that there were important quasi-inquisitorial traditions with which the United States experimented up to and including the time of the Civil War and Reconstruction. Indeed, it was only around the middle of the nineteenth century that Americans began to conceive of themselves as having a distinctively adversarial system. Of course, the period from the mid- to late nineteenth century onward represents a very substantial portion of this nation's history, encompassing some of the most seminal events in shaping modern national identity. To insist on the nineteenth-century origins of adversarial exceptionalism is thus in no way to gainsay its importance or the difficulties inherent in any attempt at real procedural change. But the fact that the United States has a significant quasi-inquisitorial past should, at least to some extent, help to reframe the boundaries of the imaginable.

Second, and perhaps more importantly, the nineteenth-century origins of our embrace of adversarialism should remind us that, as with all history, our present-day procedural landscape is a legacy of social and ideological struggle—one that determined "what is retained from the past and what is consigned to oblivion."[49] The winners of this struggle—those responsible for the turn to adversarialism as both ideology and practice—were driven by a complex combination of motivations that belie the grandiose, public-minded claims so often made in support of American adversarial justice. More particularly, they pursued three goals, each addressed, in turn, below: (1) to empower the legal profession; (2) to defend against efforts to moderate the worst excesses of market-based society; and (3) to bring an end to radical Reconstruction.

Tied to a pervasive ethos of classical republicanism, adversarialism was one of the major ways that nineteenth-century lawyers laid claim to a preeminent role in the social and political life of the nation—one that, to a remarkable extent, they have managed to preserve down to the present. Even while celebrating the many remarkable things that lawyers have done (and surely will continue to do) on behalf of the public at large, we should not blind ourselves to the substantial costs of relying so exclusively on lawyers to provide services that might also be undertaken to some extent by other professionals, such as social workers and psychologists.[50]

The link between the American commitment to adversarial procedure and the defense of a burgeoning market-based society emerged in the debates over whether to adopt European-style conciliation courts. While in no way radical anti-capitalists, those advocating for the establishment of such courts hoped that they would temper the excesses of a market-driven order—perhaps most importantly, by responding to the needs and demands of a growing urban, industrial working class. In rejecting these courts and insisting on adversarial procedure, their opponents refused even such minimal government intervention in the market—most especially the market for labor. A free, market-based society, they argued, required a procedural system in which individuals were encouraged to assert their rights and interests in free and open competition— whether in the courtroom or the marketplace. Conciliation courts and their excessively powerful judges were suited to "despotic" European states whose overweening ambitions led them to intervene excessively in private relations, including market activity. As this history suggests, adversarialism was the product of a very particular socioeconomic and political vision of the United States—one associated with notions of free contract and free labor (as later transmuted into Gilded Age laissez-faire)—pursuant to which welfare was assumed to be maximized through a minimalist government that confined itself to the enforcement of contracts imagined as freely entered and negotiated. While there is therefore some truth to the common assertion that American adversarialism is a product of our market-oriented social and economic structure, the link between the two is not set in stone, a product of some functional necessity. It is, to the contrary, an ideological construct—one that was contested from the very outset.

While the lack of a corporatist tradition in the United States meant that the deck was stacked against the conciliation court model ever taking meaningful root, race was arguably the one exception to this otherwise prevailing rule. African-Americans were long defined as a group under the law, such that membership entailed particular legal rights and (mostly) obligations. They were, as the *North American Review* insisted in the wake of the Civil War, the

American variant of the (recently freed) European serfs. It was thus imaginable that, at least as to disputes between freedpeople, the conciliation court
model might just work. And to some extent, it did. But Northern architects of
Reconstruction sought to employ the institution to resolve interracial (especially labor) disputes, hoping thereby to recognize and correct the deep-rooted
structural inequalities produced by generations of slavery. As a result, they
incurred the wrath of Southern whites and their Northern Democratic allies.
Determined to preserve their racial privilege, these men resuscitated antebellum claims about the inherently un-American nature of conciliation courts
and of non-adversarial proceedings more generally. Largely victorious, they
quickly brought an end to the Freedmen's Bureau and its courts and to Reconstruction as a whole, leaving as their legacy the rise of Jim Crow and a reinvigorated commitment to due process, now envisioned in expressly adversarial
terms.

From the vantage point of the twenty-first century, there is perhaps particular irony in the fact that adversarialism triumphed in the nineteenth century
partly because of arguments that it played an essential part in the country's
distinctive economic growth and commitment to individual freedom. As
noted above, we live in an era in which civil trials have all but vanished—
including through the successful efforts of large corporate interests to force
consumers and employees into binding, mandatory arbitration proceedings
that undermine such core adversarial values as publicity and party autonomy.
Strikingly, the turn to such arbitration is justified as vital for market growth—
as a means, more particularly, of saving costs for both corporations and individual consumers and employees, thus providing "a social good" whose effect
is to "increase[e] the size of the pie" as a whole. So too, it is defended as a cor-
ollary of our longstanding commitment to principles of free contract and thus
individual choice: "What some call 'mandatory arbitration' is better called
'contractual arbitration.' . . . Arbitration is not mandatory when it arises out of
a contract, because contracts are formed voluntarily."[51] And since the mid-
1980s, the Supreme Court has proven increasingly receptive to such claims.[52]
That at two different points in time, the same basic arguments could be so effectively deployed to justify such radically different procedural outcomes is an
important reminder of the extent to which procedure is intimately related to
social and economic context.

The inextricability of procedural practices and ideals, on the one hand, and
socioeconomic, political, and cultural context, on the other, is an overarching
message of this book—one suggesting two broader lessons. First, it is long

past time to abandon the assumption that legal history scholarship must be either internalist or externalist, rather than both, as well as the concomitant tendency of scholarship focused on procedure to adopt an exclusively internalist approach. As we have seen in studying New York Chancery's turn toward the oral and adversarial, there is much that can be learned by conceiving of procedure as an interconnected and relatively self-enclosed system of rules, practices, and institutions, such that changes in any one component tend to ramify throughout. But this heuristic must not be allowed to obscure the myriad ways that procedure is also profoundly shaped by broader nonlegal phenomena. As the nineteenth-century origins of American adversarialism demonstrate, procedure is not simply some set of rules created in top-down fashion and then recorded in books. To the contrary, it sometimes develops from the bottom up, as a matter of social practice, and is in this sense precisely the kind of endeavor on which externalist, law-and-society–oriented historians have long insisted that we ought to focus attention.[53] At the same time, debates over procedure, leading to possible rule change and reform, do not emerge ex nihilo. They instead arise in response to particular socioeconomic, political, and cultural dynamics—like the development of modern market society or the problem of remaking race relations after the Civil War—that should be of much interest to historians of all stripes.

A second lesson stemming from the fact that procedure and society are so intimately connected—one more directly tied to practice—is that it is time to acknowledge the limits (and costs) of our reigning procedural ideal of transsubstantivity. As we have seen, the notion that procedure is transsubstantive, such that the same rules should apply in all disputes, regardless of the underlying substantive law or value of the case, emerged along with the idea of procedure as distinct from substance. Indeed, a commitment to transsubstantivity was embodied in the structure of the Field Code. But despite this fact, issues of substantive law were implicated in nineteenth-century debates over procedure right from the get-go. When contemporary critics complained about excessive chancery powers, they were not thinking about the chancellor's authority to order discovery and enjoin activity in the abstract. They were focused instead on particular areas of the substantive law, such as the use of creditors' bills to support the efforts of (often commercial) creditors to collect from debtors—most especially in the wake of the financial panics of 1837 and 1839. Moreover, even beyond specific areas of substantive law as such, there were broad social and political values responsible for animating contemporary procedural debates—values like a desire to promote unfettered market activity and to preserve Southern white privilege (or instead to regulate the labor market and to promote racial equality).

Our own forgotten, non-adversarial history—our history of equity courts and conciliation courts (especially Freedmen's Bureau courts)—is an important reminder that, as argued by Robert Cover, "there are . . . demands of particular substantive objectives which cannot be served except through the purposeful shaping, indeed, the manipulation, of process to a case or to an area of law."[54] Justice, in short, sometimes requires the intermeshing of procedure and substance, especially when addressing the claims of the systematically disempowered. Equity long prided itself on developing special rules and procedures to protect women, minors, and the mentally ill. New York Chancery, for example, recognized married women as possessing an estate separate from that of their spouse, thus enabling wives to shield property from their husbands' creditors.[55] So too, as we have seen, chancery refused to enter automatic default judgments against minor defendants who had failed to file an answer and instead required the appointment of a master to investigate and establish the facts alleged in the plaintiff's complaint. Along similar lines, the Freedmen's Bureau courts addressed the risk that white planters would refuse payment to their newly freed African-American laborers at harvest time by devising such remedies as granting the freedmen a labor-based lien on the crops.

In thus deploying their authority to mitigate the effects of deep-rooted power imbalances in society, were these courts creating new substantive rights or new procedural tools? A long line of scholarship and jurisprudence teaches the difficulty of answering this question—and neither chancery nor the Freedmen's Bureau courts made any effort to do so. Throughout most of chancery's history, the distinction between procedure and substance had yet to be conceptualized. And the Bureau courts were far too busy addressing the pressing problems of Reconstruction to allow for theorizing of this sort. For both chancery and the Freedmen's Bureau courts, the goal was quite simply remedial—to do justice, where no other institution would.

So what exactly should we recover from the neglected legacy of our equity and Freedmen's Bureau courts that might help inform our effort to attend to the deficiencies of adversarialism—including, most importantly, the risk that such a lawyer-dependent legal system is likely to resolve disputes simply by reflecting disparities in wealth and power? Any attempt to restore either equity or Bureau courts in their entirety is itself a nonstarter. Equity was perennially plagued by the disjunction between its quasi-inquisitorial logic and its lack of a sizable and permanent (European-style) judicial bureaucracy. Resurrecting equity as a distinct quasi-inquisitorial system would thus require us finally to develop this bureaucracy—a possibility that the further passage of time has made only that much more improbable. As for conciliation courts, their ability to take meaningful root in the United States was repeatedly hampered by our lack of a corporatist tradition. To the extent that the Freedmen's Bureau courts were an exception to this otherwise prevailing rule, this was because of their capacity to rely on military force—an option unavailable today and, at any rate, clearly undesirable. There are, moreover, important virtues to adversarial litigation that ought to be preserved and that any attempt simply to restore equity and Freedmen's Bureau courts would jeopardize. Foremost among these is the commitment to publicity as a core component of democratic governance. The aim must thus be to mine particular features of our non-adversarial tradition with an eye toward preserving those aspects of our adversarial culture that we admire, even while correcting for its deficits.

### RECONFIGURING THE MASTER

One possibility suggested by our history of equity is to expand the role of masters. The figure of the master in many ways embodied the quasi-inquisitorial vision of equity, such that by the time New York Chancery had embraced the oral, adversarial methods of the common law, the state constitution of 1846 abolished the office. But despite abolition, masters quietly resurfaced. Although a complete account lies well beyond these pages, it appears that the Field Code's decision to authorize a "reference" to lay individuals appointed on a case-by-case basis opened the door to a partial return of the master in chancery.[56] As of today, New York courts continue to appoint referees to serve functions once performed by masters—namely, "to remove complicated and intricate issues of fact, such as the review of a long account from a judge and jury, so that such issues may be more effectively and expeditiously determined. . . ."[57] Moreover, despite the fact that there is almost no statutory authorization in New York for the appointment of masters as such, several state court judges have nonetheless appointed individuals so designated in recent years to undertake a variety of complex fact-finding endeavors. These include, for example, deciding the differing damages claims of those individuals certified to sue as a class and hearing and reporting on the evidence presented in a shareholder derivative action.[58]

The partial resurgence of masters is not unique to New York. The merger of law and equity in the federal system, (formally) accomplished through the

1938 enactment of the Federal Rules of Civil Procedure, did not lead to the abolition of masters, as did merger in New York. To the contrary, Rule 53 provided for the appointment of masters—a term expressly defined as being synonymous with "referee[s]." Pursuant to the rule, courts had the option of referring factually complex disputes to a master who would hear the evidence presented by the opposing parties and then issue a report recommending judgment.[59] As this suggests, the master envisioned by the original version of Rule 53 was to serve much like masters in New York Chancery did once lawyers had embraced the oral, adversarial methods of the common law. He was, in other words, to stand in for the judge (and jury), overseeing adversarial proceedings from a position of passive neutrality.

But with the dawn of the Civil Rights era and the concomitant rise of new kinds of complex litigation, the master's role in the federal system was reconfigured. Rather than serving as a "trial master" supervising adversarial proceedings, masters came increasingly to assume pre- and post-trial roles that in many ways reprise core aspects of their traditional quasi-inquisitorial, investigatory function.[60] In their pre-trial capacity, masters are now asked to oversee the discovery process in complex litigation, thus helping to ensure that factfinding unfolds as fairly, accurately, and efficiently as possible. And in their post-trial capacity, they are charged with monitoring the implementation of consent decrees and structural injunctions—a task often requiring them to undertake investigations of the parties' performance, sometimes on an ex parte basis. While masters serving these roles are commonly said to be performing a new "managerial" function distinct from the adversarial judicial role, the history recounted here indicates that these developments are perhaps better characterized as a restoration of their traditional, quasi-inquisitorial responsibility for factual investigation.[61]

That masters are an available resource, increasingly deployed for quasi-inquisitorial purposes, suggests that there is a possibility of further developing their role to help mitigate the effects on litigation of disparities in wealth and power—effects that adversarialism has tended to leave undisturbed (or even to magnify). As currently deployed in the federal system, masters are permitted far more independent investigative authority in the post-trial context, where they can serve as roving investigators acting on an often ex parte basis, than during the pretrial phase, where they are limited to overseeing the disputes that arise from adversarial, party-directed discovery. This distinction between the master's pre- and post-trial authority likely stems from our understanding of the judicial role in a legal system presumed to be necessarily adversarial. We assume, in short, that for the master to direct the investigation at the pre-trial discovery phase would run afoul of the passive role of judicial officers in an adversarial system. In contrast, we permit the master far greater discretion during the post-trial phase on the theory that the court has inherent authority to enforce its judgments—authority that in no way interferes with the parties' right to full adversarial control of the (pre-trial discovery) proceedings. Thus, as explained in the Advisory Committee notes to the 2003 amendments to Rule 53, "[t]he master's role in [post-trial] enforcement may extend to investigation in ways that are quite unlike the traditional role of judicial officers in an adversary system." But as the history recounted here reminds us, masters were never "officers in an adversary system" but were instead key actors within a quasi-inquisitorial one. As such, they once exercised substantial independent powers of pre-trial investigation—sometimes (though by no means always) in service of protecting the interests of the disempowered. This suggests the possibility of broadening the quasi-inquisitorial investigatory authority exercised by masters so as to ensure greater court control of pre-trial discovery.

In what kinds of suits might we want to deploy this reconfigured breed of master? The wisest path would be to permit case-by-case experimentation, thus enabling incremental change and repeated course correction. But one obvious place to start would be with the kinds of complex litigation in which today's masters already frequently serve.[62] Such suits, including but not limited to both class actions and multidistrict litigation, pit individual plaintiffs against large and wealthy defendants, including both government institutions and business corporations. They thus raise profound concerns about the potential for disparities in wealth and power to affect litigation outcomes. And while procedural tools (like the class action itself) have been devised to level the playing field, there is good reason to doubt their ultimate efficacy. Indeed, recent Supreme Court decisions aimed at toughening pleading standards and enforcing binding, mandatory arbitration agreements seem to be designed to prevent such plaintiffs from ever having their day in court.[63]

As the legal landscape is currently configured, of course, endowing masters with independent pre-trial powers of investigation would make little difference, because—due in part to the Supreme Court's recent jurisprudence on pleading and arbitration—many plaintiffs never reach the discovery stage of litigation. But the driving force behind this defendant-friendly jurisprudence has been anxiety about the potential for discovery abuse—the fear, in short, that plaintiffs with unmeritorious claims can wield the high cost of party-controlled discovery as blackmail for forcing settlement. Empowering a neutral, quasi-inquisitorial judicial officer to assume greater control over discovery should assuage precisely these fears. Such an officer would strive to protect the corporate or governmental defendant from unfair abuse, even while aiming to ensure that individual plaintiffs have a meaningful chance of obtaining the evidence necessary to support their claims. And to the extent that masters of this kind succeed in persuading others of their neutrality (and thus their commitment to preventing discovery abuse), it might be possible to reconfigure the procedural framework yet again—this time with an eye toward eliminating the various hurdles that have been constructed to prevent plaintiffs from reaching discovery.

The devil here is, of course, in the details. If we are to expand the quasi-inquisitorial authority of masters, we must first devise better mechanisms for ensuring their competence and neutrality. Under our current system, masters are selected on a largely ad hoc, case-by-case basis at the sole discretion of the judge. While in practice they are often lawyers, there are no prerequisites that they must meet concerning professional background and qualifications or the like. Moreover, in appointing the master, the judge solicits the views of the parties, thus opening the door to adversarial maneuvering—including the possibility that the wealthier, possibly repeat player will have the primary say in the master's selection. As concerns compensation, it is the parties themselves, rather than the public at large, who must pay for the master's services in the amount and proportion that the judge deems appropriate.[64] This too raises the possibility of adversarial manipulation and control by the richer, more powerful litigant.

If we are to appoint and pay masters in a manner more likely to ensure their competence and neutrality, we must confront the longstanding tension in equity between its quasi-inquisitorial logic and its lack of a sizable judicial bureaucracy. This might mean transforming masters into a permanent and salaried judicial staff. The relatively recent 1968 decision to create a new category of federal magistrate judge—one of whose functions is "to serve as a special master"—suggests at least the possibility of some development along these lines.[65] That said, given our history, any attempt to create a large new group of full-time, salaried governmental officers is likely to encounter substantial opposition. But even while continuing to rely on masters who work on a part-time, case-by-case basis, we could introduce greater regulation, such as mandating that their qualifications meet certain uniform, predetermined standards. At a minimum, we might require that judges meaningfully justify their selection of masters—perhaps by reference to an established list of criteria, such as relevant education, work experience, and the like. More difficult is the question of compensation. If we wish to ensure masters' public accountability without turning them into salaried bureaucrats, we must increase their nonfinancial, reputational incentives to serve. We already have a system in which the most talented young lawyers compete to serve in low-paying judicial clerkships. Perhaps we might extend this practice into a broader *cursus honorum,* such that later in their lives these same lawyers would vie to serve part-time as masters.

## INCREASING RELIANCE ON (COURT-CONTROLLED) EXPERTS

Are there aspects of our experimentation with conciliation courts, including especially the Freedmen's Bureau courts, on which we might also draw in an effort to temper the potential injustices of excess adversarialism? One response to this question might be to suggest that mediation is the modern-day counterpart to conciliation courts. From roughly the 1980s onward, the United States witnessed a remarkable rise in mediation, especially court-mandated mediation. And supporters of mediation rely on arguments that are strikingly reminiscent of those once advanced by nineteenth-century advocates of conciliation courts. As Deborah Hensler observes, these include (unsupported) claims of savings in time and cost; an appeal to informal, community-based norms; and an insistence on the preeminent value of social harmony (itself often framed as somehow linked to religious or spiritual ideals). But while the parallels between antebellum conciliation courts and present-day mediation are striking, it is another question entirely whether mediation as actually implemented does a better job than adversarial process at ensuring justice for those lacking in wealth and power. Indeed, as Hensler explains, "virtually nothing" is known "about the outcomes of mediation programs, about whether they change the distribution of power between the 'haves' and 'have nots.' "[66]

Rather than adopting mediation as the present-day offshoot of conciliation courts most likely to help address the limits of adversarialism, perhaps we ought to grapple more directly with the question that so confounded nineteenth-century American advocates of the institution—namely, where to locate extralegal authority in a society lacking the centuries-old tradition of European corporatist hierarchy. In certain respects, the modern-day professions can be viewed as analogs to early modern corporatist entities. Across the Atlantic at least, it is clear that there is a direct lineage between the Old Regime's communally grounded, corporatist forms of authority and today's (often state-licensed) modes of professional expertise. As James Whitman reminds us, the powerful "craft traditions" that gave rise to a strong sense of "professional identity" in countries like Germany and France are "associated with historic guild structures."[67] This suggests that translating the nineteenth-century ideal of the conciliation court into a set of practices that work in the modern-day United States might require us to embrace more fully the Progressives' commitment to harnessing the legitimating power of social and scientific expertise.

What might this increased reliance on professional expertise entail? At a very minimum, it would include reforming our approach to expert testimony. Under our current system, so shocking to much of the rest of the world, we allow parties to select and pay for their own experts, such that the presentation of expert testimony typically devolves into a battle between hired guns—one that necessarily undermines the legitimacy that might otherwise inhere in expert witnesses. The end result is a tendency to encourage the distortion of truth in ways that often redound to the benefit of the party with the deeper pockets. Although Federal Rule of Evidence 706 authorizes federal judges to appoint their own experts, very few actually make use of this authority. So too, while many states adopted evidence codes that closely track the Federal Rules of Evidence, including Rule 706, state judges appear to be similarly reluctant to appoint their own experts.[68] The causes of this reluctance are complex and include such nitty-gritty, practical concerns as the hesitancy of often overburdened judges to spend the time and effort necessary to identify and oversee appropriate experts. But at least one motivating factor appears to be judges' own adversarial self-conception. Believing that the role of a judge in an adversarial system is a necessarily passive one, judges assume that any effort to appoint their own experts would improperly interfere with the activities of counsel.[69]

That this adversarial self-conception is unduly constraining and narrow is evident from the quasi-inquisitorial tradition of equity—a tradition that teaches that American judges do have a history of playing a more active, hands-on role in guiding fact-finding (including expertise). The value, in turn, to be derived from relying more on court-appointed experts is suggested by the model of the conciliation court. As we have seen, the authority of the conciliation court judge was thought to inhere in his position of high standing within the community and thus, at least in part, in his ability to give voice to communal norms and values. So too, professional expertise today is a form of communally grounded (though often also state-recognized) authority. To the extent that a neutral, court-appointed expert would be deemed legitimate by all litigants, as well as by the public at large, reliance on such experts ought to decrease the sums spent on adversarial lawyering—including, but not limited to, those devoted to paying for a battle among *multiple* party-selected experts. This, in turn, should help to level the playing field and thereby redound to the benefit of those individuals and groups lacking substantial resources.

Important and difficult questions of implementation, of course, remain. Under our current approach to expert testimony, we focus much more on the admissibility of the proposed testimony than on the identity of the expert as such. But if we are to draw more on the communally grounded, legitimating power of the expert as an individual, we must develop more precise guidance for identifying who precisely is qualified to serve as an expert. We must, in other words, provide some specific institutional content to Federal Rule of Evidence 702's broad-brush statement that the witness must be "qualified . . . by knowledge, skill, experience, training, or education."[70] This might mean specifying as requirements particular educational degrees, forms of state accreditation, organizational memberships, and the like. So too, it might be necessary to tailor these requirements to different forms of professional expertise.

Even if we agreed on a set of criteria for ensuring the communal, institutional legitimacy of experts in particular fields, the cost of applying these criteria in each and every case would likely continue to deter overburdened judges from appointing their own experts. This suggests the need to develop a pre-identified group of experts for each court, such that a judge looking for some particular form of expertise could simply consult an available list of candidates. In appointing experts, French courts in fact rely on such pre-approved lists—a fact suggesting that we might have much to learn by studying the French example.[71] Indeed, despite the reluctance of many American judges today to consider foreign law, another important lesson taught by our experience with conciliation courts is that we have a long tradition of treating foreign law and institutions as a source of valuable guidance.

A more radical attempt to rely on expertise would be to deploy experts as lay adjudicators sitting alongside the professional judge—along the lines of the labor courts of modern-day Germany, themselves, as we have seen, derived from the original French *conseils de prud'hommes*. To the extent that litigants invest such courts with legitimacy, they will perhaps be less inclined to devote significant resources to protracted, cost-intensive litigation of the kind that tends to favor those with greater wealth and power.

It is, of course, entirely possible that specialized, expertise-based courts of this kind would ultimately fail in the United States for the same reason that the conciliation courts did in the nineteenth century—namely, our lack of a native corporatist tradition. After all, the very institutions that make possible Germany's distinctively corporatist approach to labor regulation—institutions like trade unions and employers' organizations—also play a key role in staffing its labor courts, including by nominating (and legitimizing) the lay judges who serve.[72] But professional expertise as such does carry some independent weight in the United States. Moreover, specialized, expertise-based courts might be made more readily assimilable by appealing to the parallels between their lay judges and our long tradition of relying on lay juries. This is after all precisely what Lord Mansfield famously did in devising special merchant juries to decide commercial disputes in late eighteenth-century England—a precedent that was, in turn, cited by legal realist Karl Llewellyn in his ultimately failed effort to resurrect such juries as the institutional underpinning of the Uniform Commercial Code (UCC).[73] That Llewellyn's merchant juries failed to take root is perhaps evidence in and of itself of the near-impossibility of establishing such institutions on American soil. But much has changed since Llewellyn was drafting the UCC in the early 1940s, including not least the fact that the civil jury—long in decline—has now all but disappeared. Among the factors responsible for this decline is a growing concern that juries lack the expertise necessary to resolve the kinds of complex disputes that have become increasingly common in a modern, technologically sophisticated social and economic environment.[74] To the extent that we wish to revive the jury in any fashion, our best chance of doing so might thus be to develop specialized courts calling on expert jurors to sit alongside the judge.

Any attempt to devise courts of this kind would, of course, require us to address numerous problems of implementation that lie far beyond the scope of this book. There are important questions about the kinds of expertise we attempt to represent on such courts. Would we confine ourselves to commerce and/or labor, the forms of expertise that are most prominently featured within European court systems, or would we experiment with juries of engineers, medical doctors, and others? So too, there are difficult questions about how to select the expert jurors and how to ensure the compatibility of the selection process with existing requirements that the jury pool be "selected at random from a fair cross section of the community in the district or division wherein the court convenes."[75] Moreover, how should we go about dividing responsibilities between the professional judge and lay jurors? Perhaps, most importantly, in answering these various questions, we must remain attentive to the risk that, even while such specialized courts might deploy their communally grounded legitimacy in ways that serve to decrease the costs of litigation, an overreliance on communal norms might also end up reproducing precisely those forms of social hierarchy whose influence we seek to exclude from the adjudicatory process.

As this brief exploration of the possibilities for reconfiguring masters and experts suggests, it is far from clear at this stage what precise set of reforms would be optimal. But the broader lessons of the history recounted here are readily apparent. Both equity and conciliation courts were premised on the principle that procedure is inseparable from substantive justice—a principle that has profound implications not only for how we study the history of procedure, but more importantly, for how we go about constructing our procedural system(s) and thereby delivering justice. Our present-day procedural landscape is a complex hodgepodge of forms in which traditional adversarial processes operate alongside an array of administrative, private, and other non-adversarial proceedings. But American legal actors of all stripes and, indeed, Americans as a whole continue to conceive of our legal system as fundamentally (and distinctively) adversarial. Especially as combined with a commitment to transsubstantive procedure, this continued embrace of adversarialism has led to a world in which differences in the disputants' wealth and power are all too easily reflected in outcomes—and indeed, in the ability to obtain access to a forum in the first place. But we need not throw up our hands in despair. Contrary to our most deep-rooted assumptions, the American commitment to adversarialism is not somehow encoded in our DNA but is instead the product of a particular set of socioeconomic, political, and cultural struggles. By remembering the contingent and contested nature of our nineteenth-century embrace of adversarialism, we can finally begin the hard work of freeing ourselves from its shackles.

# APPENDIX

## An Overview of the Archives

The archival holdings of the New York Court of Chancery are housed primarily at the State Archives in Albany.[1] While these holdings are sizeable, the vast majority date from the nineteenth century onward. In fact, there appears to be only one major series of chancery papers dating back prior to 1800. Unfortunately, this series—J0065—is incredibly scattered and incomplete. Although documents in the series extend from 1684 through 1800, the great majority are from the latter half of the eighteenth century.[2] Moreover, much of the documentation for these suits is missing—likely because, as discussed below, it was only in 1801 that chancery developed the practice of collecting all the records from a given suit in a single file. Within the series, case records are organized alphabetically by the first letter of the last name of the complainant. Within each of these letter groups, the initial documents that have been preserved—on the order of 7 to 12 percent of the total—consist exclusively of court decrees from the 1780s and 1790s.[3] Most of the remaining documents consist of a single pleading (usually either a bill or an answer) preserved for each suit—a small handful of which date as far back as the late seventeenth century, though most date to the period after 1750, including especially the 1780s and 1790s. Scattered among these pleadings are some records of the testimony taken—sometimes accompanied by a pleading, though often without any other documentation from the suit.

Given the vast lacunae in these pre-nineteenth-century materials, it is impossible to treat them as a comprehensive record of chancery practice. Moreover, the kinds of documents that are of particular interest in this study—namely, documents (like master's reports, interrogatories, and depositions) that reveal the distinctively quasi-inquisitorial nature of chancery practice—are precisely those that appear to be in especially short supply. While their (relative) absence from the archival records could, of course, be an indication that these documents were never created, this hypothesis makes little sense given the nature of the records that have survived. The one document that we know must have been filed in every case was a bill of complaint. But for numerous suits contained in Series J0065, there is no complaint preserved. This clearly indicates that many documents have been lost. Thus, while sufficient masters' reports, interrogatories, and depositions have been preserved to indicate that the quasi-inquisitorial practices resulting in their production were common, the surviving (pre-1800) documentation is such that it does not permit meaningful quantification of the nature and frequency of such practices.

In addition to the J0065 Series, I also examined books containing court orders and minutes of proceedings. While these books span the period from 1701 to 1770, there are enormous gaps in the time period covered.[4] Moreover, much of the documentation preserved is in the nature of a single court order from a case. Absent additional documentation to provide context, such orders provide little indication of the subject matter of the litigation, let alone the overarching procedural practice deployed to resolve it.

For all these reasons, I focused my archival research primarily on those cases filed from 1801 onward. As of that year, the New York State legislature required that all final decisions (known as "decrees") be "enrolled," meaning that these decisions would be filed along with all other papers from the case—thus making it much easier to gain an overview of the procedural mechanisms responsible for moving any one suit forward. Such enrolled decrees (available in Series J0063) date from 1801 through 1847, when—in accordance with the decision reached by the New York Constitutional Convention of 1846—chancery was abolished and its jurisdiction transferred to a newly constituted supreme court. Those cases dating from 1823 onward represent only a portion of the total number of suits filed in equity since, as we have seen, the state legislature that year created eight circuit judges endowed with jurisdiction in both law and equity. While the chancellor and the circuit judges were granted "concurrent jurisdiction" in equity, the chancellor preserved exclusive jurisdiction over those matters transcending any given circuit.[5] The J0063 Series includes those (post-1823) matters decided by the chancellor, rather than by the circuit judges.

J0063 is a very large series, encompassing approximately 120 cubic feet of records. Indeed, most of the individual case files are themselves voluminous, containing, in addition to the final decision or decree, the pleadings (including complaint, answer, and replication), additional court orders, masters' reports, depositions of testimony, and notices filed. Since the practice in preparing both pleadings and court orders was to repeat language multiple times, many of these individual documents are themselves quite lengthy. So too, they are drafted in handwriting that is often quite difficult to decipher—though from about 1830 onward, the record reflects a growing number of pre-printed forms. It bears emphasis, moreover, that even after 1801, there were many cases in which no decree was ever enrolled, either because the case settled or because it was dismissed pursuant to a court order that did not give rise to an enrolled decree as such. While papers from these cases were all filed together beginning in 1801 (and are now available in Series J0070), the lack of an enrolled decree (and usually any other court order) means that it is often impossible to determine how these suits were ulti-mately resolved.

For these reasons, I opted to approach these post-1800 materials in two different ways. First, in order to gain reliable information about standard court procedure, I pursued a systematic review of a carefully selected sample of records from J0063. Sec-ond, in an effort to supplement and broaden this review, I undertook a more informal exploration of files culled through extensive reading from both J0063 and J0070.

For purposes of the systematic review, I focused on enrolled decrees only, since these records (located in Series J0063) are the ones that provide the most comprehen-sive information for any single case—including, in particular, information about court actions. Within the series, cases are organized alphabetically by the first letter of the last name of the complainant. But within each letter group (the As, Bs, Cs, etc.), rec-ords are listed chronologically and identified by consecutive number (A1, A2, A3, etc.). Because the Archives place strict limits on the number of cartons (or reels of micro-film) one can review at any given time, sampling broadly across the entire alphabet was, as a practical matter, infeasible. Relying on the inherently arbitrary nature of al-phabetization, I opted to study those cases listed under B and S, as these are the letters under which the greatest number of cases are filed—namely, 512 B cases and 406 S ones. The index of the J0063 series (itself labeled J0064) contains a dividing line, separating cases prior to roughly mid-1823 from those decided thereafter. This line, which appears to reflect Nathan Sanford's August 1823 rise to the chancellorship, di-vides the records into two almost equal chronological periods. But notably, only about 24 percent of all the B cases and about 30 percent of all the S cases were decided in the first of these two periods.[6] Accordingly, given the relatively small proportion of B and S cases that were decided prior to mid-1823, I opted systematically to read and code all 244 of these and to reserve sampling for the 672 cases decided thereafter. As concerns the latter, I read and coded every third case, such that I was left with a sample of roughly the same size as the pre-mid-1823 cases—namely, 222.

**Table 1:  Sample of 466 Cases Filed under the Letters B and S from Series J0063**

Distribution of Types of Case

| Type of Case | Number of Cases | Percentage of Cases in Sample |
|---|---|---|
| Foreclosure & Sale | 279 | 59.9% |
| Injunction | 51 | 10.9% |
| Divorce | 27 | 5.8% |
| Distribution of Estate | 20 | 4.3% |
| Specific Performance | 17 | 3.6% |
| Rescission of K | 15 | 3.2% |
| Partition of Land | 13 | 2.8% |
| Trust | 13 | 2.8% |
| Separation of Bed and Board | 9 | 1.9% |
| Unclear | 8 | 1.7% |
| Accounting | 4 | 0.9% |
| Dower | 3 | 0.6% |
| Partnership | 3 | 0.6% |
| Agency | 1 | 0.2% |
| Maintenance of "Lunatic" | 1 | 0.2% |
| Quiet Title | 1 | 0.2% |
| Vacatur of Arbitral Award | 1 | 0.2% |

*Note:* Because chancery jurisdiction could be based on the subject matter of the dispute or on the nature of the remedy sought, the types of cases identified in this table reflect both these bases for jurisdiction. In the handful of cases in which both kinds of jurisdiction were present, I coded the case based on the subject matter at issue.

**Table 2: Sample of 466 Cases Filed under the Letters B and S from Series J0063**

Distribution of Cases (by Type) Known to Be Taken *Pro Confesso*

| Type of Case | *Pro Confesso* as to All Defendants | *Pro Confesso* as to Some Defendants |
|---|---|---|
| Accounting | 0 | 0 |
| Agency | 1 | 0 |
| Distribution of Estate | 6 | 2 |
| Divorce | 24 | 0 |
| Dower | 1 | 0 |
| Foreclosure & Sale | 222 | 17 |
| Injunction | 11 | 1 |
| Maintenance of "Lunatic" | 0 | 0 |
| Partition of Land | 8 | 0 |
| Partnership | 1 | 0 |
| Quiet Title | 0 | 0 |
| Rescission of K | 1 | 0 |
| Separation of Bed and Board | 5 | 0 |
| Specific Performance | 2 | 3 |
| Trust | 2 | 3 |
| Vacatur of Arbitral Award | 1 | 0 |
| Unclear | 0 | 0 |

*Note:* In seven of the 466 cases the surviving documentation does not permit a determination as to whether the bill was taken *pro confesso*.

**Table 3: Sample of 466 Cases Filed under the Letters B and S from Series J0063**

Distribution of Cases (by Type) Involving the Taking of Testimony

| Type of Case | Number of Cases in Which Testimony Was Taken | Percentage of Cases of a Given Type in Which Testimony Was Taken |
|---|---|---|
| Accounting | 2 | 50.0% |
| Agency | 0 | 0.0% |
| Distribution of Estate | 6 | 30.0% |
| Divorce | 25 | 92.6% |
| Dower | 1 | 33.3% |
| Foreclosure & Sale | 50 | 17.9% |
| Injunction | 21 | 41.2% |
| Maintenance of "Lunatic" | 1 | 100.0% |
| Partition of Land | 2 | 15.4% |
| Partnership | 2 | 66.7% |
| Quiet Title | 0 | 0.0% |
| Rescission of K | 10 | 66.7% |
| Separation of Bed and Board | 5 | 55.6% |
| Specific Performance | 10 | 58.8% |
| Trust | 5 | 38.5% |
| Vacatur of Arbitral Award | 0 | 0.0% |
| Unclear | 2 | 25.0% |

*Note:* As reflected in the table, there were only two suits to partition land in which testimony was procured in the normal course. That said, in an additional six suits (not reflected in the table), the court appointed a commission to partition, which can be understood as serving a function not dissimilar to that served by witness testimony.

# Notes

## Introduction

1. Stephan Landsman, *Readings on Adversarial Justice: The American Approach to Adjudication* (St. Paul, Minn.: West Publishing Co., 1988), 1.

2. There are studies of particular procedural devices that we associate with the adversarial system, such as the origins of the jury or, more recently, cross-examination. But a procedural system is much more than the sum of its parts. For example, we tend to think of the jury as a fundamental component of adversarial procedure. But despite the fact that the jury trial has become such a rarity today, few, if any, would argue that the American legal system has ceased to be adversarial.

3. See, for example, John H. Langbein, Renée Lettow Lerner, and Bruce P. Smith, *History of the Common Law: The Development of Anglo-American Legal Institutions* (Austin, Tex.: Wolters Kluwer Law & Business, 2009). See also Stephen N. Subrin, "David Dudley Field and the Field Code: A Historical Analysis of an Earlier Procedural Vision," *Law and History Review* 6 (1988): 311, 341–42 (critiquing scholars' tendency to discuss procedure "as if rules simply arrived, impelled by neither people nor ideology" and insisting that "civil procedure . . . is part of a larger socio-political universe").

4. Robert A. Ferguson, *Law and Letters in American Culture* (Cambridge: Harvard University Press, 1984), 5–8, 81–84; Daniel Hulsebosch, *Constituting Empire: New York and the Transformation of Constitutionalism in the Atlantic World, 1664–1830* (Chapel Hill: University of North Carolina Press, 2005), 204–06.

5. Mirjan R. Damaška, *The Faces of Justice and State Authority: A Comparative Approach to the Legal Process* (New Haven: Yale University Press, 1986), 3; Adhémar Esmein, *A History of Continental Criminal Procedure: With Special Reference to France*, trans. John Simpson (Boston: Little, Brown and Co., 1913), 3–12.

6. Arthur Engelmann et al., *A History of Continental Civil Procedure*, trans. Robert Wyness Millar (Boston: Little, Brown, and Company, 1927), 3–81.

7. In thirteenth-century continental Europe, the decline of the judicial ordeal was accompanied by the rise of the Roman-canon, inquisitorial system of procedure and evidence, including the quantitative system of proof. Historians widely agree that there is an important causal relation between these two developments, though there are strong disagreements concerning the precise nature of this relation. Compare, for example, John H. Langbein, *Torture and the Law of Proof: Europe and England in the Ancien Régime* (Chicago: University of Chicago Press, 1977) with James Q. Whitman, *The Origins of Reasonable Doubt: Theological Roots of the Criminal Trial* (New Haven: Yale University Press, 2008). But whichever account one adopts, there is good reason to conclude that the linkage between a system dependent on powerful judges and the use of quantitative proof was contingent on many historical particulars. It is possible to imagine a system in which powerful judges rely on free evaluation of the evidence—as is largely the case, for example, in continental Europe today.

8. Landsman, *Readings on Adversarial Justice* 1.

9. The exceptions include Christopher Columbus Langdell, *A Summary of Equity Pleading* (Cambridge, Mass.: Charles W. Sever, 1877), xix–xxvii; Michael R. T. Macnair, *The Law of Proof in Early Modern Equity* (Berlin: Duncker & Humboldt, 1999), 25–40. See also Mary Sarah Bilder, "The Origin of Appeal in America," *Hastings Law Journal* 48 (1997): 913–68 (describing the equity-based origins of American appeal).

10. Amalia D. Kessler, "Our Inquisitorial Tradition: Equity Procedure, Due Process, and the Search for an Alternative to the Adversarial," *Cornell Law Review* 90 (2005): 1239 n. 305.

11. David Alan Sklansky, "Anti-Inquisitorialism," *Harvard Law Review* 122 (2009): 1635–38.

12. Damaška, *Faces of Justice and State Authority* 4; see also Sklansky 1635, 1639.

13. Landsman, *Readings on Adversarial Justice* 41; Oscar G. Chase, "American 'Exceptionalism' and Comparative Procedure," *American Journal of Comparative Law* 50 (2002): 283–84; Monroe H. Freedman, "Our Constitutionalized Adversary System," *Chapman Law Review* 1 (1998): 57–58.

14. Jack P. Greene, *The Intellectual Construction of America: Exceptionalism and Identity from 1492 to 1800* (Chapel Hill: University of North Carolina Press, 1993), 1–161. See also Deborah L. Madsen, *American Exceptionalism* (Edinburgh: Edinburgh University Press, 1998); Seymour Martin Lipset, *American Exceptionalism: A Double-Edged Sword* (New York: W. W. Norton, 1996); Sean Wilentz, "Against Exceptionalism: Class Consciousness and the American Labor Movement, 1790–1920," *International Labor and Working Class History* 26 (1984): 1–24; Harold Hongju Koh, "On American Exceptionalism," *Stanford Law Review* 55 (2003): 1479–1527.

15. Cf. Daniel Hannan, *Inventing Freedom: How the English-Speaking Peoples Made the Modern World* (New York: Broadside Books, 2013).

16. For an overview of work in this internalist vein, see Langbein, Lerner, and Smith.

17. See, for example, Ferguson.

18. Charles M. Cook, *The American Codification Movement: A Study of Antebellum Legal Reform,* (Westport, Conn.: Greenwood Press, 1981), 3–66, 158–70; Charles E. Clark, "Code Pleading and Practice Today," in *David Dudley Field: Centenary Essays Celebrating One Hundred Years of Legal Reform,* ed. Alison Reppy (New York: New York University School of Law, 1949), 56; Daun van Ee, *David Dudley Field and the Reconstruction of the Law* (New York: Garland, 1986), 21–28. Another, more externalist version of this functionalist account suggests instead that in a country dominated by middle-class interests, procedural rationalization was vital for establishing the legal clarity and predictability required for sustained market growth. Lawrence M. Friedman, "Law Reform in Historical Perspective," *Saint Louis University Law Journal* 13 (1969): 367–70.

19. Morton J. Horwitz, *The Transformation of American Law, 1780–1860* (Cambridge: Harvard University Press, 1977), 265–66; Robert W. Gordon, "Book Review: The American Codification Movement," *Vanderbilt Law Review* 36 (1983): 437–44.

20. Horwitz 265–66; R. W. Gordon, "Book Review" 437–44.

21. R. W. Gordon, "Book Review" 432.

22. *Kring v. Missouri,* 107 U.S. 221, 231 (1883). See also Bruce A. Kimball and R. Blake Brown, " 'The Highest Legal Ability in the Nation': Langdell on Wall Street, 1855–1870," *Law and Social Inquiry* 29 (2004): 72–73 (noting the "eminence" of the various lawyers, including judges and politicians, responsible for drafting entries in *Bouvier's Law Dictionary*).

23. *Bouvier's Law Dictionary,* ed. Francis Rawle, s.v. "Procedure" (Boston: The Boston Book Co., 1897), 2:764. That a new conception of procedure had arisen, however, well before the end of the century is clear from the changing definition of *practice* that appears in earlier editions of Bouvier's and other contemporary law dictionaries. The 1843 edition of Bouvier's dictionary defined *practice* primarily as "[t]he form, manner, and order of conducting and carrying on suits. . . ." John Bouvier, *A Law Dictionary Adapted to the Constitution and Laws of the United States of America, and of the Several States of the Union, with References to the Civil Law and Other Systems of Foreign Law,* s.v. "Practice" (Philadelphia: T. & J. W. Johnson, 1843), 2:348. Evidently drawing on this language, Burrill's 1851 dictionary likewise defined *practice* as "[t]he form, manner, and order of conducting and carrying on . . . suits . . .," while also noting that "[i]n a general sense, *practice* includes *pleading,* though it is usually distinguished from it." Alexander M. Burrill, *A Law Dictionary and Glossary: Containing Full Definitions of the Principal Terms of the Common and Civil Law, Together with Translations and Explanations of the Various Technical Phrases in Different Languages, Occurring in the Ancient and Modern Reports, and Standard Treatises, Embracing, Also, All the Principal Common and Civil Law Maxims, Compiled on the Basis of Spelman's Glossary, and Adapted to the Jurisprudence of the United States, with Copious Illustrations, Critical and Historical,* s.v. "Practice" (New York: John S. Voorhies, 1851), 2:816. But the 1860 edition of Burrill's dictionary defined

*practice* primarily as "[t]he course of procedure in courts." Alexander M. Burrill, *A Law Dictionary and Glossary: Containing Full Definitions of the Principal Terms of the Common and Civil Law, Together with Translations and Explanations of the Various Technical Phrases in Different Languages, Occurring in the Ancient and Modern Reports, and Standard Treatises, Embracing, Also, All the Principal Common and Civil Law Maxims, Compiled on the Basis of Spelman's Glossary, and Adapted to the Jurisprudence of the United States, with Copious Illustrations, Critical and Historical*, 2d ed., s.v. "Practice" (New York: John S. Voorhies, 1860), 2:319.

24. Horwitz 1–30; William E. Nelson, *Americanization of the Common Law: The Impact of Legal Change on Massachusetts Society, 1760–1830*, rev. ed. (Athens: University of Georgia Press, 1994), 69–88; Thomas C. Grey, "Accidental Torts," *Vanderbilt Law Review* 54 (2001): 1231 n. 10. See also Charles Donahue Jr., " 'The Hypostasis of a Prophecy': Legal Realism and Legal History," in *Law and Legal Process: Substantive Law and Procedure in English Legal History*, ed. Matthew Dyson and David Ibbetson (Cambridge: Cambridge University Press, 2013), 12–16 (providing a comparative overview of the rise of the substance/procedure distinction).

25. Nelson xv–xvi; Daniel J. Hulsebosch, "Writs to Rights: 'Navigability' and the Transformation of the Common Law in the Nineteenth Century," *Cardozo Law Review* 23 (2002): 1050–54; John Fabian Witt, *The Accidental Republic: Crippled Workingmen, Destitute Widows, and the Remaking of American Law* (Cambridge: Harvard University Press, 2004), 1–70; William P. LaPiana, *Logic and Experience: The Origin of Modern American Legal Education* (Oxford: Oxford University Press, 1994). See also John H. Langbein, "Historical Foundations of the Law of Evidence: A View from the Ryder Sources," *Columbia Law Review* 96 (1996): 1178–79 (identifying a complex array of causes—procedural, technological, and socioeconomic—that led to a paucity of suits sounding in tort prior to the nineteenth and especially twentieth centuries). As concerns the category of contract, Brian Simpson emphasizes the important role played by the translation of continental European treatises into English, including especially the 1806 translation of Robert Pothier's *Traité des obligations*. Brian Simpson, "Innovation in Nineteenth Century Contract Law," *Law Quarterly Review* 91 (1975): 250–57.

26. Paul MacMahon, "Proceduralism, Civil Justice, and American Legal Thought," *University of Pennsylvania Journal of International Law* 34 (2013): 605–09. While the drafters of the Federal Rules of Civil Procedure espoused the notion that procedure was to be merely "the handmaid of justice," there is good reason to conclude that, as argued below, this view never in practice became dominant within American legal culture. Charles E. Clark, "The Handmaid of Justice," *Washington University Law Quarterly* 23 (1938): 297–320.

27. Oscar G. Chase, *Law, Culture, and Ritual: Disputing Systems in Cross-Cultural Context* (New York: New York University Press, 2005), 2; Laura Nader and Harry F. Todd Jr., eds., *The Disputing Process—Law in Ten Societies* (New York: Columbia University Press,

1978); Simon Roberts, *Order and Dispute: An Introduction to Legal Anthropology* (New York: St. Martin's Press, 1979).

28. James Willard Hurst, *The Growth of American Law: The Law Makers* (Boston: Little Brown and Company, 1950), 342–52; Lawrence M. Friedman, *A History of American Law*, 3d ed. (New York: Touchstone, 2005), 329–49.

29. Robert A. Kagan, *Adversarial Legalism: The American Way of Law* (Cambridge: Harvard University Press, 2001), 14–16, 34–58; John Fabian Witt, *Patriots and Cosmopolitans: Hidden Histories of American Law* (Cambridge: Harvard University Press, 2007), 209–84. In explaining why the mid-twentieth-century United States went down a unique adversarial path, Kagan emphasizes certain inherited features of the American landscape, such as the common law, fragmented government, and a political culture long fearful of a powerful state. Witt adds to these a number of more historically contingent developments, including the remarkable partnership forged in the 1950s between New Deal critic Roscoe Pound and famed tort lawyer Melvin Belli.

30. Milton M. Klein, *The Empire State: A History of New York* (Ithaca: Cornell University Press, 2001), 257–89, 307–23, 346–57; Hulsebosch, *Constituting Empire* 1–3; Herbert Hovenkamp, "The Classical Corporation in American Legal Thought," *Georgetown Law Journal* 76 (1988): 1654–59.

31. Another indication of New York's legal predominance is that after the state's constitutional convention of 1846, when many other states called their own constitutional conventions in imitation of New York practice, and in so doing, often borrowed extensively from the New York text. Jed Handelsman Shugerman, *The People's Courts: Pursuing Judicial Independence in America* (Cambridge: Harvard University Press, 2012), 100–02. But see also Nancy Buenger, "Extraordinary Remedies: The Court of Chancery and Equitable Justice in Chicago" (Ph.D. diss., University of Chicago, 2009), 3–4 (observing that efforts to quantify—and thereby establish—the influence of the Field Code have been flawed and inconsistent).

32. Kessler, "Our Inquisitorial Tradition" 1226–33.

## Chapter 1. The "Natural Elevation" of Equity

1. Stanley N. Katz, "The Politics of Law in Colonial America: Controversies over Chancery Courts and Equity Law in the Eighteenth Century," in *Law in American History*, vol. 5, *Perspectives in American History*, ed. Donald Fleming and Bernard Bailyn (Cambridge: Harvard University Press, 1971), 263–73, 282–83. While the English Revolution played a key role in catalyzing antipathy to chancery (including in colonial America and the early United States), English Parliament's distaste for the institution dates back as far as the fourteenth century—to the period when chancery's jurisdiction began significantly to expand, permitting actions where there was no applicable common law writ. Langbein, Lerner, and Smith 288–89.

2. J. G. A. Pocock, *The Ancient Constitution and the Feudal Law: A Study of English Historical Thought in the Seventeenth Century*, 2d ed. (Cambridge: Cambridge University Press, 1987); D.E.C. Yale, Introduction to *Lord Nottingham's Manual of Chancery Practice and Prolegomena of Chancery and Equity*, ed. D.E.C. Yale (Cambridge: Cambridge University Press, 1965), 7–8; Louis A. Knafla, *Law and Politics in Jacobean England: The Tracts of Lord Chancellor Ellesmere* (Cambridge: Cambridge University Press, 1977), 162–63.

3. An Act to Establish the Judicial Courts of the United States, ch. 20, 1 Stat. 73, 88, § 30 (1789). This provision of the statute was short-lived as, not long thereafter, federal courts sitting in equity resumed the traditional equitable approach to taking testimony. Kessler, "Our Inquisitorial Tradition" 1204–05.

4. Friedman, *History of American Law* 98; Henry H. Ingersoll, "Confusion of Law and Equity," *Yale Law Journal* 21 (1911): 58–71; George P. Roach, "Unjust Enrichment in Texas: Is It A Floor Wax or A Dessert Topping?" *Baylor Law Review* 65 (2013): 176 & n. 130 (noting that as of 2013, Tennessee, Mississippi, and Delaware are the only states with separate chancery courts and that New Jersey, while lacking a distinctive chancery, "maintains a separate equity division within trial courts of general jurisdiction").

5. John H. Langbein, "Chancellor Kent and the History of Legal Literature," *Columbia Law Review* 93 (1993): 571–84; Friedman, *History of American Law* 98.

6. Thomas O. Main, "Reconsidering Procedural Conformity Statutes," *Western State University Law Review* 35 (2007): 77–78; Stephen Subrin, "How Equity Conquered Common Law: The Federal Rules of Civil Procedure in Historical Perspective," *University of Pennsylvania Law Review* 135 (1987): 943–75. But see also John B. Oakley and Arthur F. Coon, "The Federal Rules in State Courts: A Survey of State Court Systems of Civil Procedure," *Washington Law Review* 61 (1986): 1369, 1425–27 (arguing that, while the Federal Rules have exerted "pervasive influence . . . on at least some part of every state's civil procedure," only twenty-three states can be said to have embraced rules that are true "federal replicas").

7. James R. Bryant, "The Office of the Master in Chancery: Colonial Development," *American Bar Association Journal* 40, no. 7 (July 1954): 595.

8. Claire Priest, "Creating an American Property Law: Alienability and Its Limits in American History," *Harvard Law Review* 120 (2006): 458–59; Winifred Barr Rothenberg, *From Market-Places to a Market Economy: The Transformation of Rural Massachusetts, 1750–1850* (Chicago: University of Chicago Press, 1992), 125–26, 242–44; Bruce H. Mann, *Republic of Debtors: Bankruptcy in the Age of American Independence* (Cambridge: Harvard University Press, 2002), 1–33; James Steven Rogers, *The Early History of the Law of Bills and Notes: A Study of the Origins of Anglo-American Commercial Law* (Cambridge: Cambridge University Press, 1995); T. H. Breen, *The Marketplace of Revolution: How Consumer Politics Shaped American Independence* (New York: Oxford University Press, 2004), xv, 36–71.

9. Charles Sellers, *The Market Revolution: Jacksonian America, 1815–1846* (New York: Oxford University Press, 1991); Daniel Walker Howe, *What Hath God Wrought: The Transformation of America, 1815–1848* (New York: Oxford University Press, 2007), 5–7, 525–69.

10. Sellers 27–28; Sean Wilentz, "Society, Politics, and the Market Revolution, 1815–1848," in *The New American History,* 2d ed., ed. Eric Foner (Philadelphia: Temple University Press, 1997), 63; Harry L. Watson, *Liberty and Power: The Politics of Jacksonian America,* rev. ed. (New York: Hill and Wang, 2006), 17–41; Bruce Laurie, *Artisans into Workers: Labor in Nineteenth-Century America* (New York: Hill and Wang, 1989), 28–43.

11. Theodore Sedgwick Jr., *A Statement of Facts in Relation to the Delays and Arrears of Business in the Court of Chancery of the State of New York, with Some Suggestions for a Change in Its Organization* (New York: Alex S. Gould, 1838), 12–15.

12. Friedman, *History of American Law* 98; Phyllis Maloney Johnson, "No Adequate Remedy at Law: Equity in Massachusetts, 1692–1877" (2012), *Student Legal History Papers,* Paper 2, available at http://digitalcommons.law.yale.edu/student_legal_history _papers/2; Antony Laussat Jr., *An Essay on Equity in Pennsylvania* (Philadelphia: Robert Desilver, 1826), 40–84, 127–33.

13. Katz 263–64.

14. *Bradwell v. Weeks,* 1 Johns. Ch. 325 (N.Y. Ch. 1814); *Hamersly v. Lambert,* 2 Johns. Ch. 432 (N.Y. Ch. 1817); *Goodrich v. Pendleton,* 3 Johns. Ch. 384 (N.Y. Ch. 1818); *Troup v. Sherwood,* 3 Johns. Ch. 558 (N.Y. Ch. 1818).

15. *Methodist Episcopal Church v. Jaques,* 1 Johns. Ch. 65 (N.Y. Ch. 1814) (cited in argument by attorney); *Woods v. Morrell,* 1 Johns. Ch. 103 (N.Y. Ch. 1814); *Brown v. Ricketts,* 2 Johns. Ch. 425 (N.Y. Ch. 1817) (cited in argument by attorney); *Hamersly v. Lambert,* 2 Johns. Ch. 432 (N.Y. Ch. 1817); *Consequa v. Fanning,* 2 Johns. Ch. 481, (N.Y. Ch. 1817); *Livingston v. Kane,* 3 Johns. Ch. 224 (N.Y. Ch. 1817) (cited in argument by attorney); *Sherwood v. Wood,* 3 Johns. Ch. 558 (N.Y. Ch. 1818); *Hood v. Inman,* 4 Johns. Ch. 437 (N.Y. Ch. 1820) (cited in argument by attorney).

16. *Fort v. Ragusin,* 2 Johns. Ch. 146 (N.Y. Ch. 1816); *Consequa v. Fanning,* 2 Johns. Ch. 481, (N.Y. Ch. 1817); *Remsen v. Remsen,* 2 Johns. Ch. 495 (N.Y. Ch. 1817); *Dale v. Cooke,* 4 Johns. Ch. 11 (N.Y. Ch. 1819); *Campbell v. Mesier,* 4 Johns. Ch. 334, N.Y. Ch. 1820; *Ferris v. Nelson,* 5 Johns. Ch. 262 (N.Y. Ch. 1821) (cited in argument by attorney); *Mason v. Codwise,* 6 Johns. Ch. 183 (N.Y. Ch. 1822) (cited in argument by attorney); *Neafie v. Neafie,* 7 Johns. Ch. 1 (N.Y. Ch. 1823); *Galatian v. Erwin,* Hopk. Ch. 48 (N.Y. Ch. 1823).

17. *Perine v. Swaine,* 1 Johns. Ch. 24 (N.Y. Ch. 1814) (cited in argument by attorney); *Methodist Episcopal Church v. Jaques,* 1 Johns. Ch. 65 (N.Y. Ch. 1814); *Woods v. Morrell,* 1 Johns. Ch. 103 (N.Y. Ch. 1814); *Wiggins v. Armstrong,* 2 Johns. Ch. 144 (N.Y. Ch. 1816); *Attorney General v. Utica Insurance Co.,* 2 Johns. Ch. 371 (N.Y. Ch. 1817); *Brown v. Ricketts,* 2 Johns. Ch. 425 (N.Y. Ch. 1817); *Livingston v. Kane,* 3 Johns. Ch. 224 (N.Y. Ch. 1817)

(cited in argument by attorney); *Goodrich v. Pendleton,* 3 Johns. Ch. 384 (N.Y. Ch. 1818); *Bregaw v. Claw,* 4 Johns. Ch. 116 (N.Y. Ch. 1819) (cited in argument by attorney); *Ferris v. Nelson,* 5 Johns. Ch. 262 (N.Y. Ch. 1821) (cited in argument by attorney); *Renwick v. Wilson,* 6 Johns. Ch. 81 (N.Y. Ch. 1822) (cited in argument by attorney); *M'Dowl v. Charles,* 6 Johns. Ch. 132 (N.Y. Ch. 1822) (cited in argument by attorney); *Galatian v. Erwin,* Hopk. Ch. 48 (N.Y. Ch. 1823) (cited in argument by attorney).

18. Geoffrey Gilbert, *The History and Practice of the High Court of Chancery in Which Is Introduced an Account of the Institution and Various Regulations of the Said Court: Showing Likewise the Ancient and Present Practice Thereof, in an Easy and Familiar Method,* ed. Samuel Tyler (Washington, D.C.: W. H. & O. H. Morrison, 1874), v. The *Forum Romanum* appears as the first half of this book (1–228). Michael Macnair, "Sir Jeffrey Gilbert and His Treatises," *Journal of Legal History* 15 (1994): 252–68. John Langbein suggests that Gilbert's various treatises were likely extracted from a larger manuscript that remained unpublished (and perhaps incomplete) at the time of his death. John H. Langbein, entry on "Gilbert, Geoffrey (or Jeffray)," in *Biographical Dictionary of the Common Law,* ed. A.W.B. Simpson (London: Butterworths, 1984), 206.

19. Joseph Harrison, *The Practice of the Court of Chancery,* 2 vols. (Philadelphia: William P. Farrand, 1807); Henry Maddock, *A Treatise on the Principles and Practice of the High Court of Chancery,* 2 vols. (New York: Clayton and Kingsland, 1817). Maddock's treatise was subsequently reissued in revised American editions in 1822, 1827, and 1832.

20. Gilbert 20.

21. John Baker, *The Oxford History of the Laws of England,* vol. 6, *1483–1558* (Oxford: Oxford University Press, 2003), 180. See also Langdell, *Summary of Equity Pleading* xix–xxvii; John P. Dawson, *A History of Lay Judges* (Cambridge: Harvard University Press, 1960), 145–71; Macnair, *Law of Proof* 25–40.

22. Gilbert 14.

23. Dawson 152–54; Michael R. T. Macnair, *Law of Proof* 173; Richard Newcombe Gresley, *A Treatise on the Law of Evidence in the Courts of Equity* (Philadelphia: P. H. Nicklin & T. Johnson, 1837), 57.

24. Harrison 1:328.

25. Ibid., 1:273, 317.

26. Joseph Parkes, *A History of the Court of Chancery, with Practical Remarks on the Recent Commission, Report, and Evidence, and on the Means of Improving the Administration of Justice in the English Courts of Equity* (London: Longman, Rees, Orme, Brown, and Green, 1828), 449–51.

27. Harrison 2:94.

28. Maddock 2:391–92; Harrison 1:321–22.

29. Harrison 2:93.

30. Harrison 1:403; Maddock 2:330.

31. Gilbert 116; Harrison 1:353.

32. Gilbert 116; R. H. Helmholz, "The Bible in the Service of the Canon Law," *Chicago-Kent Law Review* 70 (1995): 1573–74. By ensuring a rapid, concentrated trial, common-law courts also minimized the extent to which parties—having heard unfavorable testimony—could seek out new testimony to counteract it. But the common law relied first and foremost on cross-examination as its means of pursuing truth.

33. Like equity, the common-law courts also presumed that most (sworn) witnesses were truthful. George Fisher, "The Jury's Rise as Lie Detector," *Yale Law Journal* 107 (1997): 625–30. But the two types of courts derived very different implications from this shared presumption.

34. Maddock 2:330.

35. Harrison 1:371; Simon Greenleaf, *A Treatise on the Law of Evidence* (Boston: C. C. Little & J. Brown, 1853), 3:382 (sec. 378). The extent to which, in practice, common law and equity courts differed in their approach to false testimony remains an open question. While Greenleaf insisted that equity was unique in its commitment to disregarding the entirety of a witness's testimony once a single falsehood was identified, George Fisher suggests that the rule of *falsus in uno, falsus in omnibus* was also applied at common law. Fisher 654–56.

36. Harrison 1:321.

37. Ibid., 1:310, 319, 337.

38. Ibid., 1:332; Gilbert 126.

39. Harrison 1:349; Gilbert 143; Maddock 2:317.

40. Harrison 1:353, 402.

41. Maddock 2:320.

42. Harrison 1:402.

43. Fisher 659–62; Joel N. Bodansky, "The Abolition of the Party-Witness Disqualification: An Historical Survey," *Kentucky Law Journal* 70 (1981–82): 91–93; Christopher Allen, *The Law of Evidence in Victorian England* (Cambridge: Cambridge University Press, 1997); Wesley J. Campbell, "Testimonial Exclusions and Religious Freedom in Early America," *Law and History Review* 33 (forthcoming).

44. Harrison 1:402; Maddock 2:322.

45. Harrison 1:400, 402.

46. Gilbert 116, 124; Harrison 1:311, 319.

47. Harrison 1:341.

48. Ibid., 1:321–22.

49. Langbein, "Chancellor Kent" 571–84; Friedman, *History of American Law* 241–44.

50. James Kent to Thomas Washington, October 6, 1828, James Kent Papers (reel 3, container 5), United States Library of Congress (USLC).

51. Joseph Smith, "Adolph Philipse," in *Courts and Law in Early New York: Selected Essays,* ed. Leo Hershkowitz and Milton M. Klein (Port Washington, N.Y.: Kennikat Press, 1978), 30; Katz 273.

52. For an overview of Lansing's biography, see Jon L. Wakelyn, *Birth of the Bill of Rights: Encyclopedia of the Antifederalists*, s.v. "John Lansing" (Westport, Conn.: Greenwood Press, 2004), 109–11.

53. Rules 22 and 23, in John Mitford, *A Treatise on the Pleadings in Suits in the Court of Chancery, by English Bill, with an Appendix, Containing the Rules and Orders of the Court of Chancery of the State of New York, Revised and Digested by James Kent, Esq., Chancellor* (New York: R. M'Dermut & D. D. Arden, 1816), 279.

54. Rules 22 and 27, in ibid., 279, 281.

55. Rules 30, 57, and 58, in ibid., 282, 293–94.

56. Julius Goebel Jr., *The Law Practice of Alexander Hamilton: Documents and Commentary* (New York: William Nelson Cromwell Foundation by Columbia University Press, 1964), 1:170–76.

57. See appendix.

58. *Bingham v. Bingham* (N.Y. Ch. 1792), Document B22, Series J0065, New York State Archives (NYSA); *Byvanck v. Byvanck* (N.Y. Ch. 1790), B27/J0065, NYSA; *Skinner v. Gray* (N.Y. Ch. 1789), S5/J0065, NYSA; *Stewart v. Stewart* (N.Y. Ch. 1798), S20/J0065, NYSA.

59. *Moster v. Bradley* (N.Y. Ch. 1726), D1845-4/J0090, NYSA (commissioners); *Brown v. Brown* (N.Y. Ch. 1786), B112/J0065, NYSA (examiner); *Brown v. Park* (N.Y. Ch. 1788), B130/J0065, NYSA (commissioners); *Shute v. White* (N.Y. Ch. 1795), S216/J0065, NYSA (examiner); *Schoomaker v. Wood* (N.Y. Ch. 1799), S267/J0065, NYSA (commissioners).

60. *Reports of the Proceedings and Debates of the Convention of 1821 Assembled for the Purpose of Amending the Constitution of the State of New York* (Albany: E. and E. Hosford, 1821), 506.

61. Joseph Story, "Chancery Jurisdiction," in *The Miscellaneous Writings of Joseph Story*, ed. William W. Story (Boston: C. C. Little & J. Brown, 1852), 169–70 (originally published in 1820).

62. Story, "Progress of Jurisprudence," in *Miscellaneous Writings* 234 (originally published in 1821).

63. Joseph Story, *Commentaries on Equity Jurisprudence, as Administered in England and America*, 2d ed. (London: A. Maxwell, 1839), 1:23.

64. James Kent to Thomas Washington, October 6, 1828.

65. Story, "Progress of Jurisprudence" 233–34.

66. Story, "Chancery Jurisdiction" 171.

67. James Kent, *Commentaries on American Law*, 3d ed. (New York: E. B. Clayton, James Van Norden, 1836), 1:489.

68. Story, *Commentaries on Equity Jurisprudence* 1:16.

69. Story, "Chancery Jurisdiction" 150.

70. Story, "Growth of the Commercial Law," in *Miscellaneous Writings* 288 (originally published in 1825).

71. Baker, *Oxford History* 180–81.

72. Kent, *Commentaries* 1:515.

73. Story, *Commentaries on Equity Jurisprudence* 1:20.

74. Story, "Course of Legal Study," in *Miscellaneous Writings* 66; Kent, *Commentaries* 1:546.

75. Story, "Progress of Jurisprudence" 235. See also Kent, *Commentaries* 4:411–12; John Theodore Horton, *James Kent: A Study in Conservatism, 1763–1847* (New York: D. Appleton-Century Co., 1939), 89–90.

76. Story, "Progress of Jurisprudence" 234–35.

77. Ibid., 235.

78. James Gordley, "Comparative Legal Research: Its Function in the Development of Harmonized Law," *American Journal of Comparative Law* 43 (1995): 558–59.

79. Nicolaus Heinrich Julius to James Kent, April 30, 1838, James Kent Papers (reel 5, container 9), USLC.

80. James Kent to Thomas Washington, October 6, 1828.

81. Nicolaus Heinrich Julius to James Kent, April 30, 1838; Richard J. Evans, *Tales from the German Underworld: Crime and Punishment in the Nineteenth Century* (New Haven: Yale University Press, 1998), 63; Hulsebosch, *Constituting Empire* 283; Alan Watson, "Chancellor Kent's Use of Foreign Law," in *The Reception of Continental Ideas in the Common Law World, 1820–1920*, ed. Mathias Reimann (Berlin: Duncker and Humblot, 1993), 45; Alan Watson, *Joseph Story and the Comity of Errors: A Case Study in Conflicts of Law* (Athens: University of Georgia Press, 1992).

82. Charles Jerome, G. T. Curtis, and J. K. Will, Committee of Hamilton College to James Kent, October 27, 1838, James Kent Papers (reel 5, container 9), USLC. See also Angela Fernandez, "Pierson v. Post: A Great Debate, James Kent, and the Project of Building a Learned Law for New York State," *Law and Social Inquiry* 34 (2009): 301–36; Perry Miller, *The Life of the Mind in America: From the Revolution to the Civil War* (New York: Harcourt, Brace & World, 1965), 164–71.

83. Story, "Chancery Jurisdiction" 149.

84. Story, *Commentaries on Equity Jurisprudence* 2:686–87.

85. David B. Ogden, John Ducy, George Woods, Dabiel Lords Jr., George Griffens, Beverly Robinson, Benjamin F. Butler, Charles Channoy, J. Prescott Halls, Samuel B. Ruggles, Francis B. Cutting, James W. Gesard, George H. Strong, Thomas L. Ogden, David S. Jones, Samuel A. Foot, Benjamin D. Silliman, Ogden Hoffman, James R. Whiting, James S Brady, David Graham Jr., R. L. Robertson, Theodore Scogisick, John Anthow, Murray Hoffman, Abraham Priest/Crist, Joseph S. Bosworth, Ambrose L. Jordan, John W. Edmonds, Edward Sandford to James Kent, July 31, 1843, James Kent Papers (reel 5, container 10), USLC.

86. James Kent to Thomas Washington, October 6, 1828. See also Susanna L. Blumenthal, "Law and the Creative Mind," *Chicago-Kent Law Review* 74 (1998): 166–213 (discussing the nineteenth-century emergence of a "romantic judicial ideal").

87. James Kent to Thomas Washington, October 6, 1828.

88. William W. Story, *Life and Letters of Joseph Story, Associate Justice of the Supreme Court of the United States and Dane Professor of Law at Harvard University* (Boston: Charles C. Little and James Brown, 1851), 2:586.

89. Quoted in William Johnson to James Kent, November 22, 1816, James Kent Papers (reel 2, container 4), USLC.

90. Story, *Life and Letters* 180 (quoting May 15, 1834, letter from James Kent to Joseph Story).

91. James Kent to Thomas Washington, October 6, 1828.

92. James Kent to Daniel Webster, January 21, 1830, James Kent Papers (reel 3, container 6), USLC; Horton 292.

93. R. Kent Newmyer, *Supreme Court Justice Joseph Story: Statesman of the Old Republic* (Chapel Hill: University of North Carolina, Press, 1985), 53–59, 158–62, 172–73; Story, "Autobiography," in *Miscellaneous Writings* 33 (quoting January 23, 1831, letter from Joseph Story to William W. Story).

94. Miller, *Life of the Mind* 171–82 (describing how antebellum lawyers, including Kent and Story, conceived of equity as an anti-democratic force). See also Stephen Botein, "'What We Shall Meet Afterwards in Heaven': Judgeship as a Symbol for Modern American Lawyers," in *Professions and Professional Ideologies in America,* ed. Gerald L. Geison (Chapel Hill: University of North Carolina Press, 1983), 50–54 (arguing that antebellum lawyers created an idealized model of judgeship as a way of suggesting, inter alia, that the legal profession retained its elite character, despite increased democratization).

95. Benjamin L. Oliver, *The Rights of an American Citizen; with a Commentary on State Rights, and on the Constitution and Policy of the United States* (Boston: Marsh, Capen, and Lyon, 1832), 273; Conway Robinson, *The Practice in the Courts of Law and Equity in Virginia* (Richmond: Shepherd and Colin, 1839), 3:233 (citing *Commonwealth of Massachusetts v. Joseph Jenkins Knapp,* 10 Pick. 477 (1830)).

96. Newmyer 162 (quoting Story).

97. Larry Kramer, *The People Themselves: Popular Constitutionalism and Judicial Review* (New York: Oxford University Press, 2004), 116–27; Hulsebosch, *Constituting Empire* 289–92.

98. The uniqueness of the equity judge's procedural power was highlighted by the fact that, at the very time that Story was writing about equity in the mid-1830s, his common-law counterparts were beginning to lose substantial elements of their authority—including perhaps most importantly, the power to shape jury verdicts by commenting on the evidence. Kenneth A. Krasity, "Role of the Judge in Jury Trials: The Elimination of Judicial Evaluation of Fact in American State Courts from 1795 to 1913," *University of Detroit Law Review* 62 (1985): 595, 597–609; Renée Lettow Lerner, "The Transformation of the American Civil Trial: The Silent Judge," *William and Mary Law Review* 42 (2000): 242–61.

99. Story, *Commentaries on Equity Jurisprudence* 1:viii.

100. Gerald J. Postema, *Bentham and the Common Law Tradition* (Oxford: Oxford University Press, 1986), 342.

101. Joseph Story, *Commentaries on Equity Pleadings and the Incidents Thereof According to the Practice of the Courts of Equity of England and America,* 2d ed. (Boston: Charles C. Little & James Brown, 1840), 3, x.

102. Story, *Commentaries on Equity Jurisprudence* 1:1, 21.

103. Ibid., 1:21. While remedies are viewed today as distinct from both substance and procedure, this understanding emerged only gradually and as a result of the fundamental restructuring of legal categories that followed from the merger of law and equity. For many decades after merger, remedies were conceptualized primarily as a component of procedure. Douglas Laycock, "How Remedies Became a Field: A History," *Review of Litigation* 27 (2008): 161–215.

104. Story, *Commentaries on Equity Jurisprudence* 1:21–22.

105. Ibid., 1:23.

106. Ibid.

107. Ibid.

108. Ibid., 1:14–18, 22.

109. Ibid., 1:24.

110. 2 Johns. Ch. 495 (N.Y. Ch. 1817).

111. 2 Johns. Ch. 432 (N.Y. Ch. 1817).

112. 3 Johns. Ch. 558 (N.Y. Ch. 1818).

113. 7 Johns. Ch. 250 (N.Y. Ch. 1823); Robert Wyness Millar, *Civil Procedure of the Trial Court in Historical Perspective* (New York: Law Center of New York University for the National Conference of Judicial Councils, 1952), 60; Albert O. Hirschman, *The Passions and the Interests: Political Arguments for Capitalism before Its Triumph* (Princeton: Princeton University Press, 1977).

114. "Tuesday, February 6. Legislature of New York, House of Assembly, Monday, February 5. Petitions Read and Referred," *Albany Gazette,* February 9, 1821, p. 1.

115. James Kent, Report on "An Act to Alter the Mode of Taking Evidence in the Court of Chancery," in *Reports of the Proceedings and Debates,* 509–10.

116. *Reports of the Proceedings and Debates,* 506.

117. Steven Wilf, "The First Republican Revival: Virtue, Judging, and Rhetoric in the Early Republic," *Connecticut Law Review* 32 (2000): 1679–86.

118. Nicholas R. Parrillo, *Against the Profit Motive: The Salary Revolution in American Government, 1780–1940* (New Haven: Yale University Press, 2013), 9–10, 121–24.

## Chapter 2.  A Troubled Inheritance

1. Dawson 146–59; Macnair, *Law of Proof* 173; John H. Langbein, "Bifurcation and the Bench: The Influence of the Jury on English Conceptions of the Judiciary," in

*Judges and Judging in the History of the Common Law and Civil Law: From Antiquity to Modern Times*, ed. Paul Brand and Joshua Getzler (Cambridge: Cambridge University Press, 2012), 72–76; W. J. Jones, *The Elizabethan Court of Chancery* (Oxford: Clarendon Press, 1967), 103–04, 110. The court was able to rely on merely two examiners because these were responsible for taking the testimony only of those witnesses who lived in or near London. Commissioners took the testimony of all other witnesses. Dawson 152–54; Macnair, *Law of Proof* 173.

2. Macnair challenges Dawson's use of the term *lay* to describe chancery commissioners, arguing that they were comparable to justices of the peace and thus possessed the knowledge requisite for examining witnesses. Macnair, *Law of Proof* 174–75. But even if Macnair's account of their relative knowledge and sophistication is correct, chancery commissioners were laymen in the key sense that Dawson intended—namely, they were not a bureaucratic staff whose training and duties were oriented exclusively (or even primarily) to the Court of Chancery.

3. Gilbert 124; see also Harrison 1:306.

4. Macnair, *Law of Proof* 174.

5. Gilbert 129, 134–35; Harrison 1:325–26.

6. In reality, by the time that Gilbert wrote his treatise in the early eighteenth century, the more common practice was for parties to submit interrogatories directly to the commissioners upon the opening of the commission. Gilbert 124; Harrison 1:323.

7. Gilbert 124–25.

8. Ibid., 129; Harrison 1:330.

9. Gilbert 134–35, 139.

10. Ibid., 144.

11. Jones 139, 137, 108–11.

12. Michael Lobban, "Preparing for Fusion: Reforming the Nineteenth-Century Court of Chancery, Part I," *Law and History Review* 22 (2004): 394–97.

13. See table 2 in the appendix.

14. Charles Alan Wright and Arthur R. Miller, *Federal Practice and Procedure*, 3d ed. vol. 10A, sec. 2685, available at http://westlaw.com.

15. See table 1 in the appendix. The number (and percentage) may actually be higher since there are eight cases whose subject matter I have been unable to determine due to the very limited (and sometimes illegible) documentation contained in those particular files.

16. *Williams v. Corwin*, Hopk. Ch. 471, 477 (1824).

17. *Batton v. Davis* (N.Y. Ch. 1836), Document B283, Series J0063, New York State Archives (NYSA).

18. Isaac Hansen, Master's Report, in *Schuyler v. Van Rensselaer* (N.Y. Ch. 1811), S9/J0063, NYSA.

19. John G. Spencer, Master's Report, in *Brooks v. Phelps* (N.Y. Ch. 1812), B16/J0063, NYSA.

20. Benjamin Clark, Master's Report, in *Beekman v. Summers* (N.Y. Ch. 1821), B54/J0063, NYSA.

21. *Bleecker v. Staats* (N.Y. Ch. 1828), B181/J0063, NYSA.

22. *Mills v. Dennis*, 3 Johns. Ch. 367 (1818).

23. *Strickland v. Van Nostrand* (N.Y. Ch. 1822), S102/J0063, NYSA; *Bouck v. Enders* (N.Y. Ch. 1826), B163/J0063, NYSA; *St. John v. Miller* (N.Y. Ch. 1844), S364/J0063, NYSA; *Brown v. Helmkins* (N.Y. Ch. 1822), B98/J0063, NYSA.

24. "An Act Directing a Mode of Trial, and Allowing of Divorces in Cases of Adultery, Passed the 30th of March 1787," in *Laws of the State of New York, Passed at the Sessions of the Legislature Held in the Years 1785, 1786, 1787, and 1788, Inclusive, Being the Eighth, Ninth, Tenth, and Eleventh Sessions* (Albany: Weed Parsons and Co., 1886), 2:494–95 (ch. 69); "An Act Concerning Divorces, and for Other Purposes, Passed April 13, 1813," in *Laws of the State of New York, Passed at the Thirty-Sixth Session of the Legislature, Begun and Held at the City of Albany, the Second Day of November, 1812* (Albany: S. Southwick, 1813), 197–201 (ch. 102).

25. For details concerning the percentage of cases in which testimony was taken, see table 3 in the appendix.

26. *Schmelzel v. Sill* (N.Y. Ch. 1818), S23/J0063, NYSA; *Smith v. Kniskern* (N.Y. Ch. 1819), S36/J0063, NYSA; *Strickland v. Van Nostrand* (N.Y. Ch. 1822), S102/J0063, NYSA.

27. This is a conservative estimate, since in 17 percent of the cases, it is impossible to determine how testimony was taken. Note also that in a few cases, multiple methods were deployed.

28. Affidavit of James McKeen, Solicitor for the Complainant, December 14, 1831, in *Bell v. Manning* (N.Y. Ch. 1831), B494/J0070, NYSA.

29. Joseph W. Moulton, *The Chancery Practice of the State of New York* (New York: O. Halsted, 1829), 1:13.

30. In 1818, the New York legislature enacted a statute providing that only those lawyers licensed to practice before the state supreme court or before chancery could serve as masters. "An Act Authorizing the Appointment of Commissioners to Take the Acknowledgments of Deeds and Special Bail, to Take Affidavits to Be Read in Courts of Record, and to Restrict the Number of Masters in Chancery, Passed March 24, 1818" in appendix to *The Revised Statutes of the State of New-York, Passed During the Years 1827 and 1828* (Albany: Packard and Van Benthuysen, 1829), 3:37 (ch. 55, sec. 1).

31. *The Revised Statutes of the State of New York, As Altered by the Legislature, Including the Statutory Provisions of a General Nature, Passed from 1828 to 1835 Inclusive* (Albany: Packard and Van Benthuysen, 1836), 1:98. It bears emphasis, of course, that masters and examiners were not the only public officials in this period who, even while occupying their offices, continued to work as private lawyers. What would be viewed as an impermissible conflict of interest today was often more readily tolerated in the antebellum period. See, for example, Norman W. Spaulding, "Independence and Experimentalism in the Department of Justice," *Stanford Law Review* 63 (2011): 418–21, 438; Jed

Shugerman, "The Creation of the Department of Justice: Professionalization without Civil Rights or Civil Service," *Stanford Law Review* 66 (2014): 131–35, 156–60.

32. Klein 239, 301–03.

33. Art. 4, sec. XII, in *Reports of the Proceedings and Debates of the Convention of 1821 Assembled for the Purpose of Amending the Constitution of the State of New York* (Albany: E. and E. Hosford, 1821), 663. See also Moulton 1:12; Murray Hoffman, *The Office and Duties of Masters in Chancery and Practice in the Master's Office with an Appendix of Precedents* (New York: Gould & Banks, 1824), xxi.

34. Gerald Leonard, *The Invention of Party Politics: Federalism, Popular Sovereignty, and Constitutional Development in Jacksonian Illinois* (Chapel Hill: University of North Carolina Press, 2002), 35–50.

35. "Governor Elect," *The Columbian*, June 16, 1817, p. 2 (quoting the *New-York Evening Post*). See also "Multiplication of Offices," *The American*, November 29, 1820, p. 2.

36. "Executive Influence," *Jamestown Journal*, August 15, 1838, p. 2.

37. "The Journal," *The American Journal*, January 29, 1823, p. 2; "In Senate. Monday, March 24," *Saratoga Sentinel*, April 1, 1823, p. 2; "In Senate. Thursday, November 4," *Saratoga Sentinel*, November 10, 1824, p. 3.

38. *The Revised Statutes* (1829), 1:96 (pt. I, ch. V, tit. I, sec. 1, subsec. 3); Murray Hoffman, *A Treatise upon the Practice of the Court of Chancery; with an Appendix of Forms* (New York: Halsted & Voorhies, 1835), 1:20.

39. "An Act in Relation to Masters and Examiners in Chancery in the Cities of New-York and Albany, Passed April 25, 1829," in *The Revised Statutes* (1829), 3:165 (ch. 272). See also Hoffman, *Treatise* 1:20.

40. "An Act in Relation to Masters in Chancery, Passed April 13, 1835, in *The Revised Statutes* (1836), 3:433 n. * (ch. 77).

41. Herman Melville, "Bartleby," in *Bartleby and Benito Cereno* (New York: Dover Publications, 1990), 4. *Bartleby* was first published in 1853. Ibid., v.

42. *The Revised Statutes* (1829), 2:624–26.

43. Sedgwick 71.

44. Robert W. Gordon, "Lawyers as the American Aristocrats: A Nineteenth-Century Ideal that May Still be Relevant," *Stanford Lawyer* 20 (1985): 2–6; Russell G. Pearce, "Lawyers as America's Governing Class: The Formation and Dissolution of the Original Understanding of the American Lawyer's Role," *University of Chicago Law School Roundtable* 8 (2001): 384–92.

45. *Ithaca Journal*, July 23, 1823, p. 2.

46. Affidavit of David Woodcock, August 21, 1821, in *Bennet v. Woodcock* (N.Y. Ch. 1821), B511/J0070, NYSA; "Woodcock, David," in *Biographical Directory of the United States Congress 1774–Present*, available at http://bioguide.congress.gov/scripts/biodisplay.pl?index—000211.

47. Affidavit of William Lupton, September 20, 1821, in B511/J0070.

48. Notice of Motion for Defendant, September 3, 1821, in ibid.

49. Affidavit of William Lupton, September 20, 1821, in ibid.

50. Affidavit of Silas Bennet, September 20, 1821, in ibid.

51. Affidavit of Charles Bingham, September 21, 1821, in ibid.

52. Notice of Motion for Defendant, September 3, 1821, in ibid.

53. Affidavit of Henry E. Dwight, August 17, 1821, in ibid.

54. Affidavit of Emery Brown, August 27, 1821, in ibid.

55. Affidavit of Silas Bennet, September 20, 1821, in ibid.

56. James Kent, Order Denying Defendant's Motion to Suppress, September 24, 1821, in ibid.

57. *Seger v. Choumet* (N.Y. Ch. 1819), S37/J0063, NYSA.

58. "Commission, Interrogatories and Depositions," September 18, 1821, in *Bailey v. Thompson* (N.Y. Ch. 1822), B71/J0063, NYSA. See also *Strong v. Stewart* (N.Y. Ch. 1819), S38/J0063, NYSA.

59. "Depositions," December 2, 1820, in *Mechanics and Farmers Bank of Albany v. Stewart* (N.Y. Ch. 1822), B73/J0070, NYSA. See also *Bailey v. Thompson* (N.Y. Ch. 1822), B71/J0063.

60. These other files are located in the J0070 series. See the appendix.

61. There are a few occasions when individuals who served as masters were also appointed as commissioners to take testimony in particular cases and, in the latter capacity, undertook questioning on the basis of written interrogatories. But in these cases, the masters were acting as commissioners rather than as masters.

62. *Remsen v. Remsen,* 2 Johns. Ch. 495 (N.Y. Ch. 1817).

63. Hoffman, *Office and Duties* 57.

64. Samuel Andrews, Master's Report, in *Sackridger v. Sackridger* (N.Y. Ch. 1814), S25/J0063, NYSA. Similar language suggesting that it was likely the master who was responsible for questioning can also be found in: Sterling Goodenow, Master's Report, in *Betts v. Betts* (N.Y. Ch. 1814), B17/J0063, NYSA; Jeremiah Drake, Master's Report, in *Berryhill v. Berryhill* (N.Y. Ch. 1820), B40/J0063, NYSA; Gerrit Y. Lansing, Master's Report, in *Sparks v. Smock* (N.Y. Ch. 1809), S1/J0063, NYSA; Gerrit Y. Lansing, Master's Report, in *Striker v. Porter* (N.Y. Ch. 1808), S16/J0063, NYSA; Joseph B. Lathrop, Master's Report, in *Squires v. Squires* (N.Y. Ch. 1821), S58/J0063, NYSA.

65. Nearly half of the 244 cases decided prior to 1823 were foreclosure suits.

66. About 11 percent of the 244 cases decided prior to 1823 were suits for divorce or for separation of bed and board.

67. Sterling Goodenow, Master's Report, in *Betts v. Betts* (N.Y. Ch. 1814), B17/J0063.

68. *Remsen,* 2 Johns. Ch. 495.

69. Ibid.

70. Ibid.

71. Ibid.

72. Ibid.

73. Ibid.

74. "An Act Concerning Divorces," 198 (sec. 3). The master was also required to determine whether other contingencies, such as the parties' having been married in New York, were met.

75. Edmund Robert Daniell, *Pleading and Practice of the High Court of Chancery*, 5th Amer. ed. (Boston: Little Brown, 1879), 2:1300.

76. Hoffman, *Office and Duties* 382.

77. Gerrit Y. Lansing, Master's Report, in *Striker v. Porter* (N.Y. Ch. 1808), S16/J0063.

78. Gideon Frisber, Master's Report, in *Mabee v. Mabee* (N.Y. Ch. 1817), M2/J0070, NYSA.

79. Samuel Andrews, Master's Report, in *Sackridger v. Sackridger* (N.Y. Ch. 1814), S25/J0063; Horatio Gates Spafford, *A Gazetteer of the State of New York: Embracing an Ample Survey and Description of its Counties, Towns, Cities, Villages, Canals, Mountains, Lakes, Rivers, Creeks, and Natural Topography, Arranged in One Series, Alphabetically, With an Appendix* (Albany: B. D. Packard, 1824), 267 (s.v. "Kingsbury").

80. Jacob Hoighton, Master's Report, in *Ballard v. Ballard* (N.Y. Ch. 1821), B57/J0063, NYSA. See also John Scott, Master's Report, in *Stevens v. Stevens* (N.Y. Ch. 1823), S59/J0063, NYSA.

81. Joseph B. Lathrop, Master's Report, in *Snow v. Snow* (N.Y. Ch. 1818), S70/J0063, NYSA. See also John M. Macdonald, Master's Report, in *Reitz v. Reitz* (N.Y. Ch. 1821), R190/J0070, NYSA.

82. George W. Rathbun, Master's Report, in *Rexford v. Rexford* (N.Y. Ch. 1844), R246/J0070, NYSA.

83. "An Act for the Regulation of the Proceedings and Practice of Certain Offices of the High Court of Chancery in England," in S. Atkinson, *Practice of the Court of Chancery, with an Appendix, Containing All the General Orders Issued on and Since the 3rd April 1826, and Also the Recent Statutes Relative to Practice* (London: S. Sweet, V. & R. Stevens, and G. S. Norton, 1842), appendix: cxv (sec. 18).

84. Richard Newcombe Gresley, *A Treatise on the Law of Evidence in the Courts of Equity* 2d ed. (London: William Benning, 1847), 68–69 n. (d).

85. The American edition of Gresley's treatise published in 1848—but not the one issued in 1837—mentions both the 1833 statute and the 1845 rules briefly in the footnotes. Gresley, *Treatise on the Law of Evidence in the Courts of Equity* 2d ed. (Philadelphia: T. & J. W. Johnson, 1848), 72 n. (c), 103 n. (t), 511 n. (p), 541 n. (g). See also John Sidney Smith, *A Treatise on the Practice of the Court of Chancery: With an Appendix of Forms and Precedents of Costs, Adapted to the Last New Orders* (Philadelphia: P. H. Nicklin & T. Johnson, 1839), 1:40, 1:357 & n. 5, 1:367, 2:623; Daniell, *Pleading and Practice of the High Court of Chancery* 1:lvi, 2:1063, 2:1084, 2:1088, 3:1775.

86. Stephen Cambreling, Master's Report, in *Renwick v. Renwick* (N.Y. Ch. 1843), R231/J0070, NYSA; George W. Rathbun, Master's Report, in *Rexford v. Rexford* (N.Y. Ch. 1844), R246/J0070.

87. William McMurray, Master's Report, in *Belding v. Belding* (N.Y. Ch. 1846), B484/J0070, NYSA.

88. Deposition of Thomas E. Velmilyen, Annexed to Master's Report, in ibid.

89. Of the 466 cases reviewed, twenty-seven concern divorce, and in only three of these cases (or 11%) did the defendant enter an appearance.

90. "Tuesday, February 6. Legislature of New York, House of Assembly, Monday, February 5. Petitions Read and Referred," *Albany Gazette*, February 9, 1821, p. 1.

91. James Kent, Report on "An Act to Alter the Mode of Taking Evidence in the Court of Chancery," in *Reports of the Proceedings and Debates*, 507; "From Our Correspondnet [*sic*], Legislature of New-York, in Senate, Feb. 5," *New-York Spectator*, February 16, 1821, p. 4; "Legislature of New York. In Senate, Feb. 5," *Albany Gazette*, February 16, 1821, p. 1.

92. Kent, Report, 508.

93. As concerns the turn to cross-examination in mid-nineteenth-century English Chancery, John Langbein, Renée Lettow Lerner, and Bruce Smith suggest that the driving force was the new centrality of cross-examination within common-law (civil and criminal) proceedings. But in so arguing, they focus on the perspective of top-down policymakers—namely, the members of the commission appointed in 1850 to undertake chancery reform. According to Langbein, Lerner, and Smith, the commissioners came to view equity's traditional, interrogatory-based approach to taking testimony as "intolerable," because the rise of cross-examination within the common law had led to "a radical retheorization" of the way to ensure testimonial veracity—namely, a shift from oath to cross-examination. Langbein, Lerner, and Smith 376–77. Perhaps New York legislators were also influenced by such concerns, but there is no direct evidence to that effect. More importantly, in New York, the primary impetus for equity's embrace of cross-examination was the bottom-up, case-by-case actions of individual lawyers—men who, as we will see, were not universally persuaded that cross-examination was an ideal method for safeguarding against perjury and who, moreover, were positioned to focus much more on the particulars of the case before them than on systemic concerns about the theoretical underpinnings of the law.

94. Horton 249–50; Klein 250.

95. "An Act concerning the Supreme Court, for Dividing the State of New-York into Circuits," 6:214 (ch. 182, sec. 13), 6:215 (sec. 16).

96. "An Act Authorizing the Appointment of Commissioners to Digest and Report a Judicial and Equity System for the State of New-York, Passed May 15, 1837" in *Laws of the State of New York, Passed at the Sixtieth Session of the Legislature, Begun and Held at the City of Albany, the Third Day of January, 1837* (Albany: E. Croswell, 1837), 502 (ch. 436, sec. 1).

97. "Report of the Commissioners Appointed Under the Act of 15th May, 1837 (Doc. 2)," in *Documents of the Senate of the State of New-York, Sixty-First Session, 1838*, vol. 1 (Albany: E. Croswell, 1838), 8–9.

98. See also *Steer v. Steer*, Hopk. Ch. 362 (1825); *McCotter v. Hooker*, 4 Seld. 497 (N.Y. Ct. Appeals 1853).

99. "Report of the Commissioners Appointed Under the Act of 15th May, 1837 (Doc. 2)" 8, 9.

100. "An Act to Regulate the Trial by Jury, and the Taking of Testimony in Chancery, Passed April 18, 1838," in *Laws of the State of New York, Passed at the Sixty-First Session of the Legislature, Begun and Held at the City of Albany, the Second Day of January, 1838* (Albany: E. Croswell, 1838), 244–45 (ch. 258, sec. 4).

101. "An Act to Amend the Act Entitled 'An Act to Regulate the Trial by Jury, and the Taking of Testimony in Chancery,' Passed April 18, 1838, Passed May 2, 1839," in *Laws of the State of New York, Passed at the Sixty-Second Session of the Legislature, Begun and Held at the City of Albany, the First Day of January, 1839* (Albany: E. Croswell, 1839), 292 (ch. 317, sec. 1).

102. Abraham Van Vechten, Deposition Form, in *Malcomb v. Malcomb* (N.Y. Ch. 1842), M49/J0070, NYSA.

103. Deposition Testimony, in ibid.; Deposition Testimony, in *Burch v. Kent* (N.Y. Ch. 1842), B382/J0063, NYSA; Deposition Testimony, in *Burr v. Burr* (N.Y. Ch. 1842), B401/J0063; NYSA; Deposition Testimony, in *Smith v. Adams* (N.Y. Ch. 1837), S250/J0063, NYSA; Deposition Testimony, in *Starling v. Atwell* (N.Y. Ch. 1843), S349/J0063, NYSA; Deposition Testimony, in *Swift v. Hotchkins* (N.Y. Ch. 1844), S373/J0063, NYSA.

104. Deposition Testimony, in *Smith v. Adams* (N.Y. Ch. 1837), S250/J0063; Deposition Testimony, in *Swift v. Hotchkins* (N.Y. Ch. 1844), S373/J0063; Deposition Testimony, in *Burch v. Kent* (N.Y. Ch. 1842), B382/J0063.

105. Deposition Testimony, in *Malcomb v. Malcomb* (N.Y. Ch. 1842), M49/J0070.

106. Deposition Testimony, in *Billings v. Shafer* (N.Y. Ch. 1844), B487/J0070, NYSA.

107. Abraham Van Vechten, Deposition Form, in *Malcomb v. Malcomb* (N.Y. Ch. 1842), M49/J0070.

108. Godfrey Thomas Vigne, *Six Months in America* (Thomas T. Ash: Philadelphia, 1833), 69.

109. Hoffman, *Treatise* 2:270.

110. Dawson 287–304.

111. *Burch v. Kent* (N.Y. Ch. 1842), B382/J0063.

112. Deposition Testimony, in ibid.

113. New York lawyer Henry Vanderlyn discusses numerous trials in the state's common-law courts and suggests that these were often completed within the course of a single day or, at the very most, a few days. Henry Vanderlyn, *Diary*, 7 vols. (April 1827–March 1857), New-York Historical Society. See also Randolph N. Jonakait, *The American Jury System* (New Haven: Yale University Press, 2003), 97.

114. Kent, Report, 509.

115. "Rule 83," *Rules and Orders of the Court of Chancery of the State of New York* (Albany: William Gould & Co., 1829), 42.

116. *Gaul v. Miller*, 3 Paige Ch. 192 (N.Y. Ch. 1832).

117. *Blackett v. Laimbeer*, 1 Sand. Ch. 366 (N.Y. Ch. 1844).

118. Some of the linkages between nineteenth-century equity and modern-day practice are detailed in Kellen Funk, "Equity without Chancery: The Fusion of Law and Equity in the Field Code of Civil Procedure, New York 1846–76," *Journal of Legal History* 36 (2015): 176–79, 186–88; and Ezra Siller, "The Origins of the Oral Deposition in the *Federal Rules:* Who's in Charge?" *Seton Hall Circuit Review* 10 (2013): 43–109. It bears emphasis, of course, that despite the similarities between testimony-taking in nineteenth-century New York Chancery and present-day deposition practice, there are important differences as well. Testimony-taking in chancery was a means of providing the court with evidence necessary to decide the facts at issue in the dispute. In contrast, modern-day depositions serve not only this evidentiary function, but also an investigatory one—namely, helping to identify possible evidence. Siller 46. In addition, modern deposition testimony may be used at trial only for purposes of impeachment or when the witness is unavailable. Fed. R. Civ. P. 32(a). No such limits were placed on the use of testimony collected (by similar means) in nineteenth-century New York Chancery.

119. Kessler, "Our Inquisitorial Tradition" 1251–55.

120. Commission, in *Steere v. Steere* (N.Y. Ch. 1827), S161/J0063, NYSA; Commission, in *Bloodgood v. Randall* (N.Y. Ch. 1846), B503/J0063, NYSA.

121. *Brown v. Southworth*, 9 Paige Ch. 351 (N.Y. Ch. 1841).

122. Motion for Defendant, in *Reid v. Peters* (N.Y. Ch. 1847), R197/J0070, NYSA.

123. Ibid.

124. *Steer v. Steer*, Hopk. Ch. 362 (1825).

125. Jürgen Habermas, *The Structural Transformation of the Public Sphere: An Inquiry into a Category of Bourgeois Society*, trans. Thomas Burger and Frederick Lawrence (Cambridge: MIT Press, 1989); Peter Uwe Hohendahl, "The Theory of the Public Sphere Revisited," in *Sites of Discourse, Public and Private Spheres, Legal Culture: Papers from a Conference Held at the Technical University of Dresden, December 2001*, ed. Uwe Böker and Julie A. Hibbard (Amsterdam: Rodopi, 2002), 13–23.

126. Judith Resnik and Dennis Curtis, *Representing Justice: Invention, Controversy, and Rights in City-States and Democratic Courtrooms* (New Haven: Yale University Press, 2011), 295–99.

127. Jeremy Bentham, *Rationale of Judicial Evidence, Specially Applied to English Practice* (London: Hunt and Clarke, 1827), 2:189–90.

128. Norman W. Spaulding, "The Privilege of Probity: Forgotten Foundations of the Attorney-Client Privilege," *Georgetown Journal of Legal Ethics* 26 (2013): 335–36 (identifying a range of factors suggesting that Bentham's *Rationale of Judicial Evidence* likely had limited direct influence on American lawyers, including the fact that no American edition was ever published).

## Chapter 3. The Non-Revolutionary Field Code

1. Gregory S. Alexander, *Commodity and Propriety: Competing Visions of Property in American Legal Thought, 1776–1970* (Chicago: University of Chicago Press, 2008), 108–09, 114–24.

2. Mitchell Snay, *Horace Greeley and the Politics of Reform in Nineteenth-Century America* (Lanham, Md.: Rowman & Littlefield, 2011), 44; Shugerman, *People's Courts* 89–90.

3. Perry Miller, *Life of the Mind* 103, 109; Katz 257–58.

4. Francis Bergan, *The History of the New York Court of Appeals, 1847–1932* (New York: Columbia University Press, 1985), 9; Horton 217–21, 225–27.

5. Peter J. Galie, *Ordered Liberty: A Constitutional History of New York* (New York: Fordham University Press, 1996), 43.

6. Horton 231–43; David McAdam, *History of the Bench and Bar of New York* (New York: New York History Company, 1897), 1:126–28.

7. Horton 259–60.

8. *Reports of the Proceedings and Debates of the Convention of 1821 Assembled for the Purpose of Amending the Constitution of the State of New York* (Albany: E. and E. Hosford, 1821), 616.

9. *Reports of the Proceedings and Debates*, 503–04; Ralph J. Caliendo, *The Mayors of New York Before 1899*, vol. 1, *New York City Mayors* (Bloomington: Xlibris Corporation, 2010), 191–92; McAdam 1:456.

10. *Reports of the Proceedings and Debates*, 516; Jabez Delano Hammond, *The History of Political Parties in the State of New-York* (Albany: C. Van Benthuysen, 1842), 1:102; Euphemia Blake, *History of the Tammany Society; or, Columbian Order from Its Organization to the Present Time* (New York: Souvenir Publishing Company, 1901), 27.

11. *Reports of the Proceedings and Debates*, 515.

12. Ibid., 515–16, 518.

13. Langbein, "Chancellor Kent" 562–63.

14. "Report of the Committee on So Much of the Message of His Excellency the Governor, As Relates to the Judiciary, etc.," *Albany Argus*, February 4, 1823, p. 2; "In the Senate—Jan. 29, 1823," *Albany Daily Advertiser*, February 5, 1823, p. 2. See also "Gen. M'Clure's First Speech on the Judiciary Bill," *Albany Daily Advertiser*, April 14, 1823, p. 2; Wesley B. Turner, *The War of 1812: The War That Both Sides Won* (Toronto: Dundurn Press, 2000), 82.

15. Sedgwick 22.

16. *Reports of the Proceedings and Debates*, 515.

17. "New York Legislature, In Senate, Feb. 25, Mr. Wheeler's Speech, in Committee of the Whole on the Judiciary Bill," *Saratoga Sentinel*, March 11, 1823, p. 2.

18. Ibid.

19. "In Senate, March 5, 1823," *Albany Daily Advertiser*, March 5, 1823, p. 2; John Stilwell Jenkins, *History of Political Parties in the State of New-York: From the Acknowledgement of the Independence of the United States to the Close of the Presidential Election in Eighteen Hundred Forty-four* (Auburn, N.Y.: Alden & Markham, 1846), 267; "Cramer, John," in *Biographical Directory of the United States Congress 1774–Present*, available at http://bioguide.congress.gov/scripts/biodisplay.pl?index—000211 (accessed Dec. 30, 2013).

20. William H. Seward, "Annual Message to the Legislature, January 1, 1839," in *Messages from the Governors: Comprising Executive Communications to the Legislature and Other Papers Relating to Legislation from the Organization of the First Colonial Assembly in 1683 to and Including the Year 1906, with Notes*, ed. Charles Z. Lincoln (Albany: J.B. Lyon Company, 1909), 3:719.

21. "Address of the Whig Members of the Legislature to the People of the State of New York," *Albany Evening Journal*, May 15, 1839, p. 2.

22. William H. Seward, "Annual Message to the Legislature, January 5, 1841," in *Messages from the Governors* 3:871.

23. "Verplanck's Speech," *Albany Daily Advertiser*, April 1, 1839, p. 2.

24. "Verplanck's Speech," *Albany Daily Advertiser*, April 3, 1839, p. 2.

25. William Leete Stone, *Reminiscences of Saratoga and Ballston* (New York: Virtue & Yorkston, 1875), 346–49; "Anecdotes of American Lawyers," *Frank Leslie's Popular Monthly* (New York: Frank Leslie's Publishing House, 1885), 19:158; Marshall Brown, *Wit and Humor of Bench and Bar* (Chicago: T. H. Flood & Company, 1899), 517; *Memorial of the Life and Character of John Wells: With Reminiscences of the Judiciary and Members of the New York Bar* (New York: J. F. Trow & Son, 1874), 113–14; George Templeton Strong, *The Diary of George Templeton Strong, Young Man in New York, 1835–1849*, ed. Allan Nevins and Milton Halsey Thomas (New York: Macmillan Co., 1952), 1:106 & n. 3.

26. Strong 1:106–07.

27. Moulton 1:12–13.

28. "Verplanck's Speech," *Albany Daily Advertiser*, April 1, 1839, p. 2.

29. "Verplanck's Speech," *Albany Daily Advertiser*, April 2, 1839, p. 2.

30. "Verplanck's Speech," *Albany Daily Advertiser*, April 1, 1839, p. 2.

31. "Verplanck's Speech," *Albany Daily Advertiser*, April 8, 1839, p. 2. John M. Davison, Walworth's son-in-law, was the register and Hiram Walworth, the chancellor's brother, was the assistant register. *The New York State Register for 1843*, ed. Orville Luther Holley (Albany: J. Disturnell, 1843), 348; Reuben Hyde Walworth, *Hyde Genealogy: or, The Descendants, in the Female as Well as in the Male Lines, from William Hyde, of Norwich* (Albany: J. Munsell, 1864), 1:533, 536, 540.

32. Leonard, *Invention of Party Politics* 81–87; Parrillo, *Against the Profit Motive* 121–24.

33. Edward Pessen, *Jacksonian America: Society, Personality, and Politics*, rev. ed. (Chicago: University of Illinois Press, 1985), 314.

34. *Messages from the Governors* 720.

35. "Report of the Select Committee on So Much of the Governor's Message as Relates to the Fees of the Register, Assistant Register and Clerks in Chancery, and Clerks of the Supreme Court, (Doc. 186)," in *Documents of the Assembly of the State of New-York, Sixty-Second Session, 1839*, vol. 4 (Albany: E. Croswell, 1839), 1.

36. "The Legislature—It's [sic] Labors and Results," *Albany Evening Journal*, May 8, 1839, p. 2.

37. William H. Seward, "Annual Message to the Legislature, January 5, 1841," in *Messages from the Governors* 3:871.

38. Hoffman, *Treatise* 2:112; Geoffrey C. Hazard Jr., John L. Gedid, and Stephen Sowle, "An Historical Analysis of the Binding Effect of Class Suits," *University of Pennsylvania Law Review* 146 (1998): 1866–74.

39. Sedgwick 15; Sean Wilentz, *The Rise of American Democracy: Jefferson to Lincoln* (New York: W. W. Norton & Company, 2006), 474; Joshua A. T. Salzmann, "Safe Harbor: Chicago's Waterfront and the Political Economy of the Built Environment, 1847–1918" (Ph.D. diss., University of Illinois, 2008), 42

40. "Verplanck's Speech," *Albany Daily Advertiser*, April 3, 1839, p. 2; Edward J. Balleisen, *Navigating Failure: Bankruptcy and Commercial Society in Nineteenth-Century America* (Chapel Hill: University of North Carolina Press, 2001), 81.

41. Balleisen 81–82.

42. "Verplanck's Speech," *Albany Daily Advertiser*, April 1, 1839, p. 2.

43. John Lauritz Larson, *The Market Revolution in America: Liberty, Ambition, and the Eclipse of the Common Good* (New York: Cambridge University Press, 2010), 57–58; Daniel Walker Howe, "The Market Revolution and the Shaping of Identity in Whig-Jacksonian America," in *The Market Revolution in America: Social, Political, and Religious Expressions, 1800–1880*, ed. Melvyn Stokes and Stephen Conway (Charlottesville: University of Virginia Press, 1996), 259–65.

44. María Carla Sánchez, *Reforming the World: Social Activism and the Problem of Fiction in Nineteenth-Century America* (Iowa City: University of Iowa Press, 2008), 50.

45. "The Book Trade," *The Merchants' Magazine and Commercial Review* 6 (January 1842): 390; "The Victim of Chancery, or A Debtor's Experience," *The New-York Mirror: A Weekly Gazette of Literature and the Fine Arts* 18 (September 11, 1841): 295; "Literary Review," *The Ladies' Companion: A Monthly Magazine Embracing Every Department of Literature, Embellished with Original Engravings and Music Arranged for the Piano Forte, Harp and Guitar* 14 (October 1841): 310.

46. Frederick Jackson, *The Victim of Chancery, or A Debtor's Experience* (New York: University Press—John F. Trow, Printer, 1841), 30, 39.

47. Ibid., 59, 40–41.

48. Ibid., 44–46, 67.

49. Ibid., 69–72.

50. Ibid., 90–92.

51. Ibid., 92, 110.

52. Ibid., 170, 194–98.

53. Ibid., 196.

54. For an account of how the antebellum credit-based economy fostered civic, associational relations that tended to curb capitalist ambitions, see Tony A. Freyer, *Producers Versus Capitalists: Constitutional Conflict in Antebellum America* (Charlottesville: University of Virginia, 1994), 57–91.

55. William L. Marcy, "Annual Message to the Legislature, January 7, 1834," in *Messages from the Governors* 3:443.

56. William L. Marcy, "Annual Message to the Legislature, January 6, 1835," in *Messages from the Governors* 3:498; William L. Marcy, "Annual Message to the Legislature, January 5, 1836," in *Messages from the Governors* 3:536; William L. Marcy, "Annual Message to the Legislature, January 2, 1838," in *Messages from the Governors* 3:647–48; William L. Marcy, "Annual Message to the Legislature, January 3, 1837," in *Messages from the Governors* 3:609.

57. William H. Seward, "Annual Message to the Legislature, January 1, 1839," in *Messages from the Governors* 3:718; William H. Seward, "Annual Message to the Legislature, January 7, 1840," in *Messages from the Governors* 3:772; William H. Seward, "Annual Message to the Legislature, January 5, 1841," in *Messages from the Governors* 3:871.

58. William C. Bouck, "Annual Message to the Legislature, January 3, 1843," in *Messages from the Governors* 4:30; William C. Bouck, "Annual Message to the Legislature, January 2, 1844," in *Messages from the Governors* 4:54.

59. Silas Wright, "Annual Message to the Legislature, January 7, 1845," in *Messages from the Governors* 4:136.

60. "From the Commercial Advertiser," *Albany Evening Journal*, March 8, 1836, p. 2.

61. Sedgwick 46.

62. Sedgwick 7, 36; Howard Gillman, *The Constitution Besieged: The Rise and Demise of Lochner Era Police Powers Jurisprudence* (Durham: Duke University Press, 1993), 38; Edward K. Spann, *Ideals and Politics: New York Intellectuals and Liberal Democracy, 1820–1880* (Albany: State University of New York Press, 1972), 251.

63. "The Courts—The 'Law's Delay,'" *Albany Argus*, January 19, 1839, p. 2.

64. "Verplanck's Speech," *Albany Daily Advertiser*, April 1, 1839, p. 2.

65. "Memorial of the Members of the Bar of New York, for the Appointment of Commissioners for the Despatch of the Arrears of Equity Business (Doc. 36)," in *Documents of the Senate of the State of New-York, Sixty-Second Session, 1839*, vol. 2 (Albany: E. Croswell, 1839).

66. Cook 134, 195; Subrin, "How Equity Conquered Common Law" 937–38.

67. Sedgwick 64.

68. There was something of a tension between such calls to increase the number of chancery judges and complaints that equity was tyrannical. This tension was mitigated

by the fact that it was the enormous power with which the (lone) chancellor was endowed that was, in part, responsible for the view that chancery lent itself to tyranny. The very act of creating more judges in equity would therefore serve to mitigate this danger. Another means of addressing the threat posed by judges perceived to be overly powerful was to subject their rulings to appeal. The April 17, 1823, statute that endowed circuit judges with first instance jurisdiction in equity ensured that many equity cases would be subject to appeal—though the chancellor himself continued to try those matters not confined to a particular circuit. "An Act Concerning the Supreme Court, for Dividing the State of New-York into Circuits, and Concerning Circuit Courts and Courts of Oyer and Terminer, and for Vesting Equity Powers in the Circuit Judges, Passed April 17, 1823," in *Laws of the State of New York, Passed at the Forty-Fifth, Forty-Sixth and Forty-Seventh Sessions of the Legislature, Commencing January, 1822, and Ending November, 1824* (Albany: William Gould & Co., 1825), 6:212–13 (chap. 182, sec. X). Moreover, as detailed below, some of the proposals for augmenting the number of judges in chancery contemplated some form of appeal.

69. William L. Marcy, "Annual Message to the Legislature, January 7, 1834," in *Messages from the Governors* 3:443; William L. Marcy, "Annual Message to the Legislature, January 6, 1835," in ibid., 3:498.

70. William L. Marcy, "Annual Message to the Legislature, January 3, 1837," in ibid., 3:610.

71. William H. Seward, "Annual Message to the Legislature, January 1, 1839," in ibid., 3:719.

72. William H. Seward, "Annual Message to the Legislature, January 7, 1840," in ibid., 3:772–73.

73. William C. Bouck, "Annual Message to the Legislature, January 3, 1843," in ibid., 4:31.

74. William C. Bouck, "Annual Message to the Legislature, January 2, 1844," in ibid., 4:54–55; Silas Wright, "Annual Message to the Legislature, January 7, 1845," in ibid., 4:135–36.

75. "Report of the Commissioners Appointed Under the Act of 15th May, 1837 (Doc. 2)" 7.

76. Sedgwick 64.

77. "Tuesday Jan. 18," *Watch-Tower*, January 31, 1831, vol. 17, no. 879, p. 2.

78. "An Act for the appointment of a vice-chancellor for the eighth judicial circuit, and for other purposes, passed March 27, 1839," in *Laws of the State of New York, Passed at the Sixty-Second Session of the Legislature, Begun and Held at the City of Albany, the First Day of January, 1839* (Albany: E. Croswell, 1839), 85 (secs. 1–3); *Messages from the Governors* 3:720 n. 5.

79. "In Senate—Wednesday Jan. 12," *Albany Evening Journal*, January 22, 1840, p. 2.

80. See the summary of bills and constitutional amendments proposed and never enacted in *Messages from the Governors* 3:445 & n. 1 (1834); 3:536 & n. 2 (1836); 3:611 & n.2 (1837); 3:649 & n. 1 (1838); 3:720 & n. 5 (1839); 3:773 & n. 9 (1840).

81. Ibid., 4:55 n. 1.

82. Art. 8, sec. 1, in *Reports of the Proceedings and Debates*, 667; *Messages from the Governors* 4:135.

83. "The Judiciary," *Albany Argus*, March 26, 1838, p. 2; "Literature," *Putnam's Magazine: Original Papers on Literature, Science, Art, and National Interests*, vol. 1, no. 3 (March 1868): 378–79.

84. "Report of the Commissioners Appointed Under the Act of 15th May, 1837 (Doc. 2)" 8–9.

85. William L. Marcy, "Annual Message to the Legislature, January 2, 1838," in *Messages from the Governors* 3:648.

86. "An Act to Amend the Act Entitled 'An Act to Regulate the Trial by Jury, and the Taking of Testimony in Chancery,' Passed April 18, 1838, Passed May 2, 1839," in *Laws of the State of New York, Passed at the Sixty-Second Session of the Legislature, Begun and Held at the City of Albany, the First Day of January, 1839* (Albany: E. Croswell, 1839), 292 (chap. 317, sec. 1).

87. Sedgwick 61.

88. New York Constitution of 1846, art. XIV, sec. 8, in *Report of the Debates and Proceedings of the Convention for the Revision of the Constitution of the State of New York, 1846* (Albany: Evening Atlas, 1846), 14.

89. Art. VI, secs. 3, 10, in *Report of the Debates and Proceedings*, 10–11.

90. Art. XIV, sec. 8, in ibid., 14.

91. Ibid., 729; John J. Nutt, ed., *Newburgh: Her Institutions, Industries, and Leading Citizens. Historical, Descriptive and Biographical* (Newburgh, N.Y.: Ritchie & Hull, 1891), 158–59. Similar arguments were made by other delegates as well. *Report of the Debates and Proceedings* 79, 574, 594, 624, 774.

92. *Report of the Debates and Proceedings*, 783–85.

93. New York Constitution of 1821, art. IV, sec. 12, in *Reports of the Proceedings and Debates* (1821), 663.

94. Pursuant to the new constitution, a single supreme court would have jurisdiction in both law and equity and would consist of a minimum of 32 judges. Art. VI, sec. 4, in *Report of the Debates and Proceedings* (1846), 10. In contrast, under the 1821 constitution, the supreme court consisted of three justices, and there was but one chancellor. Art. V, sec. 4, in *Reports of the Proceedings and Debates* (1821), 664. Over time, these four officers were joined by eight circuit judges, two vice chancellors, and one assistant vice chancellor. *Report of the Debates and Proceedings* (1846), 580. The grand total of these judicial officers was thus 15—significantly fewer than the minimum of 32 created under the new constitution.

95. *Report of the Debates and Proceedings* (1846), 784; Judith Wellman, *Grass Roots Reform in the Burned-Over District of Upstate New York: Religion, Abolitionism, and Democracy* (New York: Garland Publishing, 2000), 121–25.

96. Shugerman, *People's Courts* 85–94; James A. Henretta, "The Strange Birth of Liberal America: Michael Hoffman and the New York Constitution of 1846," in *New York History* 77, no. 2 (April 1996): 151–76; Herbert D. A. Donovan, *The Barnburners: A Study of the Internal Movements in the Political History of New York State and of the Resulting Changes in Political Affiliation, 1830–1852* (New York: New York University Press, 1925), 14–47.

97. *Report of the Debates and Proceedings* (1846), 610; "The Representatives of the Democracy of New York and Mr. Van Buren," *Extra Globe*, vol. 7 (June 30, 1841): 100.

98. *Report of the Debates and Proceedings* (1846), 228, 582; "Angel, William," in *Directory of the United States Congress*.

99. *Report of the Debates and Proceedings* (1846), 587–88, 788; *Appleton's Cyclopædia of American Biography*, rev. ed., ed. James Grant Wilson and John Fiske (New York: The Press Association Compilers, Inc., 1918), 8:40–42.

100. *Report of the Debates and Proceedings* (1846), 55, 560.

101. Ibid., 609.

102. Ibid., 204, 601; "Nicoll, Henry," in *Biographical Directory of the United States Congress*.

103. *Report of the Debates and Proceedings* (1846), 621.

104. Ibid., 609, 560, 584.

105. Ibid., 584.

106. Ibid., 37, 590; "Loomis, Arphaxed," in *Biographical Directory of the United States Congress*. Similar arguments were voiced by delegates Kirkland, Nicoll, Chatfield, and Murphy. *Report of the Debates and Proceedings* (1846), 575, 601, 719, 775.

107. *Report of the Debates and Proceedings* (1846), 582. Similar arguments were voiced by delegates Marvin and Taylor. Ibid., 594, 629.

108. Ibid., 17, 563; George Ripley and Charles Anderson Dana, eds., *The American Cyclopaedia: A Popular Dictionary of General Knowledge* (New York: D. Appleton and Company, 1875), 576.

109. *Report of the Debates and Proceedings* (1846), 576.

110. Ibid., 621.

111. Ibid., 17, 665; "Simmons, George Abel," in *Biographical Directory of the United States Congress*.

112. New York Constitution of 1846, art. VI, sec. 24, in *Report of the Debates and Proceedings* (1846), 11.

113. "The Proposed Codification," *Spectator*, February 13, 1847, p. 1. See also "The Commissioners on Codification and Practice," *Albany Evening Journal*, April 3, 1847, p. 1; "Codification and Revision," *Albany Evening Journal*, March 10, 1847, p. 2.

114. "An Act for the Appointment of Commissioners, as Required by the Seventeenth Section, of Article First, and the Twenty-Fourth Section, of Article Sixth, of the Constitution, April 8, 1847," in *Laws of the State of New York, Passed at the First Meeting of the Seventieth Session of the Legislature, Begun and Held the Fifth Day of January, 1847, at the City of Albany* (Albany: Charles Van Benthuysen, 1847), 1:67–68 (sec. 8); "The Legal Graham Family," *The Green Bag*, vol. 6, no. 8 (August 1894), 354; "Codification and Revision," *Albany Evening Journal*, March 10, 1847, p. 2; "The Commissioners on Codification and Practice," *Albany Evening Journal*, April 3, 1847, p. 1; Alison Reppy, "The Field Codification Concept," in *David Dudley Field: Centenary Essays* 33; Henry Whittemore, *The Heroes of the American Revolution and Their Descendants: Battle of Long Island* (New York: Heroes of the Revolution Publishing Co., 1897), 101.

115. "The Commissioners on Codification and Practice," *Albany Evening Journal*, April 3, 1847, p. 1.

116. "An Act for the Appointment of Commissioners," sec. 8; see also *First Report of the Commissioners on Practice and Pleadings, Code of Procedure* (Albany: Charles Van Benthuysen, 1848), iii.

117. "Legal Pleading and Practice," *Spectator*, April 21, 1847, p. 4 (copied from the *Rochester Advertiser*).

118. "Memorial to the Legislature, February 1847," in *Speeches, Arguments, and Miscellaneous Papers of David Dudley Field*, ed. A. P. Sprague (New York: D. Appleton and Co., 1884), 1:261; David Dudley Field, "Legal System of New York," in ibid., 1:339.

119. Henry M. Field, *The Life of David Dudley Field* (New York: C. Scribner's Sons, 1898), 48.

120. *Report of the Debates and Proceedings* (1846), 11 (art. 6, sec. 24), 8 (art. 1, sec. 17).

121. "Report of the Commissioners on Practice and Pleadings, in Answer to a Resolution of the Assembly, of September 18, 1847 (Doc. 202)" 1.

122. *Journal of the Assembly of the State of New York, Seventieth Session, Begun and Held at the Capitol in the City of Albany, on the Fifth Day of January, 1847* (Albany: Charles Van Benthuysen, 1847), 2:1482.

123. "Report of the Commissioners on Practice and Pleadings" 4–5; Mildred V. Coe and Lewis W. Morse, "Chronology of the Development of the David Dudley Field Code," *Cornell Law Quarterly* 27 (1941–42), 239.

124. Field, *Life of David Dudley Field* 49; "Legal Pleading and Practice," *Spectator*, April 21, 1847, p. 4; Arphaxed Loomis, *Historic Sketch of the New York System of Law Reform in Practice and Pleadings* (Little Falls, N.Y.: J.R. & G.G. Stebbins, 1879), 15.

125. Van Ee 18–19; David S. Clark, "The Civil Law Influence on David Dudley Field's Code of Civil Procedure," in *The Reception of Continental Ideas in the Common Law World, 1820–1920*, ed. Mathias Reimann (Berlin: Duncker & Humblot, 1993), 73; Funk 189.

126. Roscoe Pound, "David Dudley Field: An Appraisal," in *David Dudley Field: Centenary Essays* 12–13; Reppy 25, 52; Cook 188, 192.

127. David Dudley Field, "What Shall Be Done with the Practice of the Courts? Questions Addressed to Lawyers, Published January 1, 1847," in *Speeches, Arguments, and Miscellaneous Papers*, 1:226–60; Field, *Life of David Dudley Field* 46–48.

128. David Marcus, "The Past, Present, and Future of Trans-Substantivity in Federal Civil Procedure," *DePaul Law Review* 59 (2010): 389. That the Field Code embraced the ideal of transsubstantive procedure does not, of course, mean that this ideal was fully implemented in practice. Charles E. Clark, "The Union of Law and Equity," *Columbia Law Review* 25 (1925): 1–10.

129. Field, "What Shall Be Done" 1:258.

130. "Report of the Commissioners on Practice and Pleadings" 11.

131. Ibid., 4.

132. "An Act for the Appointment of Commissioners," sec. 8.

133. Field, "What Shall Be Done" 1:229.

134. Subrin, "How Equity Conquered Common Law" 931–39; Subrin, "David Dudley Field and the Field Code" 327–38. In contrast to Subrin, Kellen Funk argues that the Field Code reflected more of an equitable than a common-law approach. Funk 169–86. In so arguing, however, Funk depicts discovery in pre-code equity as largely coextensive with the procedures afforded by the bill of discovery and therefore highly restricted in nature. This neglects the quasi-inquisitorial conception of chancery officials' roles (including especially that of masters), and thus their ability to undertake witness examination for investigatory purposes.

135. The commissioners did, however, strip equity pleading of the discovery function that it had traditionally served, by allowing parties to be examined just like any other witness. *First Report of the Commissioners* 242 (sec. 344); "An Act to Simplify and Abridge the Practice, Pleadings and Proceedings of the Courts of This State, Passed April 12, 1848," in *Laws of the State of New York, Passed at the Seventy-First Session of the Legislature, Begun the Fourth Day of January, and Ended the Twelfth Day of April, 1848, at the City of Albany* (Albany: Charles Van Benthuysen, 1848), 559 (chap. 379, sec. 344).

136. *First Report of the Commissioners* 76; Funk 182–85.

137. Charles Stewart Drewry, *A Treatise on the Law and Practice of Injunctions* (Philadelphia: John S. Littell, 1842), v–vii; 103–204.

138. In addition to adopting equity's approach to pleading and remedies, the code commissioners permitted greater joinder of parties and claims than had the common-law courts. Funk 172–74. In so doing, however, they also imposed significant limits on joinder, such that code procedure in this respect was a far cry from the largely open-ended approach of traditional equity. Subrin, "How Equity Conquered Common Law" 936.

139. *First Report of the Commissioners* 50 (sec. 355 [misnumbered 353]); "An Act to Simplify and Abridge the Practice, Pleadings and Proceedings," 560 (sec. 355); Subrin, "David Dudley Field and the Field Code" 332–33.

140. *First Report of the Commissioners* 184–85 (sec. 208); "An Act to Simplify and Abridge the Practice, Pleadings and Proceedings," 536 (sec. 208).

141. It was possible for the court to order such a reference on the motion of only some of the litigants and even sua sponte. Renée Lettow Lerner, "The Failure of Originalism in Preserving Constitutional Rights to Civil Jury," *William and Mary Bill of Rights Journal* 22 (2014): 848–49, 860–61; *First Report of the Commissioners* 189–90 (sec. 221), 191–92 (secs. 225–26); "An Act to Simplify and Abridge the Practice, Pleadings and Proceedings," 538 (sec. 221), 539 (secs. 225–26).

142. Funk 179–82.

## Chapter 4.  Cultural Foundations of American Adversarialism

1. Alexis De Tocqueville, *Democracy in America*, trans. George Lawrence, ed. J. P. Mayer (New York: Harper & Row, 1966), 268; Perry Miller, *The Legal Mind in America: From Independence to the Civil War* (Garden City, N.Y.: Doubleday, 1962), 109–16; Hurst 366–67; Maxwell Bloomfield, *American Lawyers in a Changing Society, 1776–1876* (Cambridge: Harvard University Press, 1976), 32–58, 136–90; Robert Stevens, *Law School: Legal Education in America from the 1850s to the 1980s* (Chapel Hill: University of North Carolina Press, 1983), 6–20; Norman W. Spaulding, "The Myth of Civic Republicanism: Interrogating the Ideology of Antebellum Legal Ethics," *Fordham Law Review* 71 (2003): 1415 & n. 65.

2. Mark C. Miller, *The High Priests of American Politics: The Role of Lawyers in American Political Institutions* (Knoxville: University of Tennessee Press, 1995), 58.

3. Charles F. Ritter and Jon L. Wakelyn, eds., *American Legislative Leaders, 1850–1910* (New York: Greenwood Press, 1989), xl.

4. Carolyn Eastman, *A Nation of Speechifiers: Making an American Public After the Revolution* (Chicago: University of Chicago Press, 2009); Christopher Looby, *Voicing America: Language, Literary Form, and the Origins of the United States* (Chicago: University of Chicago Press, 1996); Kenneth Cmiel, *Democratic Eloquence: The Fight over Popular Speech in Nineteenth-Century America* (Berkeley: University of California Press, 1990); Hulsebosch, *Constituting Empire*; Ferguson.

5. Eastman 2.

6. See, for example, Eastman; Looby; Cmiel; Jay Fliegelman, *Declaring Independence: Jefferson, Natural Language, and the Culture of Performance* (Stanford: Stanford University Press, 1993); Sandra M. Gustafson, *Eloquence Is Power: Oratory and Performance in Early America* (Chapel Hill: University of North Carolina Press / Omohundro Institute of Early American History and Culture, 2000).

7. Looby 224–29; Ruth Bloch, *Visionary Republic: Millennial Themes in American Thought, 1756–1800* (Cambridge: Cambridge University Press, 1985); Joyce Appleby, *Liberalism and Republicanism in the Historical Imagination* (Cambridge: Harvard University Press, 1992).

8. Carl J. Richard, *The Golden Age of the Classics in America: Greece, Rome, and the Antebellum United States* (Cambridge: Harvard University Press, 2009); Caroline Winterer, *The Culture of Classicism: Ancient Greece and Rome in American Intellectual Life, 1780–1910* (Baltimore: Johns Hopkins University Press, 2002), 12–43.

9. Robert W. Gordon, Oliver Wendell Holmes Lecture at Harvard Law School, February 1985; Pearce 384–92.

10. J. G. A. Pocock, *The Machiavellian Moment: Florentine Political Thought and the Atlantic Republican Tradition* (Princeton: Princeton University Press, 1975).

11. Howard Schweber, "The 'Science' of Legal Science: The Model of the Natural Sciences in Nineteenth-Century American Legal Education," *Law and History Review* 17 (1999): 438 ("Twenty years after Hoffman's book was first published, the editors of the influential Whig journal the *North American Review* said: 'If we were called upon to designate any single work, which had exercised a greater influence over the profession of the law in this country than all others . . . we should unhesitatingly select Hoffman's Course of Legal Study'").

12. David Hoffman, *A Course of Legal Study Addressed to Students and the Profession Generally*, 2d ed. (Baltimore: Joseph Neal, 1836), 2:750. See also John Finlay, preface to *Speeches of Phillips, Curran, and Grattan, and the Celebrated Irish Orators* (Philadelphia: Key and Mielke, 1831), vii–viii.

13. Such terminological slippage highlighted the extent to which antebellum lawyers seamlessly moved between and among these different institutions of governance. See, for example, "J. Q. Adams—the Right of Women," *Alexandria Gazette*, July 7, 1838, p. 2; "The Richmond Hill Barbecue," *Augusta Chronicle*, September 21, 1840, p. 2.

14. "Wheaton's Edition of Selwyn's Nisi Prius," *North American Review* 44 (1824): 157; "North American Review," *Evening Post* [New York], August 14, 1824, p. 2 (reprinting the piece from the *North American Review*).

15. "Eloquence of the United States," *Evening Post*, November 24, 1827, p. 2.

16. R. W. Gordon, Holmes Lecture.

17. Bloomfield 151.

18. R. W. Gordon, Holmes Lecture; LaPiana 29–38; Hoffman, *Course of Legal Study* 1:v, 59–63. In reality, the liberal arts ideal of legal education was the preserve of a select elite, and the rank and file of the profession learned instead through a system of apprenticeship that skipped such theoretical inquiry and focused instead on mastering the art of correct pleading. LaPiana 38–44.

19. Anthony T. Kronman, *The Lost Lawyer: Failing Ideals of the Legal Profession* (Cambridge: Belknap Press of Harvard University Press, 1993); Pearce 384–99; Spaulding, "Myth of Civic Republicanism" 1397–1407.

20. Spaulding, "Myth of Civic Republicanism" 1423.

21. Erving Goffman, *The Presentation of Self in Everyday Life*, rev. ed. (New York: Anchor Books, 1959).

22. For those familiar with the literature concerning the relationship between civic republicanism and legal ethics in the nineteenth century, the notion that the republican model of the lawyer contributed to the rise of adversarial procedure is likely to be somewhat jarring. This stems from the unfortunate fact that the term *adversarialism* has been used to convey distinctive meanings in scholarship on legal ethics, on the one hand, and procedure, on the other. In the ethics literature, adversarialism is taken to be a client-centered approach to lawyering, imagined in opposition to a more public- or justice-oriented approach. In contrast, in the procedure literature (including this book), adversarialism is understood to refer to an array of procedural devices that tend to promote (in addition to orality and publicity), lawyers', as opposed to judges', domination of the proceedings. The fact that, as Spaulding shows, nineteenth-century lawyers deployed the language of civic republicanism to justify both a client-centered (adversarial) and a justice-oriented (non-adversarial) approach to lawyering thus has no necessary implication for the relationship between civic republicanism and the rise of (procedural) adversarialism. That said, it is, of course, possible that developments in ethics and procedure influenced one another in certain respects, the specifics of which are well beyond the scope of this book.

23. Stevens 7–8; Hurst 277–83; Friedman, *History of American Law* 226–28; Cook 23–30, 69–92; Nelson xv–xvi; Hulsebosch, "Writs to Rights" 1050–54; Spaulding, "Privilege of Probity" 302–05.

24. Bloomfield 141–42.

25. James M. Altman, "Considering the A.B.A.'s 1908 Canon of Ethics," *Fordham Law Review* 71 (2003): 2480–81; Allison Marston, "Guiding the Profession: The 1887 Code of Ethics of the Alabama State Bar Association," *Alabama Law Review* 49 (1998): 501–02; George Sharswood, *An Essay on Professional Ethics*, 5th ed., Vol. 32, *Reports of the American Bar Association* (Philadelphia: T. J. & W. Johnson, Co., 1907), 145.

26. Hulsebosch, *Constituting Empire* 28–32; J. H. Baker, *An Introduction to English Legal History* (London: Butterworths, 2002), 26–27, 130–32, 169–72.

27. Ferguson 78–80; Richard 1–29, 42–45; Garry Wills, *Lincoln at Gettysburg: The Words That Remade America* (New York: Simon & Schuster, 1992), 41–89.

28. Miller, *Life of the Mind* 151–55. See the discussion below of Henry Vanderlyn's diary. So too, George Templeton Strong devoted great energy to critiquing contemporary oratory in religion, politics, and law. Strong 1:83, 1:134 (religion); 1:93, 1:147 (politics); and 1:131, 1:225–26 (law).

29. Ferguson 74.

30. Looby 158–74.

31. Richard 18–19; R. W. Gordon, Holmes Lecture; Stephen Botein, "Cicero as Role Model for Early American Lawyers: A Case Study in Classical 'Influence,'" *Classical Journal* 73 (1978): 313–21.

32. Hoffman, *Course of Legal Study* 2:602.

33. Story, "Inaugural Address," in *Miscellaneous Writings* 461.

34. Strong 1:179.

35. See the discussion in the conclusion.

36. John Williams, *A Treatise on the Study and Practice of the Law; with Directions for a Course of Law Studies* (London: T. H. Coe, 1823), 154–67; "On the Profession of the Bar," *The Port-Folio* (1801–1827), June 1, 1825, 473 (republishing portions of an article that originally appeared in *London Magazine*); "The Law Student: Letter II," *The Analectic Magazine* (1813–1820), October 1, 1814, 326 (republishing a piece from *The Reflector*).

37. Compare "For the Northern Whig. No. IV—The Bar," *The Northern Whig*, March 25, 1817, vol. 9, p. 3 (criticizing American oratory), with "Communication: The Drama—Mr. Pelby," *Baltimore Patriot and Mercantile Advertiser*, May 16, 1822, vol. 19, p. 2 (praising it).

38. Hoffman, *Course of Legal Study* 2:619, 608, 620.

39. Hugh Blair, *Lectures on Rhetoric and Belles Lettres* (Philadelphia: T. Ellwood Zell, 1866), 341, 358–64; Michael H. Frost, *Introduction to Classical Legal Rhetoric: A Lost Heritage* (Aldershot, U.K.: Ashgate Publishing Limited, 2005), 12–13, 44–54, 70–78.

40. David Hume, "Of Eloquence," *Essay and Treatises on Several Subjects* (Edinburgh: Bell and Bradfute, 1825), 1:95.

41. Sarah Barringer Gordon, "Blasphemy and the Law of Religious Liberty in Nineteenth-Century America," *American Quarterly* 52 (2000): 687.

42. Hoffman, *Course of Legal Study* 2:769.

43. David Paul Brown, *The Forum; or Forty Full Years of Practice at the Philadelphia Bar* (Philadelphia: Robert H. Small, 1856), 1:xxxii–xxxiii, xlviii, 137–38.

44. Ibid., 2:603, 607, 621, 603, 604–05, 607.

45. Blair 281–82; "Bar Oratory," *The New Monthly Magazine and Literary Journal*, August 1, 1825 (London), reprinted in *The New Monthly Magazine and Literary Journal* (Boston: Cummings, Hilliard & Co., 1825), 167; *The Museum of Foreign Literature, Science, and Art*, October 1, 1825 (Philadelphia: E. Littell; and New York: G. & C. Carvill), 7:359.

46. "On Forensic Eloquence," *The Enquirer* [Richmond, Va.], November 10, 1804, p. 4; "New Books," *The Newport Mercury* [Rhode Island], January 18, 1806, p. 3; "Forensic Eloquence," *The Weekly Inspector* [New York], January 17, 1807, vol. 1, p. 232; "Curran's Speeches," *The Public Advertiser* [New York], March 3, 1807, v. 1, p. 3; *American Commercial Daily Advertiser* [Baltimore, Md.], March 15, 1817, vol. 35, p. 3.

47. "Curran's Speeches," *The Public Advertiser*. See also Finlay vi.

48. "Wirt's Speeches, British Spy, etc.," *The New-York Evening Post*, July 26, 1808, p. 4; "Wirt's Speeches, British Spy, etc.," *The Public Advertiser*, July 26, 1808, vol. 2, p. 4. See also "Literary Intelligence," *The Weekly Inspector*, January 17, 1807, vol. 1, p. 232; "Selfridge's Trial," *The Balance, and Columbian Repository* [Hudson, N.Y.], January 27, 1807, vol. 6, p. 32.

49. Gregory Lansing Paine, ed., *Southern Prose Writers: Representative Selections* (New York: American Book Company, 1947), 28.

50. "On Forensic Eloquence," *The Rainbow: Second Series,* in *The Enquirer* [Richmond, Va.], November 10, 1804, p. 4.

51. Eastman 53–111.

52. Hulsebosch, *Constituting Empire* 204–05; Ferguson 24–33.

53. John H. Langbein, *The Origins of Adversary Criminal Trial* (Oxford: Oxford University Press, 2003), 10–66; Langbein, "Historical Foundations of the Law of Evidence" 1201; T. P. Gallanis, "The Rise of Modern Evidence Law," *Iowa Law Review* 84 (1999): 503, 538. While the "Confrontation Clause" of the U.S. Constitution and similar provisions in state constitutions reflect a longstanding common-law practice of permitting criminal defendants to confront their accusers in court, this "altercation" differed notably from the later arising practice of cross-examination in that it did not involve lawyers. Langbein, *Origins of Adversary Criminal Trial* 10–15, 233–34 n. 241.

54. Baker, *Introduction to English Legal History* 183–84.

55. Langbein, "Historical Foundations of the Law of Evidence" 1174–76, 1194–1202; Gallanis.

56. While cross-examination—a lawyer driven process of questioning (routinized as an essential part of all cases)—was new, the oral questioning of witnesses was not. Writing in the 1760s, before cross-examination became an established feature of common-law civil litigation, Blackstone distinguished between the common-law and equity methods of taking testimony, arguing that the former was superior because it relied on oral, and most importantly, public questioning. But such questioning was primarily by judge and jury, rather than by counsel. William Blackstone, *Commentaries on the Laws of England* (Chicago: University of Chicago Press, 1979), 2:373. Writing about thirty years later, in the very last years of the eighteenth century, English barrister Charles Barton argued for the superiority of the common-law approach to taking testimony in nearly identical terms. Charles Barton, *An Historical Treatise of a Suit in Equity: In Which Is Attempted a Scientific Deduction of the Proceedings Used on the Equity Sides of the Courts of Chancery and Exchequer, from the Commencement of the Suit to the Decree and Appeal, with Occasional Remarks on Their Import and Efficacy; and an Introductory Discourse on the Rise and Progress of the Equitable Jurisdiction of Those Courts* (Dublin: P. Byrne, 1796), 156–58 n. 1.

57. Langbein, *Origins of Adversary Criminal Trial* 246–47.

58. Hortensius [pseud.], *Deinology; or the Union of Reason and Eloquence, Being Instructions to a Young Barrister, With a Postcript Suggesting Some Considerations for the Viva Voce Examination of Witnesses at the English Bar* (London: G.G.C. Robinson, 1789), 232–33.

59. Oliver 310, 312.

60. James Kent, Report on "An Act to Alter the Mode of Taking Evidence in the Court of Chancery," in *Reports of the Proceedings and Debates of the Convention of 1821 Assembled for the Purpose of Amending the Constitution of the State of New York* (Albany: E. and E. Hosford, 1821), 508.

61. Langbein, Lerner, and Smith 459–64; Conor Hanly, "The Decline of Civil Jury Trial in Nineteenth-Century England," *Journal of Legal History* 26 (2005): 258. Moreover, around the mid-nineteenth century, a number of procedural developments served further to weaken (and perhaps also reflected the growing weakness of) American judges vis-à-vis the lawyers litigating before them. These included new restrictions on common-law judges' ability to comment on the evidence and to craft (without lawyers' input) jury instructions. Krasity, "Role of the Judge in Jury Trials" 595, 597–609; Lerner, "Transformation of the American Civil Trial" 242–61; John Leubsdorf, "The Surprising History of the Preponderance Standard of Civil Proof," *Florida Law Review* 67 (2015): 1615–17.

62. Ferguson 78; John Quincy Adams, *Lectures on Rhetoric and Oratory, Delivered to the Classes of Senior and Junior Sophisters in Harvard University* (Cambridge: Hilliard and Metcalf, 1810), 1:315–17. See also Brown, *Forum* lxxiii.

63. Brown, *Forum* lxxiii.

64. Hoffman, *Course of Legal Study* 2:742.

65. Finlay vi.

66. Oliver 314.

67. Blackstone 2:379.

68. Lerner, "Failure of Originalism" 812–13, 817–20.

69. John Phillip Reid, *Controlling the Law: Legal Politics in Early National New Hampshire* (DeKalb: Northern Illinois University Press, 10), 18–32, 95–130; Horwitz 28–30; Nelson 165–74.

70. Lerner, "Failure of Originalism" 821–69; Renée B. Lettow, "New Trial for Verdict against Law: Judge-Jury Relations in Early Nineteenth-Century America," *Notre Dame Law Review* 71 (1996): 505–52; Renée Lettow Lerner, "The Rise of Directed Verdict: Jury Power in Civil Cases Before the Federal Rules of 1938," *George Washington Law Review* 81 (2013): 457–74.

71. Langbein, Lerner, and Smith 529–32; Lerner, "Rise of Directed Verdict," 518–24.

72. It is also important to recognize that the general trend toward increased judicial control did not unfold at the same pace in all institutions. The lower tier of trial courts—including especially the justices of the peace before whom the rank and file of the legal profession regularly argued—were much slower to become dominated by legally trained judges. There is therefore reason to suspect that juries called before such courts retained significantly more lawmaking authority. John A. Dunlap, *The New York Justice; or, a Digest of the Law Relative to Justices of the Peace in the State of New-York* (New York: Isaac Riley, 1815), 237; *The New York Civil and Criminal Justice: A Complete Treatise on the Civil, Criminal, and Special Powers and Duties of Justices of the Peace in the State of New York, with Numerous Forms,* 2d ed. (New York: C. M. Saxton, 1859), 281.

73. Resnik and Curtis, *Representing Justice* 293–94; Judith Resnik, "Courts In and Out of Sight, Site, and Cite," *Villanova Law Review* 53 (2008): 785 & n. 35; Judith Resnik,

"Whither and Whether Adjudication?" *Boston University Law Review* 86 (2006): 1111–13 & n. 43.

74. Lerner, "Transformation of the American Civil Trial" 233–39.

75. Strong 2:84 (January 26, 1852).

76. "Court of Oyer and Terminer," *Commerical Advertiser* [New York], October 19, 1826, p. 2; "Court of Oyer and Terminer," *National Advocate* [New York], November 21, 1826, vol. 14, p. 2; "Forensic Eloquence," *Commercial Advertiser* [New York], February 15, 1834, p. 1; "Forensic Eloquence," *New London Democrat,* September 20, 1845, p. 2.

77. Hurst 302–07.

78. Ibid., 286.

79. Ibid., 311–12.

80. See, for example, Walter Theodore Hitchcock, *Timothy Walker: Antebellum Lawyer* (New York: Garland Publishing, Inc., 1990), 44–47, 139–40 (discussing the life and career of Vanderlyn's contemporary, noted lawyer and treatise-writer Timothy Walker, and emphasizing, inter alia, Walker's obsession with oratory).

81. Vanderlyn.

82. Horatio Gates Spafford, *A Gazetteer of the State of New York: Embracing an Ample Survey and Description of its Counties, Towns, Cities, Villages, Canals, Mountains, Lakes, Rivers, Creeks, and Natural Topography, Arranged in One Series, Alphabetically, With an Appendix* (Albany: B. D. Packard, 1824), 396 (s.v. "Oxford").

83. *Supplement to the Annual Report of the State Engineer and Surveyor of the State of New York for the Fiscal Year Ending September 30, 1905* (Albany: Brandow Printing Co., 1906), 683; J. Disturnell, *A Gazetteer of the State of New York: Comprising Its Topography, Geology, Mineralogical Resources, Civil Divisions, Canals, Railroads, and Public Institutions, Together with General Statistics, the Whole Alphabetically Arranged, Also Statistical Tables, Including the Census of 1840, and Tables of Distances* (Albany: C. Van Benthuysen & Co., 1843), 314 (s.v. "Oxford").

84. In 1843, for example, a gazetteer reported that, as of 1840, the town contained "about 1,300 inhabitants," or 3,179, if residents of the surrounding countryside were included. Disturnell 314.

85. Compare, for example, Vanderlyn's account of his practice with that of the Manhattan firm that George Templeton Strong was to join in the 1840s. For a description of the latter, see Henry W. Taft, *A Century and a Half at the New York Bar, Being the Annals of a Law Firm and Sketches of Its Members, with Brief References to Collateral Events of Historical Interest* (New York: privately printed, 1938).

86. Klein 310.

87. Friedman, *History of American Law* 167–79, 193–97; Mann, *Republic of Debtors* 6–33; Freyer 57–91.

88. Hurst 302–07; LaPiana 91–92; Stevens 22; Wayne K. Hobson, *The American Legal Profession and the Organizational Society, 1890–1930* (New York: Garland Publishing, Inc., 1986), 142–44, 164, 196–99.

89. Vanderlyn 3:61 (January 18, 1833). Volumes 1, 4, 6, and 7 appear to belong to the former category—and volumes 2, 3, and 5 to the latter.

90. Henry J. Galpin, *Annals of Oxford, New York, with Illustrations and Biographical Sketches of Some of Its Prominent Men and Early Pioneers* (Oxford, N.Y.: Times Book and Job Printing House, 1906), 395.

91. See, for example, Vanderlyn 2:48 (December 1, 1829), 2:77 (March 6, 1830), 3:34 (November 2, 1832), 3:181 (January 22, 1834), 5:232 (April 17, 1839), 5:291 (April 28, 1841).

92. Nancy Isenberg, *Fallen Founder: The Life of Aaron Burr* (New York: Viking, 2007), 158–59.

93. Vanderlyn 1:8 (April 22, 1827); 1:14–15 (May 6, 1827); 1:17 (May 6, 1827).

94. Ibid., 1:8 (April 22, 1827); 1:22–25 (May 13, 1827); 1:29–30 (May 20, 1827).

95. Ibid., 1:27–28 (May 13, 1827).

96. Ibid., 6:130 (November 27, 1846).

97. Ibid., 1:266 (June 19, 1831); 1:288 (January 22, 1832); 1:222 (April 4, 1830); J. H. French, *Gazetteer of the State of New York, Embracing a Comprehensive View of the Geography, Geology, and General History of the State, and a Complete History and Description of Every County, City, Town, Village, and Locality, with Full Tables of Statistics* (Syracuse, N.Y.: R. Pearsall Smith, 1860), 229 n. 1 (s.v. "Oxford").

98. Vanderlyn 1:222 (April 4, 1830); 1:248 (December 2, 1830); 1:289 (January 22, 1832).

99. Ibid., 3:126 (August 15, 1833); 3:242 (August 12, 1834).

100. Ibid., 6:70 (October 29, 1844); 4:182 (February 10, 1832).

101. Timothy Walker expressed similar ambivalence regarding politics. Hitchcock 47–55.

102. Vanderlyn 4:155 (copy of letter from Henry Vanderlyn to Eliza Chester, March 27, 1837); 6:444–45 (October 8, 1852).

103. Ibid., 4:68–69 (August 27, 1834).

104. Ibid., 5:311 (October 23, 1841); Bloomfield 142–50 (discussing how Jacksonian-era lawyers sought to divorce law from politics in order to present themselves as "benevolently neutral technocrat[s]," rather than "designing cryptopolitician[s]").

105. Vanderlyn, 1:263 (May 22, 1831).

106. For a discussion of how lawyers (in a later period) managed to combine commitments to an ideal of legal science and reform, on the one hand, and to the real-world, material interests of their clients (and themselves), on the other, see Robert W. Gordon, " 'The Ideal and the Actual in the Law': Fantasies and Practices of New York City Lawyers, 1870–1910," in *The New High Priests: Lawyers in Post–Civil War America,* ed. Gerald W. Gawalt (Westport, Conn.: Greenwood Press, 1984), 51–74; Samuel Haber, *The Quest for Authority and Honor in the American Professions, 1750–1900* (Chicago: University of Chicago Press, 1991), 72–76.

107. Vanderlyn 1:263 (May 22, 1831); 5:258 (February 21, 1840).

108. Ibid., 1:204 (December 21, 1829); 1:210 (February 9, 1830); 6:246 (September 10, 1848).

109. Ibid., 3:101 (May 20 and 21, 1833); 3:106 (June 6, 1833); 2:132 (September 9, 1830); 3:156 (November 12, 1833); 3:104 (May 30, 1831).

110. Ibid., 1:74, 79 (September 30, 1827).

111. Ibid., 1:79.

112. Ibid., 1:110 (February 16, 1828); 1:243–44 (October 12, 1830). See also Vanderlyn's account of the oratory he delivered at a trial held at the Norwich Circuit Court on October 17, 1831. Ibid., 1:273–75 (October 17, 1831).

113. Ibid., 1:200 (October 18, 1829).

114. The longstanding common-law doctrine of coverture prevented married women from filing suit in their own names. Norma Basch, *In the Eyes of the Law: Women, Marriage, and Property in Nineteenth-Century New York* (Ithaca: Cornell University Press, 1982).

115. Vanderlyn 1:106, 105 (January 2, 1828).

116. Ibid., 1:275 (October 17, 1831).

117. Ibid., 1:243 (October 12, 1830).

118. Ibid., 1:243 (October 12, 1830); 6:261 (entry entitled "Scences at the Court on the 19th, 21st, and 22nd Dec., 1848," but not dated). See also ibid., 4:184 (March 22, 1838).

119. Ibid., 6:209 (January 23, 1848). See also ibid., 4:143 (entry entitled "Copy of Letter sent to Argill Gibbs, esq. of Ovid, Seneca County, 19 June 1836").

120. Ibid., 6:209 (January 23, 1848). See also ibid., 6:261 (entry entitled "Scenes at the Court on the 19th, 21st, and 22nd Dec., 1848," but not dated).

121. Ibid., 4:131 (February 9, 1836).

122. Ibid., 1:30 (May 20, 1827).

123. Ibid., 1:82 (October 13, 1827); 1:80 (October 2, 1827); 6:108 (June 8, 1846).

124. Under New York's first constitution, the highest common-law court was the supreme court, which sat in New York City, Albany, and Utica and whose judges rode circuit to hold trials in different counties. The only court then authorized to hear suits in equity was chancery, whose permanent seat was in Albany—though the chancellor typically held two sessions annually in New York City. As a result, during this period, lawyers had ample occasion to travel to attend sessions of the supreme court and chancery. Under the Constitution of 1821, eight circuit judges were established to try cases at both law and equity in eight different districts in the state. The common-law and equity decisions of these circuit judges could then be appealed to the supreme court and chancery, respectively. This reduced the need to travel as far (at least in the case of first-instance litigation), but it was still necessary to travel to the circuit court, which was typically held in the county seat—a town that was also usually the location of the common pleas court. Alden Chester, *Courts and Lawyers of New York: A History, 1609–1925* (New York: American Historical Society, 1925), 2:829–76; Charles P. Daly,

"History of the Court of Common Pleas for the City and County of New York, with an Account of the Judicial Organization of the State and of Its Tribunals, from the Time of Its Settlement by the Dutch in 1623, Until the Adoption of the State Constitution in 1846," in E. Delafield Smith, ed., *Report of Cases Argued and Determined in the Court of Common Pleas for the City and County of New York, with Notes, References, and an Index* (New York: Jacob R. Halsted, 1855), 1:lxxi–lxxii; Langbein, "Chancellor Kent" 562–63.

125. Vanderlyn 2:48 (December 1, 1829); 1:152 (December 18, 1828); 5:380 (January 22, 1844); 6:423 (April 5, 1852); 6:419 (March 3, 1852).

126. Haber 78.

127. Vanderlyn 6:376 (November 30, 1843).

128. Ibid., 1:81 (October 13, 1827); 6:202 (December 22, 1847).

129. Ibid., 1:154 (December 18, 1828).

130. Ibid., 1:242 (November 1, 1830).

131. Arbitration and reference were both modes of extrajudicial dispute resolution. In the case of arbitration, however, the parties pursued the extrajudicial path prior to filing suit, while in the case of reference, they did so (either on their own initiative or in response to a court order) after the suit was already filed. Goebel, ed., *Law Practice of Alexander Hamilton* 2:375–77.

132. Goebel 2:379–80; Eben Moglen, "Commercial Arbitration in the Eighteenth Century: Searching for the Transformation of American Law," *Yale Law Journal* 93 (1983): 143–44. Scholars disagree about whether, beginning in the early 1800s, there was a decline in New York merchants' reliance on arbitration. Compare Horwitz 149–50 (arguing that such a decline occurred), with Moglen 147–49 (questioning whether the evidence proves such a decline).

133. New York enacted a general arbitration statute in 1791. This permitted arbitration of any kind of dispute (rather than exclusively those concerning merchants' accounts) and allowed the arbitral report to be entered as a rule of court, such that it could be subsequently enforced through the court's contempt power. Horwitz 149 & n. 53; Moglen 147.

134. Vanderlyn 1:122 (April 22, 1828). Since the plaintiff initially filed suit in the supreme court, this case was technically a reference. Vanderlyn, however, referred to it as an arbitration.

135. Because April 20 was a Sunday, proceedings were paused then.

136. Ibid., 1:122–24.

137. Ibid., 1:124.

138. Ibid., 1:123–24.

139. Ibid., 1:124.

140. When Kent was chancellor, the court held only two sessions annually outside of Albany, and these were both in New York City. Langbein, "Chancellor Kent" 562–63. By the time that Theodore Sedgwick Jr. published his 1838 critique of chancery, the court also held sessions in Saratoga. See Sedgwick 21.

141. While appeals to the Supreme Court from circuit-court decisions were themselves common, the Supreme Court sat in three different cities, thus facilitating the ability of lawyers to travel to court and argue cases themselves. Chester 2:850–51 & n. 21.

142. Lawrence M. Friedman, *American Law: An Introduction* (New York: W. W. Norton, 1998), 268.

143. Vanderlyn 1:204–05 (December 21, 1829); 1:105 (entry entitled "Achorn Chancery Suit," but not dated; located between entries for January 2 and 13, 1828). The suit is reported at *Prentice v. Achorn*, 2 Paige Ch. 30 (1830).

144. That this is the case is suggested, for example, by Vanderlyn's October 1841 account of the "examination of witnesses in chancery in the suit of Winsor versus Abner Wood and alia." Ibid., 5:311 (October 19, 1841). Testimony in this case was taken by an examiner in the town of Unadilla, located in neighboring Otsego County. According to Vanderlyn, when he arrived at "the place of examination," he "found the examiner engaged in another ponderous cause with a barroom of witnesses to be examined." Ibid., 5:311 (October 19, 1841).

145. Ibid., 1:205 (December 21, 1829).

146. Joel Munsell, *The Annals of Albany*, 2d ed. (Albany: Joel Munsell, 1869), 1: 299–301.

147. Vanderlyn 1:105, 106 (entry entitled "Achorn Chancery Suit," but not dated; located between entries for January 2 and 13, 1828).

148. N.Y. Laws 1847, c. 59, Act of April 8, § 8 (statute establishing a three-person commission to create a unified mode of procedure).

149. Cook 192–93.

150. Strong 1:301 (September 28, 1847); 1:334 (November 9, 1848).

151. Cook 163–64, 185–88.

152. Vanderlyn 5:376, 377 (December 1, 1843); 6:54 (March 11, 1844); 6:140 (January 16, 1847).

153. Indeed, as of the late eighteenth century, the (statutorily established) fees that lawyers were able to charge clients were somewhat higher in chancery than in the supreme court. Herbert Alan Johnson, "John Jay: Lawyer in a Time of Transition, 1764–1775," in *Essays on New York Colonial Legal History*, 145.

154. Basch 131.

## Chapter 5. Market Freedom and Adversarial Adjudication

1. On the intermeshing of republican and liberal ideologies in the antebellum era, see, for example, G. Edward White, *The Marshall Court and Cultural Change, 1815–35*, vols. 3–4 of *The Oliver Wendell Holmes Devise History of the Supreme Court of the United States* (New York: Macmillan Publishing Co., 1988), 1–10. Many sought to justify an individualist, market-based order by appealing to older, more civic republican or

communalist ideals of the public good. Harry L. Watson, "'The Common Rights of Mankind': Subsistence, Shad, and Commerce in the Early Republican South," *Journal of American History* 83 (1996): 41. See also Amalia D. Kessler, *A Revolution in Commerce: The Parisian Merchant Court and the Rise of Commercial Society in Eighteenth-Century France* (New Haven: Yale University Press, 2007), 188–285.

2. Daniel T. Rodgers, *Atlantic Crossings: Social Politics in a Progressive Age* (Cambridge: Belknap Press of Harvard University Press, 1998), 3–4.

3. Amalia D. Kessler, "Marginalization and Myth: The Corporatist Roots of France's Forgotten Elective Judiciary," *American Journal of Comparative Law* 58 (2010): 698–701; Jean Léonnet, "Une creation de l'Assemblée Constituante: La conciliation judiciaire," in *Une autre justice: Contributions à l'histoire de la justice sous la Révolution française* (Paris: Fayard, 1989), 273; Anthony Crubaugh, *Balancing the Scales of Justice: Local Courts and Rural Society in Southwest France, 1750–1800* (University Park: Pennsylvania State University Press, 2001), 132, 135–36, 141–42, 146–47; Richard M. Andrews, "The Justices of the Peace of Revolutionary Paris, September 1792–November 1794 (Frimaire Year III)," *Past and Present* 52 (1971): 58–61; George Martin, *Les justices de paix en France: manuel pratique des juges de paix, précis raisonné et complet de leurs attributions judiciaires, extrajudiciaires, civiles, administratives, de police et d'instruction criminelle en suite de tous les changements de législation* (Paris: Garnier frères, 1880), 2; Isser Woloch, *The New Regime: Transformations of the French Civic Order, 1789–1820s* (New York: W.W. Norton, 1994), 307–08.

4. Henrion de Pansey, *De la compétence des juges de paix*, 2d ed. (Paris: chez Théophile Barrois pere libraire, 1812), 3 (quoting Deputy Thourette); D. Dalloz, *Jurisprudence générale: Répertoire méthodique et alphabetique de législation de doctrine et de jurisprudence en matière de droit civil, commercial, criminel, administratif, de droit des gens et de droit public, nouvelle edition*, ed. A. Pougin, s.v. "compétence civile des tribunaux de paix" (Paris: Bureau de la jurisprudence générale, 1849), 11:88–89 (art. 5).

5. Martin 405–06; Woloch 319; Jean-Claude Farcy, "Les juges de paix et la politique au XIXe siècle," in *Une justice de proximité: la justice de paix, 1790–1958*, ed. Jacques-Guy Petit (Paris: Presses Universitaires de France, 2003), 143, 161; Serge Defois and Vincent Bernaudeau, "Les juges de paix de Loire-Atlantique (1895–1958): une magistrature de proximité?" in *Une justice de proximité*, 195, 200–01.

6. "Décret contentant réglement sur les conseils de prud'hommes (11 juin 1809)," in *Collection complète des lois, décrets, ordonnances, réglemens, avis du conseil-d'état*, ed. J. B. Duvergier (Paris: Guyot et Scribe, 1836), 387–88 (Tit. III: "Mode de nomination et d'installation des prud'hommes"); William H. McPherson and Frederic Meyers, *The French Labor Courts: Judgment by Peers* (Urbana: Institute of Labor and Industrial Relations, University of Illinois, 1966), 16; Alain Cottereau, "Justice et injustice ordinaire sur les lieux de travail d'après les audiences prud'hommales (1806–1866)," *Le mouvement social* 141 (Oct.–Dec. 1987): 35; "Décret contentant réglement sur les conseils de prud'hommes," 388 (Tit. IV, art. 22); ibid., 389 (Tit. V, art. 36); Monique Kieffer,

"La législation prud'hommale de 1806 à 1907," *Le Mouvement social* 141 (Oct.–Dec. 1987): 12.

7. Kessler, *Revolution in Commerce* 68–80; Claire Lemercier, "The Judge, the Expert, and the Arbitrator: The Strange Case of the Paris Court of Commerce (ca. 1800–ca. 1880)," in *Fields of Expertise: A Comparative History of Expert Procedures in Paris and London, 1600 to Present*, ed. Christelle Rabier (Newcastle, U.K.: Cambridge Scholars Pub., 2007), 117, 130–35.

8. "III. Arbitration in Trade Disputes," in *Companion to the Almanac; or Year-book of General Information for 1857* (London: Knight & Co., 1857), 42.

9. Annemarie Højer Pedersen, "'Skranker for Lovtrækkeriets Krumveie': De Danske Forligskommissioner Deres Nedlaæggelse Og Genopstaen" (Ph.D. diss., Copenhagen University, 2005), Section 1.2.

10. Antoine Follain, "De la justice seigneuriale à la justice de paix," in *Une justice de proximité,* 19–33; Serge Bianchi, "La justice de paix pendant la Révolution, acquis et perspectives," in *Une justice de proximité,* 39; Gilles Rouet, "La justice de paix en France entre 1834 et 1950: une exploration spatiale," in *Une justice de proximité,* 98–99; Steven G. Reinhardt, *Justice in the Sarladais, 1770–1790* (Baton Rouge: Louisiana State University Press, 1991), 150–52.

11. Norma Landau, *The Justices of the Peace, 1679–1760* (Berkeley: University of California Press, 1984), 173–208.

12. A leading mid-nineteenth-century Spanish treatise on civil procedure, for example, framed much of its analysis of conciliation and conciliation courts by explicating (and critiquing) the views of a "celebrated writer"—namely, Bentham. José de Vicente y Caravantes, *Tratado histórico, crítico, filosófico de los procedimientos judiciales en material civil, segun la nueva ley de enjuiciamiento; con suscorrespondientes formularios* (Madrid: Imprenta de Gaspar y Roig, 1856), 1:450, 453–55.

13. Henry Peter Brougham, *Speeches of Henry Lord Brougham, Upon Questions Relating to Public Rights, Duties, and Interests; with Historical Introductions, and a Critical Dissertation upon the Eloquence of the Ancients* (Edinburgh: Adam & Charles Black et al., 1838), 2:287–88; Paul D. Carrington, "'Substance' and 'Procedure' in the Rules Enabling Act," *Duke Law Journal* (1989): 299 & n.123; Michael Lobban, "Henry Brougham and Law Reform," *English Historical Review* 115 (2000): 1186 & n.3.

14. Amalia D. Kessler, "Deciding against Conciliation: The Nineteenth-Century Rejection of a European Transplant and the Rise of a Distinctively American Ideal of Adversarial Adjudication," *Theoretical Inquiries in Law* 10 (2009): 432–42.

15. Paul E. Johnson, *A Shopkeeper's Millennium: Society and Revivals in Rochester, New York, 1815–1837* (New York: Hill and Wang, 1978), 37–42.

16. Wilentz, "Society, Politics, and the Market Revolution, 1815–1848" 63–64; Sellers 17–19.

17. Karen Haltunen, *Confidence Men and Painted Women: A Study of Middle-Class Culture in America, 1830–1870* (New Haven: Yale University Press, 1982); Patricia Cline

Cohen, *The Murder of Helen Jewett: The Life and Death of a Prostitute in Nineteenth-Century New York* (New York: Alfred A. Knopf, Inc., 1998).

18. Mary P. Ryan, *Cradle of the Middle Class: The Family in Oneida County, 1790–1865* (Cambridge: Cambridge University Press, 1981).

19. Ibid.; Johnson, *Shopkeeper's Millennium.*

20. For an exploration of the interrelationship between these transformations in the family and the labor market, on the one hand, and tort law, on the other, see John Fabian Witt, "From Loss of Services to Loss of Support: The Wrongful Death Statutes, the Origins of Modern Tort Law, and the Making of the Nineteenth-Century Family," *Law and Social Inquiry* 25 (2000): 717–50.

21. Chase, *Law, Culture, and Ritual* 2; Nader and Todd, eds., *Disputing Process;* Roberts, *Order and Dispute.*

22. Hurst; William J. Novak, *The People's Welfare: Law and Regulation in Nineteenth-Century America* (Chapel Hill: University of North Carolina Press, 1996), 84–88; Christopher L. Tomlins, *Law, Labor, and Ideology in the Early American Republic* (Cambridge: Cambridge University Press, 1993), 294–97.

23. Harry N. Scheiber, "Private Rights and Public Power: American Law, Capitalism, and the Republican Polity in Nineteenth-Century America," *Yale Law Journal* 107 (1997): 859.

24. Walter W. Manley II, E. Canter Brown Jr., and Eric W. Rise, *The Supreme Court of Florida and Its Predecessor Courts, 1821–1917* (Gainesville: University Press of Florida, 1997), 4–14, 20–24; Charles D. Farris, "The Courts of Territorial Florida," *Florida Historical Quarterly* 19 (1941): 346–48.

25. "Legislative Council of Florida," *East Florida Herald,* May 31, 1823, p. 3; "Orders of the Day," *East Florida Herald,* June 28, 1823, p. 2.

26. Y. C. [pseud.], letter to the editor, *East Florida Herald,* August 2, 1823, p. 3; "Courts of Conciliation," *East Florida Herald,* June 28, 1823, p. 3; R. [pseud.], "Answer to S.," *East Florida Herald,* July 26, 1823, p. 2.

27. Jose Sanchez-Arcilla Bernal, *Historia de las instituciones politico-administrativas contemporaneas, 1808–1975* (Madrid: Dykinson, 1994), 5–7, 405.

28. Ibid., 9–28, 405; Enrique Orduño Rebollo, "El municipio y la organización territorial del Estado constitucional," in *El municipio constitucional* (Madrid: Instituto nacional de administración pública, 2003), 86; José de Vicente y Caravantes, *Tratado histórico, critico, filosófico de los procedimientos judiciales en material civil, segun la nueva ley de enjuiciamiento; con suscorrespondientes formularios* (Madrid: Imprenta de Gaspar y Roig, 1856), 1:450; Patricio de la Escosura, *Diccionario universal de derecho español constituido,* s.v. "alcalde municipal" (Madrid: Imprenta del diccionario univeral del derecho español constituido, 1853), 4:832–33 (discussing March 19, 1812 Constitution, Tit. 5, chap. 2, arts. 282–83); Langum, *Law and Community,* 132 n. 5. For an overview of the Cádiz Constitution and its influence in Spanish America, see M. C. Mirow, *Latin Amer-*

*ican Constitutions: The Constitution of Cádiz and its Legacy in Spanish America* (Cambridge: Cambridge University Press, 2015).

29. Vicente y Caravantes 1:453.

30. Tamar Herzog, *Upholding Justice: Society, State, and the Penal System in Quito (1650–1750)* (Ann Arbor: University of Michigan Press, 2004), 243–45.

31. M. C. Mirow, "The Constitution of Cádiz in Florida," *Florida Journal of International Law* 24 (2012): 271–329; Duvon Clough Corbitt, "The Administrative System in the Floridas, 1783–1821, II: The Government of East Florida, 1782–1821," *Tequesta: The Journal of the Historical Association of Southern Florida* 1 (1943): 61; Amy Bushnell, *The King's Coffer: Proprietors of the Spanish Florida Treasury, 1565–1702* (Gainesville: University Presses of Florida, 1981), 107–08; Duvon Clough Corbitt, "The Return of Spanish Rule to the St. Marys and the St. Johns," *Florida Historical Quarterly* 20 (1941): 58.

32. Charles Gibson, *Spain in America* (New York: Harper & Row, 1966), 170–73; Donald Eugene Smith, *The Viceroy of New Spain* (Berkeley: University of California Press, 1913), 1:258; Corbitt, "The Return of Spanish Rule," 53–58.

33. Allen Morris and Amelia Rea Maguire, "Beginnings of Popular Government in Florida," *Florida Historical Quarterly* 57 (1978): 22–29; "Legislative Council of Florida," May 31, 1823, p. 3.

34. Corbitt, "The Return of Spanish Rule," 55–56; Morris and Maguire 25.

35. Louise Biles Hill, "George J. F. Clarke, 1774–1836," *Florida Historical Quarterly* 21 (1943): 197, 204, 209; George J. F. Clarke [A Native Floridian, pseud.], letter to the editor, *East Florida Herald*, July 19, 1823, p. 2.

36. Reinhard Zimmermann, *The Law of Obligations: Roman Foundations of the Civilian Tradition* (Oxford: Clarendon Press, 1996), 528–30.

37. Clarke, letter to the editor, p. 2.

38. Leon Huhner, "Moses Elias Levy: An Early Florida Pioneer and the Father of Florida's First Senator," *Florida Historical Quarterly* 19 (1941): 319–229, 336–37; C. S. Monaco, *Moses Levy of Florida: Jewish Utopian and Antebellum Reformer* (Baton Rouge: Louisiana State University Press, 2005), 12–51, 95–114.

39. Moses E. Levy [Youlee, pseud.], letter to the editor, *East Florida Herald*, June 14, 1823, p. 3.

40. Ibid.

41. Wilentz, "Society, Politics, and the Market Revolution, 1815–1848" 66–68; Mark M. Smith, *Debating Slavery: Economy and Society in the Antebellum American South* (Cambridge: Cambridge University Press, 1998), 12–30, 87–94; Jonathan Daniel Wells, *The Origins of the Southern Middle Class, 1800–1861* (Chapel Hill: University of North Carolina Press, 2004); Tom Downey, *Planting a Capitalist South: Masters, Merchants, and Manufacturers in the Southern Interior, 1790–1860* (Baton Rouge: Louisiana State University Press, 2006).

42. Edward E. Baptist, *Creating an Old South: Middle Florida's Plantation Frontier Before the Civil War* (Chapel Hill: University of North Carolina Press, 2002), 18.

43. Y. C., letter to the editor, p. 3.

44. Clarke, letter to the editor, p. 2.

45. Amicus Curiae [pseud.], "Courts of Conciliation," *East Florida Herald*, June 7, 1823, p. 3.

46. Ibid.

47. Verus [pseud.], letter to the editor, *East Florida Herald*, June 14, 1823, p. 3.

48. Ibid.

49. "Courts of Conciliation," *East Florida Herald*, June 28, 1823, pp. 2–3; "Territorial Laws," *East Florida Herald*, July 19, 1823, p. 1.

50. "An Act to Provide for the Conciliation of Private Controversies," in *East Florida Herald*, "Territorial Laws," p. 1.

51. Langum, *Law and Community*, 32–33; Brian R. Hamnett, *A Concise History of Mexico*, 2d ed. (Cambridge: Cambridge University Press, 2006), 138, 141.

52. Langum, *Law and Community*, 35–40, 101, 132 & n. 5; March 20, 1837 statute, in *Report of the Debates in the Convention of California on the Formation of the State Constitution in September and October, 1849*, ed. J. Ross Browne (Washington, D.C.: John T. Towers, 1850), appendix, xxxi–xxxiv; May 23, 1837 statute, in *Report of the Debates in the Convention of California*, appendix, xxxviii–xxxix.

53. *American Ins. Co. v. 356 Bales of Cotton*, 26 U.S. 511, 542 (1828); David J. Langum, "California Rejects the Mandatory Conciliation Formerly Required Under Mexican Law," in *Historic U.S. Cases: An Encyclopedia*, 2d ed., ed. John W. Johnson (New York: Routledge, 2001), 211; *Report of the Debates in the Convention of California*, appendix, xxiv–xxv.

54. *Von Schmidt v. Huntington*, 1 Cal. 55, 59 (1850).

55. Stephen J. Field, *Personal Reminiscences of Early Days in California, with Other Sketches* (Washington, D.C.: n.p., 1893); Walter Colton, *Three Years in California* (New York: A. S. Barnes, 1850; reprint, New York: Arno Press, 1976); Edwin Bryant, *What I Saw in California: Being the Journal of a Tour, by the Emigrant Route and South Pass of the Rocky Mountains, Across the Continent of North America, The Great Desert Basin, and Through California, in the Years 1846, 1847*, 3d ed. (New York: D. Appleton & Co., 1849); James Rand Robertson, "From Alcalde to Mayor: A History of the Change from the Mexican to the American Local Institutions in California" (Ph.D. diss., University of California, Berkeley, 1908), 209.

56. See art. VI, Sec. 13 of Constitution of 1850, cited in *Report of the Debates in the Convention of California*, appendix, ix.

57. James Robertson argued that this provision was designed to preserve the Spanish-Mexican conciliation courts, but he failed to recognize that this language was lifted directly from the New York Constitution. Robertson 267.

58. George Hamlin Fitch, "How California Came Into the Union," *The Century: Illustrated Monthly Magazine* 40 (September 1890): 788; 1 Cal. 58.

59. 1 Cal. 65, 64.

60. Robertson 209.

61. Max Weber, *Economy and Society: An Outline of Interpretive Sociology,* ed. Guenther Roth and Claus Wittich (Berkeley: University of California Press, 1978), 2:976.

62. Langum, *Law and Community* 135, 138.

63. Ibid., 131–52, 138.

64. Field's narrative, unlike the others, was not published around the time of the Gold Rush. Originally written in July 1877 as a "campaign biography," designed to assist in Field's 1880 run for the presidency, the narrative was widely used during the campaign. But the entire work did not appear in print as a single whole until 1893. Paul Kens, *Justice Stephen Field: Shaping Liberty from the Gold Rush to the Gilded Age* (Lawrence: University Press of Kansas, 1997), 177 & n. 31.

65. Brian Roberts, *American Alchemy: The California Gold Rush and Middle-Class Culture* (Chapel Hill: University of North Carolina Press, 2000).

66. Carl Brent Swisher, *Stephen J. Field: Craftsman of the Law* (Washington, D.C.: The Brookings Institution, 1930), 5; Charles W. McCurdy, "Prelude to Civil War: A Snapshot of the California Supreme Court at Work in 1858," *California Supreme Court Historical Society* 1 (1994): 5; Stephen A. Siegel, "The Revision Thickens," *Law and History Review* 20 (Fall 2002): 631–37; Manuel Cachán, "Justice Stephen Field and 'Free Soil, Free Labor Constitutionalism': Reconsidering Revisionism," *Law and History Review* 20 (Fall 2002): 541–76.

67. Field, *Personal Reminiscences* 1–6, 20–22; Swisher 20–24; McCurdy 3.

68. Field, *Personal Reminiscences* 36–37, 27. For an account of the lawlessness (both real and perceived) of California in this period, see Roger D. McGrath, "A Violent Birth: Disorder, Crime, and Law Enforcement, 1849–1890," in *Taming the Elephant: Politics, Government, and Law in Pioneer California,* ed. John F. Burns and Richard J. Orsi (Berkeley: University of California Press, 2003), 27–73; and Gordon Morris Bakken, "The Courts, the Legal Profession, and the Development of Law in Early California," in *Taming the Elephant,* 74–95.

69. Field, *Personal Reminiscences* 35–36.

70. Ibid., 36.

71. Steven Wilf, "The Invention of Legal Primitivism," *Theoretical Inquiries in Law* 10 (2009): 499.

72. M. D. Gilman, *The Bibliography of Vermont, or a List of Books and Pamphlets Relating in Any Way to the State, with Biographical and Other Notes* (Burlington: The Free Press Association, 1897), 61; Colton 13–17, 55; David Brion Davis, *Antebellum American Culture: An Interpretive Anthology* (University Park: Pennsylvania State University Press, 1997), 116.

73. R. John Brockmann, *Commodore Robert F. Stockton, 1795–1866: Protean Man for a Protean Nation* (Amherst, N.Y.: Cambria Press, 2009), 140.

74. Colton 33, 44, 50–51, 63–64, 75–76, 195–97, 236, 356.

75. For an account of the many negative stereotypes of the Californios held by newly arriving migrants from the East (and from Europe), see Shirley Ann Wilson Moore, "'We Feel the Want of Protection': The Politics of Law and Race in California, 1848–1878," in *Taming the Elephant*, 99–102.

76. Colton 112–13.

77. Ibid., 357, 249, 55, 197, 236.

78. Ibid., 236 (referencing Heb. 11:21).

79. John Hughes and John Breckinridge, *A Discussion of the Question Is the Roman Catholic Religion, in Any or in All Its Principles or Doctrines, Inimical to Civil or Religious Liberty?, and of the Question Is the Presbyterian Religion, in Any or in All Its Principles or Doctrines, Inimical to Civil or Religious Liberty?* (Philadelphia: Carey, Lea, and Blanchard, 1836), 428; J. Endell Tyler, *The Image-Worship of the Church of Rome Proved to Be Contrary to Holy Scripture and the Faith and Discipline of the Primitive Church, and to Involve Contradictory and Irreconcilable Doctrines Within the Church of Rome Itself* (London: Francis and John Rivington, 1847), 103–04.

80. Brockmann 140.

81. Ibid.

82. Consider also the account published by Edwin Bryant, which proved to be an enormous success, going through six American editions (as well as separate English, French, and Swedish editions) by 1850. Jack Hicks et al., eds., *The Literature of California: Writing from the Golden State (Native American Beginnings to 1945)*, (Berkeley: University of California Press, 2000), 129.

83. "Courts of Conciliation," *Connecticut Mirror*, July 28, 1823, p. 3; "Domestic," *Boston Recorder*, July 26, 1823, vol. 8, p. 119.

84. *Report of the Debates and Proceedings of the Convention for the Revision of the Constitution of the State of New York* (Albany: Evening Atlas, 1846), 588.

85. "Lord Brougham's Local Court Bill, with Full Particulars Relating to the Inferior Courts of Scotland, and the Continental Courts of Conciliation," *Law Magazine, or Quarterly Review of Jurisprudence* 5 (1831): 36–37 (citing and discussing *Edinburgh Review* no. 102, p. 495). See also "Literary Intelligence: The Law Magazine and Quarterly Review of Jurisprudence, No. XI, London—Saunders and Benning," *United States Law Intelligencer and Review* 3 (1831): 225, 225 (discussing the aforementioned piece in the *Law Magazine, or Quarterly Review of Jurisprudence*); Joanne Shattock, "Spheres of Influence: The Quarterlies and Their Readers," *Yearbook of English Studies: Literature and Its Audience* 10 (1980): 95–104.

86. Jean-Pierre Catteau-Calville, *Tableau des états danois, envisagés sous les rapports du mécanisme social* (Paris: Treuttel et Würtz, 1802), 1:298.

87. Sydney Smith, "Catteau, Tableau des états danois (*Edinburgh Review*, 1803)," in *The Works of the Reverend Sydney Smith* (Boston, Phillips, Sampson & Co. 1858), 270–79.

88. *Weekly Visitor, or Ladies' Miscellany* [New York], "From the Present State of Denmark, by Catteau, 1802," June 29, 1805, p. 5; "Tribunal of Conciliation," *Enquirer* [Richmond], July 5, 1805, p. 3; *Suffolk Gazette* [Sag Harbor, N.Y.], "From the Present State of Denmark, by Catteau, 1802," July 22, 1805, p. 1; *Political Observatory* [Walpole, N.H.], "Extract from the Present State of Denmark, by Catteau, Written in 1802," August 3, 1805, p. 4; *Green Mountain Patriot* [Peacham, Vt.], "Historical Extract from the Present State of Denmark, by Catteau, Written in 1802," May 13, 1806, p. 1; *Post-Boy* [Windsor, Vt.], "Extract from the Present State of Denmark, by Catteau, Written in 1802," June 3, 1806, p. 172.

89. Miller, *Life of the Mind* 96–116; Richard E. Ellis, *The Jeffersonian Crisis: Courts and Politics in the Young Republic* (New York: Oxford University Press, 1971), 111–22, 157–70.

90. Horwitz 140–59. But see Moglen 147–51; Carli N. Conklin, "Transformed, Not Transcended: The Role of Extrajudicial Dispute Resolution in Antebellum Kentucky and New Jersey," *American Journal of Legal History* 48 (2006): 39–98.

91. Jesse Higgins, *Sampson against the Philistines, or, The Reformation of Lawsuits: and Justice Made Cheap, Speedy, and Brought Home to Every Man's Door: Agreeably to the Principles of the Ancient Trial by Jury, Before the Same was Innovated by Judges and Lawyers,* 2d ed. (Philadelphia: B. Graves, 1805), 31.

92. "Tribunal of Conciliation," *Enquirer* [Richmond], p. 3.

93. Lobban, "Henry Brougham and Law Reform" 1184–85, 1204. That Brougham played such a significant role in promoting conciliation courts may be surprising because he is widely remembered as a champion of zealous advocacy—of the principle that a lawyer's duty is to place the (adversarial) vindication of his client's interests over and above all other, more public-minded concerns. Spaulding, "Myth of Civic Republicanism" 1420 & n. 90; Fred C. Zacharias and Bruce A. Green, "Conceptualizing Advocacy Ethics," *George Washington Law Review* 74 (2005): 2–3. But as one scholar has suggested—and as Brougham's advocacy of conciliation courts would seem to confirm—this traditional portrait of the chancellor may well be overdrawn. Monroe H. Freedman, "Henry Lord Brougham, Written by Himself," *Georgetown Journal of Legal Ethics* 19 (2006): 1213–19.

94. Brougham 2:408.

95. Ibid., 2:408, 2:523–24.

96. Vanderlyn 4:169 (entry not dated, but located between those for July 25, 1837 and August 26, 1837).

97. *Report of the Debates and Proceedings* (1846), 589.

98. Jessica M. Lepler, "1837: Anatomy of a Panic" (Ph.D. diss., Brandeis University, 2008), 8–12, 329; John Joseph Wallis, "What Caused the Crisis of 1839?" *National Bureau of Economic Research Historical Paper* 133 (April 2001): 1; Ballard C. Campbell, *Disasters, Accidents, and Crises in American History: A Reference Guide to the Nation's Most Catastrophic Events* (New York: Facts on File, 2008), 78; Claudia Goldin and Robert A.

Margo, "Wages, Prices, and Labor Markets Before the Civil War," in *Strategic Factors in Nineteenth-Century American Economic History: A Volume to Honor Robert W. Fogel,* ed. Claudia Goldin and Hugh Rockoff (Chicago: University of Chicago Press, 1992), 67–69; Sean Wilentz, *Chants Democratic: New York City and the Rise of the American Working Class, 1788–1850,* 20th anniversary ed. (London: Oxford University Press, 2004), 294, 95, 299–300.

99. Jan M. Saltzgaber, "For the Salvation of the World! Revivalism and Reform in Seneca Falls, New York," in Glenn C. Altschuler and Jan M. Saltzgaber, *Revivalism, Social Conscience, and Community in the Burned-Over District: The Trial of Rhoda Bement* (Ithaca: Cornell University Press, 1983), 32.

100. Freyer 76–83.

101. Whitney R. Cross, *The Burned-Over District: The Social and Intellectual History of Enthusiastic Religion in Western New York, 1800–1850* (Ithaca: Cornell University Press, 1950), 268–71; Michael Barkun, *Crucible of the Millennium: The Burned-Over District of New York in the 1840s* (Syracuse, N.Y.: Syracuse University Press, 1986), 119–20; Wilentz, *Chants Democratic* 300, 305.

102. Henry M. Baird, *The Life of the Reverend Robert Baird, D.D.* (New York: Anson D. F. Randolph, 1866), 200–07, 287–88; "Lecture on Norway, Sweden, and Denmark by Dr. Baird," May 9, 1846, *Friends' Weekly Intelligencer* [Philadelphia], p. 41; "The World Abroad, Lectures on Europe by the Rev. Dr. Baird: No. 3, Russia (Continued)—Scandinavia—Holland—Belgium—Germany," *Saturday Evening Post* [Philadelphia], May 12, 1849, p. 2; "Original Lectures, Rev. Dr. Baird's Historical Lectures on Europe: The Scandinavian Countries, Norway, Sweden, Denmark, and Germany," *Saturday Evening Post* [Philadelphia], May 25, 1850, p. 2.

103. "Original Lectures," *Saturday Evening Post* [Philadelphia], p. 2.

104. "Lecture on Norway, Sweden, and Denmark," *Friends' Weekly Intelligencer* [Philadelphia], p. 41.

105. *Report of the Debates and Proceedings* (1846), 833.

106. Wellman, *Grass Roots Reform* 149.

107. *Report of the Debates and Proceedings* (1846), 588.

108. Jabez D. Hammond, *Political History of the State of New York from Jan. 1, 1841 to Jan. 1, 1847* (Syracuse: L. W. Hall, 1849), 3:513.

109. *Report of the Debates and Proceedings* (1846), 589.

110. Ibid., 588, 658.

111. Ibid., 658, 589.

112. Ibid., 588–89, 611.

113. Ibid., 589, 612, 658.

114. Jane Rendall, "Recovering Lost Political Cultures: British Feminisms, 1860–1900," in *Women's Emancipation Movements in the Nineteenth Century,* ed. Sylvia Paletschek and Bianka Pietrow-Ennker (Stanford: Stanford University Press, 2004), 45.

115. Judith Wellman, *The Road to Seneca Falls: Elizabeth Cady Stanton and the First Woman's Rights Convention* (Urbana: University of Illinois Press, 2004), 8, 80, 86, 121, 148.

116. Jerold S. Auerbach, *Justice Without Law? Non-Legal Dispute Settlement in American History* (New York: Oxford University Press, 1983), 101–02; Claire Lemercier, *Un modèle français des jugement des pairs: les tribunaux de commerce, 1790–1880* (Paris: Université Paris VIII Vincennes-Saint Denis, 2012), 302–49, available at http://tel.archives-ouvertes.fr/tel-00685544/.

117. *Report of the Debates and Proceedings* (1846), 658–59.

118. Ibid., 799–800.

119. Wilentz, *Chants Democratic* 214–15.

120. Ibid., 219–53, 299–359, 363–89.

121. *Report of the Debates and Proceedings* (1846), 589.

122. Richard E. Quest, *Images of America: Tioga County New York* (Charleston: Arcadia Publishing, 1999), 92.

123. *Report of the Debates and Proceedings* (1846), 738.

124. Saltzgaber 26; Wellman, *Road to Seneca Falls*, 75.

125. David McAdam, ed., *History of the Bench and Bar of New York* (New York: New York History Co., 1897), 1:522.

126. L. B. Proctor, *The Bench and Bar of New-York, Containing Biographical Sketches of Eminent Judges, and Lawyers of the New-York Bar, Incidents of the Important Trials in which They Were Engaged, and Anecdotes Connected with Their Professional, Political, and Judicial Career* (New York: Diossy and Co., 1870), 588–89.

127. *Biographical Directory of the United States Congress, 1774–2005, The Continental Congress, September 5, 1774, to October 21, 1788, and The Congress of the United States from the First Through the One Hundred Eighth Congresses, March 4, 1789, to January 3, 2005, Inclusive* (Washington, D.C.: United States Government Printing Office, 2005), 2021–22 (s.v. "John James Taylor").

128. *History of the Bench and Bar*, 1:414.

129. *Report of the Debates and Proceedings* (1846), 593.

130. McCurdy 280, 282.

131. *Report of the Debates and Proceedings* (1846), 589.

132. "Henry Nicoll's Defalcation: Progress of the Investigation of His Affairs—Matters Not Believed to Be So Bad As Reported," *New York Times*, January 24, 1875.

133. "Death of James C. Forsyth Confirmed," *New York Times*, March 19, 1856.

134. *Report of the Debates and Proceedings* (1846), 799–800, 590.

135. Ibid., 799.

136. "Political Portraits with Pen and Pencil: Robert H. Morris," *The United States Magazine and Democratic Review* 20, no. 58 (June 1847): 551–56.

137. *Report of the Debates and Proceedings* (1846), 813.

138. Art. vi, Sec. 23 of the 1846 Constitution, in ibid., 11.

139. "Domestic: Court of Conciliation," *New York Observer and Chronicle*, April 10, 1847, p. 59; D. M. Mahon, "Tribunals of Conciliation," *Christian Inquirer* [New York], September 18, 1852, p. 1; An Observer [pseud.], "Litigation," *Cultivator* [Albany] 6 (October 1849): 315.

140. "A Good Recommendation," *Saturday Evening Post* [Philadelphia], February 9, 1850, p. 2. See also "Governor's Message," *New York Daily Times*, January 17, 1856, p. 2 (message of Governor Myron Clark).

141. S. Lindsey, "A Court of Conciliation," *Boston Cultivator*, March 30, 1850, p. 101.

142. For a discussion of the Indiana provision, see chapter 6. Steven H. Steinglass and Gino J. Scarselli, *The Ohio State Constitution: A Reference Guide* (Westport, Conn.: Praeger, 2004), 193; *Small Claims and Conciliation Court, Hearings Before the Comm. on D.C., U.S. Senate, Seventy-Fifth Cong., First Sess. on S. 1835 ("A Bill Establishing a Small Claims and Conciliation Branch in the Municipal Court of D.C. for Improving the Administration of Justice in Small Cases and Providing Assistance to Needy Litigants, and for Other Purposes")* 70 (n.p.: n.p., 1937); Frank Ravitch, "The Four Michigan Constitutions," in *The History of Michigan Law*, ed. Paul Finkelman and Martin J. Hershock (Athens: Ohio University Press, 2006), 134 & n. 81; John B. Winslow, "Tribunals of Conciliation," *Report of the Proceedings of Meetings of the State Bar Association of Wisconsin*, for the years 1912–1913–1914 (1915), 10:206.

143. Indiana and North Dakota both adopted conciliation courts, but these quickly failed. Indiana's experience is discussed in chapter 6. North Dakota established conciliation courts in 1893, shortly after its admission to statehood. Such conciliation proceedings, however, were to be brought only after a formal lawsuit had been commenced and, as established by an 1895 statute, upon the consent of both parties. These courts thus rapidly fell into disuse. *Small Claims and Conciliation Court*, 70; Eric H. Steele, "The Historical Context of Small Claims Courts," *American Bar Foundation Research Journal* 6 (1981): 312; Winslow 224.

144. "Adjournment of the Legislature," *New York Evangelist*, May 20, 1847, p. 79; "State Affairs: Courts of Conciliation," *New York Daily Times*, January 29, 1855, p. 1; "Courts of Conciliation," *New York Evangelist*, February 15, 1855, p. 26.

145. Augustin-Amant-Constant-Fidèle Edouart, *Silhouettes of Eminent Americans, 1839–1844*, ed. Andrew Oliver (Charlottesville: University Press of Virginia, 1977), 169.

146. Document no. 98, Apr. 28, 1847, "Letter of Steen Bille, relative to Conciliation Courts," in *Documents of the Senate of the State of New York, Seventieth Session, 1847* (Albany: Charles Van Benthuysen, 1847), 3:1, 6

147. Ibid., 4–5.

148. Ibid., 294.

149. *The Code of Civil Procedure of the State of New-York, Reported by the Commissioners on Practice and Pleading* (Albany: Weed, Parsons, & Co., 1850), 642.

150. Ibid., 643 (tit. VII, sec. 1528 and sec. 1530).

151. Ibid., 644 (tit. VII, sec. 1532).

152. Ibid., 641; *Report of the Debates and Proceedings* (1846), 836.

153. *Code of Civil Procedure*, 641–42 (tit. VII, sec. 1523).

154. Document no. 72, Feb. 14, 1862, of the Committe of the Judiciary, on the Bill Entitled "An Act to Establish a Tribunal of Conciliation in the County of Delaware," in *Documents of the Assembly of the State of New York, Eighty-Fifth Session, 1862* (Albany: Charles Van Benthuysen, 1862), 4:1–2.

155. An Act to Establish a Tribunal of Conciliation in the Sixth Judicial District, in *Statutes at Large of the State of New York, Comprising the Revised Statutes, as They Existed on the 1st Day of July, 1862*, ed. John W. Edmonds (Albany: Weare C. Little, 1863), 4:603, 605 (ch. 451, sec. 7).

156. Letter from Deborah Lambrecht, Records Management, Delaware County Clerk's Office, Delhi, New York to author (Oct. 12, 2007); e-mail from James Folts, head of Reference Services, New York State Archives, Albany, New York to author (Oct. 1, 2007).

157. Amalia D. Kessler, "Arbitration and Americanization: The Paternalism of Progressive Procedural Reform," *Yale Law Journal* 124 (2015): 2961–73; Barbara Yngvesson and Patricia Hennessey, "Small Claims, Complex Disputes: A Review of the Small Claims Literature," *Law and Society Review* 9 (1975): 219–74: Steele 348–55.

158. Cook 69–118.

159. Consider, for example, Francis Lieber, a German immigrant. John Arkas Hawgood, *The Tragedy of German-America: The Germans in the United States of America During the Nineteenth Century—and After* (New York: G.P. Putnam's Sons, 1940; reprint, n.p.: Arno Press, 1970), 239.

160. Many of those arguing both for and against conciliation courts were the elite lawyers who belonged to the Convention's thirteen-member Judiciary Committee. Charles Z. Lincoln, *The Constitutional History of New York: From the Beginning of the Colonial Period to the Year 1905, Showing the Origin, Development, and Judicial Construction of the Constitution* (1906), 2:140; Hammond, 3:622.

161. Wilentz, *Chants Democratic* 306–14.

162. Ibid., 308.

163. *Report of the Debates and Proceedings* (1846), 611.

164. Francis Lieber, *On Civil Liberty and Self-Government*, 2d ed. (Philadelphia: J. B. Lippincott, 1859), 232–34.

165. Bianchi 39; Rouet 98–99.

166. Laura F. Edwards, *The People and Their Peace: Legal Culture and the Transformation of Inequality in the Post-Revolutionary South* (Chapel Hill: University of North Carolina, 2009), 6–7, 74.

167. *Report of the Debates and Proceedings* (1846) 880, 800, 836.

168. Ibid., 589.

169. "Courts of Conciliation," *Alexandria Gazette*, January 21, 1856, p. 2.

## Chapter 6. The Freedmen's Bureau Exception

1. George R. Bentley, *A History of the Freedmen's Bureau* (Philadelphia: University of Pennsylvania Press, 1955), 16–26; Ira Berlin et al., *Free at Last: A Documentary History of Slavery, Freedom, and the Civil War* (New York: The New Press, 1992), xxxi; Michael W. Fitzgerald, "Emancipation and Military Pacification: The Freedmen's Bureau and Social Control in Alabama," in *The Freedmen's Bureau and Reconstruction: Reconsiderations*, ed. Paul A. Cimbala and Randall M. Miller (New York: Fordham University Press, 1999), 46; Robert J. Kaczorowski, *The Politics of Judicial Interpretation: The Federal Courts, Department of Justice, and Civil Rights, 1866–1876* (New York: Fordham University Press, 2005), 21.

2. "General Howard's Report on the Freedmen's Bureau," *New York Times*, December 25, 1865, p. 4. See also "Speech of Hon. J. H. Ela," *New Hampshire Statesman*, January 31, 1868, col. E.

3. American Freedmen's Inquiry Commission, *Preliminary Report Touching the Condition and Management of Emancipated Refugees, June 30, 1863* (New York: John F. Trow, 1863), 27. See also Bentley 25; Eric Foner, *Reconstruction: America's Unfinished Revolution, 1863–1877* (New York: Harper & Row, 1988), 68; John W. Blassingame, ed., *Slave Testimony: Two Centuries of Letters, Speeches, Interviews, and Autobiographies* (Baton Rouge: Louisiana State University Press, 1977), 370; John G. Sproat, "Blueprint for Radical Reconstruction," *Journal of Southern History* vol. 23, no. 1 (February 1957): 34.

4. Cong. Globe, 38th Cong., 1st Sess. 3285–86 (1864); Richard William Leopold, *Robert Dale Owen: A Biography* (Cambridge: Harvard University Press, 1940), 361–62.

5. *Preliminary Report*, 33.

6. E. Anthony Rotundo, *American Manhood: Transformations in Masculinity from the Revolution to the Modern Era* (New York: Basic Books, 1993); Jonathan Levy, *Freaks of Fortune: The Emerging World of Capitalism and Risk in America* (Cambridge: Harvard University Press, 2012).

7. Robert Dale Owen, J. McKaye, and Saml. G. Howe, "Final Report of the American Freedmen's Inquiry Commission to the Secretary of War," in *Index to the Senate Executive Documents for the First Session of the Thirty-Eighth Congress of the United States of America, 1863–64* (Washington, D.C.: Government Printing Office, 1864), 110.

8. *Preliminary Report*, 33.

9. "Final Report," 25.

10. *Preliminary Report*, 30–31.

11. Ibid., 32–33.

12. Ibid., 31.

13. Final Report, 110.

14. David S. Clark, ed., *Comparative Law and Society* (Cheltenham, U.K.: Edward Elgar Publishing, 2012), 79.

15. *Preliminary Report*, 31.

16. Ibid., 71, 109.

17. Leopold 65–84, 321–39.

18. Robert Dale Owen, "One of the Problems of the Age," *The United States Magazine, and Democratic Review* (New York: Henry G. Langley, 1844), 14:156.

19. Robert Dale Owen, *Twenty-Seven Years of Autobiography: Threading My Way* (New York: G. W. Carleton, 1874), 260; Leopold 6–46.

20. Leopold 19–23, 31–34; Owen, *Autobiography* 286; "Abstract of the Proceedings of the Convention Instituted for the Formation of a Constitution of Government for the New-Harmony Community of Equality," *The New-Harmony Gazette*, February 15, 1826, vol. 1, no. 21, p. 161.

21. "Constitution of the New-Harmony Community of Equality," *The New-Harmony Gazette*, February 15, 1826, vol. 1, no. 21, p. 163 (art. 13).

22. Thomas Edlyne Tomlins, *The Law Dictionary, Explaining the Rise, Progress, and Present State of the British Law: Defining and Interpreting the Terms or Words of Art, and Comprising Also Copious Information on the Subjects of Trade and Government*, 4th ed., s.v. "Compromise" (1835), 1, n.p.; Alexander M. Burrill, *A New Law Dictionary and Glossary: Containing Full Definitions of the Principal Terms of the Common and Civil Law*, s.v. "Compromise" (1850; repr., Clark, N.J.: The Lawbook Exchange, 2008), 249.

23. Leopold 27–28, 43–44.

24. Owen, *Autobiography* 89, 44–45.

25. Leopold 65–102; Wilentz, *Chants Democratic* 176–216.

26. Owen, "One of the Problems of the Age."

27. Leopold 123–235, 268–303.

28. Robert Dale Owen, "Tract No. 10, Situations," in *Popular Tracts* (New York: Free Enquirer, 1830), 2–3.

29. Leopold 270 (quoting *Madison Courier*, February 10, 1851).

30. "The West: Western Travel—Railroad Management—State of Indiana—Indianapolis—Agriculture," *New York Daily Times*, September 22, 1852, p. 2.

31. *Report of the Debates and Proceedings of the Convention for the Revision of the Constitution of the State of Indiana* (Indianapolis: A. H. Brown, 1850), 2:1906, 2:2073 (Art. VII, sec. 19).

32. Law of June 11, 1852, ch. 2, Ind. Laws, 224–26 (secs. 6–7, 14) (repealed 1865).

33. *Report of the Debates and Proceedings of the [Indiana] Convention*, 2:1912.

34. "Address to the Electors of the State (February 8, 1851)," in Charles Kettleborough, *Constitution Making in Indiana: A Source Book of Constitutional Documents with Historical Introduction and Critical Notes* (Indianapolis: Indiana Historical Commission, 1916), 1:409–10, see also 1:404; Jacob Piatt Dunn, *Indiana and Indians: A History of Aboriginal and Territorial Indiana and the Century of Statehood* (Chicago: American Historical Society, 1919), 1:451.

35. "Courts of Conciliation," *Chicago Inter-Ocean*, Nov. 12, 1887, in *Public Opinion: A Comprehensive Survey of the Press Throughout the World on All Important Current Topics* (Washington, D.C.: The Public Opinion Company, 1887–1888), 4:127.

36. *Journal of the House of Representatives, of the State of Indiana, during the Thirty-Ninth Session of the General Assembly of the State of Indiana, Commencing Thursday, January 8, 1857* (Indianapolis: Joseph J. Bingham, 1857), 98; *Journal of the House of Representatives of the State of Indiana, during the Forty-First Regular Session of the General Assembly, Commencing Thursday, January 10, 1861* (Indianapolis: Berry R. Sulgrove, 1861), 50, 301; *Journal of the House of Representatives of the State of Indiana, during the Forty-Third Session of the General Assembly, Commencing Thursday, January 8, 1863* (Indianapolis: Joseph J. Bingham, 1863), 217, 360; Law of Nov. 30, 1865, ch. 62, Ind. Laws, 163.

37. J. H. Binford, *History of Hancock County Indiana, from Its Earliest Settlement by the "Pale Face" in 1818 down to 1882* (Greenfield, Ind.: King and Binford, 1882), 392; Thomas B. Helm, ed., *History of Cass County, Indiana, from the Earliest Time to the Present* (Chicago: Brant and Fuller, 1886), 324.

38. "Courts of Conciliation," *Chicago Inter-Ocean*.

39. *Report of the Debates and Proceedings of the [Indiana] Convention*, 2:1906.

40. "Final Report," 106–07.

41. *Preliminary Report*, 23.

42. Paul Skeels Peirce, *The Freedmen's Bureau: A Chapter in the History of Reconstruction* (Iowa City: University of Iowa Press, 1904), 34; James M. McPherson, *The Struggle for Equality: Abolitionists and the Negro in the Civil War and Reconstruction* (Princeton: Princeton University Press, 1964), 186.

43. John G. Sproat, "Blueprint for Radical Reconstruction," *Journal of Southern History* 23 (1957): 34–35, 38; Cong. Globe, 38th Cong., 1st Sess. 3285–86 (1864).

44. Barry A. Crouch, *The Freedmen's Bureau and Black Texans* (Austin: University of Texas Press, 1992), 67; Williamjames Hull Hoffer, *To Enlarge the Machinery of Government: Congressional Debates and the Growth of the American State, 1858–1891* (Baltimore: Johns Hopkins University Press, 2007), 65–82.

45. An Act to Establish a Bureau of Emancipation, H.R. 51, 38th Cong. § 6 (1863).

46. An Act to Establish a Bureau of Freedmen's Affairs, S. Rep. No. 137 at § 6 (1864).

47. An Act to Establish a Department of Freedmen and Abandoned Lands, H.R. Rep. No. 38–9 at § 6 (1865) (Conf. Rep).

48. Cong. Globe, 38th Cong., 2nd Sess. 2973 (1864).

49. Peirce 38–43.

50. An Act to Establish a Bureau for the Relief of Freedmen and Refugees of 1865, § 90, 13 stat. 507, 508 (secs. 2, 4) (1866).

51. Mary Farmer-Kaiser, *Freedwomen and the Freedmen's Bureau: Race, Gender, and Public Policy in the Age of Emancipation* (New York: Fordham University Press, 2010), 15.

52. Owen, *Autobiography* 44–45.

53. Oliver Otis Howard, *Autobiography of Oliver Otis Howard: Major General United States Army* (New York: Baker & Taylor Co., 1908), 2:207–08.

54. William S. McFeely, *Yankee Stepfather: General O. O. Howard and the Freedmen* (New Haven: Yale University Press, 1968), 26–39; Howard, *Autobiography* 1:3–16, 44–58, 74–89; Oliver Otis Howard, *Major General Howard's Address at the Second Anniversary of the U.S. Christian Commission* (Philadelphia: Caxton Press of C. Sherman, Son & Co., 1864), 10.

55. John A. Carpenter, *Sword and Olive Branch: Oliver Otis Howard* (Pittsburgh: University of Pittsburgh Press, 1964), 24–25; Bentley 50–56; McFeely 9, 26, 61, 85.

56. "The Freedmen's Bureau," *New York Tribune*, August 22, 1865, p. 6; parts of speech also excerpted at "Speech of Gen. Howard at Kennebec, ME," *Philadelphia Inquirer*, August 18, 1865, p. 2.

57. E. Allen Richardson, "Architects of a Benevolent Empire: The Relationship Between the American Missionary Association and the Freedmen's Bureau in Virginia, 1865–1872," in *The Freedmen's Bureau and Reconstruction: Reconsiderations*, 119–21.

58. Circular No. 5 of May 30, 1865, H.R. Ex. Doc. No. 11, at 45 (39th Cong., 1st Sess. 1866); Bentley 152; Donald G. Nieman, *To Set the Law in Motion: The Freedmen's Bureau and the Legal Rights of Blacks, 1865–1868* (Millwood, N.Y.: KTO Press, 1979), 5–8.

59. Howard, *Autobiography* 2:198–99, 201.

60. "Report of the Commissioner of the Bureau of Refugees, Freedmen, and Abandoned Lands," H.R. Exec. Doc. No. 11, 39th Cong., 1st Sess. at 32–33 (1866).

61. Howard, *Autobiography* 2:251.

62. "Items of Interest," *Colored Tennessean*, October 7, 1865, p. 2; "Freedmen's Bureau in Virginia," *Lowell Daily Citizen and News*, October 5, 1865, p. 2; "Consultation," *Norfolk Post*, October 14, 1865.

63. "Consultation," *Norfolk Post*.

64. Howard, *Autobiography* 2:252.

65. Nieman 103–32, 143–45; "Report of the Commissioner of the Bureau of Refugees, Freedmen, and Abandoned Lands," H.R. Doc. No. 1, at 719 (39th Cong., 2d Sess. 1867).

66. H.R. Doc. No. 1, at 719 (39th Cong., 2d Sess. 1867).

67. "Proclamation Suspending the Writ of *Habeas Corpus* (September 24, 1862)," in *Lincoln: Political Writings and Speeches*, ed. Terence Ball (Cambridge: Cambridge University Press, 2013), 153–54.

68. Paul A. Cimbala, *The Freedmen's Bureau: Reconstructing the American South after the Civil War* (Malabar, Fla.: Krieger Publishing Co., 2005), 98–102; William L. Richter, *Overreached on All Sides: The Freedmen's Bureau Administrators in Texas, 1865–1868* (College Station: Texas A&M University Press, 1991), 71–72.

69. William Winthrop, *Military Law and Precedents*, 2d ed. (Boston: Little, Brown and Co., 1896), 2:1303–04; Mark E. Neely, *The Fate of Liberty: Abraham Lincoln and Civil Liberties* (New York: Oxford University Press, 1991), 162–63.

70. *Major General Howard's Address* 10, 11.

71. The Bureau courts (qua conciliation courts) must be distinguished from the "Court of Conciliation" that General Henry Halleck established in Richmond, Virginia, in May 1865 to address disputes regarding property and the payment of debt "where contracts were made upon the basis of confederate currency." "General Order No. 5, Military Division of the James (May 3, 1865)," in Walter L. Fleming, *Documentary History of Reconstruction: Political, Military, Social, Religious, Educational & Industrial, 1865 to the Present Time* (Cleveland: Arthur H. Clark Co., 1906), 1:203.

72. McPherson and Meyers 15–16; Kieffer 9–10; Cottereau 33–34; Amalia D. Kessler, "Marginalization and Myth: The Corporatist Roots of France's Forgotten Elective Judiciary," *American Journal of Comparative Law* 58 (2010): 679–720.

73. "Décret contentant réglement sur les conseils de prud'hommes (11 juin 1809)," in *Collection complète des lois, décrets, ordonnances, réglements, avis du conseil d'état*, ed. J. B. Duvergier (Paris: Guyot et Scribe, 1836), 386–88 (Tit. I, art. 1; Tit. III); Kieffer 11. It was only in 1880 that employers and employees were definitively guaranteed equal representation on the court. Kieffer 15–19; Alain Supiot, *Droit du travail* (Paris: Dalloz, 1987), 7–9.

74. D. Dalloz & Armand Dalloz, *Jurisprudence générale, répertoire méthodique et alphabétique de legislation, de doctrine et de jurisprudence en matière de droit civil, commercial, criminel, administratif, de droit des gens et de droit public* (Paris: Bureau de la jurisprudence générale, 1857), 38:539.

75. McPherson and Meyers 16; Cottereau 35; "Décret contentant réglement sur les conseils de prud'hommes," 388 (tit. IV, art. 22); ibid., 389 (tit. V, art. 36); Kieffer 12; Kessler, "Marginalization and Myth" 702–03.

76. George Bartle, *An Old Radical and His Brood: A Portrait of Sir John Bowring and His Family* (London: Janus Publishing, Co. 1994); Joyce Youings, ed., *Sir John Bowring, 1792–1872: Aspects of His Life and Career* (Plymouth: Devonshire Association, 1993); David Todd, "John Bowring and the Global Dissemination of Free Trade," *Historical Journal* 51 (2008): 375–82.

77. *Report from Select Committee on the Silk Trade with the Minutes of Evidence, an Appendix and Index* (n.p.: n.p., 1832), 542.

78. Ibid., 855–56.

79. E. P. Thompson, *The Making of the English Working Class* (New York: Vintage Books, 1966), 269–313; "Report from Select Committee on Hand-Loom Weavers' Petitions; with the Minutes of Evidence, and Index," *Reports from Committees: Sixteen Volumes* 13 (1835), iii.

80. "Report from Select Committee on Hand-Loom Weavers' Petitions," xix.

81. Ibid., 10, 20.

82. "Parliamentary Proceedings: House of Commons, Tuesday, March 6," *The Manchester Guardian*, March 10, 1855, p. 8; "Tuesday, March 6," *The Observer*, March 11, 1855, p. 11; "Report of the Select Committee on Masters and Operatives—Equitable

Councils of Conciliation," *The Observer*, August 3, 1856, p. 5; "Report from the Select Committee on Masters and Operatives; Together with the Proceedings of the Committee, Minutes of Evidence, Appendix and Index," in *Reports from Committees: Sixteen Volumes* 22 (1860), vii.

83. "Lords Sitting of Tuesday, August 2, 1859," in 155 *House of Lords Hansard* (3rd ser., 1859), at Col. 844–45 (Eng).

84. "Tuesday, August 2; The Strike in the Building Trades," *The Observer*, August 8, 1859, p. 2; "Report from the Select Committee on Masters and Operatives," vii.

85. Alexander Macdonald, *Handybook of the Law Relative to Masters, Workmen, Servants, and Apprentices* (London: W. Mackenzie, 1868), 275.

86. "Industrial Arbitration and Conciliation," in *Cyclopaedia of Political Science, Political Economy, and the Political History of the United States,* ed. John J. Lalor, available at http://econlib.org/library/YPDBooks/Lalor); Caroll D. Wright, *Industrial Conciliation and Arbitration* (Boston: Rand, Abery and Co., 1991), 50–53.

87. "Councils of Trade," *Friends' Weekly Intelligencer*, April 6, 1844, p. 10; "Councils of Trade," *The Penny Magazine of the Society for the Diffusion of Useful Knowledge* (London: Charles Knight, 1833), 83; Merle Curti, *The Growth of American Thought*, 3d ed. (New Brunswick, N.J.: Transaction Publishers, 1982), 340–41; S. M. Waddams, *Law, Politics, and the Church of England: The Career of Stephen Lushington, 1782–1873* (Cambridge: Cambridge University Press, 1992), 34.

88. "Councils of Trade," *Friends' Weekly Intelligencer;* "Councils of Trade," *The Penny Magazine.*

89. "Les Conseils de Prud'hommes," *Mechanic's Advocate*, February 4, 1847, p. 77.

90. "From Our London Correspondent," *Daily National Intelligencer,* June 26, 1860, p. 2; "Article 14—No Title," *Scientific American*, May 18, 1861, p. 317; "Workmen's Courts of Conciliation," *American Railway Review*, May 16, 1861, p. 304; "Courts of Conciliation," *Street and Smith's New York Weekly,* June 6, 1861, p. 4.

91. Michael Crutcher, "Historical Geographies of Race in a New Orleans Afro-Creole Landscape," in *Landscape and Race in the United States,* ed. Richard H. Schein (New York: Routledge, 2006), 29; "Observations on General Hurlbut's Answer; No. 1," *New Orleans Tribune,* March 28, 1865, p. 2.

92. "Official, Headquarters, Department of the Gulf, March 11, 1865," *New Orleans Tribune,* March 25, 1865, p. 1.

93. "Observations on General Hurlbut's Answer; No. 1"; "Observations on General Hurlbut's Answer; No. 3," *New Orleans Tribune,* March 30, 1865, p. 2.

94. Ibid.

95. "From Gen. Hurlbut," *New Orleans Tribune,* March 28, 1865, p. 1; "Observations on General Hurlbut's Answer; No. 3."

96. Howard, *Autobiography* 2:252.

97. Gregory P. Downs, *After Appomattox: Military Occupation and the Ends of War* (Cambridge: Harvard University Press, 2015), 46–47, 89–90.

98. Foner 169; James Oakes, "A Failure of Vision: The Collapse of the Freedmen's Bureau Courts," *Civil War History* 25 (1979): 75–76.

99. Bentley 152.

100. "Art. V: Mémoire sur l'origine et l'organisation des committés conciliateurs en Dannemarc, par A. B. Rothe, Copenhague, 1803, 16 mo., pp. 126," *North American Review* 102 (1866): 141.

101. George Steinmetz, *Regulating the Social: The Welfare State and Local Politics in Imperial Germany* (Princeton: Princeton University Press, 1993), 132.

102. Anthony Crubaugh, *Balancing the Scales: Local Courts and Rural Society in Southwest France, 1750–1800* (University Park: Pennsylvania State University Press, 2001), 191, 196; *Revue des conseils de prud'hommes: Recueil périodique de législation ouvrière, jurisprudence, législation, travaux parlementaires, informations, chroniques, bibliographie*, eds. Charles Strauss & Raymond Daly (Paris: Muzard & Ebin, 1899), 115–16.

103. Nieman; Farmer-Kaiser; Leslie A. Schwalm, *A Hard Fight for We: Women's Transition from Slavery to Freedom in South Carolina* (Urbana: University of Illinois Press, 1997); Laura F. Edwards, *Gendered Strife and Confusion: The Political Culture of Reconstruction* (Urbana: University of Illinois Press, 1997).

104. René Hayden et al., eds., *Land and Labor, 1866–1867*, ser. 3, vol. 2 of *Freedom: A Documentary History of Emancipation, 1861–1867* (Chapel Hill: University of North Carolina Press, 2013), 420.

105. "The Freedmen," *New York Herald*, March 27, 1866.

106. Thomas Franklin Philip Crandon, "Register of Correspondence, 1865–1866," Manuscript, Stanford University Special Collections, 272, 273, 275 (entries for May 9 and 10, 1866).

107. Hayden et al., eds., *Land and Labor, 1866–1867*, 169.

108. Ibid., 168–69, 445, 448.

109. Ibid., 484; "Document 141: Freedmen's Bureau Special Agent for Jackson County, Florida, to the Headquarters of the Florida Freedmen's Bureau Assistant Commissioner (February 28, 1867)," in ibid., 481.

110. "Document 174: Georgia Freedwoman to the Freedmen's Bureau Subassistant Commissioner at Macon, Georgia; Wife of the Freedwoman's Employer to the Freedmen's Bureau Agent for Houston County, Georgia; and Proceedings in a Case between the Freedwoman and Her Employer (March 2 and 5, 1867)," in ibid. 545–48.

111. Ibid., 152–54; Peirce 144; Nieman 17–22; Bentley 152–54; Schwalm 260–61.

112. Circular No. 5.

113. Nieman 8–9.

114. "Report of the Commissioner of the Bureau of Refugees, Freedmen, and Abandoned Lands," H.R. Doc. No. 1, at 719 (39th Cong., 2d Sess. 1867); Nieman 145–46.

115. "Freedmen's Bureau," *New York Herald Tribune*, May 18, 1866, p. 5.

116. Bureau records do not specify that lawyers were absent. But many fail to note that parties were represented by counsel, thus suggesting that these parties likely represented themselves.

117. Crandon 46–47 (December 15 and 16, 1865).

118. "General Steedman's Tour," *New York Times*, May 25, 1866, p. 5.

119. "Document 102: Freedmen's Bureau Officer in Mississippi to the Headquarters of the Mississippi Freedmen's Bureau Assistant Commissioner (April 9, 1866)," in Hayden et al., eds., *Land and Labor, 1866–1867*, 407–08.

120. Ibid., 409.

121. "The Freedmen," *New York Herald Tribune*, March 27, 1866, p. 9; "Hitting All Around," *Daily Constitutionalist* [Georgia], May 4, 1866, p. 3.

122. "Freedmen's Court," *Savannah Daily Herald*, March 7, 1866, col. B. See also "Freedmen's Court," *Savannah Daily Herald*, March 9, 1866, Col. A; "Freedmen's Court," *Savannah Daily Herald*, March 5, 1866, col. B; "Important Case in a Freedmen's Court," *Colored Citizen* [Ohio], May 19, 1866, p. 2; "The Use of the Freedmen's Bureau," *New York Tribune*, May 18, 1866, p. 8.

123. Crandon 52–53 (December 18 and 19, 1865). See also ibid., 72–73 (January 19, 20, and 22, 1866).

124. Crandon 52–53 (December 18 and 19, 1865). On some occasions, moreover, defendants opted to submit an answer to the complaint in writing. "Freedmen's Court," *Savannah Daily Herald*, February 27, 1866, Col. B.

125. "Document 174," in Hayden et al., eds., *Land and Labor, 1866–1867*, 545–46.

126. "The Freedmen," *New York Herald*, March 27, 1866, p. 9.

127. "Freedmen's Court," *Savannah Daily Herald*, February 27, 1866, Col. B.

128. Farmer-Kaiser 8–12, 16–17; Hayden et al., eds., *Land and Labor, 1866–1867*, 72–73; Foner 69–70, 155–70; Schwalm 263–68; Nieman 59–60.

129. In this respect, they resembled the version of the *conseils* adopted in Germany. Steinmetz 132.

130. "The Freedmen," *New York Herald*, March 27, 1866, p. 9.

131. Crandon 42, 43, 45, 47 (November 27, December 15, and December 16, 1865).

132. Ibid. See also Crandon 62–63 (January 9, 1866).

133. Oakes 75–76.

134. Ibid., 73–74; Farmer-Kaiser 148–66; Schwalm 260–66; Edwards, *Gendered Strife and Confusion* 63–65, 96–98; Edwards, *People and Their Peace* 287–89.

135. In the rare circumstances in which freedpeople did turn to the model of the conciliation court, they seem to have imagined it in much less paternalistic terms than did Northern whites. This was the case, for example, of the African-American community of New Orleans in its above-described discussion of the French *conseils de prud'hommes*.

136. "The Freedmen's Bureau," *New York Times*, June 26, 1865, p. 2. See also "The True Condition of the Freedmen—Reports of the Freedmen's Bureau," *New York Times*,

December 27, 1865, p. 4; "Freemen and Freedmen in West Tennessee," *The Independent . . . Devoted to the Consideration of Politics, Social and Economic Tendencies, History, Literature, and the Arts,* September 7, 1865, p. 1; "The Progress of Reconstruction," *The Independent . . . Devoted to the Consideration of Politics, Social and Economic Tendencies, History, Literature, and the Arts,* September 28, 1865, p. 2.

137. "The Freedmen's Bureau," *Harper's Weekly,* July 25, 1868, pp. 467, 473.

138. "Scene in a Freedmen's Court," *Liberator,* August 25, 1865, p. 135; "Scene in a Freedmen's Court," *Bangor Daily Whig and Courier,* August 26, 1865, col. D; "Scene in a Freedmen's Court," *Lowell Daily Citizen and News,* August 29, 1865, p. 2; "Scene in a Freedmen's Court," *Zion's Herald and Wesleyan Journal,* August 30, 1865, p. 140; "The Progress of Reconstruction in the Southwest," *The Independent . . . Devoted to the Consideration of Politics, Social and Economic Tendencies, History, Literature, and the Arts,* August 24, 1865, p. 3.

139. "Scene in a Freedmen's Court," *Bangor Daily Whig and Courier;* "The Progress of Reconstruction in the Southwest," *The Independent.*

140. "Scene in a Freedmen's Court," *Lowell Daily Citizen and News.*

141. Ibid.

142. Ibid.

143. John W. Frick, *Theatre, Culture, and Temperance Reform in Nineteenth-Century America* (Cambridge: Cambridge University Press, 2003), 48–77.

144. "Grenada—A Reign of Terror—Thugs—Murder of a Bureau Officer—The Bureau and the Freedmen—Conflict of Labor—Changed Conditions—Gideon J. Pillow, etc.," *New York Times,* July 2, 1866, p. 1.

145. "Art. V: Mémoire sur l'origine et l'organisation des committés conciliateurs en Dannemarc, par A. B. Rothe, Copenhague, 1803, 16 mo., pp. 126," *North American Review* 102 (1866): 135–46.

146. "North American Review," *Bangor Daily Whig and Courier,* January 17, 1866, col. A; "North American Review for January," *Evening Star* [Washington, D.C.], January 10, 1866, p. 2; "Sundries to Sundries," *National Republican* [Washington, D.C.], January 10, 1866, p. 2; "The North American Review," *Jackson Citizen Patriot,* April 13, 1866, p. 2.

147. Nieman 4, 103–21, 143–47; Bentley 162–63.

148. "Art. V: Mémoire sur l'origine," *North American Review,* 141.

149. Ibid., 143–44.

150. Ibid., 146.

151. Ibid., 144–45.

152. "Mixed Metaphor," *The Daily Phoenix,* September 8, 1865, p. 1; *Colored Tennessean,* October 14, 1865, p. 2 (citing *The Jackson News*).

153. "A Freedmen's Court in Mobile," *Patriot* [Penn.], February 23, 1866, p. 1.

154. "Obscenity of a Freedmen's Court," *Memphis Daily Avalanche,* January 20, 1866, p. 1.

155. "North Carolina," *New York Times,* January 25, 1866, p. 2.

156. "Speech of Hon. Montgomery Blair," *Daily National Intelligencer* [Washington, D.C.], June 23, 1866, p. 1; William L. Barney, *Oxford Encyclopedia of the Civil War* (Oxford: Oxford University Press, 2001), 34–35.

157. "Democratic Platform," *The Constitution* [Atlanta], September 8, 1868, p. 1.

158. Ibid.

159. Ibid.

160. "Speech of Hon. Montgomery Blair," *Daily National Intelligencer.*

161. "The Freedmen's Bureau," *New Orleans Times,* October 15, 1865, p. 4; Bentley 154.

162. "The South," *Daily Morning Chronicle* [Washington, D.C.], November 13, 1865, p. 1 (citing *The Richmond Sentinel*).

163. "The Freedmen's Court Discontinued in Nashville," *Columbus Daily Enquirer* [Georgia], June 1, 1866, p. 3 (citing the *Nashville Dispatch*).

164. "The Freedmen's Bureau," *New Orleans Times,* October 15, 1865, p. 4.

165. "The Apathy and Apparent Indifference of the People of the United States to the Violations of Their Constitution, and the Causes of It," *Crisis* [Ohio], May 13, 1868, p. 122.

166. "Tragedy at Pine Bluff," *Little Rock Evening Republic,* June 8, 1867, col. A.

167. "Announcing that the Rebellion has ended, April 2, 1866," in Edward McPherson, *A Handbook of Politics for 1866* (Washington, D.C.: Philp & Solomons, 1868), 16–17.

168. Brooks D. Simpson, "Ulysses S. Grant and the Freedmen's Bureau," in *The Freedmen's Bureau and Reconstruction: Reconsiderations,* 15.

169. *Ex parte Milligan,* 71 U.S. 2 (1866); Simpson, "Ulysses S. Grant and the Freedmen's Bureau" 15.

170. "Veto of the Second Freedmen's Bureau Bill, July 16, 1866," in Edward McPherson, *The Political History of the United States during the Period of Reconstruction (from April 15, 1866, to July 15, 1870)* (Washington, D.C.: Philp & Solomons, 1871), 147–48.

171. Donna L. Dickerson, ed., *The Reconstruction Era: Primary Documents on Events from 1865 to 1877* (Westport, Conn.: Greenwood Press, 2003), 87.

172. 71 U.S. at 127, 136–37.

173. Ibid., 127.

174. John Fabian Witt, *Lincoln's Code: The Laws of War in American History* (New York: Free Press, 2012), 313; Aziz Rana, "Freedom Struggles and the Limits of Constitutional Continuity," *Maryland Law Review* 71 (2012): 1041–45; Simpson, "Ulysses S. Grant and the Freedmen's Bureau" 21.

175. "Veto of the Reconstruction Bills, March 2, 1867," in McPherson, *Political History of the United States,* 170.

176. Nieman 196–208; Act of March 2, 1867, ch. 153, 14 Stat. 428; Simpson, "Ulysses S. Grant and the Freedmen's Bureau" 23. This potential jurisdiction was

limited, moreover, to criminal suits, thus failing to revive the Bureau courts' once substantial civil jurisdiction.

177. *Ex parte McCardle,* 74 U.S. 506 (1868); *Ex parte Yerger,* 75 U.S. 85 (1868). Shortly before the Court was to decide *Ex parte McCardle,* Congress repealed the Habeas Corpus Act of 1867 pursuant to which McCardle had sought review, leading the Court to conclude that it lacked jurisdiction. The Court thereafter held in *Ex parte Yerger* that it could review Yerger's petition for release pursuant to the much older habeas provision of the Judiciary Act of 1789. But just as it was poised to review the constitutionality of Yerger's conviction, the attorney general arranged for his release, leading him to withdraw his petition. Witt, *Lincoln's Code* 316; Barry Friedman, "The History of the Countermajoritarian Difficulty, Part II: Reconstruction's Political Court," *Georgetown Law Journal* 91 (2002): 25–39.

178. Nieman 198–99; Act of March 2, 1867, ch. 153, 14 Stat. 428.

179. Preface to *The Freedmen's Bureau and Reconstruction: Reconsiderations,* ix; Nieman 11; Edwards, *Gendered Strife and Confusion* 63–64, 97–98; Schwalm 260–68.

180. Nieman 15–16; Peter W. Bardaglio, *Reconstructing the Household: Families, Sex, and the Law in the Nineteenth-Century South* (Chapel Hill: University of North Carolina Press, 1995), 127; Jerold S. Auerbach, *Justice Without Law? Non-Legal Dispute Settlement in American History* (New York: Oxford University Press, 1983), 58–60; Leon F. Litwack, *Been in the Storm So Long: The Aftermath of Slavery* (New York: Vintage Books, 1979), 379–86.

181. *The Constitution of the United States of America as Amended: Unratified Amendments, Analytical Index,* ed. Robert A. Brady (Washington, D.C.: U.S. Government Printing Office, 2007), 17; Witt, *Lincoln's Code* 315; *Slaughterhouse Cases,* 83 U.S. 36, 83 (1872).

182. Nieman 221; Bentley 165–67; Owen, "One of the Problems of the Age," 14:156.

## Conclusion. The Question of American Exceptionalism and the Lessons of History

1. Marc Galanter, "Predators and Parasites: Lawyer-Bashing and Civil Justice," *Georgia Law Review* 28 (1994): 645–47, 669–75; Basil Markesinis, "Litigation-Mania in England, Germany and the USA: Are We So Very Different?" *Cambridge Law Journal* 49 (1990): 273–74.

2. Kagan 9, 11–14.

3. Ibid., 14–16, 34–58; Witt, *Patriots and Cosmopolitans* 209–84.

4. Dawson 39–115; Engelmann et al. 432–37, 455–92, 507–602, 645–768.

5. Engelmann et al. 750.

6. Ibid., 508, 532–86; P. Oberhammer and T. Domej, "Germany, Switzerland, and Austria (ca. 1800–2005)," in *European Traditions in Civil Procedure,* ed. C. H. van

Rhee (Oxford: Intersentia, 2005), 108–13; James M. Donovan, *Juries and the Transformation of Criminal Justice in France in the Nineteenth and Twentieth Centuries* (Chapel Hill: University of North Carolina Press, 2010), 23–48.

7. David A. Bell, *Lawyers and Citizens: The Making of a Political Elite in Old Regime France* (New York: Oxford University Press, 1994); Lucien Karpik, *French Lawyers: A Study in Collective Action, 1274 to 1994*, trans. Nora Scott (Oxford: Clarendon Press, 1999), 36–156.

8. Hurst 286–88; Hobson 65.

9. For an overview of the transatlantic parallels, see Langbein, Lerner, and Smith 377–78. For English developments, see Lobban, "Preparing for Fusion: Reforming the Nineteenth-Century Court of Chancery, Part I," *Law and History Review* 22 (2004); Michael Lobban, "Preparing for Fusion: Reforming the Nineteenth-Century Court of Chancery, Part II," *Law and History Review* 22 (2004).

10. There is reason to suspect that enthusiasm for oral, adversarial procedure—and especially for cross-examination—played a greater role in spurring the procedural reform of New York Chancery than of the latter's English counterpart. As we have seen, the path leading to the merger of law and equity in New York began with Kent's 1817 decision in *Remsen,* authorizing oral testimony before masters in the presence of parties and their counsel. David Dudley Field himself would later assert that it was New York Chancery's embrace of the common law's oral, adversarial approach to taking testimony that led to the creation of a uniform approach to pleading and trial practice—and thus to the Field Code of Procedure. In contrast, in England, it was concerns about delays in chancery, combined with a Whig-led campaign against Lord Chancellor Eldon and his Tory allies that seem to have sparked initial efforts at reform. Indeed, the primary focus of the 1824 commission appointed to consider possible reforms of English Chancery practice was not on introducing oral, adversarial cross-examination, but instead on curbing abuses of the fee system for paying masters. Field, "What Shall Be Done" 1:258; Lobban, "Preparing for Fusion, Part I" 409–14.

11. "Minutes of Evidence Taken Before the Commissioners Appointed to Inquire into the Process, Practice, and System of Pleading, in the Court of Chancery (Dec. 22, 1851)," in *Supplement to Appendix to the First Report of Her Majesty's Commissioners Appointed to Inquire Into the Process, Practice, and System of Pleading in the Court of Chancery, etc.* (London: W. Clowes and Sons, 1852).

12. Samuel Miller, *The Orders of the High Court of Chancery from Hilary V. 1828 to Mich. T. 1842, with the Statutes Relating to Pleading and Practice in That Court* (London: Butterworth, 1842), 78–79 (Order 69).

13. *Copy of the First Report of Her Majesty's Commissioners Appointed to Inquire Into the Process, Practice, and System of Pleading in the Court of Chancery, etc.* (London: W. Clowes and Sons, 1852), 21, 40.

14. "An Act to Amend the Practice and Course of Proceeding in the High Court of Chancery (July 1, 1852)," ch. 86, in *A Collection of the Public General Statutes Passed in*

*the Fifteenth and Sixteenth Year of the Reign of Her Majesty Queen Victoria, 1852* (London: George Edward Eyre and William Spottiswoode, 1852), 897–916.

15. Chancery Commissioners, "Memorandum as to the Mode of Taking Evidence in Chancery (Aug. 1854)," in *The Third Report of Her Majesty's Commissioners Appointed to Inquire Into the Process, Practice, and System of Pleading in the Court of Chancery, etc.* (London: George Edward Eyre and William Spottiswoode, 1856), 23–24; "Order of 13th January 1855," in C. Stewart Drewry, *The New Practice of the Court of Chancery* (London: Law Times Office, 1856), 331–32; "Report to the Queen's Most Excellent Majesty," in *Report of Her Majesty's Commissioners Appointed to Inquire Into the Mode of Taking Evidence in Chancery, and Its Effects* (London: George Edward Eyre and William Spottiswoode, 1860), 7–10; "Order of 5th February 1861," in Edmund Powell et al., *The Principles and Practice of the Law of Evidence*, 3d ed. (London: Butterworths, 1868), 617–19.

16. J. M. Lely and D. I. Foulkes, *The Judicature Acts, 1873 and 1875: Containing the Statutes, Rules of Court and Orders in Council, with Notes; Forming a Practice of the Supreme Court*, 2d ed. (London: H. Sweet, 1877), lx.

17. David Lemmings, *Professors of Law: Barristers and English Legal Culture in the Eighteenth Century* (Oxford: Oxford University Press, 2000), 295–304, 308. From the late eighteenth century through the nineteenth, barristers were recruited almost exclusively from the upper echelons of British society—the sons primarily of urban businessmen, but also of the landed gentry. Daniel Duman, *The English and Colonial Bars in the Nineteenth Century* (London: Croom Helm, 1983), 16–19. But over the course of the nineteenth century, and beginning especially in the 1830s, there was a significant expansion in the number of barristers called to the bar. Ibid., 26–29, 206–07; J. R. Lewis, *The Victorian Bar* (London: Robert Hale Limited, 1982), 39–41. This expansion exerted less competitive pressure than sheer numbers would suggest, however, in that many of these men had good career options other than litigating in the English courts. These included practicing in the colonies, joining the civil service, and returning to their family estates. Duman 26–29, 206–07. See also Wendie Ellen Schneider, *Engines of Truth: Producing Veracity in the Victorian Courtroom* (New Haven: Yale University Press, 2015), 52 (suggesting that Victorian barristers depicted cross-examination as being rooted in "norms of aristocratic conduct").

18. Lemmings 248–90, 304–19, 323–24.

19. Langbein et al., 459–64; Hanly 258.

20. Michael Lobban argues that the Field Code provided the "key political impetus" for the merger of law and equity in England. Lobban, "Preparing for Fusion, Part II" 584. See also Langbein et al., 384–85.

21. New York authorized oral testimony before masters in *Remsen*, decided in 1817. England did so through an order promulgated in 1828. Miller, *Orders of the High Court of Chancery* 78–79 (Order 69). While New York authorized oral examination before examiners in a statute passed on April 17, 1823, England did not enact a statute to this

effect until July 1, 1852. "An Act to Amend the Practice and Course of Proceeding in the High Court of Chancery (July 1, 1852)," ch. 86 (secs. 30 and 31), in *A Collection of the Public General Statutes Passed in the Fifteenth and Sixteenth Year of the Reign of Her Majesty Queen Victoria, 1852* (London: George Edward Eyre and William Spottiswoode, 1852), 905. New York abolished masters in its constitution of 1846, while England did so through a statute enacted in 1852. Lobban, "Preparing for Fusion, Part II" 581–82. New York abolished examiners in its 1846 constitution, but England did not dispense with its examiners in chancery until 1884 (at which time these officers were replaced with a new group of examiners, responsible for taking out-of-court testimony for all divisions of the newly established supreme court). Samuel Rosenbaum, *The Rule-Making Authority in the English Supreme Court* (Boston: Boston Book Company, 1917), 192–93. New York opted to create a unified supreme court in its Constitution of 1846 and to establish a unified mode of procedure through the Field Code of 1848. England, however, did not adopt these changes until the Judicature Acts of 1873 and 1875. Patrick Polden, "Mingling the Waters: Personalities, Politics and the Making of the Supreme Court of Judicature," *Cambridge Law Journal* 61 (2002); Baker, *Introduction to English Legal History* 49–51.

22. "Minutes of Evidence Taken Before the Commissioners Appointed to Inquire into the Process, Practice, and System of Pleading, in the Court of Chancery (Dec. 22, 1851)," 1–10. The commissioners also asked many New York lawyers other than Field to answer questions concerning the code. As Henry Vanderlyn noted in his diary in March 1851, "H.R. Mygatt and James Clapp were in my office this evening. We wrote answers to the law reform circular of London issued by the committee, requesting answers to the questions 19 in toto respecting the working of our code of procedure...." Vanderlyn 6:381 (entry for March 25, 1851).

23. David Dudley Field, *Law Reform in the United States and Its Influence Abroad* (St. Louis: Review Publishing Co., 1891), 13–14.

24. Lobban, "Preparing for Fusion, Part I" 390–414.

25. As Joseph Story wrote to an English friend in 1836, "We have not yet become votaries to the notions of Jeremy Bentham." Newmyer 280.

26. John Dinwiddy, *Bentham* (Oxford: Oxford University Press, 1989), 14; Fisher 659–60; Lobban, "Henry Brougham and Law Reform" 1186–91; Bentham, *Rationale of Judicial Evidence* 2:202–20, 2:345–79; 5:328–73.

27. Hurst 340–43; Hobson 197–201.

28. Hurst 339, 342–52; Friedman, *History of American Law* 329–49.

29. Thomas C. Grey, "Modern American Legal Thought," *Yale Law Journal* 106 (1996): 497–500; Jerry L. Mashaw, *Creating the Administrative Constitution: The Lost One Hundred Years of American Administrative Law* (New Haven: Yale University Press, 2012), 256–63, 278.

30. John H. Langbein, "The Disappearance of Civil Trial in the United States," *Yale Law Journal* 122 (2012): 524 (quoting Samuel R. Gross and Kent D. Syverud, "Don't

Try: Civil Jury Verdicts in a System Geared to Settlement," *UCLA Law Review* 44 (1996): 51).

31. Marc Galanter, "The Vanishing Trial: An Examination of Trials and Related Matters in Federal and State Courts," *Journal of Empirical Legal Studies* 1 (2004): 459–570; Marc Galanter and Angela M. Frozena, "A Grin without a Cat: The Continuing Decline and Displacement of Trials in American Courts," *Daedalus* (2014): 115–28; Langbein, "Disappearance of Civil Trial" 522–72.

32. Owen M. Fiss, "Against Settlement," *Yale Law Journal* 93 (1984): 1077–78; Judith Resnik, "The Privatization of Process: Requiem for and Celebration of the Federal Rules of Civil Procedure at 75," *University of Pennsylvania Law Review* 162 (2014): 1803–23.

33. Margaret Jane Radin, *Boilerplate: The Fine Print, Vanishing Rights and the Rule of Law* (Princeton: Princeton University Press, 2011), 130–35; Imre Szlai, *Outsourcing Justice: The Rise of Modern Arbitration Laws in America* (Durham, N.C.: Carolina Academic Press, 2013), 7–9; Jean R. Sternlight, "Creeping Mandatory Arbitration: Is It Just?" *Stanford Law Review* 57 (2005): 1636–53, 1661–65.

34. MacMahon 563–74; Kevin M. Clermont and Emily Sherwin, "A Comparative View of Standards of Proof," *American Journal of Comparative Law* 50 (2002): 259; Mirjan Damaška, "A Continental Lawyer in an American Law School: Trials and Tribulations of Adjustment," *University of Pennsylvania Law Review* 116 (1968): 1368.

35. Bruce A. Kimball and Pedro Reyes, "The 'First Modern Civil Procedure Course' As Taught by C. C. Langdell, 1870–78," *American Journal of Legal History* 47 (2005): 266–77; John Henry Merryman, "Legal Education There and Here: A Comparison," *Stanford Law Review* 27 (1975): 867.

36. Kagan 56; MacMahon 567–68.

37. Kagan 56; Michael S. Greve, "The Non-Reformation of Administrative Law: Standing to Sue and Public Interest Litigation in West German Environmental Law," *Cornell International Law Journal* 22 (1989): 231.

38. Freedman, "Our Constitutionalized Adversary System" 57, 90; Stephan Landsman, *The Adversary System: A Description and Defense* (Washington, D.C.: American Enterprise Institute for Public Policy Research, 1984), 45–46.

39. Richard A. Posner, *Economic Analysis of Law* (Boston: Little, Brown and Company, 1972), 321; Frank B. Cross, "America the Adversarial," *University of Virginia Law Review* 89 (2003): 205. See also Paul T. Wangerin, "The Political and Economic Roots of the 'Adversary System' of Justice and 'Alternative Dispute Resolution,'" *Ohio State Journal on Dispute Resolution* 9 (1994): 224–25.

40. Ellen E. Sward, "Values, Ideology and the Evolution of the Adversary System," *Indiana Law Journal* 64 (1988/1989): 302; Monroe H. Freedman, "Judge Frankel's Search for Truth," *University of Pennsylvania Law Review* 123 (1975): 1065.

41. As concerns discovery, in particular, there is evidence suggesting that abuses today are much more common in certain high stakes cases, including especially those

concerning antitrust, securities, patents, and trademarks. Bryant G. Garth, "Two Worlds of Civil Discovery: From Studies of Cost and Delay to the Markets in Legal Services and Legal Reform," *Boston College Law Review* 39 (1998).

42. Kessler, "Our Inquisitorial Tradition" 1251–60.

43. Deborah L. Rhode, *Access to Justice* (New York: Oxford University Press, 2004), 3, 6–7; Justice Earl Johnson Jr., "Equal Access to Justice: Comparing Access to Justice in the United States and Other Industrial Democracies," *Fordham International Law Journal* 24 (2000); Rebecca L. Sandefur, "The Fulcrum Point of Equal Access to Justice: Legal and Nonlegal Institutions of Remedy," *Loyola of Los Angeles Law Review* 42 (2009); Sande L. Buhai, "Access to Justice for Unrepresented Litigants: A Comparative Perspective," *Loyola of Los Angeles Law Review* 42 (2009).

44. Resnik and Curtis, *Representing Justice* 303–08.

45. Gillian K. Hadfield, "Higher Demand, Lower Supply? A Comparative Assessment of the Legal Resource Landscape for Ordinary Americans," 37 *Fordham Urban Law Journal* (2010): 151–52.

46. Johnson, "Equal Access to Justice" S83–S98.

47. Kessler, "Our Inquisitorial Tradition" 1251–73; Hadfield 152–53.

48. Sandefur 962–76; Hazel Genn, *Paths to Justice: What People Do and Think About Going to Law* (Oxford: Hart Publishing, 1999), 75–78. See also William J. Stuntz, "The Uneasy Relationship between Criminal Procedure and Criminal Justice," *Yale Law Journal* 107 (1997) (discussing the unappreciated costs of adversarial procedure in the criminal context); "Citizens Advice Bureaux Funding Cut by 10 Per Cent on Average," *Third Sector*, September 6, 2011.

49. Christopher Prendergast, "The Price of the Modern: Walter Benjamin and Counterfactuals," in *Tradition, Translation, Trauma: The Classic and the Modern*, ed. Jan Parker and Timothy Mathews (New York: Oxford University Press, 2011), 146.

50. Carrie Menkel-Meadow, "Crisis in Legal Education or the Other Things Law Students Should Be Learning and Doing," *McGeorge Law Review* 45 (2013): 135–37.

51. *"Mandatory Binding Arbitration—Is It Fair and Voluntary?" Hearing before the Subcommittee on Commercial and Administrative Law of the House Committee on the Judiciary*, 111th Cong. 83 (2009), 78 (statement of Stephen J. Ware, Professor of Law, University of Kansas School of Law).

52. Judith Resnik, "Fairness in Numbers: A Comment on AT&T v. Concepcion, Wal-Mart v. Dukes, and Turner v. Rogers," *Harvard Law Review* 125 (2011): 113–18.

53. Judith Resnik, "Changing Practices, Changing Rules: Judicial and Congressional Rulemaking on Civil Juries, Civil Justice, and Civil Judging," *Alabama Law Review* 49 (1997): 147–48 (identifying such bottom-up rule-making during the twentieth century).

54. Robert M. Cover, "For James Wm. Moore: Some Reflections on a Reading of the Rules," *Yale Law Journal* 84 (1975): 718.

55. Marylynn Salmon, *Women and the Law of Property in Early America* (Chapel Hill: University of North Carolina Press, 1986), 81–120.

56. As envisioned by the Code commissioners, the parties themselves could consent to have the case decided by referees and thereby secure "the advantages of an arbitration." But referees could also be appointed on the motion of only some of the litigants or by the court "of its own motion" in those cases necessitating an accounting or "[w]here a question of fact, other than upon the pleadings, shall arise, upon motion or otherwise, in any stage of the action." Moreover, the code's broad authorization of fact-finding—not simply in response to the parties' own motion but "otherwise" (and thus presumably on the judge's sua sponte order)—suggests at least the possibility of a return to a more quasi-inquisitorial tradition of court-directed investigation. *First Report of the Commissioners* 191–92 (secs. 225–26); "An Act to Simplify and Abridge the Practice, Pleadings and Proceedings of the Courts of This State, Passed April 12, 1848," in *Laws of the State of New York, Passed at the Seventy-First Session of the Legislature, Begun the Fourth Day of January, and Ended the Twelfth Day of April, 1848, at the City of Albany* (Albany: Charles Van Benthuysen, 1848), 539 (chap. 379, secs. 225–26). See also James Oldham and Su Jin Kim, "Arbitration in America: The Early History," *Law and History Review* 31 (2013): 253–54 (explaining that common-law courts long identified those individuals to whom cases were referred for arbitration as referees).

57. *Commercial Litigation in New York State Courts: New York Practice Series,* ed. Robert L. Haig, 3d ed. (2013), vol. 3, chap. 32, p. 2.

58. Ibid., 2, 4.

59. "Rule 53," in *Rules of Civil Procedure for the District Courts of the United States* (Washington, D.C.: United States Government Printing Office, 1938), 65–66.

60. As explained in the advisory committee notes to the 2003 amendments to Rule 53, "Use of masters for the core functions of trial has been progressively limited." 2003 Amendments to Federal Rule of Civil Procedure 53, available at www.law.cornell.edu/rules/frcp/rule_53. The dominant function of masters is now instead to "address pretrial and posttrial matters that cannot be effectively and timely addressed by an available district judge or magistrate judge of the district." Rule 53(a)(C), available at www.law.cornell.edu/rules/frcp/rule_53.

61. Kessler, "Our Inquisitorial Tradition" 1194–98, 1247–50.

62. Thomas E. Willging et al., *Special Masters' Incidence and Activity: Report to the Judicial Conference's Advisory Committee on Civil Rules and Its Subcommittee on Special Masters* (Washington, D.C.: Federal Judicial Center, 2000), 9

63. Resnik, "Fairness in Numbers" 113–18; *Bell Atlantic Corporation v. Twombly,* 550 U.S. 544 (2007); *Ashcroft v. Iqbal,* 556 U.S. 662 (2009); Jonah B. Gelbach, "Locking the Doors to Discovery? Assessing the Effects of Twombly and Iqbal on Access to Discovery," *Yale Law Journal* 121 (2012): 2270–2345. Cf. David Freeman Engstrom, "The Twiqbal Puzzle and Empirical Study of Civil Procedure," *Stanford Law Review* 65 (2013): 1203–48 (questioning the reliability of many of the empirical studies claiming to identify the consequences of *Twombly* and *Iqbal*).

64. Rule 53; Kessler, "Our Inquisitorial Tradition" 1254–57.

65. 28 U.S.C. §636(b)(2), available at www.law.cornell.edu/uscode/text/28/636. See also Linda J. Silberman, "Masters and Magistrates, Part II: The American Analogue," *New York University Law Review* 50 (1975): 1297–1372; Judith Resnik, "'Uncle Sam Modernizes His Justice': Inventing the Federal District Courts of the Twentieth-Century for the District Court of Columbia and the Nation," *Georgetown Law Journal* 90 (2002): 607–84.

66. Deborah R. Hensler, "Our Courts, Ourselves: How the Alternative Dispute Resolution Movement is Re-Shaping Our Legal System," *Penn State Law Review* 108 (2003): 165–97, 188.

67. James Q. Whitman, "Consumerism Versus Producerism: A Study in Comparative Law," *Yale Law Journal* 117 (2007): 391.

68. Federal Rule of Evidence 706, available at www.law.cornell.edu/rules/fre/rule_706; Edward J. Imwinkelried, "Impoverishing the Trier of Fact: Excluding the Proponent's Expert Testimony Due to the Opponent's Inability to Afford Rebuttal Evidence," *Connecticut Law Review* 40 (2007): 325–28.

69. Tahirih V. Lee, "Court-Appointed Experts and Judicial Reluctance: A Proposal to Amend Rule 706 of the Federal Rules of Evidence," *Yale Law and Policy Review* 6 (1988): 480–82, 494–99.

70. Federal Rule of Evidence 702, available at www.law.cornell.edu/rules/fre/rule_702.

71. Kessler, "Our Inquisitorial Tradition" 1267.

72. Pete Burgess, Susan Corby, and Paul L. Latreille, "Lay Judges and Labor Courts: A Question of Legitimacy," *Comparative Labor Law and Policy Journal* 35 (2014): 208.

73. James Oldham, "On the Question of a Complexity Exception to the Seventh Amendment Guarantee of Trial by Jury," *Ohio State Law Journal* 71 (2010): 1041–52; Zipporah Batshaw Wiseman, "The Limits of Vision: Karl Llewellyn and the Merchant Rules," *Harvard Law Review* 100 (1987): 512–21 & n. 218, 527–30; James Q. Whitman, "Commercial Law and the American Volk: A Note on Llewellyn's German Sources for the Uniform Commercial Code," *Yale Law Journal* 97 (1987): 170–74.

74. Langbein, "Disappearance of Civil Trial" 524; Lerner, "Failure of Originalism" 831, 846–51.

75. 28 U.S.C. § 1861, available at www.law.cornell.edu/uscode/text/28/1861; Oldham 1032–33.

## Appendix. An Overview of the Archives

1. Some records of the various circuit courts created in 1823 are based elsewhere.

2. A review of the 319 suits filed under the letter B and the 284 suits filed under the letter S suggests that about 85 to 90 percent date from roughly 1750 onward. I chose to review the cases filed under these letters because they were the most numerous.

3. This estimate is based on a review of the cases filed under the letters B and S.

4. The first volume covers 1701 and 1702; the second, 1705 to 1708; the third, 1720 to 1735; and the fourth, 1748 to 1770.

5. The circuit courts' jurisdiction was "confined to matters and causes arising within their circuits only, or where the subject matter in controversy shall be situated within such circuit, or where the defendant or party proceeded against, shall reside within such circuit." "An Act concerning the Supreme Court, for dividing the State of New-York into Circuits, and concerning Circuit Courts and Courts of Oyer and Terminer, and for Vesting Equity Powers in the Circuit Judges, Passed April 17, 1823," in *Laws of the State of New York, Passed at the Forty-Fifth, Forty-Sixth and Forty-Seventh Sessions of the Legislature, Commencing January, 1822, and Ending November, 1824* (Albany: William Gould & Co., 1825), 6:213 (chap. 182, sec. X). While some of these circuit-court suits were thereafter appealed to the chancellor and therefore appear within J0063, the vast majority of cases preserved in this series are ones that were originally filed directly with the chancellor. Only 8 of the 222 post-1823 cases that I reviewed (or 4%) were appeals from circuit-court decisions.

6. These numbers themselves understate the extent of the docket expansion that occurred after 1823 in that that year marked the creation of the circuit courts, which were granted concurrent jurisdiction with the chancellor over suits in equity.

# INDEX

*Note: Page numbers in italic type indicate illustrations.*